HERE'S TO THE
LADIES

Also by Eddie Shapiro

Nothing Like a Dame: Conversations With The Great Women
of Musical Theater

A Wonderful Guy: Conversations with the Great Men of Musical Theater

EDDIE SHAPIRO

HERE'S TO THE LADIES

CONVERSATIONS WITH MORE OF THE GREAT WOMEN OF MUSICAL THEATER

OXFORD
UNIVERSITY PRESS

OXFORD
UNIVERSITY PRESS

Oxford University Press is a department of the University of Oxford. It furthers the University's objective of excellence in research, scholarship, and education by publishing worldwide. Oxford is a registered trade mark of Oxford University Press in the UK and certain other countries.

Published in the United States of America by Oxford University Press
198 Madison Avenue, New York, NY 10016, United States of America.

Library of Congress Cataloging-in-Publication Data
Names: Shapiro, Eddie, 1969– interviewer.
Title: Here's to the ladies : conversations with more of the great women of musical theater / [interviews by] Eddie Shapiro.
Description: New York : Oxford University Press, 2023. |
Includes bibliographical references and index.
Identifiers: LCCN 2023021180 (print) | LCCN 2023021181 (ebook) |
ISBN 9780197585535 (hardback) | ISBN 9780197585559 (epub)
Subjects: LCSH: Women singers—Interviews. | Singers—Interviews. |
Actresses—Interviews. | Musicals—History and criticism.
Classification: LCC ML400 .S479 2023 (print) | LCC ML400 (ebook) |
DDC 782.1/409252—dc23/eng/20230503
LC record available at https://lccn.loc.gov/2023021180
LC ebook record available at https://lccn.loc.gov/2023021181

Printed by Sheridan Books, Inc., United States of America

Dedicated to all the greats who are still to come. May this book and others like it inspire you. And also for others I hope to inspire: Noa, Hallel, Max, and Audrey.

Contents

Foreword

I was a musical theater late-bloomer. I came into it knowing pretty much nothing and was lucky enough to get work in this industry without really understanding what it all entailed. I recognized a lot of the names I was working with, but I didn't know their stories. It's funny—you can share a stage with someone over the course of a year and know them intimately on some levels, but not know them at all on others.

This industry has come to mean so much to me. It's my church as well as my vocation. So when Eddie Shapiro wrote *Nothing Like a Dame* and *A Wonderful Guy*, I couldn't wait to dive in and see what my peers had to say. So many of these people I had known for years, but I didn't know their process or what made them tick. It was fascinating to read how similar some of us are in the ways we approach the business, and equally fascinating to read how different some of us are in our thinking about the work and the industry.

I have sat opposite Eddie many, many times, both on the record and off. What makes him so easy to talk to in either setting, and what makes these books so compelling, is his ability to really listen. He hears what is said, and also what's not said, and then, using his encyclopedic knowledge of theater (it's terrifying, actually), he immediately understands context. I've been interviewed many times over the years, but the ease I experience with Eddie, whether we're talking Broadway or talking about our love lives, is unusual. I felt it as soon as we met. It's what makes great stars willing to open up, and therefore makes these books essential reading for anyone who enjoys the theater, aspires to the theater, or just wants to hear about how some really interesting people ended up doing what they ended up doing at the highest level of their profession.

So now I invite you to sit back, relax, and dive into these great women and their stories. Welcome to my church and to Eddie's gift to theater lovers.

Norm Lewis

Introduction

When I wrote *Nothing Like a Dame: Conversations with the Great Women of Musical Theater*, and then its follow up, *A Wonderful Guy: Conversations with . . .* (you get the picture), I hadn't considered that I'd get to do a third volume. But a confluence of factors led to the book you hold in your hands.

First, I simply wasn't ready to be done. These are the kinds of books that I devoured as I was growing up; anything that helped me pull back the curtain was like catnip to me. It still is. I loved that what I was doing with these books could spark the imagination of the next generation of theater geeks. And I delighted in celebrating (not to mention talking to) the artists who had given me so much.

Second, another book on Broadway's women would allow me to feature people I wasn't able to include the first time. Some of the women in this volume were, in fact, interviewed years ago for *Nothing Like a Dame*, but for one reason or another, their chapters weren't included. Others had agreed to participate in *Dame*, but as you might well imagine, dames don't always have the clearest of calendars and we ran out of time. And still others who were just cutting their teeth twelve years ago when I first started working on *Dame* have since blossomed into full-fledged Broadway stars.

And finally, 2020, which took so much from us, unexpectedly gave many of us something, too: time. I saw an opportunity and I jumped. For those first two books, the availability of all of the actors was one of the challenges, but now everyone I wanted to talk to was stuck at home and learning their best webcam lighting.

These Zoom conversations meandered, in several instances, for twelve or thirteen hours. That was, of course, likely due to the aforementioned clear calendars, but I think that there was something else at play; being on a universal pause gave many people an opportunity to contemplate and discuss their careers in ways that they might not have if they had been in the middle of a show's run or on break from a rehearsal. The sudden stop opened the door to greater objectivity as we all found ourselves at home, considering why we do what we do and how we do it.

As I look back on the conversations that fill these pages, I am once again so, so grateful. These women trusted me with their hopes, their fears, their insecurities, and their triumphs. I am honored to be their chronicler, and I hope you feel some of the giddiness I experienced as you dive into their stories of what it was like for each of them to deliver the gifts they have shared with us, show after show after show.

Barbara Cook

June, September 2009

Author's note: This conversation was one of the first that took place for Nothing Like a Dame. By 2012, when the book was ready for publication, Cook was working on her own autobiography and apologetically asked me to hold off on publishing. She died in 2017, but with the blessing of her son, I am pleased to be able offer it now.

Barbara Cook likes her art. And no, I don't mean the art she practices (although she likes that, too), I mean the art she collects. She has so much of it, in fact, that the walls in her Upper West Side apartment can't hold it all. Cook proudly shows off her collection, whose theme, appropriately, is "stuff I like." It all amounts to an incredibly varied array of expression, the very thing for which Cook is adored. For while her voice is one of the purest, most celebrated (and some would say the best) ever to grace a Broadway stage, it's her deep, deep skill as an interpreter that make her a legend.

She'll be the first to tell you that it was not always thus. When Cook came to New York from Atlanta in 1948, she was "greener than green." But with her clear soprano, blue eyes, and long blonde hair, it took her very little time to start amassing credits. First came *Flahooley, Plain and Fancy*, and a couple of memorable Rodgers and Hammerstein revivals before a landmark: *Candide*, with a Leonard Bernstein score that would come to be known as one of his finest. *Candide* was not a hit, but Cook's next show sure was. As Marian the Librarian in *The Music Man*, Cook was irresistible, taking home the Tony Award. Her subsequent musicals—*The Gay Life*, *Something More*, *She Loves Me*, and *The Grass Harp*—were all disappointments, and in the early 70s, Cook took a hiatus from the stage. When she re-emerged, most markedly with a legendary Carnegie Hall concert in 1975, it was as a cabaret and concert performer, the career she's so successfully embraced ever since. Although she's mounted several of her concerts as extended engagements on Broadway, there have been only two other shows: the legendary *Carrie*, which Cook was wise enough to abandon after its pre-Broadway, London run ("Honey, I felt like I was on the Titanic," she said) and *Sondheim on Sondheim* in 2010. In 2011, Cook was the recipient of The Kennedy Center Honors.

Sitting with Cook in her home is an intimate experience despite the ongoing squawking of her two parakeets, George and Ira. She spends virtually the entire conversation leaning forward, bringing her face to mine, making sure that her points land. She is relaxed and breezy, laughing liberally. But occasionally, when she starts to sing to demonstrate a point, it's as if a switch effortlessly is flicked and this otherworldly sound comes from her. She switches it off just as quickly, but in that fleeting moment there is the feeling of being in the presence of true greatness. Then she sighs, laughs, and says something irreverent just to remind you that she's really just a simple Georgia girl.

As Amalia in *She Loves Me*.
(Photofest)

You have seriously devout fans. You have been designated as a living landmark in New York. How does it feel being idolized that way?
I know people talk about it and I am not a dope, I know some of it is true. But there's a kind of separation about it. When I am in a big venue and there are a couple of thousand people applauding, it's hard to take it in. It's almost as if it's happening to "her." I'm me and that's "her." I don't know if you've heard other people talk about that separation but I think it's pretty common. I go home and I am alone with my art and my stuff and my problems. It's very nice to hear all that

but it's hard to take it in. I used to have the tendency to feel that people gave me compliments just because they were being nice. My friend Harvey Evans is always saying to me, "You don't understand how much people love you." I do but I don't, if that makes any sense at all.

It would seem to me very hard to internalize, to understand. After all, to you, you're just you.

You got it. I'm better at taking it in than I used to be. But that's in the moment. And I am much better at saying "thank you" when someone says, "I loved you in *The Apple Tree*." And of course, I was never in *The Apple Tree*. But gosh Barabra Harris was wonderful in that. That song she did? "I want to be a mooooovie star?" I never touched that. I thought, there ain't no way I can even come close to that, it just isn't in my bones the way it is hers.

That reminds me of something you mentioned in your most recent show; you said that you never did Cole Porter because it just wasn't right on you.

Can you imagine me singing, "I get no kick from champagne/flying too high with some guy in the sky … ?" It ain't who I am. I don't know, it's not that I don't have my own kind of sophistica-

Barbara Cook	
Flahooley	Broadway, 1951
Oklahoma!	City Center, National Tour 1953
Carousel	City Center, 1954
Plain and Fancy	Broadway, 1955
Candide	Broadway, 1956
Carousel	City Center, 1957
The Music Man (Tony Award)	Broadway, 1957
The King and I	City Center, 1960
The Gay Life	Broadway, 1961
She Loves Me	Broadway, 1963
Something More	Broadway, 1964
The Unsinkable Molly Brown	National Tour, 1964
Show Boat	Lincoln Center, 1966
Funny Girl	National Tour, 1967
The Grass Harp	Broadway, 1971
Follies in Concert	Lincoln Center, 1985
Barbara Cook: A Concert for Theatre	Broadway, 1987
Carrie	Stratford on Avon, 1988
Mostly Sondheim	Broadway, 2002
Barbara Cook's Broadway	Broadway, 2004
Sondheim on Sondheim	Broadway, 2010

tion but it's just not me. That whole world, the long gloves and the champagne? I'm this shit-kickin' girl from Georgia. It's not where I live.

You're very clear about who you are and where you fit. Not everybody is.

Yeah! It's amazing to me how often it is that young people starting out don't understand how to choose songs for themselves. They don't have any idea how much of themselves they have to put into a song and how to do that. Seventeen-year-olds singing "Can't Help Lovin' That Man of Mine." I had a seventeen-year-old sing that for me and I said, "You can attempt that song, but there's no way you can know what this song is about. It's just not appropriate." Occasionally you come across an old soul who can do that, but that's rare.

Is there a single thing you try to achieve every time you perform?

You know, when I go to the theater, I really want to be moved. So I just try to let people in.

Is that the hardest thing?
It is. It's also very hard not to worry about sound or how I look. I'm fat, I'm old, I'm this, I'm that. Whatever. It's hard to let that go. But when I am really inside a song, there's nothing but the song.

Some of your choices seem to be in flagrant disregard of any of that self-consciousness. When you sing "A Wonderful Guy"—I think you started doing that in your mid-seventies.
I keep doing it because people seem to love it so much. There's a line [about being a girl] and it used to bother me. And I don't think about it at all now. It's about that wonderful exuberance of being in love no matter how old you are.

One of the things you said about your own work is "I think I act these songs as well as they've been acted."
I think I'm getting better at it. It's a process. I didn't start out doing this. I think SOME of it I do better than I did five years ago and SOME of it I'll do better in five years than I do now. Because I have more courage. In rehearsals I am very cautious. I dip my toe in and then I get in up to my ankles, then my knees, and finally I am in the water. Some people just throw themselves in and don't care what they look like in rehearsal. I can't do that. Very cautious. How far do I go? Do I really, really get into this lyric? Then I think, "Boy, if I am not willing to do it than I better not sing that song." Just recently I'm doing a song that I have loved for years but I had never ever done before. I think I just wasn't ready to do it. It's a very emotional song, "Goodbye John" by Alec Wilder. The first time I sang it in front of an audience, I had gone so far emotionally, I had opened up so much, I thought, "My god, do I look like a fool? Do I look stupid?" So I made a flip remark afterward. My son was so angry with me. He said, "I can't believe you did that. You sang the song so well and then you made this remark and took everybody down. Don't ever do that!"

You grew up in Atlanta and you started singing . . .
I don't remember when I didn't sing. It's like I breathed and I sang. I ALWAYS sang. My mother and father would take me to shows and I would come home and do the shows for them. I was like four years old. I'd do all the dances, getting on top of the tables, singing and carrying on. I had a pretty little voice. I was always the angel in the Christmas pageant. I always sang. And I was always nervous, too.

But the compulsion to sing was greater than the nerves?
I guess so. I never thought about it that way. I used to be asked by friends to sing at their weddings and I was incredibly nervous singing in church because I figured in church it had to be perfect. And I had this nervous thing that would happen: I would be singing and I would swallow involuntarily so it would stop the sound. That was something I had to deal with. When people would ask me to sing at their weddings I said, "OK, I'll do it if you don't see me. If I am behind a column or something." You know, how I managed, with all of my fears, to do what I've done, I'll never know.

But you kept going. . . .
I have always had this fear of not doing it right. When I was growing up, if you needed to make a long-distance telephone call, you had to get the long-distance operator to put the call through. You had to tell them the number. My hands would sweat so. My mother and father had divorced and I had to call my father long-distance. I was so fearful of seeming to be a fool

before this totally unknown person on the other end of the line. I would sweat so profusely that the phone would slip out of my hands. And in school, if I had to write on the blackboard, the perspiration from my hands would smear my writing. When I did a test, I always had to have a couple of pieces of paper under the test because it would be soaked with the perspiration from my hands.

Given that, how on earth did you decide to perform?
For years I was fascinated with the idea of New York. And when people would ask me what I wanted to do, I would say "musical comedy." I meant the kind of musical comedy they do in movies. I loved movies. But rather than be in movies, I wanted to be in the shows that were depicted in them, somehow. My mother had a very close friend whose brother lived here, so the three of us came to visit him. It was supposedly a two-week trip but before we left I told my mother that I was going to stay and see what I could do. I don't think she believed me. I never came home again and I never wanted to. You know, as I think of it now, as a parent, I realize that my mother must have been terrified. I was twenty years old. 1948. A girl in the big bad city. She must have been devastated.

Why do you think she let you?
She probably couldn't stop me. There was no question in my mind that I belonged here and not in Atlanta.

The first show you saw was *Oklahoma!* right?
Yeah. You would think that I would have been overjoyed to see it and I was, but the other side of me was terrified because I thought, "This is what I've come to do and I cannot imagine that I could ever be up on stage with people like that doing it. How could I ever do that?" I was absolutely terrified. These people were not human, they were superhuman.

What did you do to try to become that?
I started studying. There used to be a larger community with a lot more to do. All sorts of periodicals came out once a week about who's auditioning for this, that, and the other. I started reading all of that stuff. You meet people, you know? And I did it. And pretty soon, too. I had a show in three years. But I was also a complete nervous wreck. By then I had contacted an agent, Charlie Baker. And he had sent me out right away. I went to see him with my scrapbook under my arm. It's just so silly but there it was, with all my clippings and things, right? And that very day without ever having heard me sing, he sent me out for auditions. Later I said to him, "How did you do that?" He said, "I just knew. I didn't have to hear you, I knew." Isn't that wild? So obviously I was showing something that I didn't know I was showing, right? For one thing, physically, I was a really good type. I had nice reviews and a pretty voice or something. Vernon Duke, the composer, had sort of taken me under his wing. I don't know how I got to sing for Vernon Duke. I don't remember. But he befriended me and tried to take some of the rough Georgia edges off. Never a hint of anything other than helping. Nothing. Just total belief in my talent and trying to help me in any way he could. Personally, as well. He taught me how to eat artichokes. I had never even seen an artichoke before. We forget that before jet travel, there wasn't interest in that kind of food in this country. I am from Georgia. I had never seen an avocado! Herbs? No one cooked with herbs. You just didn't do it. It's hard to remember. I'm eighty fucking years old, you know?

Did you ever have to hold down a survival job?

From time to time. When I came here, I got a job with a subsidiary of Shell Oil. I would write letters to Venezuela all day. Or I'd type numbers. They had statistical typists because there were no computers then. All of that had to be done by hand. Then of course they had to be proofed. But once I did *Flahooley*, I never did have to go back. There were lean times but I never went back. I met Jack Cassidy in 1950. His uncle was the postmaster in Flushing, New York, and he got me a job as temporary Christmas help. We both worked there. But other than that…. And I never did waitressing. I think I'd be really bad at that.

You got *Flahooley* in 1951.

It was also 1951 when I worked at the Blue Angel, after I had done *Flahooley*. Orson Bean was on the bill and we became friends. I remember him saying to me, "God Barbara, you've done a Broadway show. You're not ever going to have to worry about anything ever again."

Do you think that's the way it was then for a lot of people? That once you did a featured part on Broadway, your career was set?

I don't know. I don't remember what I thought about that. I didn't trust what he said because … I'm not a pessimist but I also didn't believe in myself.

How could you? All you knew at that point was that you had a pretty voice. You didn't know if you could act.

I believed I could act even though I had never studied. In high school I didn't have a drama class but we had Spoken English. We had to do little short plays in front of the class. I was supposed to do something with other people but I didn't like the thing so I didn't show up for rehearsals. So I did something on my own. I found this little scene, an older woman and her husband is dying. He's in the next room. He loves the sound of the cuckoo bird in the springtime and he wants to hear the sound of the cuckoo bird one last time before he dies. She knows that's impossible so she goes out into the garden and imitates a cuckoo bird. I'm going, "cuckoo, cuckoo." Do you know how laughable that would be in most high school classes? And do you know that I had everybody in tears? I came home and I was thinking, "Jesus, I've got something." I couldn't wait to tell my mother. When she came home from work, I said, "Mom, I have something really important to tell you. I found out today in school that I can act!" And she said, "That's fine, dear, now let's do the dishes." It didn't mean a thing to her! But I knew I had something. I just knew. I knew I was talented, but I never studied acting at all or had any kind of training back then.

***Flahooley* was your first show. At your audition, the director came running up to the stage to give you a hug. That doesn't happen too often.**

No, it doesn't. It ruined me. This is the way I thought it was always gonna be. It never happened again.

What do you remember?

I remember that Sammy Fain, the composer, was such a gentleman. I remember watching auditions was painful for him because he hated the idea that he was going to have to say "no" to most people. I remember sitting out in the house with him while auditions were on after I had already been chosen and I thought everybody sang better than I did. I was scared I was going to be fired. We tried out in Pennsylvania and I remember going back to my hotel room one evening after the performance and saying to myself, "If this is what it takes to do musical theater, I don't want any part of it. I can't put myself through this." I developed all sorts of nervous ailments. And when I hear the dialogue that I did on the album, it's not very good. And Yipper [lyricist/librettist Yip Harburg] started out directing, but he was not very good at it so they brought in a man named Danny Mann. Jerry Cortland and I were the ingénues, if you will. I remember Danny taking us downstairs in the theater and trying to give us quick acting lessons. I didn't get it. Now it seems obvious but it certainly didn't then. What he told us—now remember this is my first show, never had an acting class in my life—you know how in rehearsal you pretend to pick up a glass or you pretend to open a door? God, this is embarrassing—even that, I found very hard to do. It was all so foreign, it was excruciating. I was miserable a lot of the time. I didn't want to do it again. But I don't know, something happened I guess, because I got a lot better. People kept hiring me because I sang nicely and I looked good. That's the luck of the gene pool and all that stuff.

Flahooley **didn't last long. Was that hard?**
Yeah, it was. But I never saw the show. You cannot judge a show from the stage. You CANNOT. I never saw that show so I don't know how it looked.

Your next show after *Flahooley* **was touring in** *Oklahoma!* **as Ado Annie. You were in a production of the first Broadway show you saw, only three years after saying, "I can't be those people."**
I don't remember thinking about it that way. I was still quite unsure of myself. This man Jerry White used to stage these things for the Hammerstein office and he was a son of a bitch. Some of it is not his fault; the Hammerstein office wanted the shows to be put on exactly the way they had been originally done. I get that. But you can't tell someone twelve years or more after the fact to sing "I Cain't Say No" the way that Celeste Holm did. But I tried. I was doing the gestures she did. I was miserable and I was not very good. One day before we started at City Center, I thought, "This is terrible. I have to do something. I know I can do this better." So at a technical rehearsal I did it with my sensibilities and what I thought it meant. I was convinced it was fine but he was livid. He came backstage and said, "Don't think that just because you are going on the road you can pull this kind of shit because I will turn up when you don't know I'm there." That kind of shit. So, I did what they said to do. And then I was having vocal trouble. I was getting hoarse and I went to doctors. I went to a very wise man. He said, "You know what's wrong? You hate doing this role. You have to come to terms with the fact that this is the way it is right now." And it really helped. It's amazing how things work, isn't it? That man in Chicago helped me in ways he could never know.

After Ado Annie, you played Carrie in *Carousel*. **It's interesting that you were playing the character roles.**
I didn't play the leads. In those days I didn't have confidence in those high notes. I could sing Q over X but when I did it, it felt like a trick: me pretending to be an opera singer. Believe me, the shock of my life was to find myself in *Candide*. Talk about scared to death.

But first was *Plain and Fancy,* **in which you used more soprano.**
Yeah. During "I'll Show Him." In rehearsal I thought I did it so badly I went to the choreographer and the director and said, "Please take this number away from me." And they were like, "You're out of your mind!" Let me tell you one thing about *Plain and Fancy* that you might be interested in: it has to do with the McCarthy era. A man named Stefan Schnabel played my father. He

heard that I had planned to go to an Equity meeting and he came to my dressing room and said, "Barbara, I'd advise you not to go to that meeting. But if you go, whatever you do don't vote on anything. There are people there tracking how you vote. You can be blacklisted." Now if I had been born two years earlier there's no question I would have been blacklisted. Can you believe you couldn't go to your own union meeting? You had to be careful. It happened. It really happened.

After *Plain and Fancy* came *Candide*. Was it terrifying being in the presence of Leonard Bernstein?
Yeah. He was great, though. He was very supportive. I didn't have the kind of background that most people [in the cast] did. I had never sung anything even remotely that difficult or that high. I had to find out if I could do it. And they had to find out. This tells you a lot about Leonard Bernstein: I had been working on the aria with the conductor for a couple of weeks and he said that Lenny was going to be looking in that day to see how we were doing. Honey, the highest note I had ever sung in public before was the G just over the top of the staff. And now E flat over high C. A lot of them. There were twenty-one high C's written for that role! Anyway, there is a line in "Glitter and Be Gay": "Here I droop my wings ..." and you sing a high C. Bernstein had written it to stop on that note. I asked to do a drop-down. It makes it easier to sing. That was the main reason I wanted to sing it, but it also makes sense. The wings are drooping. But this is Leonard Bernstein! I didn't know Leonard Bernstein, it was the second day I had ever been with him. And I am telling him to change the score? And he did! That tells you something about Leonard Bernstein. I am a nobody, you know? And I am telling him to do this phrase. Come on! Is that wild? For both of us! I just heard some interviews with Stephen Sondheim and he said Bernstein was a great collaborator and that's a perfect example of collaboration. The thing is written that way now. Isn't that amazing?

When you get your hands on material like that . . .
There is no material like that!

I always wonder if the first time you are hearing something so unusual . . .
I think most of the company understood that we were involved in something that was really good. Tricky, but very good. Don't forget that this was still the McCarthy era and Lillian Hellman, who wrote the book, was very political. We had a book-burning scene in there. They were making very strong comments that a lot of people were afraid to make in that era. They were being very courageous. I was very proud to be part of it and I am sure I was not the only one. I am still very proud to have been part of this group who had the courage to say that what was going on in this country was really bad. It was a major piece in that sense.

Too bad that the piece can't carry that context with it. When you see it now, you can't possibly know what it was like for a 1956 audience.
It would be nice if there was some discussion of that in the programs. What they did was very courageous. You know that great thing that Lillian Hellman said before the House Un-American Activities Committee? "I cannot and will not cut my conscience to fit this year's fashions." I loved her. I'm sure people thought she was difficult. Perhaps she was. There were all sorts of fights going on behind closed doors. At one point before we opened, she took over direction. That meant that there was a big power struggle going on. That didn't last long. I guess they didn't really collaborate well together. And I don't think [director] Tony Guthrie's work

was his best. In New York when we used to do a show, it was like this was our life, to make this show work. Tony Guthrie came from the whole English rep thing and on opening night he said, "Remember darling, it's just a play. Only a play." I loved him too. He was so funny.

What about Lillian Hellman?

I think of her as very kind. And very sensitive to what was going on around her. Much, much, much later, when I had gotten heavy and I was playing at Reno Sweeney's downtown, my manager made Tuesday nights "Celebrity Nights" to try to help with business. We'd ask a particular celebrity if they would come. By then she was quite ill. She had bad emphysema and it was hard for her to breathe, but she showed up. She got dressed, she looked great, and she showed up just to be there for me. She was a woman of her word. I admired her tremendously.

What about Bernstein? Do you have particular memories of him?

He was so kind. And supportive. And sexy? Holy shit! He'd walk in to rehearsal and you'd hear all this twittering. Very sexy man. My God. Very charismatic. Tremendous positive force. Always very thoughtful. On opening night, he was not so thoughtful. He came back to wish me good luck and said, "Oh, guess what? Callas is out front." I said, "Oh God, Lenny, I didn't need to hear that!" And he said, "Oh don't be silly, she would kill for your E flat."

After *Candide*, you were working a lot.

But you know, every time, you think you'll never work again. That's all I did at that time. Now, leading people on Broadway also have acts. They do concerts. They have to because there are not a lot of shows. But then people didn't do that because there would be another show to go to. They didn't feel they had to do television, or this, that, or the other. That part has really changed. It's good, in a way, to have more control over your life. You have to. You can't sit around waiting for the next show. Years can go by. When I first met Jack Cassidy, one of the things that intimidated me so much about working with him was that I had heard that he had already been in twenty-one musicals. And he was a young guy! And that's because in those days, you could sign for six months and you'd go from one show to the next. Or your show closes but there's always another. I hadn't done any. Scared to death.

Even after playing the lead in *Candide*, you still thought you'd never work again?

Always. And also, I think this is quite common: you pick up a script and you think, "Oh my God, this is the one I won't be able to do." You know? "Oh God, how did I do those others?" That's part of the fun in a way, but it's scary.

Then the next thing you did was *The Music Man*. You just described being daunted by scripts. Did that happen when you read *The Music Man*?

I heard the score first and I thought it was really sensational. I loved all of that talking in rhythm stuff. No one had done that before except [composer] Meredith Willson. I think he did it on radio. One of the last big radio shows was called *The Big Show* and it starred Tallullah Bankhead. He was the music director. He had this all-male chorus speak the commercials using that rhythm/speech that he did. And that's the first time anybody heard that. He took that and used it in *Music Man*. I thought it was good right from the beginning, a knockout. And it was great working with Bob Preston. It's interesting about the music: I am not inclined to sing that music now. It's kind of what I call "presentational."

Resisting the "extraordinarily sexual" Robert Preston in *The Music Man*.
(Photofest)

What do you mean by "presentational"?
I never wore a body mic. When I first started out we didn't have mics at all, but in *Music Man*, we had mics in the foots, so you had to keep your face out front. The songs had to be written in keys to support your natural power. That kind of singing is not right in an intimate place. It's written theatrically because you had to be heard. There is something to be said for all of the micing that's done now. Because that gives you the opportunity to do different kinds of songs and also the ability to sing in a more natural, believable way, to come out of dialogue and sing. It's easier in that sense. I don't mind the mics as much as some people do. And I understand the complaints, I get all of that. But there's something to be said for it, too.

But obviously you know that power of singing without the mic because you do it at the end of every concert.
I stole that from Tony Bennett.

It's a good steal.
That's what I thought.

***The Music Man* was your first big hit and you finally got to settle into a long a run. How did that success feel?**
I remember coming home on opening night. Somehow, I have a vision of opening the door and my husband saying, "Barbara, you're a hit in a hit!" And I thought, "Oh jeez, am I going

to want to do this for a year and a half?" What used to happen was that around 5:00, I would think the last thing on earth I want to do is get to the theater. But once I got started, I'd get lost and the time just flew. But thinking about doing it again, it's like, "OH MY GOD!"

How did you get through?

I used to give myself little tasks. I would think, "Do you think you can sing this song and just stand there and do it without all kinds of gestures and stuff?" Just to see if I could do it simply.

Simplicity is what you're known for now. You were working on that even then?

Well, it's not easy to stand in front of a big crowd and sing and not gesture or do something. Now obviously I chose a song that I thought it could work in. But I found it was hard. I learned a lot doing a long run.

How was working with Robert Preston?

He was wonderful to work with. Everybody felt that way. God, he had so much energy. He just sparked the whole company. He'd get on the loudspeaker and say, "How is everybody tonight?" sort of pulling us together. He was a tremendous force for good in that company. No question.

Do you remember reading the *Music Man* reviews?

Yeah, kind of. That's when people still went to Sardi's. Those were the days when you had to wait. The publicity people would call the *Times* to get the reviews. They were great, great, great reviews, And, if I remember correctly, in the Sunday, secondary reviews, Bob Preston didn't get the great, great reviews. They were good reviews, don't get me wrong, but they weren't star reviews in the way that you'd expect.

That's so odd because it's considered one of the legendary performances.

It truly is. It truly is. We watched it happen. It was extraordinary.

When you are in the toast of the town . . .

Well, we opened the same time as *West Side Story*. One of my best friends, Harvey Evans, who was in *West Side*, said, "We HATED *The Music Man*! They got the Tony." And we did. We beat *West Side*. Who knows. It's mind-blowing now. It was an extraordinarily well put together show, structured just beautifully. When we did the gypsy runthrough, the reception was unbelievable. People were stamping their feet. It was the first time we heard that rhythmic clapping over "76 Trombones" and I never failed to hear it the whole time I was in the show. People were not only standing on the seats, they were standing on the arms of the seats, screaming and yelling. Teak DeCosta, the director, said it really made him nervous because he wanted to be sure that we didn't just rest on our laurels. We worked out of town just as hard on that show as on any show I ever worked on that was in trouble. They tried new songs. He tried a whole new song for "Iowa Stubborn" that was in for maybe a few days and out. I did twelve different versions of my song, "My White Knight." Originally it was a big long song. . . . But as far as the size and weight of the song, Meredith told me that he intended it to be for Marian what the pool song was for Harold. But the scene it was in couldn't hold it. It was too much. So I did twelve different versions! I remember counting at the time. "Today Barbara, do this, but when you get here, go to version B, then back to A." Oh, Mama!

Did you see the revival?
Yes I did.

What is it like to watch a show . . .
It's odd. It's always odd. I thought that show was too loud. And it was edgy. I don't think ours was edgy. Maybe I am wrong. There was a softness that I remember feeling when I saw the show when I was on vacation. I must have seen it without Bob, though, because he insisted that our vacations would be together so that we didn't have to play it with anybody else. I remember being surprised when the Buffalo Bills sang "Lida Rose" and "Sweet and Low." When you put them together, it was just magic. That moment almost stopped the show every night. I would be on stage and think, "What the hell is going on?" It didn't seem that good to me. Not bad, but not so good as to get that kind of response. But then when I saw it from the front, I understood.

You thought this one was loud. . . .
I thought it was loud and every production I have seen of *Music Man* suffered in this sense: Bob Preston was an extraordinarily sexual guy. He had sexual power, Honey. That's one of the reasons the show worked. He could seduce the wallpaper off the wall. And in effect, he seduced every man, woman, child, and beast in the town, so it worked. It made sense that all these people got flabbergasted around him. He was this huge sexual magnet. All of the people I've seen play it since . . . there aren't that many people who have that kind of— Richard Burton had it. Leonard Bernstein, Hugh Jackman. They are few and far between. It's not that Craig Bierko was not good. I thought he was. Very good. But that super-duper element has been missing from everyone else I've seen. I can't tell you how many women wanted to meet Bob and wanted to know what it was like working with him. They went nuts about him.

You mentioned the show winning the Tony. So did you. What do you remember?
Well, it wasn't televised then. It was a dinner in the ballroom of the old Astor Hotel. It was very nice and my God I was so pleased to get it, but it was not the kind of big deal that it is now. However, I must say that it was more difficult to get a Tony in those days because there was so much more competition. And I don't mean to take anything away from people who win three and four now. I don't mean to do that at all. It's just that you were far less likely to do that then.

During *The Music Man* you got pregnant and took some time off, and then you did a show that you thought was the best thing you ever did.
The King and I. It was really good. Really, really, really good. Farley [Granger] thinks it's the best thing he ever did, too.

Richard Rodgers was also impressed, right?
Dick Rodgers always liked to see the City Center things. He'd like come in at the end and give notes. He was so bowled over. It was just great. Arthur Laurents wrote Dick Rodgers a note about the production, saying that he had not liked *The King and I* so much [originally] and he felt now it was the best thing [Rodgers had] ever done and he wished he could see it at least once a year. And he went on and on about the two of us. And Dick Rodgers wrote

back saying, that Barbara and Farley did the show much better than the originals. It was really amazing.

What made it feel like the best thing you had done?
Well, first of all, Farley and I were sensational together. We just had this wonderful, sexual thing between us that was so good. It was very sexy. And that's important in this show because you really can see what happens with them. And I don't think that happened so much with Yul Brynner and Gertrude Lawrence. No, it was kind of . . . clean. I hadn't been cast in an adult role like that. A real grown-up. And I was surprised that I was asked to do it. And Farley had a kind of sensitivity that he brought to the role that Yul Brynner didn't. Now I ain't gonna fault Yul Brynner, don't get me wrong, it's just something else. You know that, just before they dance, that moment? Oscar Hammerstein said that it was the best scene that I've ever done. I sang the bejesus out of it.

That was your third time to do a Rodgers and Hammerstein show with Rodgers and Hammerstein present. What was your relationship with them?
Well, I found them very easy to deal with. First of all, they appreciated my talent. I don't remember them so much in *Oklahoma!,* but when I first did *Carousel,* when I did Carrie Pipperidge, there's an exit that she does. Jean Darling, the original, got a laugh because when she walked off, she did some kind of flouncy little walk that made her bustle bounce. Well, when we did it, Dick said, "I want you to do [the walk]" and I said, "Why? She never walks like that any other time." "You want to get the laugh, don't you?" "I'll get the laugh, but I don't have to do it that way." And I did. And he respected me for that.

So you got Richard Rodgers to accept your staging changes, you had Bernstein change notes for you. And allegedly, when Sondheim asked you to change the phrasing on something during a rehearsal for *Follies* . . .
I said I'd think about it.

Gutsy!
Well, you know about the *Flahooley* one? When we had our first orchestra rehearsal and the conductor said to me, "You're going to have to change your phrasing here because it interferes with the saxophone," guess what I said? "Change your sax." I was twenty-three years old. I had two lives, in a sense: one was "I'm going be fired any minute," and the second was "You've gotta serve me." It doesn't make sense to me, but I know that's what happened. I said, "You have to change this number because you hired me to do what I do and I can't do it if that's in my way. So change it." Wild, isn't it? Very early on I had a very clear idea of how I wanted to present a song. Very early on, it was mine. I think a lot of that came from Mabel [Mercer] and really studying and stealing what she did. I still do. I learned a lot from her.

What did you steal from her?
The way I use consonants. The way I really, really dig into certain important words. [And what you sing] has to be backed up emotionally. As I've gotten older, I've had more courage to go farther and farther with that stuff. I wonder if people really understand the kind of courage it takes to keep doing this. Like Chita, you have to give her tremendous credit because she puts it on the line again and again.

Let's go back to the 60s. After *The King and I*, your next show, the next year, was *The Gay Life*.
Oh yeah. I'm sorry that didn't work. There were good things. [Leading man] Walter Chiari was a mistake. He was adorable, I loved him. Darling, darling man but they hired him because he was thought of as this Latin lover type. He was having this international affair with Ava Gardner. So he was this lover, right? I think he was sexy, but I think women wanted to mother him. And his English was very difficult. He didn't sing well, couldn't understand a damn thing he said. And because he didn't really have technique, if something worked, he couldn't necessarily repeat it. He was used to everything being off-the-cuff. That's what he did and obviously he was very good at it. But he was a big mistake. The original director, Gerry Freedman, was replaced by the choreographer, my friend, Herbie Ross. It just didn't work.

And they changed the show after opening. There were rewrites going . . .
Oh, it got crazy. They were trying to make it work. I remember closing night. Kermit Bloomgarden, the producer, came into my dressing room and practically cried because so much money was lost—$400,000. Of course, it's almost nothing now. You can't do anything for $400,000 these days.

That show was notable for you career-wise, because your name was above the title.
The first time, yeah. That used to mean something. That doesn't mean anything anymore.

You don't think it means something anymore?
No. People get put above the title instantly. Because producers want people to think they've got stars in the show. You really used to have to earn that.

It was the first play where you didn't have to audition—which was a big deal at the time. Did you ever audition for a musical again?
I don't remember. What did I do?

***She Loves Me, Something More, Show Boat, Funny Girl, Molly Brown*. By the way, if I hadn't done the research, I never would have known that you had done those last two shows. And I never would have conceived of you doing either of those roles.**
I was such a good Molly Brown. That again is one of the better things I did.

What about *Funny Girl*? Because a Jewish girl from Brooklyn, you're not.
I have a friend who had seen me do *Funny Girl*, but he had never seen Barbra Streisand do it. And of course, everything I did was perfect no matter what, right? I was already getting a little chubby then, too. When the movie came out, he called me and said, "Well, she's too thin and too Jewish."

How did you pull it off?
I don't know, maybe I didn't. I did it with George Hamilton. He was so good. We had wonderful chemistry. And we liked each other. He gets a bad rap, I think. He had a very clear idea of who he was as a commodity. He saw himself as a commodity. A real businessman. And

he knew what he could sell. He worked his ass off. He rehearsed as hard as anybody I've ever worked with in my life. Hard, hard worker. Not at all what you think of George Hamilton.

The next show you did after *The Gay Life* was *She Loves Me*.
It is a jewel, I'm sorry it didn't last longer. It didn't pay back, so, that's why they say it didn't work. But it was during the time of big blockbuster shows like *Hello, Dolly!*, right? And that's not what it is. Some people loved the score, some people didn't get the score. It was unusual in that there was a lot more music and a lot more sung than is typical. I think it's extremely melodic. In fact, when they played the score for me, I was sitting on a piano bench next to [composer] Jerry Bock and I practically fell off the bench. It was just one extraordinary thing after another. Hal Prince was one of the best producers I ever worked with and in some ways a really, really fine director. The one thing that I missed and that I think would have improved [the show] was a time of discovery. He sets it out in his mind and sets you into his vision and it works to a certain extent because he's so talented and so good. But who knows what would have happened if we had had that time in rehearsal to explore. We'll never know what we might have found. And you feel kind of boxed in that way. As far as I'm concerned it worked. I remember being very surprised when closing notices went up.

After that, you tried your hand at straight plays. You did *Any Wednesday* and then *Little Murders* before your next musical, *Something More*.
Something More really didn't work. It's not good.

And that's your first show with Jule Styne?
I love Jule Styne. Oh my God, he was a trip and a half. He started out directing, which was kind of a joke. And he pretty soon realized, I think, that he was not up to it. But rather than say, "Ok I can't really do this, I'm calling in somebody else," he sort of feigned fainting in rehearsal one day and said, "I can't do this because of health reasons." He couldn't do it because he couldn't do it. But he, of course, stuck around the whole time. When we were out of town and we were doing tech rehearsals, this guy who played a small role was chewing the scenery. So Jule yells out, "No George, no! Don't act, just rehearse!" He was like the cartoon of a film director in the 30s. We expected him to have a megaphone and jodhpurs and the beret. One day we were on a little break and he says, "Ok folks, ok, we're going to do twenty-one." Act 2, Scene 1. I'd never heard anybody call it twenty-one. He always called us by the names of our character. So he says to Arthur Hill, "Bill, you're going to do twenty-one, alright? And in this scene, in twenty-one … in twenty-one, in this scene … you're … offstage." When I did the *Follies* concert, the first night after curtain, he says, "Barbara baby, goddamn, you're looking great. You walked out there and you sang eight bars before you opened your mouth." He was very Damon Runyon-esque. What a trip!

Did you always read your reviews?
Oh yeah, I've always read them. I know some people don't, but to each his own. There's just no way I could not read the review. Gotta know. And now it's about business. I mean, my God, if you don't get a good review from Stephen [Holden, *New York Times* music critic], you've had it! Some reviews are so good. Rex Reed, when I did *The Grass Harp*, said, "If she was selling germ warfare, I'd buy it."

In 1966 you did *Show Boat*. You said later that during that run you came to the realization that you were getting older and couldn't keep doing the kinds of roles you had been playing.
It's very hard to describe this. I can tell you what I felt, but I can't totally explain it. It's kind of like adolescence, when you don't know who you are and you don't know where to go. It's a big transitional time. Well, the same thing is true when you're getting older. I coined the phrase "middle-essence." I didn't know where to aim myself, I didn't know what to do. And at that time, there was a big slump on Broadway. I turned down an awful lot of stuff. But I was also beginning to be an alcoholic and I was not aware of that. I just had problems. Divorce and this and that and God knows what. It was an unhappy time for me. The drinking certainly didn't help. But I thought I drank because I had problems; if I get rid of the problems I won't have to drink. But then you get to the point where you cross over and you drink because you drink and you can't fix anything 'til you stop drinking. But that's very common and that's certainly what happened with me. I just didn't know, I did not know that I was an alcoholic. I was constantly depressed.

You said you turned down a bunch of stuff....
Yes, scripts came in to me and I didn't throw them out. I turned them down and years later I would look at them and think, "This wasn't that bad. It would have been work, why the hell didn't I do it?" I didn't want to work. I needed to get my ducks in a row and I didn't know what row to put them in. And I needed some time off, but I think if I had consciously done that, I would've felt guilty, so I decided there were all sorts of reasons why I shouldn't do this, that, or the other. But a lot of it had to do with that I just didn't want to work. I wanted to step back and regroup.

In the middle of this middle-essence, you did one more book show, *The Grass Harp*.
That was a labor of love in a lot of ways. The main part of the scenery was this big tree that we all went to live in. And it was beautiful, it was a wonderful tree. We all fell in love with the tree. Truly. Just fell in love with it. I can't explain that. We felt so safe and comfortable up in that tree. It took up the whole stage. I'm sorry it didn't work. Wonderful score. And really, really great singers. Everybody could sing like crazy. There were some really good things in that show. But again, I didn't see the show. I don't know why it didn't work.

After *The Grass Harp*, you went through the period of depression and alcoholism that you mentioned. And then you started performing in cabaret at Brothers and Sisters. You once said that you didn't plan to have this whole cabaret thing become a second career.
No. There wasn't that much cabaret when we started this thing in the beginning. We [she and longtime musical director Wally Harper] just felt we'd get together and see what we could come up with. It went really well. And then Herbert Breslin saw us there and put us into Carnegie Hall. I didn't like the idea of a second career. That meant I wasn't going to continue with the theater. And I wonder sometimes why I didn't. I loved the fact that I was much more in control of my life and in control of my work. That was so appealing and I didn't want to give it up.

That's the only reason?
Well, a lot of the time I was too fat, I think. There were times when my weight was down at a good level, but people would ask me to do *Tugboat Annie* for Christ's sake. That was some musical they were going to write. *Tugboat Annie?* It was about as far from me as ... maybe not

my body but my soul. You get the picture. You know, the other thing that shocked me was when I was looking at the clippings from right around the time of the Carnegie Hall concert: every single piece is about fat. It wasn't about the work.

When you're launching something as big as a debut concert at Carnegie Hall, how do you tune that out?

It ain't easy. Somebody who I didn't even know very well sent me two photographs [of myself, thin and heavy] and he said, "How could you allow this to happen?" And another woman—I was walking in a mall in a town where I was touring, and this total stranger came up to me and she said, "Are you Barbara Cook? What have you done to yourself? How could you let yourself do this?" It's just awful. Can you imagine saying that to anybody, for any reason whatsoever?

An unexpected return to Broadway in *Sondheim on Sondheim.*
(Joan Marcus)

One of the reviews of the Carnegie Hall concert describes you twirling on the stage and really owning it. They describe you as an Earth Goddess. With all of this chatter about weight, to then be onstage and take ownership of it that way . . .

That's what I do. You know, you can stay at home and hide or you can live. Every single time in my life when I've had a choice toward life or not, what do you do? Life. I had put off saying that I would do this Carnegie concert, I was scared to death. And the day came when if I didn't say "yes," they were going to lose the date. It was so clear to me that death lay one way and life lay another way. Even before Carnegie Hall, I remember performing and I was so concerned about clothes and what I was going to wear to rehearsal and everything. I weighed like 160 pounds, it's nothing. I was crying one afternoon and my son, who was fourteen or fifteen or something, he put his arm around me and he mothered me. He shouldn't have had to do that. He said, "Mom, let's go out and we'll find something for you to wear to rehearsal. And when you sing, you'll be beautiful." My darling son did that for me.

You performed a second Carnegie Hall concert and made several recordings, but in 1985, you took on another show, if only for two nights; the all-star *Follies* concert at Lincoln Center.

Oh, that was extraordinary. When I was asked to do it, I thought, "Well now, ok, I've never done a Sondheim show. It'll be nice, I guess." I didn't really realize we had five days of rehearsal to stage all of this, all these people. And I think, maybe on the second day, it hit me that it was gonna be really good. I got really excited. Oh my goodness! I'm telling you the excitement of the audience, you'd think the place was going to levitate. It was really amazing. I just got chills.

And, of course, that began a long association with you and Sondheim.

Stephen has told me something really nice about "Buddy's Eyes." He said that was kind of a forgotten song and he said, "Barbara you've given this song a life that it wouldn't have had otherwise."

You said *Follies* made you want to do a musical again.

Yeah, it did. But it didn't happen.

Three years later . . .

Oh God, *Carrie*! Well, Terry Hands was a very seductive guy. And I really thought he had more expertise than he did. As far as musicals go, he had very little. But I figured, my God, he's been with the R.S.C. all these years, he's directed everything. And I assumed that he'd see what I saw and that it would be fixed. It was so obvious to me. It wasn't obvious to Terry Hands. But in talking with him [before rehearsals began], I could imagine myself being inside certain moments and seeing them work. So that's why I finally decided to do it. Man, they just didn't know how to put it together. They didn't understand which moments to musicalize, and that's really ABC. And nobody involved in that thing had ever done a musical from scratch. So, for instance, at one point I said, "Ok here's the kind of song that my character [needs]. This woman, this mother has to kill her child for the good of the earth. Carrie's going to destroy the world, so in order to save the world, I have to kill my child. Write me a song that talks about the pain of having to make a decision like that. And the best thing is, if the decision is made within the song. If you can do that, it would be great." So, they came back to me and said, "We've got it, we've got it, you're going to love this, Honey, we've got it."

It was a song that talks about how quiet the house is going to be when Carrie is gone. "When There's No One." That's a very pretty song, but it sure as hell didn't do anything close to what I asked for. First of all, the idea that they wouldn't know that that's something to musicalize.... Just one mistake after another. I thought, "They can't open a show like this." In the early part of the show, the girls are taking their shower and they've got their bras and underpants on. People don't keep their underclothes on in the shower! I couldn't fucking believe it. I thought, "They're just opening like this in England, they'll work it out." But no, they never worked it out. This is a good one: when Terry Hands left the R.S.C., in one of the big London papers there was this long interview with him. He said he thought he'd really made a lot of mistakes with *Carrie*. Probably the biggest mistake was deciding that it was a Greek tragedy. He said, "I was totally wrong: it's a Roman tragedy." This is for real! This is not a joke! Now this is a bright man, it absolutely boggles anybody's brain, doesn't it? That he was that obtuse? And the reason we got into Greek tragedy in the first place—here's a lovely story: the Weisslers were originally going to produce it and a year or so after it closed I ran into Fran Weissler and she said, "Did I ever tell you the story about some of those first meetings with Terry? The first meeting we had, I said it really ought to have this feeling of *Grease*. So, he came back the next time with all these drawings of everybody in togas and so forth and so on." She meant G-R-E-A-S-E [the musical] and he heard G-R-E-E-C-E! That's how he came up with the idea of Greek tragedy in the first place.

And that's why the set was all white and those clothes . . .
All of it. Also, this was cut out, but early on when the high school kids go to Farmer Brown's place to get the pig's blood, they had Trojan helmets with the bristly things [on top]. They were wearing Trojan-fucking-helmets! Well, they cut that because nobody understood what the hell that was about.

So, you're at the center of this and you see it going on around you. You've been in things that aren't working before but probably never of this magnitude.
Never. At least some of the music was very beautiful. It didn't have a hell of a lot to do with the show sometimes, but it was really beautiful. It was a hard score for me. A lot of it's belty kind of stuff that I can't do, I had to be very careful with that stuff. I did it ok, but man I had to work at it. I think Betty [Buckley, who replaced Cook after she quit] was very good for it. Better than me. I saw it several times in New York. Oh, and there was a producer there, Fritz Kurz. I said, "Fritz whatever deutschmarks you got, put the rest of them in your pocket and go! This is going to be a phenomenal failure. There's no way it cannot be. I beg you, cut and run, I'm telling you it just ain't gonna work." I would have hated for that to be the thing I came back to New York in.

Your success in later life eclipsed your earlier success. You're iconic.
That's because if you live long enough you get to be an icon. In my old age I've come to think that we allow ourselves only the amount of success that we think we deserve on some unconscious level. I think that's true for most people.

Does that mean something shifted in you wherein you gave yourself greater permission?
Well, I think something has, since I've gotten older. I've given myself a really nice place to live. It took me ages to give myself that. Having this apartment has liberated me in ways that

I would never have expected. It's cheerful and I bought all this art. There were times when I could have afforded to live in a better place than I did. I don't know why I couldn't do it. I think part of it is getting older. Things kind of settle in. You find out who you are and you stop trying to change yourself. I've gotten to the point I finally said, "This is it folks, take it or leave it. I've done about all the changing I'm gonna do." I just have a lot more self-confidence than I had for a long time and I don't feel that I need to apologize to people about who I am at all.

You never stop working. Obviously you don't need the work anymore, so what is it that keeps you going?
Oh, I feel like I need to work.

For your soul?
Because it's an important part of my life, yeah.

So there's no part of you that wants to slow down or do less?
I don't enjoy the travel so much. But I love the work and love doing it. And, you know, I don't have any desire to really stop.

Tonya Pinkins

October 2008

Most actors spend a lifetime dreaming of career success. According to Tonya Pinkins, success was her undoing. In 1992 Pinkins's career was taking off. She was appearing on the soap opera *As the World Turns*, and she had just won rave reviews and a Tony Award for *Jelly's Last Jam*. That success, says Pinkins, was too much for the ego of her then-husband. "When you're coming from a house full of women," she says, "you really don't know anything about men and have no basis for picking and choosing. I just picked a string of really bad ones." This one not only sued for divorce, he fought for and won sole custody of Pinkins's two children. She had to leave the show to focus on the court proceedings, spent years in battle, going bankrupt in the process, and found that for the rest of her career to date, despite artistic success, she'd be dealing with the fallout.

Tonya Pinkins was born in Chicago into a home inhabited by her mother, grandmother, great-grandmother, and aunts, none of whom was especially interested in the arts. A junior high school teacher saw Pinkins's talent, however, and lobbied the St. Nicholas Theater Company to allow her to study in their professional program. By age nineteen she was in New York, having been cast in the legendary flop *Merrily We Roll Along*. Her next Broadway musical was *Jelly's Last Jam*, followed by the disappointments *Chronicle of a Death Foretold*, *Play On!*, and *The Wild Party*. Then, in 2003, at The Public Theater, she took on the role of Caroline Thibodeaux in *Caroline, or Change*, one of the most fascinating anti-heroes in the history of musicals. She was a maid in 1962 Louisiana, supporting four children on $30 a week, surviving by suppressing her feelings. It was an astonishing performance that Pinkins was able to repeat on Broadway, on tour, and in the West End. After this conversation, Pinkins performed in the short-lived Tupac Shakur musical, *Holler if Ya Hear Me*, and spent the next decade focused primarily on straight plays and a great deal of TV work. In 2020, she wrote, directed, and starred in the film *Red Pill*.

In 2006, Pinkins penned a self-help book, *Get Over Yourself!: How to Drop the Drama and Claim the Life You Deserve*. She appears to have taken her own lessons to heart, because despite a litany of difficulties that could sour the best of us, Pinkins is warm, with an open, smiling face and an easy laugh. Though she describes herself as "constantly pessimistic," her aspect totally belies that.

You started studying acting in eighth grade. Did it occur to you at that point that you would want to pursue acting?
Not really. It was always sort of disappointing in a way. I always wanted it to be more than it was.

So what made you stay?
My teacher, Harris Goldenberg. He made me stay. He would take me to auditions. He was totally my stage mother.

Duke Ellington and Shakespeare combined in *Play On!*
(Photofest)

At some point you transitioned into thinking "Maybe I do want to do this. . . ."
No, that didn't happen. It was something that would come up, and I would do it. I remember when I was selecting my colleges, I got a full scholarship to Yale, but because of his influence I ended up picking Carnegie Mellon.

But you weren't there for very long.
No, because I auditioned for *Merrily We Roll Along* over the Christmas break. I didn't want to do that, either. I was on my way to Puerto Rico, and Harris said, "No, there's an open call." He was very persuasive. So I came back for the open call and ended up getting cast and going to New York, knowing the show would not happen for almost another year. But these were the gods of the theater [Stephen Sondheim and director Hal Prince].

Did that you lead you to finally embrace acting as a career?
I didn't ever feel like this was "it" or going to be "it." I probably spent the majority of my career trying to leave it, but jobs kept coming and I knew that work is such a precious thing. I knew so many people who didn't have it, so if it was offered, I would take it.

Were you able to really believe in yourself if you weren't committed to it?
I used to think, "I don't know what they're seeing. I don't get it." It didn't feel very secure because they were responding to something that I was not doing, and I wasn't in control of. They were responding to something about which I felt, "I don't know why it's here today, and

I can't tell you I'm going to be able to create this tomorrow," so that was a very scary thing. [I just never got excited about these things] and my agent used to say, "Nothing ever affects you," because I would just say, "Oh, I got this job? OK. Thank you."

You got to New York in 1981 and got a place on 47th and Broadway. That was the heart of Times Square at its seediest.
Oh, yeah, I lived in it. I remember visiting New York; it was a scary place. I didn't really like it. I turned Juilliard down because it was in New York. I remember one of the first days I was in New York I was on a bus and I saw a car almost run over a biker, who threw down his bike, got off, started bashing the car's windshield and meanwhile somebody stole the bike. I'm thinking, "OK, this is New York."

Tonya Pinkins	
Merrily We Roll Along	Broadway, 1981
A My Name Is Alice	off-Broadway, 1984
Jelly's Last Jam (Tony Award)	Broadway, 1992
Chronicle of a Death Foretold	Broadway, 1995
Play On!	Broadway, 1997
The Wild Party	Broadway, 2000
House of Flowers	Encores!, 2003
Caroline, or Change	off-Broadway, 2003; Broadway, 2004; National Tour, 2005; West End, 2006
Holler if Ya Hear Me	Broadway, 2014

What do you remember about working on *Merrily*?
It was probably one of the most devastating experiences of my life but also one of the most educational. Everything that could possibly go wrong went wrong. [But later] when I'd go to other shows and things would go wrong, I would be unfazed. I was sort of just watching because it was a world I didn't know anything about. It was completely alien and foreign to me so I was just observing the politics, the rules. I've always been a very anti-clique person, so that always made me an outsider in a lot of ways. I would just watch a lot of things. Very bizarre, strange things happened on that show. You'd show up to rehearse your scene, and somebody else would be doing your part.

Since you had no context for having done a Broadway show before, did it feel like maybe that's how it works?
No, it never felt like this is how it works. It felt chaotic and like, "What are these people doing?"

Could you tell that the show was not working, or could you not be objective about it at that time?
I knew very early that it wasn't working and as I watched the changes that were being made I knew they weren't going to work. But I was nineteen years old so who cares. The day they cut all the costumes and the wigs, that was like, "OK, maybe this is a tax write-off or something."

Do you have a specific recollection of working with Sondheim?
No, because we didn't really work with him. But we got invited to his home for a party and he showed us his working room. I remember he opened the door where he housed his scores and there were all the empty shelves for the ones yet to be written. I loved that. At Hal's house, they had a rotunda foyer with one of his many Tonys spotlit.

Where do you keep your Tony?
I don't have my Tony.

Where's your Tony?
I don't know. It's a long story. I don't know where it is. I may never see it again.

You said before that it was one of the most devastating experiences. It got you to New York and then it was over in a couple months.
I don't know if that was the devastating part of it. It was more, "What have I gotten myself into?"

You decided to go to Yale at that point....
Yeah, but I didn't. I was up for *All My Children*, which was my favorite show in the whole wide world. I turned down a show at Actors Theater of Louisville because I had a screen test for *All My Children*. I didn't get it but shortly after I ended up on *As the World Turns*. The thought of being on a soap was really exciting to me. I think I quit in my third year.

Why?
I wasn't in a happy place. I'm like the most negative interview you're getting, right? But those people were so unhappy. It was the most cutthroat place I'd ever been.

After you left...
I had two kids. And I started studying acting with Bill Esper. I'd do a scene and my son, Max, would be there with me on my fanny thing.

So if you went back to class, had you decided to really commit to acting?
Yes, I did. I wanted to be really good, and I wanted to know how to produce this thing that people were so fascinated by. I wanted to have a craft to do that with. You're here, this is what you do, get good at it. I was there for two years, but I left in the second year because I did *The Piano Lesson*. That was my greatest failure. I remember I did a great audition. I almost intuitively did Lloyd Richards's blocking, but then when I got there, I always felt like I just didn't fit. Something was wrong. I never felt like I was giving them what they wanted. I didn't get it, I didn't bring it, I didn't fit. I think there are the August Wilson actors, and I'm not one of them. The August Wilson actors were this whole crop of character actors who would never get to Broadway were it not for August writing all these amazing roles. They're so good at the character thing. At the risk of sounding conceited, I have a star quality that doesn't fit into that. I think the plays went awry when they started sticking stars in the mix of that ensemble thing. I think that all those character actors in August's plays, in terms of the work, they're special, but they're lacking ... what would I call it? Graciela Daniele once told me that Bernie Jacobs closed *Once on This Island* when it was still playing at 80 percent capacity. He said, "It's just not a limousine play." I think that that's the quality beyond talent that makes stars. Can we see you getting out of a limousine and coming and hanging out at our party? That's my feeling.

So that said, having the career that you've had, do you think that you've been chosen?
Absolutely.

And what do you think made the difference for you?

That I'm articulate. That my teacher taught me early on how to be in the room and so I'm poised. I'm someone that people with that kind of wealth and power feel comfortable having in the room.

It sounds classist.

I think it is.

At what point did you realize that you were chosen?

I think the first time that I became really aware of it was working on a show called *Play On!* We were trying to work as a team of actors to make our contracts be the same. The producers had sort of put me in the position of the star and were offering me better. I remember that at that point it was the first time I realized, "Oh, they aren't going to value certain people." Others were brilliant, talented, just not valued. I don't even know how to describe it. It's just the kind of sense that I have. I knew I was getting chosen to have opportunities and that it didn't have anything to do with my talent, so I wanted my talent to match the opportunities that I was going to get to have that other people weren't.

You did a number of straight plays in the late 80s and early 90s, and then *Jelly's Last Jam*.

Jelly was supposed to start on Monday. I auditioned on the Friday and the Saturday before it started. I had just come off *The Caucasian Chalk Circle* at The Public with George C. Wolfe and I think it was like, "What about her? Let's give her a try." That's the show that I earned my stripes on. I really came to trust my talent and ability to be a good actor. For the audition, I only got to see some sides, and [the role] was written like your typical sassy Black girl. It wasn't until I was on the plane [on the way to L.A. to take the job] that I got to read the whole script. I realized that this woman is amazing and powerful and like my grandmothers and aunts. I didn't even know if I had it in me. I went into that show just paralyzed, paralyzed. I felt I had something extraordinary and I did not know that I had the capacity. I was just scared. And then to top it off, I was in a room with actors who had played my role before and were now in the chorus. So I'm in a room full of all these people who know each other and have worked together, and then I come in. I'm not one to try to impress people—the way I work in rehearsals—I don't do anything. I just come in, and I read. I'm just taking in and researching. Some people come in and what they give you at a first read-through is what their first performance is going to be. In TV if you don't give it to them on the first read, you're fired. I would work on all the things I wanted to do at home, but I didn't have enough confidence in them that if I tried them, and I'd gotten a note, that I'd be able to trust myself to do them again. So I had decided that I was not going to do any of my ideas until I had a run-through where I knew I could get through the whole thing without a note. I just felt like one note and I'd be like, "I was wrong. I can't do this." So that's what I did.

But you hadn't communicated that?

No.

So for all they knew . . .

She sucks.

It didn't occur to you to say, "Trust me"?

No, because I didn't trust me. I knew I was working on stuff, but I didn't know that it was going to work.

So you get to do it at the run-through, you unleash.

And all hell broke loose. I don't really know the backstage of what happened, but people were so blown away, although unhappily. It was almost like they had all plotted that I was going to be gone, and suddenly it was like, not only was I not what they thought, I was so much more. The whole show was going to have to adjust to that. It was not a happy moment.

You'd think they'd be thrilled that you finally came through.

The lead actor, Obba Babatunde, was very unhappy with me. There were five women principals at the time and nobody ever thought that my character was that important. So I'm shifting the balance of the play, and I'm now getting all the notes. But once I did it at that run-through, and I experienced how it worked and how the room took it, I knew I found this and I could not ever back off of it. Everybody was ready for my ship to sink.

Well, I can understand why people would be upset. You're getting close to opening, and suddenly you've just shifted the balance of the show, and everything that they were working on.

But I couldn't do it any other way. I was too afraid.

Were you apologetic at all?

No.

Do you have the sense that if someone else had done that in your show you might be a little uneasy about it?

No. No. Bring it. I want you to bring something new every day. Let's do it. We're creating it right here in the spot. When Gregory Hines came into the show he had the opposite problem; he had a forty-year career already and he knew how to have an audience eating out of the palm of his hand. George essentially said, "This is not Gregory Hines. You have to pull all of that." Ultimately he embraced it, but it was rough going through the rehearsals because he did not want to give up what he knew worked. Working with him was fantastic once he knew he could trust me.

Was it an adjustment singing again after so long?

It was definitely. The singing thing was awkward. When I came to New York, Black women were supposed to sing gospel. I don't do that. I don't riff. I'm Catholic. We don't sing like that. So that was another place where I always felt fake and inauthentic. Whenever I'd play the sassy Black woman, that just didn't feel like my truth. Going into *Jelly*, I was also working with a lot of riffers, some of the most amazing singers. There was always a sense of insecurity about the fact that I don't do that. And then there was [musical director] Luther Henderson, who very much wanted my character, Anita, to be like Lena Horne. So I was getting coached on how to have that quality and I didn't know that I definitely wanted her to be that. It was interesting because he's a god of the theater as well....

Recording *Jelly's Last Jam* with Gregory Hines.
(Photofest)

It sounds like you were being bombarded with all kinds of mixed signals that you had to synthesize.

I think that's what growing up is. The world is always going to be giving you input and it's your job to see what's meaningful and throw away what isn't. So *Jelly* was the place where I found out that I was a good actor and that I knew how to make good choices. I didn't question it in that same way ever again.

And it paid off, obviously. You got the Tony.

I can't say it was because I deserved the Tony. I lobbied and worked really hard for that Tony.

What did you do?

I hired a publicist who was charging me $250 a month. Leonard Fink. We would get together in the evenings, and we would come up with what we were going to be selling about Tonya Pinkins because nobody knew who Tonya Pinkins was and nobody cared. Len Fink and I would write articles. We'd get new press. I'd get new pictures and we'd just send them and everybody would say, "No." We'd come up with a new story, and we'd just keep sending packages. Every night we'd come up with some angle. And the way it felt—because I don't know what's going on inside the workings of the business—is that when the reviews finally came out, and they were good, suddenly I got a bunch of press, but I got it because they already had all the materials about me for months. It was all there, in place for them to run all kinds of stories. When those nominations started coming, I was in *People* magazine six weeks in a row, but that was because of Leonard and me.

What were you coming up with to be sending?
I don't know. We'd think of a personal interest story. We'd just come up with things and kept doing it. And still, *The New York Times* said I wasn't going to win the Tony that year. I hadn't been chosen yet.

So these nominations start happening, and at that point you feel like it was because you'd been campaigning?
Absolutely. I didn't have some idea that, "Oh, I'm so good." At that point, I knew that the work I was doing was work that I was proud of but I had no illusions beyond that.

So was there a feeling of inauthenticity when you got the nomination? Like you had won the con?
No, because that's how you get the awards. And then once you're in the club of people who get awards, you get nominated more because you're already in the club. That's a different thing. But being good was my personal thing and I had to do that for me. The rest of that, if I can play that game right, then that may play into some other things.

But the awards part is business?
That's business.

During your run in the show, as you were signing autographs one night . . .
I said, "Oh, where do you want me to sign. What's your name?" And the guy says, "No, this is for you." I open it and it's a divorce summons. I was getting a little big and my husband wasn't about to let that happen. I won every award you could win. I'm having meetings with Woody Allen, James Brooks. It was like my career was about to happen and he didn't like it.

And when you got home that night?
He just sits there. To this day he will say that I divorced him. I had to walk away from all the work stuff to focus on my divorce and I end up losing. I ended up losing custody of my kids a year later.

So you left the show and the soap [Pinkins was also on *All My Children* at the same time] and spent your life savings . . .
More than my life's savings because it's still going on today. My last child isn't twenty-one yet.

You walked away from everything you had been working toward to try to sort this out.
I didn't care. I didn't care at all.

And you spent how many years caught up in this battle?
The next six or seven.

You represented yourself in court.
Well, that's after I lost. I didn't have any more money. This is the first time where the game didn't work. And I think that had a lot to do with me being a very successful Black woman. That was actually my first experience with racism because I know [that] I know how to play the game. I'm in court every day with the pearls and the ponytail and the shoes. My

ex-husband's playing, "She's an angry Black woman, and I fear for my life from her." Here's a White judge looking at a White guy and a Black woman, and he says, "On balance, it goes to the father." And they get to do that. They don't answer to anyone.

Well, you go through the appeal process?
Right. I went through more than that. I actually was able to prove that the entire case should have been thrown out, but nothing ever changed.

Your next show in New York was *The Merry Wives of Windsor* at Shakespeare in the Park.
That went badly because I had to go to court for something and there was a chain of command issue at the theater where whomever was supposed to tell whomever didn't tell whomever. They just threw me under the bus and acted like I never told anybody. They acted like I just walked out of a dress rehearsal. Everybody was mad at me and my reputation was bad. For the last performance, I got stuck in traffic, and I got there late. They didn't let me do the show. It was ugly, but I was doing my life, and ultimately there was nothing else that was any more important than me doing my life.

After *Merry*, you did *Chronicle of a Death Foretold*.
What a fab experience. I love Graciela Daniele, just love her. But I had to leave that show because they started garnishing my wages without ever having a trial to determine what I owed. They just started taking money. So I said, "Then I'm not working." And I left the show. I wasn't getting paid. They were taking 65 percent.

That was your first time working with Graciela, right?
I love Graciela. She's brilliantly talented, and she's loving and nurturing, and it's about the people. For a lot of directors, it is all about the show and forget the humans. She's all about the people. I think that can have its good side and its bad side. I watch directors who will abuse people in the name of their vision. Gracie's like, screw the vision. If the actor can't do it, oh, well, that's who we hired. We're not firing anybody. We will make it work.

Two years later you did *Play On!*
First I went back to finish college. I get pregnant and what am I going to do with myself? Everybody's telling me I should be a lawyer and then I get accepted with a full scholarship to a two-year law school in San Diego. And right at the same time I get an offer to do *Play On!* at The Old Globe in San Diego. I call [director] Sheldon Epps, and I say, "Sheldon, these Erte gowns.… Is that locked in stone because I'm pregnant." "How pregnant?" "Oh, you know, just a little." I don't tell them that on the day we start rehearsal I'm seven months pregnant, wearing a girdle to keep everything in and working out vigorously. They're designing these costumes to grow and grow and grow. They don't know it ain't going to be growing much longer.

Did you give birth while you're doing the show at The Old Globe?
Yes. During the run.

What happened to law school when you went to New York with the show?
I had to leave law school, which was very disappointing. *Play On!* was another rough one. I mean I have had rough experiences but they taught me great lessons. I've always been trying

to help everybody. I'm the union organizer. On *Play On!* [we tried to organize favored nations contracts and it went badly]. But I loved the show, and I loved the cast so much.

That show closed pretty quickly, and you went through a lot for it. You moved back to New York with a newborn, you gave up law....
That one was really disappointing. To this day I've been trying to get people to bring that show back or take it to London. That show was fantastic. It broke every box office record at all the regional theaters. That was just bad producing. And that was the point at which I started thinking I should be a producer. But let me tell you, I have learned I am not producer material.

Why?
It's 24/7 and it requires a lot of manipulation.

You're good at playing the game.
I used to be. Not anymore.

When did that change?
Probably when I got my [dread] locks. I didn't want to play the game anymore. [I knew not having] white girl hair was going to substantially cut probably 75 percent of my opportunities. But I don't want to spend five hours a week in the hairdresser. And at that point in time I don't think I had any shows going on anyway. It wasn't like I was working. We do *Play On!* on the road and I get pregnant again. I have my last son, and I moved to Mexico.

Mexico?
Well, I knew it was either Mexico or Canada. Canada you get free health insurance. Mexico you can buy oceanfront property if you're a citizen. So I decided to go to Mexico and raise my child. Manuel was born there.

What got you out of Mexico?
Manuel almost died. He got some illness and nobody ever figured out what it was, but he lost half of his body weight. So I came back to L.A. I was school teaching, substituting, trying to get some voiceovers.

And then *The Wild Party* happens?
Yes. I was very bad on that one.

What do you mean?
First they take like four months to negotiate because George Wolfe thinks I'm too heavy. They don't know how to tell me. So the negotiations are dragging on for four months because nobody will tell me that they think I need to lose weight. George is actually very, very sensitive about things like that. You know, he can seem very glib about some things, and then other things ... he really didn't like confrontation. Really and truly. Finally we work that out, and I do it.

And your experience on that show?
I'm just such a busybody, know-it-all. I looked at the script, and I said, "I'll do this because the play doesn't begin until I walk in the room. Obviously they're going to develop me." But that

wasn't the intention. They were creating something new, and I'm always on board to create something new. It just wasn't the right combination, in my opinion, to create something new.

How do you mean? The right combination of artists?
I don't know, but we didn't create something new. Well, we did do something new, and now you see a lot of shows that are kind of like that. So, we did break ground, and it was the most incredible, artistic thing to ever work on because you had to be on stage nonstop and you had to create that life continuously. No going off stage ever. Amazing. Just amazing. And people did some extraordinary work.

Do you have a specific recollection of working with Eartha Kitt on that?
She would act all old, like she can't do anything, and then she steps onto the stage and she knocks it out! She's just great. She's just the loveliest, loveliest woman. And so simple—so not her character. The woman is not [what people think of as] Eartha Kitt.

What about Toni Collette?
They loved her. I, on the other hand, thought that she was why the show died and told her.

You told her that?
I'm bad. And of course she'll never speak to me again. The experience that I would have right here with Toni [face to face] oh, my God, she's brilliant. Amazing. I just never felt it went across footlights. Now, she's a star. She's a movie star, and they kept rewriting to accommodate her. We never did the same show twice and that largely had to do with the fact there were things that Toni just wouldn't do. Like conflict. So here we have a poem [the original source material] that doesn't have any conflict, and every time they try to impose it, Toni says things like, "Well, if she did that to me, I'd just leave," and she would leave. And so they'd have to write a new number. So I'm watching a show that's getting worse and worse because they're writing the material that the actress will do and trying to tell a story that ain't a great story to begin with and doesn't have any conflict. And then the actress won't play conflict. It wasn't like I said, "You're bad," I was just trying to say, "This is what the theater is. It's conflict. Movies are the look, the reaction. In theater we want to see what happens when you can't do what you want to do. Conflict."

And you told her this?
Mm-hmm.

In what context and what made you decide that you were going to do that?
I think I was frustrated because I really needed the job and I wanted this show to work. I loved this show and I knew she was the star. The show was her. She was going to make that show. I knew she'd be loved, and I knew she'd get nominated. All of that was guaranteed. But I also knew what that character had to be to make the show work. Mandy Patinkin is a force to be reckoned with. To me, that's what you get on the stage for. He's going to give you something every day, and if you walk away from it, then we're missing why we're at the theater.

So when you say you were bad on that show—
Well, I feel like that was just none of my business and not my place to do. But at that point I needed the job! I hadn't done anything in forever, and Toni was it. This show was going to rise and fall on her.

So when that didn't work either, how is it that you never lost faith in the business?
I never had any faith in the business. I still don't have any faith in the business. But the work itself. . . . Because when you're doing the work itself, it's like good sex. It's like an orgasm. All of the rest is a nightmare. I don't think it's ever going to be anything but a nightmare. But the work itself is worth it.

When *The Wild Party* closed, you were offered *Thoroughly Modern Millie* in San Diego, pre-Broadway.
I thought, "I just got offered a part with all these great people. I should be happy, but [I'm wary because they] just fired Yvette Cason who is brilliant." It was not a fit for me. I haven't yet mastered—and I'm working on it right now—light with no depth, just fun and silly. So it wasn't a fit because my anchor, my security blanket to being an actress, is to step in the technique. And Yvette told me that she tore it up, and that it was great and a great role for her. I could see that because Yvette is one of the most astonishing jazz singers on the planet. I don't do that so I needed to be able to do something else. What I ultimately decided was they wanted somebody in the club in that role. That's why they picked me. She wasn't yet in the club.

So you're saying talent-wise, you weren't bringing anything to the table that she didn't have? They just wanted somebody in the club?
That's what I think. But I wasn't a fit. I'm not interested in playing light and frothy but that was what that show was about. I gave them all the notes, and they took my notes, and they fired me. That's my story. They took all my notes, but they got rid of me.

But that was a role you were perfectly happy not to continue on in?
Absolutely. I thought it was just weak. I know what a show-stopping song is. I know what you get a Tony for. Neither of those songs were it. And Sheryl Lee Ralph [who replaced Pinkins] didn't even get nominated. Even with the new material. You know as an artist when someone's giving you material that will stop a show. Give me the material. I know how to stop a show.

***Caroline, or Change* came next.**
That was just a great gift of a show for me. I didn't know what it was when I got in it. I just wanted to be in the room with those people, and as a general rule, that's how I take projects. Is it a bunch of people who I respect and I want to be in the room with? I don't even care if they succeed. I want to be in the room with them. When I first read it, I didn't understand it. I was thinking, "This is completely unlike what we are accustomed to drama being. Show me how you do this."

Every single show that you'd done up until now, you have described as a "tough one." Here's one that was perfect. You're creating something, it was your role, your show. This was the role of a lifetime in a show that you loved being in, and yet when it was moving to Broadway, you were prepared to walk away during negotiations. That's hugely brave.
Not to me. To me it was just simple. I understand the game, and I'll play the game with you, but don't think I don't understand that we're playing a game. I understand what the game is, I understand what you have to do, but don't think I'm stupid. I wrote the producers a letter: "You are the smartest producers in the whole world. You put this budget together and you

With Chandra Wilson in the heartbreaking *Caroline, or Change*.
(Photofest)

obviously know what you need. I am sure it will be a success without me. Good luck." We got exactly what we asked for, which was not anything unreasonable. Not even half of what the other ladies on Broadway were getting at the time. But if that's the game, that's the game.

When the show opened on Broadway, you were back on *All My Children*.
It was the most-perfect fit for me. I get to go do the fun stuff and play with all the cute actors during the day and then go do the hard stuff at night, and it was just perfect. Like in a certain sense, if I don't ever do anything else again, I got to have the best time. I've had some great opportunities in my life.

This was your first time carrying a show. How did that feel?
It was great, and that was when I finally got the lesson: you have a responsibility to other people. When I was nominated for the Tony, all of the producers and so many people were out there making calls, lobbying for me to get these nominations. The sense of responsibility to them, and the awareness that not winning was as painful for them as for me.... I know how hard they worked. [But in the end] it's politics. It's not about work.

Was that Tony experience different for you this time?
Absolutely. I'd never been invited to as many parties. Every day. Breakfast, lunch, dinner, after-show drinks. That six weeks I felt like this must be what a presidential campaign is like. You are glad-handing, smiling, parties. And I knew what the voters' problem was with me. I'd been told that they didn't like my curtain call. They wanted me to come out and be happy and smiling and a different person [than I had been on stage]. It was like "the Black girl scared us

and we need to know she's safe." I wouldn't give to them. It was kind of a choice. I'm not giving you that.

Do you have any regret about that?
No, because it wouldn't have made a difference. They were going to close our show no matter what. My winning a Tony—they would have closed our show, and I'd have been more pissed.

Playing the show, you've said having gone through what you went through with your own battles, you already knew Caroline so well—
I did. Oh, it was so satisfying. Here I'm walking around with all this rage, all this horrible stuff that's still having me in the courtroom, and I have a place every night where I can go and let it all come out.

You started to have vocal trouble during the run, didn't you?
They didn't trust me vocally. It had been this effortless vocal thing, and they put me with Joan Lader, who was extraordinary, extraordinary. She's got an amazing gift. But if you teach me something, I'm going to try to learn it 1,000 percent. Joan is a teacher for someone who's in trouble. She teaches all these in-trouble techniques. So I'm trying her in-trouble techniques, and I get in trouble. I start to lose my voice. And honestly, it's probably for the better, I never recovered the facility and skill that I had before because I completely lost the ability to know what I used to do. I always just had a natural ability to do what I did. I made up voices and characters, and I just did it. There was no technique involved in it. And suddenly, I'm trying all these techniques and I forget how to just naturally sing.

Do you still feel that way?
I lost my voice completely, and when the show was going to London, they didn't think I could sing it. They weren't going to bring me to London. I had to audition. Also, when I got to London, I was no longer the person—all that rage and stuff was gone. I was lighter, happier. When I would try to do the rage, my body would just reject it. I had this amazing teacher there, Annemette Verspeak, who had to teach me a technique whereby I could still produce what I did, because before I was just living it.

What changed?
Well, after doing it and going on the road and the reception in L.A. and San Francisco, it was just a great time, and I just cried all those tears. I had money saved and didn't have to worry about it, so I was living a way I had never lived in my entire life.

Happily?
Never lived that way in my entire life. It was a lovely time. So going back to it, my body was like "no, we're not doing that." I had to work hard to find a physical posture for her.

After *Caroline*—your next Broadway show was *Radio Golf*, and since then you've only done straight plays. What do you want to be doing, or what do you think it looks like next?
I don't know. I am trying to figure out what I'm going to do with the rest of my life because acting isn't enough. I know what I like. I know what I want. I know what I think. I have a sense of a whole play. And so I have made decisions to not even take meetings on certain projects

where I felt that my personality and the fact that I have so much to say would not be a fit for that group.

Do you feel part of the community?

Absolutely. But you know we don't see each other very often except during award seasons when we're at the damn parties. When we did that yearbook picture of all the Tony winners that were still alive and could get there, it was just like, "Oh, my God, I'm in the club." Yeah, that's thrilling. Forever, I'm in that club. If I never do anything ever again in my whole life, I'm in that club.

Faith Prince

April 2022

"It's always the hard way for me," says Faith Prince without a whiff of self-pity, as she describes that everything she's achieved has been a struggle. It's not what I expected from a woman whose career exploded in 1992 when, all sniffles and squeals, she captivated New York as Miss Adelaide in *Guys and Dolls*, taking home every award they could throw at her. But she was hardly an overnight sensation. "It took me ten years to get a Broadway show," she says. Nor was she happy with all that attention. What she was happy about was the work. Miss Adelaide made her a star and that stardom has ensured a steady career on Broadway in both musicals and straight plays, on TV, and in concert halls across the country. If she ever wrote a book, Prince laughs, it would be called "Just Famous Enough."

Faith Prince grew up in Lynchburg, Virginia, and found out in church, as so many do, that she enjoyed an audience. That realization eventually took her to the Cincinnati Conservatory of Music, and then New York. Her pre-Broadway decade was prolific, full of off-Broadway and regional credits, including the original production of *Little Shop of Horrors*. Her Broadway debut came in *Jerome Robbins' Broadway*, where, in a show composed of showstoppers, she, along with Debbie Gravitte and Susann Fletcher, blew the roof off the Imperial Theater with "You've Got to Get a Gimmick." In that one scene, Prince deployed that unique combination of characteristics that would define her career: razor-sharp timing, daffy physicality, a nasal yet clarion belt, and delicious unscripted giggles, chirps, sighs, and utterances of joy. (Think of the sounds she makes during her "Gimmick" "ballet," or the "ah-ha" moments she finds in "Adelaide's Lament" from *Guys and Dolls* as she figures out the words "see note."). Prince references Madeline Kahn when we talk, and it's an apt comparison. Like Kahn's, Prince's comedy doesn't stem from trying to be funny per se, it just is, when there are stakes to commit to and the material is right. Her comedic gifts were on display most famously in *Guys and Dolls*, and many of the shows that followed (*Little Me*, *Bells Are Ringing*, *Noises Off*, *The Little Mermaid*, *Billy Elliot*, *Annie*, and *Disaster!*). But Prince was no less compelling in dramatic roles (*The King and I*, *A Man of No Importance*, and *James Joyce's The Dead*), where that effervescence was calibrated, whittled down to a glint in the eye or a sly smile. *A Catered Affair* presented the one opportunity (to date) to step into the shoes of a character whose light had been all but completely extinguished. Prince rose to the occasion, with an unfussy, egoless, and utterly heartbreaking performance that should quell any notion that she can't dig deep.

"I'm not the woman you aspire to be," Prince told me in our first conversation. "I'm somebody you relate to. I'm every woman. And I like that about myself. I know what I am. I've never been, 'Oh, woe is me. I'm not the beauty.' Fuck that. When people say, 'You could be thinner,' yeah, I could, but I'm not. I still like myself. I've got a cute and talented husband as well as a great and talented son. I like that I'm quirky. I can have pink hair at sixty-four. I'm working it how I need to work it." And we, the audience, get to be the lucky spectators, watching her "work it" in a career spanning four decades—and counting!

"Someday I'll land in the nuthouse. . . ." As Miss Hannigan in *Annie*.
(Joan Marcus)

As I understand it, your earliest theatrical influences were playing Raggedy Ann at six in school and then performing in *The King and I* in Lynchburg. Is that when the bug bit?

It actually happened earlier than all of that. My first recollections were when I was three. In church they asked me to do the welcome before a Sunday supper or something like that. I was really proud because I had just learned to be potty-trained. And I said, "My bowels moved three times today!" My mother was going, "Hush now! Hush, Faith. We don't need to tell that." But I could feel the power of commanding an audience just from that. I remember noting that I really enjoyed being in front of people. That stuck with me. My mother was more tentative than I am. My dad was kind of a piece of work. He was a really smart man, a nuclear engineer. My mother is also extremely bright. They both made really good grades in school and their work ethic was an example and set the bar for me. I remember that anything they did, they did extremely well. They both had great personalities. They were funny: she was tall, he

Faith Prince	
Scrambled Feet	off-Broadway, 1980
Tintypes	National Tour, 1980
Little Shop of Horrors	off-Broadway, 1983
Groucho: A Life in Revue	off-Broadway, 1986
Jerome Robbins' Broadway	Broadway, 1989
Falsettoland	off-Broadway, 1990
Nick and Nora	Broadway, 1991
Guys and Dolls (Tony Award)	Broadway, 1992
Fiorello!	Encores!, 1994
Du Barry Was a Lady	Encores!, 1996
The King and I	Broadway, 1997
Little Me	Broadway, 1998
James Joyce's The Dead	Broadway, 2000
Bells Are Ringing	Broadway, 2001
A Man of No Importance	off-Broadway, 2002
A Catered Affair	Broadway, 2008
The Little Mermaid	Broadway, 2009
Billy Elliot	National Tour, 2010
Annie	Broadway, 2013
Disaster!	Broadway, 2016

was short. She was kind of soft and elegant and he was … I would describe him as a fire hydrant. A little Mickey Rooney when he was sort of good-looking. Tight, and maybe with a little Napoleon complex. My timing comes from both of them in different ways. My mother has this cackle laugh and is kind of wacky, and my dad is just rapid-fire. He was a real entertainer. A vaudevillian, of sorts! I think that's how I came to understand and appreciate that particular style of performing. I was really marinating in being part of both of them. I remember him entertaining people when they'd come over and I'd always think, "I could do that," as a kid sitting on the sidelines. The storytelling is just epic in my family. Very Southern. So, all that contributed to this sort of amalgamation of the beginning of me. There is a logic to how any performer, or any person, for that matter, becomes who they become. And it starts the moment you're born. That's the raw material, and then it's on you to do something with it. There is a lot more you can do for yourself than one might imagine. It's not just like, "Oh gee, I hope the world sees me." No. I knew I was going to have to get out there and make it happen, both in career and love. I was not going to be a person that was just going to be picked from the side. I didn't have that kind of energy and I didn't mind. I'm a slow mover. Not everybody has the same way into this business. I knew I was going to have to create my way in.

Well, you did. Your first show happened because you raised your hand during a post-performance Q & A.
I made it happen. I asked. And I asked nicely. I wasn't pushy. I always tell my students, "Nudge gently."

So there you are, having gotten out of conservatory, newly in New York...
After getting my Equity card in Washington. I had met a choreographer at the Wagon Wheel Playhouse where I had done three summers of shows [and she suggested me] for a revue at a hotel. Nobody ever came. There was no one in the audience but it did give me my Equity card. During the day I was waitressing on this little seafood boat, and I just thought that was magical. People would just leave me money and I couldn't wait to see what they left me! I was pretty good at it. I've always been good with people. I was camp counselor, R.A. at college ... I love people, I really do. Not so much anymore. Now, I'm like Elaine Stritch; I'm a little crabby. [Anyway], Jimmy Walton, who had gone to CCM, was going on in *Scrambled Feet*, this little revue with three men, a woman, a piano, and a duck. My mom was coming to see me for the first time, [so we went]. They had a [Q & A for a college group] afterwards and I still to this day don't know what possessed me, but I raised my hand. "Do you need another girl?" One of the guys in the show happened to be the director and writer and he said, "As a matter of fact we do, for our cast in Boston. Talk to the stage manager and we'll get you an audition." It was actually my mother who turned to me at intermission and said, "You'd be really great in this." I hadn't been thinking that way. And she's not Mama Rose at all.

So you auditioned and you got it!
In Boston, to replace Evalyn Baron. I was thrilled. I was coming in with so much energy, but I was scared to death. I had been scared to death to go to CCM, too. I think I cried every night my freshman year, but I just went, "I'm not going home, I'm just not fucking going home."

Were you also terrified when you got to New York?
I wasn't freaking out. I think Cincinnati really prepared me. And I was still studying in New York. I was so determined to be a success—and let me be clear: not famous. It was about the work. I wanted to do great work, work with great people, and be respected. That's what I was after.

Well, your *Scrambled Feet* co-star, Hermione the duck, wasn't exactly respectful.
The duck didn't like me, which really upset me because usually animals and kids love me. But I think Hermione was missing Evalyn. That first night the duck made a beeline for my hemline and bit the shit out of me. I hurled the duck and it went off the stage [with its fully extended] six-foot wingspan. It was a big duck. I thought, "Oh my God, I'm going to be fired." The producer came back and he had tears in his eyes. He yells, "Faaaaaaith Priiiiince!" And I thought, "Oh God, here it comes." He says, "That is the funniest thing I've ever seen in my life. Could you do that every night?"

No, no, I can't.
No! Absolutely not. I showed him my bruise. But Hermione and I found our space together. I ended up doing the show in New York for a couple of weeks and then I opened it in L.A. I got a pilot with Suzanne Somers. I played her roommate. And I was on *Remington Steel....*

So you were cooking! What made you go back to New York?

I didn't like L.A. It was too vast and I really didn't know that many people. I liked L.A. much better later on, when I moved there with my family and we had friends. It was a different kind of experience for me. But at that time, I was by myself, living with Judy Norton, who was on *The Waltons*. We had done *Cinderella* at Pittsburgh Civic Light Opera and she was great. I was there for five or six months.

And then you went back to New York. Were you working survival jobs?

I always had a job going. My parents didn't really have the money [to help me] which can be hard but also golden. It makes you strive. I worked at McHale's Bar and Grill on Forty-sixth and Eighth, and let me tell you that was a brutal place. Those girls were hardcore. I wasn't the best waitress but I got better. I remember Peggy McHale—she'd be behind that Lucite, smoking a cigarette which would steam up the Lucite. She'd go, "You're gonna make it kid," in that low voice. And I said, "You think so? Why do you say that? You just get a feeling about me?" And she said, "No. You're a lousy fucking waitress." But I kept getting jobs intermittently—summer stock, regional theaters, a mini-national tour of *Tintypes*. Then I started getting pre-Broadway things, like the *Carousel* that went to The Kennedy Center with Tom Wopat. That never came in.

You were Carrie in *Carousel*?

Yeah. I even did Julie at one point and when they sing, "You're a queer one, Julie Jordan," they really meant it. I really wasn't a soprano but I acted the hell out of it. Terrence McNally came up to me during that *Carousel* and he said, "You're an actor. I see a lot in you. I'm going to have you start coming to the Manhattan Theater Club and doing stuff for us." I started getting in with [that off-Broadway crowd].

Which takes us to *Little Shop of Horrors*.

Yes. I was the first Audrey chosen for that. But I had a contract with IBM [doing an industrial] and couldn't get out of it. The rest is history. Ellen Greene went on to do it. I remember being at the Goodspeed doing *Leave It to Jane* and Ellen had a Hirschfeld in the *Times*. People were like, "Don't show Faith!" They were talking about the wrong girl. I'm not like that. I said, "I can be happy for other people, I really can. And you should be too. It's just not my time." And I really do think that had I originated Audrey, I probably would not have been Adelaide.

And you did get to ultimately play Audrey.

I did! For a long time.

Did it feel like, "I'm making it! It's happening!"

I felt like I was making a living. I was paying my rent. It was a little hand-to-mouth because I wasn't getting big-paying jobs. Some of the TV was good. Yeah, I felt like I was doing it. I felt like I made a good choice. I don't even know if I ever said, "I have to do a Broadway show." I don't even think I felt like that, which is probably why it just kind of made its way there naturally.

That show was *Jerome Robbins' Broadway*, in 1989. How did you get that?

I did a production of *Guys and Dolls* at the Seattle Rep. and I met William Whitener. He's a choreographer and he was working with Jerome Robbins. He put my name in the pot. They called me and we had five or six auditions for that show, and I got in. I really got on with Jerry. I loved him. I loved his intensity, the way he thought. Stakes. The life and death sort of thing. I was looking to be with somebody that was that intense. Musical theater, for me, had always been serious business. That was the way I was taught at Cincinnati. I didn't really know I was funny.

So you didn't even fully appreciate what you were bringing to the table?
In my teaching now, people say, "Let's have Faith do comedy classes." And I say, "You're not going to like what I have to say." I don't think in terms of comedy. I understand the push/pull of things. If it's good writing, if you accomplish the dilemma and you commit to whatever's in front of you, the funny will come. Nathan Lane and I are very different like that. I don't dream about bits [like he does]. I'm never worried about it being funny.

He's of the Jerry Zaks school, where comedy is scientific, you plot it, you calculate it.
Yeah, and Jerry's direction was so, so, precisely calibrated. Like a surgeon. He would take things apart. When it's dissected like that … I understood the notes, but it was hard to reconcile the science of his rhythms with organic responses, which is the way I like to work. Sometimes too much dissection can stop the natural flow, and things that might be discovered get squelched before there is an opportunity to discover them. But at the same time, I had great admiration for his skill at that. It just wasn't always great for me. [During previews, when] I knew the critics were coming, I pulled Jerry into my dressing room, and I knew I was potentially ruining a relationship, but I said, "I can't have any more notes now. I got this. I need to be free. And I'm going to hit it out of the park for you." You didn't just say that to him. Sadly, I felt like our relationship was never quite the same. But if I hadn't had that, I don't think I could have done it. I couldn't think anymore. I'm not calculated. That isn't to say that I don't work things out, or that I don't think of things, or that I don't listen to an audience. But there's a natural thing that happens; I just kind of know what to do and when it's played with too much, it messes with my head. But I do want to say that Jerry was a master at pulling a company together and being a real leader. We were in safe hands. He knew what he was doing. I haven't always felt that.

In _Jerome Robbins'_ you appreciated the discipline.
Even with him, that rehearsal process was so long that it was almost on the verge of detriment. We had words one day because of it. He would snap his fingers in the middle of a scene, telling you to move on. I said, "No! it needs a pause!" He said, "It doesn't." "Yes it does, Sir. But you wouldn't know that because we haven't had an audience for five months!" But I learned so much, especially watching him work with other people. His focus and the way he would focus a scene or a number kind of ruined me for anything less. He was truly a genius.

Can you pinpoint some of what you learned from him?
No movement was without storytelling. Nothing extraneous. His choreography was so specific. Anything he did, he thought about it a long time. You had to be able to hang with him in the intensity. I'll give you an example of something that stayed with me: we did the "Moo Cow" number [from _Gypsy_] a couple of times and I played Mama Rose. My line was, "Sing out, Louise!" I did it and he looked at me and said, "She's not mad. She needs her to get the job." I said, "Could you do it for me?" [She says the line again, encouragingly]. I thought, "Man, I'm going to put that away because maybe someday I am going to do Mama Rose." To him, that was the tragedy—she was doing everything to get food on the table and she thought

she was doing it right. He said, "That's why I loved Ethel Merman. She didn't know she had a problem." A lot of times it is played angrily. He thought Angela Lansbury had too much complexity. I really loved him.

I've been told that he was much harder on the dancers, that he was more respectful of the actors.
That's true. He was. I think it was because it was a world he didn't feel as comfortable in. He knew expression through movement, but articulating acting beats was much more foreign to him.

What was it like making your Broadway debut in that massive show with a company of sixty-five?
Just perfect. It was such a great ensemble. Great people. We've still managed to stay in touch. He had impeccable taste in humans and humanity. Being in the Imperial with all those people, it was always, "Excuse me. I'm sorry. Sorry. Sorry. Excuse me." It was just so jam-packed.

But being on stage with that many people, and part of that ensemble . . .
It was thrilling. I got into theater to be collaborative with other people. I am a team player. It's very upsetting sometimes when people are competitive. In *Jerome Robbins'*, because it was number after number after number, you'd feel the energy in the wings and you had to match it and take it somewhere else. You just wanted to make sure your stuff was up to snuff. It wasn't about who's better. It was making sure you were up to the bar. I would say that show, *Falsettoland*, and *Disaster!* were some of my favorites because of the ensemble feeling.

How did *Falsettoland* come into your world?
I had auditioned for James Lapine a couple times for other things. He really wanted me to be Trina. I thought I was right for the lesbians from next door. James called me and said, "Forget that. I want you to be Trina." I said, "I'm not Jewish." He said, "Don't worry about it. Just do it." And I did. I didn't even audition.

You were joining a cast where the creators and the three male leads had so much history together.
These guys had this huge history with each other. I was observing. I certainly keep my own nose clean. But it's like playing piano duets: if you're on the bottom, and you're too loud and not blending, it doesn't work. And I noticed how they did the music. I'd never seen people sing into the next measure, back-phrasing, and they all did it. They had this family-like energy, bickering around the dinner table. They could kid and josh and kvetch and no one was offended. Chip Zien turned to me one day and said, "How come you're not fighting and yelling [like the rest of us]?" And I said, "I don't have to. You guys will do it for me. I'm picking up the caboose on this one." It's like guest-starring on a TV show where the cast all knows each other. "What tones are going on here? Oh, I see. All right. Yeah." And then I can just jump into the pool and start swimming like everybody else.

Trina brought all kinds of opportunities to stretch. You played real heartbreak and drama.
But you know, that's always inside a comedian. Always. Make no mind. That's what's driving the comedy. Always. I can't even think of a more stupid remark than when somebody says,

"But they're a comedian." And? What is your point? There's a reason the comedy comes forward. Always. Always.

Audiences wept nightly. It was a real catharsis.
I loved it, loved it. I was so happy to go to work, make people feel, affect people. It meant something. I remember [early in rehearsals] James saying, "I'm not sure what we have here, but I know it's special." I've never felt so confident. With that experience and also *A Catered Affair* because of John Doyle, I didn't think in terms of being nervous. It was more, "I'm here to share. I'm here to do my job to allow people the space to heal." I don't like the fame thing. I don't like any of that. Never have. Annoys me.

I've heard you say it gets in the way.
It does. It really does.

So, as your fame is growing during this period, did that make you uncomfortable?
It didn't in that because we were an ensemble. What I don't like is the feeling that you're doing a show together and then you get called out [for excellence, with reviews or award nominations] and suddenly, you're the outsider. You can feel it in the company.

You got even more attention in *Nick and Nora*. That was one where the show was panned but your reviews were solid.
Well, I was playing this bizarre little character. But Arthur Laurents just laid me out during the workshop. I was asking so many questions because she was a complex role. She went from being this little mousy secretary to sleeping with the producer to [using] cocaine to sleeping with a woman. I was curious what was driving that. I was asking, like anybody else in the situation would. He was just mad as fire at me one day. He was trying to get backers. We were not there to work on the piece, [the workshop] was to get money—but nobody told me! I frustrated him. He just wanted me to just say the fucking words. And I mean, there were great people in that cast: Joanna Gleason, Christine Baranski, Chris Sarandon, Debra Monk, Josie de Guzman, and he just snapped at me in rehearsal one day in front of everyone. "Who do you think you are? Do you see them asking all these questions, taking up my time?" I just sat there. "Just do your job. Don't ask so many questions." In my head I was going, "You little, short, fuck." I think he expected me to cry, but I didn't. I said, "I've had harder. My dad was worse than you are right now." I walked out of the room and went to a pay phone. I called my therapist and said, "We've got work to do." He was brutal. I think he was a scared little man. An unhappy, scared, little man and he wore it like armor.

Could you tell in rehearsals that the show was in trouble?
I think when somebody writes something and directs it, it's tricky. I have my theories; I think Arthur Laurents wasn't a particular fan of musical theater. He cared about the words, but he didn't want everything so musical.

That's an incredible theory given that his career is built on *West Side Story* and *Gypsy*.
Isn't it? But he wrote the BOOKS for those. He would rather you not sing that much. I kind of got that feeling with [director] Joe Mantello as well. I said to him, "Do you really want *Man of No Importance* to be a kitchen sink drama? It's a musical, after all." We were trying to find

the right tone. It's dark. I give you that. With *Nick and Nora*, I remember thinking, "This is on the wrong track." It had many issues, though. I kept my mouth shut after I had been slapped down so hard during the workshop.

So, when that show closed . . .
I already had my sights set on *Guys and Dolls*. In fact [when I gave notice], Arthur came into my room and said, "You're making a big mistake, the biggest mistake of your life." I said, "Sorry, I disagree."

But you didn't have to leave in the end, because the show closed. How did *Guys and Dolls* even happen in the middle of *Nick and Nora*?
Jerry Zaks came to see *Nick and Nora*. And Frank Rich had written in his review in the *Times*, something like "the best thing in it is the cadaver." That was me.

What he wrote was, "We can look forward to hearing a lot more from Ms. Prince. In the meantime, there's no escaping the unfortunate fact that the liveliest thing in *Nick and Nora* is a corpse."
There you go.

So, Jerry Zaks saw you in it . . .
I had to go in and audition and I kept thinking that I really better think about what to pick for my audition song. After a lot of consideration, I decided I needed to take a risk. I had Scott Frankel arrange "Something Wonderful" for me. He put in some chords that made it sound so different. I did it as Miss Adelaide so that I could show the depth of what I think this role is about. I had my gloves, a handkerchief, and a pillbox hat. [She performs the song as Adelaide, punctuating with sneezes.] It was a huge gamble, but I just put so much depth into it. I thought, "This woman has a big quandary. I can't imagine being engaged for fourteen years, and lying to my mother. And I fucking love this guy and he will not fucking do this." That was my point of view on it. Jerry asked me about working with Nathan because we had done a show together, *Bad Habits*. I knew that Nathan and I could be great together. I think we're like George and Gracie. I knew we had the chemistry and timing; it just has to be the perfect project and we needed to be given the right space to play.

In the rehearsal process, you and Nathan, as I understand it, went a little rogue with "Sue Me."
It's usually a given that actors come to rehearsal with ideas about how they want to play a scene, but Jerry worked differently. He wanted everything to be discovered in the room. He said at the beginning that he didn't like it when people talked about the process outside of rehearsal. I'm a person that tends to go with the rules until I can't, and I was trying to play by the rules. But Nathan had worked with him before and Nathan always has ideas. I trusted him to know how far he could go and how to work that. One day, we were outside the rehearsal room and he scanned the hallways to make sure the coast was clear. He said, "I have an idea. When you hit me with the purse, just smack the shit out of me. I'll just keep going down, down, down, to the floor." So, I did. I thought, "This is going to be different from the last time we did it and Jerry will know. Daddy is going to yell at us!" But I was willing to risk it. We did it and I looked over at Jerry, tentatively. He looked at us and said, "OK then." So what I got from that was, you can sneak and do it, but it better be fucking great. And it was.

The show exploded. The rave review and your picture were on the front page of *The New York Times*. Unheard of. You've said repeatedly that all that attention was a bit of an albatross.
When you're doing a Broadway show and you're in the thick of it, they've got you out every day off, promoting, so that your show will be Tony-nominated. It is so incredibly exhausting. I've never been as tired in my life. And you're trying to keep yourself well for eight shows a week. I got vertigo right after the Tonys and it lasted for three months. It was horrible. Between the nerves and the interviews and all the TV, it's incredibly difficult. You know, when you do those TV segments, you're doing a different version than what you are doing eight times a week. It's truncated, or the staging is different, or you're alone instead of standing with the company. You have to adjust and it's not easy. After that I started saying "no" a lot more. You learn. I remember the time I performed live on *The View* [during *The Little Mermaid*]. I said to my manager, "Did you like that?" She said, "Loved it! It was great!" I said, "Good. Because I'm not doing that ever again. It's taken five years off my life." Winning a Tony—your life doesn't really get back on proper track. Because now, you're not just a character actress. Things have to be "worthy" of you doing them. We had big meetings about what I could be doing or should be doing and all of that. I didn't like it. I'm grateful for it, but I missed the days when I would look at things and think, "that sounds like fun to do. That sounds like good work." It just became about something else.

Once all of that abated, were you able to relax into the joy of doing the show?
Well, my brother died of a drug overdose. So, no. I just felt under pressure. It was like the best of times/the worst of times.

Does it make you at all sad that you weren't able to bask in the excitement of being in the season's smash hit?
That's what I'm trying to tell you: I think that's the myth. It's really hard to bask—particularly for theater people. I certainly did enjoy it. I had moments. I did it for a year and a half—close to two with rehearsals, but by [the end of that] I was tired and sad. I wanted to go out before I really was dragging it. Being present is really important to me, and I wasn't willing to go on stage feeling anything less than fully alive.

You said that after the show, it took five years to get in sync with yourself.
It really did.

We've talked about why some of that was. How did you get yourself grounded again?
I had a family. I had a baby in '95. I think that was very helpful for me. I'm much better when I have a lot going on personally. It's like, "I can be worried about things in my career for a day, but then I've got to change diapers and figure out the groceries." I think it was very helpful having another life.

Your next Broadway outing was the play *What's Wrong with This Picture?* And then you went into *The King and I,* replacing Donna Murphy, so it seems like what you effectively did was say, "Whatever the expectations are ... comedic leading lady in a star vehicle.... Nope. I'm going to replace and I'm going to replace in something that you wouldn't necessarily think of for me."
Those were very thought-out choices. Peter Strain, my agent at the time, was really good at thinking in those terms. Mary Rodgers was instrumental in making *The King and I* happen.

She was the one that said, "Hey, what about you as Mrs. Anna?" I was like, "Me?" She said, "Well, Gertrude Lawrence [the original Mrs. Anna] was a comedian." That helped me see myself in the role. Mary was a mentor of mine and I think saw more in me than [others did]. It is unusual to think that someone who played Adelaide could be Mrs. Anna, but for me, it's about the work. That's what I got from Jerome Robbins. That's what I got from Arthur Laurents, as hard as it was, and people like James Lapine and Jerry Zaks. They take it so seriously. Beyond seriously. And that's [how you get] exceptional musical theater.

It was a reinvention of the role from what Donna had done. That there was that latitude is pretty unusual.
True, and that felt very fulfilling.

You showed a lot of restraint in your portrayal.
And that was my goal as an actor, to try different things and put myself in different situations. To me, that's why you do the work. It's exciting—not to be the most famous person, but to really commit to and enjoy the work. I still enjoy the work so much. I love bringing everything to it.

Anything you want to say about your co-star, Lou Diamond Phillips?
I could eat him up. Just loved him to pieces. He was so loved. Even the ushers gave him presents when he left. I've never seen anybody so adored. I have felt that love in the theater, but not like that. I've never seen anything like it.

Your next show was back to high comedy: *Little Me*, with Martin Short.
I loved [director] Rob Marshall. He's incredibly charming and smart. It seemed like a good show, but it turned out to be an odd fit and not quite what they promised. They were going to re-write it. The original novel was about her [Prince's character, Belle] and I was led to believe that would be addressed. It was kind of all about Marty, through no fault of his own, just as the original was all about Sid Caesar. Marty's form of comedy changed everything tonally. It becomes something different with a comedian, and that's not terrible. I resigned myself that that's what it was. Ben Brantley thought I was miscast. I don't totally agree. On the album, I think I come off well. Usually the role is played by two different women. Here, it was just me, and you hear me go from fifteen to fifty-six. I'm really proud of it. But there were also inherent challenges at Roundabout, which was new to producing on Broadway at that time. The backstage was not unionized and I really had a problem with it. They had some major safety issues. I'm a big union person. I went through two dressers, who were lovely and well-meaning, but not up to the job of fourteen costume changes. Finally, I said, "This is really not working for me. I need to bring in my own union dresser, who I can count on." When I did, my dresser Leon and I got the union in there, and they unionized the backstage. I was never hired there again. That's OK.

You left an important legacy.
I was on the cover of the IATSE newspaper.

That must have felt rewarding.
It was very rewarding. You're getting to know the real me. I care about certain things, I don't care about other things. I'm not your typical actress.

On a show that felt otherwise disappointing, you got to have a different kind of triumph and feel like you made a really important contribution.

Exactly. It didn't occur to me that I was miscast but maybe I was.

Well, Belle, as written, is all boob.

And I am really not. That's not my vibe. I think of Judy Holliday—she was a very smart dumb blond. I guess I always go that way. She wasn't really a beauty, she just was interesting. Barbara Harris was interesting. She put the boobs on in *The Apple Tree*, like me. Those are the women I was patterning myself on.

How was it working with Cy Coleman?

I loved him. He was a sexy guy. There was an inner sexuality about him that I really appreciated. And I loved Carolyn Leigh's lyrics. They were so, so sophisticated. I liked their songs on every level. It really matched my voice. It all seemed good on paper.

You next went into *The Dead*. What made you do it?

[Playwright/director] Richard Nelson asked me and I wanted to work for him. And again, I like really different roles and that one was very different. I've never been to Ireland, but Irish, Scottish, and English—I have that inside me. It's like when I did *Billy Elliot*, I thought, "I know these people." Richard Nelson, I thought, could really help me in this part. But this cast was very distraught that Blair Brown was leaving. I sensed it immediately. I didn't take it personally, but it was difficult. I just kept working, working, working, and Richard Nelson was my guide. And Alice Ripley and Emily Skinner were really good to me. They knew it was going to be a tough situation. Marni Nixon wanted me to stand the way that Blair would, so she literally, physically moved me around in the space. Emily and Alice would go, "Marni! Leave her alone!" I said, "It's OK." "No!" And Marni said, "Well, Blair would do it. . . ." In perfect harmony like the *Side Show* twins, "She's not Blair!" It was almost like I was observing it. And then you had Christopher Walken. He didn't want to rehearse. Richard said, "He has to do the put-in rehearsal, but he does not want to rehearse beyond that." So we did our run-through. And then Christopher came to my dressing room and said [doing a Walken impersonation], "We … should maybe … talk about some of these things … because we … have never put them together … and I'm thinking we need to … have a meeting." So, we talked it through and that night I went on. At one point I reached over and I touched him on the leg while I was saying something to somebody else. Everybody [looked horrified]. I came offstage and I said, "What just happened?" I was told, "He doesn't like to be touched!" "But I'm his wife." And they said, "He doesn't like to be touched." I said, "You know what? He can tell me himself." He never said anything.

Did you keep doing it?

I did. I loved doing the role. I went on to open it at the Ahmanson and then at The Kennedy Center.

In 2001, you took on the first Broadway revival of *Bells Are Ringing*.

I still like that piece a lot. When people ask me who my favorite director is, it's always Tina Landau. I loved working with her. She was marvelous to work with, and I think she was so hurt by that situation.

What makes her your favorite?

Such positivity. She and John Doyle. They never come from a place of good or bad, right or wrong. They never use words like that. She always makes you feel like a million bucks, like the smartest person in the room. The way she would stage things, she would make you think you made it up. It was so much fun. Playing. Like being a child again. It was a marvelous feeling. But [producer] Mitchell Maxwell was disastrous. Like the mob, coming in his black car to hand over the money. He had bounced I don't know how many weeks of checks. The whole experience was really tough. And when I'm the lead in something, I take that very personally. You feel responsible. Or I did.

How did you get into *Bells* to begin with?

I did a staged reading of it with Tina Landau at The Kennedy Center. But then *Little Me* happened before we got it to New York. The Dodgers [producers] were supposed to do it, but they were dragging their feet and I didn't know when they would do it, so I took *Little Me*. Betty Comden did not like that. She was very upset at me. So when the time came and they finally got the money together, the Dodgers had left it. They got Mitchell Maxwell to produce and they went looking for another Ella. I was devastated. That went on for like nine months. They looked and looked. Tina would call me and say, "Just hang in there. Don't lose faith." At one point Kristin Chenoweth was going to do it and I was really sad about that, not because I don't love Kristin, but she wasn't the right age. This woman has [spent her life holed up in this answering service] and she's kind of past her prime. [Finally] I get a call from Tina and she said, "Betty says she'll see you." I had to audition again. I was like, "You're fucking kidding me. Any words of advice?" She said, "Go in with love." I went in and did like two or three numbers, and Mitchell Maxwell said, "What have we been doing for nine months? This is Ella." So, I got to do it, but then it was difficult.

Why?

You know, sometimes I think it was the wrong season for it. It's like *Disaster!* opening during the season of *Hamilton*. *Disaster!* was a great show. It should have run. I've never heard people laugh that hard in the theater. Ever. Ever! EVER! Wrong season. Wrong theater. All those things matter. *Bells Are Ringing* had a white floor. I don't mean to diss the scenic designer, but it's hard to have a white floor. And Mitchell Maxwell was a hot mess of a producer. I had never before felt, "Oh my God, my people are not going to get paid!" There was such stress. And then the reviews were mixed. It had a lot of issues.

***The New York Times* reviewer thought that Tina Landau's choices made the piece feel dated. Was that your experience, or is that even something about which you can be objective?**

I think I can't be. I honestly don't know, but I could tell by the reaction that it was just not quite working. It was really difficult. After it closed, I stayed home and just painted my house. I was miffed! The experience at The Kennedy Center was so joyous, how could the two be so different? I was weary. I loved Marc Kudisch. He was the perfect foil for me. We had a great time on stage. And I loved the cast—David Garrison and Beth Fowler? They were stellar! That's the sad thing—it had all the elements and just wasn't quite gelling. I'm sure somebody on the outside could tell me more. It felt like winning every battle, but losing the war. It happens a lot. *A Catered Affair* seemed like a really good idea, too. And *A Man of No Importance.*

An exploration of simplicity in *A Man of No Importance*.
(Paul Kolnik)

But you can see why those two shows aren't necessarily going to be everybody's cup of tea. They are dark and intimate. More provocative than entertaining.
I feel like we need a place on Broadway other than Lincoln Center for that kind of work. It's like going to the foreign film theater. Those kinds of shows are important.

How did *A Man of No Importance* come about for you?
Terrence McNally wrote the part for me. But I had done a play with [director] Joe Mantello called *What's Wrong with This Picture?* and it was not a great experience. I am not questioning his talent, but we didn't gel. My agents said, "Do the workshop. If you hate it you don't have to do it." So I did it and Joe pretty much left me alone. And then we got into the production

and—he always wanted something from me and I was never quite sure what it was. He had fired one of the other leads, a young man who had been with the project since its inception. He had done every workshop, every demo—how do you decide after two years that this guy is not right? Roger Rees and I were both very upset. I stood up and said, "Joe, honestly, if you had fired me yesterday, I wouldn't have been a bit surprised." The cast gasped. I said, "No, really. Sometimes you're hard to read. It's not clear what you want. This decision at this time is extremely difficult for all of us." You know, every director has a different approach, but I always work best with people who attempt to give notes from a positive perspective. John Doyle and Tina Landau had a way of saying, "Try the window this time instead of the door. Let's see what that's like." As opposed to some people saying, "Wrong, wrong!," or in Joe's case, under-communicating, in my opinion.

What about composers Steven Flaherty and Lynn Ahrens?
Love, love, love, love. I love their stuff. And Terrace!

So, working in the room with those three people, were you feeling creative?
Fantastic. [Musical director] Ted Sperling was there, and [conductor] Rob Berman…. Just great people. Roger Rees: what a dear and a mensch. Andre Bishop [Lincoln Center artistic director]! He always made me feel great at Playwrights Horizons and at Lincoln Center, just really proud of the work we were doing. But I've never been in another Joe Mantello show, and that's ok. Sometimes the alchemy in a relationship doesn't always jibe.

It's like deciding that you're not a match for somebody in a relationship. You're just not a fit.
Exactly. That's exactly the way I look at it. That's why I think it's so important to understand yourself as yourself, separate from your career and being a performer. It's so important to do that work as well as your craft. It's part of your craft.

You made a choice after *Man of No Importance* to move to L.A.
I did. For my son. It wasn't working. He really wanted somebody at home and we heard him. We thought, "Well, he's not going to want to be with us that much longer. Soon he'll be grown and out of the house. Let's be with him while he still wants to be with us!" We still worked, I did concerts and some TV, but we were both home with Henry more.

You were persuaded back to New York five years later with *A Catered Affair*.
I was. Henry was older by then. When I read it and saw the movie [I identified with it]. I could understand [the character of] Aggie through my grandmother. Not that she was from the Bronx, she was a Southerner. But she cared for her family. It was about taking care of other people [before herself.] She had a really hard life; her twins died at a very young age. But she didn't make you feel it. I had a really special relationship with my grand-mother. And I liked being somebody that was joyless. I never experienced that. What if this was my life? Aggie came alive when she finally got a chance to use her imagination about something for her own life. She had never had that opportunity. I think a lot of people don't even get the chance to imagine, they just do what's expected and focus on what needs to get done, and to me, that's the tragedy. You live a certain way and nobody shows you the possibilities.

What was the rehearsal like?
I was so excited to be working with John Doyle and Harvey Fierstein. Harvey and I had done a benefit together and had really gotten along. And Tom Wopat and I had done several things together. Tom Wopat and Nathan Lane—there's like a pain body we share. We've never talked about it, it's just something deep between us and it always works. We don't even really talk that much offstage, but with both of those relationships there's something inherent that we understand that just makes beautiful chemistry together. It's something that's just felt. I really dig that and it works for the work. Harvey had a hard time with that experience. It was difficult being on stage with somebody who was writing it, too. That was kind of a note to self: maybe don't do that again. Because you can feel when the two sides of someone's brain are working. Harvey recently wrote his own memoir and I got a call from my manager saying, "They want to mail us a book." I said, "Why?" She said, "Don't you think he'd say nice things?" I said, "I can't imagine that he would." And she said, "You think he'd really send you a book if it wasn't nice?" And I said, "Yup. It would be just like Harvey to let you know first." The book came and there was a whole chapter on *A Catered Affair*. He didn't name one cast member. How would you feel?

Why was it difficult between the two of you?
I don't know what he was feeling. We were not close once it came to New York [after the tryout]. I felt something shift. He experienced bad reviews in San Diego and I think his impetus was to try to control everything more. He wanted to put himself as the narrator and he tried to take out the one moment that I thought was really the most interesting moment I had ever experienced in musical theater, which was that sort of burst of pain [when Aggie has a wordless breakdown].

How would you describe that moment?
She just finally lets go. I think it's the first time in her life she's ever done it. It's for her [dead] son, it's for her own life, the possibilities lost, what she could see for her daughter … it had been a hard life, just a fucking hard life.

And he wanted to lose that?
He did. And I thought, "Wow. You're that hurt that you would remove what I think is the best thing about the show?" So I just depended on John Doyle to fight that fight, and he did. But it got worse between the two of us.

As the writer of the piece, I would think that he saw that you were serving his piece well.
I never was told that.

So, how does that manifest? You're getting rave reviews and a Tony nomination for what you're bringing to his piece and he was just chilly?
That's why I say it's tricky being in something and writing it. I think that's a great conflict. It's what I said about Arthur Laurents, who wasn't in *Nick and Nora*, but he was writing and directing it. I am not saying it can't be done. But even Howard Ashman writing and directing *Little Shop*—I think it was difficult for him. And he managed to pull it off brilliantly, but working on it was hard. I think it's hard to keep your feelings out of it. Harvey was hurt. He didn't understand what went wrong and I understand that. I still don't know what

went wrong with *Bells Are Ringing*. It's very hard to see when you're in it. So, on this one, I just kept it clean and took notes from John Doyle and tried to keep in my own lane. When the nominations came out [Wopat and Prince were both nominated for Tonys, Prince for an Outer Critics Circle Award, and both of them, along with Doyle and Leslie Kritzer, for Drama Desk Awards; Fierstein's book was also Drama Desk nominated, but not his performance], I thought, "Oh, God, this is not going to be good." And it wasn't, so much so that he wrote an entire chapter and doesn't mention the cast. He said, "Our show won accolades and nominations," but he never says who. I mean, it's pointed. It's just sad. He wasn't nice to John Doyle.

What did he expect of John Doyle that he didn't get?
They had differences about tone. I think John Doyle saw it as a darker piece. The movie is definitely dark. And they were selling it like *Father of the Bride* with the three of us as musical comedy people. [The ads] did a disservice to it. *Caroline, or Change* hadn't sold as well as they had hoped and they had presented it as what it was [the ads featured art of a beleaguered housekeeper, looking unhappy]. So, the marketing people were trying another thing, but you can't do that. And that puts a lot on the actors. It's like having a candy store and selling weapons.

Was it satisfying to you, ultimately?
Definitely! After that I would take the chance to do Tennessee Williams or William Inge. It was great for me personally.

You learned more about your own chops?
Yes. It can be hard and still be good. But you have to be a very, very strong person. Strength doesn't come from just being strong, it's doing something even though you're scared. Things can be really hard, but there's always a takeaway. Performing that show was also emotionally hard. I started to think I was depressed. My husband said, after a couple of months, "Baby, it's that woman you're playing." It hadn't even occurred to me. But when Elizabeth Franz was in *Death of a Salesman*, she started feeling bad and the doctor said, "So what are you doing?" She said, "*Death of a Salesman*." He said, "What happens in that?" "My husband kills himself every night." He said, "Your body doesn't know it's acting." His advice was to take any opportunity to enjoy yourself. It's got to balance out.

Did you do that?
Yeah, I did. It was hard to go there every night. That life was hard.

Your next role went from very drab to full-on technicolor; you did Ursula in *The Little Mermaid*.
She was a joy. I enjoyed scaring children. Who knew? I really loved working on the material. I knew Alan Menken from *Little Shop*, so I understand him a lot. It was fun finding the push/ pull of her. I gave a lot to that part. Evil people are usually the most charismatic people in the room. It's that kind of thing that I find really interesting: luring people in until they get really close and then you devour them. Playing with that was great. The costume isn't what I would have imagined; there were lots of the pieces that were clunky and I wanted it to be more flowing and undulating.

"I enjoyed scaring children. Who knew?" confessed Prince. As Ursula in *The Little Mermaid.* (Joan Marcus)

That's a costume that I could see wearing you instead of you wearing it, if you're not careful. I used those tentacles like a boa and I actually snapped one of them because I was trying to work it. That's how hard I tried to control it. One night the entire tentacle [portion of the costume] fell off the apparatus [supporting it]. It was pretty funny. I used my fingernails to sort of waffle my way through the end of the song after the eels hurled the apparatus offstage. I love it when things like that happen. Everything slows down. But I had a ball on that show. I made it mine and I really went through the beats of it. When Alan Menken came to see it, he got on his knees and kissed my feet.

The following year, you did your first tour since *Tintypes*. You went out with *Billy Elliot*. What made you decide to tour?
Money. And it came at a time that worked. Henry was finishing high school and it seemed like a good time. And I really like the role. I love Julie Walters [who played it in the movie] and I thought that it was a really good piece to do. I enjoyed the work a lot—not the machine element of it—some shows have this machine. . . . Disney stuff is kind of a machine, although they gave me latitude. On *Billy Elliot*, they tried to pour me into what was there. I don't do well with that. I kind of make things my own. I do care what the director thinks immensely, but I tend to put my stamp on it. When I first go in, they have the template and, yeah, OK, I'll start with that. And then as it goes on, I try new things and see if they work. I'm very malleable, but I still have a thinking brain and I come to the table with a lot. Replacing and finding all that out has been interesting. And I'm pretty strong-headed. You've got to tell me why [you need it a certain way] and you've got to make me understand. So, it was tough on *Billy Elliot* because they had a lot of, "It's been done this way." I got a lot of memos. I said, "We're

going to Dallas and [associate director] Julian Webber's going to be there. If he doesn't like what I'm doing, I'll throw it out and try something else." I have no problem doing that and that seemed to calm them down a little bit. But Julian said, "I've never seen it done like that but it works. It's a go."

I could see that particular conundrum being pronounced on a tour, where you're being put into the show by stage managers and it's their job to maintain the director's blocking and intentions as written. They don't have the latitude to say, "It's OK for you to go in that different direction."
Exactly. They're worried about their jobs and I'm not doing it exactly like my predecessor. And if Webber didn't like it, I would have changed it.

You did that show for a long time, so you must have enjoyed it.
I really did. I got out because they sold [the production] to another company and [the pay and the production] were going to be less. That's not what I signed on for. It went from fifteen trucks to five. They were slimming it down and it wasn't working for me.

After the tour, you got an offer to replace Jane Lynch in *Annie*, and you were directed by James Lapine again.
When I heard he was doing *Annie* I thought, "I am not sure I would have put those two together." Lapine, and also Doyle, both seem to be wary of broad humor. I think they are afraid it will upset the tone and they seem nervous about things getting too big. My theory is that it can be big all day long, as long as it's rooted in reality.

There was nothing small and nothing not rooted about Dorothy Loudon when she did it originally.
Exactly. And she was my template. It was vaudevillian [in style], that's how that piece was written. Miss Hannigan has the same dilemma as Annie. She needs and wants just like Annie does. She's not getting. There is a real desperation in this woman. The more Annie gets, the more she's clamoring. I loved doing it. I enjoyed that so much. When I came into it, Lilla Crawford—talented kid—[playing Annie] upstaged me on my very first line. She walked right up behind me, so, if I were to talk to her, I'd cut myself off from the audience. But I know how to cure that: I [delivered my line out to the audience, rather than turning to face her.] She understood immediately and came scurrying around back into my sight line. She never did it again. She learned. We were only together a week but she asked me to be on her podcast. I said, "I'd love to." I wish I'd been there with her longer, because I could have shown her some different ropes.

After that, *Disaster!* comes along out of the blue.
I got a text from Seth Rudetsky. "Hey, Lady," that's what he calls me, "You want to do my show?"

What was it like in that ensemble? Roger Bart, Rachel York, Adam Pascal, Kevin Chamberlain, Kerry Butler, Jennifer Simard, Seth Rudetsky . . .
I love when strong, talented people are standing together. Let's go! And we feed off of each other: you go, now I'll go. . . . And it becomes this incredible thing that we've created together. It's my favorite thing. They all were fan-fucking-tastic! I loved it. I loved the character and

finding her sexuality. I enjoyed helping with the costume. And then really coming in with the realism of the death scene. Jen Simard—I can weep when I talk about her. She's such a genius comedy-wise. There's something so unexpected. I just die to be on stage with people like that. Everybody worked well together. And honestly, I was never in my dressing room; I was usually watching the show if I wasn't in a scene. And to hear people LAUGH and LAUGH … I loved every single person.

If we're looking at the aggregate of all of the shows that we've talked about, there are only a couple that sound like they were pure joy, and this was one of them.
Pure joy. Bliss. Time of my life. So fulfilling.

What is it that you think that you want now?
The thing I've always wanted: an interesting character. Being in the room with great people. Being respected. Having a good payoff—you've got to feel good at the end of the night. And feeling like you still have the talents to deliver. I have no regrets or anything like that. Am I finished? No. It just depends on what's coming my way, what I'm interested in, what catches my fancy. Could I see myself going through those doors? Could I contribute? I certainly enjoy other aspects of my life and if somebody said, "You can't do it anymore. You're done," I'd be OK with that, too. I really would. There are other ways I can express myself. And I like that. I feel like I have so much inside of me. My girlfriend said to me, "You know, you really have a bulk of work." I guess I do, I just don't think about it. I'm in the moment. What's next? I'm looking to what's next, but I'd love for it to add up in a way that I thought it could. To be somebody like Judi Dench—she wasn't a looker, just a damned good actress. Jean Stapleton. Or Maureen Stapleton! Or Shirley Booth. These are interesting women to me. That's kind of where I thought it was going.

Isn't it?
Maybe. I'm still positive and open. I know I belong here. I've proven that. Now, what else you got? How can I use it to help somebody? Where do we go from here? I still love the work terribly. I still have the passion and I find the puzzles intriguing. I'm never bored. That word rarely comes out of my mouth.

Charlotte d'Amboise

January, March 2021

Charlotte d'Amboise is a goofball. She is silly, irreverent, playful, profane. A delight. That's not to say she is without discipline or drive. She grew up in the stately halls of City Ballet, after all, the daughter of Jacques d'Amboise, one of the all-time great ballet dancers. When she's working, she works incredibly hard and appreciates that ethic in her peers. She just refuses to take herself too, too seriously.

That was true from the time she was a young ballerina, training at the School of American Ballet. She had the technique, but found herself drawn to Broadway more than the barre. At nineteen she originated the role of Cassandra in the first national tour of *Cats*, before joining the Broadway company. It was there that she first fell for her future husband Terrence Mann, strutting his stuff as the Rum Tum Tugger. She also became part of an elite group of Broadway dancers who seemed to be on the same circuit, all going from *Cats* to *Song and Dance* to the ill-fated *Carrie* to the landmark *Jerome Robbins' Broadway* for which d'Amboise was nominated for a Tony Award. *Damn Yankees* and *Company* followed before the show that changed everything—*Chicago*. When d'Amboise originated the role of Roxie in the first national tour, she stepped into jazz shoes she would slip in and out of for more than twenty years. To date, d'Amboise has appeared in the Broadway production for engagements of varying lengths a whopping twenty-four times, a feat made possible by the intersection of a set of unusual circumstances (the show's longevity, the producers' willingness to swap out cast members regularly, the role's unspecified age), but an amazing feat nonetheless. Her subsequent work in *Sweet Charity*, *A Chorus Line* (another Tony nomination), and *Pippin* all happened between stints in *Chicago*. Although *Pippin* was her third show with Mann, it was the first that they played opposite one another, Lunt/Fontanne style, and she loved it. Their collaboration also includes two daughters and Triple Arts Musical Theater Summer Camp, an annual intensive which they founded, making teachers out of both of them and a bevy of their friends and colleagues.

Mann hovers in the background during some of my talks with d'Amboise, interjecting corrections or jokes, just as she did when I met with him. Theirs is an easy and enviable rapport. Their longevity defies the show biz couple odds, but then, despite d'Amboise's claim that she's easily bored, she does have a history of long runs. And as a dancer who, well into her career, still stuns with a perfect pirouette, defying odds seems to be a d'Amboise specialty.

I often ask people when the theater bug bit, but you grew up in a household of performers. I was raised watching a lot of Judy Garland movies. And Fred Astaire, Ginger Rogers. I guess the bug started with *H. R. Pufnstuf*, if I think about it. Jack Wild. I fell in love with him. I was always into the singing. But I remember always thinking, "Oh, Judy Garland's dead," or "These people are really old," and I didn't connect with them. Then I saw *Hello, Dolly!* with Barbra Streisand. I fell in love with her and I said to my mom, "Is she dead?" Because it seemed like one

"The name on everybody's lips is gonna be . . . ROXIE!" In *Chicago*.
(Photofest)

of those old MGM movies. She's like, "Oh no. This is her now." And I started to follow her and her life and career. I got obsessed with musicals because she was alive and doing it, and then I just started singing. My dad really encouraged that.

When did you figure out that musicals were not just in the movie theater but twenty blocks south, on Broadway?
We didn't see many musicals when I was little because we didn't have money. Four kids. The first musical I remember seeing was *Fiddler on the Roof* with Zero Mostel. I remember him sticking his tongue out at the audience. He was such a clown. I wanted to be an actress/singer because of Barbra Streisand. I loved dancing but not the technical part, the acting part of it. To this day, when I dance, I like it to be in a story. I always wanted a reason [to dance]. I think I was just born with that.

At sixteen you went to Luigi [a renowned teacher of jazz dance, real name Eugene Louis Daccuito], which was a big step.

Charlotte d'Amboise	
Non Pasquale	off-Broadway, 1983
Cats	National Tour, 1983; Broadway, 1984
Song and Dance	Broadway, 1985
Carrie	Broadway, 1988
Jerome Robbins' Broadway	Broadway, 1989
Damn Yankees	Broadway, 1994
Company	Broadway, 1995
Chicago	National Tour, 1997; Broadway, 1999, 2003, 2004, 2006, 2008, 2009, 2010, 2011, 2015, 2016, 2017, 2018, 2019, 2020, 2022, 2023
Contact	Broadway, 2001
Can-Can	Encores!, 2004
Sweet Charity	Broadway, 2005
A Chorus Line	Broadway, 2006
Pippin	Broadway, 2013

I knew that I wasn't going to be a ballet dancer. Now mind you, if I had gorgeous feet and the perfect body, I might have stayed with it. But I could see that that wasn't going to be my thing. Plus I was bored. I preferred jazz dancing. Jazz dancing was more like those old MGM movies. I made a choice. I knew I had all this technique and I wanted to branch out. At fourteen and fifteen, I was going to dance studios, taking classes all by myself after school. In ninth grade, I was like, "I could go to [School of] Performing Arts and get my dance classes done in the morning, and then after school, I could go take acting and singing classes." It was all about trying to get it all in and learn everything. I hated school so much. The dance classes didn't compare to what I was used to and the academics weren't strong enough, so I left there and went to Professional Children's School for tenth and eleventh grade and that was when I started to audition. I started getting trade papers and going on random auditions just to practice. I knew I sucked at auditioning, but I knew that I was meant to do this and I would get better and better and better. I was terrified. All these people were so good and so much better than me. I was clueless, a little ballerina. I knew that I needed to learn, so I would throw myself in there and fail. I failed a lot. I knew that I had better technique than everyone and I knew that I had more passion than anyone, I just didn't know how to dance jazz. But I knew that if I could pick it up, I'd be better than everybody in the room and that's what kept me going. I knew I couldn't sing [as well], so I went to every jazz class in New York City, so I could learn every style, and I taught myself how to pick things up quickly. I had to work at it. But I always knew I could.

Do you think that confidence came from ballet training and learning there that if you drill, you grow?

Yes, exactly. I knew that. And that's the same way I approached everything in life. I was very insecure about my acting. I had to study a lot. Shit, I mean, I remember being in Washington, DC, with *Cats* doing eight shows a week—I was nineteen years old. I signed up for an acting class at the Arena Stage from 9:00 to 6:00 every day, and then I would run to the theater and do the show. I knew I needed acting. I was so scared and insecure but I knew that I had to do it. I just I threw myself into it.

Cats was your first big show.

I auditioned for the original cast of *Cats* on Easter Sunday when I was seventeen. I got all the way to the end. There were five of us there that morning and they were casting three. Cynthia Onrubia walked in and I was like, "That's it. It's over." I didn't get cast but I was like, "I am going to get the first national." I just had that focus in my mind. Meantime, I got my Equity card at the New York Shakespeare Festival in a show called *Non Pasquale*. I was so excited to get that show because I was obsessed with *Pirates of Penzance* which I saw so many times. I would sneak into the second act. *Non Pasquale* was like a fucking dream come true because it was the same director and musical director as *Pirates* and all the women had been in it. All these incredible singers! I was thinking, "I can't believe I'm with these people and doing this show!"

You were in the Cats original cast of the first national tour, so you had Gillian Lynne choreographing and Trevor Nunn directing?

Yes! It was amazing. I played Cassandra. They re-staged everything [since the tour would be on proscenium stages while the Broadway stage was a thrust]. Gillian put me up in the front the whole time. I was featured in that first national company, and then when eventually they moved me to Broadway, Cassandra was in the back the whole time. I was so upset. I was so much happier in the tour! It was the most exciting thing in my life. I have to say, nothing tops that moment. I'm doing that show with Gillian Lynne and Trevor Nunn and all these people who I admired. It was a dream come true, a dream come true. And to dance that ball! I gave a hundred and fifty percent with that show. I loved every second of it.

Was working with Gillian Lynne different from what you had experienced in training?

I think choreographers loved me because I was quick. I took direction really fast. I wasn't confrontational. They saw me working overtime. I would learn the combination and then I'm in the back doing it twenty million times. Choreographers always loved me because of that. I'm the same way when I teach or choreograph; when I see the people in the back working their asses off and going that extra step, I love them. I was that kid. And also, I'll do anything you tell me. I'll do a back-flip. I'll do the cartwheel. I was just fearless and eager and joyful and happy to be in the room. It was always full-out with full passion. Gillian loved me and I loved her. Cassandra was all sleek. She was the only one that didn't wear leg warmers. I was very self-conscious about my feet, so I somehow managed to talk Gillian Lynne into talking to John Napier, the designer, about redesigning my costume and giving me little leg warmers. I was the only Cassandra in the history of *Cats* that ever had little semi-leg warmers.

Your husband described the *Cats* rehearsal process with Trevor Nunn as a lot of crawling around, exploring, all of that stuff. Did you do that for the tour?
Yep. We did the whole thing. Had to improvise for like a week. It makes me laugh to think that I met my husband when he had full cat makeup on. We all improvised being cats and our relationships with each other. That was very valuable because there's nothing in that show [that spells out the relationships between the cats]. You have to make it interesting. You have to have so much shit going on to make some of that stuff work. There was so much stuff that you had to fill in with your own individuality. It made me realize how much you can take charge of your performance and bring it to another level. I added so much for that character. Even when I was in the dark in the corner, I had shit going on. I was not going to waste one second. I would not feel good if I didn't give my all. I'm such a performer. I care about being good.

Tell me about Trevor Nunn.
He believes, like Robbie Marshall, that you are as important as the lead in the show even if you have the tiniest part. Your contribution is as valuable as Betty Buckley's. He made you feel that important. He had a relationship with each person and he would come and talk to you very quietly. He'd whisper, like it was really important and you were special. He's really good with actors. Once you have that, you only want to work with those kinds of people. He was brilliant.

This was when *Cats* was the hottest ticket in town and they were casting the crème de la crème of dancers. As a newbie, did you feel intimidated?
I always felt I had something to prove. Did I feel intimidated? I felt intimidated about the singing, not about my dancing. Ever. But I never took it for granted. I never stopped working and making every moment more special or more interesting. I think they saw that, which is why they moved me to Broadway. It's not just being able to be the best, it's the mindset of going for more. Tom Reed oversaw all the companies. I had auditioned for him years before for *A Chorus Line* when I was like fourteen. I had braces. I came in ballet slippers for that audition! Pink tights. So wrong! But he never forgot me [and helped get me seen for *Cats*]. So much of auditioning is about people knowing you and recognizing you. Those years of auditioning paid off for me. I was lucky.

So they move you to Broadway. That must have felt huge.
Amazing! I moved back home at that point because I didn't have an apartment. I remember feeling that this is exactly where I should be and exactly where I want to be. This is my purpose. You feel that a few times in your life. That was one of them for sure.

Did you feel yourself becoming part of that world of Broadway dancers?
I remember when I came into that Broadway company, they were tough! At my put in, you had to go through the whole "Jellicle Ball." Everyone's marking. They don't want to be there. I did that fucking ball full-out! Everybody thought I was crazy, but I didn't know any other way. I remember there was a little attitude. You have to work your way into every company. The new girl. But once you get into the circle, it's a small world.

There were lots of injuries during *Cats*.
I did get kicked and shattered all the bones in my hand in the middle of the ball. I wouldn't go off stage. I was determined to finish the fucking ball. I finish, and then I went to the hospital. I had to have a pin put in and I was out for six weeks.

You stayed in *Cats* until *Song and Dance* came up?

Yes. I workshopped that during the day and then at night I did the show. And finally, they were going to go into production and I went right into *Song and Dance*. It was a great experience in every way. It was a very, very small cast. My brother was the lead, my best friend got cast, also. It was a dream. Peter Martins choreographed and he was like, "Take your own classes or do whatever you want in the morning and we'll start rehearsal at 1:00." It was fun and very collaborative. We all got along so well. The cast loved each other and Bernadette Peters led that beautifully. She loved that company. To watch her was a big lesson—how she worked, how she managed people, how she dealt with things. I was so impressed with her. For instance, I would see the director give her something to do which was really wrong. You just knew that it was the wrong direction, that it wasn't going to work. She would never say "no," even though she knew it was wrong. She would do it a hundred and fifty percent and never say "no." She would give everything a try. She'd ultimately get her way, but she didn't ever object to anything in front of people. I also remember she could be sick as a dog but she would not miss. She would do the show and sneeze and cough during the whole first act and she wouldn't make any excuses. I believe she had such confidence in herself as an actress, she knew that even if she wasn't going to sing those notes perfectly and she would crack, it didn't matter. I was so impressed with that because I was like, "Oh my God, if I don't hit that double pirouette…." And then you realize that maybe it's not that important; it's who you are, your essence, what you bring. Bernadette taught me that. I was amazed by her. Really, really amazed. She was an incredible leader, plus she would throw great parties. She was just a class act. I learned so much watching her perform, watching her succeed, watching her fail, watching her get back up again—watching her was amazing.

That was 1985, when AIDS was hitting the Broadway community of dancers hard. And you were twenty-one.

We were all confused. Nobody knew what the hell was going on. We knew people were dying, but nobody knew why. Everybody was just terrified. You got it and you were dead. Fast. A lot of that original company of *Cats* died. Everybody was afraid you would get it from saliva. People didn't know how it was transmitted. And at that time the world was much less accepting of gay people. It was such a stigma and so many of these men were battling with their identity. It just breaks my heart. It was very hidden. People were afraid to say they had AIDS. They didn't tell you. I'll never forget Michael Scott Gregory during *Jerome Robbins'*. He suddenly became angry, just really angry, mad at the world. This guy who was such a light…. No one knew. He performed for the longest time during *Robbins'*. and then he died quickly. People hid it as long as they could. And then they were suddenly in the hospital or gone. All the art that got lost, that would have been produced. Chris Chadman was on his way to being huge. I think Michael Scott Gregory would have ended up a huge choreographer and director. He would have been like Casey Nicholaw. Who knows. Such potential and talent.

You went from *Song and Dance* to the infamous *Carrie*.

I auditioned for that show and got all the way to the end. [Choreographer] Debbie Allen loved me because I'm a dancer, but [director] Terry Hands did not really care for me. He was madly in love with Mary Ellen Stuart and she got cast. She would have been fabulous, actually, but she was very uptight. She was a born-again Christian and the show had a shitload of curse words. She called me up and she's like, "I am going to turn it down. I can't say these words." I'm like, "Thank God! I can say those words! I can say those words, no problem!" So that's how I got cast. We went to London and rehearsed. Debbie Allen gave us the fucking hardest warm-up, which I loved. It was a crazy experience, just wacky. [I had seen and loved other work directed by Terry Hands] but he wasn't great with actors. He kind of wanted you to do it and he didn't give much direction. He was all about the look and the lighting.

The rumor was that Debbie Allen was more at the helm. Was that true?
Definitely with us. Debbie was the one that would hold my hand and took care of us.

Did you have a sense that it was not coming together?
Not during it. You're just kind of thrown into it, and it was all so separated; I didn't really see what [the leads] Barbara Cook and Linzi Hately were doing, so I didn't know how anything fit together. But once we started performing in the costumes it was like, "Oh." You knew that things were weird. Terry didn't want us wearing stockings at all in "In" [the opening, set in the gym] and we were in these little briefs that, if you kicked your legs, they could see your insides. But he was really adamant because stockings didn't look real. We all hated it and we were like, "Why are we in these Grecian outfits?" He saw it as a Greek tragedy. He stuck by it. He was determined. We got horrible reviews, scathing. So we all knew. And then when it moved to Broadway, Terry Hands thought, "I'll just put Betty Buckley in and everything's going to be great." Nothing else changed. We were going to get killed. Slaughtered. This was the same season as *Phantom*. They had already opened and we were the last show of the season, right before Tony nominations. Terry was very competitive with Andrew Lloyd Webber and during tech, sitting in the house, he said to me, "Wait till they see this show! *Phantom* doesn't even know what's going to hit them." I was like, "Oh my God, he's absolutely delusional." He had it in his mind that this show was amazing. But Betty Buckley's performance was one of the best performances I've ever seen on stage. Crazy unbelievable. It was mind-boggling. I can't say enough about it. Brilliant in every way.

You had also seen Barbara Cook play it.
I love Barbara Cook, but she was never invested in it. She didn't take it to the level that Betty Buckley did. It was very different with Betty. The intensity. She was scary but vulnerable. She really went there. Barbara Cook was not willing to go there, or wanting to, which I totally understand. And she had no direction. Betty Buckley really knew how to do it on her own. I remember her calling me in the middle of the night, when she first came into the company, and she wanted to talk about character—my character, her character. Talk, talk, talk. I didn't want to talk about my character. In retrospect, I wonder if she was trying to help me out, because I didn't know what the fuck I was doing. I'd love to think that that's true.

Here you were a principal with lines and solo singing. Everything that you wanted. . . .
It was great. I was terrified, too. It was slightly embarrassing. I remember calling my mom and saying, "They're booing." It was scary. But there was a confidence boost in that, yes, I can say lines on stage. Yes, I can do this. Yes, I can get new pages and have something new thrown at me [right before I go on]. It was a step up in the right direction. I remember Mary Ellen Stuart coming to see the show. She didn't even come backstage! I'm sure she was like, "Oh thank God I didn't do that show!" But for me, it was a great experience. It was my first flop. I tried my best and that's all I could do. It's painful because you love everybody and you give your heart and soul to something that gets crapped on. Reviews are so painful. But you move

on to the next thing. That's what it's about. You can't get stuck on something. You let it go. Plus, it was a hard-ass show for me physically. It was a bit of a relief when it closed.

The very next season . . .
Was *Jerome Robbins' Broadway.* I auditioned for Jerome Robbins while we were doing *Carrie,* in the two weeks that we were previewing. I was barely hanging on because physically, I was worn out and my throat was a mess. Then add the stress of audiences laughing at us and boo-ing. . . . At nine o'clock in the morning me, Scott Wise, Joey McKneely, and Mary Ann Lamb [all *Carrie* cast mates, and Wise and Lamb had been in *Song and Dance*] go to audition for Jerome Robbins. He gave us a dance combination and he showed it to us once or twice. We did it and I thought we were marking it. All of us did. I didn't even do the pirouettes. I was just doing it in my head. Barely did it. I thought we were then going to do it full out. And he said, "OK, that's it. That's all I need to see." Mary Ann and I were like, "What the fuck?" I realize now in retrospect that he had seen us all in everything. Especially *Song and Dance,* because that was Peter Martins's choreography. He saw *Carrie.* So he knew. He knew he wanted us all. "Dreams Come True" [a ballet from *Billion Dollar Baby*] was what he really wanted me for. That was a big chunk of the show that was important to him. I was really good at that kind of physical comedy.

That rehearsal process was six months long! And as I understand it, even though he had a company, you were still auditioning for your individual roles throughout the process. People were moved around throughout.
I had Anita [from *West Side Story*] and "Dreams Come True" in my contract. But he looked at everybody for every role.

So it's impossible to relax into your role, because it can be taken away at any time. And then, famously, Jerome Robbins could be ruthless to performers. I realize that he comes from ballet and in the ballet world, that's frequently how directors get results, but it seems rough.
Yes, that's how he was inspired. He loved to see different people do the roles and it would in-spire him to get ideas, and then he would also decide who he thought was best. How lovely for him, but painful for the actors. You always felt like you were in a constant audition. I always felt a little security because I knew I had those two roles in my contract. He would switch out my guys in "Dreams Come True" all the time. I finally said to him, "Stop it. Stop it." And he did. "Dreams Come True" was a particularly intimate rehearsal process, just the four of us, because for that number he didn't have any footage of the original choreography, so it was just from memory and recreation. We rehearsed it a lot because he was trying to remember what he did, and he'd take our input.

It's interesting that he took input and that he built it on you, because he was recreating, not just the original choreography, but the original costumes, the original set design. I'd have assumed that he was strictly adhering to the original steps.
You could come up with something and if he liked it, you would keep it, but you were still al-ways under his control. He loved actors. He was much nicer to actors then he was to dancers. And maybe he was nicer to me because "Dreams Come True" was more about acting than dance steps.

Do you think your lineage helped? Not only was your father with him at City Ballet, but your mother had danced for him.

Let me tell you about my lineage with him: my father wouldn't dance with him. Of course Jerry wanted my dad because my dad was gorgeous and big and was great with partnering. But my dad hated working with him because Jerry rehearsed and rehearsed and rehearsed. He refused. My brother worked with him and it was a horrible, horrible experience. He abused my brother so badly that my brother ended up quitting City Ballet. Jerome Robbins was fucked-up. My mother had a good relationship with him. She was in the corps de ballet and he called her "Twinkles." But I don't think it helped me at all. If he doesn't like you, he doesn't like you. He liked me because I was quick and fast. I was ahead of him. If he wanted something, I saw it, I was there, and I could do it fast. He loved those people. He also loved people that had a sense of humor. I was in most of the acting pieces. He was harder on the people who were just technically dancing. He would pick on certain people.

So what kind of dynamic did that create for you guys as a company?

Oh terrible. You had your friends that you felt close with, and Jason Alexander was fantastic, a real leader and a wonderful person. He tried to help us all during the process. You had a lot of personalities that were very competitive with each other because Jerry set it up that way. A lot of people that were very talented didn't get used enough. They were really angry. They thought they were going to have bigger parts. So there was just a lot of competitive unhappiness. And yet everybody knew they were doing something brilliant. Everybody knew that we were working with a genius. So you were happy, in a way, too. It was a weird combination of things. Every week we had to perform for people like Stephen Sondheim or Leonard Bernstein or old movie stars who had done the roles before. We were performing for all those people and he'd listen to what everybody had to say. He wanted everybody's opinions. He was not somebody that was cut off and only listening to himself. He was smart in that way.

Once you opened, after that long rehearsal process, did the drama die down?

On opening night three people gave their notice. It was exhaustion. After six months rehearsing, we were already sick of the show when we opened. But once it opened, people did feel the "hit" of it all. Everybody was very proud of the show, but people had their own demons with it and with him. I remember every single person in the company had a run-in with him. Every single person. I never did and I remember thinking, "I can't believe it." And then in previews I got sick. I missed like four shows and my understudy went on for "Dreams Come True." When I came back, there was a different feeling around the theater. Something was weird. I remember Jason Alexander saying that they had to cut a number. I was worried they were going to cut *Peter Pan* [in which d'Amboise played Peter] because he never liked *Peter Pan*. It wasn't really about Jerry's work, it was about flying, even though his direction on it is perfect. He knew that the flying got the attention, not his brilliant direction. He was wanting to cut it but then, at first preview, the audience went nuts for it. Thank God. But I never thought in a million years he would cut "Dreams Come True" because it was his baby. We'd worked that thing so hard. I am told, "Oh, no 'Dreams Come True' today." It was just cut. It never went back in the show and he never spoke to me about it. He never came up to me, he never said anything to me. A week goes by and not a word to each other. I was hating him so fucking much. Then I remember running into him in the wings. I think he said, "I'm sorry."

We hugged and that was it. On opening night he gave me a picture of "Dreams Come True." It shows you how he just couldn't deal with intimacy.

Cutting "Dreams Come True" must have been awful for you.
It was devastating. I really felt part of that because it was our creation together. For Anita and Peter Pan, I was just doing what I was told. We rehearsed that number every day for six months. Every day. Just him and me in the room with the three guys, so it was really my piece. It was why I got hired. It was devastating. It was just cut away so fast, out of nowhere.

You performed Peter Pan in front of Mary Martin and Anita in front of Chita Rivera....
Peter Gennaro [who had assisted Robbins throughout his career and, though uncredited, originally choreographed "America"] came and worked with me privately, which was so fantastic. He pulled me aside and asked if he could work with me. "Oh yes, please God!" Jerry didn't care that much about that number because it wasn't really his. Any direction that I got was from Peter. Jerry didn't know he worked with me. I would never be cast as Anita nowadays, but in those days, it was accepted, somehow. As much as I get it and I totally understand, I really feel lucky that I did get to do it.

You received a Tony nomination.
That was amazing, but I remember being terrified. Wide-eyed and thrown into it. I didn't feel in my body.

So you didn't enjoy it?
I think it's hard with Tonys. I don't know, do people ever really enjoy it? Maybe some people do. I mean, it's exciting, but you're performing every night and people are coming and judging you. You're trying to give your best performance. And then you're going to all these events during the day with all these other stars. Some of them are really interesting. But you're just kind of overwhelmed and feeling judged the whole time.

Did it feel like you had done the thing you set out to do? A moment of arrival?
Yes, it did. It totally did. It didn't feel quite as good as *Cats* did. Nothing felt better than getting *Cats*. I was doing everything I'd wanted to do. I was working with the masters, incredible actors and performers that were the best at what they do. And I was doing Broadway, which was my dream. But it was a hard show. It was hard on the body. Icing all the time. People weren't happy, it wasn't a happy cast.

I heard that there were times that Peter didn't fly.
Oh, yeah. There were a lot of times I'd just have to jump out the window, or run around the stage. It was horrifying.

You said that his direction of that number was ...
Brilliant. He was brilliant and truthfully, to this day, when I see any production ... those three kids, and I mean, they were adults, but how good were they? He was so brilliant at human connection and honesty on stage. You couldn't be dishonest because he could see it a mile away. Even if you were doing big broad comedy, it still had to come from a place of honesty and truthfulness and storytelling. He was very particular about the honesty of

it all. And focus. He was brilliant at knowing where everybody had to focus to make it all seem natural and real. He was incredibly brilliant at humanity. He couldn't do it himself. He couldn't, as a person, show it or talk to you that way, but he knew how to get it out of you. He knew how to direct it and bring it out. That's what his brilliance was. The thing I learned most from that show was how to focus on stage. If you focus on this person, they get the laugh. Don't upstage. It doesn't help you. You want to send your focus to the person that it needs to be sent to [in order] to tell the story. Then it helps everybody. I learned that in a big way from him.

And then during the run, Terrence Mann came into the show.
Terry came in and we got together immediately. But I left not long after he came in. I just had enough. I didn't have another job to go to, I was just like, "I'm done." In those days I did that a lot. Nowadays you hold on to your job. That's probably because I'm older. When you're younger you're trying to grow.

Up until then you had really hopped from show to show, but then you didn't work for a while.
Jerome Robbins burnt me out. We all felt burnt out after that experience—exhausted. I said to my agents, "I don't want to go up for musicals. I only want to do plays." I wanted to be a better actress and not rely on my dancing and singing. I did a lot of regional theater: *Speed the Plow, Italian-American Reconciliation.* I was going to try to do some more film and television stuff and we moved to L.A. We were there a month and I said, "We're going home. I can't stand it here." It just was not my scene. I'm such a New Yorker and I felt isolated there. New York City makes me want to be in theater, you know? I have to be around it. Otherwise, I'll just be a hermit. In Los Angeles, nothing inspired me. I didn't work for nine months. I did a couple of commercials and an industrial. It was me, Jimmy Newman, Jackie Patterson, for McDonald's. I was a tap-dancing hamburger. Jim Newman was a Coca-Cola. We totally went down notches. But it was a great gig for the whole summer. We'd work like one week out of a month and get paid the whole month. But I remember thinking, "Shit, maybe I've got to get out of the business and do something else." That was a really weird time. But then *Damn Yankees* happened [replacing Bebe Neuwirth in the lead role]. Jack O'Brien and Robbie Marshall were at the audition, and Cynthia Onrubia was teaching. They were like, "You don't have to dance," and I was like, "Oh no, I'm dancing!" Because I always knew that would always be the thing [that set me apart]. It was an all-day thing, down in the basement of the theater. We were called up one at a time. Nerve-wracking as all hell.

And you got it!
Yes! Robbie Marshall wanted to re-choreograph a few things for me, so he worked with me privately and we redid a few of the numbers. It was an incredible experience. They were so happy to have me and I couldn't believe I was doing this big lead on Broadway. It was thrilling. I did it with Victor Garber, who I had the biggest crush on. I had such a good time with him. Then he left and Jerry Lewis came in. I loved him, too. Loved him. Working with Robbie Marshall—he's on top of my list besides Jerome Robbins. I was in love with him, too.

Why did you love working with him?
Because Robbie makes you feel like a million bucks. He made you feel special, like you were the only person in the room. And he didn't just do that to me. You just walked across the stage

and he made you feel that way. He was really brilliant and very different than Robbins. He catered to you. He wanted to see what you could bring to the role, and who you were.

Tell me about working with Jerry Lewis.
It was a dream come true. I watched Jerry Lewis [when I was] growing up. He was an icon to me. He really was respectful of the piece and he loved it, loved being there. He treated us all like gold. The cast loved him. We knew we were running because of him. He kept the show going. It was a really happy time. I used to watch him do his number every night. He had the audience in the palm of his hand. Him dialing the phone number to hell on a rotary phone went on for ten minutes. He could make shit up and it was hilarious—watching somebody make something out of nothing. He was just brilliant.

The next season you worked with Rob Marshall again in *Company*.
That was partially because of Robbie. He wanted to choreograph me in that role. I actually played Kathy at Surflight Theater when I was eighteen. I missed my high school graduation and went straight there and did twelve shows in twelve weeks. We got $30 a week. David Loud was the assistant musical director. I wasn't happy with the choreography for my dance and I remember waking him up in the middle of the night to make him come look at what I had re-choreographed. "Do you think I can do this instead?" Cut to years later, *Company* on Broadway, David's the musical director and I'm going in to audition for David and Sondheim and Scott Ellis and Robbie. That was amazing. That's when I met Deb Monk and Kate Burton who I literally fell in love with. LaChanze and Jane Krakowski and I shared a dressing room and became best friends. I hit the jackpot with those actors.

When you're going in for an audition full of people you know like David Loud and Rob Marshall, is it comforting because it's people who you know, or is it more stressful because they expect so much?
It's a combination of both. They know you and they want you to be good. I don't want to disappoint them if I suck, which so many times I do. Auditioning is not my forte, never has been. Every once in a while, I nail them, but I can't tell you how many I have not, how many I fucked up. I mean I still fuck up a lot. The only thing that did make me feel better was having Veanne Cox in the waiting room before me. So neurotic. Ten million times more nervous. I remember thinking, "OK, I can do this." She was brilliant, by the way.

You stopped the show twice, with "Tick Tock" and "You Could Drive a Person Crazy."
Robbie choreographed "Tick Tock" on me, to the way I moved. That was everything I ever wanted. And the song ... we practiced it every day. We would meet before the show and go through it. When I did it at Surflight, I wasn't fucking doing the harmonies, I'll tell you that!

Shortly thereafter, *Chicago* opened. Were you salivating for that show?
Salivating! I saw it at Encores! A lot of my friends were doing it. It was like the best thing I'd ever seen. Ann Reinking was on fire! I knew, "I gotta do that show. I gotta do that show." When they were doing the first national, I got the call that they wanted me to come in for Velma. I knew I wasn't a Velma. I knew that I could play it, but there was somebody that was gonna walk in and be Velma. Like Jasmine Guy—she just has to stand there and say the lines and she's it. I'd have to act at it and I didn't want to do it even though I could dance and sing it. Roxie was the part I felt I could bring something to. So I worked on the Roxie stuff with

my acting coach and I went to the audition and I started to do Roxie. They went, "No, no, no, you're here for Velma." I was like, "I was told Roxie! I don't know the Velma stuff." So they said, "OK, just do Roxie." So I did my whole thing. [Director] Walter Bobbie still asked me to read Velma. I pretended I had never looked at it even though I had. I did the scene, but I'm not a Velma. I know it. They pretty much cast me that day.

What do you remember about the rehearsal process?
It was a weird experience. Annie was kind of tense. It was not good, actually. All the creative people were freaked out. They hired Jasmine Guy and me and we were the youngest Velma and Roxie. It was always cast kind of older. This was not the norm. I always felt like they weren't sure they made the right decision with us. Walter didn't really know the roles that well then. He was just learning them himself. When they did Encores!, Bebe and Annie kind of threw up the show that they had done in California with Rob Marshall. I think Walter was still figuring it out. Walter Bobbie knows this show like nobody else at this point. He's so fucking brilliant. But at that time he didn't know the show that well. I felt like I didn't have that much help and I took my time. I wasn't the kind of actress that was like, "I'm going to walk in and do this." I knew that I would get there, but it was going to be a process and I felt like they didn't want to see that process. They don't want to see you not be ready. I remember doing the first run-through and at intermission [producer] Barry Weissler came up to me and said, "I'm hoping the second act is going to be better." The whole Broadway cast was watching us. It was tense between Walter and Annie. She was in a really bad place. She was in a lot of pain with her back and doing eight shows a week on Broadway. It was just not a healthy thing and they were freaked out about us. We opened in Cincinnati, and I remember getting a great review, thank God. Barry was really happy, really positive, even though I still didn't know what the fuck I was doing. But then I got injured. I hurt my knee really badly—tore a ligament tendon and I was out. The tour's big opening was Washington, DC. We were supposed to be there for like six months and I was gone. Belle Calloway, my understudy, opened it. I remember being at home, fucking miserable. I get a call from Barry Weissler: "Charlotte, this show was fantastic and Belle was fantastic! So listen, I'm going to be opening up a new one. This is the Roxie company but in about six months, I'm going to be bringing out the Velma Tour. Why don't you do that?" I was like, "No!" Anyway, I went back to Washington and ended up doing it. They re-reviewed and I got a really great review. It was a rocky road but it ended up great and they were very happy with me.

You said that Walter Bobbie and Ann Reinking weren't in a good place?
There was just a lot of tension initially with them. Everybody was just so stressed out. Annie had a lot of pain. She was really struggling. I don't know what the agreement was with how much she was going to be involved but I think there was a misunderstanding about that. When Annie came in, she gave incredible direction. But you needed them both. Walter sees the whole picture, Annie sees little bits and pieces. He cut a third out of that book. It needed that much. It had a lot of fat. When you see that original script, you're like, "what?" It's night and day. He streamlined it perfectly. Just enough for each character to be fully established with the least amount of words. Walter also put together the whole ending.

Do you remember learning from Ann, despite her unhappiness?
It took me a long time to find that monologue. It's brilliant. You have to find the confidence. I was young. I needed a little bit of Jerry Lewis—taking control and knowing that you can just hold that stage. I was just barely hanging on. Annie helped me a lot with that. She was also

very much about giving you a lot of freedom. She's not nitpicky. She really likes you to come up with it. Walter too.

It's really interesting that you say she encouraged freedom, because the Fosse style is so precise and fine-tuned.
She knows I'm going to improvise in the Fosse style. She was also always adamant that Roxie had a certain classiness to her. As much as it can be raunchy, there is always a certain class.

You and Jasmine Guy were dropped into another company for the Los Angeles run and I think that was the beginning of that show really becoming a revolving door of ins and outs. It's very unusual for companies to change as often as the companies of *Chicago* do.
Yes, that's when it started. When I first went to Broadway, that company—they were assholes. They were really cold to me. They were cold to anybody coming in. Now, of course, that's all changed. It's like the exact opposite because it has happened so many times. You'll have the worst people come in and it doesn't matter. Nobody's actually that judgmental anymore. Which is kind of lovely.

Is it lovely? I mean, I understand that could be lovely backstage, but is there ever the feeling that "Wow, this used to be something really, really sharp. And now the standard has slipped."
Absolutely. And that happens. And then suddenly it'll all kind of come back again when the regulars are back in. One weak link of any of those main characters and the show does suffer, but it still holds. The Weisslers have sort of worked it out that they have a supporting team around, so when they bring in somebody that's less strong, they usually make sure all the support is solid. They figured that out. I've gotten used to it. And the moving around of the leads has kept the show going.

You described being sick of *Jerome Robbins'* and sick of *Cats*. With this show, you have come and gone so many times. Do the breaks keep you from getting sick of it?
Exactly. For starters, it's is a great role and I'm allowed a lot of freedom with it. It just grows and changes. There are so many different ways to play it and they all work. And I did get sick of doing Roxie, but you break for a year and then you come back. With long runs, I wish they'd do that all the time. I wish they would do it with everybody in that cast. I get a chance to leave but the ensemble does not. It would make a huge difference if they would give them all breaks. It would help the show and the morale. Otherwise, it becomes a grind and that's when the negativity starts.

Do you try to influence it?
I like to bring joy around as much as I can. My dressing room door is always open. I used to have tons of candy. . . . I want everybody in my dressing room. But that has to do with coming from the chorus. I don't like to be alone. I like people in my dressing room, unless I have to vocalize or whatever. I like to put my makeup on with the girls. I like to hang out with the cast. I'm not going to let negativity bring me down.

Have you ever gone into the show and been surprised in a good way? Have you ever learned something unexpected from a new Velma?
Absolutely! I loved Ruthie Henschel. She was fucking unbelievable and you just never knew what she was going to throw at you. She was just a powerhouse in every way. And Vicki Lewis, too. She was always interesting, always surprising.

How did the role change for you as you evolved in it and how has the role also changed you?
Well, the one thing I realized is that I don't have to dance perfectly or sing perfectly every time and I can still be good. I started to trust what I brought to the role and that's what mattered more than my dancing ability or my singing ability. Even though that's important, there were times when I wasn't able to dance well because I was injured. I could still do the show and walk out of the theater feeling good. I used to not feel that way ever.

The first time you left *Chicago*, you went into *Contact*.
That was an acting/dancing role, not a singing role. Acting with dance ... I've always been able to do that, so it was easy for me to go right into that show. But it was a lot of hard dancing. Exhausting! I recently saw the PBS taping we did and I was like, "Fuck! That is twenty minutes of me non-stop dancing." But it was a really good acting role and I loved that. I knew everybody in that cast. It was a great time. Lincoln Center was really respectful. I was treated really well.

And then you did *Can-Can* at Encores! *The New York Times* called you "the always delectable Charlotte d'Amboise."
Aw. I had just had a baby! That was one of the first things back. That was great. I loved Patti LuPone! She works her ass off! She came in and she knew every line. She's a workhorse. Takes her work very seriously—no nonsense. What you see is what you get. She's really honest and straightforward. If you don't fuck with her, she won't fuck with you. We only had two weeks and I had all these numbers. I don't know how we got through that. I was so stressed out that I broke out with all these fever blisters on my face. Horrible! And I had to kiss this poor guy ... I was bleeding! And he was so nice about it. But it was fun.

The following year the Weisslers asked you to stand by for Christina Applegate in *Sweet Charity*.
I had read that show was going to come in and I was like, "I want that part!" And then I heard Walter Bobbie was doing it! I got an audition before they had signed Christina. It was one of those things where I knew I nailed it. I just knew it was one of the best auditions I've had in my life. That part is just me. I could tell Walter was really happy. Then I heard that Christina Applegate got it and I was devastated. I was in *Chicago* at the time and I get a call from Barry Weissler. He takes me out to lunch and he offers me the chance to continue doing Roxie in New York and to cover Christina. He says, "I don't know if she's gonna be able to do eight shows a week. She's fantastic but we don't know her. We want a strong backup in case she can't do it. You would get paid double and be ready to go on when you need to go on." So, of course I said yes because why wouldn't I? My other choice was to say no and never get a chance to do the role. I was fine about it. I wasn't angry or anything. I was happy to be in the room. Christina was fantastic. I have only amazing things to say about her. More amazing than I ever expected. Hard worker, knew what she was up against, respectful, talented. She was brilliant. Then they go on tour and I get a call that she broke her foot. I was in New York doing *Chicago* and they had changed the show on the road. I didn't know any of the changes. "Hey Char, you're on, Baby." I did it in Boston and ended up doing the first week of previews in New York. I wish I could have gone on more. I finally remember feeling like I had it and then I didn't get to go on much more. Because she was solid. She was really determined after she broke her foot. Really professional. I had two little kids at home and I don't even know how I did it. Four months would go by and they'd

be like, "You're on tonight." They never rehearsed me. But that was a perfect example of my realizing, "Hey, if I fuck up these dance steps, who cares? Who is going to know? [The dancers] are behind me. I am the lead! I can do whatever I want. I can just make it up!" I remember that feeling of freedom, so it was fun. I loved that role and I got better later in the run because I was able to bring more of my essence.

Your next show was *A Chorus Line*. There were only a handful of really strong triple threats at the right age for Cassie. Did you think it was yours to lose?
I did. I always think it's mine to lose! But you don't ever know. You have to nail it, always. I never felt I was a shoo-in.

Dancing "The Music and the Mirror" in *A Chorus Line.*
(Paul Kolnik)

And you got it.

It was great but also stressful. They were very much doing the [original] show. Not too much input. They didn't mess around with my acting, but for the dancing, they wanted the original. They didn't want anybody to go out on a limb and be really different. When we were in San Francisco, just before we left for New York, [director] Bob Avian sat us down and said, "I want you to remember exactly what you did here. This is the show I want when we go." And I remember thinking, "Oh, you can't tell people to stay the same." They were afraid of people doing too much.

It really did look like a museum piece and I don't mean that pejoratively. It was a recreation, as much as possible, not just of Michael Bennett's original work, but Tharon Musser's lighting and Theoni Aldredge's costumes—a recreation, except in the acting choices.

I don't know how much they allowed the acting to really change that much, either. It was so clean! At an audition, no one would be that clean!

Did you feel constricted by that sort of slavish devotion to recreation?

I did feel restricted. But they never gave me acting notes. Except one. It was a good note—not to be too kooky. Cassie is straight and if you try to do something different with it, it doesn't work as well. It's much better just straight and honest. And that's what was hard to do with that part; I get bored quickly. I want to be funny or I want to try something new. It was easy to do for the first three months and then it's hard to stick with it. I wanted to do more with it acting-wise. You're stuck with the choreography. It's fine, but I did feel stuck.

"The Music and the Mirror" is almost a danced monologue. Cassie is speaking volumes, all physically. It was built on Donna McKechnie's body and to fill each of those moves, her moves, with your emotional choices, would seem to be a particular challenge.

Baayork Lee [who reconstructed the choreography] didn't give me any intentions, just the moves. You've got to just fill it. I also struggled a lot physically because I had a herniated disc in my neck. They wanted to operate and put a rod in right before opening. It was bad. So here I am doing the Cassie dance and I can't move my neck and I'm scared of being paralyzed. It was a really stressful time. Pain. But I got through it and luckily I never had to get a rod. Thank God I didn't take advice from that guy. But it was a struggle, the whole time. It's hard to do that dance in your mid-forties eight shows a week. Cassie was written to be thirty-two! I think I would have been a little happier doing it in my thirties! That show was hard.

You got a Tony nomination. How was that?

It was good. It was OK. After opening, I went through a period of stage fright for the first time in my life. I would have panic attacks and I couldn't sing, I couldn't talk, I would sing off pitch. I could dance only because I could let out the energy. It was a nightmare, I started getting letters from people, like, "What are you doing up there?" It was weird! First time in my life experiencing that. And then I somehow pulled through after I started to talk about it. I knew the cast members were like, "What is wrong with her? What is she doing?" All day long I lived in terror of what was going to happen at night. And then I went past it. Then the Tonys came and I got nominated. It was just stressful. I felt such pressure with that show. Once in a blue moon I felt good about a performance.

So being nominated, did you feel like a phony?
I didn't feel like a phony, but I didn't feel like I really deserved it. I didn't feel really proud.

Do you feel differently about it now, looking back on it?
No. I still feel the same. I was not happy with most of my performances.

So when it closed, it was a bit of a relief?
Oh yeah.

You spent a few years in and out of *Chicago* and then, according to your husband, when they auditioned him for *Pippin* they asked, "And what's Charlotte doing?"
Yeah! But still, they made me fucking audition for that! I remember Fran Weissler calling: "Charlotte darling, wouldn't it be fun? We could all go up to Cambridge together with the kids. But, you know, you have to audition." They saw everybody for that role. So, what am I going to do that's different? I remember feeling that pressure. I remember them saying, "You don't have to dance," and I said, "Oh yeah, I do." I felt like I had to win over Diane Paulus even though she had seen me in things. It was an awesome audition. They had Terry come in and do one of the scenes with me. That was magic. The whole experience of *Pippin* was magic and such a surprise. It came out of nowhere. And Broadway parts that we were both right for and we could play husband and wife? I loved every minute. So many things got changed and fixed. It was like a dream. There are so many shows that are like, "If they'd only fix that number…." And here, they did!

For example?
The ending. Diane Paulus had this idea about a ladder and fire … it cost a lot of money. We did like two performances and it didn't work. So they cut it, even with all the money they put into it. They never do that. That's just one example. It was like that with every scene, every song. They streamlined it and made it all work. And they listened to us. The team was brilliant. Everybody came together in a positive, thoughtful, creative way. It was a give-and-take the whole time and everybody felt important.

What was it like working with your husband? Did you give each other notes?
Usually, it's me saying, "Honey, would you look at me? Will you stop upstaging me for God's sake?" No, we had a ball. I loved working with him. We had met each other working together and it was nice to work together again because it was a reminder of what we fell in love with in each other. I love watching him work. It was fun and sexy. He was so good! He was just so full of ideas and he made something out of that part. It was one of the high points of our life as a couple, during that show.

Dancers on Broadway have a shelf-life and so many of your friends and peers no longer perform. How do you feel about that?
I feel, truthfully, that I hit that shelf-life ages ago, but somehow I keep dancing. It's a dancer's life. Dancing is not as fun anymore because it hurts. They forget to tell you that. You have to take a lot of Advil, and use a lot of Bengay. It just doesn't feel as fun. It's a loss. For a lot of people it's a loss of identity. I don't feel that way because I've still been dancing. And I have to

"I'm just an ordinary housewife and mother, just like all you housewives and mothers out there." In *Pippin*.
(Joan Marcus)

tell you the truth: I don't want to dance like that anymore. I don't have that desire. Because I did it. I love acting. I like acting that has dance in it and luckily I've been able to do that a lot. I still love a musical comedy number!

What do you want now?
I don't know. I kept thinking I'm gonna figure it out during this [COVID] time and instead I got a dog. I feel like I've had a really nice break. I don't know how much I really care about being an actress anymore. I don't have that desire. I'm not like a Chita, wanting to be performing until I'm eighty. I wish I did. I don't think I have that drive.

So if someone offered you *Kiss of the Spider Woman*, which Chita did when she was older than you, you wouldn't want it?

Well, first I'd say I'm not right for that part. But I don't want to carry any show now. I'd like a nice sidekick role. I do still love to perform. And it is me. I teach a lot and I love teaching and mentoring. I love making a difference with people that are talented. I can really help them. I used to always be focused on achieving particular goals; I have none of that now, which is ok. I don't feel I have to prove anything anymore and I feel so lucky I got to do as much as I got to do. I'm amazed by it and thrilled and there's not an ego in me that feels a need to do more. If it's here and it happens, I'll still enjoy it.

Mary Beth Peil

January 2022

Careers can suddenly take totally unexpected turns that change everything. Angela Lansbury was a Hollywood actor with three Oscar nominations under her belt when, at the age of forty, she was offered her first musical by Arthur Laurents. Barbara Cook spent the first half of her career as a successful stage actor, only to enjoy even greater success as a cabaret performer for the second half of her life. And then there's Mary Beth Peil, who trained as an opera singer and for the first two decades of her professional life sang soprano at major opera companies across the country. It was only when those opera companies started adding musicals to their repertoire that she found herself performing in one. She was petrified, but *Kiss Me, Kate* provided a moment of epiphany from which she never looked back. She realized, she says with a chortle, that she was an actor who can sing, not a singer who can act.

What followed was a non-stop career that staunchly refuses easy categorization and, forty years later, continues to astonish even Peil. In 1985 (right after that fateful *Kiss Me, Kate*) she made her Broadway debut as Mrs. Anna opposite Yul Brynner in his final tour of *The King and I* (nabbing a Tony nomination for her efforts, thank you). That was the first on a path of shows she shared with musical theater giants, including Stephen Sondheim (*A Little Night Music*, *Sweeney Todd, Sunday in the Park with George, Follies, Road Show*), John Kander, Terrence McNally and John Doyle (*The Visit*), David Leveaux (*Nine*), McNally again with Ahrens and Flaherty (*Anastasia*), Michael John LaChiusa (*First Lady Suite*), and Bartlett Sher and David Yazbek (*Women on the Verge of a Nervous Breakdown*). Unwilling to settle for just a single paradigm shift, Peil became a staple in straight plays, too, appearing both on and off-Broadway in over twenty shows. And—why not—she conquered television as well, first domineering as Michelle Williams's grandmother on *Dawson's Creek* and then as Chris Noth's mother on *The Good Wife*.

Throughout one of our conversations, Peil's phone rings repeatedly, much to her annoyance. It's the costume designer for a new film she's starting while she simultaneously goes into rehearsal for the workshop of a new musical. Ask her to account for her jam-packed résumé and Peil self-effacingly cites the diminished competition for roles in her age bracket. Don't believe her. What Peil brings to any role, even when she's the fourth or fifth lead, is that indescribable "it" factor that absolutely commands attention. With her ramrod posture (often expertly deployed to signal patrician condescension) and her inquisitive eyes, which can alternatively exude warmth and wisdom or shoot icy darts of judgment, Peil is indelible, standing out even as she shares the stage with the likes of Chita Rivera, F. Murray Abraham, Antonio Banderas, Bernadette Peters, Liev Schreiber, and Patti LuPone, to name just a few of her co-stars. Her Upper West Side apartment, doused in light and overlooking the Hudson, overflows with books and memories, including wall sconces and a set of rolling pins from the *Dawson's* set. Though she's often cast as imperious matriarchs, Peil is anything but. She speaks of Rivera as "one of the girls," but Peil could just as easily be describing herself. "We need to get a drink," she tells me as we wrap up our chat. I get the immediate feeling that Peil knows the city's best watering holes and has laughed heartily and conspiratorially in all of them.

"Shall We Dance?" With Yul Brynner in *The King and I*.
(Photofest)

When you were cast in the Minneapolis Opera Company's *Kiss Me, Kate*, did you feel like you were slumming it?
Musical theater was always a no-no. I never considered it. It was verboten. I was terrified because I had always been told that if you abuse your voice, you could lose it. I was concerned that eight hours a day of rehearsal—which never happens in the opera—in a show like *Kiss Me, Kate*, where not only are you speaking and singing legitimately, but you're also screaming, I would lose

my voice. I went in with great fear. My savior was a wonderful baritone named John Reardon, who had been back and forth doing musicals and opera. He helped me get over the fear. Day by day, I would come home thinking, "Well, that's probably it. I won't be able to speak tomorrow." And the next day I felt stronger and freer. It was crazy. I had no idea. It was a light-bulb moment, a revelation. How freeing it was to know that I wasn't going to hurt myself.

What about that first time just uttering lines?

I'm sure it was hilarious for anyone in the room. I had started taking acting class with Frank Cusarro and I had done some work on some scenes, so I was not shockingly awful. I can only imagine.

Of all roles in the musical theater canon, to start with one that includes Shakespeare . . .

Yes! But it was the perfect segue, because it's so classically rooted.

Mary Beth Peil

The King and I	National Tour, 1984; Broadway, 1985
Birds of Paradise	off-Broadway, 1987
Sweeney Todd	Milburn, NJ, 1992
As Thousands Cheer	off-Broadway, 1998
Sweeney Todd	Washington, DC, 2002
Nine	Broadway, 2003
First Lady Suite	off-Broadway, 2004
Sunday in the Park with George	Broadway, 2008
Women on the Verge of a Nervous Breakdown	Broadway, 2010
Follies	Broadway, 2012
The Threepenny Opera	off-Broadway, 2014
The Visit	Broadway, 2015
Anastasia	Broadway, 2017
Road Show	Encores!, 2019
A Man of No Importance	off-Broadway, 2022
Cornelia Street	off-Broadway, 2023

You decided to seek out more musical theater. How did that happen?

I came back to New York with this light bulb still over my head. I said to everyone I know, "I think I'm going to try to do some musical theater." It was like "fools rush in." I had no idea how you do this. I rented a space, now it's called the Kaufman, a couple of blocks north of Lincoln Center. When I think about it now, I can't comprehend doing that. That's just not who I am. I hired a pianist, I pulled out some musical theater stuff, some opera arias, and some art songs, and I invited everyone I know. I just talked and told my story, interspersed with songs, and by the end of that afternoon I had three jobs: two more *Kiss Me, Kate*s and a *Most Happy Fella* at opera companies. And I had some management interest. Within a couple of weeks, [I heard from] a friend of mine that her friend knew the casting director for *The King and I*, and they were looking for a Mrs. Anna for the Los Angeles run with Yul Brynner. So [ultimately] I had to turn down the other three jobs that I got! I talked to the casting director and she said, "Come to the Equity Lounge." I had no idea what that was. She took me in a room and I sang, "Hello, Young Lovers" and read some lines. She asked me to come back that afternoon to the Uris Theater. I sang for Mitch Leigh, the producer. Everybody got very excited and they said, "Can you be on a plane to L.A. tonight at 6:00 [to sing for Yul Brynner tomorrow]? "Mitch Leigh says, 'You have to wear white and black. Brynner doesn't care for colors. Do not wear heels because you're tall and he's not. Wear your hair back. Look like an English tea rose.'" He gave his credit card to the casting director and said, "Go to Bonwit's for a white top, black skirt, black flats." We flew up to Bonwit's, headed straight for Ralph Lauren, and she pulled out a black linen skirt and white linen top. I got in my car and drove back to New Jersey. I had called my kids and said, "Pack a bag with a toothbrush and my nightie, meet me on the front porch." I pulled into the driveway, my kids hand me the bag, and off I go to the airport. I pull into Newark at 5:40 for a 6:00 p.m. flight, run to the gate—it couldn't happen now—fabulous first-class flight, land, pick me up, take me to the Hilton, room service. I have breakfast in the morning, get dressed, try to look like an English tea rose, go to the Beverly theater. There are four ladies auditioning for Mrs. Anna, and a bunch of other people for other parts. We're all backstage in a little room. I go out and I sing "Hello, Young Lovers." It's totally dark except for the ghost light and a pin spot. From the darkened house I hear, "Brrrravo," from a distinct and deep voice. So I thought, "Well, at least Brynner liked it." And then they had me read some lines with the stage manager and I was terrible. I thought I just sucked. I left and flew home on the red-eye that night. And by the time I got to my house in New Jersey I started thinking about what had actually happened in the last twenty-four hours and how this could possibly change my life. Up until then it had just been a lark. I didn't really think about how much I might possibly want it. The next few hours were excruciating. But then the call came about 2:00 in the afternoon.

As you were talking about dressing to Yul Brynner's tastes, it occurred to me that even though the King was originally a supporting part, this production existed because of him and he had control of everything down to the carpeting backstage [to accommodate a largely barefoot cast] and the brown paint in his dressing rooms at every tour stop [to cover shabby walls]. I would imagine that with a star so entrenched in that level of control, your being a neophyte really served you. You were open and ready to learn.
Yes! He was totally the King. It was a perfect setup for both of us. He couldn't have been kinder and more encouraging right from start. I was told silly things like, "When you first meet him, don't look him in the eye. Don't touch him," all this kind of stuff. And, of course, he walked in the room, looked me right in the eye, gave me a big hug, and said, "Welcome aboard." The things that people perpetuate.... But he was a tough master. I mean if you weren't doing what he felt needed to be done, he let you know he was not pleased. After about a month, I remember coming into his dressing room and saying, "I feel like I now know the part, I know the blocking, and I can start developing my Mrs. Anna." He smiled at me and said, "Yes, yes, of course." I would try things and then, maybe two days later—we always met during the ballet. He would come to my dressing room or I would come to his and he would tell stories, or we would talk about what we were doing on stage—and he would say, "You know, I see what you did last night. I know what you were thinking, but you know, we have tried that many times. It doesn't work as well."

He was probably right, right? They probably did try it.
Oh, I am sure they did try. He had how many Mrs. Annas? Maybe thirty? And he was a great director. I mean, he had a career as a director. He had a wonderful eye for detail. He knew what worked. So it was a real shortcut, a speed course in musical theater.

The two of you had a real sexual tension that I don't think existed in the original.
Before I left for L.A., I had people who said, "You really shouldn't do this because he'll eat you up and spit you out. He's a formidable force and not a nice person." Everybody has their own stories and their own experiences, so I'm not saying that they were wrong, but

I met him at a time when he was just at the beginning of his fourth marriage to this beautiful young Chinese/British dancer [Kathy Lee Brynner]. They were quite extraordinary together. There was no hanky-panky. Not even a question of it. And then, the day after I had gone to his dressing room to say, "I am ready to work on my Mrs. Anna," he came to my dressing room and told me that he was terminally ill with inoperable lung cancer. So we were immediately joined at the hip. I remember the date: October 4th. I was sworn to secrecy. The only people who knew his situation were me, his dresser, and his wife. And so, there was that really deep bond, right from the beginning. Maybe one would say that's not sexual, but a bond is a bond and I think it reads on stage. He also told me many stories about how he and Gertie [original Anna, Gertrude Lawrence] came upon a solution to what was, up until some point in Boston or New Haven, a relatively dry book. They both were trying to figure out what was wrong with it. It was talky. The story, as he told it, is that one night he and Gertie cooked up some stuff that could happen in a couple of the scenes prior to the ballroom scene. Most of it had to do with hooking eyes. He was a big believer in eyes and taking long pauses. Oscar Hammerstein came backstage and said, "What was going on there? What was happening? It was fantastic." Within a day or two he and Rodgers wrote "Shall We Dance." The secret to that scene is that he's at one end of the stage and she's at the other and the music starts and they just look at each other. He said, "The secret is do not take your eyes off of my eyes. I'm going to move slowly towards you and you do not move. Do not breathe. Do not take your eyes off of me." By the time he gets to her and puts his hand on her waist, it's like [gasps].

With him being somewhat tyrannical, how was that for company morale?
The company itself was such a family. Pat Weber had been with Brynner in some form of *The King and I* since she was fifteen. She was even in the movie as one of the young wives. [Some people] had been with him either in the '77 incarnation and [had] come back again, or [had been] with him for the two or three years that he had been touring. He was like Papa. He was kind and generous to a fault with everyone.

Did you ever feel out of your element? Or did you feel like you took to it well?
I took to it well. He had my back. The whole company had my back.

I heard you say once that he taught you stillness.
Yes, he did. And that was another part of the sexual thing, as well. I would just watch him. He would just stand. But it wasn't like a statue. Just the act of listening made him so powerful.

Did you have to unlearn what you had known and relied upon in opera?
I hadn't really thought about that, but for sure. The way I was trained, the job of the opera singer is not only to sing beautifully, but to make the most of the movement or the motion— your movement, your thought, your emotion is what makes the music happen, rather than the music acting on you. They called it musical motivation. You don't let the music do it for you, you create the music, you create the need for the music. It's very subtle. Your body is always slightly ahead of the music so that the music seems inevitable rather than you being the result of the music. The music dictated everything in the opera world. There was never a moment of stillness. Whereas as an actor, you could control the timing of what the next beat was in a scene.

So you come to New York with the show.

I think I'm fortunate in that I was never overwhelmed by being in awe of or overly impressed by him or his fame. I think I was spared that kind of thing of "Broadway." Maybe it's because I was older. I wasn't a kid.

While I can buy that as a theory, you literally had done one musical and decided to try doing more of them. Next thing you know you're a leading lady on Broadway. How was that not kind of heady?

I don't know. I think because I'm always just so much in what needs to be done. I go to the heady part when I look back, but in the moment, I'm not easily made heady.

There are moments, like a Tony Award nomination, that might give one pause.

You know what happened with the Tony Award nomination, though? It was sort of the opposite of heady. I was embarrassed. I didn't know anybody. I didn't know what the hell it was. There was a meet-and-greet with the press and I remember I had no idea what was expected of me or who these people were. Hal Prince was ushering his leading lady [Leilani Jones] around the room, meeting people, but I had no one to take me around. What am I supposed to do? Why am I here? What is this about? And then by the time we got to the night of the Tonys and seeing all these wonderful actors running up and down the aisles hugging each other and saying, "hi," I was embarrassed. I didn't belong there. I wasn't part of the family. I said to myself, "If I'm ever back here again, I am going to belong. I'm going to feel what I'm not feeling. I'm going to feel celebratory." It was a strong, strong feeling. Not heady at all. Quite uncomfortable. It was thrilling to be at a table with Brynner and Kathy Lee and John Lithgow, and his wife and son. That was fun. I was actually talking to a famous actor and he was talking to me and I thought, "Oh, well, there's a start."

Watching his health decline, I imagine you learned what it meant to support somebody on stage.

In every sense of the word. Physically, emotionally … I'll probably be processing those last two or three months for the rest of my life because it was so intense and so deep. As I've gotten older, I've experienced dying friends and parents, I'm not a stranger to it now. But then … the process of watching someone go…. And yet when he was on stage … in the wings, he's in a director's chair and they literally lift him out of the chair and head him toward the stage, and the minute the light hits he's [alive]. I think it was his way of connecting with himself and the world. Yes, there was a lot of ego involved, but it was more than that. He really knew he had a limited amount of time.

When the show closed, you were a newly Tony-nominated fish out of water.

Yeah. Now what? I had a couple of years of finding my way. I did another *King and I* with Minnesota Opera, I did some workshops, and I met people. By then I was forty-six or -seven. I didn't know enough about musical theater to even know how many other roles were out there. I started acting class with Michael Howard. It was the best thing I ever did.

Did you think that, if you had to, you could always go back to opera if musical theater didn't work out?

It never occurred to me to go back to opera. I loved it when I was doing it, but it was so clearly, not my world. I fit in the world with actors. Because I wasn't working, I could really concentrate on the classes and that was helpful. I was learning how to audition, I was meeting people, I was doing a lot of workshops. I had saved a lot of money from *King and I* and I didn't have to really worry about paying bills yet. I was very driven and very focused on learning.

In 1987 you got *Birds of Paradise*.

That was such a special show. And such an amazing cast [including J. K. Simmons, Donna Murphy, Barbara Walsh, John Cunningham]! We had so much fun.

And Arthur Laurents directing.

He was intense. I learned so much from him. He wanted us to do Chekhov. We began to see his weakness in his need to be cruel. He took it out on Donna, which shocked all of us because Donna was the best thing in the show and had the most to offer. He kept saying that she reminded him of Kim Stanley and in his mind that was not a good thing. Donna didn't do anything to deserve it. But, you know, years later I was with Donna when he gave her a big hug, and he didn't exactly apologize, but he talked about how he knew that she always had it. I learned since then that she was in good company.

Then came your first in a long line of Sondheim shows: *A Little Night Music*.

That little company was run by a guy who was sort of ahead of his time. He saw the possibility for opera and musical theater crossover. I just happened to be the epitome of the opera/musical theater crossover person. That was thrilling. That wasn't actually my first meeting of Sondheim: when *King and I* closed in Los Angeles, Brynner needed to go back to Germany to do cancer treatments. I get a call from my agent saying that they wanted me to fly to New York and sing for Sondheim because they're looking to replace Christine Baranski [for *Sunday in the Park with George*'s Broadway transfer]. I had a chance to sing for Sondheim! So I get on a plane and I fly to New York and I sing some Bernstein songs and read a couple of scenes. They know that I'm flying back to L.A. and they're very, very lovely, and very encouraging. James Lapine comes up on stage and hands me a manuscript of the show and says in sort of whispered tones, "Don't tell anybody I gave you this, but take this back to L.A. and read it," and he gave me notes about the character. January comes and there's a callback and I sing. I do the scene [implementing] the notes James had given me. He comes downstage and looks up at me and whispers, "What the hell are you doing?" I said, "I'm trying to do the notes you gave me." "No, I didn't. No, no, no, no." Then he gave me another note that was totally the opposite of what he had told me. I tried that but obviously I didn't do it very well. I knew that I had failed, but that was OK. I knew I was going to go back on the road with Brynner. I told my agent what happened and she called John Lyons, the casting director, and said, "What happened with Mary Beth and James? Was there some misunderstanding?" They got me another audition. By now, I'm thinking, "Well, I have no idea how I'm supposed to do this part. I'll just show up. It all goes OK but I still am assuming I'm never going to get this, they are just being nice because they kind of screwed me up. I get home. It's a Friday. I get a call from Brynner: "I hear you are singing for a Sondheim show. Are you leaving?" "No. No, I'm not going to do a Sondheim show. I couldn't turn down an opportunity to sing for him but they're not going to cast me. No way." He said, "I cannot do this show without you. You know that. Are you deserting me?" I said, "No. I'm not. It's not going to happen." Ten minutes later I get a call from Mitch Leigh. He's not happy. "What the fuck are you doing? Are you leaving? If you want to do this show you have to come into the office right now and sign the contract [for the continuation of the tour]. Sign your contract right now, or I'm having auditions tomorrow to replace you." So I got back in the car, went to his office, and signed the contract, which I wanted to do. And then Monday morning comes. I get a call from my agent: "I have good news!" They made the offer. Now I have to tell my agent that I have already gone ahead and signed a contract without her knowledge. She was not happy. By June of that year, I'm in the wings with Brynner watching the '84 Tonys on a tiny TV backstage. Dana Ivy's coming up on stage to get her Tony, and he looks at me and says, "Do you have regrets?" I didn't. All was supposed to be. You get to the revival of *Sunday in the Park* and I'm doing a much better part!

Wow. Well, back to *Night Music* . . .
[Sondheim] was lovely. He came to rehearsal and he couldn't have been nicer to everyone. He said to me, "Why do you sing 'Send in the Clowns' like you're sad?" And I said, "Because I'm sad this romance is not going to work." He said, "You are not sad. You're pissed off. Everybody sings it like a sad song. She is pissed." The review called me an angry Desiré. I thought, "Well, he might not like it, but I bet Sondheim did."

We are focusing on your musical career, but you next made another big pivot, jumping into the unknown by doing *Cymbeline* at The Public.
The miracle [of breaking from opera] had already happened, so I was game for whatever. I have to thank Michael Howard for a lot of that because he taught me how to trust my instincts. Half of your talent is your instincts.

I also don't usually talk much about regional theater productions, but you got to do another *King and I* with Stacy Keach. The review said that you went from a production in which Brynner's King set the tone to being "a prima donna in charge."
Stacy's King was very childlike, so we complemented each other. He was in no way going to even begin to try to be the Brynner King with arms akimbo. When he had a tantrum, it was like a kid stamping his foot. And I had that much more experience by then. I did own the part.

In 1992, you did another notable regional performance, as the Beggar Woman in *Sweeney Todd* at the Paper Mill Playhouse with Judy Kaye and George Hearn.
That was really fun. I love that part so much. I remember when I first saw the original, I kept thinking, "Who's that woman over there? Who's that?" I tracked her right from the beginning. So by the time we got to the end, I was like, "Oh my God, that's the part! She's the secret weapon. She's what weaves the whole story together." Doing Mrs. Lovett never interested me. Isn't that funny? I thought that the Beggar Woman had great comic potential and I made her really dotty. I remember thinking, "There's gold here, comic gold."

Your next moves continue to surprise given that you were really interested in pursuing a career in musicals and still relatively new to it. You turned down originating Mrs. Potts in *Beauty and the Beast* on Broadway to take a small off-Broadway play.
Well, I had been trying to get cast in a play. Just to get me an audition for a straight play was a big deal. The role wasn't even a role, it was the understudy in *Later Life* at Playwrights Horizons. The play had already opened and it was a success. There were two women's parts played by Maureen Anderman and Carole Shelley, and Carole played twelve characters. Perfect for Carole

Shelley, brilliant. The understudy had to cover both women. The audition was so much fun! Don Scardino cast me as the understudy and that was what I'd been hoping for—THAT door, so I could go play with those people. I'd been doing really well and having a great time playing with music theater people, but I really wanted to play with the people in the straight theater room, too.

Most actors would not have made the choice to do an understudy part in a limited run off-Broadway instead of a lead on Broadway, even if just from a financial stability standpoint.
This was what I'd been taking acting classes for and what my agents had been trying to get me in the door for. The understudy seemed a way to get experience and meet the people and see what that world was like without any pressure. Little did I realize what the pressure was when you have to go on, and I did have to go on and eventually take over.

Well, while it may look to many like a counterintuitive move, that led you to greater confidence doing straight roles, which then led to a host of off-Broadway shows and then television work, and all of that might not have happened had you gone the Mrs. Potts route.
There were years there, when I started with *Dawson's Creek*, when I thought, "Maybe I won't sing again. I don't know." There was an almost ten-year period of time when I basically did straight, off-Broadway plays. I did *Triumph of Love* regionally [pre-Broadway] but I got an offer to do *Dawson's Creek* and I remember this long phone call with [director] Michael Mayer. We were both just weeping about the fact that I felt like I had to again turn down a musical to do something I'd never done before, a TV series. It was learning something new, even though I couldn't imagine that this little TV series with these teenage kids was going to go anywhere. Who knew?

Right after *Dawson's*, you got to revisit the Beggar Woman in *Sweeney Todd* at the Sondheim Celebration, starring Christine Baranski and Brian Stokes Mitchell. What was it like being part of Camp Sondheim?
It was heaven. It was like going to church every day. That's all we were doing—living, breathing, sleeping, eating, talking, singing Sondheim. We all felt anointed. To just sit in rehearsals and watch [director] Chris Ashley try to get the darkness out of Stokes, who is this shiny positive being. And to watch Christine be given permission to be as sexy and [primal] as she was.... I sat in rehearsals, [staring], cross-legged, knitting. I was knitting an afghan for J. Smith Cameron's baby that got longer and longer over the months that we were there. I never went home from rehearsals, I just sat and watched Chris work with these two gigantic talents. Watching that particular Sweeney/Mrs. Lovett relationship come to life—I have goosebumps just talking about it. Talk about chemistry! They both worked so hard to get out of their own way. And Celia Keenan-Bolger as Johanna! Oh my God, she was like this little bird-creature. I just sat and watched everybody's rehearsal and soaked it up, so much so that Chris ended up finding ways for the Beggar Woman to be lurking in every scene. He told me years later, because of all those rehearsals with me sitting there on the floor, he couldn't imagine those scenes without me in the corner somewhere. That made that particular Beggar Woman not so comic.

What was your experience of Sondheim during that period?
He was so appreciative and supportive. He would just look at me and give that kind of smile. His face was full of so many colors, always. I remember him saying, "We have to do something about your look. You're too beautiful." I said, "Well I can put some more lines under my

eyes." And he said "Pockmarks!" Just like Donna in *Passion*. In her case it was moles. That's the answer if you're too beautiful! We all felt very protected by him. He was happy with what was being served. At least with *Sweeney*.

The next year you were in a company of all women and Antonio Banderas in *Nine*.
Let the games begin! I have to say, I was nervous going into that room. I knew that [director] David Leveaux liked me and the audition process with him was so exciting and wonderful, but I knew that [composer] Maury Yeston didn't like me. In the old days, I could sing those high A's like it was nothing, but that part of my voice was no longer accessible to me. I didn't want to go crazy to try to make it accessible. So, David put the screws on Maury to transpose the song down a step and a half and Maury was not happy. That's what he wrote and I understand that. He finally gave way and, in the end, he was happy, but going into the first few days of rehearsal, I was sheepish. Antonio is such a mensch and gentleman that he found a way, with the help of Jonathan Butterell, the choreographer and assistant director, to make a company feel like a company immediately. That's the kind of person he is. Antonio made it his mission to get to know just enough about each of the women that he had a special kind of language or contact with each one of us. We all felt like we knew him—every woman in the ensemble, every swing. And the fact that he took the time and effort to do that when he himself was insecure … because he'd never sung before! He just kept doing the work, and at the same time making each one of us feel important.

The company really had to support each other on that show. You all served as ensemble when it wasn't your scene. How was that?
We really were Antonio's women. There wasn't nearly the amount of backstabbing and gossiping that there could have been.

What do you remember about working with Chita Rivera?
She was the queen. Everybody was around her and I remember purposely thinking, "I don't feel like being part of the group of acolytes and worshippers." I mean, I really respect her so much, but I was never buzzing around her like many of the girls were. But once we got into the theater—I'm one of those people that always gets there at least two hours early, and so is Chita. My dressing room was up the stairs from hers, so I started checking in with her before I went upstairs and that's where our friendship started, really, because nobody else was around. It was just the two old broads talking. It was great. She would say things to me like, "Are you wearing those sneakers again? Get yourself some shoes!" We would laugh! I love her to death. I have images of myself [during that run] sitting on the stairs that went to the dressing rooms with several of the younger women in the cast. I wouldn't go so far as to say they were therapy sessions, but consultations. As much as I am shocked at how little the younger generation is interested in advice or stories from the older people, that cast [was different]. It was a really sweet and a very special time. Leaving the show was sad. It felt like I was leaving my family.

Well, you had never left a show before.
Yeah, I had never had that experience. In one way, it felt very cheeky, in another way, sort of liberating. "I can do this if I want to." I left to do a very interesting play at the Atlantic called *Frame 312*. It was a really interesting part and I just thought, "I think this is what I need to do." And I remember [writer] Arthur Kopit saying to me, "Why would you leave a Broadway show that you love to do an unknown, short-lived, off-Broadway experiment?" I have a history.

I imagine that with *Dawson's Creek* money in the bank, that put you in a position of being able to choose roles because they interested you, without having to consider the financial security of the job.

That was amazing. And in that same period of time, I got a couple of films. It was quite a year.

Your next musical gig was playing Eleanor Roosevelt in *First Lady Suite*.

I had had a falling-out with [composer] Michael John LaChiusa ten or eleven years earlier; I was in one of the *First Lady Suite*s [when they were individual pieces] at E.S.T., and it was my first time working with him. It was just heaven! For me, he was the epitome—obviously Sondheim is, but Michael John took the idea of conversational song one step further. You know, where you can't tell when the song begins and when the conversation ends. He was a master of it and he was getting better and better. He writes character music with little signature flourishes, little sounds, that to me are little punctuation marks that are clues to the character. I played JFK's secretary in that early version and Michael John said to me, "Eventually, this is going to be a first lady suite. I'm going to do several of the first ladies and I want you to be in in them." But [because of commitments] I didn't do the premier of *First Lady Suite* at The Public and he didn't speak to me for ten years. I adore him and I had deep, deep love of his talent, but … Anyway, years later, Jack Cumming decides to do this piece and he has no idea that Michael John hasn't spoken to me for ten years. He asked me to do it and it was fine. I love those kinds of off-Broadway, rehearse in a basement, throw it on the wall and see what it's about, situations. No real pressure to make money. Who cares what the critics say? I love that. And mostly everybody behaves because there's no pressure.

In 2008 you were in the first Broadway revival of *Sunday in the Park with George*.

There is nothing in the world as thrilling as singing "Sunday." I get goosebumps thinking about it. The very first day of rehearsal when we just sat around and read through it, we got to that number and it's like the creation of the world or something. It's like, "and then on the seventh day, God created…." He taps into something that is so deep. Something about the way the harmonies rub against each other…. When we were in DC for Camp Sondheim, Christine Baranski and I were leaving a rehearsal and they were rehearsing *Sunday in the Park* [across the hall] and the two of us sort of looked at each other—she didn't know my story about almost replacing her—and we went over next to the door and just stood there and listened to them singing. She was a mess because she had loved doing that so much and it had meant so much to her. [The revival] was one of the happiest, richest experiences of everything I've done. I was at the right place at the right time. I think it is his most meaningful show. It says everything about family, about art, about everything. It's full of such bittersweetness. The alchemy of that production at that time with those people…. It almost felt *b'shert* [Yiddish: meant to be].

Talk to me about working with Sondheim on this particular show.

I have on my wall a piece of the score that I asked him to sign. I caught him in the hallway or something. And he wrote, "You are wonderful," exclamation point, exclamation point. That's like gold.

Did he give you any notes you can recall?

You could always tell when he's not happy. He gave me many notes. "You missed a word. Look at your punctuation. Look at your lyrics again." I would think, "What is he talking about? I sang the right lyric." But there would be something tiny. A preposition. He was always aware of the details.

Did he give you any notes that helped you access the song?
You know what helped me access the song was something that [actor] Jessica Molaskey said. She said, "When I hear you sing that, I hear both the old lady, the tiredness and the disappointment in her, but then you go into the higher voice and I hear what she's missing. I hear her youth."

So instead of just regret about what is, she heard memory of what was?
Yes, memory in a visceral, sound way. And I had never thought of it that way. But I ran with it. Our director loved the part of the mother so much. He let those scenes and especially the song be something. Every time I'd ever seen it, the song ["Beautiful"] was done upstage, under the tree, not really taking center. He really let me try different things.

In *Women on the Verge of a Nervous Breakdown*. "That was the perfect title," says Peil.
(Paul Kolnik)

Well, then came *The Good Wife* and while you were shooting that, you were in *Women on the Verge of a Nervous Breakdown*.

That was the perfect title! It was so not *Nine!* It was, "What the fuck is going on here?" until the day it closed. I had done two workshops and it was one of the most beautiful pieces of music—David Yazbek captured the place, the time period in music so beautifully. You knew where you were immediately, just from the sound. The workshops were so much fun. I was playing the Concierge. In the movie, her awareness of what was going on, and of people coming and going was very important. In the workshop, there were killer lines, but my concern was that [she] might get lost in the shuffle. Bart [director Bartlett Sher] assured me that this character was very important to the integrity of the piece and she wouldn't get lost. And then the first day of rehearsal there was a whole other vibe than in the workshops, mostly because Patti LuPone was in the room. She's Patti. She's legendary and she has opinions. She's strong, both on and off stage. I remember, first or second day, a lunch break. Everybody had brought their own lunch and a bunch of the ladies headed for the window and sat. She looked up and said, "I am just so happy to be here. I'm so excited to not have the burden of a show on me. I'm so happy to just be one of the girls." And it flashed before me how hard life probably is for Patti.

And she was just coming off *Gypsy*.

Yup. I just thought, "This is going to be really interesting. It will be good for her and it'll be good for all of us." And then it didn't happen that way.

In what way?

I got an infection and I had to miss a couple of days. When I came back, I was in the hallway and Danny Burstein was outside. I could hear Patti singing some of Sherie Rene Scott's music. I said, "What happened?" Danny looked at me and said, "Patti had some ideas." I remember just sort of watching how both Yazbek and Bart—it's not that she was dictating things or telling them what to do, but they were checking with her, sometimes in obvious ways, other times in more passive-aggressive ways. Sherie [who had the leading role] could see that they were checking with Patti and it started affecting Sherie early on. That feeling that she wasn't being looked to.... She felt—and I'm not putting words in her mouth, I heard her say it many times—she never felt listened to or heard from early on. Early in rehearsal she started asking about the bed on fire. "Well, what's going to happen? Is it going to be real fire? How close am I going to stand to it? Is it going to be hot? When I breathe, is it going to affect me? Is it chemical?" Bart just kept saying, "Don't worry about it. You will be protected; you will be OK." She started asking those questions about the bed early in rehearsal and they all acted like it was only happening once we were in tech. No. She never felt heard about anything, and I think she could see that Patti was heard about everything. And then, little by little, we all start to feel not heard. I remember sitting in tech for hours because it was a huge show with all these moving parts. Wonderful dance numbers kept getting cut because there were tracks everywhere for all these sets to move in and out. There must have been at least four tracks on the stage, so the dancers could only dance [horizontally, without any depth]. They had been rehearsing these fantastic flamenco numbers and had some of the best Broadway dancers. Kept getting cut. They were so frustrated. And I remember sitting in the tech rehearsal behind Sarna Lapine, who was Bart's assistant at the time, and just shaking my head and saying, "What is going on?" She had been in the room when Bart had said to me, "Don't worry, the Concierge won't get lost in this production." And I said to Sarna, "The Concierge might as well be written out of this piece." She said, "No, no, no. We'll figure it out." [We didn't.] And then we got into previews and we're at the Belasco. Stokes and I not only visited the Belasco apartment [legendary producer David Belasco had an apartment above the stage and is said to haunt the theater], but we took our sage and we saged every nook and cranny of that theater. Every day. Stokes did it every night for the whole run. We tried. People would come to the dressing room that I shared with De'Adre Aziza. They would sit on the carpet and just moan and bitch and let it all out. I would take note and listen. They just needed to be heard. And everybody knew this thing was going on between Patti and Sherie so the whole theater was vibrating already. I got a legal yellow pad and I started taking notes from all of these observations and complaints that people were coming to my dressing room with. One night after a preview, I sat down and I wrote a letter to Bart and in a frank and not too aggressive way I let him know what was going on in the ranks of his company. I also made a few suggestions. I signed my name, "as dictated by David Belasco." The next day he stuck his head in the dressing room and said, "And don't think any of the changes in today's rehearsal came from David Belasco." But he did change things.

When you look at all the elements, while the goal isn't to place blame...
Bart knows that I do hold him accountable. For the mood in the room, for allowing that rift between Patti and Sherie to happen.... He saw it happen, he watched it happen, and Sherie was the most vulnerable one. She was the one who carried it and she wasn't a star.

But apart from their rift, is it possible to be objective about whether or not this show ever would have worked?
That particular production, I don't think would ever have worked. It was too big and things hadn't been worked out. The storytelling wasn't clear. I was very sad but I'm grateful that I wasn't the only one. Stokes would look at me all the time like, "What is happening here?" It was never going to work. They needed to do it out of town. They needed to rethink the orchestra so that you could hear the words and follow the story better. The orchestra was beautiful but it was just too much.

How did you find your own way?
I just did the work. I was always glad to be there because it was a Broadway show and Broadway family. I loved Stokes and Danny. I learned to love Sherie. I tried to love Patti. I would watch her sit with some of the kids in the wings when Sherie was onstage and she would be saying not good things about Sherie's performance. That's not good. It was like she was enlisting the kids to agree with her. I didn't ever get to know Patti and kind of stayed out of her way.

Hard to know what was going on with her. People frequently talk about this or that person's behavior but I believe context is everything. Who knows if under different circumstances...
John Doyle and I have had this conversation. His relationship with Patti is fabulous. He worked with her in an ensemble and she loved it and loved working with him. And maybe, to her credit, because she is such a pro and such a veteran, she smelled that the show was going to be in trouble and that Sherie wasn't up to holding her own without some help.

One wonders if, with Patti's support, Sherie might have soared.

The production would always have been in trouble, but with Patti's support, and had Sherie been supported by the director, she would have soared, I have no doubt.

You say you were never not happy to be there, but going to work every day, was that fraught?

I walked in happy because I couldn't wait to see what's gonna happen. Something was always going to happen! So much intrigue! I felt badly about the show but no, it was fun. The horror stories are the ones that make good stories.

It's not just because we all sort of rub our hands at the deliciousness of strife. A large number of people believed in this piece and all of its elements from script to score to creative team to cast. There's a lot of talent to buoy the piece and then, to watch it deflate, you can't help but think there has to a be a story there.

It's fascinating! On paper, this show was gold. Check, check, check, check. I remember Andre Bishop coming to announce that we were closing. These are his exact words: "Well, you know, we are an off-Broadway, not-for-profit theater, and it is our business to make and lose money." My whole body started going [shaking]. What did he just say? I looked at Danny. "Did he just say what I thought he said?" What does that mean? I think it was his way of saying it's not your fault. I had a drink with Bart maybe a month later. He said, "I know you think it was my fault, but it wasn't. I cast the wrong leading woman." And I said, "I'm not so sure that you cast the wrong woman, but I do think it's your fault."

You went immediately to another show with Danny Burstein, *Follies*. It's not a role for which you'd be an obvious choice.

I could not imagine what made them think of me and I still don't know. I never could get a straight answer from [director] Eric Schaeffer, but I'm so glad they did. I had seen lots of different versions of *Follies*, and I always thought Solange was the stupidest character with the stupidest number, the most annoying person. But it's *Follies* and it's Sondheim and this great group of actors, and I said, "Yeah, I'll do it." But then I started looking at the lyrics and I thought, "Oh, she's not yucky. She's actually delicious." I love the lyrics and I realized that part of the reason I never liked it was because I could never understand them! They [usually] cast real French women with heavy accents! It was fun! It was fun to be in a show that everybody talks about with such awe.

The cast was so interesting; Jan Maxwell, Bernadette Peters, Danny Burstein, Elaine Paige . . . do you remember learning anything new from watching them?

It was interesting, especially after the experience with *Women on the Verge*, to observe Jan and Bernadette and how they handled the dynamic of two leading women, one a star and one a brilliant actress, but not a star, and watch how that dance went. It was not at all like the dance between Patti and Sherie, but it was a dance. [For example,] at the end of the show, for the last scene we used to go into the wings and watch the two of them as everybody's leaving the party. I know Jan started it because Bernadette would never do this; Jan started taking longer and longer to leave and having more and more of an emotional moment. We would stand in the wings and start counting how long it was going to be before it was Bernadette's turn. It was horrifying, but it was fabulous to watch. All of a sudden, there's a whole new show going. I thought, "Are they friends now [the characters]? Do they hate each other? What happened? I want to see the next act of that show!" Then Bernadette starts. There was one night when she fell to her knees like she fainted. It was just too much. Danny had to help her up and try to get her out because she was a mess. I'm thinking, "Oh my God. It's a whole new show."

So they were competing with each other to see who could have the greater breakdown?
Yes! And we were all in the wings just watching, counting! "She broke the record tonight: thirteen seconds!" We'd pass it around: "Thirteen!" "Nineteen." "Twenty." A friend of mine once said about Jan, who was such a brilliant actress and a really, really good person, "Her fatal flaw is that everything has to be an event. If things are going really well and everybody's happy, that just makes her crazy. She needs to make an event. It doesn't even have to be about her, just something has to happen."

Does it ever cross your mind that someone might think of you as a great actress and good person and that you might be unknowingly overindulging on stage or taking thirteen seconds to exit?
I tend to do just the opposite and I've been encouraged to be more like that, to own the stage more. "Take your time." "Acknowledge!" "Demand it." Mitch Leigh used to say to me, "You have to make your entrance! When Gertie Lawrence did this part, she was a star and her entrance brought the house down. You have to make your entrance like that." I had no idea what he was talking about. Anyway, Jan always redeemed herself with the company at the curtain call; she would come out and—the dress that she wore had a totally bare back, practically down to her butt. She always had something on her back for the company to see when she made her curtain call. She'd paint things on it, she'd glue pieces of hair to it. Once, between shows, she'd been hit by a taxi and had to go to the emergency room, but she came back and did the show that night. She had her dresser paint tire tracks on her back. In so many ways she didn't take anything seriously. She was always cutting up before going on stage. She was fascinating. Bernadette was humble. She's not self-effacing but she's not self-aggrandizing either. She's authentic. She lets her insecurities show as much as anybody. I remember sitting in her dressing room and she was quizzing me about singing and vocal technique. I love that she's still searching for it. She doesn't think of herself as a star. She's so hard working and so sincere

You went from *Follies* into *Threepenny Opera* and then *The Visit*. You were in a real period of darkness.
I was. It was fabulous to be able to do *Threepenny*. Earlier when I was still really singing, Kurt Weill would have been great for me but I wasn't aware of it and it just passed me by. But then *Threepenny*! That was fun. It was another situation where the actors had to rescue the show. I wanted to do the show because of [director] Martha Clarke. The things of hers that I had seen were so singular and visually so stunning and intellectually stimulating. And then we got into the rehearsal room and it seemed like there were two different casts; there were the downtown actors/improv people and then there were Laura Osnes and Michael Park and Sally Murphy and me—the Broadway people. It made it interesting for both groups. We were fascinated by what the other ones were doing and trying to learn from each other during rehearsal. But it became quite clear that Martha was more comfortable with the downtown tribe and a lot of that had to do with making pictures, which was very interesting, but she didn't know how to work with the actors. I remember Michael Park saying, "Stop, stop, stop. What are we doing

"Beirut has sunshine. That's all it has." *Follies.*
(Joan Marcus)

here? What story are we telling?" Martha said, "Story? There is no story. Don't worry about it."
She lost us. Rehearsals were kind of a waste of time. We learned the music and we spent a lot
of time with a dog licking peanut butter off of someone's leg. We spent a lot of time with props.
We got into the theater and the set wasn't finished. The set designer's wife was dying, so he was

not around. The lighting designer took a Broadway job, so he was in two techs at the same time. We kind of had to re-stage everything. It was so frustrating because that score is so fabulous and we had this fabulous band. And the potential of the sets, if they had just been finished, was so perfect. So the company started [acting from] survival mode. We were all going to die if we didn't help each other, so we actually bonded over this lack of leadership. Every time she tried to have a rehearsal it got worse because she was clearly not capable of handling this group. Nobody was happy with the way the show went and the way it ended up. But I had some interesting experiences with this group of downtown actors that I got to know and learn from.

***The Visit* was a year later. What was what was the experience like?**
I have to say, I was in awe of being with Terrence McNally and John Kander and John Doyle. I'm not given to being in awe. But because of the work of John and Terrence and their age, you can't take this for granted. You're not going to walk into a room like this again. And watching them work with Chita—Chita worked on the show as though she hadn't done it before. She doesn't run the room. She's a gypsy. She's sits in her chair and gets up when it's her turn and goes back to her chair just like the rest of us do. And John Doyle—I used to say that John should charge admission because people would pay to witness his rehearsals. Chita and I call him "Father John." It's like going to church. There's a reason why in a lot of his things people are on stage all the time. He wants everybody in the rehearsal all the time. You are asked to watch everybody work and after a scene has been worked on, we would all gather around and you'd never know who he was going to call on: "What did you see? What do you think? What do you think happened there? Do you think she's going to agree to that? Did you buy that?" We were always on our toes. We also learned the [whole] show. I've never felt so prepared for a show by opening night as I did with *The Visit* because we were all in on every single moment of every decision that was made, every moment of the show, everybody's part, everybody's choices, everybody's process. And we helped each other right from day one of rehearsal because that's how he guides the [process]. There was such a feeling of trust and caretaking created in that room.

I can see why there would be reverence. Plus the fact that you were delivering the final Kander and Ebb musical, and that it was Chita Rivera closing her long Kander and Ebb chapter by finally bringing this show to Broadway.
When we were doing *Nine*, in those dressing room talks with Chita, she was telling me about this show and how she was going to do it in Chicago. She was so excited about it. So I was aware of it and of her journey with Kander and Ebb and this particular piece. It was hallowed ground. And Roger Rees brought something to it that I can't even describe it. I wish I had known him before. He was such a joyous, good person and dedicated to the work. Chita couldn't wait to get on stage. After the show we would sit on her floor and have drinks and food in her dressing room. She had a full bar. Nobody wanted to go out, we just wanted to go to Chita's room. We'd have the best time. There were a couple of door people who were not happy about it. We tipped them.

When a show that you love doing isn't doing well, what's that like?
I think everybody sort of knew that this was not going to be everybody's cup of tea and that it was not going to be a hit. It was poetry. It's too poetic for tourists. We never thought of it as faltering as far as the production and what everybody was bringing to it. We were aware of the box

office. But you know, I always just say that's not my job. I loved every day of rehearsal and every day in that theater, but throughout, we were all aware of our mortality. With the story, you're already in that world. And then Roger [who was dying of cancer], and the inevitability of closing, it felt like all of a piece. It was a moment in time that I just feel lucky to have been a part of.

And that led you to your next Terrence McNally collaboration, *Anastasia*.
This also was *b'shert*. [She shows me her library of Russian books and literature.] They're my favorite shelves. Are you kidding? A musical about the Romanovs? Heaven! To this day, I've never seen the film. I thought I'd see it after the show closed but I still haven't.

Tell me about the experience of doing it.
Well, it started like a fairy tale. We started rehearsals the first week of April, and we were all on the train, taking Amtrak up to Hartford. About an hour outside of Hartford, it started snowing. By the time we got to Hartford, it was like we were in Russia. We were "Once upon a December." I mean, it was ridiculous. And then there were the costumes that Linda Cho built on me. They were like museum pieces. So authentically real … the fabrics, and the care, and the choices. In all the years of opera I had worn some fabulous costumes by fabulous designers, but I've never had an experience like that. I was part of making art with the costume.

Tell me about Stephen Flaherty and Lynn Ahrens.
Yum, yum, yum, yum, yum. I just love both of them on and off stage. They're consummate. They both sort of work the way actors do. They get into the skin of the culture, the background story of the characters. None of their shows sound the same. They do their homework and they are both channelers. For *Anastasia* what Stephen did—and probably not that many people in the audience would even realize it—but he found a way to channel some iconic rhythms and colors of Tchaikovsky, Rachmaninoff, very singular, Russian kind of sounds, and yet they weren't terrifically on the nose. And at the same time, he wrote his own music. Lynn's lyrics were never hard to learn because they always felt inevitable.

I heard you say that more than any other show you had done, the audiences showed how excited they were to be there nightly.
Oh totally. Totally, totally, totally. And Christy Altomare, God love her, not only delivered every night and in a way that was pretty extraordinary vocally, but after the show there would be these lines at the stage door and she would be there till 1:00 in the morning. If there were two people left, [she stayed]. It drove security crazy. People came back and back and back because they felt like they were coming to see a friend. It's admirable in many ways but I used to scold her all the time because she'd be out there in the freezing cold. But it kept the show going. She felt that it was part of her job to do that. It's just the opposite of when we were doing *Liaisons*; Janet McTeer would do everything she could to avoid the backstage line. She was exhausted and she said, "They got their money's worth. I do not owe them anything."

You received another Tony nomination for *Anastasia*.
I felt so special, like royalty. I soaked up every minute of it. Everyone complained about all the press and all the stuff and I thought, "You guys are fifty years younger than I am. What are you complaining about?" I loved every minute of it. I did not take any second of it for granted. The only drawback was that I could not be too vocal about my joy because I was the only one

in our cast nominated. I thought there were some nomination-worthy performances that were overlooked. As a company, they were all very supportive, but I felt a little guilty.

You got to do the last Sondheim, *Road Show,* at Encores!
I mean talk about not expecting it. Just a gift. I had seen almost every incarnation of that show and I thought, "This is fantastic!" Trying to remember how I used to feel with Sondheim—it was a weird combination of walking a tightrope because the detail and precision of every-thing was so important to making the whole piece that there was always this sort of fear and trembling, and yet, the ethos or the Gestalt of the piece, whatever show it is, you always had a net. Every cast member felt the same way, that we were all on the same tightrope. Somebody would catch you. You didn't feel like the only one who didn't really know what they were doing. Everybody was always aware, especially in that that abbreviated rehearsal at Encores!, that you are really sticking it out there.

Raúl Esparza told me he wasn't interested in doing it. He did it because Sondheim called him and asked him personally, and then he said it was one of the best things he's ever done in his life. He was just blown away by how rewarding the experience was. You're nodding . . .
I watched him. I watched him change from fear and dread. First day of rehearsal, I mean—he's Raúl and he always has tremblings going on, but he doesn't hide them, he battles them. He takes them on. I am a great, great admirer of him and his talent and his generosity as a colleague. I was always rooting for him and always felt like we were in this together. And then Brandon Uranowitz: he's one of the most gifted, talented people and he's almost too good of a person to make performing his life. I just found him to be one of the purest, most interesting performers I've ever been on stage with. To look at him on stage, you see into him. He and Raúl together were such an interesting mix because they work so differently. Raúl lets you know what he's trying to conquer, and Brandon is working it out himself, and then he brings it. Sondheim was so emotional. He and [writer] John Weidman were both so happy that it was being done and they were so happy to be in the rehearsal room. I remember how emo-tional Sondheim was. He said to me once, "You sing it so beautifully. It's never been sung so beautifully, but you've got to look at the lyrics again." I was missing a word. I had no idea, but he heard it! That's that tightrope. You get involved in the music and the character. The pre-cision of the language in the lyrics is crucial. So he gave me a couple of scolds, all the while letting me know that he loved what I was doing.

There was a feeling, at least from this audience member's point of view, about that produc-tion redeeming the reputation of the show and giving it back to Sondheim and Weidman.
It was tremendously rewarding and I think Sondheim actually said that in so many words to Raúl. I think that was definitely the feeling that we all had.

At this stage of your vast and varied career, what do you want?
I'm still right where I always have been. It's like, what's next? I'm game for whatever. I mean, what more could there be really? When the phone rings, I never know what it's going to be and I love it. And you know what? Even if it doesn't keep ringing, it's OK. I have a beautiful family, two delicious granddaughters. If the phone doesn't ring, I'm still OK. Grateful is the word.

Judy Kuhn

September, October 2020; February 2022

There's a 1998 video, much-loved in theater circles, of Judy Kuhn performing a trio of Andrew Lloyd Webber songs at Carnegie Hall with Marin Mazzie and Audra McDonald. The three of them, all at the peak of their powers, blend sublimely, despite their three decidedly unique sounds. Kuhn hates watching it. "I had a terrible, raw sore throat," she says. "I gave everything I had to 'Don't Rain on My Parade,'" which she had sung earlier in the evening. "I had no voice left. It was the first and maybe the only time I ever walked on stage not knowing if I was going to be able to produce any sound. I had a fever, I was all sweaty, and my hair was kind of plastered to my head. I felt like I couldn't really sing the way I can sing and I looked like a little sweaty gnome next to those two statuesque beautiful women." Such is the chasm between audience perception and that of the artist, as well as the very, very high standard to which Judy Kuhn holds herself.

Born in Manhattan and raised in Bethesda, Maryland, Kuhn grew up with music. Her mother played clarinet in a local orchestra, and both parents regularly exposed Kuhn and her brother to the arts. Kuhn wasn't exclusively into musicals ("I was just as happy seeing a musical as I was a Tennessee Williams play," she says), but as soon as she hit Broadway in the mid-80s, musical theater couldn't get enough of her. After an ensemble/understudy track in *The Mystery of Edwin Drood*, she was featured as the doomed Bella in the doomed *Rags*; then, in the same season, *Les Misérables*, in which Kuhn originated the role of Cosette in the Broadway production, winning a Tony nomination. When her contract was up, her *Les Mis* director, Trevor Nunn, cast her as Florence, the bear of a role at the center of the highly anticipated (though ultimately unsuccessful) *Chess*. Another massive show, *Metropolis* in the West End, followed, before *She Loves Me* and then *Sunset Boulevard* (again with Nunn). After so many big, commercial musicals, Kuhn did an unexpected about-face with her next succession of shows. She did smaller plays and musicals off-Broadway and regionally (made financially viable, in part, by her casting as the singing voice of Disney's titular *Pocahontas*), including *As Thousands Cheer*, *Eli's Comin'*, *Dream True*, *Three Sisters*, *The Ballad of Little Jo*, *The Glass Menagerie*, and John Doyle's production of *Passion*. In 2013 she originated the role of Helen Bechdel in *Fun Home*, winning a Tony nomination (her fourth) for her searing, heartbreaking portrait of repressed emotion. *Fiddler on the Roof* followed, first on Broadway and then (yet again with Nunn) in a separate production in London. And most recently, *Assassins*, reuniting her with Doyle.

Kuhn is a smart woman, totally unassuming and not especially impressed with herself. She'll concede, if pressed, that her résumé is strong, but mostly, she considers herself lucky. I consider her uniquely gifted. The evidence is actually in her first Broadway credit; in *Edwin Drood*, she understudied both Betty Buckley's Drood, all belting and bravado, and Patti Coheneur's Rosa Budd, the virginal ingenue with the lyric high G. Buckley couldn't have played Budd, and Coheneur couldn't have played Drood, but Kuhn played them both. Very well, at that. What other Cosette also played Florence? What Amalia can also pull off Golde? Who else has both the acting range and the singing chops for that kind of diverse résumé? Damn few.

"Will he like me?" In *She Loves Me*.
(Martha Swope, ©Billy Rose Theatre Division, New York Public Library for the Performing Arts)

When do you remember being bitten by the theater bug?
When I was little, I always thought the theater was magical. There was some part of me that understood that it wasn't real, and yet it felt so real. [I knew] that somebody was making it real for me. I loved that. We lived in New York for a year when I was in grade school. That was the first time my parents took us to see some Broadway shows and that's when that really hit me profoundly. I was so moved, but I understood I was watching actors on a stage. I couldn't believe that those people could instill that kind of belief in me and move me so much. My mother's first cousin is Stuart Ostrow, who produced the original production of *Pippin*. When it played out of town in Washington before it went to Broadway, he took us backstage afterwards. It made real that magic because all the sets and costumes that were so glittery on-stage were just on racks. Flats that looked so colorful on stage now leaned up against the wall, looking lifeless. It was this whole other layer. I still have that feeling when I walk backstage and see all the stuff that helps create that magic. It looks totally different backstage. Without the light, without the context, [sets are] just wood, leaning up against a pole in this kind of dingy backstage. I was thrilled by that.

At what point did you decide to pursue it?
My dad was such a role model for me. He was an activist and a civil rights lawyer and he believed deeply in social justice. He took us to marches, and there was all kinds of community organizing going on in my house. I always thought I should follow in his footsteps, although I never really wanted to go to law school. I love reading and I love school to a certain extent, but studying and writing papers was never my thing. I loved theater and music. I was so torn about that as I grew up and started thinking about what my future was going to look like. One of the most profound things my father ever said to me was when I said, "I like the performing arts but

I feel a little guilty. I should do what you do and help change the world." He said, "You should not feel guilty about doing what you want to do. You have to do what you love and what you're good at or you won't do anybody any good. But a little bit of guilt about the privilege that you've had and the gifts you've been given is good, because that'll make you give back and you will find ways to contribute." I have tried to live by that motto. I can always be better, but that was a gift.

Prior to studying at Oberlin, were you aware that your voice was special?
I was a junior hippie. I sang folk songs with my guitar. When I went to Oberlin, I didn't know what I was going to major in. I auditioned for the Oberlin College Chorus and didn't get in. I was so devastated! I am a terrible sight-reader; that might have had something to do with it. At that moment I was determined to learn how to be a better singer. I knew that I loved singing and I thought I should be better at it. I eventually found a voice student in the conservatory and I took some lessons from him. It was great. He taught me a lot. I was trying to figure out my major. In my deep, dark, secret soul I wanted to do theater, but I was also afraid. I was afraid to go to auditions; I was afraid of

Judy Kuhn	
The King and I	National Tour, 1984
The Mystery of Edwin Drood	off-Broadway, Broadway, 1985
Rags	Broadway, 1986
Les Misérables (as Cosette)	Broadway, 1987
Chess	Broadway, 1988
Metropolis	West End, 1989
She Loves Me	Broadway, 1993
Sunset Boulevard	West End, 1993
King David	Broadway, 1997
Strike Up the Band	Encores!, 1998
As Thousands Cheer	off-Broadway, 1998
Dream True	off-Broadway, 1999
Eli's Coming	off-Broadway, 2001
Passion	Washington, DC, 2002
Les Misérables (as Fantine)	Broadway, 2006
Passion	off-Broadway, 2013
The Cradle Will Rock	Encores!, 2013
Fun Home	off-Broadway, 2013; Broadway, 2014
Fiddler on the Roof	Broadway, 2016
Hey, Look Me Over	Encores!, 2018
Fiddler on the Roof	West End, 2019
Assassins	off-Broadway, 2021

acting classes. I was a very shy and scared person back then. I'm not sure how I survived in this business. But I was really enjoying my voice lessons, so I started thinking that maybe I should major in music. I auditioned for the conservatory and was admitted. So, as a sophomore, I was a conservatory student all of a sudden. I knew the whole time I was there that classical music wasn't going to be my career. I never felt like my voice was big enough for an opera house, and I knew it wasn't my path, but I loved doing it there. I wound up in the studio of one of the great voice teachers of the twentieth century, Richard Miller. I actually made that happen because I was assigned to a teacher who I wasn't crazy about. Somehow, I got the courage to go knock on Mr. Miller's door and say, "I want to study with you." It took a little work, but eventually he said, "OK, I'll take you on." He was someone who really loved language and I think he saw in me someone who was interested in language and not just making pretty sounds. I learned so much from him. I would not be able to do what I do now without the training that he gave me. I spent a lot of time in the library translating text and trying to understand why the composer set this poem in the way that he did and what he was telling me as an interpreter. There was one lesson I'll never forget: he looked at me and said, "You hear a lot of great voices in this Conservatory, don't you? But not a lot of music." I sort of felt like he was telling me, not to worry about how big my voice is or whether it was as good as somebody else's in his studio. I was making music and that's what I should feel good about.

You graduated, and then what happened?

I wound up moving to Boston and lived in Somerville for a year. My brother and some friends were there. I found a voice teacher. I volunteered with these teachers, teaching theater in public schools. I waited tables. At some point, someone suggested summer stock. I was offered a spot at The New London Barn Playhouse and I went up there for the summer. I was so happy! I loved every minute of being there and making theater. All the sewing of costumes and painting of scenery, staying up all night and then being on stage and telling stories ... I just loved it. A couple of people there said, "You really should move to New York." I went back to Somerville and I thought, "If I don't do this now, I never will." So I packed my bags and I moved to New York. I was waiting tables and working checkout at the original Dean & DeLuca down in SoHo. I was going to open calls. A very close friend of my parents was the head of the Juilliard School. [He connected me] to John Stix, a wonderful acting teacher. I went to his class every week for a few years and it was really eye-opening to me. I didn't really know what it was to be an actor. I actually thought about going back to school to get some actual training but then I got a job. John said, "Take the job. Make the rehearsal room your classroom." [While I am not sorry,] there is a part of me that always wishes that I had gone back to school. I really do wish I'd had a formal conservatory training. I think it might have opened up more opportunities for me, but it's not like I haven't done lots of wonderful things that I loved and am proud of. And certainly, there have been a lot of rehearsal rooms that were classrooms for me, where directors taught me so much. I've worked with amazing actors. Just watching them work—they taught me. I always say to students, "Never stop being a student. Don't ever think you know it. When you're in a rehearsal room, look around. Who knows stuff that you don't know? Who's doing stuff that you're not sure how to do? Who has advice or wisdom to pass on? Always be learning."

That job was in Yul Brynner's last tour of *The King and I*. What was the experience on the road like?

It was fun and challenging. It wasn't the easiest company to be in, but I found my home in it. I found some lovely people, not the least of whom was Mary Beth Peil. She is one of my favorite people I've ever met in this business. She was really supportive and appreciative of me.

Yul Brynner was known to use his stardom in a way that is not necessarily great for the rest of the cast.

Well, you said it, not me. I guess I learned something about how not to lead a company. When you do things like you host a party for 60 percent of the company and let the other 40 percent know that it's happening but they're not invited ... I feel you always set the mood from the top. It's nice to be treated like you're part of a company. The people backstage, the crew, everybody's part of making a show happen, whether they're in the spotlight or not. I found people who were warm and welcoming.

I understand that you would not know from night to night whether or not he was going to sing "A Puzzlement," so you did not know when your entrance was going to be.
Yeah, that was true. Sometimes he would sing that song and sometimes he wouldn't. I think it depended on how he was feeling and whether he liked the audience. I don't really know, I just knew that we had to hang around backstage during the scene before "A Puzzlement," because there was always a chance he wasn't going to do it and we might have to go on. To me, that tour was an adventure. It was fun to do something like that. I was young, unattached, making real money for the first time in my life.

Did you learn a lot?
Absolutely. Absolutely. And that show is beautiful! I was not unappreciative of the fact that I was watching someone who had created that role and who was kind of brilliant. I loved being part of that production. I may be the first Jewish wife he ever had. I got to see all these cities. I was a kid, trying to figure out how to be.

You were cast pretty soon after in the ensemble of *The Mystery of Edwin Drood* in Central Park and then on Broadway.
I got *Drood* by going to an open call! I went to my audition and I had to sing something belty and something soprano-y. At the final callback, I walk into the room and there were Rupert Holmes, Wilford Leach, Joe Papp, and Graciela Daniele. Rob Marshall was her assistant and the dance captain. It was a room full of important theater people. I had to do the Act 2 Alice Nutting speech. Wilford directs me and says, "She tells everybody off and storms out of the room. I want you to tell us all off and storm out." I gave them what for and I just thought, "Did he mean really storm out? OK, I'm just going to go for it." I finish the speech, I grab my bag, march out, and I slam the door. And then, of course, I was in the hallway with all the other people waiting for their audition. They looked up at me like, "Oh my god what happened?" I just started to laugh. I was outside the room with my bag, thinking, "What do I do now? Should I go back in, or should I just leave?" Then Rob opened the door and said, "That was great. You can go."

But you got it!
That was a classroom. There were so many extraordinary artists in that company. Different approaches, different skills. It was remarkable to be a part of that and it was just fun. When we were in the park, it was like a party every night. Rob Marshall taught me the show and I watched a lot. George Rose was the company leader. He set the tone onstage. Such a funny, funny man. Oh my God, all the improvisation he did, playing around with the audience.... It was about being adventurous and creative and fun. Everyone was so inventive. Betty Buckley, Howard McGillin, Joe Grifasi, Cleo Laine ... it was an incredible group of people to have had that first kind of big show experience with.

You were understudying two of the leads and you went on as Rosa Budd early in Broadway previews.
That was an out-of-body experience. I had not had understudy rehearsals. It was crazy. Everybody helped me through that night.

You were chosen as the murderer.

That was a shock. I will never forget coming offstage after the voting and the stage manager saying, "It's you." I was sure she was pulling my leg just to scare me, and I was like, "Yeah, yeah." "No. It's you." And then I had to go right back on stage. I was looking up at the great Cleo Laine, listening to her sing and thinking, "Oh my God, what are the lyrics to my song?" The next day I woke up and I was like, "I don't remember what happened." Donna Murphy was the other swing. She [ultimately] took over for the role of Drood but she was not the Drood understudy. She was probably a much better Drood than I was. I'm a small person. Betty is much taller than me. When she got dressed as a boy, she was sort of a match for Howard, who is very tall. But when I put on that garb, I looked tiny. Apparently, when I went on for Betty, George would say to Joe, "There goes the bar mitzvah boy." I looked like a twelve-year-old Jewish boy!

You left *Edwin Drood* to do *Rags*.

The director, Joan Micklin Silver, was a wonderful filmmaker who's famous for having made *Hester Street* and *Crossing Delancey*. Her daughter is also responsible for my marriage! She set me up with my husband on a blind date. I was doing this off-off-Broadway show called *Pearls* which Joan had seen. After that, I was asked to audition for *Rags*. I remember going to Charles Strouse's apartment on Central Park South and he and Stephen Schwartz taught me the title song. I had to kind of go, "OK, don't be overwhelmed by this thing that's happening to you right now. Just learn the song." I did the audition and they offered it to me. I didn't have an agent to negotiate it for me. I was still doing *Drood* and [cast member] Joe Grifasi told his agent that he should come see me when I went on for Patti Cohenour. He signed me and then he negotiated the contract for *Rags*.

That sounds magical.

Absolutely. I'm with all these major, major people [Strouse, Schwartz, Joseph Stein]. I'm doing my first featured role in a big show in New York. Super exciting. But there was tension in the room because Joan had never directed a big musical. I think she's amazing, but she was with these very experienced writers who wanted to tell her how to direct it. I have no idea what went on behind the scenes, but I could sense there was tension in the room. It wasn't a great situation for her or for anybody. After two weeks of rehearsal, we showed up and she was gone. I can't remember what the explanation was. Charles and Stephen were going to direct. It wasn't ideal since they were the writers and should have been focused on the writing. I was so young and green. Thank God I had Lonny Price, Dick Latessa, and Teresa Stratas as my scene partners. But Teresa had also never done anything like this before. It scared her not to have a real director helping her. It was complicated. Lonny would sometimes say to me, "Come on. Let's go to the lobby and rehearse." Then we'd come back and Lonny would say, "This is how we're going to do it." It was baptism by fire. I learned a lot. I was grateful to be there but it was unnerving because there was a certain amount of chaos going on. I didn't know how to react to it except to just try to listen, do my best, and take what came my way. Teresa would often sit out of the show to watch it when new things went in because she felt like she needed to keep an eye on things. She is an extraordinary artist and has very good instincts. It wasn't like there was a person in charge who you could go to and say, "I'm not sure about this," or "I feel uncomfortable with this." The writers were writing and directing and re-staging. I knew it wasn't the way it was supposed to be. And it's a shame because I think it had the potential of being brilliant. There were all the ingredients to be amazing. It was sad the way it worked out.

Do you remember moments of learning?
Oh, yes. There's one that I think about all the time. There's a great song that Teresa sang called "Blame It on the Summer Night." The way it was staged, she just kind of moves slowly across the stage and encounters people as if she is walking down a New York street. She ends up on the other end of the stage. We were rehearsing and she didn't want to sing out. She was preserving her voice. So, she did the staging and barely made any sound. And yet, she was riveting. You could just feel everyone in the room leaning forward, looking at her, hanging on everything. I remember thinking, "What is it that makes that so riveting?" I carry that with me. Over time I understood it was about the commitment she brought to everything she did. There wasn't any part of her left behind. It wasn't like, "I'm marking this." She committed herself. I learned so much from watching her.

And then, after opening . . .
The day after we opened, I was just thrilled with it all. I was home vacuuming, planning to have dinner and go to work. I see the *Rags* logo on TV and I turn up the volume, thinking it's a review. I hear, "*Rags*, which opened last night at the Mark Hellinger Theater, will close tomorrow after four performances." I was stunned. We went into the theater and there were the producers who were a little chagrined. They'd sent out a press release but hadn't told us. I was devastated. I loved the show. And I had done bad shows. I knew what a bad show was and I didn't think it was a bad show. Everyone in the cast was furious. It just felt like everything had been badly handled and it shouldn't have happened that way. But there was a silver lining. . . .

You had already auditioned for *Les Misérables* while you were up in Boston with *Rags*.
Four of us had auditioned while we were in rehearsal in New York, and then when we went to Boston, we all got callbacks. So, we all took the train to New York together on our day off. I'll never forget that. I was so nervous. I walked in the room and Trevor Nunn jumped up from behind the table and came running over to me. He put his arm around me and said, "Thank you, thank you for coming!" My first thought was, "I have never met this man and he thinks I'm somebody else. How am I going to tell him that we've never met?" And then I realized that that's just what Trevor does. He puts actors at ease because he knows that's the only way he's going to see who they truly are and therefore find out if they're the right person for the role. It's remarkable. He'll tell women who come in with super high heels, "Why don't you kick those shoes off and pull up a chair?" Anyway, we did that audition and went back to Boston. Right after *Rags* closed, I got a call that they wanted me to come back in and [learn some of the *Les Mis* music] and I got the offer to do Cosette. Again, "Wow! How is this happening to me?"

***Les Misérables* was a Royal Shakespeare Production. Their rehearsal process is notoriously very unusual as compared to an American approach.**
I have now worked with Trevor four times. The thing that you learn with Trevor is that it is all necessary work and as you build on that work, you know it in the deepest way. It's hard to explain but he works very slowly and very fast at the same time. And when you arrive at that

first performance, you absolutely know where all your guideposts are, you know exactly what to do and where to go, but you also continue to have permission to explore and to make new choices and discoveries. With *Les Mis*, we were doing a production they'd already done [in London], but we were never made to feel like we were doing something they'd already done. They made us feel like we were coming up with it in the room. It felt very organic, like we owned the work that we were doing. It was amazing. We did theater games, improvisation, crazy stuff. We had to pick a cartoon character and make a little play [featuring that character], and then we each had to get up and do it for each other. We sat in a big circle and everyone got up and did their thing and people tried to guess your cartoon character. Everyone thought they were going to be fired, which Trevor thought was hilarious because why would he fire you for not being good as a cartoon character? The point wasn't to be good! At the end of it, he said, "Now that you have jumped through the ring of fire, you know there's nothing you can do wrong. Now we're just going to get to work." It was a way for us to each [realize] we're going to be able to take risks and do what we need to do. It was great. Now we're a company. The other very clever thing that Trevor did—when we were in Washington, he had every single person in the company sit out one night and watch the show. He wanted to give all the swings and understudies a chance to go on so that they were confident, and he also wanted every person in the company to understand what they were a part of—to see the entire story in front of them and understand that it was an ensemble show and what our particular role in telling that story was. We did it again after six months on Broadway because he wanted us to be reminded of what the show was and not get lazy or complacent. It was just amazing to see the sweep of the whole show and how beautiful it was. It's funny—people talk about the British invasion, the mega musicals, the chandelier, the helicopter—*Les Mis* was really a very simple production. The only big set piece was the barricade. It's basically a turntable and actors moving pieces of furniture—boxes, benches, whatever. It was an ensemble creating the space. People would leave the theater and think they'd been in all these different locations, but really the only scenery was the gate and the barricade. Props, amazing lighting and actors on a stage. To me that was theater magic.

And that year at the Tonys, you were nominated and you performed twice!
It was insane, no question about it. [*Les Mis* was] performing on the Tony night. *Rags* was also nominated as best musical so they asked Teresa to sing. She declined and, because I sang the title song, they asked me, very last minute, to sing the title song. I hadn't done the show for almost a year! They had to cut a fifteen-minute song down to a three-minute version. They cut a bridge and at some point, they decided to put the bridge back. I barely had any rehearsal and I was doing eight shows a week. I was so nervous. I had never sung on live TV before. That night I was told that my category would be first and after that was done, somebody would come and get me and bring me backstage so I could get dressed for *Rags*. I knew I wasn't going to win, so I was really just focused on the song. There was actually going to be a semi-quick change between *Rags* and the *Les Mis* number and they were going to have a booth set up backstage with my costume and wig and everything. My category came and went and I just wanted to get backstage and get ready. On the commercial break, I looked around for somebody to come get me. Nobody came. A few more awards and numbers, and then another commercial break. I looked around for someone to come get me and nobody came. It's a live show and you don't know what the order of events are. I had no idea if I was on in an hour or if I had ten minutes. Finally, I just couldn't take it anymore and I found my

own way backstage. Some PA saw me and said, "Oh my God, where have you been!" I had just enough time to get changed and into mic and wig and the next thing I knew there was Angela Lansbury introducing me. I did the first verse and then I said in my head, "This is where they made the cut." I went on and the orchestra was playing something different. "Oh my God, what's happening?" And then I realize—they put that section of music back in. I'm wrong. Dick Latessa just went with me. It was a beautiful thing. After, I went backstage and I was asking people if they could tell I messed up. They were like, "You don't have time for this! We need to get you changed!" And they pushed me back out on stage and I was in nineteenth-century France. The next day I felt like I'd been hit by a truck. I had nightmares after that of Angela Lansbury introducing me while I was still sitting in my seat.

How was it being in such a huge hit?
It was just fun. It was exciting. I was young. I was in a big hit on Broadway. I was living a dream that I'd never really had. It wasn't like that was my goal, but there I was living it.

What made you decide to leave?
I had been offered *Chess*. It coincided with the end of my contract. Trevor Nunn told me that when he saw me do the *Rags* number on the Tonys, that was the first time he had the idea that maybe I could be Florence. I'd been doing Cosette, a soprano, and that's how he thought of me. Of course I went through a whole audition process. They asked everyone to come in with a song and a Shakespeare monologue. The way he re-did the show from the London production, it was going [to have spoken dialogue, which the London production didn't]. The great playwright, Richard Nelson, was working on a new book, but there wasn't anything to read at that point. Trevor wanted to see people handle language. I chose a Juliet monologue, "Gallop apace you fiery-footed steeds...." I worked on it with an acting coach in this really visceral way to the point where I was rolling around on the floor. I was not a very courageous person back then, but I just remember him looking at me at the end and saying, "Very brave." I got offered the job, the leading role! Another dream that I had never imagined.

What was rehearsal like?
It was different than for *Les Mis*. Trevor really treated this one more like a play. We did a week of table work, just reading scenes, talking about it, really digging into the history of it. It was really exciting. And, of course, the most exciting moment of rehearsal for me was the day I walked in and Benny and Björn said, "We wrote you a song!" Benny sat down and played "Someone Else's Story." It was very exciting. Another dream that I had never dreamed before, that anyone would ever write me a song, let alone the ABBA boys.

As you know, they have revised the book again and again since that production. Was there the sense then that it was not working?
Maybe I'm in the minority but I don't think the problem with the show was ever the book. We had a lot of issues with the set. It was a big, complicated set. When it worked, it was unbelievable, visually magical. But it didn't always work. There were twelve towers that were moving around the stage, on and off the turntable. We spent most of rehearsal staging the set as opposed to working on the show and dealing with any problems that existed in the book or the music. In a way, it was a show that was eaten by the set, and that's not to diss [designer] Robin Wagner, who's brilliant. Trevor wanted to do the show with no blackouts. He wanted it to feel

cinematic and naturalistic. He wanted characters to be able to walk and talk down a hall and then walk into a room. He wanted this sense of constant movement. It was a great idea but it was unmanageable. Maybe if we had done an out-of-town run, which the producers had wanted to do, those issues could have been fixed. Our first preview was more than four hours long. The intermission took forty-five minutes because to change over from Act 1 to Act 2 they had to fly all this furniture. We had a whole technical rehearsal for the intermission. So, we just lost a lot of time. I don't have any perspective on the show. And the Cold War was over; it felt a little dated. I thought the story that they invented was actually quite beautiful and brilliant. There's a reason that people keep trying to do it again. They always blame the book. I don't think it's the book. I think it's more complicated than that. I don't know.

What can you tell me about working with David Carroll?
Oh my God, he was a dream. He was that rare, rare leading man who was tall and handsome, incredible voice, a really good actor, no vanity, really humble, and wickedly funny. It's so rare to find that combination in leading men. We had fun together. There was a scene where we're sightseeing and I have a camera around my neck and I take a picture of him. On our closing night, at that moment, he pulled a camera out of his pocket and took a picture of me taking a picture of him so I would have a souvenir of that moment. He was trying to make me laugh, but he also wanted to do something generous for me. I still get a little choked up when I think about him. God, when I think about all the work we could have had from him. He was only forty-one when he died.

Were you aware of the *Chess* reviews?
I really tried to avoid reading reviews by this point. My then boyfriend/now husband would go to our deli and buy the papers. He would summarize for me. That night we got home from the opening night party, which was at the UN, he went to the deli to get the reviews and he came back and said, "They didn't have the papers in yet." It wasn't until years later that he admitted to me that he had been lying. He read the reviews and he thought, "Judy doesn't need to hear about this now."

The show closed two and a half months later.
We figured out we were closing when we came into work and there were people measuring the dressing rooms. They said, "We're working for *Jerome Robbins' Broadway*, and we're coming into this theater." Another shocking way to find out that I was losing my job.

Your next show, *Metropolis,* took you to London.
My agent just got an offer to do this show. I didn't know anyone involved. I don't actually know how that happened. I was really torn. My husband had just moved to New York to live with me. I was like, "Eeeek. Should I go to London?" There wasn't much of a show then, so I didn't really understand what it was. Seemed like an interesting idea. They said, "Come to London, meet with the director and producers and you can decide." I had tea with Trevor and he told me that the director, Jérôme Savary, had had this highly regarded company in France. He sounded like a really interesting person and that, combined with this idea of doing a stage adaptation of a really out-there silent film, sounded exciting. I knew nothing about Joe Brooks [composer, later indicted for multiple counts of sexual assault], who now we know way too much about. They were treating me like I was something really special. I

saw some amazing theater in London, and I thought, "I want to be in a place that makes theater like that." I went home and I was still really torn, and then my agent said, "Listen, I'll just ask for [a lot of] money." It was more money than I had ever made, and they said, "Yes." So, I went. It was a very complicated experience. Jérôme Savary turned out to no longer be an interesting, talented director, but an alcoholic who had no idea how to stage a big musical. Joe Brooks really didn't know how to write a musical. It was a nightmare. We were in tech and they hadn't figured out how to end the show yet. We literally got to a point where there was nothing written. The cast was wonderful. I loved them. That was the moment I realized what being in my position meant. I had to be a kind of leader because I was the lead, the American they had brought over. Everybody in the company was sort of desperate. Nobody knew what the hell was going on. I had this one diva-ish moment onstage, two days from our first preview. I had a script in my hand because they were still handing us pages. They were all arguing about how the show should end. I finally said, "You know what? I'm going to my dressing room. When you figure out how to end this show you can come get me, but I'm not going to stand here anymore." And I walked offstage. My cast mates in the wings were saying "Thank you! You were the only person who could say that!" I realized that they had been looking to me to lead. That was a lesson to me—that they needed me to be the voice. I also remember during tech, we were on break and Jérôme Savary saying, "How much longer on this break?" Five more minutes. "OK. I'll be in the bar." And he'd go next door and drink. Finally, they fired him and they had to put security guards at all the doors so he wouldn't come back in the theater. I just thought, "It's going to be a failure and I'm going to get to go home." We opened and got slammed, but there was this very wealthy Texan who had invested a lot of money in it and thought it was going to be the next *Les Mis*. Joe Brooks kept convincing him to pour more money into it, so we kept running. Sometimes there was hardly anybody in the audience. I was like, "This can't go on," but somehow, we kept running—not only to the end of my contract, they hired a replacement for me. I loved being in London. By the time we opened it was springtime and it was maybe the most beautiful spring London had ever experienced. It was sunny every day. I saw a ton of theater. I lived right by Kensington Gardens and I would take a blanket to the park and read. All these very pale English actors had never seen such beautiful weather and they came in every night with these terrible sunburns. We were doing a show about people who live underground and never see the sun, so the poor stage managers were putting notes up on the callboard every day, saying, "Please do not go in the sun! Wear sunscreen!"

When you came home . . .
I did *The Glass Menagerie* at the McCarter Theater. I told my agents I wanted to do something different. I wanted to do a play.

You said you regretted not having formal training and that you might have had other opportunities. Was this the kind of thing you were looking for?
Totally. Shirley Knight played Amanda. She knew Tennessee Williams personally! She had worked with him! She taught me so much. Dylan McDermott was Tom. [Director] Emily Mann was wonderful. After *Les Mis* and *Chess* and *Metropolis*, there I was in a four-person cast with one, non-moving set and a dead playwright. No one was coming in with pages. Tech rehearsal was not about moving scenery. It was wonderful. I learned things about the play that I never knew were there.

Did that production help inform what you wanted to do next?

I don't know. I never really shot for anything in particular. I've never been strategic about my career and that may have been a mistake.

You did a piece with Martha Clarke at BAM and you did *Martin Guerre* at the Hartford Stage.

I loved doing both of them. The Martha Clarke piece, *Endangered Species*, was dance theater, unique and wild and exciting. It had dancers and poetry and live animals—an elephant named Flora! Just glorious. There was a monkey, but he got fired. And *Martin Guerre* had things in it that worked stunningly, beautifully, and there were things that didn't work at all. One of the writers wasn't really willing to change those things. It's kind of sad. It was actually during that time that Andrew Lloyd Webber jetted in to talk to me about doing *Sunset Boulevard*. He wanted to hear me sing some of the score and I was like, "OK, but I'm doing a show. I can't come to London." So, he said, "We'll come to you." I remember one afternoon, Andrew trotting into the theater with his entourage. We went down into the orchestra pit and Andrew sat at the piano. I sang "Too Much in Love to Care" with him playing. [Later] I got an offer for the London production, but I had just gotten married. I couldn't go back to London. They asked if I'd be interested [in the upcoming Los Angeles production, which would commence roughly nine months later]. There was no contract signed, but I said I'd be interested. And then I went back to New York and that's when I auditioned for *She Loves Me*.

That production had an amazing cast: you, Boyd Gaines, Howard McGillin, Sally Mayes. . . .

That was just fantastic! It was early in Scott Ellis's directing career and *She Loves Me* was the first musical that Roundabout had ever done. For me, [I was so excited that] it was comedy! Scott really put together the best pieces of a puzzle to make that production what it was. He hired all the right people. It was an all-around great experience and also the beginning of Rob Marshall's career on the other side of the footlights. He was choreographing and it was clear he had a future as a director. He and I would go off in another room and work on "Ice Cream," and he gave me great direction. His sister, Kathleen, was his assistant. She had just moved to New York. All those people were just about to be launched into these big careers. It was such a beautifully directed production and Scott just hit a home run with that company, with the designers, with everything. On opening night, a package arrived for me. Inside this gift bag was a note from Barbara Cook, wishing me well and a happy opening. She explained that in the original production, Guerlain had given them all these beautiful antique perfume bottles to decorate the set. On closing night, she took one as a souvenir of the show and she wanted me to have it. And inside the gift bag was this beautiful crystal perfume bottle. It must have been a precious memento for her. That she would give it up at all was such an act of generosity, but I also felt like symbolically she was saying, "The role is yours now. I'm giving it to you." It's the most beautiful thing anyone's ever done for me.

When the show was transferring, you did not stay because of *Sunset*.

That was another complicated thing. At that point I was also thinking about other life things. I really wanted to have a child. I also needed health insurance. I was torn about leaving town. And then something weird happened with the commercial producers of *She Loves Me*; they started making offers to all the actors and they didn't come to me. I think they knew I had another job and they were afraid of what I would ask for. I'm not going to play one job off another. I actually really wanted to stay with the show because I loved it so much. Meanwhile the *Sunset Boulevard* people caught wind of this transfer and they were calling my agent saying, "Are we going to lose Judy?" We found out that *She Loves Me* hadn't posted bond with Equity yet and people in the company started feeling insecure about whether the show was really going to transfer. Something just felt off and the *Sunset* people were going, "What does she want? What does she need? We're here." I got a little scared that if I turned them down, I'd be out of a job. And, of course, agents always want you to go to L.A. *Sunset* was a chance to work with Trevor Nunn again. It was a chance to work with Glenn Close. I decided to go. To do this crazy Hollywood story in Hollywood just seemed like another adventure. I had the terrible task of sitting down with Scott and saying, "I'm not going to transfer with *She Loves Me.*" That was really hard. I think a lot of people were displeased with me. There were times I wished that I had stayed with the show because I just loved doing it so much. But then, I wouldn't have had my daughter. I got pregnant while I was out in L.A.

What can you tell me about *Sunset Boulevard*?

It was very heady being in Hollywood, working on a show about Hollywood, starring a Hollywood movie star. I would walk out of my dressing room and there, outside Glenn's dressing room, is Tom Cruise or Harrison Ford. One night there was a knock on my door and there was Meryl Streep. But then we had God's wrath; first there were fires in Malibu, then torrential rain which led to mud slides, and then a huge earthquake, which was one of the most terrifying things I've experienced and that's saying a lot because I live ten blocks from the World Trade Center. [But] I loved working with Glenn Close. She still gets in touch. I did a Kickstarter campaign to make a CD and she made a donation to my campaign that put me over my goal, and this was twenty years after *Sunset*. When I got pregnant and I told my various representatives, they said, "Please don't say anything to anybody yet," because sometimes pregnancies don't work out and you don't want to be replaced until they need to replace you. Of course, there were some physical complications with that. The costumes had these little cinched waists! I got to the point where I said, "I have to tell them now because I need my costumes to be let out." I suddenly had these boobs! I was really worried that everyone was noticing how my body was changing.

Were you sad to leave the show before Broadway?

Not for a second. I was happy being part of that production, but I had been wanting to have a child for a really long time and I was getting to the age that was now or never. That was the priority. I was thrilled. And in the middle of it, I got a Tony nomination for *She Loves Me*. All these great things were happening to me and there was just no room for being disappointed about not going to New York. The timing was perfect because I couldn't have done another day or they were going to have to write something new about her relationship with Joe! The cast was so wonderful; they threw me a surprise baby shower. One of the women in the company was a quilt maker and each of the women in the cast and crew made a square which she quilted into this beautiful baby blanket. I still have it. It was really moving.

Were your next several career choices informed by being a new mom?

Yeah, totally. I had a really hard time kind of figuring out how to balance my sense of devotion and responsibility to this creature that we'd made and my desire to still have an independent life. Every mother handles it differently, but it was complicated for me. I also had a lucky bonus [in that] while I was in L.A., I recorded my first solo album and that came out a couple of months after my daughter was born. I also recorded the songs for *Pocahontas* and Disney started doing the pre-release publicity for that. So, for a good chunk of the first year of my daughter's life, Disney was keeping me busy and they were paying me. They would pay me to fly places and sing these songs, and they made sure that I had at least three plane tickets so I could bring my husband and a sitter. I was well taken care of. It made me feel like I was still a working person.

Did *Pocahontas* come about because Stephen Schwartz knew you from *Rags*?
I don't know. I just know that when he and Alan Menken wrote "Colors of the Wind" and they wanted to demo it as part of the pitch to Disney to do a Pocahontas movie, they asked me. I went up to Alan's house and recorded it in his home studio with him playing the piano. Months after that, Stephen told me they couldn't hire me because they were going to look for a Native American actress to do it. I am not sure what happened, but I was later told that Joe Roth, who was head of the studio at the time, got very attached to my re-cording of the song and they ultimately decided to use me and look for a Native American actress whose speaking voice matched my singing voice. I guess it usually works the other way around.

Your next series of shows were smaller, off-Broadway productions with shorter runs. You did *Strike Up the Band* at Encores!, *As Thousands Cheer*, and then the two musicals at The Vineyard, *Eli's Coming* and *Dream True*. Was that a conscious choice or just the way things evolved?
I wish I could say everything is a choice. I think it's just the way it happened. I don't have a memory of turning Broadway shows down. I did check out for a little while when my baby was a baby. I look at women who are bringing their babies to theaters and I just didn't feel capable of doing that. I was exhausted! During the first several years after my daughter was born, a lot of the stuff that I got offered was out of town and that was complicated. At that point in my life, I wanted to just do work that had meaning to me. If it was going to take me away from my family, I needed it to feel artistically important in some way. It wasn't like I was making any money on those shows.

Thank you, *Pocahontas*.
Yes, thank you, *Pocahontas*. That was the gift that kept on giving. And it keeps on giving. It's an incredible thing to be part of that legacy. It's going to be there forever.

After working at The Vineyard, you ended up joining their board.
There are so many ways to contribute and to be active in things that I really care about, and I love The Vineyard. I think it's one of the most extraordinary theater companies in our country that produces incredible work. I just love what they do. To be able to help an or-ganization that I really care about, and bring my circle into the fold by becoming donors or audience members, it's very gratifying. I used to host the season kickoff party at my house for many years. It's been fun and it's also just a way to be engaged in the theater community that I care about in a different way.

In 2002 you were asked to be part of The Kennedy Center's Sondheim Celebration [in which six Sondheim shows played in repertory], playing Fosca in *Passion*.
That was incredible. I had never done a Sondheim show and always wanted to. And then out of the blue I got an offer. I was sort of taken aback. It was this extraordinary journey, working on that show with Rebecca Luker and Michael Cerveris. The show had so much meaning for Sondheim and he loved that production. That was really gratifying. I don't read reviews very often, but I was told that Ben Brantley [in *The New York Times*] called our production "the jewel of the festival." When the curtain came down, Sondheim walked on stage and just embraced the three of us and thanked us for the work we'd done. I mean, what's better than that, right?

What was it like working with him?
I didn't really work with him so much, but he did come to our first run-through and he gave us some incredible notes. He said to me, "I just want you to remember that she is a nineteenth-century woman and her center is down here [indicates her core]." I went back to my room and I thought about how to work on that. I used some exercises that I had learned in a Shakespeare class to work on the text. We did another run through and apparently the assistant director said, "Is Judy OK?" She thought for a second that something was wrong with me, not realizing that I was just bringing something new to Fosca. That one note had such a profound impact on what my performance became, it was really extraordinary. All the rest of his notes were about contemporary vowel sounds [and things like that].

Are you able to articulate what it was that changed in you in the performance?
I don't know if I can. This idea of being nineteenth century… it just changed my physicality, changed the sense of my center, my power. It was a way of seeing the world through her eyes in a different way. It very much jibed with the research I'd been doing on trying to understand what was actually wrong with her. This idea that somehow she's just ugly isn't right. That was the point of view of these particular men on this military base. And they're always talking about how she was ill. What does that mean? I started reading about the nineteenth-century point of view of depression and melancholy. I also read William Styron's extraordinary memoir about his own depression, *Darkness Visible*. He describes, in the first person, what depression does to you physically. And being an intellect would have seemed to those soldiers like she was just weird. She was laughable. So all of that, with Sondheim's note, just made sense to me. And, of course, it's in that music and lyrics. It's an extraordinary piece of writing. I feel so lucky that I got to do it. Rebecca and Michael and I were called in to meet with Sondheim and he said to us that we were all so good but that we were too careful with his music. And he said the whole thing should be rubato. "Don't be so strict with it." We sang through a lot of the score with him conducting us through it to show us what he meant. That was amazing. The three of us had such a great time together.

Your next Broadway show was a return to *Les Misérables*, in the revival.
That was weird. I had been working regionally. There were many times that Cameron Mackintosh asked me if I wanted to come back and play Fantine and I always said, "No, thank you." At that point, I hadn't been working for a little while and I thought I could use the money. The whole thing was very odd. It was fun to play that part but it was like going back

"Judy played Fosca like a hungry, starved, rotting girl," said Melissa Errico of her co-star in *Passion*. With Ryan Silverman.
(Joan Marcus)

to a childhood home; everything looks a little different or smaller than you remember. There were all these people who were toddlers when I did the show originally.

You said that you hadn't been working for a while before you went into that.
There were times when I was being offered things that I really didn't want to do. I've had many times in my career when I thought, "Is this really what I want to be doing anymore?" And then something would come along and, "Oh, that sounds really interesting to me. I'd like to do that." So that would kind of pull me back. And then there were times when it seemed like nothing interesting was coming my way.

So when it seemed like nothing interesting was coming your way, what did you think to yourself?
I'd think, "What else can I be doing with my life besides this?" I've thought about going back to school. I've thought about other ways to be engaged in the world. I started doing some teaching and I found that I really love it. That felt like a way of giving and engaging my craft in a different way. I've been really lucky that I've been able to mostly do work that really does matter to me. I am incredibly grateful for that. And I've been lucky in that I have been able to make choices for artistic reasons and not for the economics. There was a period of time where I thought, "Well, if I keep getting offered things I don't want to do…." And I've always had a conflict about family versus work. Maybe it would be such a relief to work the way normal people work. You're home in the evening, you have time for your friends, you're able to go to the movies with your husband. And as I got older, I had this feeling that I wasn't going

to get roles that were interesting anymore. My self-esteem was lower. I thought, "Life doesn't have to be like this." I sort of moved away a little bit. I felt very conflicted about the business and about my place in it and whether it was really filling me up. I did a lot of soul-searching and I did a very interesting thing on my brother's recommendation; I talked to this business consultant. She was really extraordinary—part career counselor, part life coach, part cognitive therapist. She got me to this place where I started to understand that the reasons that I got into the business in the first place were not the reasons that I wanted to be in it anymore. But I also recognized what I love about what I do and that I still love doing that. As a result of my conversations with her, I started asking myself, "What is it that I want to do? And how can I make that happen and not sit around waiting for someone to make that happen for me?" So I did things like raising money to make a new recording, and I started doing more concerts, which I felt like I had creative control over. I started putting myself out there. I just started saying "yes" to everything and all of a sudden everything changed. It was an amazing transformation for me. At that same time, my daughter was getting older and didn't need me in the same way. At one point, she said something extraordinary: "Mom, you sacrificed so much for me and now it's your time."

You said that you started to realize that the reasons you got into the business were no longer important to you?
When I was young, I got a lot of positive reinforcement from performing. We all need to be reassured. "You're OK. We like what you do." There comes a point in life where we just don't need that. The getting is not as important as the giving. It's not like I don't care whether people appreciate what I have to offer; of course I still do. But if somebody doesn't, I'm not going to go home and cry about it. I'm more interested in what I can give than what I get and I think that that is about just growing up, really. Becoming a more confident person. It's unfortunate, especially for women in this business, that the better you get at what you do, the more you understand about it, the more you have to give, the less work there is. But I've been lucky in that, too. I've been able to play roles that are a little more ageless.

And then *Fun Home* came into your life.
I got this email from my manager, an offer to do this reading at The Public Theater for a new musical based on a graphic novel by Alison Bechdel, written by Jeanine Tesori and Lisa Kron, directed by Sam Gold. Yes! I want to be in a room with those people! I don't care what it is. I've always felt that way—who you get to work with is key. It wasn't that I had not been working all this time. I had done some other things [out of town], but I look at this moment as a kind of turning point. It was a relaunch of something. It was just extraordinary to be in that room with those people. I knew that there was something really, really special in that piece and I loved working on it.

It was a five-year process from workshop to Broadway, with lots of gaps.
Yes. And during that process my daughter was applying to college. I remember [director] Mark Lamos offered a play to me that I really wanted to do, but it would have meant that I wouldn't have been able to go on college tours with my daughter. I was like, "I have one child and one chance to experience this with her. That's what I'm doing this spring. I'm going on college tours." Maybe doing that play would have been a great experience, but I don't regret not doing. it. Not going through that with my daughter would have been a regret. Anyway,

we did our *Fun Home* presentation and then at Sundance and that was the beginning of a multi-year journey with those great artists and that piece. It will always be one of the most extraordinary experiences, not only of my working life, but life in general. It was bigger than just a piece of theater to me.

Why?
It was deeply fulfilling creatively and artistically. I'd never been involved in something from such an early stage of its development. I felt very involved in creating the role. Sam, Lisa, and Jeanine are extraordinary collaborators with each other and with all of us. I learned so much from working with each of them. They are such brave artists and when you're with brave people like that, it gives you permission to be braver. I don't think I've ever worked with writers like Lisa and Jeanine who are so willing to take great material and throw it out because they didn't think it was serving the story well enough. Usually people get very precious about their work. "That's my favorite song!" Doesn't matter if it's your favorite song if it does not work right there. I mean, they even made changes from The Public to Broadway. The Public Theater production was hugely successful and they threw out one of the great songs in the show that had actually been there from that very first workshop! They cut it because they felt like that scene wasn't telling the story that needed to be told there. To watch them work on getting it right, always in the search for the greater truth and the better storytelling … to be around that is so incredible. And the piece itself, aside from being a beautiful piece of art that deeply moved audiences, meant so much in terms of the world at large. We were doing the show when the Supreme Court made marriage equality the law of the land. It was a show that met the cultural moment and had such an important thing to say. The conversations we had at the stage door … we felt like we were changing people's lives. My passion about social justice and activism and my passion about the theater and storytelling were coming together in one piece and one experience. Samantha Power, who was the US ambassador to the UN at the time, came to the show and brought fifteen ambassadors from countries all around the world where being gay was illegal and, in some cases, punishable by death. They didn't know what they were seeing. They just knew that she was bringing them to a Broadway show and that they were going to have a discussion with the cast afterwards and a reception across the street. The conversation was extraordinary. The ambassador from Ecuador said, "I was sitting here thinking, 'What are you trying to say to me,' and then I finally realized you were saying, 'you are me and I am you and we are all together.'" Yes! That's exactly what we were saying! This show had an impact on those people and it may affect what they say to the leaders of their countries and that's extraordinary. That is what theater can do. It is a place where people can build empathy and where people can look at something that is different from their experience and understand it in a different way. That experience encapsulates why it was more than just doing a show that I loved.

You had a significant break between The Public and Broadway. Do you remember coming to the character anew when you came back to it?
For sure. Also, I did other things in between. It's always good to go and do something different and stretch other muscles and then come back. You find these things again. But also, going from proscenium to performing in the round changed the dynamic and the texture of it in an interesting way. It made it feel more real, in a way. It felt like we lived in that house. Anything that was presentational was gone. You could move anywhere you wanted [without

worrying if you were facing the audience. The character of] Adult Alison became the center of it in a way that she hadn't been before, because she didn't have to stand off to the side. She could literally stand in the middle and watch her past. The transformation was incredible. I understood how the show was functioning in a whole new way.

Your song, "Days and Days," is such a benchmark moment in the show. Did you feel that weight?

When we did that very first reading, Helen was barely on the page. There was some of that speech before "Days and Days" and it just said, "song to come." They knew they wanted Helen to have something to say there. Two days before the presentation, Jeanine came running in and she played it for me. That song was worth waiting for! There was one part of it that is in this tricky part of my voice. I said, "Do you think this is the right key?" And she said, "Oh, yeah. I put it there because I knew it would be hard for you and I felt that would be good for the song, for Helen." After that, I remember saying, "This scene and this song are so incredible, but right now it doesn't feel like it's earned." [The hard part to me] wasn't so much the responsibility of that moment, it was earning it. I knew she had to be quiet. I knew I wasn't gonna have any big scenes. We had to understand who she was and what her place was in the family, so that it didn't feel like the song was coming out of nowhere. The responsibility was less about that song, but making sure that the seeds for it were planted throughout the show, in teeny little moments. Small Alison coming over to the piano and saying, "So Mom, you and Dad came back from Germany, right?" And I had just one line: "Yes." But in that one word I had play how Helen's fantasy of what her life was supposed to be collapsed. She had to come back to Beech Creek and be the wife of the funeral director. That was really what my responsibility was. It's an extraordinary piece of writing. I'm not saying it's not hard or that it doesn't take work to make that come alive, but to be held up by writing like that makes it a lot easier.

People say that about Sondheim's work. "If you get out of the way it's all there."

Absolutely! Just get out of the way. Just … get … out … of … the … way. Fosca is like that; look at the song, "I Read." Once you've actually learned how to count it—because every measure is in a different meter—once you learn that, you realize he's telling you what Fosca's emotional state is, how her mind works. It's like Shakespeare; once you understand the rhythm of it—he gives you so much information. You have a road map. It's all there in the writing.

You got a Tony nomination for *Fun Home*. Did it feel gratifying?

What was amazing is that all five of the leading actors were nominated. No one was really left out. And the show got so much love. [Award season] has turned into such a circus. It's exhausting. Especially when you have to do your eight shows a week and especially when we were told that if we didn't win Best Musical we weren't going to be around for very long. We were getting up early and spending the entire day, every day, doing press and going to luncheons and doing other award things. By the time we got to Tony night we were all like, "Thank God it's going to be over and we can just go back to doing our show." It's so different now than when I started out, and with social media and everybody taking your picture, you know that your picture is going to show up everywhere. You've got to have a thousand outfits. The press people have a chart of what all the events and press things are and what outfit you're going to wear to each. Everything's planned out. It's a lot and it's not really my thing. It's not

"Don't you come back here." As Helen in *Fun Home.*
(Joan Marcus)

what I love about what I do. And there was also an extra special pressure on me during that time because at every fucking interview I did, they'd say, "It's your year. You're going to win." Don't say that! Even *The New York Times* said I was going to win and that kind of pressure is just awful. Especially when you don't win because then you feel a sense of failure. But the show got so much love that night! That we swept all the top awards was extraordinary. And then we ran for another fifteen months.

What was it like when you closed?
I have a picture of me at curtain call on closing night. I don't think I've ever sobbed so much. I'm often ready when a show closes after a healthy run. I'm ready to say goodbye and go on to the next adventure. I knew that this was just a unique experience and that I would never have anything like it again. I knew I'd have other jobs that I loved, but it was very hard to say goodbye.

One of the shows you did between *Fun Home*'s two productions was *The Visit* in Williamstown. You were there with John Kander and Chita Rivera and Roger Rees and Terrence McNally and John Doyle and Graciela Daniele.
So many legends! Such amazing people and amazing artists. I knew I couldn't come to Broadway with it because of *Fun Home*, but it was a great experience. Watching Chita and Roger play those scenes with each other was beautiful. It was fun for me to play someone who's kind of ugly as a human. It was such a weird, interesting piece and I love that kind of stuff. You just wanted to be in a room with artists of that caliber. That's how you learn and grow. When I said I was trying to figure out what I really wanted, that's what I really wanted—to be in a room with people like that. And I got to play the wife of the late, great Roger Rees. I was always a massive fan, but then to work with him—one of the kindest, most generous, most loving people you could ever hope to share a stage with. And wickedly funny!

You went directly from *Fun Home* into *Fiddler on the Roof.*
In a way, that saved me from going into a deep depression after *Fun Home* closed. Jessica Hecht was leaving and they asked me if I would want to come in and finish the run. I thought, "Yeah, actually, because otherwise I'm going to go into a mourning period." So it was actually kind of perfect. I'd never done the show and I love Danny Burstein. It seemed like fun. I had two or three weeks off and then I started rehearsing. I had never seen myself as a Golde but I fell in love with her as I figured out how to play her. I am such a process person; I want to invent. But your job, when you replace, is to go in and not mess with the show that's been playing. Danny's so generous. I would say, "Tell me if there's anything you need from me in this scene. I don't want to shake things up." He was like, "No, no, no, do whatever you want."

You did get the opportunity to build the character from the ground up when you did Trevor Nunn's production in London.
In the summer of 2018, [I had just done a lot of things and I wanted to take the summer off and be with my family]. We were at the house of close friends for Labor Day weekend, sitting on their porch, drinking coffee, and I thought to myself, "Oh, wow, summer's over as of tomorrow. I'm unemployed. I really have to think about what I am going to do." It was the first time in a very long time that I really didn't know what was coming next. And reflexively, I picked up my phone and opened up my email and there was a message from Trevor Nunn.

Had he seen you do it in New York?

No, he didn't even know I had done it. When he was doing the casting, he brought it up with Sheldon Harnick and he said, "Oh, she just played it in New York." In his email, Trevor said, "I thought it was such a brilliant idea, but apparently I wasn't the first one to have it."

What was that like?

Oh, it was great! I had such a good time. It was challenging because I had to get the other production out of my head. I didn't want to give up the things that I'd learned that I thought were useful, but with Trevor you have to start from the beginning. It was a completely different approach, done at the teeny, tiny Menier Chocolate Factory. It was so intimate, a gorgeous production. The audience were made to feel like they were part of the village. We did a lot of improv around what a day in the life of these characters was like. He was really going for the reality of these people's lives. He steered us away from playing schtick. You always felt the life of the village and how the family is part of the fabric of it. And then what he did at the end, emptying the village, made it so powerful and relevant with what's going on in Syria and with the migrants coming from South America. Leaving the stage empty in the snow, in silence, was a stroke of genius. It was a wonderful company and it was really thrilling that that production was so well received. We moved to the West End and won the Olivier for best revival and I got to spend an additional three months in London.

In 2020, you were getting ready to do *Assassins* off-Broadway when COVID hit, but you did get to do it in late 2021.

Yes, we got shut down, and it was rough. But doing that show was the most fun experience. And meaningful! First of all, it's a masterpiece. It's a show that you can't believe was written thirty years ago. Doing it now, in the climate that we're living in, between our obsession with guns and gun culture, the way we're dealing with all this political violence, the divisions in our country, the economic resentments, the racism … everything that's making our country really lose its mind—it feels like it was written about this country right now. So it felt incredibly gratifying and important to be doing it now. Also, a little depressing. The show is a bit of a Rorschach test in that people have different responses to it and take away different messages. It doesn't tell you what to think or how you should feel about America. It just puts a mirror up to the country and the people sitting in the audience and says, "You think about it. You think about what it means and what you should do about it." I really admire that as a piece of theater.

It was, of course, especially significant as Stephen Sondheim passed shortly after you opened.

It was the last opening he attended of one of his shows. Sondheim had had an ankle injury so he hadn't been able to see the show before that, much to his dismay, because he loves to come early to dress rehearsal and previews. I was told he was definitely coming to the opening, so I sent him an email inviting him to a celebration I was hosting at my house. I thought he would say, "It's a little much," or whatever. I mean, he was ninety-one. But he wrote back immediately saying, "I'd be delighted to come! Can I bring my husband, Jeff?" He sat on my couch and held court and drank wine. He looked so happy, and I think he was thrilled by the production and just thrilled to be there. It was very moving and of course it was the last time we saw him because he died less than two weeks later. Then, to be able to go on stage every night and pay tribute to him by doing his work…. You could feel the change in the audience. They felt very privileged. I think, to be there, listening to his music. And also, for his collaborators, one of them being John Weidman, who wrote *Assassins*, it gave them a place to go and grieve. John came to the show a lot. That made it even that more special and meaningful. I feel like the show found its time. People were on their feet at the end. They were desperate to talk about it and what it meant. I hope that this is the last time it has that kind of meaning, but sadly I think it won't, given what's going on. I don't see things getting better anytime soon.

There hasn't been a major Stephen Sondheim production in New York or London that hasn't had his fingerprints on it. It's very sad to think about that loss and that future productions will no longer have the benefit of his notes.

The first time I did *Passion*, his fingerprints were on my performance. He gave me amazing notes. And to think, "Wow, anyone who does Sondheim now won't have that opportunity," makes me feel so unbelievably lucky. I always felt sad that I never got to originate a role in a new Sondheim show, but I got to be in the room with him and got to hear his thoughts and feedback. I got his support and that's extraordinary. After he died, John Doyle said, "We knew Mozart." That's true.

Anything else you want to say about doing the show?

I've never gotten to play a real comic role before. I was so anxious about doing it. When we started rehearsals before the pandemic, I went to rehearsal so anxious every day. I came home feeling like I didn't know what I was doing. But something happened to me in that year and a half off when everything seemed lost. When we got it back, I thought, "You know what? Fuck it." I said to John, "I'm going to risk being ridiculous," and he said, "Go for it." That's the kind of director he is; he encourages you to fail on the way to finding your performance. As soon as I let go, I found certain keys to unlock her for myself. I just started having fun! I got really good feedback from the writer, which was also really helpful. It felt like such a personal triumph for me. I just loved doing it. And it was such an extraordinary company! There's nothing I love more than being in an ensemble show with a lot of really talented people. And on top of that, they're also really great fun, interesting people. We were all crammed into one tiny dressing room backstage and it was such a good hang. To be with a group of people that you admire so much onstage and as humans offstage is just a gift. Every day I felt so lucky.

You said earlier that you don't think you're all that interesting. Having just done this with me, on reflection, do you think your life is interesting?

I don't think that I am especially interesting, no, but I have been really lucky; I have had a lot of interesting experiences and a really interesting life and for that I am very grateful.

Beth Leavel

September 2020

"There's no scenery left when I do Miss Hannigan," admits Beth Leavel of her own performance in a regional production of *Annie*. She confesses this shamelessly. Giddily, even. That's because Beth Leavel, versatile though she may be, knows her not-so-secret weapon: size. Subtle nuance may be in her grasp, but it's not where she lives. In the great tradition of women like Bette Midler, Dorothy Loudon, Pearl Bailey, Carol Burnett, and Ethel Merman, Leavel is a broad. She made her Broadway debut as the sassy, brassy Anytime Annie in the original production of *42nd Street* before winning a Tony for creating the title character in *The Drowsy Chaperone*, an egomaniacal, wildly gesticulating, slightly tipsy, huge-voiced (and definitely not drowsy) diva. More recently in *The Prom*, her Dee Dee Allen (a role written for Leavel) was so over the top, she had a song called "It's Not About Me" (P.S.: it was). There are other big belters on Broadway, but is there anyone else who plants her feet and lets fly with more relish than Leavel? Is there anyone less tentative?

Born in Raleigh, North Carolina, to Lynn and Ruby Leavel, she grew up without any real context for theater. But once she landed in her high school production of *Brigadoon*, Leavel was obsessed. Still, she was Southern and, though it's hard to imagine, shy. It took her some time to work up the courage to head north, but once she did, she was unstoppable. Thirteen Broadway shows followed, including the aforementioned trio, plus *Crazy for You*, *Young Frankenstein*, *Elf*, *Baby It's You*, *Bandstand*, and *Mamma Mia!* Her many regional performances include almost annual visits to the St. Louis MUNY, where she played roles like Dolly, Hannigan, and Mama Rose.

In person, Leavel is what one might expect. She is playful and bawdy, self-effacing and uninhibited. More than once, she feels the need to get up and physically demonstrate what she's attempting to convey. The hallmark of a Leavel performance is a keen instinct for "the line"; she sees it, knows it, dances awfully close to it, but she never crosses it. It's a tightrope she's been successfully navigating for thirty-five years.

Given that you didn't care about theater growing up, how did you end up in *Brigadoon* in high school?
My best friend at the time, Jan Herndon, said, "Why don't you audition for the spring musical?" I'm like, "Why?" It just wasn't in my DNA. She said, "Well, it's a great way to meet guys." [Yes. Gay guys.] My people ever since. I remember the first day of rehearsal—and you know, in high school you rehearse for six months before you actually do four shows over a weekend. I remember sitting in that band room and thinking, "Who are these people? Where have they been? How can I be in this oxygen for the rest of my life?" Because we were all just a little left of center. Wore our emotions on the outside. I just wanted to be with these people for the rest of my life. But I hear Ruby and Lynn going, "An actor? In North Carolina? You do want to eat, don't you? You do want to get married and have children, don't you?"

"He vas my boyfriend!" In *Young Frankenstein*.
(Paul Kolnik)

Did you listen to those voices for a while? I ask because in school you only minored in theater.
There was no major. That's the only reason. I was so immature and chicken. I went to Meredith College, which actually is in the town where I grew up. I met this teacher, Linda Bamford. She pushed me and I auditioned for every piece of theater I could get my hands on. She just

kept encouraging me and making me uncomfortable in a good way, getting me to acknowledge that this was something I should really think about doing. At the end of the four years, she encouraged me to move to New York. I had been to New York twice. The first time was with Lynn and Ruby for the International Lions Club Convention. I had the chance to ride the subway out to a Yankees game or to see Angela Lansbury in *Mame.* The subway ride seemed much more entertaining than seeing Angela Lansbury. Idiot! God only knows … if I had seen Angela Lansbury instead of the Yankees losing, possibly my whole trajectory would have been different! But the thought of moving to that city as a pseudo-adult was like, "Are you kidding me? I'll die! I don't have the chutzpah, I don't have the skills. No, no, just let me stay here." So I went and got an MFA at University of North Carolina at Greensboro and those two years changed my life again. I realized then, "Oh my gosh, I'm going

Beth Leavel	
42nd Street	National Tour, Broadway, 1985
Grease	National Tour, 1988
Crazy for You	Broadway, 1992
Show Boat	Broadway, 1994
The Civil War	Broadway, 1999
42nd Street	Broadway, 2001
Lone Star Love	off-Broadway, 2004
The Drowsy Chaperone (Tony Award)	Broadway, 2005
Dancing in the Dark	San Diego, 2008
No, No, Nanette	Encores!, 2008
Young Frankenstein	Broadway, 2008
Minsky's	Los Angeles, 2009
Mamma Mia!	Broadway, 2009
Elf	Broadway, 2010, 2012
Baby It's You	Broadway, 2011
Bandstand	Broadway, 2017
Annie	Milburn, NJ, 2017
The Prom	Broadway, 2018

to do this!" I did *Dolly* for the first time as my thesis production. My director, John Joy, wore leather pants, so I worshipped the ground he walked on. He was the kindest man and again, thank you teachers! What a difference they made in my life! He came over to my parents sitting in the middle of the auditorium and he said, "You must be so proud right now." My parents were very withholding when it came to compliments and they could hardly sit still, they were so excited. I think, after that moment, they decided to let me try. They supported me financially until I started getting a paycheck. And then when I was getting a really nice paycheck, they really approved. [In a smug, Southern accent, as Ruby] "My daughter is an actress!"

They had sent you tap school, so even before that, they saw value in your performing, no?
I'm not sure that's why they sent me to tap school because they also sent me to cotillion. I think it was just the correct, proper thing for a Southern girl to do. I hated ballet. I just wasn't flexible enough. But tap … Betty Kovach's School of Dance for three or four years until I thought it was uncool. I don't have many regrets but I wish I had stuck it out a little bit more. I knew the vocabulary. And thanks to cotillion, I knew what a samba and foxtrot were. I had minor skills.

So after you got your MFA . . .
I was cast as an intern at the Pennsylvania Stage Company in Allentown, Pennsylvania. And I decided to go with that even though it was literally no money. My parents would have to help support me, but I would get my Equity card at the end of my internship. I was there for

eight months. Worked the box office in the morning, struck sets. I was like third sword carrier from the left in *Taming of the Shrew*. And then I was literally on the bus to New York from Allentown, like Peggy Sawyer [in *42nd Street*]. I shared a fifth-floor walk-up on 45th between 10th and 11th. 1982. It was great. I was where I was supposed to be.

No vocal training at all? Your vocals just came naturally?
Isn't that terrible? Natural? I still feel like I'm being trained. I still feel like a perpetual student in that. Particularly as I age. My vocal teachings have come from musical directors. I learned by doing. You just have to learn to take care of yourself. But I never really studied voice. I've learned to listen to other people [and copy their warmups]. I've stolen from the best.

So you just ... realized you could sing?
Yes, I think so much of it is a matter of confidence. The more I worked and the more successful I was, the better singer I became. I think they kind of go hand in hand. At like twenty-five, I learned how to belt. That's been a very handy skill. You just keep practicing.

Did you get a survival job?
I had a few temp jobs. This was when word processing was starting and that's not one of my special skills. But I was highly communicative and entertaining, which, I guess, got me paid. I got work pretty quickly. I did a showcase for a friend of mine. They rented out South Street Theater on Theater Row. I got so many agent offers from that. I went with an associate, Mark Redanty, and I am still with him today! Longer than any other man in my life. Every Thursday I would get *Backstage*. It was biblical. I would circle every audition coming up and each week was a new adventure, a new opportunity. And then I auditioned for the national tour of *42nd Street*, onstage at the Majestic Theater. I was in my fuchsia suit that my mother bought me because she said it would pop. She wasn't wrong. I sang "I Got Rhythm." That was my go-to song because it just kept getting me work. There was a row of suits sitting at the table: [Writer/director] Mark Bramble, [Writer] Michael Stewart ... I sang the song and apparently that went well. They gave me the sides for Anytime Annie and apparently, I was funny. And I hear, "Do you mind just doing some tap steps?" I'm thinking, "I studied at Betty Kovach's; I'm gonna nail this." I remember Karen Baker, who was Gower Champion's assistant, coming up from the audience. I was terrified. She shows me, like I am a dancer who can pick things up, the tap break. It could have been Mandarin. I had no earthly idea. I did not do well. I could tell I had broken her heart. I asked her to do it slower and then I finally got my Walkman out and recorded her feet, while talking into it [calling out the steps]. "Shuffle step, step...." She told me I had a week to essentially get better. My husband at the time, John, was a much better dancer than I was, so we rented a room at Harlequin Studios. The other steps [from the lobby at Harlequin] led to a gay porn shop. How do I know that? [In her highest pitch, happening upon the imaginary customers accidentally] "Hey! OK! So ..." in my little dance clothes. Anyway, I worked my ass off and I got back a week later and I did it so much better. I think she saw a trainability in there, and I got Anytime Annie. To this day people still think I am a tapper. I can do what I learn in shows. But I can still do the Anytime Annie choreo.

What was your experience on the road?
It was so much fun and we became so close. A lot of those people are still very, very dear to me. There's nothing like a national tour to really bond a bunch of storytellers. Thank goodness I

had comic chops and could sing, because I had to get better at the tap. I was in the room with Karen Baker for weeks, just her and me doing my number. I'd finish with my vagina on the floor and she'd go, "let's do it again." She whipped my ass into shape. I worked hard.

So the role opens up on Broadway . . .
I was the fourth replacement for Anytime Annie and I stayed for four years. I was so happy there. Nothing else was really coming up and I thought, "Why would I leave?" If I get in a show, I'm going to stay there until I get another job. It was nice making money.

People often describe getting really tired of doing a long run. How did you manage?
I always, always, always think about my responsibility to the audience. I can never mark. If I am tired I just have to get over it. It's my job. I know there's someone in the audience seeing their first Broadway show. That is a huge responsibility to me and I am not going to sidestep that in any way, shape, or form. Theater changes lives and I'm going to do my part and do what I have to do to be a part of that experience for people. I'm going to go out there every night and give a hundred and fifty percent. I can't not. And I learned so much watching some of the women that came through—Peggy Cass, Bobo Lewis ... to me she was like the quintessential, New York, strong, independent, feminist, beer-drinking woman. A group of us would go out every Thursday night to Bangkok Cuisine on Eighth Avenue. It was almost like huddling around a campfire with her and we would just listen to her stories. "Come on girls, we are gonna go out and get some beers." I'm so glad to be a small part of that theater history, even if I was the fourth replacement. It was Gower Champion's *42nd Street*! Then this *Grease* audition opened up with Jack Wagner as Danny. I was Rizzo. It went on a mini tour, then we went to Washington, D.C., with plans of coming to New York. We closed in Washington. It got terrible reviews.

You had a bit of a break between *Grease* and *Crazy for You*.
I must have done something ... [thinks—eyes go wide] I had a baby! Don't tell him I forgot! I gave birth in 1989. I did *Broadway Jukebox* off-Broadway. I did a couple of regional things. *Hello, Dolly!* And I did Anita in *West Side Story*. Because, you know, when you think of Anita ... I apologize to everyone right now! I'm so sorry. My heart was in the right place. It was a job. And then I had eight auditions for *Crazy for You*. I was Tess and I covered Jodi Benson. She could dance! I am not a dancer, people! I feel personally responsible for Susan Stroman's career.

Tell me about working with Susan Stroman.
She's brilliant. She's such a pro. I'm so terrified that I'm going to let someone down because they're going to make me dance. Fortunately, they made Tess the dance captain, which is code for "I don't have the technique that those fabulous women did." I walked into one of the rehearsals and literally the women were on pickaxes! Just watching her, thinking, "How did you visualize that? How did you come up with that?" So cool. She kept adjusting for me. I remember during rehearsal, she said, "Beth, can you not breathe so hard at the end of that number?" I was [gasping for air] dying. So, at the end of the number I would just kind of hold my breath, thinking, "please don't faint, don't faint." She is always super prepared. A kind person, but in her rehearsals you're there to work! It was thrilling because we could feel how special it was.

I always wonder if actors can have perspective during rehearsals and if they can tell how the show is—good or bad.

You sure can. Even if you're like [unconvincingly], "No, no, this is good. Just wait till we get costumes!" With this, everyone knew. You never want to go, "Oh my gosh, this is such a hit," because that's the kiss of death, but we just felt it.

Did you feel like you were "making it"?

I was originating a role for the first time. First cast album. First Tonys. The commercial. Everything was new. Being an original cast member in an original Broadway show is spectacular. I felt like it was the first time I had a real blip in the New York Broadway scene. I felt like I finally kind of earned my place here. [During the run] I got pregnant again. I stayed as long as I could lay on my stomach [in "I Can't Be Bothered Now." I left when] they could no longer take the costumes out anymore. I had planned to go back in, but right towards the end [of my maternity leave] Stro calls and says, "Would you be able to come in and do Ellie in *Show Boat*?" I went for a costume fitting in Toronto three weeks after Sam was born. Then I went into *Show Boat*, just lactating. There were three or four of us that went in at the same time. Carole Shelley went in to replace Elaine Stritch, Hugh Panaro went in. One of my favorite Stro stories: I got a note that when I'm holding my dance partner, not to have my pinky out. "That's the wrong period." I'm like, "Wow, that is attention to detail!" That's Broadway. It matters.

When you speak of detail, you are reminding me that I saw you do a video tour backstage at *Mamma Mia!* The level of detail work on your costumes was extraordinary and virtually imperceptible to most of the audience, and yet . . .

Everyone's artistry is represented. During *Drowsy Chaperone*, I would make people come backstage to celebrate Gregg Barnes's costumes and point out details; "Do you see what he did here? The beading work? There are hieroglyphics on the bottom of my costume and they're drinking martinis and smoking! Do you even see that? Well look!" The pinky—that's perfectionism. That show had a cast of seventy. So much of my energy was spent not getting lost and trying to get to know people's names! I shared a dressing room with Gretha Boston. To watch her process of warming up . . . I sponged! I learned by just being in the room. "Oh, I'm going to steal that!" She had this huge warmup that she had learned to produce those fabulous vocals that she had. And in between shows, my kids would come and play. The crew would let them go on the boat. And I remember TJ running up and down the aisles of the Gershwin Theater. That's what *Show Boat* was to me: a great job, I got to know a whole new set of family members, and I was in a Hal Prince show.

Your next show was *The Civil War*. We already discussed that you can tell when a show is or isn't working.

When there's not one voice . . . there were five people giving notes, five people making decisions. I don't think there was a cohesive point of view as to what the story should be. The book was actually based on letters written during the Civil War and some of the lyrics are taken from actual letters. At the Alley [in Houston, where the show premiered] there were no guns, there was no fighting. It was all about storytelling the relationships and what happened to the soldiers and the people they left behind. It was much simpler. And then they started to [makes air quotes] "improve it" for Broadway. And I remember thinking, "Is this a good idea?" It just felt unsettled. Things didn't feel good. But I thought some of the music was just beautiful. The cast was magnificent and the orchestrations and the singing— hearing those men sing like that? I'm such a Pollyanna, thinking, "This is going to work." I never saw the show, so I can't speak from an audience perspective. I had a song called "Five Boys." Funny, funny song [she is being sarcastic—the song is about a woman who loses her five sons]. I don't read reviews but I heard they were terrible. You'd go out and you'd see half an audience. You know when you're not in a hit. You feel it in the community. You hear people sidestepping: "Oh, you're in *Civil War*. Beautiful costumes!" But we were nominated for a Best Musical Tony. After we did our number at the Tonys, we get on the bus [back to the show's theater] and I couldn't fit because I was in costume. I had to stand up and put the dress on its side. I took up like nine seats. Then we went and watched the broadcast and when we didn't win anything, I heard one of the guys say, "You can kiss this show goodbye." We closed the following week. I remember [the announcement before a show], "Cast on stage please, cast on stage." They told us we were closing that weekend and I remember watching one of the actors who had two small children drop to his knees on the stage. That was awful. You give birth to something. It's a very personal thing and you have to grieve it. Even if the show wasn't successful, there was so much of our DNA in there. It feels awful, feels awful. But now it's time for the next thing. I got two kids and a mortgage and insurance I have to keep, so let's figure it out and see what's next. My feelings were really hurt and I felt like I had let someone down, which was ridiculous, but....

There was a big gap between that and your next show, the revival of *42nd Street*.
There was. I was auditioning a lot. I did a slew of commercials. I went to the *42nd Street* audition and Mark Bramble said, "You're just right in the middle. You're too young for this, too old for that. Would you consider standing by for Christine Ebersole and Mary Testa?" Absolutely. That was the first time I stood by and I liked a lot of it. I could go home at 9:30! But then I started going on a lot because Christine had some health hurdles. I went on for two weeks of previews and they didn't have costumes for me, so they went to Lord & Taylor to the mother-of-the-bride shop. The swings developed a very close-knit group. We called ourselves "Lurky" because we just lurked. We would sit there and watch movies when we weren't on. I've never seen so much TV in my life. That was an interesting experience. You don't feel as much a part of the community. You're not invited to the Tony Awards, you're not on the cast album. But you're still on Broadway. Such enthusiastic, young dancers. Their energy was so amazing. When you're in a room with all these Broadway debuts, it makes you see things again through their eyes. They work their butts off. Then Christine left and they offered me the job. I did it for maybe a year and then they hired Shirley Jones to replace me [to boost sales. I got that call when I was] at Disney World with my family and I remember being like, "Put that down! We can't afford it!" But I had a good run. The night I left, at curtain call, David Elder gave the most emotional, eloquent speech about how I was going to be missed. That was one of those imprinted moments in my life. I just remember sobbing on stage. That was a really beautiful thing.

What did he say?
I get very flustered having to repeat compliments. He talked about leading the company with love and kindness, how my dressing room was like the therapy room. Everyone wanted to

come to the room. It was really sweet. The audience was probably going, "Come on already! I have a dinner reservation!"

That's the first time you describe yourself as a company leader.
If you're the leading lady in the show, energy trickles down through the entire cast and I take that responsibility seriously. I like to lead with my best self when I come to the theater. I have my dressing room door open all the time. I like to go around and check on people. I like to make sure the crew is OK. If it's possible for me to affect an energy change just by bringing joy into the room, let's do it. We'd play games. I'd have a question of the day on a bulletin board. That kind of thing. Eight shows a week is hard, so anything we can do to keep people happy.... Just one person can sometimes shift something, just by trying to lead with joy and love.

You went on to *Lone Star Love*.
Oh, I forgot about that. It was a fun show to do. We got paid so little it was ridiculous. I could get more on unemployment. But that was just that [off-Broadway] contract at the time.

And then *The Drowsy Chaperone*.
You know I didn't get the part, right? [Then my agent called, months after my audition, and] he said, "I have a job offer. *Drowsy Chaperone*." I literally made him call the casting person again because [director] Casey Nicholaw told me I didn't get it. He and I knew each other from *Crazy for You* and he called me. I said, "I don't think I'm the right person to lift this person off the page." They truly didn't know who the character was yet. I think they were just trying to find someone to give it a spark: "That's where it needs to go! That's the age. That's the energy!" They looked at Joan Van Ark, Eartha Kitt, Tina Louise.... Honestly, I think they gave up. Rumor has it Casey said, "Just give it to Beth. Let's see what happens." When we got to L.A., we spent every morning from 10:00 to noon basically doing research, watching films from that era, just so everyone would have the same storytelling tone. Then Casey said, "Now we're going to start doing improv games." I remember thinking, "I HATE this!" But that's where I found the character of Beatrice Stockwell, in the game Hot Seat. We had to write a bio and I just made something up. Just bullshit, bullshit, bullshit. I didn't know who she was. But in Hot Seat you sit on a stool and the cast and creatives throw questions about your character at you and you respond in character. It's very difficult to do if you don't really know who your character is. But in one of the last days, Casey said, "Ladies and gentlemen, Dame Beatrice Stockwell." He had never said "Dame" before. Everyone stood up and applauded. It just changed the way I walked. And then, going to the stool [she demonstrates a bow in which she bends all the way to the floor, still beckoning for more applause with her hands]. It was like a light went off. "There she is! There she is! This narcissistic, fabulous, drowsy, diva!"

With a show as calibrated as that one, I am curious to know about the specificity of the work.
How about having the author [Bob Martin] with you on stage every night, clocking every laugh? With Casey and Bob particularly, every day in previews you're going to come in and there's going to be huge script changes. They will refine and rewrite until it's absolutely what they think is perfect. One of my early lines had something like ninety choices. Eddie Korbich's character asks, "Say, isn't it a little early in the day to be drinking?" And my favorite response was, "Not in Burma." What we ended up with was, "I don't understand the

"Champagne makes me drowsy!" With Danny Burstein in *The Drowsy Chaperone*.
(Joan Marcus)

question." And that line, "Why in the world would anyone put olives in a Gibson?"—that line went through so many different cocktails. But being in a room with Casey, I can always do my best work because I feel so taken care of and so safe. That makes all the difference in the world. When I can go in a room and throw everything I have up against the wall and have someone go, "Yes. No. Yes. Yes. No. Yes," I am happy. Don't ever yell at me, please, or I will Southern girl right down on you. With Casey and some other directors like Andy Blankenbuehler, you always feel taken care of and therefore you are able to risk and make choices and not lead with fear. You lead with your artistry. If you are trying to make everybody happy, you won't get there. That's like my Achilles heel. Please don't yell at me. Don't be angry. I just won't work. I shut down.

You must have had instances where you've had to figure out a way around that.
Absolutely. I think that's probably one of the reasons I'm so funny. I'm telling you, you can change a room like that. Even at the DMV—if you can make somebody laugh.... Anything to avoid confrontation.

You won the Tony.
It was amazing. I mean, good God! I got so many people that said I had won that award for them, for the worker bees, the people that are just working and working and trying to get the next job. That meant so much to me. I was grateful that the shoes finally fit so brilliantly. It feels so good to have originated something that's loved so much and that has so much of my DNA all over it. I felt like it was the first time I really, really, really gave birth to something. It comes with age, too. You have a little more wisdom, you have a lot more confidence. People

love *The Drowsy Chaperone.* I had done the Tony Award show for *Crazy for You* and *Civil War* but this was the first time I was nominated, so, getting into costume and wig, getting into Beth red carpet [clothes], getting back in the costume.... It's one of those experiences that is hard to just articulate. They told us that [if you win] we'd have ninety seconds from when they say your name. So I remember, when they said my name, after I go out of shock, I'm running up that aisle like a linebacker. I don't really remember the rest of it except that my voice was really high. And I remember thinking, "Please don't curse. Please don't fall." At the end I thanked Ruby and Lynn Leavel in Raleigh, North Carolina, and my parents' phone started ringing—radio stations, TV stations, relatives. Days later, my mother said [in the heaviest drawl], "Well now I just take the phone to the bathroom because it just rings all the time and I don't want to miss anybody." [I was so happy to] give that little gift to them.

Let's talk about that amazing cast.
Again, Casey sets the tone, but they were not company members, they were family. When you go through the opening of a new show, the amount we need each other to stay sane and happy and connected? I don't know what we would have done without each other. We're still so close. I truly believe that Tony Award was for the entire company because nothing would have happened without Danny, Sutton, Bob, without everybody. We were such a good group and we took such good care of each other. I think that showed on stage. I think it showed in the development, too, because we all loved each other and were able to take those risks. How far can we push and still play, and still be truthful to the story? You can't do that without the support of other people, and damn they were talented. If you look at our set ... all of us were asked to bring a piece of ourselves to the set. So, there was a picture of my boys at Thanksgiving. And if you look on Man in Chair's table, there's Sutton's cast [she broke her arm in Los Angeles]. It's hidden back there. There are some tacky plates that Casey's family gave him. It's just like, wow, that's how you lead a company. We were all so invested in this and it was so personal. Boy, when it lifts like that, when it's a celebration, like *Drowsy* and like *Prom*, I'll do theater until they kick me off the stage.

So what happens as cast members start to leave?
That's the business. When an original company starts to dissipate, you have to grieve and it's an adjustment. I've been that new person [coming in] and I'm like, "I'm so sorry I'm not that person." I'm trying to be sensitive, bringing my own stuff, but yet you have to respect those boundaries until you develop your own relationships and you can bring your singularity to the storytelling. Because that's why you've been hired. But it's tough.

What was it like closing?
I don't think I've ever cried so hard in my life, except the night that David Elder made that speech at *42nd Street.* It changed my life so much, so to have to say goodbye to it was heartbreaking. I thought it needed to be around a little longer. It was difficult to let that one go.

You went into *Dancing in the Dark* in San Diego, which had its eye on Broadway.
That was another show where no one had the best idea. I had a great time doing it, I loved the cast, I met my fiancé, Adam Heller, but there wasn't a lot of joy in the room, except between us principals. We made each other laugh. You feel an energy when something's not working. There's a lot of pressure and a lot of money on the line. It's just not happening, not working.

You try to change it, you fix it, you cut it. And then you still get bad reviews and the producers are upset.

On *Civil War* you said you felt personal responsibility....
On this one I didn't feel personal responsibility. I felt my stuff was working—not because of my brilliance, just because that part of things wasn't really broken. It just never came together completely.

You next did *No, No, Nanette* at Encores!
It was great. The wig I wore was my *Drowsy Chaperone* wig. They rejiggered it.

And then Susan Stroman called to ask you to do *Young Frankenstein*.
That was interesting, joining a company that, I felt their soul had died. It was just palpable. I think they had such success in Seattle and then were so slammed here. They felt broken and people were leaving left and right. When I auditioned, I didn't have time to rehearse it but I got the CD. I don't read music but I have a very good ear. So, I listened all night. I come into the audition thinking it's just going to be [casual]. There's twenty people behind the table! Sue Stroman, the producers, Mel Brooks! Something I forgot—sometimes when they record the CD, it's not the entire song, is it? I was awful! I was just awful and so flustered that I hadn't better prepared. I wish I'd asked for more time. Mel Brooks stood up and he said, "Now, I know you're better than that." Because thank GOD he had seen me in *Drowsy*. They asked me to come back and maybe do a little more work on it. I was off book and in a costume the next time I auditioned. They offered me the job, but talk about a learning curve! At my put in rehearsal—the set was designed for Andrea Martin, who's 5′1″ [Leavel is 5′8″]. And the wig and boots ... I'm supposed to go through the arch and went [mimes crashing into wall]. "Hold please. Hold." I had to figure out how to get in there and still try to get the laugh. I had to limbo. I about wet my pants. But I certainly learned something from the show, taking over from someone as brilliant as Andrea Martin, trying to steal from her as kindly as I could. I watched her. I trailed her. She wrote me a letter for my opening night, thanking me for taking care of something that she had given birth to and meant so much to her. It was so lovely. And then I got *Minsky's* so I didn't even stay until it closed.

Back to Los Angeles. That had a Charles Strouse score.
He wrote me this beautiful note on opening night, about how wonderful it was to hear his songs sung by me. I had some great tunes in that show. *Minsky's* was—again, you could tell something wasn't working. You can just feel it. We would try to fix it but the reviews were not good enough to let us move to Broadway. It's so disappointing but that's show business.

You had just come from working with Christopher Fitzgerald in *Young Frankenstein*, and now he's the lead.
I wish I had his courage. He doesn't have an edit button in his body, which is so refreshing. He will throw everything up against the wall. He's such a good actor and a singer and a comedian and I wish this show had worked for him. I wish he could have brought that to New York and everyone could have seen him do that.

You came back and stepped into *Mamma Mia!*

They let me rehearse for four weeks! They had a mock-up of some of the set at Ripley Grier Studios and the stage manager was like, "just do what you want." There were eight of us going in. He gave us permission to kind of re-block it or do whatever we were comfortable with. That never happens. I think we ended up doing the same thing [as their predecessors], but just to have permission to do that! We couldn't do our own thing with the music. From what I understand the rights were [contingent on faithful interpretations]. It needed to sound like the original recordings. No riffing. Except "Winner Takes It All." There I could do whatever I wanted. So, "no straight tone here … now vibrato after four counts.…" I ended up doing so much homework. I remember being tan for a year. That was one of the big things that you had to maintain because we were in Greece. You had to be tan. I remember getting a spray thing and smelling like Burger King for two days. Doing that show every night was like doing a rock concert. People love ABBA and their music. To know that the audience is going to sing along with you, and at the end, it's really like being at a club. They're screaming at the stage door. It was really kind of thrilling that way. I was tan and I was a rock star.

You did that punishing score for a year. Did you ever have vocal issues?

I had a big issue. I popped something in my neck during "The Winner Takes It All" and I'm like, "there's my career. Going to be working at Macy's." My voice came back by the finale but that started what must have been a four-month-long journey of trying to figure out what had happened. Because of the rake in the stage [I compressed something in my spine]. There were nights when I couldn't hit the note and I just started doing alternate notes. I thought I'd ruined my voice forever. But once I got off the stage and straightened back up, it came back. It was terrifying. And I was separating [from my husband] at the time which probably contributed, as well. Stress has to go someplace. There were a lot of injuries in *Mamma Mia!* because of that stage. But aside from that it was a rock concert and the company was so much fun. There were so many extracurricular activities. The stage managers really knew how to just keep it going, keep it happy backstage, because that shows onstage.

You got to wear your own hair.

Your hair gets damaged under the lights and they had to dye it and highlight it every three weeks, but it made going home a lot easier. One night, they were making my hair look like it's been in the sun, and there was something wrong with the product. This was between a Sunday night and a Sunday matinee. My hair came out dark purple. There wasn't enough time to fix it, so it was like goth Donna that night. The next morning, I was doing a photo shoot with Joan Marcus for *Elf.* They had to triage my hair!

Let's talk about *Elf.* You were working with Casey Nicholaw again, and this was your first time working with composers Chad Beguelin and Matthew Sklar.

Some of the best people on the planet. And their work! I think *The Prom* is the best thing they've ever written. I just can't wait to watch them grow. They can ask me to do anything and I cannot say "yes" quick enough. They're just great. Untalented sons of bitches, but great. *Elf* was such a blast. Partially because I had so little to do! I had two great songs and a lot of time to play with the girls upstairs. I wasn't responsible for driving the train like with Donna. I was just doing my part, serving the story the way I knew how. It took me about a month not to be tan [from *Mamma Mia!*].

You did have to drive the next one. . . .
Oh God, *Baby It's You*. This show had been a thing in L.A. The writer/director was interesting. We were speaking of the tone of the room? It's complicated; it takes a certain amount of skill to communicate to an actor what you would like, to develop communication as opposed to having a dictatorship or giving line readings. It was a very difficult rehearsal period. Floyd Mutrux is not a director. He wrote it and had such a personal investment in the story, but he just didn't know how to communicate with actors. We would sit around at the table read and he would literally yell, "No! Why would you do it like that?" I was on the defensive so much. I was so nervous and yet I had to carry this whole show. Since Floyd didn't have that ability, they hired Sheldon Epps, so there were two directors. But Floyd had all the power. Everything trickled down from that energy, which was crazy. It was a little crazy in the room.

You already described yourself as someone who shuts down when faced with that kind of approach, so what did you do?
I had to get my big girl panties on. I remember having a conversation with the producer, saying that I needed help, I needed to feel safe in the room. If I was expected to drive the train and do my work, I needed to be allowed to make mistakes as an actor. Let me grow. There were constantly changes and lots of talking and yelling. [It was clear] the show was not going to work. To our credit as a company, from where the show opened and where we ended when we closed, we had learned so much. By then I think we had personalized it and made it our own show. People were really enjoying it. But boy, the rehearsal process … I learned a lot! I have to stand up for myself and ask for what I need if you want me to do this ginormous thing. I had twenty-five costume changes! I've never been so spent in my life. It was exhausting. There wasn't a settled energy in the theater even though the cast was lovely. It was crazy time, a lot of drama.

But aside from rough rehearsals, the piece was still the piece. What did you think when you first saw the script?
I thought, "Oh great! A great paying job." The book needed work but that's what you do in a rehearsal process. That didn't happen. The material had become precious [to the writer] and was not changeable. To achieve any kind of change took an act of Congress. So, let's just get to the song and try to make the book as truthful as possible. The [real life] woman I was playing was so fascinating. That has to sail through. It didn't happen. In certain people's minds it was a big hit in L.A., so [the thinking was] if it's not broken, don't fix it. I felt like I could only do what I could do.

Your name was above the title. Did you feel the stress of being responsible for it?
I never felt that. I just didn't have time to even think about that. There was my picture on the marquee, but I didn't put that pressure on myself. I'm not a miracle worker. I can only achieve what I can do. I can't rewrite the book. I can only be responsible for me.

You got another Tony nomination.
Well, they were so sorry for me. I loved singing that music. I felt very proud of what I did. But the show had already closed. My dresser should have gotten the Tony nomination.

Your dresser . . .
Kay Gowenlock. Oh my God, she worked so hard in that show. She'd leave at night, like, [gasping], "Where's the cocktail?" Dressers become your therapist, your lifesaver, they keep you from going onstage nude. Sometimes they actually keep you fed. She really saved my life during that show. During all the changes, she would literally have the script in her hand and read me my entrance line for the next scene. I'd have no idea what was next.

Your next show was supposed to be *Something Rotten!* until they decided that the character needed to get pregnant. So first you have to a leave *Crazy for You* because you're pregnant, then you have to leave this because you can't get pregnant!
Casey took me to dinner to tell me. God bless the writers. They wrote me the sweetest letter about how they tried to take the pregnancy out of the story. I understood. I have no control over how old I am, but wah-wah. I was glad to see it succeeded. But, "Dear diary: Today, I was told I'm old." I did have to grieve about *Something Rotten!* and I understood it. I love Heidi Blickenstaff [who took over]. We had a phone conversation and I said, "I'm so glad that someone so capable is going to take care of the part."

You went on to *Bandstand*.
We did a lab and a workshop and Paper Mill Playhouse. And then out of the blue it comes to Broadway. It was really lovely that they just reached out and offered me this role of June Adams.

It's particularly interesting that they just reached out and offered you this role because it is not a typical Beth Leavel role.
At all! Why would you think of me for that part? But they did want to find someone that could bring some comedic chops to a show that doesn't have a lot of laughs, yet not lead with that. Andy Blankenbuehler was so flattering and he's so great. It's a different energy than Casey, but again, you feel so safe. He's so smart. You just feel like you can come in and throw everything you have up against the wall and figure out what sticks. I had even less to do than in *Elf*, so my dressing room became the green room. I was responsible for the socializing and snacks and the entertainment of the entire company. It was a great job. So many [military] veterans said that for the first time they found themselves represented truthfully on stage. Wow, what an honor that was! Every night before the show, we would round up before half hour and dedicate the show to a veteran. We'd find out their history, who they were. That was cool and gratifying and important. We had a whole wall on the second floor dedicated to [company members' family who were veterans]. I learned a lot. I am very thankful for that show. And I knew *The Prom* was right around the corner.

It was written for you!
Casey calls, casually, "Bob Martin, Chad and Matt and I wrote something for you and Brooks Ashmanskas and Chris Sieber and Angie Schworer." We went up to Casey's Studio and sat

"It's not about me!" flanked by (clockwise from right) Josh Lamon, Brooks Ashmanskas, Angie Schworer, and Christopher Sieber in *The Prom*.
(Deen van Meer)

around a table and read it. It was night and day from what it eventually ended up being, but its heart was there, and its comedy. They just had to figure out how to make it work. So we did that, then another table read, then we did a lab, then we did a workshop, then we went to Atlanta. Then *Mean Girls* got a theater [which tied up Nicholaw], so everything was on hold. During all that I'm just praying to the theater gods, "Please let it come to New York. Please let people get to know Dee Dee Allen. Please let these songs be heard." I go to the MUNY. I'm all over the place. All of a sudden, *A Bronx Tale* closed and we had the Longacre. We went back into rehearsals.

Did the show change a lot?
The first scene of *The Prom* was so problematic, trying to set the tone. That changed so many times in Atlanta that I kept my lines in my bra. I couldn't remember. "Which version is it tonight?" Because if Casey and Bob and Chad and Matt don't like it, it gets changed and, "here are the new lyrics for tonight." The biggest change that they made in Atlanta … [the creators decided that] you have to like us, me, Chris, Brooks, and Angie. We call ourselves "the olds." Trying to find that tone in the comedy so that you're willing to journey with us for the rest of the show was a real challenge to the writers and to Casey. I think they came up with it in New

York, but it was blood, sweat, and tears for a while. It's like, "Nope! Here's a new scene." Act two pretty much never changed.

The four of you, plus a few other actors playing adults, were surrounded by a company of young people. Thirteen Broadway debuts. How did that make you feel?
It made me feel old, and it made me very grateful that I didn't have to do hip-hop. I remember in Atlanta watching Casey Hudson and John McGinnis, who were Casey's assistants, teaching this combination, thinking, "Oh my God! Thank God I don't have to do that!" All of a sudden. Casey wants everyone doing it. Dammit! So in Atlanta "the olds" would go into what I called "a time-out rehearsal room." Every day we would deconstruct that hip-hop. I mean, I'm a pretty good mover, but that was sometimes … even uncountable in my tap head. We struggled with that like nobody's business. It was actually fun once we got it. The kids would sit in our rehearsal and watch us work because they saw it as an opportunity, and conversely, we would sit and watch them after they learned a number because we wanted to experience their skill and their enthusiasm. Like *Drowsy*, it was a real love fest.

Brooks Ashmanskas is known to be unpredictable.
He's so dangerous. It's so thrilling because when Brooks makes a mistake, he can't just let it go. He has to point it up, comment on it, correct himself, and try again. I have never laughed or covered a laugh so much on stage as I did during *The Prom*. Mostly I blame Brooks.

And Chris Sieber never breaks. . . .
Until the time he did! And when he broke, we literally had to stop the show. Fortunately, it was a scene that wasn't too deep, but the audience caught on to it and they were applauding and laughing. None of us could get our shit together. I'm looking down and … tears. I mean, I've never laughed like that. We were so exhausted. We had done a photo shoot all day and we had zero brains. Chris broke and we were done. The only reason I don't feel so guilty is that the audience loved it so much.

You knew the show was playing like gangbusters and that people loved it, but you also knew that it was struggling. How was it managing that?
It's so frustrating. I think the first graphics that were introduced were a little misleading as to what our show was about. But reviews [I was told] were great. So now it's a matter of doing so much publicity to try to convey how much people loved it once they were there. How do we get them in the seats? Show business can become so frustrating. Of all the shows I've done, this one had the most impact. It literally changed people's lives, kids and their parents. I believed so much in *The Prom* that it was joyous for me to share it in any way that I could. I knew that they needed us to do press and be joyous and enthusiastic to get people in the seats. So 6:00 a.m. interview? Let's go! Sure, I'll sing. Whatever it takes to keep this baby alive. It was frustrating to look at the numbers. What do you do now? The producers believed in us so deeply. They got us through the Tony Awards. When [we didn't win anything] we knew it was going to be tough. And it was. I am glad that it's now going to be a movie because at least the message will get out there.

There's a funny coincidence that Meryl Streep got your role in the movie but that you are playing her role in the upcoming *The Devil Wears Prada*.

I had to grieve but I'm not an idiot. They're not going to hire us when they can get Meryl Streep. But when you've REALLY given birth to someone and it's so much your creation, to relinquish that ... it was a journey. But if I'm going to relinquish it to anyone.... It's like, "Oh that's why they were all in the audience!" Meryl was there, Nicole Kidman. I am hoping that the producers can make a lot of money. They put their hearts, souls, and wallets in that show.

So when the show ultimately closed . . .

Thankfully the producers had given us five weeks to prepare. And again, after the Tonys we saw the writing on the wall. But what made this closing a little different was the fans. They loved the show so much that the closing performance was like twelve *Mamma Mia!* rock concerts put together. I swear it was almost three and a half hours long. That took away a lot of the pain until the very end when Brooks ... one of my favorite moments of the show was when I cross over to Brooks at the end and I say, "So this is what not failing feels like." Closing show, walking over him to say the line, he looks at me and says, "You can do this." And I started crying. It was a good cry, a letting go cry. [She starts to cry again as she repeats the line]. And he cried. That to me was the essence of that show. "So this is what not failing feels like." I can't believe you made me cry.

You talked about the importance of the piece, the joy of creating Dee Dee and the collegiality of being in the room with those people. . . .

That's the trifecta of success right there. Now that bar has been set it's like, how am I ever going to top *The Prom*? How is it ever going to be better than that? But for the stars to align and for me to be going into my fourteenth Broadway show? I do have a reverence for that. I'm really lucky. It's a privilege I work very hard at. I'm still kind of in awe about the whole thing. If you told me this would be my life when I was in *Brigadoon* I'd have said you are out of your mind. And yet it feels so right in ways I can't really explain. This is what I'm supposed to do. I'm still learning how to do it. You get me talking about this, and talking about *Prada* and I realize I got one more chapter in me. I got another ten to fifteen years in me to tell some more stories and we'll just see how that happens. I love surprises. *Devil Wears Prada* was like, "What?" I didn't even know it was in the ether. It was just out of the blue! So bring on the next one. Can we please get through a plague and let the storytellers get back to work?

Carolee Carmello

August 2020

Ethel Merman was a stenographer in Astoria, Queens, who, quite famously, never took a singing lesson but whose clarion bell of a voice and massively powerful belt propelled her to Broadway stardom. Carolee Carmello graduated from the State University at Albany (where she was born) with a degree in business administration. She also never took a singing lesson but, like Merman, found herself in possession of a big, amazingly durable (and even more versatile), brassy vocal instrument that was destined for Broadway. In another era, she would have given Merman some serious competition.

But while Merman dreamed of the footlights, Carmello never planned on a life in the theater. She came to New York thinking she'd "get it out of [her] system and then go back to real life," but quickly found herself a hot commodity. After a couple of national tours (*Big River* and *Les Misérables*) and her one and only ensemble performance on Broadway (*City of Angels*) she was cast in the very big, very belty role of Florence in the national tour of *Chess*. Then came a whopping twenty-one shows in New York alone (sixteen on Broadway and five off), two other tours, and three Tony nominations (for *Parade*, *Lestat*, and *Scandalous*). Her robust résumé includes multiple at-bats in which she replaced another actor during a show's run. That's unusual for an actor at her level (Merman did it once), suggesting that Carmello was always more interested in the work than in the cachet of press and opening nights. She didn't always need to have her fingerprints on the creation of a role; she told me, "I could always manage to put my stamp on it." While she is undisputedly a Broadway star, she is, not incidentally, also a Broadway stalwart. Throughout much of her career she was married to the equally prolific actor Gregg Edelman, with whom she has two children.

Talking with Carmello, it's impossible not to smile broadly and frequently. She exudes positivity, laughing freely and often, even as she pokes at unease about her future. Recently, Carmello began to question how many more Broadway opportunities she'd have, expressing pragmatism more than despair. "The roles are getting further and further apart," she confessed. "They just don't write parts for women who are on the down slide." But just as she considered slowing down, along came the national tour of *Hello, Dolly!*, which she took over from Betty Buckley, earning her unanimously euphoric reviews. Like Dolly herself, triumphant at the top of the staircase, only a fool would count Carmello out.

The theater bug bit you relatively late.
I'd say it was late compared to a lot of people. I didn't get exposed to much musical theater until college. I was studying business administration. I was taking classes in accounting, economics, and stuff like that. I did a couple of shows in my dormitory and that was the first time I played a part in a show. I did *Fiddler on the Roof* and *Oliver!* in my dorm cafeteria. After college I was trying to figure out what to do and I got offered this summer stock job. That was the first professional theater thing that I did. 1983.

Mamma Mia, here she goes again.
(Joan Marcus)

But even before that, playing Nancy in *Oliver!* must have given you a sense that you had a voice, an unusually good instrument.

I don't think I felt like it was that special. I don't know how many people I was competing against, you know? It was just my dorm, so I didn't think, "Oh, I'm really good at this." It was just fun. But the people that I was exposed to in that world became more and more interesting to me. Theater people are funny and smart. They were a lot more interesting than the people in my business classes.

So at what point did you decide to make it your profession?

It was more that I just didn't know which way to go at that point. I was finishing my degree and I was sort of thinking about law school, and thinking about maybe an MBA. This job came along and I thought, "This will be good. I'll do this for the summer. I can clear my head and figure out what to do next." Then I met all these New York actors and they encouraged me. More than being thrilled by the possibility of starring on Broadway, I thought, "I don't want to be forty-five or fifty years old and wonder what would have happened if I'd moved to New York in 1983." So I did it to prove to myself that I could never make it. I gave myself a deadline and tried it for a year. I got a couple of little jobs—enough to convince me to try it for another year. So it was more like my pragmatic self was saying, "Just do this now because you don't have responsibilities. I'll try this for as long as it's enjoyable and if it's not enjoyable anymore, I'll do something else."

Carolee Carmello	
Big River	National Tour, 1987
Les Misérables	National Tour, 1987
City of Angels (Ensemble in 1989, Oolie in 1991)	Broadway, 1989, 1991
Chess	National Tour, 1990
Falsettos (as Cordelia)	Broadway, 1992
Falsettos (as Trina)	National Tour, 1993
Hello Again	off-Broadway, 1993
Das Barbecü	off-Broadway, 1994
john and jen	off-Broadway, 1995
1776 (as Abigail)	Broadway, 1997
Parade	Broadway, 1998
The Scarlet Pimpernel	Broadway, 1999
A Class Act	off-Broadway, 2000
Kiss Me, Kate	Broadway, 2001
Elegies	off-Broadway, 2003
Urinetown	Broadway, 2003
Mamma Mia!	Broadway, 2004, 2006, 2007
Lestat	Broadway, 2005
The Addams Family	Broadway, 2009
Sister Act	Broadway, 2011
Scandalous	Broadway, 2012
Finding Neverland	Broadway, 2015, 2016
Tuck Everlasting	Broadway, 2016
Sweeney Todd	off-Broadway, 2017
Hello, Dolly!	National Tour, 2019
1776 (as Dickinson)	Broadway, 2022
Bad Cinderella	Broadway, 2023

What were you doing with yourself?

I was living way out in Flushing, Queens, because a friend of my parents offered me a little basement room that she had. She had a daughter and she said, "If you babysit for me sometimes, I will let you stay." I was way, way out. I had to take a long bus ride even to get to the end of the subway line to get into Manhattan, but I went to auditions.

Were you taking classes?

I started to go to auditions and they would have me sing a little bit or read some lines, and then they would put a bunch of us into a dance call. I didn't know any of the terminology, so I went to some dance classes just to learn what they were talking about. I am not a dancer but [I learned] a basic understanding of what those choreographers were asking me to do. Just enough to get through.

So you were driven to class, not so much by a desire to become better, but to learn the basics.

It was more like self-preservation. I didn't want to be humiliated. I was feeling really embarrassed at those auditions because all the girls probably went to college for musical theater, or at least knew dance steps.

Were you working beyond the babysitting?

I was one of those girls at department stores who sold perfume—a fragrance model. That was a good job; ten dollars an hour which, at the time, was decent, and it was flexible. I did that for a few years. The first big role I got was a production of *Little Shop of Horrors* that I did in Boston. I did that for a whole year. That was a great learning experience. That was the same director who I had worked with in summer stock in '83, Victor Valentine. Sounds made up, doesn't it? It was. He was the first professional in theater who saw something in me that I didn't know was there. He saw more in me than I did myself. And I was YOUNG to be playing Audrey, twenty-three. He was a great communicator. He died of AIDS a couple of years later. I still think about him and the work he might have had in front of him. And he was my first real friend that I lost during that horrible time.

And then you went out on tour in *Big River* in 1987.

And then I left that. I don't know if it was a good decision or not. It was one of those decisions that really tore me up because [I left to do the original company of the] *Les Mis* first national tour, which is a big deal. I got cast in the ensemble, which was not so fun for me. I was playing a nice role in *Big River* [Mary Jane Wilkes] and I left that to go do *Les Mis* because that show was like *Hamilton* at the time. Everyone was like, "Oh my God, you have to do *Les Mis*!" People really thought it was a good move. So, I went and did that for a year and I was miserable.

Backing up for a second, did getting the *Big River* tour feel like a significant moment?

I think so. I'm trying to remember.

The fact that that's your response suggests that you didn't see it as a big step in your career or your confidence. More like you were just going a step at a time. You weren't especially impressed with yourself.

Yeah, I think that's true. I'm still not impressed with myself. I remember in the last ten years or so, I would do Q and A's after Broadway shows, and people would say, "When did you finally decide that you were going to stay in theater?" after I had told my story about not studying and kind of getting into the business ass-backwards. "When did you make the decision 'this is my career'?" My response was always that I haven't decided yet. I think there are some people that just feel like they won't be happy doing anything else and therefore they are going to find a way to make it work no matter what. I don't necessarily feel like that. It was always like, "I'll try this for as long as it's enjoyable and if it's not enjoyable anymore, I'll do something else."

During *Big River*, do you have any recollections of what you learned or experienced?

The road is fun. I liked exploring new cities, staying in hotels. And I did like the show. I didn't do it all that long. It was maybe five or six months before I left for *Les Mis*, I think. *Les Mis* was one of those experiences that really altered my self-awareness. I thought, "Maybe I'll be happy because it's the big popular 'it' show of the day." But I realized over the course of that year that I didn't want to do ensemble work. I would rather play a fun role in a community theater than be in the chorus of *Les Mis*. I just couldn't be happy. I saw people around me in the show who were happy doing that and I was always amazed. They just enjoyed the work. They enjoyed the process. I couldn't do it. It was a nice and really talented group of people that I had a lot of respect for, but I just didn't like my job. I was happy when I got to go on as Fantine. Except maybe that first time—in Act 1, one of Fantine's, shall we say, paramours, grabs her. Diane Fratantoni, who was playing the role, is much shorter than I am. So when Bamatabois—we called him "Bam-Bam"—grabbed me, he was used to a smaller person. My head didn't hit his chest like hers did. Our faces smashed together. We both ended up bleeding. He got to leave the stage, but I had to sing to Javert with blood literally dripping down my chin.

You did take another ensemble job, in the original company of *City of Angels*.
I was miserable there too! There's another one! In that show, ensemble was nothing. I literally had one line and I was on stage for maybe ten minutes of the whole show. But I left that show a few weeks after opening. I remember sitting with a buddy in the show, at the opening night party. We were just so unhappy. Everybody was celebrating and we were like, "The reviews are good? Shit! This is going to run!" But then I got cast in the national tour of *Chess*.

Before we jump to that, anything you remember about rehearsing *City of Angels* with the likes of Cy Coleman and Larry Gelbart and Michael Blakemore and David Zippel?
I wasn't really involved. I was always an observer and that was frustrating. I remember a lot of time sitting in the house with David Zippel, who became a really good friend of mine, and just watching other people work. I wanted to be up there doing what they were doing. I was sitting on my ass watching other people do fun stuff.

You did get to watch the guy you married.
That's true. We had so little contact in that. It's funny—he barely remembered me because I left the show so quickly. It wasn't like I was watching Gregg Edelman and going, "Oh, he's dreamy!" I mean, he is. But that wasn't where my head was at. It was just me being frustrated and ambitious and not wanting to stay on the sidelines.

And then *Chess*. Did that feel like a milestone?
Des McAnuff directed it and he rearranged a lot of things so it was sort of a combination of the London and Broadway versions. They've been trying to fix the book of that show for like thirty years, so that was the version that Des came up with. Tim Rice wrote some new lyrics and that was very exciting. It was, like you said, a milestone, and I did feel like I kind of found a happy place. I got to sing great music and play with Steven Bogardus and John Herrera and Barbara Walsh. It was a great company and I think it was the first time I really went, "OK, this is where I'm supposed to be."

Did you feel ready? It's a lot of score to sing and a lot of acting.
I don't remember feeling intimidated or like I didn't deserve to be there. I felt like it was within my reach. It felt fun! When you get to sing great music with great people and a really good orchestra and you have beautiful costumes—I finally felt like all the pieces came together. And I think when I came back from that I felt more confident. I mean, I still never walk into a room and go, "You'd be a fool not to hire me," but I think that show did boost me.

It's amazing to me that you never trained as a singer and you were able to handle a score that dense. Did you have to learn how to sustain? Or did it just come naturally?
I think I'm just really lucky that way. During the run of that show I only missed one performance and that was because I was giving my understudy a chance to go on since we were in her hometown. I never blew my voice out or anything, which was a good thing to find out about myself. If you're not in those situations you don't really know how you're going to hold up. Energy-wise, it was a real eye-opener. How much energy it takes to do that every night. But I was young. Nowadays it's like, "Oh boy, lemme catch my breath."

When you came back, you went back into *City of Angels*, this time as a lead.
Yes, it was much more fun! I remember not wanting it to close because I was having a good time. It was with Michael Rupert. I think I have done more shows with him than any other leading man. We did *City of Angels, Falsettos, Elegies, Baby* twice, a concert of *Rags*.... He and I have in common, I think, that [for us] this is a job and it's a job that I do well and I like it most of the time, but if I didn't get to do it anymore, it wouldn't be the end of the world.

In your next show, *Falsettos*, you were reuniting not only with him, but with Stephen Bogardus and Barbara Walsh from *Chess*.
That was an amazing experience. The show was so emotionally powerful. I think it was the first time I ever experienced a show like that where people would just be weeping. After the show audiences could not get up out of their seats. Being on stage for that was very powerful. I remember feeling like this was an important story to tell. Bill Finn has such an amazing ability to tap into emotions in his writing.

What do you remember about rehearsals, being directed by James Lapine?
James doesn't hold your hand. I have a vivid memory of being in previews and he had given me notes about this one line practically every single day. Finally, I was like, "Just give me a line reading!" And he says, "Just keep trying. I don't know. That's not it." It was that kind of direction. He expects you to find it. He is a tough cookie. One of the things that James does so well is to take an audience to the brink of something. You want [the characters] to touch or kiss and they don't and it's almost more powerful. I remember him saying at one point—because I would get very emotional at the end after Whizzer dies—"if you cry, the audiences won't. You have to hold on to it and allow them to have the emotional experience. This is not about you." That was fascinating to me, and I think he's right about that.

I imagine the stage door became really important.
Yeah, people had such emotional reactions and it was very moving. There would be people waiting to tell us how much it meant, and "I lost this friend," or "I lost my lover." There were always a few people that wanted to talk to us, but it wasn't like it is now with a hundred people waiting outside. It was more about, "let me just hold your hands while you tell me about the loss that you experienced," and I was more than willing to do that. It was a privilege.

When you took the show on the road, did you find that it was received differently?
Oh, yeah. I have a distinct memory of playing The Jackie Gleason Theater in Florida. The lights come up on Marvin and Whizzer in bed, and you heard this old man from the back of the house going, "Oy, again with the boys." These seventy- and eighty-year-old people in Florida

didn't know what they were getting. They had season tickets to the Broadway series and they wanted to see *The Music Man* and *Hello, Dolly!* So yeah, that was a show that got very different responses depending on what city we were in. We knew it was going to be difficult for some audiences. But there was also a sense that this was a story they needed to hear. "Try to hang on if you can." But it was always a show that was a pleasure to do. I loved that material so much.

That show marked your first performance on the Tony Awards. Do you have any memories?
I thought the performance part of it was really fun. I remember being surprised by the fact that we were pulled into the theater and sort of kept in a corner, and then as soon as the number was over, we were kicked out of the theater. There was no sense of, "You're a nominated cast! You're performing on the Tony Awards. This is a big deal!" It was like, "All right, get out of the way, you're done." And then we had to leave and go to Gallagher's or something to watch. I remember feeling like the hired help. "Get out and make it fast because someone else is coming in right after you."

Your next show in New York was *Hello Again*, which is actually the first time you played a role no one else had played.
Yes, it was a show that was being changed and written as we went, and that was the first time I was really involved in that process. There were scenes that didn't change at all from the first day, and there were other scenes that changed every day. I was pretty lucky that I was in two scenes that were working fairly well. But I have memories of Michelle Pawk, John Dossett, and John Cameron Mitchell being in rehearsal every day, trying to figure out a couple of scenes that just weren't landing, through no fault of their own. It was just the luck of the draw that I got a song that didn't need a lot of futzing.

"Tom." It's an amazing song. What were your impressions of Michael John LaChiusa who was really at the beginning of his career?
I thought he was brilliant. A lot of people have said they find his music difficult to learn. But somehow for me, it came fairly easily. It all made sense to me. I guess we spoke the same language. And he's such a good storyteller, his lyrics are really easy to act.

That cast was an embarrassment of riches. The people you mentioned plus Donna Murphy, Michael Park, Malcolm Gets, Judy Blazer . . .
Oh my God, I know! And [director] Graciela Daniele was a dream. I love her more than almost anybody else I've ever worked with. She's really smart and she knows how to talk to actors. She loves it so much. You could just feel that she loves it. She's one of those really rare directors who is encouraging and loving in the room and yet is able to get the best out of everybody. You need [someone in] command but at least for me as an actor, I enjoy that nurturing, supportive energy that she brings. I've certainly worked with brilliant directors and lots of people that get the end result, but they don't always make you feel good in the process. And sometimes you feel good just because you're part of the end result and you're like, "Hey, look what has been created and I'm a part of it!" But I'm a person who doesn't really like rehearsal—I know it's blasphemy for an actress to say—but I don't like it. Grazie is one of the few people that I've ever worked with who makes me enjoy the process. I like the repetition of the run of the show. I like it when it's all figured out. I've tried to analyze what it is that I don't like about it. I think there's a certain discomfort in not having it all figured out. That's why it's easier to go into a show that is established. You know where the laughs are, you know where you're supposed to stand, you

know when the lights are going to come up on you, and you just have to fit yourself into that. But when it's a new piece, it's exciting but it's also kind of unsettling because you don't know what's going to work and what's not. You don't know if the choices that you're making are good ones or bad ones. You really need an audience to help you. The audience is the biggest factor for me to tell me what's working and what's not. That's the part that I enjoy.

So you don't need to be part of the development of the character, you just want to serve the piece?
Yes, I think you're right. I think that my job is to be an interpreter and a storyteller, which is why I've never really enjoyed doing a club act. That's just you being you. I like the characters. I like the costumes and the wigs.

You did a couple of other off-Broadway musicals in quick succession: *Das Barbecü* and *john and jen.*
I just listened to the whole *john and jen* score and I don't ever do that. I never listen to recordings of myself or even shows in general. It's so beautiful and it really holds up. I can understand why it gets done by colleges and different theater companies. I loved doing that show. And then I got pregnant. I couldn't finish the run, which was sad because we had done readings and a workshop.... It had taken a long time to get it to New York. But they let me open the show and they made costumes that would hide me for a little while, until I was about six and a half months or something, and I couldn't hide it anymore. It was a little frustrating to be that involved from the beginning of something and then not be able to finish it out.

You have done a lot of readings and workshops throughout the years.
I think this is a pretty universal feeling among actors—you always feel like it's a giant audition. Sometimes they keep you on for the next leg of the process and sometimes they don't. I did all the readings and workshops that led up to the Broadway production of *Scarlet Pimpernel* and then I did not get cast in the original company. I was devastated.

Many times, in workshops, the quality is not there.
Most times it's not. You think, "Well, that's never going to happen." At least I do. There are some people that feel like they have to really believe in every single project that they start. But I look at it from a more pragmatic point of view. That's why when something like *Parade* comes along—I remember at the very first reading of *Parade*, I started looking around at some of the other actors, like, "This is really good! Isn't it good? Or am I crazy?" It's so rare.

After your maternity break, you joined the company of *1776* with your husband.
1776 was one of my favorite shows of all time, even before I got that job. I fell in love with it as a kid, never really thinking, "I'm going to be in this someday." I loved the show from day one. It was a great experience. There was this giant chorus dressing room that wasn't being used and we used to bring our daughter, Zoe, into the theater to play in that room. I wasn't on stage all that much so I could be backstage with her. That was a great time. I still love that show.

And then came the show you have often referred to as your big breakthrough: *Parade*.
I remember being in awe of this Jason Robert Brown, who was twenty-five or something. I was like, "How is this music coming out of this kid? Where is this coming from?" It was so deep and

soulful, so powerful. And I was so impressed with [writer] Alfred Uhry. I just thought he was to die for. And that was the first time I worked with Hal Prince. It was an amazing experience. The only negative thing that I would say about it was that we never knew if there was going to be a next step. I always believed in the show, but I never knew if it was going to be picked up by anyone. When we finally made it to Broadway, Garth Drabinsky was co-producing and all of his money got pulled out. Lincoln Center couldn't afford to do the show anymore. We just couldn't keep going. It was devastating. I remember [commuting] during that last week, and I would cry in my car the whole way to work because I knew it was going to be over and I just loved it so much.

What about it did you love so much?
I think it was a combination of things. Like *Falsettos*, it was powerful and emotional and something that people would be really affected by, not just entertained by. The writing was so good. There was so much to sink my teeth into that it was a pleasure to do those scenes and sing those songs. It felt like wearing a really perfectly tailored suit. It just felt good. You just felt good doing it. And the cast was so great. There was nothing bad about it except that I wanted it to last longer. I knew that without a good *New York Times* review that it was probably going to be hard. I am a person who reads reviews. I know a lot of actors don't, but I generally read them because it's going to affect whether or not I have a job. I try not to take them personally. We almost didn't make the cast album and thank God we did because at least that's something to pass on.

What do you remember about working with Hal Prince?
He was such an amazing leader because he just loved it so much. He was so animated. This was his lifeblood. As I said, I don't particularly like rehearsals, but he was just so fun when he was there. He didn't stay around that long. He would come in the morning for a few hours and then he'd go home to watch *Judge Judy* every day and we'd work on other things. He was amazing. I remember one moment: he was watching a run-through and he was talking through a lighting cue. I remember him sitting there and watching us work and then saying, "The spot light is getting dimmer … and dimmer … and closing in … and closing in. …" He was seeing it in his mind and I was watching him, amazed by his vision. He was not someone who really talks to actors about their process, necessarily. He was a producer. He came at things from the big picture. I think he liked actors—and there are directors who don't like actors very much—but he just didn't speak the same language.

What can you tell me about Brent Carver?
Brent was so brilliant, so brilliant. I watched and learned from him. Every night, watching him in the trial scene, I was blown away. And singing with him was great. He had such a unique sound. It was really satisfying doing that show. You know, sometimes if I'm doing a show that I'm not that connected to, or if I don't feel like I'm that much a part of the story-telling, I get to the end of the night and I'm like, "Oh! Did I even do anything? I guess it's time to go home now." But that show was exhilarating and exhausting and draining, and at the end of the night, I felt like I had done something.

You got your first Tony nomination.
That was thrilling … except that the show had closed. I've been nominated three times and every time the show has already closed. I've never had that experience of going to work every

night and wondering if there are Tony voters in the house, or going to the Tonys right after a matinee. So it was bittersweet. It had ended a couple months before and so it was exciting to reunite with everybody and put that Tony Award performance together. [And] it was satisfying to feel like now I'm in this club of people who got nominated. But if you were to ask me if I would trade the nomination to have another year to do that show, I probably would have traded it. I bought a dress at the mall—in fact, for all my Tony Awards, I never got dressed by designers or anything.

So you gave yourself the treat of buying a new dress, but you didn't make a huge deal out of it and set your expectations too high.
Yes! Because every time I was nominated, I was positive I wasn't going win. But it was exciting! I had never done anything like that before. It's thrilling to go through that whole process and feel like you're one of the lucky ones.

After *Parade*, you finally got your Broadway chance at *The Scarlet Pimpernel*. This was version 3.0 [the show had opened and closed and been revamped twice]. That's interesting because even though they were "improving" it, you knew you were going into a troubled show that had had a very mixed reaction.
I did. I think it's actually Frank Wildhorn's best score. It was fun. I got really beautiful songs to sing and romantic escapades. It ends with a big wedding and a big kiss! There was a lot to recommend it. And I had a three-year-old, so playing a glamorous beautiful person on stage was a nice break from being a mom. I was happy with what we ended up with. I thought it was a fun story. I felt so glamorous in such beautiful costumes.

You went from that into another original off-Broadway musical, *A Class Act*.
That was a tricky kind of experience. That was one of those shows that didn't ever feel like it gelled. They had cast someone as Ed Kleban who became suddenly unavailable. For a while we were rehearsing without anyone in the lead and then finally they decided Lonny [Price, the director] should play it. That was hard for the rest of us. I don't know how to talk about it except to say that it just became like a dysfunctional family when we were rehearsing. Him having to step out of the role all the time so he could watch . . . it just wasn't a happy family. Although I made some really great friends. I didn't get to do the Broadway run because I was having another baby. I was pregnant, so that might have colored my experience.

Adversity sometimes brings people together.
I hadn't thought about that in regard to this show, but I think you're absolutely right. David Hibbard is still one of my really good friends and Julia Murney and Jonathan Freeman. . . . It was a good group of really nice, talented folks. It just was a problematic show, and then having a director who was also the star made it even more problematic.

So maybe your pregnancy gave you an excuse to exit.
I would have done it on Broadway if I hadn't been pregnant. I'm not independently wealthy so I can't turn down a Broadway show. Gregg and I weren't living paycheck to paycheck, but I think we always felt like we're never going to work again, like so many actors feel. We had responsibilities: a kid and another one on the way and a mortgage.

So did you ever take work that you would not have otherwise taken had it not been for the paycheck?

Absolutely. The one that really became a job because I was supporting my family was *Mamma Mia!* I probably would have done the show anyway that first year [that I did it], but then I left. When *Lestat* fell apart, I called my agent and I said, "See if they'll take me back at *Mamma Mia!*" I knew that that show was going to run for a long time. That was really about the money. But if another Broadway show had come along . . . I just didn't feel like I could walk away. But I was losing my mind after four years. Then I said, "I don't know if I can do this any longer."

Do you think that might have been true of any show you did for that long?

No. That was a particularly hard time. I struggled on and off with depression at different times in my life and I remember reading that different jobs were more prone to creating an environment that might contribute to depression. They used flight attendants as an example. They said that trying to be cheerful and happy all the time in front of your audience is exhausting. That's how I felt in *Mamma Mia!* I felt like I had to always be "on" and it really wore me down. I don't want to say bad things about the show because people love it and find so much joy in it, but it wasn't my thing. I remember sitting in the back row of the theater when they offered me the show, deciding whether I could take the job. But they paid me good money and I had two kids. I remember in rehearsal—Judy McLane still kids me about this— we were working on "Super Trouper" and I kept saying to her, "Don't look at me, don't look at me. This is embarrassing." She was like, "I'm in the scene with you! I have to look at you!"

They kept bringing you back, though, so you obviously sold it.

I think people can be good at something without enjoying it. It brings up one of my favorite stories about my son, Ethan. He was maybe five years old at the time, backstage one night. Gregg was in the dressing room with him. I was not feeling well and I was doing the show, but every time I came back to the dressing room he saw me holding on to the table, moving slowly and kind of moaning. He would say, "Are you OK, Mommy?" And I would say, "I don't feel good. I just want to go home." And then I would go out and do the next scene. Gregg took Ethan to watch the finale. Afterward, I'm taking my costume off and moaning. Ethan was like, "Mommy, what's the matter?" I said, "Honey, I just don't feel good." And he said, "But you were out there, singing and dancing." I said, "Yeah honey. That's my job. I have to do that. People paid a lot of money to watch the show and I have to do my job." He sat there for probably five minutes, silent, as I was taking my makeup off. Then he said, "So they pay you to pretend you're having a good time?"

After he was born in 2001, you went right into *Kiss Me, Kate*, replacing Marin Mazzie. That was a call that came from Michael Blakemore after working with him in *City of Angels*?

Michael Blakemore called me and I had to tell him, "I would love to but I'm pregnant!" But luckily the timing worked out. He's one of those directors that, once he finds people he likes, he just keeps hiring them. He's very loyal that way. It felt really hard, coming off of childbirth. I was exhausted and pumping breast milk at intermission and all that. It was an exhausting time. But I loved it. When September 11 happened, as an actor I felt useless. What could I possibly contribute that would be meaningful? But I came to realize that people really need experiences like theater in order to process and heal. I realized that we do serve an important purpose. In the weeks after the attacks we played to empty houses. Literally 100 people in a

1,500-person house. But we felt like what we were doing was needed by those people. Our cast actually bought tickets out of our own pockets to give to first-responders and volunteers. They would tell us how grateful they were for the escape. They needed to laugh.

You took *Kiss Me, Kate* to the West End. What was that experience like?

Kiss Me, Kate closed shortly after September 11, so it was great to have a chance to do it again, and I had always wanted to work on the West End. The thing that really surprised me about that whole experience was finding out that West End ensemble people and crew don't really make enough money to survive on that one job. It just doesn't pay very well and most of them had second jobs. You want to do it for the artistic experience, but you can't really afford to live in an expensive city on that salary. I just found that fascinating. I was happy in London. I lived right near Buckingham Palace, which was totally cool. The hardest part was being away from my kids. Gregg was not doing a show at that time so he was able to be home. We kind of took turns that way. But actors don't get to choose when these jobs come along. Whenever one of us got an offer to do something, there was always a big discussion about what it would mean for the family. When I went to do *Addams Family* in Chicago for three months, I made a deal with myself that I would fly home every day off to be with the kids. We just tried to do whatever we could to have as a normal a life as we could for the kids.

Kiss Me, Kate was some broad comedy, but then you went even broader in *Urinetown*.

What a fun show! That was one of the funniest shows I've ever done. I just think that show is brilliant. I never thought a show could be that funny.

And then you went into the polar opposite: *Elegies*.

That was perfect because whenever I'm doing something that's comedy for comedy's sake, I always crave doing something that's got a little more gravitas after that, and vice versa. I like the variety. It doesn't always work out that way. But when it does, it's nice because you can switch gears.

***Elegies* actually had the combination of laugh-out-loud funny and then the gut punch, in succession.**

Sometimes in the same song. That's what Bill Finn is so good at—using humor to make an emotional punch. I think no one does it better than he does. I would cry every night watching Betty Buckley doing "Just One." She was just brilliant. And Bill's lyrics, his storytelling, so good. And I had beautiful stuff to sing. "Anytime," the song that he wrote about his friend who was dying—he had her singing to her children after she was gone. That song is probably the hardest thing I've ever had to get through in a performance in my whole career. The idea of a mom dying and leaving her children has always been so hard for me. In rehearsal, I never got through it without sobbing. And I remember Grazie and Bill going, "You've GOT to get through this song!" I would stand there in performance and do anything I could to distract myself. I wanted to invest it with what I thought it deserved, but at the same time I knew if I took myself to that place that I wouldn't be able to sing it anymore. I remember standing there and trying to be peaceful and calm and just digging my fingernail into the pad of my other finger, just to feel pain so I wouldn't get caught up in the tears and the emotion of the song. I just had to distract myself. It was so hard. And I know there were times that I didn't sing it as well as I wanted to because I would get choked up. Betty Buckley tried to teach me how to sing through tears because she saw me struggling. She's a teacher at heart. But I could never do it. I mean, she has that ability to just let the tears roll down her face, but it doesn't affect her cords. I don't know if that's something she's figured out over the years or if it just naturally comes to her, but she would always tell me, "Just let the emotion come. Don't fight it, don't fight it." And I'm like, "If I don't fight it, I'm going to sound like [makes frog sound]." We shared a dressing room and we got along. She's fascinating, Betty.

After *Elegies*, you began your *Mamma Mia!* years. Anything positive that you can remember?
Ummmmm … I was really thin? That was nice. And there was a chunk of the show in the second act where it was ballads and storytelling, culminating with "Winner Takes It All." That felt good to me as an actor. I felt like I was able to carve some kind of story out of that song. Those lyrics are so obtuse. I did feel pretty proud of myself to be able to justify something out of that song. And it was fun to sing. The thing about that show that was amazing to me was how much people loved it. I just remember feeling like, "Is this what people want to see now?" [I guess] there is definitely room for all kinds of shows. I just don't necessarily want to be in all those shows.

At least you knew that it was making people happy and that you were providing some joy.
That's true. And it supported my family for a lot of years.

You left the first time to do *Lestat*.
At that point, I hadn't originated a big role in a new musical that many times. So even though I had done some of the workshops and I knew it had problems … I knew what I was getting into but I also thought, in the same way that *Mamma Mia!* has this kind of built-in fan base because of the ABBA songs, Anne Rice has got a bazillion fans around the world. I thought that between her and Elton John there would be enough curious people. But that didn't happen. I don't know why. I can't sit here and say it was a good show, but it wasn't the worst show I've ever done. There was some good music. I'm really sad that they never released the cast album. We recorded it, but Elton John didn't want it out there for whatever reason. There were some great singers in *Lestat*, belting their faces off.

So when you go into a rehearsal process already knowing that the show doesn't work, are you just optimistic that they'll get it fixed? They certainly had resources. . . .
I knew that even if it was going to fall on its face like it did, I still wanted to try it. It was a new original show and I felt like I had to be doing more of that rather than just staying in *Mamma Mia!* It was a gamble.

And you got another Tony nomination.
And the show was closed again.

This time, was that a relief?
No, I would rather it lasted a little longer. It's not that I loved doing it, but there were fun things about it. I got to sing that crazy duet with Hugh Panaro, and he got to bite my neck and turn me into a vampire. It was a fun character. Could I have done it for four years? Probably not, but I would have liked to have had a year with it instead of whatever it was—six weeks or something.

Pensive in *Lestat*.
(Paul Kolnik)

Given the name recognition of the title, I am surprised they didn't give it longer to find its audience.

I'm surprised too. It was Warner Brothers producing their very first show on Broadway, and I think that a big corporation can do that: "This isn't working, pull the plug." The Warner rep was really dedicated, and he was there all the time working on it, but it wasn't his call, it was corporate. I think if they had been scrappier producers, they might have tried a little harder.

What was it like working with Elton John?

Elton John was never there.

Well, that's a problem for a new musical, don't you think?

Yep. Never there. He came to one performance at our San Francisco tryout and then he came to one preview and opening night and that was it. He never came to rehearsal. And according to what I've heard—and this may be just rumor—he didn't want to change anything. I heard that when the director or when Bernie Taupin—who did come around a bit and was very nice—would call him or ask him to redo something or think about it in a different way, he wasn't available. So that was a problem.

You went back to *Mamma Mia!* and then *The Addams Family*.
Again, a troubled show right from the get-go. The part didn't turn out to be what they sold me on, and the vibe in the rehearsal room was difficult. Nathan Lane and Bebe Neuwirth work very differently. And then the directors—they wanted to direct a different kind of show, which they kind of did for the out-of-town tryout in Chicago. They saw a kind of macabre fantasy, very visual. Then they were replaced, although Julian Crouch was kept on as the designer. When they brought in Jerry Zaks, it was a whole different thing. He's about the comedy first. And of course, Jerry is nothing if not focused on what he wants. He knows what he wants to do and it was completely the opposite of the two guys that preceded him. We were all like this group of foster kids who now had a new stepfather. We had to adjust. He whipped the show into shape as best he could. And then, from what I understand, he changed it again for the tour. People told me that the tour was very different from what we did in New York. I think he didn't have as much time as he wanted to make all the changes before we opened on Broadway. I left at the end of my contract, which was a year and a half. I was ready to move on. I just didn't know if I could do it. My marriage was ending and I was having a really tough time. I just couldn't put myself through an unpleasant experience any longer than I had to.

The concept of toxicity backstage always interests me. Because you're all still having to do the show every day, so the challenge is finding a way to transcend the environment. What makes that so hard? Is it the piece? Is it the actors? Is there a way out? Who's responsible for making it better? It does all seem so fragile. But coming into work doesn't have to be terrible.
Oh, it wasn't. I mean, I made great friends in that. Wesley Taylor is still one of my good friends and Zachary James. And I love Terry Mann. There were a lot of great reasons to be there. But I don't know that anybody could have really fixed the whole dynamic of the dysfunctional family. I suppose Jerry might have been the only one who could have done it, but he had so little time to do so much work. And he's not the kind of director who gets involved in backstage drama. But I love working with him because he knows what he wants. He's quick. He doesn't fool around.

How did you personally navigate those waters?
Breaststroke! I tried to stay under the radar. I tried not to make waves with anybody. I tried to be pleasant to everyone and not stir up any unnecessary bad feelings. Like you said earlier, it's one of those things that bonds the other people together. A lot of my memories of that time period are tied into my personal life during that time, which was really a mess. So, I don't know if I would have had a better experience and maybe been able to rise above it a little better if I hadn't been going through stuff at home.

Your next show was also with Jerry Zaks: *Sister Act*.
That was fun. Jerry just asked me to step into it. Except that was the beginning of my menopause hot flashes, so I would be in that costume where every part of my body was covered except for from my chin to my eyebrows. I was burning up! My dresser bought one of those water bottle/fans like they have at Disneyland. She would squirt me to try to calm me down. But that was a fun show to do. I was grateful to have that job. I was really grateful to Jerry because he just offered it to me. And he helped put me in the show. Normally, when you're

replacing, you really only get a stage manager. Jerry came in for a few days and worked with me, which was really nice. Except for the hot flashes, it was a good experience. With that costume, that would have been a good show to be pregnant in!

Throughout that whole period, you were doing the workshops that became *Scandalous*. It was *Saving Aimee*, then *Hurricane Aimee*.... The show was troubled but you stayed throughout, so the character spoke to you?

Yeah, absolutely. [For all seven years of workshops] it wasn't quite working and yet I felt like the story of this woman's life was so fascinating. I thought if we could mold this to have even a fraction of the interest that her actual life had, it would work. But Kathie Lee Gifford had an image of what she wanted to say about this woman because Kathy's so passionate about her faith, as was Aimee. I think she was reluctant to show anything really negative about this woman for fear that it would shine a bad light on religion or people of faith. And these things are really alchemy, right? The right composers, writers, director, cast, designers, and producers have to be telling a story that the public wants to hear at that particular time—and they have to be on the same page about what that story is and the way they're going to tell it. Frankly, I'm not sure all of our ingredients added up. I really think there could have been a show about Aimee, because she's such an interesting character. Obviously, I don't know what the truth is about her disappearance or her drug addiction or any of that, but I do think that it's possible for someone to really be a person of faith but also be incredibly flawed. I think that's an interesting story to tell. But this particular telling wasn't coming together.

So what was that like for you, with your name above the title, knowing it's flawed and not improving?

It's exhausting. Look, I never saw it and I don't know what it looked like from the audience, but I know how it felt. I had endless conversations with the team, and I ended up going to some of the production meetings at the end of the night because I just wanted to have my voice in the mix. I tried to do the best with what I had.

Did that make you sad? Did it feel like rearranging the deck chairs on the Titanic? Did you sometimes question yourself, thinking maybe you were wrong and it was good?

No, I knew I wasn't wrong. Yes, to both of the other questions. It did make me sad and I did feel like we were rearranging deck chairs. Everyone is doing their best and working hard, but sometimes the correct fix is elusive. You can't always find it. At some point, you run out of time for fixing things. You have to somehow fill in the holes, and if the holes are too big for spackle, there's not a lot you can do. You can stuff paper towels in them, but it's just a losing battle. You start to worry that you look like a bad actor. I am not pointing fingers because there are so many elements that can contribute to why a show isn't working. But this wasn't working. But, like you said, I was above the title for the first time in my life and I felt like this was the role of a lifetime, in a way. I like having those challenging parts that have a big age range and a big emotional range. So there were things about it that still appealed to me. I was the oldest teenager on Broadway, I used to say. When I was doing *john and jen* I was playing six [for part of the show], but I was actually thirty-two. When I was doing Aimee, I was playing seventeen, but I was actually fifty, so it was an even bigger gap!

You had to put on a happy face and promote it a lot.

That was completely exhausting. We were rehearsing every day during previews because they knew things had to be fixed. I sang every song in the show, which was ridiculous. There was one song that George Hearn sang in the second act and I could go offstage and sit down for two minutes. They cut it. I was only offstage to change my clothes, which is why I lost my voice the day after we opened. I missed one show and that doesn't happen to me very often. The stress of it.... And because we were doing rehearsals all day before every show, plus the amount of singing, and all the press, I just couldn't make it. We had to cancel the performance.

You seem to have lungs of steel, but we seem to be in an age where every leading lady is asked to sing at the top of their range and to the rafters multiple times in every show. It didn't used to be that way.

Yeah, and the audience gets tired of it, too. I appreciated all the material they gave me, but it loses its power after a while. It just doesn't have the same impact when you see this character belting D's and E's in every song. The vocals in *Scandalous* were some of the hardest I've ever sung. It was the hardest vocal workout I've ever had in a show. I don't think I'll ever have anything like that again.

Had you ever had vocal trouble before?

I have lost my voice a couple times for a day or two, mostly when I'm fighting a cold. Or if I'm doing a workshop of one show during the day and then trying to do *Mamma Mia!* at night. But I'm really lucky that way. I haven't had a lot of issues.

In your next show, *Finding Neverland*, you got more downtime....

Yeah, and some people love those kinds of roles. I talk to a lot of actors, especially my age, who say, "This is great. Give me half of a reprise and a couple of scenes and I'm happy as a clam." But I always felt like I wanted more to do. I liked that show, but I had an hour [off between scenes], and that's a long time to sit in your dressing room while other people are working. It doesn't feel like you're part of the experience anymore. I was glad to have that job, but it was kind of a frustrating artistic experience. As it happens, it ran longer than I thought it would.

You actually left to do *Tuck Everlasting*, and then returned after that closed.

Right. And the part was even smaller when I came back. They made some cuts after I left and then when I came back I was like, "Can they put it back the way it was?" "Nope. Sorry." Because to change it again would have meant changing lights and orchestrations and they didn't want to spend the money. So I ended up finishing the show with a version of it that had even less for me to do than when I started! But the saving grace of that show was all those kids. I loved all those boys that came and went during the run. I really like working with kids a lot, and that was a show that gave me a lot of time offstage, so I could play with them and make silly videos. I know there are people who don't like working with kids, but if you have good kids in a show it really brings so much energy and light into the room. They're just so excited to be there.

Tuck Everlasting . . .

That one, again, was one of those long, drawn-out processes. I think we had seven years of workshops of that show. It was a long road to get there and I still believe that if we were not in the season of *Hamilton* that it may have stood a chance. It was not good timing.

You think that's all it was?

I think it was on a par with *Finding Neverland* as far as the quality of the material. So I think it should have had a year.

You have done several shows that closed quickly. You told me you wept through the last week of *Parade*, but I never asked you if the closing of any of the others was heartbreaking.

As we get older and we have more of these experiences, I think they're less devastating each time. I can see it coming. You learn how to not take it personally. *Parade* was the one that devastated me and I think after that I was certainly disappointed and sad when things closed, but it didn't destroy me or send me into a tailspin.

Is that, in part, because you are confident there will be another show soon? Your trajectory has really been from show to show with very few lulls.

I would say no. And I've heard other actors saying this, too: there's always that fear that it's the last time, unless I already have other irons in the fire. No one's writing a show for me. No one's coming up with ideas of what project they could do next to include me. I don't take it personally; I just think people aren't writing shows for middle-aged women. It's just not happening. I could probably do regional productions of *Mame* and *Gypsy* for the next ten years. Although there's a little part of me that worries that might be disappointing, just because the production values won't be as good, there's not as much budget. If it's going to be an experience that feels like a diminished version of the experiences I have had, I am not sure I want to end my career [that way]. It's a big question hanging over me right now, honestly. I am really grappling with what am I going to do for the next few years to make money until I can collect my pension. Once I can do that and I'm not worried about paying my rent, what am I going to do to occupy my time? Maybe I'll work once in a while if somebody calls me, but I don't envision me doing Broadway shows for the next fifteen years. I just don't think it's going to come my way. Would I want to? Maybe. Depending on the project. But I think I might have to find something else to do. I just don't think the roles are there. I'm not interested in directing, and not especially interested in teaching musical theater. I might be interested in teaching something else. It's really what I've been struggling with for the last year or two.

How does it make you feel?

Sort of unsettled in a way. Luckily, I've had enough good jobs in my career that I have been able to save some money. I'm not panicking. But we all want to feel useful and productive in our lives. In order for me to get that back, I'm probably going to have to shift to doing something else. I'm not really sure what that is yet. I'm not saying that no one's ever going to call again. I think there will be little things here and there. But that might not be enough to sustain my soul. So, I need to find something else that's going to do that.

Well, your next show required middle-aged stars: *Sweeney Todd.*

I did *Sweeney Todd* for a year. That was a fun show. I mean, I went broke doing it [off Broadway] for a year, but it was such a unique production and I was so grateful to have that experience. It was really unlike anything I'd ever done before, and we only had three weeks to learn it. Sondheim came to our very first show! Norm Lewis lost his voice in the middle of the show and didn't do the second act. The understudy, David Michael Garry, who had never been on before, had to go on. I was talking to him at intermission, like, "Don't worry, I got you." And I was thinking, "What am I talking about? I barely know this show myself!" Sondheim sitting there that night was unbelievable. But he came back one other time, so that was good. He said, "I knew you could sing it, but I didn't know you were so funny." I can't ask for any higher praise. I can die now. I keep telling the producers that they should do it again in another city. It made money! And so few theater productions do.

And after that, *Hello, Dolly!*

I feel like with *Dolly* the writing was there to support me and I didn't have to do that much in order for it to be successful. It was a really good experience. The show is beautiful. Those Thornton Wilder monologues are beautifully written. John Bolton was a dream to work with. It was the first time I had done that kind of touring in a while. And it was encouraging in the sense that I was like, "Oh, I can still do this." A big part, eight times a week. But I think I always felt like this is the exception not the rule for what's going to be coming down the pike. Maybe that sounds pessimistic, but I feel like it's realistic. I love getting laughs and there are so many great laughs built into that show, especially the way Jerry directed it. It's a really fast-paced musical comedy. It's like jumping on a merry-go-round and just trying to hold on.

"You're looking swell . . . ," in *Hello, Dolly!*
(Julieta Cervantes)

What do you think you want now?

I always said, "I don't really care if I'm a big star, I just want to be a working actor," and that's sort of what happened. I'm realistic about my career. I feel like I'm good at what I do, but I also know that there are so many people that are good at what they do. This business is so competitive that I feel lucky to have done fourteen [as of publication, that number is now sixteen] Broadway shows. It doesn't happen to most people, so I feel very fortunate. And I also know that there's so much luck involved. I was lucky to work and I worked with a lot of great people. That *Dolly* offer was a big surprise to me. So maybe there'll be other surprises, right?

Rachel York

July 2021

Rachel York is a terrifyingly good mimic. Julie Andrews, Marilyn Monroe, and Lucille Ball all made cameos during our conversations with a specificity that would make Rich Little jealous. It comes, says York, from a childhood as a latchkey kid, left alone in the house. York would study her favorite singers, training herself to create their sound. It got the appreciation of her mother, who had wanted to perform, but instead married at nineteen and became a working parent to four kids. When the younger York was nineteen, she set herself on a very different course, marching into the office of agent Bill Timms. She sang from *Evita*, did a monologue from *Sophie's Choice*, was immediately signed and, within two years, made her Broadway debut—clad in nothing but a sheet—in *City of Angels*.

From then on, the work was non-stop, with leading roles on Broadway (*Les Misérables*, *Victor/Victoria*, *The Scarlet Pimpernel*, *Dirty Rotten Scoundrels*, and the straight play *Sly Fox*), off-Broadway (*Putting It Together*, *Dessa Rose*, *The Best Is Yet to Come*), national tours (*Kiss Me, Kate*, *Anything Goes*, *101 Dalmatians*, *Camelot*), London (*Kiss Me, Kate*), and regionally (*Grey Gardens*, *Ragtime*, *Hello, Dolly!*, *The King and I*, *The Addams Family*, *Into the Woods*, and *Spamalot*). Most recently, she held her own in a company of scenery chewers in *Disaster!*, ruled a medieval kingdom while doing fan kicks and splits in *Head Over Heels*, and reprised her Reno Sweeney almost a decade after first playing her in a London run of *Anything Goes*. She also married, gave birth to her daughter, Olivia, and moved back and forth between the coasts a dizzying number of times.

The year 2022 found York living unexpectedly on neither coast, but in Orlando, Florida, where she has the benefit of space and easy access to New York when Broadway calls. Our conversations are long and meandering, with York just as passionately discussing her family dynamics or her zodiacal makeup as her career. Like any actor, she's had a number of disappointments, but York laughs at the absurdity rather than wallow. The tears come when she talks about loved ones lost, not career challenges. She has a home studio from which she records self-tape auditions and voiceovers, and where she's been writing and reflecting. "Maybe at the end of this, you can tell me what my purpose is," she jokes. Rest assured, Rachel York, who never stops creating, doesn't need my help with that.

When did you decide you wanted to perform?
As a kid I enjoyed dancing and singing with my mother in the living room while she played the piano. I started dance classes at eight. I was the youngest in my family and a clown with endless energy. In fact, it was tough shutting me up. But, when my family and I moved to Boulder, Colorado, when I was nine, things changed. My brothers and sister were away at school and my parents began working out of town more often. Adjusting to a new school was difficult and I developed reading problems, mostly because my new school was much more advanced than my old school. I felt alone and couldn't let people know I was behind, so I pretended to read. I was in that awkward stage of life, with an overbite. The kids were mean and called me "dog." I wore the wrong clothes, became shy in school, and was petrified of reading aloud in class. I also remember the first ballet class I attended in Boulder. The teacher

"What's with the soap?" in *Victor/Victoria*.
(Photofest)

stopped the class halfway through and told me I wasn't good enough for the class, humiliating me in front of everyone. By the time I was twelve and in middle school, things were better. I had braces and started sneaking into my mother's makeup bag. My reading improved. But, when I went to audition for the school play, I found out they were having everyone read the script cold and I chickened out. Though my reading improved, I still carried that fear of reading aloud, along with the ridicule, panic, and shame that went with it. It was when I got into choir that I realized my singing voice was my strength. I felt I had something special. So, it was through singing in choir that I found my literal and figurative "voice." But, damn it, I wanted to act! I had to get over this reading aloud thing. I would spend countless hours reading plays out loud, alone in my empty house, to the detriment of my homework, I would also sing for hours after school, trying to sound like different singing artists I admired. I was a relentless perfectionist when it came to singing. I immersed myself in choir and theater, my escape from my sad life in Boulder. When I was a sophomore in high school, I won the lead, typically given to the senior, in *Inherit the Wind*, and

Rachel York	
City of Angels	Broadway, 1989
Les Misérables	Broadway, 1992
Putting It Together	off-Broadway, 1993
Victor/Victoria	Broadway, 1995
The Scarlet Pimpernel	Broadway, 1998
Kiss Me, Kate	National Tour, 2001; West End, 2002
Dessa Rose	off-Broadway, 2005
Dirty Rotten Scoundrels	Broadway, 2006
Camelot	National Tour, 2007
101 Dalmatians	National Tour, 2009
The Best Is Yet to Come	off-Broadway, 2011
Gentlemen Prefer Blondes	Encores!, 2012
Anything Goes	National Tour, 2012; West End, 2021
Little Me	Encores!, 2014
Disaster!	Broadway, 2016
Grey Gardens	Los Angeles, 2016
Head Over Heels	Broadway, 2019

continued to be a part of every production after that. I understudied all the female roles in *Godspell*, and it was then that I decided, "I don't ever want to be an understudy again." I mean, understudies are amazing, and God knows in the last year we've seen how vital they are, but I just didn't have the skill set. I have to say I was very proud of myself when, in *Summer and Smoke*, I got cast as Rosa Gonzales and I really wanted Alma—I had memorized all of her lines—so, I had to coach myself that there were no small parts! In my senior year, we moved to San Clemente, California, and I beat out the girl who was "supposed to play" the role of Evita in *Evita* and won the Macy Award for Best Actress in Southern California. Acting became my passion and singing my healing. I wanted to uncover the meaning of life by walking in other people's shoes, so to speak. I was fascinated by the complexities of people. And I had this knack for impressions. I could listen to different singing artists and be able to hear and mimic the intricate nuances in their voices. These artists were my vocal teachers for the most part. I loved transforming into another human being, voice and all. The voice of a human being and how they express themselves says a great deal about a person. It is important not to leave that detail out when interpreting a character. I loved to research and analyze every aspect of a character, finding all the pieces to the puzzle, covering every base. Around this time, I watched Meryl Streep in *Sophie's Choice* and I thought, "That's what I want to do!" I wanted to be a chameleon actress.

When your family moved to California, you began studying professionally.
I received a scholarship to attend the American Center for Music Theater at the Dorothy Chandler Pavilion and was taking scene study with Aaron Speiser at that time. He has since become a well-known acting coach to some very big Hollywood folks. At the time, I was one of his first students and he was a wonderful mentor to me. He was the one who suggested that I move to New York because it offered what I was missing: "life experience." When I moved there, I was very courageous but not incredibly wise. I sometimes wound up in some really dangerous situations. Luckily, I had my angels watching over me. I was living with my best friend from San Clemente in a studio apartment and we didn't know how to be adults yet, much less survive in the city and succeed in the acting biz. We had never paid bills before. We were so scared even though we were trying to act like we knew everything, as teenagers do. When my BFF and I went our separate ways after six months, I was devastated and alone, but I refused to give up and go back home to California. I survived somehow. At one point, there was an accompanist in one of my classes at HB Studios, Brad Ross, who introduced me to an agent he knew and that agent signed me, but there were many hard lessons to learn ahead of me. It was intense.

And you were a bartender, right?
And a cocktail waitress at the Palladium. I was the worst bartender in the world. I wasn't even twenty-one. I didn't know anything about bartending. I didn't even drink. But you know, when you're desperate, you're like, "Yeah, OK, I'll do it." I remember my auditions were terrible at the time. My confidence was in the toilet. My mom flew out and saved me by helping me to start a practice of meditating, yoga, and listening to these positive-thinking tapes, day and night. That practice changed my life. I was afraid I would end up homeless. I remember at one point I lived in a ground-floor apartment and the air conditioner was being repaired. There was only a piece of cardboard [put in place of the air-conditioner] between me and the homeless people going through the trash on the other side of the wall. It was empathy building. My mom helped me rediscover my light, which soon led to a fun job in Monte Carlo.

And then, shortly after you got back, you booked your first Broadway show, *City of Angels*.
Yes … after I tried my stab as a solo pop recording artist in New York and later, briefly with a French rock band in the South of France. But that's the road not taken. *City of Angels* was so exciting. They don't do musicals like that anymore with two months to develop a new show in New York before previews. I was so enormously grateful, but also very "green." It was awesome working with greats like Cy Coleman, Michael Blakemore, and Larry Gelbart, and my dear friend, David Zippel, who, like me, was new to the scene at that time. I grew up watching old movies and listening to Ella Fitzgerald and Manhattan Transfer. I was very familiar with that time period and its music and I made sure to be super prepared for the audition. I booked it then and there. But during previews I got weird vibes from some people in show, and I let that alter my performance. Sometimes the vibe of a play can get into people's psyche. *City of Angels* is a bit about deception, distrust, illusion, and that was part of my experience. That's not to say anything bad about anybody in the show. The cast was amazing. I was just so optimistic and naïve, I was like, "This is gonna be the biggest hit ever! Yay! I'm Pollyanna!" I think it rubbed members of the cast the wrong way because the word around town was that it wasn't going to be a big hit and there was this fear looming backstage. I can't tell you how many times we changed the finale. People were on edge. I didn't understand it at the time. I did get a good amount of publicity and I think that there was some resentment about that, too. I made many mistakes and I grew up a lot during that show. I will always remember my

first Broadway opening night. And we got amazing reviews! So much for rumors. We were stunned. I kept saying to myself, "Oh my God, I'm on cloud nine!"

Do you remember learning anything specific from director Michael Blakemore?
Pace. He taught me pace, which is integral to comedy.

Did you feel like you were now positioned for the next thing?
I was getting a lot of offers to play dumb blondes. You do something very well and all of a sudden folks begin typecasting. I wanted to be a character actress.

You made a splash with that role, but for your next step you chose to go to L.A.
Yes, I did. My family was there. Living in New York City was always challenging for me and I set out to be a film actress, after all. I wanted to be the next Meryl Streep. I did a couple of films, one in Moscow, which was an adventure, and some episodics. Then Broadway came calling again with an offer to play Fantine in *Les Misérables* and I couldn't say no. It was a role I had always wanted to play. I had auditioned five times for it prior, so getting this call was huge! Annoyingly, several people said that I was too young, but I was twenty-three and, in the book, she dies at twenty-six. I was the perfect age. It was just such a meaningful experience to be involved with that show and that particular company. It was professionally, emotionally, and spiritually fulfilling.

You went straight from that into *Putting It Together.*
That was a difficult experience, which means I grew a lot. The director [Julia McKenzie] was not great with people and it was odd to me, because she was an actor and actors usually have a certain insight into people. I'm sure there was a great deal of pressure on her.

Well, in New York it became a vehicle for Julie Andrews's return to the stage for the first time in thirty years. It became star-driven.
Understandably, the producers and creatives wanted to make Julie happy. But I soon learned that, as the youngest in the cast, I was the bottom man on the totem pole. There was no script for this piece. It was a Sondheim revue and the director had the "story," including the characters and relationships, in her head. Look, it all comes down to one thing: communication. And she didn't seem to have the time nor the desire to communicate to me what she wanted. I'd get up and sing and [in a heavy British accent], "No, no, no, no, no, no, no! You're doing it all wrong." "Um, OK. What should I do?" "Just do it better. Let's move on to Julie's number." And it happened every time! [Laughing] It was absurd, actually. Can you imagine the pressure of trying to create in that atmosphere? I tried to approach her directly several times and she never had time. When we got to my number "Lovely," as if on cue, "No, no, no, no, no, Rachel! Let's go on to Julie's number!" I was able to sing my songs all the way through maybe once or twice during the entire rehearsal process. I was convinced that I was going to be terrible in this production and the anxiety resulted in my being sick and out for four days. Upon my return, the cast had already blocked the entire second act. They were going to do a run-through of the whole show and I had barely rehearsed any of my moments. I thought, "I guess I have to wing this!" I thought I was doing a pretty decent job, all things considered, until we get to this one point during a sequence when the characters are playing a party game and I improvised a bit to add some humor. It was teeny. Not a big deal. The director stopped the run-through yelling *"What are you doing?!"* She tore me to pieces in front of everybody, including Julie Andrews, Cameron Mackintosh.... I explained that I was

simply trying something different because everything I was doing seemed to be wrong in her opinion. If she would just tell me what she wanted I would be happy to oblige. At the end of the run-through the director complimented everyone and then looked at me and said pointedly, "We'll work on it." I felt like dirt and just wanted to get out of there. Julie came up to me as I'm trying to sneak out [in a flawless Andrews impersonation], "Oh, Rachel, Rachel, I just want you to know that I think you're doing a wonderful job." I said, "I don't think the director thinks so." I'm trying not to cry, but failing as Julie puts her arms around me and says, "Oh I think what you're doing is so funny and creative—things I never would have thought to do. Everything's going to be all right." Fortunately, I wasn't fired. As opening night neared, I just kept my head low and did the best that I could. I approached the director once again trying to glean some insight about the character. I said, "I've tried the dumb blonde, the innocent, and the vamp approach. None of them seem to work for you." And she fired back, "She's dumb but she's not dumb." OK. Fine. I'll take it, but what the heck does that mean? I went home that night and turned on the TV and Goldie Hawn in *Private Benjamin* was staring back at me. I thought, "I'll try it. I'll give her a Goldie Hawn flair." The next day in tech, I received a note from Stephen Sondheim. It said, "Think Goldie Hawn." Hallelujah! Thank you, Stephen!

Once it opened did you ever feel like it was coalescing?
Yeah, I was able to find my rhythm after the director left.

Did you learn anything from Julie Andrews?
So much! Julie is a beautiful person; always gracious and kind. She's wonderfully witty and sharp and possesses an amazing memory. We shared a dressing room during *Putting It Together* and she taught me the essentials of decorating. [As Julie] "Always use creams, whites and taupes. They make every room appear fresh clean and open." At the end of a tough eight-show-week, she'd sometimes come into our dressing room and say, "Oh, Rachel, I am just exhausted. I don't think I have it in me tonight." And I would say, "Julie, am I going to have to sing the song?" "Oh no! Rachel, please don't." [singing, imitating Julie's voice] "Oh, it's a Jolly Holiday with Julie...." "Oh honestly, Rachel." "Julie makes your heart so light." "Oh fuck it. All right, I'll do the show!"

Obviously, she liked you because she asked you to do *Victor/Victoria*.
Julie was like a second mom to me. She often called me "cheeky." And I adored Blake Edwards. It was wonderful working with him, too. We had a great rapport. He let me go out on stage and be free to explore. It was euphoric and so much fun to have a director that supports you, letting his actors play, discover, and have fun on stage. He fed my creativity. Blake is still very close to my heart. He is on the other side now, but I still talk to him now and again.

The show did not work as well as anticipated. What was the atmosphere like as you were putting it together? Was it evident that there were issues?
The atmosphere was wonderful, but the show was tough on Julie. She had so much responsibility to carry on her shoulders and she didn't want to let anybody down. Julie created a very welcoming, motherly, and nurturing atmosphere and Blake created an inspiring and creative environment to play in. One of the things I learned as far as comedy is concerned is that you never know for sure if it's funny until you do it in front of an audience. I think the show grew enormously from when we opened to the end. What was captured on video during previews is

not what it was seven or eight months later. Sometimes he'd bring in something we all thought was hilarious and we'd go out there and do it and it's crickets. So that was cut. Then he'd have another new scene the next night and we'd be like, "It's bad." And he would say, "Just try it, let's see." And boom! People are laughing hysterically and it stops the show. You just never know.

Julie's Broadway return was embraced by the Broadway community, but the show was not well received. Did that bring the company closer together?

Reviews were mixed and many elements of the show, including my performance, were greatly praised. We were always a very close company. Not a bad egg in the group.

You had Liza Minnelli as your leading lady for a bit while Julie took a leave.

Liza came in to help us while Julie recovered from laryngitis and vocal strain. Julie's dressing room was all whites and creams and taupes and Liza splashed red all over the walls. She hung a Warhol painting in her dressing room … of herself. I thought it was hilarious. Liza was a hoot. The energy in the company was weird because Julie was like everyone's mum and now we had a step-mum. But I love Liza and we became friends. Liza was dealing with a lot. She had just had hip surgery and was on medication, she's coming into a cast that's already a family, stepping into Julie's shoes … it was enormous pressure. So, when it came to opening night, we were kind of nervous because she hadn't had enough rehearsal and we all knew it. We figured we would just steer her around. And that's exactly what we did. It was rather sur-real and magical sharing the stage with her. I felt honored she wanted to be my friend. She hugged me every single night during the bows. It was a ball working with her. No one can ever describe Liza as a bore. She will forever be brilliant.

Quite famously, when Julie was nominated for a Tony but the rest of the show's elements were not, she made a curtain speech, declining the nomination and defending the "egre-giously overlooked." What do you remember about being on stage during that moment?

It was a really big moment. We had all worked very hard and put all of our love and creativity into that show. I think it was very hurtful to the whole company. Everything was snubbed. Rob Marshall's amazing choreography? Willa Kim's brilliant costumes? There were folks out there that thought my performance was pretty swell, too. Julie was the only company member to be recognized by the committee. That night Julie stopped the bows and gave her speech even though our producers advised against it. That just goes to show you who Julie is. She wanted to do right by the company. What a ride … I was in that sweet spot. I remember being onstage and feeling that incredible connection with the audience that whatever I did, they were with me. It was a beautiful gift and Blake and Julie gave me the opportunity.

When the show closed, you went back to L.A. again.

I did. I was hoping to build more momentum in film and television. Producers Craig Zadan and Neil Meron encouraged me to move back west. Sadly, when I got out there … crickets. Years later, though, when they were looking for somebody to play Lucille Ball, they managed to find my number again. I felt honored to play Lucille Ball and wanted to do her justice, make her proud. She was a perfectionist and loved rehearsal, much like I do. It was all in the details with her. But in TV, unless you are an A-lister, most decisions are out of your hands, so you have to hope that those in power make the right ones. There were inaccurate choices made in the film that bothered me, but ultimately, I was proud of my work. I believe I was able

to channel Lucy's essence. After *Lucy*, I was very down on Hollywood and the inherent super-
ficiality. My drive and passion were running on empty and my priorities began to shift. I was
tired of being so obsessive about my career. The *Lucy* experience also reinforced my appreciation for the wonderful opportunities I had been given in theater. Onstage, you are able to sink
your teeth into a character and own it. It's yours! The director can direct you until opening,
but when you're onstage you are free to express your being and to sing your heart out. I had
a new and profound gratitude for being a theater performer. A few months after *Lucy*, I was
offered the lead in a musical version of *Summer of '42* in Texas and I jumped at the opportunity to get out of town. Did I necessarily want to go to Texas? No. But I wanted to get out of
L.A. It would be the first regional show I had done in fourteen years, but I just knew it was the
right decision for me. And it ended up being where I met my husband!

Before you shot *Lucy*, you had a brief return to New York in *The Scarlet Pimpernel*.
I auditioned for *The Scarlet Pimpernel* version two and was cast as Margarite. The show would
be retooled and reopened with a new director, new costumes, new lighting, new songs ... and
Rex Smith. I was taking care of my sister at the time who was suffering from rheumatoid ar-
thritis and so we both moved to New York. This one was a unique experience—I mean how
many times do you get to watch a show before going into rehearsals with a new director who
is making changes? I was able to objectively weigh in about what I thought worked and didn't
work from version one, and I was on fire with ideas about how to improve it. Ultimately, *The
Scarlet Pimpernel* was a delightful experience and working with Douglas Sills was pure joy.
He's absolutely brilliant.

You went into the show with Rex Smith, with whom you also co-starred in *Kiss Me, Kate*.
Yes. Rex had a Jack Russell terrier and Rex *is* a Jack Russell terrier: he's smart, but he could get
a bit hyper and self-involved at times. While Rex worked hard and is hugely talented, his ego
got in his way at times. Rex and I worked well together, but I kept a professional distance. He
had that matinee idol reputation after all.

In taking *Kiss Me, Kate*, you made the decision to embark on your first national tour.
Kate was a role I had always wanted to play. It fit me like a glove. But on tour, people's worst
sides can come out. Morale, especially in a long-term run, is very important and I strive to
lead by example. Toxic energy can destroy a company. In my experience, it is often the least
experienced individuals with the biggest insecurities and competitive egos that have not
learned to keep said egos and insecurities in check. They just haven't done the work on themselves. While most of the company was really sweet and respectful and didn't indulge in the
backstage bickering, there were a few people poisoning the well, talking negatively about
other people and creating some toxic energy, which was unfortunate. It doesn't have to be
like that. I make a point of treating every single person in the company with the same level
of respect. We all need each other, and I never indulge in gossip. Two-faced behavior and
cattiness—there's just no room for it. It's my pet peeve. Come to my dressing room anytime,
but if it's to gossip, please don't.

You had the opportunity to join the London company.
Yes. I replaced the late great Marin Mazzie on the West End. It's not always easy to step into
a show that's been running for a while and has its own groove. The same show can evolve

differently with different companies. What Rex and I were doing on tour was different than what Brent Barrett and Marin were doing in London. It took some adjusting and finesse, but eventually Brent and I developed our own chemistry. Brent is so consistent and a pleasure to work with. His voice never faltered, which is quite rare and unbelievable actually. How do you sound that good every single time? In London weather? I remember watching the show in London before put-in rehearsals and I was like, "Oh no. They're not going to make me do that, are they?" [Actors were doing] little bits that didn't have any basis in reality. Lots of upstaging and milking that just wasn't funny in my opinion. For instance, the gangsters developed a bit where they literally started barking at Lilli out of nowhere. They wanted me to bark back. In my opinion, Lilli had too much dignity to bark, period. Listen, I love absurd humor and as actors we want to continually perfect and enhance the scene and our character. But there is a fine line between a funny bit that comes out of being in the moment and a bit that is contrived to make people laugh. I couldn't bring myself to participate in a bit that didn't make sense to me or my character. This is something that can happen in a longer run: actors will try to outdo each other by coming up with comic bits in addition to the clever comic bits already written in the script. This is when you need a director to come back and reel it in.

A few years after you came back from the West End, you did the underrated off-Broadway musical *Dessa Rose*.
Dessa Rose was a beautiful piece of art gifted to us by the brilliant composers Ahrens and Flaherty and director Graciela Daniele. At the time, I was wanting to portray a kind of salt of the earth, plain woman and then Ruth showed up. I relished playing her from ages nineteen to eighty-six. Growing up, I spent many hours observing my Southern grandmother and so I connected deeply with old Ruth. Ruth's story starts out very lost, fearful … bigoted, because that's what she'd been taught. As an actor, one of the most interesting journeys to take with any character is one that goes from ignorance to a new realization and expanded perception of truth, love, and understanding. Acting can be enlightening when we approach our character with nonjudgment. Walking in an ignorant character's shoes can be liberating when that character lets go of their fear and hate. It was very satisfying to bring *Dessa Rose* to the world. I find that every role that I play is an education. LaChanze and I did *Lucy* together prior to *Dessa Rose*. She is a lovely human being and we had a great connection onstage and off. It's glorious when you can work with somebody who truly knows how to act, give, and receive. You don't always get that, and you don't always get those layers and depth in a character. I was honored to be a part of that story.

When a show means that much to you, what's it like when it closes?
A terrible shame. But so many people who came to the show talked about how meaningful it was to them, how much it just affected them. There were many tears of joy.

Your next show can't be called "meaningful," but it sure was fun: *Dirty Rotten Scoundrels*.
Jonathan Pryce and I both went into the show at the same time and rehearsed together. I find it fascinating to observe how the greats approach their craft. I have been fortunate to have had a front-row seat to learn from some of the best. Jonathan Pryce and Norbert Leo Butz were no different. Two more amazing talents that invited me to play in their sandbox. We were a wonderfully creative trio. Norbert seemed to be excited about the new blood and

trying out new things. The two of them played and played. It was a joy to watch. Especially after the show I had just come off of, *Sly Fox*. That was fucking mind-boggling. There were these master comedic actors in the room—Bob Dishy, Bronson Pinchot, Richard Dreyfuss, René Auberjonois, Peter Scolari.... The director, Arthur Penn, made it clear on day one that he didn't want us to ever go for the laugh. I appreciated what his approach seemed to be, letting the comedy build naturally and organically. I was on board. This was going to be a great experiment in making sure that everything we did was rooted in truth. But, when we began rehearsing, whenever any actor had an instinct to do basically anything during their scenes, he stopped them cold in their tracks and told them to do nothing. "Don't move unless you have to." It was perplexing, and then imprisoning. These were comedic geniuses being told to ignore and silence their comedic instincts! So much time was wasted doing "nothing." He was controlling and restraining our creative impulses, thereby strangling the comedy right out of the play. It's so odd to think about it. It brought back memories of *Putting It Together*. Life never ceases to throw you curveballs every so often. That said, I still enjoyed it, and I am grateful for the experience. There was frustration, but there was laughter, there was camaraderie, and I got to observe so much. Bronson Pinchot has idea after idea after idea. It's inspiring to watch, even if he didn't get to actualize his full potential. I got to work with amazing people and watch them essentially have the experience I had in *Putting It Together*—how do you create when a director tells you not to? So watching Jonathan and Norbert cut loose—that was a breath of fresh air.

After *Dirty Rotten Scoundrels,* you took a tour of *Camelot*.
I'm so glad you're reminding me because I'm like, "What happened after that?" One of the reasons I chose to do *Camelot* was that my beloved cat, Romeo, was dying of bladder cancer. I got the offer to go on this tour, and I thought, "What am I going to do with myself after he passes? I'll just be sitting around, devastated. If I can channel the emotion into this character, it will be a cathartic experience." Years earlier, I had done *Anything Goes* in Los Angeles, directed by Glenn Casale. He and I talked about *Camelot* and how they've always cast these really old men as Arthur. We agreed that he needs to be young and masculine for the audience to believe in the love triangle. Arthur is by nature a strong brute, but wants to be civilized. He wants to create a world that is just, fair, reasonable, mindful. Lancelot is gorgeous, loyal, pure of heart, and his most gifted knight. Guinevere falls in love with both of them. [Fast forward], Glenn Casale is directing, and I decide to do it. And then I found out they cast Michael York who was seventy-two. Even though he has done great film work in the past, I was like, "Oh. That's completely NOT what we discussed." They wanted Michael York to do it because they thought that he would sell tickets. Not only did he not sell tickets, but reviewers took aim at him. I chose to make the most of it, though. I expressed a great deal of the emotional pain I was holding inside, which was healing for me.

After *Camelot,* you started a family.
I actually had a miscarriage during *Camelot*. I went up during one of my solos and started making up words. Something was happening to my mind and my body. I thought I was dying. Then I did a show at The Goodman in Chicago called *Turn-of-the-Century*, directed by Tommy Tune, with Jeff Daniels. It was wonderful working with both of them. I had high expectations for this show, but it died in Chicago. Such a shame given the pedigree behind it.

The concept was brilliant, but the execution fell short. When we were in tech, I was pregnant, unbeknownst to everyone. I was in this really, really tight dress, it was hot, and I was standing around for hours. And when you're pregnant you have to really be careful about temperatures and tight clothing. I lost the pregnancy that night.

But you did manage to get pregnant during your next show, which was another new show with high hopes, *101 Dalmatians.*
That was another great company, just sweet as can be. I love them all. The children were great. And the dogs were adorable but a bit of a problem. We had a creative team comprised of all men. No slight against men, but there is something to look at here. [Choreographer] Warren Carlyle and [director] Jerry Zaks came up with the concept to have the humans on stilts, to differentiate between the people and the dogs. The show incorporated human dogs, real dogs, and children as dogs. A whimsical concept to be sure, and the cast was all game. Actors are always game, aren't they? I was really good on those stilts but from the audience perspective, they seemed unstable. It took people out of the moment. And there are limitations to being on stilts. But I relished playing Cruella de Vil. I would love to play Cruella again someday because frankly, I'm a brilliant Cruella! I had a great time. The script had a lot of heart, but it was way too long. Dennis DeYoung wrote this fabulous music. He would see things that could be improved and he would go to Jerry, but Jerry didn't especially like being told what to do. Dennis just wanted it to be good. He was watching it every single night. His heart was so invested in that show. As the creative team worked to improve the script, they sadly ended up cutting the best and most heartfelt parts of the show. They couldn't decide whether it was a Broadway show or a children's show. Then I got pregnant. I'm on stilts, dancing eight shows a week, and I have a history of miscarriages. So I chose to leave the show. Unfortunately, I lost that child. But not much later I did get pregnant again and I became engrossed in the joys of motherhood.

Until David Zippel asked you to do his Cy Coleman revue off-Broadway, *The Best Is Yet to Come.*
Well before that, when my daughter was just six weeks old, I did a Broadway workshop for a new musical about Marilyn Monroe. It was a project that an ex-agent royally botched for me a few years earlier, but it came back around. This time John Rando was directing, who I absolutely adore. I was just getting back into my body, still breastfeeding. You just do it. You just do it because you're so happy. You have brought this new child into the world and you just make it work. It was a happy time. I felt very blessed. The book and the music had problems and the composer didn't want to change or modify anything he had written, so it was frustrating for John. While I was in New York I received the offer to do the Cy Colman revue right after the workshop and I had a lovely time. David has become a dear friend over the years and it was a joy to have him direct the show. During the run, Liza came to the show and kissed my daughter's feet! A few weeks later, I did a reading with Chita Rivera, who did the same. I have a Broadway baby in the making!

And then you did a pair of excellent shows at Encores!, *Gentleman Prefer Blondes* and then *Little Me.*
Yes, both with John Rando. What a joy! He's one of the good ones and he has a great sense of humor. Christian Borle, John, and I had a blast. Even with limited rehearsal, he's never

too short of time to try new stuff and play. As a side note, I'm glad Encores! exists, but they are really making out. *Little Me* is a really big show. We delved into it and had a great time, but it was a lot of work; a full-fledged Broadway show put up in eleven days. Those shows are NOT staged readings. Who are we kidding? As actors, we are taught from the beginning to be a trooper. I never complained. But I observed and I was slightly horrified. Josh Bergasse's choreography was amazing. I think he's a real visionary. The problem was his choreography was super quick paced and difficult—one time I was watching one of the male dancers toss a female dancer in the air, quick spin, and he caught her by the skin of his teeth. That could have been a broken neck. They were doing such difficult choreography [without the proper rehearsal time]. It scared me to death. We're a dime a dozen so we've got to be amazing to work with and give 110 percent every show. It's all about the actor/dancer bringing it. And we want to be the best we can be, we *want* to be exceptional at what we do, but all it takes is one bad fall and that person never dances again. One burst vocal cord and that person may never sing the way they used to sing before. On a positive note, Christian Borle is such a gifted actor to work with in every way. And I was blessed to work with John Rando once again. Perfection....

Between your two Encores! shows you did the national tour of *Anything Goes*. This production of the show was dance-heavy and you describe yourself as a clutzy, non-dancer.
Tap dancing was always my forte. I just have too much respect for professional dancers to call myself a real dancer. That said, I had just had a baby and hadn't tapped in twenty years. I feel very confident in saying that Reno is a perfect fit for me. The company was just a dream. We had a ball. My daughter was with me the entire time. I did have an experience which others might find helpful: about halfway through the run, I started developing really bad acid reflux which caused hoarseness, and it got worse and worse. Vincent Rodriguez III was a good friend in the show and he said, "It might be a food sensitivity." It turns out I had a major allergy to eggs. I cut them out and within two weeks my voice was back to normal. So I think to myself, all of these singers out there who are plagued with acid reflux may actually have a food allergy. My advice to anybody with acid reflux is to get a sensitivity test! *Anything Goes* was my second show working with Kathleen Marshall. She had choreographed *Kiss Me, Kate* and directed *Anything Goes*. The great thing about Kathleen is that she is straightforward and to the point. She's consistent, efficient, she respects her actors, and she has good judgment and taste. Her specialty is period work, of course. She may have watched even more old movies than I did as a kid. When you work with Kathleen, you know it will be a good environment and most likely a good show.

In 2014, you joined Betty Buckley at Bay Street Theater for a production of *Grey Gardens*, and then you had the opportunity to revisit it for a longer run in Los Angeles in 2016.
I was very excited to work with Betty, and Michael Wilson is the best director I've ever worked with—and I've worked with some really great directors. He is very insightful. A great communicator. He's a visionary. He is a student of humanity and he really understands the process. He respects actors and what they have to go through. I can't say enough great things about him. Working with Betty was very meaningful. We both like to delve deeply into our characters. She was very protective of me, too, because I was playing this very demanding

With Betty Buckley (Right) in *Grey Gardens*.
(Craig Schwartz)

role and juggling a five-year-old. We were in tech, onstage, and she's like, "Rachel needs an assistant." They had an intern serving as Michael's assistant and she demanded that Michael give me his assistant. I was grateful because I am the kind of person that doesn't ask for help when I should. "Don't worry about me. I'm OK." And so, I greatly appreciate Betty looking out for me and for being the strong woman she is. She is no pushover. She has learned to speak her mind. We made a great team.

You came back to Broadway in *Disaster!* in 2016.
I could do a show like *Disaster!* forever, because it was so much fun. It was just a wonderful creative atmosphere with all these veteran actors. "Broadway Royalty," as Faith Prince liked to call us. We all knew our craft, we're all past any kind of competitive nonsense, nobody's a diva. We loved each other and it was just an awesome experience. I'm grateful to Seth Rudetsky for writing it, along with Jack Plotnik, the director. I really enjoyed working with both of them. When I wasn't onstage, I would sometimes watch the audience from the wings because they were having such a good time, just rolling over in laughter. What a sight to behold. It made me proud to be a part of something giving so much joy. But the marketing just wasn't there. There were a lot of reasons it didn't last longer, but it was a great show. And a healthy atmosphere. I ended up with neck problems from doing some of those disco moves,

and I'd still go back into it tomorrow if I could. It isn't often that you can't wait to get to work every day, but that was one of those.

Later, that same year, you ended up in *Head Over Heels* workshop.
Yeah, I was intimidated. It's in iambic pentameter! I had to trust my craft. I entered this piece thinking, "This is going to be an ensemble show, so I won't have too much pressure." Boy, was I wrong. I remember feeling more stressed out and more exhausted after each show than in any show I'd ever done. It was puzzling to me. I was so stressed I developed an eye twitch. My eye would not stop twitching and I realized then that I needed to try a different approach, an antidote to the inherent, frenetic energy of the show. My character, Gynecia, was the voice of reason, the true leader and the calm in the storm. I had to find MY peace and Gynecia's peace in this cacophony. Once I finally realized that, I knew that I could still honor the pace that Michael Mayer wanted, but trust that my power is in my stillness. That informed everything else and Michael was supportive of the choice. I think *Head Over Heels* is really special; the message was powerful and beautiful: love is love. The music of the Go-Go's was incredible and every member of the cast was divine. It was a very timely piece that unfortunately did not fly. As much as it was a celebration of the gay and trans communities, a queer show, as the marketing team was selling it, the message applied to everyone else, too. The themes are universal. It's a show about inclusion, female empowerment, tolerance, celebration of life, family, love. Everybody! My daughter was seven and she took friend after friend to see the show. She loved it! It is her favorite show over *Matilda, Wizard of Oz, Wicked, Annie, The Lion King*.... Parents were not aware that this was a show for kids. The show was a joyous fairytale and the marketing missed the boat. It was too narrow in its focus.

It seemed like that company was a very tight company and very appreciative of one another. When you're in a company like that, and you're also looking at half-empty houses and you're having to play broad comedy and sing for the rafters, what's that like?
It's a shame. But the show's message and content had its own satisfaction for us. We knew it was awesome and audiences were charged and filled with joy. Much like *Diaster!*, there's nothing better than providing that kind of joy and laughter. I have a sort of mixed feeling about *Head Over Heels* in that I wanted it to go on forever, yet my body was utterly exhausted. And the back pain.... That took a while to fix. Ultimately, the *Head Over Heels* company continues to be my family. Peppermint and Bonnie Milligan are two of my besties.

What do you see for yourself looking forward?
I love New York and I love the Broadway community, but New York is intense. I used to find a lot of creative energy in New York, but because I have a family now and there are so many other layers to my life, I need space. I want to do more TV and I'm writing a series at the moment. I love theater and I have come to appreciate it more than ever. I will always consider Broadway if she calls me back. I remember when I saw Jessica Tandy on the Broadway stage years ago, and she was, I think, eighty-six. I thought, "That's me. I'm going to be doing this till I'm eighty-six years old." I have projects in the works. One is about Marilyn Monroe. And this series I'm creating could be brilliant if I can just crack the code. I need time. Lots of time, with no distractions. Ha! Wish me luck with that. I like to think I am being inspired by a higher power, because I don't know what the hell I'm doing! But I'm wiser and more informed now.

As Gynecia, the calm in the storm in *Head Over Heels*.
(Joan Marcus)

I'm not interested in superficial fluff projects. I want to create and be a part of projects that have deeper meaning, positive messages. We are at an interesting moment in history. I want to be present and informed. I want to do what I can to inspire, empower, and inform in my work, while at the same time encourage people to laugh and lighten up. I do believe that levity and gratitude are the keys to life.

Melissa Errico

January 2021

"I was up really late last night reading pre-Raphaelite history," confesses Melissa Errico as we embark on one of our chats. "There's a Bohemian kind of artist's life that I think I would have been suited for. People are always dumbfounded by how much art history there is around my house and how many books there are." I am dumbfounded by the notion that people would be dumbfounded. Anyone who knows Errico even a little understands her to be an inquisitive creature with a voracious appetite for exploration and a vocabulary that would make Roget proud. Over the course of our conversations, she'd regularly grab a book and read me relevant passages from the likes of T. H. White, Glennon Doyle, or even Melissa Errico, *New York Times* columnist who was asked to chronicle the life of the actress over a series of ongoing pieces. She is an intellectual. When I suggest that she comes from privilege, she works hard to disabuse me of the notion. "I am a Bohemian," she insists. "In another time, I might have ended up in some painter's studio, undressed."

Melissa Errico grew up on Long Island with art surrounding her. Her father is a surgeon, but also a classical pianist who, at four years old, slept under the piano rather than leave it. Her mother is a painter and sculptor. And her maternal grandmother, discovered by Florenz Ziegfeld, was an opera singer who learned piano so that she could accompany herself. That Errico became who she became should surprise exactly no one. But it wasn't easy. After a youth spent practicing gymnastics, a dream killed by puberty ("Gymnastics was immediately canceled by my ass," she laughs), Errico found theater. She gained admittance to Yale with an application she styled to look like a Playbill. She majored in art history, taking a year off to play Cosette in the national tour of *Les Misérables*. Upon graduation, she went straight to Broadway with another musicalized classic, albeit a less well-adapted one, *Anna Karenina*. It flopped, but that led directly to the starring role in a major revival of *My Fair Lady* alongside Richard Chamberlain. At Encores!, she shone as a princess in *Call Me Madam*, and then seduced audiences and critics alike as a goddess in *One Touch of Venus*. It was the performance of the season, catapulting her to the top of every director's wish list. *High Society*, another disappointment, was next before a moving *Sunday in the Park with George* at The Kennedy Center. That was a palate cleanser before she was back on Broadway, struggling to fill in the blanks in archetypal roles whose chief characteristic was prettiness. "Because of my looks I wasn't given a whole wide range of characters to play," she sighs. "I was always playing the perfect, petticoated ingenue." In an attempt to change that, she sought training with Howard Guskin, who told her, "My job is to get the word 'lovely' out of your reviews." Still, her next two shows offered her more of the same, but they both had their upsides: *Amour* introduced her to the composer Michel Legrand with whom Errico became quite close. They collaborated on a definitive album, *The Legrand Affair*. And *Dracula* introduced her to Kelli O'Hara, who talked Errico into the merits of motherhood. Three daughters in two years followed, and Errico shifted her priorities. With her husband, tennis player Patrick McEnroe, often on the road, the only musicals she'd agree to were limited runs so as to minimize her time away from family. Off-Broadway gave her those opportunities in acclaimed runs of *Passion*, *On a Clear Day You Can See Forever*, and two

"I've never worked so hard in my life," said Errico of *Sunday in the Park with George* at The Kennedy Center.

(Joan Marcus)

separate productions of *Finian's Rainbow.*
She also explored television, more concert
work, and recorded *Sondheim Sublime,* another esteemed album combining her intellect with her sensuality. As she said to me
more than once, "What goes on between
my ears goes on between my legs."

When Errico was twelve years old,
while having lunch with her mother at
Manhattan's tony Café des Artistes, they
spied the legendary actress Marian Seldes at
a nearby table. "Go talk to her," her mother
prodded. "Do you have any advice for a
young actress?" asked the shy Errico. Seldes
offered one word: "Live." Everything about
Errico suggests she took that advice to heart,
even if the wisdom "felt like the riddle of the
Sphinx." She never stops finding new ways
to create. "Meaning arrives when you make
things." The myriad numbers of people she
describes as "good friends" range from legendary designer Tony Walton to *New Yorker*
writer Adam Gopnik to her cab driver on a

Melissa Errico	
Les Misérables	National Tour, 1988
Anna Karenina	Broadway, 1992
My Fair Lady	Broadway, 1993
Call Me Madam	Encores! 1995
One Touch of Venus	Encores!, 1996
High Society	Broadway, 1998
Sunday in the Park with George	Washington, DC, 2002
Amour	Broadway, 2002
Dracula	Broadway, 2004
Finian's Rainbow	off-Broadway, 2004
White Christmas	Broadway, 2009
Passion	off-Broadway, 2013
Do I Hear a Waltz?	Encores! 2016
Finian's Rainbow	off-Broadway, 2016
On a Clear Day You Can See Forever	off-Broadway, 2017

Greek Island with whom she stays in touch. Her kids mean everything to her. Her art means everything to her—even when it bombs. "The principle about tennis," she instructs (tennis meta-
phors, learned during a life with McEnroe, are unsurprisingly frequent), "is not to concentrate on
the ball you just missed, but to concentrate on the next ball. The actual percentages of things you
miss in a game you win are incredibly high. You miss almost all the balls and you still win. Success
is made of hundreds and hundreds of mistakes."

You have said that seeing *On Your Toes* on Broadway lit the performing spark in you.
On Your Toes was my Conversion of St. Paul. I asked my mother, "Who are these people? How
did they get there?" My parents went out and bought a book called "How to Get Your Child into
Show Business." We didn't really have a lot to go by. By eighth grade I did start to go to the city
on Saturdays [to take class]. My mother would go to the Art Students League and take art class,
and I went to Steps and would take dance class until I couldn't walk. I loved it beyond words.
Plus, it created a bond with my mother. We were putting an artistic date aside. I do credit my
mom with understanding my desire and feeding it. Getting to French Woods [performing arts
summer camp] really helped. French Woods just crowned me. I got every part. Drove people
up a wall. Jason Robert Brown and I were in everything together. I played Evita, he was Che. We
learned all of it in three weeks. Nothing on Earth could make me want to go swim in the lake; I
wanted to go to rehearsal. I used to ask my mother to send costumes because I didn't trust that
the costume person was going to [do the role justice]. So just in case, she used to mail me costumes. She sent me her nightgown for my death scene. She mailed me a brooch so I'd look like a
very together fascist. At intermission, my mother ran backstage and did my bun, made me look
unbelievable. We had fun. I never associated the theater with hard process, I always associated it
with an alleviation of stress. I was good at it—cute, funny, sexy—I was good. I could work hard.

Nothing about it was anything short of exciting and fun. I got straight A's in school because it was the only way to get my father, who is a tough guy, to give me more freedom to do theater.

You made your professional debut while you were at Yale.
[At the end of freshman year] I started looking at *Backstage* magazine, thinking of the summer coming up. I circled all the things that interested me. I circled the Ringling Brothers Barnum & Bailey Circus. I guess I had a kind of wanderlust, and maybe an impatient nature. I auditioned for *George M!* at Rhode Island Theater by the Sea and I had little shorts and big curly hair. [Director] Richard Jay-Alexander saw me in the hallway changing my shoes and he asked if he could please bring me across the hall [to audition for the *Les Misérables* national tour]. The guys from Theater by the Sea [told me later], "We knew we'd lost you." So I went in and auditioned for *Les Mis*. I did know "In My Life," but I feigned that I didn't, so as they were teaching it to me [it seemed like] I was picking it up really fast. Richard Jay says that I tried to talk him out of casting me. He said, "Can you start in ten days?" And I said, "Are you sure? That wasn't very good." He was laughing his ass off and we have been friends since then. I did it for fifteen months. There was some talk of my doing Christine [in *The Phantom of the Opera*] after, but I said no. I did want to go back to college and have a college education. And I did know how high the singing is and I didn't think I could do it.

Let's go back a bit. You got cast as the first replacement for Cosette and you had ten days to go into the show?
I had to organize my studies to be a correspondence student—I called it "Yale by mail." I asked a guy on the football team if he could help me pack my car and he got the entire football team to do it in one swoop if I would go out to dinner with him when I got back. I picked up the tour in Chicago. I was eighteen so I couldn't go out to drink with the cast. I was really taken good care of by that company. They were all so nice. I was a kid. I gained a lot of weight on the tour. I figured out that you can't eat pasta all night. No one had told me this. Barbara Walsh and I were roommates for a significant portion of it and she taught me how to exercise and eat well. She was really kind.

What was it like being in the hottest show at that time?
I was everywhere I wanted to be. I was really happy to be there and I wanted to live up to my character. I read the Victor Hugo. Michael McCormick was very kind to me, teaching me not to over-practice in my room. He used to say, "Don't leave it in the dressing room." That was a big thing for me to discover. I was so under-rehearsed, and I so wanted to do a good job, that I would warm up and warm up and warm up. I probably drove myself too hard and people like Michael were sort of saying to just relax. I got looser as it went along. I did learn a lot about social dynamics, and I also learned a lot about repetition. I wanted to do a good job so badly. I had access to that sort of idealized maiden. I really could make her real. When my father died onstage, I cried almost every performance. [One night, though,] he's dying and I came running in and tripped. I dropped the carafe and all the glasses. It was real glass. Shattered. He's dying and on his last breath, meanwhile, the stagehands are coming out, dressed like French peasants, their ass cracks hanging out, and they have Dustbusters, sucking up all these little crystals.

You finished Yale, but you had a show before you even graduated.
Before graduation I auditioned for the workshop of *Anna Karenina*. I went to my mother's house, borrowed a green dress, buttons all the way down, turtleneck, long sleeves, cameo, hair back, a piece of luggage. I got the part [of Anna.] They said it would just be for the workshop. I

drove back and forth from New Haven and I had the best time. Pat Birch, the choreographer, said, "You were some conundrum. We could not believe a twenty-two-year-old could do what you did. Feel it like that." I don't know what it was. I was completely in love with that show. I loved the music. I loved the tragedy of it. I found it emotionally demanding and easy as pie.

So, during the workshops, it never felt like the show wasn't working?
No. I don't have a well-developed critical gear. I am very focused on what people are giving me and I make the most of it. That may or may not have served me, as different things that I did were rocky. I really believed who Anna was and I really believed I told that story. It may have worked when I did it, I don't know. It is possible that a really loony actor can justify some crappy material. When it went to Broadway, I became the understudy and played Kitty. I don't remember it not being good. I had a great time; I was living my dream, I loved the character, I got really good reviews except for John Simon, who killed me. I never forgot his every word. So, I was calm, I didn't feel in danger. I was sorry for the show not getting great reviews. I was really proud of it. I didn't want to feel unsafe and the times in this business where I have felt unsafe have concerned me, really concerned me. I just want to be in the circus, you see, and so long as I was in the circus, I didn't need it to be [bigger than it was]. I was really happy to do it, and happy to go to work in something I felt was the right kind of thing for me. It not being a hit wasn't running me down. I was just so happy to be there.

And that show led directly to your being cast in *My Fair Lady*.
I got called back and then I didn't get called back. And then the Weisslers [producers] came to see *Anna Karenina*. The night that they came, my big, Russian hoop skirt got stuck on my wig and I got the giggles. I was able to sell the song because she's supposed to be stupid anyway, but I was acting crazy with the hoop skirt over my head. The Weisslers described it as "entropic." It was really lively and they put me into final callbacks for *My Fair Lady* right away. That began a really long war to get that role. [Actor/director/teacher Austin Pendleton coached me] and I worked as hard as I could to really understand Eliza so I could be ready for [director] Howard Davies. He was explaining to me that this is not an idealized maiden, this is a politicized maiden. I've been sort of blessed and cursed by my conventional beauty; you're playing all these characters and it's very hard to say how are they different from each other.

You said it was a war to get the role?
That was the first time that I saw that this was not going to be that easy. Show business is hell. I had to keep going back [to audition, repeatedly for musical director] Jack Lee, then I would go and dance for Donald Sadler. I had private sessions with Howard and Fran Weissler. The whole concept that Howard had, which was quite fascinating, was that Eliza looked masculine, resembled Charlie Chaplin. They wanted big boots and black pants. They wanted the girl to look like one of the boys. When she says, "I've come to have lessons, I have, and to pay for 'em, too, make no mistake," she's buying something. She has no cuteness. Howard was very, very demanding that I don't suffer at all. He never wanted the character to fret. He used to say, "Anytime you make a decision that brings your eyebrows together and you fret, you must make another decision."

That's a great direction.
It's a great direction. I was prone to suffering. [When she says] "I'm a good girl, I am," it's a positive, not defensive. "I am not a prostitute. I have taken care of myself, thank you very much." This other powerful intellectual was supposed to be Richard Chamberlain, which

is completely, no offense, not the right casting. To seduce me under the terms that [Howard wanted for Eliza] it's the wrong casting. His hands were tied, though. It's just one of those commercial decisions that was made. I'm not much of an aerial view critic; I didn't come in and say, "This guy's gonna suck." [But] I don't think that Richard liked Howard's interpretation at all. I don't think he understood it. And I don't think he understood how a domineering, brilliant man could fall for this super smart, mouthy girl. The sex vibe comes together and these two are drawn to each other sort of hungrily, but not because he's overpowering her, it's because of matched intellect. I was a great student and super psyched to do it and Howard was impossibly attractive to me. The Weisslers paid for me to go to London for two weeks to work with Joan Washington, who was the Henry Higgins of London. She wore Edwardian clothes and she would teach me phonetics. She had this natural androgyny about her and that was exactly what Eliza was supposed to have. I loved working and she taught me phonetics to a degree that—there's just no way that many Elizas have ever had that kind of training. She beat me down and she was amazing. I learned how the tongue works because she saw I was interested: what is a lateral plosion? Where does it come from historically? Where do these sounds come from? The history of Cockney rhyming slang, the music of it, the humor. And that humor is a method to survive. It comes from hardship. I got so much information and I loved my sessions with her. My days were ideal and I would then go to Howard later in the day and do script analysis at his apartment. You've never seen a script more written in. I loved taking notes. The chemistry [between me and Howard] was incredible but nothing was said. We began rehearsals in New York and we worked our asses off. Howard had ideas about political and social engineering—the phrenological head [which was prominent on the set] was part of another idea that he had. There was a lot of science at the time, that you could socially engineer a person in the same way that Frankenstein's monster was created by a scientist. *Frankenstein* was written at the same time as Shaw. So, the feminist ideas of Shaw, and the social engineering concepts, pulling the power of modern science into the science of phrenology, was an idea that Howard had which would create this kind of intense smartness. To be the victim of that, to be Frankenstein's monster, to be Eliza, being maneuvered socially, is a very strong and interesting idea and it's scary. I think he wanted to give it a scary quality. It was not a fairy tale of this girl becoming a princess in Howard's mind. Howard was a Welsh, intellectual, socialist. So you give him Shaw and this heady Yale graduate and [it's a perfect match]. He asked me if I would go to a sound studio to record the scream [in the first act] so that when Eliza is taken offstage and stripped of her clothes, there's this kind of raw, physical, terrifying, stripping down of her pride. I was so committed to this idea. I went to the sound studio alone and I screamed. I screamed in different ways because the engineer didn't know what they wanted. So we did all kinds of things and I hurt my voice. I did it too much. I gave too much. Did I have a preexisting vein on the vocal cord? We will never know. I have a daughter who has a slightly hoarse voice. She has a little cyst. It's actually called a verax. It's not a big thing but it creates hoarseness. It's a small injury with a large impact on your singing. All the women you've spoken to have had it—they're never going to tell you, trust me. The amount of shame associated with vocal injuries is crazy. They will all tell me, but they won't tell you. This is a common reason why people have a sprained ankle or a bad back. They actually had none of those things, they had a vocal injury. It's a setback that's often hidden. I can't hide it because it haunted me again later in my career. So many actresses have been so kind and told me, "It happened to me, too," and told me I'd get over it. And they were right, I did get over it, but it was harsh. I didn't open the show out of town and I got repaired. I was out for a couple months and then I came and did the second half of the tour. By that point I had definitely lost Richard Chamberlain's support.

What does that mean? How did that manifest?
He wasn't terribly pleased to see me and didn't look me in the eyes. He had gotten used to the understudy. He needed support and he had insecurities. I liked him. And I have more compassion for him now, realizing how difficult it is to star in a show.

One can imagine that Richard Chamberlain, a big star whose one musical theater experience, *Breakfast at Tiffany's,* **had been a huge flop almost thirty years prior, would feel the pressure of carrying the show. Add a virtually unknown Eliza and a director's vision that plays against his charm and looks . . .**
Exactly. It didn't feed his audience. I have lots of sympathies for him in retrospect. We both had decencies but we were opposing, in some ways. I was in love with the director. The director fell in love with me and I wanted to serve his vision. I was willing to fight my way back to health to do it. I really wanted to get well and play that part.

Of course you did! It was an iconic part with gorgeous songs being directed intellectually.
Let's also add the word *erotic*; it was really erotic to me. The teacher/student relationship with a very strong sense of the girl knowing her worth . . . I think something really powerful was going on between Eliza and Higgins and concurrently with me and Howard, to be honest. We were together for like five years.

That could be another reason Chamberlain might have had issues.
Yeah, I get it. We were on the edge of getting married. It was really a huge, huge love, and so *My Fair Lady* is entangled with the dynamics of his genius. I got to do it again [at the Hollywood Bowl] with John Lithgow. It was so amazing. I got to do the girl again and work on my interpretation. It never got to Broadway the way it was meant to be.

That whole Charlie Chaplin thing that you described was gone by the time it hit New York.
Yeah. When I came back into the show, my costumes were pink and purple.

That wasn't Howard's vision as you described it, so how did that happen?
Tommy Tune [who was working regularly with the Weisslers]: "Pretty this up." And Heidi Landesman was brought in to pretty up the set. I came back and my scarf was pink and the coat was purple. I was like, "Fuck, this makes no sense." I think the whole thing became a complicated compromise.

So how did that affect your performance?
I was being redirected by my environment, but not by the director.

But the given circumstances are that she's wearing a pink scarf and a purple coat. So you have to justify those choices and become the character who wears those things.
I didn't. I just kept playing it, but it didn't feel as good. I think she just felt juvenile at that point. I had to kind of lighten up her reasoning. I was uncomfortable, for sure. The whole thing became uncomfortable. I found comfort in the *Tommy* company. I became really good

friends with them. I just kind of found my way. I was taking care of my voice a lot and getting through. It wasn't as inspiring an experience as it could have been. *The New York Times* said I was "frisky." I did gymnastics, I did cartwheels, I did a back walkover. The headboard of the bed was four and a half inches wide, exactly the width of a traditional professional balance beam. So when the housekeepers were chasing me, I jumped up on the top of the headboard and I was balancing. It gave people a heart attack but I had perfect balance from gymnastics and I loved it. It was a tricky time, but the reviews were good and I didn't feel disappointed. And I fell wildly in love with Howard. We had a wonderful, intellectual relationship. Constantly reading. We got an apartment, we traveled. It was a wonderful period in my life. *My Fair Lady* was my first big thing. It was like the dream, but then tempered by reality. I found comrades along the way. I fell in love. Every theater production is some kind of catastrophe. The people who survive are the ones that make lifeboats out of the floating pieces. You know how I said I wanted to join the circus? I have a nature of finding the fun in things even when they've gone awry. It's the resilience of the girl on the elephant. You have to stay on the elephant. You wobble, and then you've got to look pretty again. I have the girl on the elephant resilience. I think it's one of my great strengths. Immediately after we closed, I did the *Busker Alley* workshop with Tommy Tune and the Weisslers. We worked like a month or more at the Nederlander Theatre. It was another cockney character for me. Tommy is a little bit of a peacock. He likes to see himself. He hung twenty feet of mirror from the balcony, in the house, so he could be on stage looking at himself. Sheets of mirror. I think I was really like a tennis partner; I had to get the ball going back so he could practice. They never drew me in as a partner. We were working more from the outside in and Howard had taught me to work from the inside out. I just had to be soft and playful. One day my mother and father called to tell me that my mother had been diagnosed with cancer and it was bad. [Designer] Tony Walton was in the room when I hung up the phone. I just started weeping and we were bound to each other forever. Tony and I are very close. So always, when he was doing sets and costumes at the Irish Rep., I was in those.

That's how you ended up there! It seemed curious that at the peak of your musical theater power, you were doing Shaw and Wilde at a tiny off-Broadway theater.
Tony Walton is the link. I wanted to do it all. I had an unquenchable kind of creativity on all fronts. I didn't want to do a long run of a play. Off-Broadway means you can do three or four months. Anyway, Tommy knew [what was going on with my mother] and I remember him saying, "You have to differentiate between your life and the show. The show's the thing." That wasn't going to work for me. Life was happening. [When Tune broke his foot] the whole thing just kind of fell apart. It never happened.

After *Busker Alley*, you did *Call Me Madam* at Encores! With Tyne Daly.
That couldn't have been more fun. Nothing went awry there. Everything was crazy though. We didn't have any idea what we were doing. But I think what we were being paid for was our willingness to play. Not to be prepared and perfect, but to make progress with every sentence, every scene. I think our world has gotten so mechanized and perfectionistic. People are so steely about their vocal choices. Their high notes are perfect. Progress was what we wanted over perfectionism. We were playing and the directors were so wonderful and relaxed. I didn't even have an accent until opening night. We were in the wings and Tyne Daly said, "I think you need an accent. You're supposed to be Eastern Europe." I said, "Oh. Like Dracula,

maybe?" I never practiced. So every scene I was like [demonstrates heavy Dracula accent]. I was in my own clothes, this gorgeous green dress I got at Henri Bendel's in Columbus, Ohio, right before we opened on Broadway in *My Fair Lady*. Tyne Daly loved me and she was so generous, and brought out the best in me as a result. She wasn't threatened by me. I got the reviews of a lifetime with that. Those reviews got me [the series] *Central Park West*.

The next season, you were back at Encores! With *One Touch of Venus*.
The minute I heard about *One Touch of Venus* it totally appealed to my sense of the glamorous and absurd. I loved that. The formidable elegance of a statue who really wants a man was a nice duality for me to play because I had access to both. I knew how to be cool and elegant. Howard gave me wonderful advice: to play the role as if I had a bowler hat on my head over one eye. Play the role with a little bit of yourself hidden so the audience always feels like there's something withheld. That's maybe something I wouldn't have done intuitively and I trusted where that would take me. I think it gave me a kind of feeling that there was a percentage of me that was held back. I think a lot of great actresses know how to do that. It was a wonderful experience and I had such a great time. I looked like a million dollars. I remember the dresses were rather long and we were going to hem one, but I said, "Let me go get some shoes." I went down to Eighth Street where all the drag queens buy their stuff and I bought huge, white, platform, patent leather sandal shoes. Under the gown, so you had no idea how I was so tall. It gave me the feeling of being a statue. It was just like a $17 pair of shoes.

Those reviews were so rapturous, that it propelled you forward in a way that is really uncommon for such a short run. *The New York Times* said, "Where, you may ask, has Melissa Errico been all our lives?"
It was beautifully generous. After that review, I got entrance applause. Applause for doing nothing. I found that super curious. That was the first time I ever felt that your reputation precedes you. I've always felt that it's "game on" every game, like a tennis player. It's zero/zero at the start of every match. Fame is a luxury because you have them on your side right away. There were producers who wanted it to go to Broadway. There was a lot of buzz. It just didn't go forward.

But you found yourself in extremely high demand.
I did workshops of everything. I did *Triumph of Love*, *High Society*, and *The Sound of Music* and then I got asked to do all three of them on Broadway that year. There was a bidding war for me. From a decision standpoint, that was a really hard year. People, like my parents, for example, like to replay that decision; "You did the wrong thing." I guess I thought that *The Philadelphia Story* [the basis for *High Society*] had a little more of that urbane [sensibility]. I was not Rodgers and Hammerstein as much as Rodgers and Hart. It seemed like a good idea. I actually liked all three parts. That was tough. I think I pissed a lot of people off. Rebecca Luker had also workshopped *High Society*, so in retrospect, it's nice to know we changed roles: I took her *High Society* and she took my *Sound of Music*. *High Society* is probably where I learned that my theater instincts were maybe sounder than those of the creative team. I knew that "I Am Loved," which was the opening number in San Francisco, was where the show ought to have started. I just should have affirmed my own intellect. They changed it because they said the audience is going to be really excited to see Melissa, so she should do something fun in the beginning. They changed my wig from blonde to

brown because they said no one knew it was me. I came in singing "Ridin' High." I believe if we had opened it differently and kept more of *The Philadelphia Story*, which is the way it was in San Francisco ... I loved the play and the play helped a lot. But they kept cutting lines. They got rid of Jere Shea, which made no sense. Jere was freaking great. I have no idea why they did that. Randy Graff was an angel. Stephen Bogardus came in. He was solid as a rock. We're all pals. I guess [director] Christopher Renshaw getting fired seemed necessary to [producers]. Right before he got fired, in rehearsals, there was a day he asked all of us to come back from lunch a little early. We were going to have a ceremony. A bunch of Tibetan monks were coming up on a bus from Chinatown to bless the stage. They set up a big cauldron and a really large Buddha, like three and a half feet tall, on a pedestal. Christopher was praying and kneeling. He wanted to bless the theater. Well, the bus broke down, so we were all there waiting. I'll never forget [producers] Michael David, Lauren Mitchell, all these men in suits, in the wings and looking pissed off. The monks were late and we were on company time. Then all these monks started to come down the aisle. They did a ceremony with lots of incense coming out of this bowl. It was quite beautiful, a whole ceremony with singing and gongs. The producers were enraged and Christopher was fired pretty soon after that. Des McAnuff came in and cut forty-five minutes from the show. He kept saying we have to work on "musical theater time, not straight play time." I thought that Des was completely wrong, and I should have fought for that. There were great lines [being cut] and that really would have set up the allure. [Musical director] Paul Gemignani said he'd never seen a show attacked like that. I was devastated by the show being changed so much and then suddenly not working. It was hugely successful in San Francisco. I was really disappointed for all of us and I was really bummed about the show. It was the first time I felt the commercial pressure to be the star and I wanted it to succeed. I know my reviews were good, but I took very little comfort in that. That was probably the experience that I didn't survive that well because I didn't make a lifeboat out of the floating pieces.

There was also the challenge of the show's logo and artwork. I think people sometimes discount how important that can be.
The artwork was so beautiful in San Francisco. It had a wonderful kind of witty elegance. It made the show look like an elegant romp, like it was going to be smart and definitely beautiful. I remember being in my studio apartment when the fax came through of *The New York Times* advertisement, which was the new poster. Three cats in the boat. Turns out the in-house graphic artist—his cat had died that week. It was an homage to his cat. I get dizzy thinking about it. It was so wrong. I think they wanted to make it playful, but the show wasn't playful. It was sophisticated and intelligent. I was a rock. My voice was a rock. I looked like a model. I had been killing my body to look like that. I looked the role and that was hard for me because I'm Italian. I'm shapelier. I tamed my body to look more square. No breasts, no hips. It's hard to change yourself for a part and I did. Randy was pissed about the changes in the script. She used to say to me, "Melissa if it ain't on the page it ain't on the stage." I got worn out crying and trying to make it better. Anybody who gave me input—I had a lot of famous people come—Donald Sadler, Tony Walton, Roger Rees, even Celeste Holm [who was in the original film]—and they would give me thoughts about my performance. I had yellow Post-it notes and anytime I got advice, I put it on my mirror. My mirror got so full, you could hardly see my face. And it was a big mirror. There was no winning. It ran for another six or seven months and we had to keep selling it. It was a long slog.

When it closed, you moved out to Los Angeles.

I couldn't go straight into another musical. I needed a minute. I deliberately wanted to try something new. I did feel burned out by the efforts of the Broadway musicals and I already knew how much I enjoyed television.

What got you back?

A phone call from The Carlyle, actually. They offered a month-long engagement. I was, at the time, the youngest person to ever sing there. I hired Lee Roy Reams to direct and he taught me the difference between the theater and the cabaret: "You don't look over their heads. You look in their eyes. Your manner has to be very direct and eye-to-eye. You have to drop all your fear of who you are." I did that and I loved it. I had two black beautiful Morgan Le Fay dresses. I would sit in the bar and wait for the late show, not drinking—that's just poison to me. Lee Musiker, my musical director, would look at me and say, "You love this." It was my idea of real decadence. Elaine Stritch would come to my show. She'd be in the back with this huge [yelling] "Yeah! Yeah!" And then one night, she left me a note on a napkin, which she had a waiter deliver: "Sondheim will love you." I still have the napkin.

And you decided to stay in New York?

I went back to L.A., bought an apartment, and never stayed there for a day. I got a fax from my big Hollywood manager: "There's an audition in New York. *Le Passe Muraille* [later renamed *Amour*] directed by James Lapine." Boom! "Coming over from Paris with music by Michel Legrand!" I had just sung a bunch of Michel Legrand at The Carlyle. I loved him. I said to the manager, "Michel Legrand wrote a musical?" And she says, "I know, I know. I love her." That moment was a turning point, where I realized that L.A. and me were [not a match]. I flew to New York and I auditioned for James Lapine and all these big casting people. It was a perfect marriage of both of my personalities; James Lapine was highly analytical and wants everything to make sense and he's really witty and edgy, while Michel Legrand is so affirmative and sensual. I was happy in every department. I loved Malcolm Gets. We were friends from Yale. I was just in heaven. L.A. went away. Of course, when you buy an apartment in L.A., that's when you're bound to get a leading role on Broadway. If you want a job in L.A., all you have to do is sign a lease in New York! Stephen Sondheim saw the *Amour* workshop and that's how I got *Sunday in the Park with George*.

Which you did that summer, after the workshop, as part of the Sondheim Celebration.

My father called me six weeks before I was going to The Kennedy Center and said, "I know you're good, but you're not this good." I'll never forget that sentence. "You need to get to work." And he was right. I've never worked so hard in my life. I called Paul Ford, who taught Bernadette Peters the part and who played the piano in the original production. Paul trained me. He was warning me about particular pauses and changes in tempo and why they were happening. I don't think I had a waking moment when I wasn't studying that score. When I got to The Kennedy Center, I was ready. I got very, very interested in the second act. I loved playing Marie [the daughter of her first act character, Dot]. There was an old age home near my apartment and I studied people outside, sitting in their wheelchairs for hours. I had an idea about Marie that tied the whole show together for me. I saw her as an elderly woman with a silk scarf, a very fine person. Someone who had gone to Smith College, in my mind. She's from South Carolina so I got a coach to teach me that very specific accent. I made myself as flat-chested as possible. I wanted to look like a very refined person who appreciated art. I didn't want to look at all sassy or stylish, like she'd inherited her mother's sensuality. Dot's lusty, desirous, impetuous, impatient, all of that. I wanted Marie to be a cool figure, delicately appreciative of the painting and able to give George really valuable advice. "Children and Art." She really understands what her mother represents, being so alive in that painting forever and the importance of having a life. I think this older woman is the perfect person to bring all the themes of the story together: personal life and creativity. I wanted to put equal value on both themes. "Children and Art" is the most important song.

And you were immersed in the entire Sondheim celebration.
We all lived together in an apartment complex and you could hear people singing and rehearsing. Christine Baranski and I used to share groceries. It was like intense camp. My soul was on its knees with gratitude. That was where I really saw what I'd been missing in terms of being in something fabulous that works and that suits me. It was everything. I was so happy. That was when I first did nudity.

It was your idea to set your part of "Color and Light" naked, in a tub, right?
It was. It's impressionist painting.... And I was thinking how to make it more desperate. I wanted to amp up the vulnerability of the rejection when he says, "I have to finish the hat." I spoke to our amazing designer, Derek McLane, about putting a bathtub in the space where George is working because that's how it would have been [in 1885]. All of it would have been in one space. There was no discussion. Everybody said, "Sure!" [I was in the tub] kicking bubbles. It was very complicated from a technical standpoint because of the microphone. They had to put the batteries and everything in my hair for that section of the show and I had to make sure to have my head tilted when I kicked or I would short the mic. I loved being able to interpret a great piece, but I wasn't trying to improve it. There were many, many years when I didn't get everything I ever wanted, but there are moments when I got everything I ever wanted. I really identified with Dot—her search for love, her desire for connection....

And you were partnered with Raúl Esparza.
The best. The best. Raúl's like meeting fire. He was young, it's not like he was famous or anything, but he was a firebrand. We were easy friends immediately and never had a minute of discord. Nothing. I would do anything for him and he would do anything for me and we would do anything for Sondheim. We were acolytes at the Church of Sondheim together.

So what was it like working with Sondheim?
Incomparable. Me and Raúl were new to him and we were happy and hyper and ahead of the game. Accurate: that's one way to have a good time with Mr. Sondheim. I was playing a muse and I love admiring the master. But I had a lot of discipline and Mr. Sondheim loves discipline. It's not comfortable to deal with Sondheim. You never know what you're going to get back. An email could be just poisonous, completely judgmental and full of harsh advice, but that's okay. Our relationship was good but it got even better other times when he was able to play around with my obsessive love of detail. It really happened in *Passion*. He started throwing weird shit at me, like telling me that when there's an apostrophe, you don't sing the "ent." You have to sing the apostrophe. I said, "But it's an exclusion by definition. You're losing the word 'not,' so it's a silence. It's a caesura." He says, "Yes, you have to sing the caesura." "I have to sing

the silence?" "Yes." We loved each other. There were apostrophic phrases throughout *Passion* and, at the sitzprobe, every time that someone had to say "don't" or "wouldn't" or "couldn't," I would look at him and he would look at me. It was my little secret joy that he knew that the second it was to be clocked, I had clocked it. Little victories, you see, with Mr. Sondheim, are like humongous victories. If you care over the small stuff, the entire play comes together for him. I had a wonderful experience. Total birds of a feather. And Raúl felt the same way. Raúl was crazy in love with the whole project. I have deeply spiritual feelings about Sondheim. His birthday concert during the pandemic [*Take Me to the World*, produced by Esparza, in which Errico sang "Children and Art"] was like an act of solidarity and renewal that we all needed desperately. I can't say enough about the rays of light that come off of his page for me.

And then back to New York for *Amour* on Broadway. Did working with James Lapine meet your expectations?
It was perfect in every way. I hit it off with James immediately. I am happy to say I'm still good friends with James. *Amour* was a real winner for me. I realize that it was a bomb, but we had a lovely six weeks or so. James wasn't happy doing the show. He felt it was a naturally off-Broadway show. [Producer] Gerry Schoenfeld really wanted it on Broadway. My enthusiasm made James laugh. He's very logical and he was always trying to make some sense. Michel didn't understand why something that's already surrealistic in nature needed to have so much narrative sense. I understood both so I think maybe I helped. Maybe it would have been even worse if I wasn't in it. I was someone who could come in and make something weird makes sense. James worked really hard to make it good. I think that the show might work one day if someone keeps going with it. I saw the London production last year and they were getting there.

You had an amazing cast. Malcolm Gets, Norm Lewis, Christian Borle . . .
They're all awesome. We all looked gorgeous. I didn't have a single day where I had to warm up even though I sang for the whole show; my voice loved that music, it was a pleasure to do. Though the set was dangerous. The boulangerie fell on the front row and that was super scary. It was in the newspaper. My balcony, in one of the very early performances, got stuck on a wire and I was tilting. It was terrifying. It sounded like the Titanic. They closed the curtain. That was bad. It's not like we didn't try. It was special and French and odd and it didn't capture a commercial audience. But we made the album and the album was adored. I still hear about that album. And then the phone call that I got nominated for a Tony Award! It got several nominations. So not all bad.

So given that you loved it so much, were you saddened by its early closure?
I saw Joel Grey on the street one day and he said, "We all have bomb after bomb after bomb. That's the game." You just carry on. Plus, there was so much good in it. We were proud of it. It wasn't a hurtful thing. And Michel Legrand and I were like electricity. We knew we were going to work together again [and they did. Errico became one of Legrand's favorite interpreters of his music].

So even though *Amour* had closed, you went to the Tonys.
My husband was playing the French Open. I flew there to watch him play and I realized, "When we get home, it's the Tony Awards. I need a dress!" I remember running around Paris

and I went to some unbelievably shitty place. I found a dress for like $100. It was very pretty, a nude kind of a fabric with some shimmer on it. It was an absolute rag from nowhere. At the Tonys: "Who are you wearing?" I was like, "A French designer. It's vintage." It wasn't vintage. I got a diamond necklace through the production. They called Harry Winston and they lent me something. Everything was all about *Hairspray* that night.

The following year you did *Aunt Dan and Lemon* off-Broadway and *Dracula* workshops. But before you took that to Broadway, you did *Finian's Rainbow* at Irish Rep. for the first time.
Finian's Rainbow was a wonderful experience, both in terms of its goals, but also the *Brigadoon* quality of it. The idea that these people have a leprechaun that's following them around and that wishes are happening—it has this Gaelic charm and these great ideas. This was a winner for me. The girl is like a fairy. She doesn't exist, really. Glocca Morra is a symbol. "It's that faraway place in everyone's heart, a little beyond one's reach, but never beyond one's hope." I loved working with Max von Essen and Jonathan Freeman. I loved the cast. I love singing "How Are Things in Glocca Morra." I've never stopped singing it. I don't know ... something about that song really suits me. And [I loved exploring all of writer/lyricist] Yip Harburg's ideals. I mean this man's goal was, he said, "to laugh racism out of existence." It was very successful at the Irish Rep. Sometimes the Irish Rep. is the perfect jewel of a place to put over things that are a little quaint. We took really good care of it.

You went from that almost immediately into *Dracula*.
Dracula. Madness. More nudity. This is when I invented the term "ingenue-dity." I do think that as an ingenue evolves, you go looking for some way to make each character a little different. They're all so similar, archetypes. As you age, you sort of shed the petticoat.

How did it come into your world?
Des McAnuff called me. [Composer] Frank Wildhorn was not a good match for me. I'm not the voice in his head. Michel Legrand used to tell me, "Melissa, when I compose, it is your voice in my head." I know I'm not the voice that Frank Wildhorn hears in his head. But in the original workshop, that worked to my advantage. I was the delicate Mina, and Lauren Kennedy was very robust in her performance as Lucy. She's very breasty and rough and athletic in the way she sings. Two women essentially being stalked by a monster that they want because he's sexy. It's a Victorian, sexual awakening story, a fear that all the women are having sex and the men are freaking out. I found my way into it. I didn't mind doing the show. I just didn't think that I was the muse that Frank really wished for. But he worked to adapt and he wrote "The Heart Is Slow to Learn," which was a good song for me. Lauren got pregnant and dropped out, and [Kelli O'Hara replaced her]. She's a genius. She can sing anything. I didn't want to do the show and I told Des that I didn't think it was going to be good. They offered me so much money and he also brought in [playwright] Christopher Hampton to have a meeting with me. Christopher was right up my tree and he's the kind of person I want to be around. I would follow Christopher across any train track. They promised that Christopher's hand was going to be all over it and that it was going to feel like a Victorian story and from a visual standpoint, they really sold me. They said, "You're going to look like a pre-Raphaelite painting." And that would be very correct—to look kind of pale and have this flowing hair. The idea of those rich, wine colors and the aesthetics of that. So, from a visual standpoint, I was intrigued. I remember those costume fittings for *Dracula*. If you could only have seen the

quality of my corsets and the lace and the beautiful things that were put into it. And I trusted Christopher to understand the sexual hunt and not make it vulgar. One of the things Howard used to tell me was that *Les Liaisons Dangereuses* [by Hampton] was the sexiest thing he ever directed and no one in it ever touched. The tension that was created … I have a real attraction to the idea of eroticism. There really was a disjuncture between the high ideals and the nature of Frank Wildhorn. It should have been a bodice-ripper. That's what Frank does, so in his defense, we may have done the wrong thing. Frank is a pretty nice person and not easy to intimidate, but I think he was intimidated by some of those people. He was willing to try. I think my voice doesn't want to sing Frank's music. My voice just didn't want to do it. I didn't feel moved to sing it.

So, you were led to believe that it was going to be one thing and then, as you're rehearsing it, it was another. How did you manage?
I loved the cast. I loved Tom Hewitt. I loved Darren Ritchie. But to be honest, if it weren't for Kelli, I wouldn't have survived it. I loved working with her. I never heard someone who rides their vocal track that easily. Her training was unbelievable. My husband used to say that she' like Roger Federer. I think she had a really good self-protective quality. She knew what her job was and she was preparing *Light in the Piazza* backstage. She was disciplined and she had herself on other things. I felt like I had to fix this show and so I was a little more stressed about *Dracula* than maybe she was. She was good for me because she was calm. Very professional. If I didn't have her, I think I might have gone nuts. She stayed in my room all the time. She advised me to have a family. I think she could see that I was the kind of person to immerse myself in things and really care. Like, if the show wasn't working, it wasn't working. I kept caring and trying to fix or improve it. I think she knew it was what it was. She had a natural sense of wisdom at that time.

During rehearsals, how did you handle it when the show was obviously not coming together?
It wasn't obviously not coming together. We didn't have a set and we were supposed to have a lot of special effects. You can't really tell until the special effects come in, and the costumes. The set [pieces would disappear into the floor] and that meant that there were gaping holes on the stage. They never dealt with the fact that if we fell in them, we would die. Stephen Henderson, the man playing Van Helsing, says, "Melissa Errico saved my life." He lost his balance and I saw it and pulled the back of his jacket. I had to sing a whole song surrounded by holes that closed gradually. At some point I was to walk where a hole had been and I had to trust that that trap was closed. It was horrifying. I should have been pissed. I did workshops and workshops. I'm very good in a workshop. I'm good with the script on a music stand, making commitments and using my imagination. The workshop was good. It was a clear story. I didn't think it was going to be an epic disaster.

I always marvel at having to keep selling a show that you know isn't working.
We amused ourselves. We weren't tortured. Some of the stuff that's bad about *Dracula*, I found funny. Tom is a pretty funny guy and I had to lick blood that tasted like strawberry off his chest every night. I took great solace in my friendship with Kelli. And I believe I saw David Belasco's ghost [which is said to haunt that theater]! Crazy stuff was going on. Right before we opened, a pipe broke and the entire show was flooded. The fire department had to come and they were like, "David Belasco strikes again." I saw him near my dressing room,

walking into the mirror. And then in my room, I had turned the light off and I left. I forgot my coat and I went back into the room and someone turned on my lamp. It freaked me out. I was really calm. I got the coat, turned off the light, and I intended to close the door. I felt the door close behind me. I ran out of there.

After *Dracula*, you focused on motherhood for a bit. Three kids in two years!
I had Victoria, and then [I lost a baby, late term]. I had had an operation to take the baby out. Then I conceived the twins immediately. My body had advanced weight and I already had a stomach. I got pregnant on top of that body with twins. I was wrecked. That's when I started my charity. I began a mothers' community for pregnant women and new mothers, Bowery Babes. I got myself involved in social work.

In 2003, 2005, and 2006, at the Hollywood Bowl, you took on three separate shows, all famously played by Julie Andrews; *My Fair Lady, Camelot*, and *The Sound of Music*.
My Fair Lady was the first one and I absolutely loved John Lithgow. He's just so funny and fast. Quick mind. And Rosemary Harris was incredible as Mrs. Higgins. I was glad to revisit it, because, like I said, it wasn't a totally relaxed experience on Broadway. I was unencumbered by the complications of my Broadway production and the stops and starts and my relationship with Richard Chamberlain. Playing in that huge house with people who just love to play, I was really pleased to be able to just bring the fire. The laughs we got were crazy. At the Hollywood Bowl, people get the laughs first in the front, and then you hear the laughs go up the mountain. The timing for 20,000 people on a hill is a lot different. You have to wait for the whole mountain to get it. It was an incredible experience. I got my man pants. I looked like

"What Do the Simple Folk Do?" With Jeremy Irons in *Camelot*.
(James Higgins)

Chaplin. I loved Roger Daltrey, who played my dad. [I came out of an interview and he says,] "How'd it go darlin'?" I said, "It was great. They really just wanted to know what it was like to work with you." Which is true; they were asking questions about Roger because he wouldn't do interviews. He says, "Well, tell 'em I'm a really great shag." *Camelot* was bizarre because I didn't know I was pregnant. Nobody works as hard as Jeremy Irons. He wanted to be really, really good. We went to voice lessons together. He picked me up before rehearsals on his motorcycle and we would go up to Eric Vetro's house and take lessons. And then we'd go to rehearsal. The combination of the discipline and the motorcycle felt so right. You have to let go. I love that renegade energy I learned from Jeremy. [I figured out that] Guinevere is really a woman of appetite, not so much the lovely character [people think of]. One day we did a run through, then notes, and we had a break before the show. After the break, Jeremy turns to me and he goes, "Oh darling, we had our break. We should have had sex, but I forgot." He was so funny. *The Sound of Music* was a magical time. Victoria was a newborn. I was breastfeeding backstage, dressed like a nun. I was in a habit with my tits out. You can't make this up. "The Sound of Music" is a spiritual song for me. The hills are alive. I took that song really seriously. I've always wondered why that song is not mystical to everyone. I loved the opportunity to sing it coming down the mountain. [From the top of the Hollywood Bowl] you can't hear the orchestra [without a sound delay]. So I had to actually follow the visuals of the conductor and sing. Once you see the hands of the conductor, you just had to start. [I'd hear] the orchestra like two seconds later. As I came down, I got closer to the accuracy of the orchestra. I really enjoyed working with John Schneider. He was great.

In 2009, you came back to Broadway with *White Christmas*.
I had my figure back somewhat.

You looked fantastic!
That's because I'd made great friends with the costume maker. He was epic. He had dressed people like Rosalind Russell and he had every trick in the book for making your figure look good. Everything from widening the bodice to make the waist look smaller, or padding the hips. In my winter coat, I had huge pillows underneath. He said, "You'll look like a stick. They're never going to know." Richard Jay-Alexander came and said, "You should kiss that costumer on the mouth. You look like a million dollars." But I had been through hell and back. I had a little vertigo. I was very uncomfortable with the porch set. I used to feel like I was going to fall, so I used to hold the poles. I never really acted without holding something. I would go from one to another because my body had been through so much.

So why do the show?
The twins were eight months old or something. I was excited to give it a whirl. But I was definitely really vulnerable, not the Melissa that I had been—not strong and thin and overly beautiful. I'd been through a rough time. My body had changed; it had a different function. I was very, very humbled by what my body had to do to create children. I was a very different person when I auditioned for that show. I was nursing and I was caretaking for other people. I guess that's when I started to notice that my whole approach to things changed. Gone was the feeling of life or death about everything in the theater. Life or death was at home. Life or death was in the women at Bowery Babes. I was reaching out to find out the blood type of every child to help another child who needed that blood type. I was

literally like an operator. I killed myself for my neighborhood. This is before Facebook. People didn't know how to reach each other. I did it in my house. So Broadway be damned, I had other things to do. I had a different mission. [She tears up] I saw real life. I also needed to work really hard to learn how to be a mother. I think it was hard for my parents because they were very much used to seeing me as a star and then suddenly, I'm this mother with three little kids and my husband's all over the world trying to scramble money for us to live. So *White Christmas* was a whole different Melissa starring on Broadway. I had my first panic attack doing that show. I thought it was food poisoning. I didn't know. I had gone home [between shows] to feed the kids. I came back and people would say, "Did you nap?" Nap? I'd taken the subway all the way down to Soho, nursed twins, fed a cranky two-year-old, dealt with total mayhem, ate whatever was on the floor that they didn't eat, and then got back in time to do a Broadway show. I mean, I literally lived like that. I wanted to be with them. I didn't just check out. I had a panic attack and I didn't know what was going on. I'd never heard of a panic attack. Stage management had to take me outside at intermission to breathe. I took half an Ativan from someone and I did the show fine, and then I got some sleep. So that was humbling.

Were you able to enjoy the show at all?
Yes. I did my damnedest to do a good job and I had a lot of satisfaction that I'd done it. I never missed a show. To sing that score was great, that cast was great. Being back with Rob Berman [conductor of *Sunday in the Park*] was great. That's when Richard Jay-Alexander came into my life and [pushed me to do more cabaret]. Richard was a total champion. We put on some seriously good shows.

You were very much on a chanteuse track, doing cabaret and concert work until *Passion* in 2013.
Passion was great until I caught a cold. It was like the best thing ever. I worked my ass off to be ready and to know those songs. My body was, like, sick. I was really fit. I had the sensual confidence, I had curls for days, I was really ready. I love the music and I love [director] John Doyle. I think I carried with me a melancholy understanding of Clara's choices. She's a mother and she wants personal space. She wants to be with this man in this room. And that's enough—to have a small room where she can fuck this guy. To love and be loved and then go home. It's not enough for Giorgio. He accuses her of not giving enough. I was willing to be completely broken by it. The show demands that you live on the edge and I brought, I think, a melancholy understanding to a mother's choice. I was really, really, happy to get the part and I did everything John wanted. He has a real process. Everyone stays on stage and everyone listens to everyone. Everyone's in everyone's mind. Every time a piece of paper, a letter—because it's an epistolary musical, it's all letters—every time a letter is passed, every actor on that stage has to know that that letter is the most important focal point. Your energy is on this letter, whoever's reading it. I loved that. The communal obsession over focusing on the plot, but not leaving the stage much—I barely ever left the stage. Wonderful. John is a genius. I read *Julie* in my spare time, which was a novel that's referred to [in the play]. It's Fosca's book. It's an incredibly important book to understanding the women in that show.

John Doyle, I've been told, likes to rehearse individual beats again and again and again in immediate succession.

I loved the repetition. It's good for me because I have a lot going on in my head. So it gives me a chance to have like seven hundred rehearsals of the seven hundred ideas that could pass through Clara's mind. I loved the way it drained me of energy, and it made me more present. I loved working with Judy Kuhn. Judy is like dark chocolate to me. She's smart and centered and intellectual. I loved her performance. Judy played Fosca like a hungry, starved, rotting girl. She wasn't a big drama queen. I thought Clara was needy. Some people think she should just be played pretty, not needy, to contrast the neediness of Fosca. Well, I challenge that because if you're really a mother who wants sex with a soldier, you're taking chances. If you're risking divorce and losing your child, you're an edgy woman. I was happy to be back and I was overcome with gratitude to be in this little dressing room with Judy. I loved it. We were like shoulder to shoulder in that little room and it was cold. We had snow coming in under the door. I had bronchitis and that's when I hurt my voice. My voice was hoarse in the middle of a show. I was really coughing a lot but singing well, so I remember thinking, "I got this. I'm actually singing on a cold." But I was also crying and singing. I hemorrhaged a vocal cord. [My doctor] took me out of the show. I was pretty sure I'd just get over the cold and everything would resolve. I actually ended up never coming back. We had like five weeks left. I recovered from my cold and I had a vocal bruise around the corner of the vocal cord. It's like a sprained ankle in the world of sports. I was resting my voice and doing Reiki and praying. I didn't talk to my kids. I didn't open my mouth to my children. I was hugging them a lot. There were like eleven shows left and I was cleared to go back. I get a phone call from [my agent]. "They're letting you go. They terminated your Equity contract." But they didn't call me. I would have liked a phone call. I wrote to John. Nobody called me. Nobody made an effort at that time. The day that I got that news, I cried so hard. I was so sad and I felt really betrayed. The vocal cord bled again, merely from crying. The doctor said I broke the blood vessel. I mean, I cried really hard. I was devastated. So when even the tiniest capillary breaks twice, you need to get it fixed. I went and had surgery. I went to Mass General Hospital, to the guy who did Adele's voice. All of it was planned and overseen by Julie Andrews, through Tony Walton [Andrews's ex-husband]. I got fixed. It took a little bit of a process. And $26,000. It's the most expensive day of our life. All the stars you've ever seen in your whole life are on the wall in Mass General Hospital. Nobody wants you to know that they're on that wall. These things happen. If you are working 18,000 performances in your lifetime and you injure yourself twice, that's not so bad. It was a very difficult time and I was heartbroken. I blogged about it. I blogged about what goes on in your mind when you're separated from your art, why I love theater, what I would do for Sondheim, what Clara was struggling with, children and art. I was absolutely impassioned. It wasn't long after that *The New York Times* asked me to write for them. What's it like to be an actor? What goes on under the surface? I wouldn't be writing now if I hadn't done the blog. So hopefully I'll be able to write a book. If not, I'll be writing essays and things. In a weird way, I lost one voice and gained another. I got well but the show was done and I was really bruised. I felt like I [had given everything and] hadn't been cared for in return. You can't just cut someone loose and say, "you're not coming back." I don't know what happened. I've had meals with John Doyle since and we just move on. I think we have to be careful, though, about how we treat each other when we're down.

In *Passion*, "Love that fills every waking moment."
(Joan Marcus)

That first *New York Times* piece was about navigating the theatrical landscape as a forty-six-year-old ingenue.
I got the call and the editor-in-chief asks me, "How's your career going?" I said, "I just got asked to do *Finian's Rainbow* again. I am way too old for this!" And he says, "That's funny! Would you be willing to unpack that?" I did it. I'm not even sure if I took the part because of *The New York Times*. I may have taken the part on assignment! I felt the experience was grounded not only by the opportunity to write about my own aging, but the idea of the surface skin—green, black, older—what's the difference? We are who we are inside. It was very empowering to have the opportunity to organize that show in an essay in *The New York Times*. I was pleasantly surprised that Trump's election [which happened during the run] breathed new life into the piece because the country was going backward. So even though I felt like I was definitely not advancing my career by revisiting something that was safe, it suddenly became important.

In your writing, you really poke at what you've learned as a woman in the business.
Women actors are expected to show so much passion and confidence, but you also have to accept so much powerlessness in the everyday reality of it. There's so much powerlessness. I always thought that passion was power until recently. My instinctual reflex was to apologize. I've been inclined to present myself as a hot mess when, in fact, I possess a really accurate eye for folly and B.S. For example, in *High Society*, my instincts were very sound, but the creative team made decisions and I stayed out of it. I could see that affirming my intellect wasn't going to get me anywhere. I wanted to be liked. And I thought it was the way to move forward. I never had a hissy fit in my life, never raised my voice. I cried. I cried a lot. My reflex was to

turn myself into someone weak. The growth I needed to make was to transfer those tears into words and ideas and voice.

When you did *Do I Hear a Waltz?* at Encores! in 2016, you played your first fully mature woman.

I loved playing Leona. She was like my coming out party as a complicated person assessing choices she'd made. I brought something to Leona that I couldn't define. I felt all of her contradictions. She's kind of self-destructive. There's an edginess that I started to feel on stage and I didn't hide it. Leona is not the easiest person to be around. Maybe I'm not always, either. I feel like every character I've ever played … I feel like they're all me. I am Venus, the warm goddess who wants the little nerdy guy; I am Guinevere, who wants both men and who has a fantasy of romance in her life; I felt like I was Clara, who had to give up her child if she was going to go any further and wouldn't do that; I felt like Eliza, a learner, a student. Leona was where I could continue that instinct that all these women are me. And now I'm older and I've suffered. I'm ready to play those *Dear World* and *Grey Gardens* parts. I was so loaded up. I had so much to bring. I had no problem finding feelings, contradictions, charm, aggravation, sex, fantasy. "Do I hear a waltz?" What, is she nuts? You have to work with the idea that she's actually going to hear a waltz. Like, what is that? She's cuckoo. I felt like it was a new turn for me.

In 2018, you got still more complicated in *On a Clear Day You Can See Forever* at Irish Rep.

Daisy spends a lot of time as this other person. [The play depicts the character's past life as well as her present.] I didn't just play them as two separate characters. I was marrying them in my own mind. I saw one's losses as related [to the other]. I don't think all of that was on the page. I think Alan Jay Lerner was into past life regression therapy and far-out shit at that time. It was the 60s. He fucked so many women, he wanted to justify it. Somebody asked him, "Why do you keep getting married?" And he said, "It's just my way of saying goodbye." And he wrote "If Ever I Would Leave You!" He had eight wives! I didn't want that show to close. We were getting better every day. I've never been on such an upward line, like every single day. I got much more ridiculous by the end. I played the extremes more. I just got more free. Everyone did. We were making it great. We were getting there. I'm ready to handle a longer run now. My children are twelve; they're OK with me being around less. I have been asked to replace in a few shows but [until recently] I really couldn't do that with kids. Once your kids are in school, you want your nights. So I did television, concerts. I got way into the process to take over in *The Band's Visit*. Five callbacks, and then they closed the show. They gave me excellent coaching in Hebrew. I would have loved that. But to take over *Sweeney Todd* downtown for no money for eight shows a week, and they wanted a year contract? It's different at the Irish Rep. where they only want a few months. And the Irish Rep. doesn't do Tuesday nights, so you get a little bit more time with your family. As much as I love Broadway, and I do want to do more of it, I've found new work. I've found other avenues.

So what do you think you want now?

I came back into the business with a different fragility and vulnerability that happens from the way I experience motherhood. Now I feel so well restored and my children are doing so well. I am surrounded by three graces every day. I learned in my house to let go of perfectionism. I learned to allow things to be more ordinary. I used to want to improve every day. Everything could be improved, to be more wonderful. I've learned that's not a healthy way for children, and by extension, it's changed the way I work. I hold on less tightly to things. It allows room for failure; it allows room for exploration. It puts a premium on the effort and progress and action over perfectionism. That's something that I didn't know and I think that's why I was so hard on myself in *High Society*. I was such a perfectionist. I wanted to live up to my reputation from *One Touch of Venus*, which really had just been a lark. Suddenly I was goddess. OK. Then I wanted to do the right thing and make the right moves. Everything had a right and a wrong hovering over me. Parenting gave me a chance to repair myself and learn new patterns. I think I have come into the healthiest, happiest, time moving forward in my whole career. I thank my three graces for that. I've somehow managed to give them a belief that their flexibility in life is what matters more than their accomplishments. I feel like I've had a very happy kind of arc overall. I did have a sort of astounding early success. I was young. And I had an inevitable midcareer period of uncertainty. I feel like I found the right path. I'm at a point in my career now, starting to understand what I could bring. I rode the elephant. I did. I got here. My tombstone should say, "She loved what she did." And then, maybe on the back, "Oh. And she's still waiting for her Tony."

Alice Ripley

August, September, December 2020; February, March 2021

Chatting with Alice Ripley is a bit of a wild ride; she wanders off-topic frequently, and she knows it. It can be both charming as hell and equally maddening when the word count is tight. But the fact that Ripley never seems to feel rushed to get to the point or edit or censor whatever ideas our many talks conjure is not just endearing, it's at the root of what makes her great. She is, she says, like Kokopelli, the Native American deity. "He's got his hair going crazy, and you can't tell if he's playing sax or if he's dancing or if it's hair. It's like the image of the wild spirit of the artist. I feel like that was me."

Alice Ripley's early career consisted of ingenue roles that made the most of her blonde hair, mile-high cheekbones, and lithe figure. (She was a *Hee-Haw* girl in Nashville!) It's what she did with them that made her special. Look at Betty Schaeffer in *Sunset Boulevard*, a role that, on paper, is more plot device than character. Ripley filled her with an intelligence and wit that made her a truly formidable threat to Glenn Close's Norma Desmond. And then, as Violet Hilton in *Side Show*, Ripley doubled down, digging deep and bringing more of those same qualities to what would be her breakout role. As conjoined twins, she and Emily Skinner created performances so heartbreaking and so intrinsically connected, they were nominated for the first ever joint Tony award. In *The Rocky Horror Show*, she got to play with that ingenue image while also showcasing her other superpower: an uncommonly powerful rock and roll belt. But it was as Diana Goodman, a bipolar mother, in *Next to Normal* that Ripley achieved that all too rare alchemy of the perfect actor for the perfect role in the perfect moment. Ben Brantley, in his *New York Time*s review, called her "astounding," adding, "Ms. Ripley is giving what promises to be the musical performance of the season. Her achingly exposed-seeming face and sweet, rawness-tinged voice capture every glimmer in Diana's kaleidoscope of feelings." It was a Tony-winning performance that helped make *Next to Normal* a must-see show, and also made audiences profoundly uncomfortable. So real was Ripley that, to this day, people have trouble understanding that Diana and Ripley are, in fact, distinct from one another.

Do you remember when you knew you wanted to perform?
The Flying Monkey [in *The Wizard of Oz*] was the first time I was on stage in a musical with other kids. Everybody wants to be Dorothy, of course, but that's not me. That's my story. I'm not Dorothy. The answer to that big question is never as exciting as I want it to be. I just knew that it was my way into so many things: ways of discovering myself, coping, finding a vocation, finding a family. [Performing] was my ticket out. That's how you feel when you're a teenager. I just knew everything I didn't want to do, and it was everything else but this. I saw it as a way to be heard and have the floor. When you have ten brothers and sisters, you don't really get it very often. It's just part of the deal. My dad always used to say that we were the best show on earth. I wanted to be a real actress—Shaw, Shakespeare, Ibsen, Chekhov— those playwrights. But I would sing and then the room would get quiet and I liked that a lot. Singing feels like a psychic bath or something. It feels like a massage when you're really in the

"I will never leave you." With Emily Skinner (left) in *Side Show*.
(Photofest)

zone because you have to want to sing to make something happen. You have to want to sound beautiful to sound beautiful. So, to get to that place where you want to sing sometimes is the challenge. We have to be as ready as you can all the time.

In college, you majored in vocal performance, so by then you knew you were focusing on singing.
I thought, "Let me legitimize myself." I got a scholarship, and I got some loans. I was serious. And my family didn't get in my way.

After you graduated, you went to L.A.
I had this fantasy: Linda Ronstadt, moving there when she was eighteen, about to meet The Eagles—that's how I wanted to move to L.A. That wasn't how it went. I was like twenty-two, right out of college, and I had just gotten married, so it was the opposite of moving to L.A. to start a rock band. My husband was in the Navy, so, San Diego. I was always very serious about doing this, I just didn't know what the path was going to be. Nothing's ever going to stop me from expressing my art and being an artist. I know that. The marriage didn't last because he didn't know that. He didn't take it seriously. But I always knew that it was just going to be me. I always knew I would end up here.

Living in San Diego—that's how you got your Equity card at the La Jolla Playhouse? And that ultimately led to *Tommy*.
I worked as a singing telegram performer, just like Bette Midler in *Beaches* except you add a scooter on Highway 163, in tap shoes and fishnets. A construction site with nothing but concrete, me with the Hershey's Kiss and a champagne bottle. Shoes going click, click, click,

looking for the guy. I had an agent in San Diego, but I was calling the Equity hotline to learn about auditions. I was going to Los Angeles and standing on the sidewalk for open calls for three hours. You'd get there at 5:00 a.m, so you leave home at 2:00 in the morning. And I was doing that kind of thing because I figured, "If I'm going to do this, it's going to be now." Some things I make harder for myself than I need to. But when I'm doing hard work and I know that I'm going to get there, it feels great. I got my Equity card and I worked at every theater in San Diego: The Rep, the Lawrence Welk Resort Theatre, small little theaters, the college theaters, the Globe. But I couldn't get on the main stage at the La Jolla Playhouse. Remember, I wanted to do *Titus Andronicus*, *Romeo and Juliet*, and stuff like that. I got my Equity card in '88 and I moved to New York in '91. I started auditioning. Audition, audition, audition, audition. And then I got cast in *Tommy*. Once I moved to New York, La Jolla Playhouse finally wanted me. That's how the business works, kids. I mean, I was the same Alice that I had been a year before. So I found myself

Alice Ripley	
Tommy	Broadway, 1993
Les Misérables	National Tour, 1993; Broadway, 1998
Sunset Boulevard	Los Angeles, 1993
King David	Broadway, 1997
Side Show	Broadway, 1997
Li'l Abner	Encores! 1998
The Dead	off-Broadway, 1999; Broadway, 2000
The Rocky Horror Show	Broadway, 2000
Company	Washington, DC, 2002
Little Shop of Horrors	Coral Gables, FL, 2003
The Baker's Wife	Milburn, NJ, 2005
Next to Normal (Tony Award)	off-Broadway, 2008; Broadway, 2009; National Tour, 2010
American Psycho	Broadway, 2016
The Pink Unicorn	off-Broadway, 2019
Baby	off-Broadway, 2019

back in San Diego. It was really, really amazing. One of the golden moments in my life. I met people like Michael Cerveris and Norm Lewis—these are like the best people that I know. The show ended up transferring and we had to re-audition. That's how it works, and I think that's how you put together a fantastic cast—you make them jump through the hoops again. [I found out that] the ensemble is a really powerful place to be. You learn so much more about yourself because of the things that are demanded of you. The kind of ensemble work that I did in *Tommy* set me up for being able to do *Side Show* and *Next to Normal* as far as just physical endurance. To be able to run offstage and make way for somebody who's coming by with a clothesbasket, and to take the stairs two steps at a time, that's all part of what makes it that beautiful illusion that you see onstage in the light. [I understudied Mrs. Walker.] I was always on for the role because Marcia Mitzman.... It was the beginning of the Rosco Fog story; the fog that they used to use in *Les Mis* and *Phantom*, it deposits itself on your cords and some people were having lots of physical problems. That's all been worked out, but back in the day, it was a thing, and Marcia was having trouble. I really hope I get to play Mrs. Walker again. *Tommy* is a perfect show. It's right up there with *Next to Normal*. The action is led by the music. You just jump on it, and it takes you like a magic carpet ride.

What do you remember about that rehearsal room?
My [director] Des McAnuff imitation is, "You guys, you guys, you guys need to just focus, focus!" He's always rubbing his hands on his face. I had never worked with Wayne Cilento

before, our choreographer. When he won his Tony, I cried. I was so excited and happy for him. If anybody ever deserved it…. He kicked my ass. He kicked our collective asses. You don't stop moving for the whole first act when you're in the ensemble. I used to look forward to playing Mrs. Walker because it was like a vacation. The swings—they work harder than anybody else. They could totally do anything that anybody else does. I was the first one to leave the show. Partially because Des wouldn't cast me as Mrs. Walker. He thought I looked too young. Marcia was perfect in that role. She got a Tony nomination, which I thought was amazing because she was hardly ever there. [I went on a lot] and I was getting some good recognition. Tom Flynn—he's one of those swings that does everything—said to me, "Do you want to play the role, or are you happy being the understudy?" I said, "I want to play the role." And he said, "Well then, you've got to nip this in the bud. You can't ever accept another understudy role." And I realized that the people that stand by or understudy are just as right for the role. They could easily do the role. I didn't want to be somebody who wasn't allowed to play the role because I was such a good understudy. So I decided to leave the show.

Before we leave *Tommy,* what can you say about singing a rock score like that on Broadway?
You have to rock out. You don't think about looking attractive. Its balls to the wall and that's really the only way that you can do rock music. The piece needs you to get a little crazy. After a while your ear starts to be affected by it. By the end of the week, we were all hoarse. We all had to learn how to pull it in a little bit—not just the singers but the orchestra and the sound guys. I think that now we're really hitting our stride with that. It's a completely different way of making music on a Broadway stage. Linda Ronstadt taught me how to belt. Listening to Elaine Paige and Patti LuPone and Laurie Beechman—I tried to copy that. I had never heard anybody sing like that. The constant amping up is not necessarily rock and roll. No, it doesn't have to be in a dog's realm of hearing. It has to be emotional. But if we have men writing rock and roll, they're writing in their range. This is my theory of why everything is so high. It doesn't have to be high to be emotional. Just because we're on stage doesn't mean we have to belt all the time.

Although now, it seems that that's become the expectation of leading ladies even if it's not a rock score. The ladies of *Wicked* or *Waitress* are expected to sing their faces off.
That's true. You have to find your own sound. We all learned the hard way how to conserve and not over-sing, how to recover, how to get yourself back to a state of whole to do the next show. *Next to Normal* really perplexed me to no end, and I never really figured it out. But if I ever went back and played that role now, I would know how to do it. I have grown so much and I've been through so much. My heart is so much stronger, my instrument stronger. I think that it would be an incredible experience to play her now because I wouldn't have to do as much. [Ripley did indeed play the role again, in Barcelona in 2022.] It did feel like getting hit by a bus, and if you get hit by a bus eight times a week, by the time the eighth show comes around, how do you put those pieces back together? We need some vocal rest, which takes time.

It was a bold move for you to decide to leave *Tommy.*
I mean now, to think about leaving a hit Broadway show right after the Tonys … I would never do that. If that job is going to keep going, you don't quit. But Tom Flynn—I took him seriously and I think he was right about it. It was right in line with what I always thought about myself. I didn't know how good I had it. I really didn't know how good it would have

been to be employed by a Broadway show for a whole year. But I was leaving to go play a dream role of mine: Fantine in *Les Misérables*. I left *Tommy* to go play a role on the road, which seems kinda crazy, but it was Fantine. I loved it. It was my first time being on the road. I love traveling. I love seeing the different audiences. When I came back, I got cast in *Sunset Boulevard*. It all just came full-circle because I played Norma last fall [in Massachusetts]. I'm more like Norma, maybe, than any character that I've ever played. People are always surprised. They think that I'm like Diana Goodman [in *Next to Normal*], but I don't have anything in common with Diana. She's an architect, married, mother of two. She lost a child. Tries to kill herself several times. Takes pharmaceuticals all day every day for years and years. Doesn't really communicate with people. Doesn't really know herself. Doesn't really know her husband. And bipolar. I'm not any of those things. But if you look at Norma, everything about her is like me. She lives alone. She wears sunglasses inside the house. There's a guy in the picture but he's in the periphery somewhere in the shadows. I want to be a star at all costs. It's all about me all the time. At the end of the play when Norma goes in that free fall in the Salome outfit, that was the easiest thing I've ever done.

Tell me about auditioning for *Sunset Boulevard*.
Judy Kuhn was playing Betty Schaefer in Los Angeles [with the pre-Broadway company. Kuhn got pregnant and decided not to continue]. I'm her fan. I'll never shrug that. I always have to kind of act normal around her. We're friends now, but before I came to New York I was listening to her on the *Les Mis* and *Chess* albums and I was mesmerized by her voice. So anyway, the audition process was just like any other. I would go in and sing, I had a couple of callbacks. It was one of those Last Supper auditions, meaning there are twelve people on the other side of the table. Then I was being flown to Los Angeles because that's where the company was at the time. I auditioned in a studio in the Shubert Theater, where the show was playing. All cement. No windows. Andrew Lloyd Webber is sitting right in the middle of the table with Trevor Nunn and David Caddick, the musical director. I sang "Unexpected Song" [by Lloyd Webber]. When I finished, he stood up and applauded. It was just one of those moments where you go, "This is great! Wow!" I got goosebumps right now, thinking about it. I will never forget that moment. I went back to my room at the hotel across the street and flopped down on my bed. There were mirrors on the ceiling. I called my agent and he told me I got the part! And then I got to go see the show that night. I have been asked several times about moments where you [saw a performance and] were never the same after. I think I've maybe had three or four moments like that in my life. When I saw Glenn Close play this role from the fourth row of the orchestra … captivating. There was magic happening every time she's played it. I saw the revival and it was different, but it was just as amazing. It's changed because she's changed and the character changes with her. I'll never forget the effect of the house coming down after the opening. Sidebar: when Elaine Paige took over the role on Broadway, they lowered the bannister on the staircase [Paige is significantly shorter]. We had to have a put-in rehearsal because the bannister was now lowered for Elaine! It was just a golden little bubble of time. I got engaged right after *Sunset* started. I took my vacation for two weeks to get married and while I was gone, the show closed. I was there for the whole run.

Let's talk about rehearsing *Sunset*.
We were at 890 Broadway. It was one of those big, big rooms. Bigger than the stage. That's what it needs to be so you can tape out the whole stage and have a green space for people to

actually sit in chairs and at tables, not in the hallway on the floor, which is what we do now because there's no room. The art was really upheld because of the space. It really starts with the rehearsal space. And that was part of what made it feel huge once we got on the set and saw what [designer] John Napier had done. I think that the piece is phenomenal. Andrew Lloyd Webber comes up to me after opening night, bows, looks me right in the eye: "Bravo." I just felt like, "This is why I did everything I did up until now. Andrew Lloyd Webber felt like I told his story." That's what I think my function is now. The two years at *Sunset* were relatively uneventful. I was so happy to be a working actor in a hit show. Alan Campbell and Glenn Close and George Hearn—these people were amazing and perfect for me to look up to and try to come up to their level. I feel like I got my legs in *Sunset Boulevard*.

Did you watch Glenn Close leading a company?
Yeah! Oh my God, yes! Glenn and Elaine and Betty Buckley, they all had their own way of doing Norma and they were all terrific.

So backstage, and keeping the company morale up . . .
It was really George and Alan. They were the hosts. George's door was always open. If you walked in, it was never the wrong time. That was the atmosphere backstage and everybody contributes to it. George was one of the major leaders of the tone, how everybody conducted themselves backstage. And Glenn—she was there before everybody else. She showed me how to be a leader for sure. I'm not sure that I'll ever live up to what I think she is. But I've done my best to be how Glenn embodies a leader. She's tough, [but] she is the most gentle, gentle soul.

You worked with three megawatt stars. . . .
I mean to me they're all different parts of Norma Desmond, all different sides of her. But when Betty Buckley played the role, something happened, something shifted. Betty was Norma; Norma was Betty. Watching Glenn, watching Betty, watching Karen Mason, they all stuck to me. They all contributed together to help me become more real. But it was different with Betty Buckley. Maybe it's because she approached the role the way that I would. You just devour it and then you live inside it. It's you. I didn't realize it back then, but *Next to Normal* taught me that I'm a method actor. You live the role all the time. Your work is about beating back the role and carving out yourself again, re-establishing that boundary all the time. I'm getting better and better at that, but I didn't even know I was still living Diana's life the next morning, you know? And I think that's maybe how Betty does it. I don't know. I think that Betty and me and Norma are a lot alike in a lot of ways. I'm honored to be in that category, whatever that energy is. That bright, chaotic energy. My job is to keep it [together] because Norma doesn't do that and look what happens. They were all really good and they all had different approaches and I would steal as much as I could.

Tell me about rehearsing with Trevor Nunn.
I wish I could go back because I would do everything at my highest level all the time, which I didn't. I was really focused on my relationship and life outside of rehearsal as much as rehearsal. I was getting married, I was starting a band, I was writing music. [If I could] I would go back and get there early every day, know when to shut up, when to make suggestions and then shut up again, be the first one off book, and have awesome opening night presents early!

Are you saying that you didn't know professionalism?

It's not that I didn't take the work seriously. It's that I was still as concerned about what I wore to rehearsal as anything else. It's just that level of appreciation and regard for the actual work process. I've changed a lot since then. I should have gotten to the Rainbow Room earlier on opening night. I showed up really late and people were already gone. The person who did my hair and makeup took too long. That's who I'm blaming. But now I would just go with a bare face like Glenn would. I wouldn't worry about that. Sutton shows up at the Tonys with a ponytail and no makeup. Every opening night, you walk in and you spend the entire three hours trying to get to your family. When we came in the door for *Side Show*, it was all flashes going off. It was like Hollywood. My waist was [tiny], and I was wearing this Chanel dress, one of my favorites I've ever borrowed, and I had jewelry. My mother took me by the hands and she's just crying and crying, and she says, "I can't believe you're mine." I felt so happy because that's who I always wanted to be for my mother. She saw me as a star that night. I can't ask for much more than that. I grew up in the suburbs, but I walked around barefoot on the farm in Ohio. Big city was not something that I ever even knew. And I ended up coming here because I decided you have to be here to work with people that you want to work with. Right. Because they all come here. But I was a country girl. I was barefoot and a tomboy. I love to joke, but it's serious: I didn't have my own socks till I was in my twenties. And my mother had that dream, too, to be a star. I didn't have kids on purpose because I wanted to get down to me right away. I didn't have time or support to do it any other way except to just get right to the center of what I needed to realize about myself. Part of why I was doing it was so that my dad and my mother could see me do it. I didn't want to do it through a kid or anything else. I wanted to do it for me. [Anyway] I didn't really realize what a foundation that show built for me. And it was the longest run I've been in on Broadway. Two years. There was a foundation that was built throughout every square foot of my life, and that felt really good. And I felt like I was ready for the next big task, which would be *Side Show*. Halfway through the *Sunset* run, the first summer, I double-dutied shows, rehearsing the *Side Show* workshop during the day. My husband was on the road at the time, so luckily I didn't have to take care of anybody but my cat. I just put everything toward the work. Doing those two together galvanized something in me that was really good. *Sunset* left me feeling hungry to show everybody how deep I can go. Little did I know what was coming. Tom Kitt told me that when he saw me in *Side Show* while he was a student at Columbia, he decided to write *Next to Normal* for me.

After *Sunset* closed, you did *King David* for a week.

Talk about luxurious! When you're doing a Disney show, it doesn't get any better than that. I got to share a dressing room with Judy Kuhn. She's super cool. Every single time she got out onstage, it was perfect. She has this luminous thing going on. Judy's up there in the dressing room with a transistor radio and one of those little ear buds from Radio Shack—this is before WiFi or anything—and she's listening to the Mets, going, "Oh, God, oh, God, oh, crap, oh...." And she had to stop listening because she had to go onstage. I was like, "I just love this! This is so New York!"

After *King David*, you were waiting for *Side Show* to come together?

I was doing a lot of workshops. I was doing my band. I was starting to work on some songs for an album called *Everything's Fine*. We were just waiting by the phone [for *Side Show*]. That feeling where you wait up all night for somebody and they never show? Where are they, they said they'd be here. That kind of feeling.

And then it finally got the green light. Rehearsals start . . .
I have never had a more difficult rehearsal period. We worked our asses off. Starting from trying to look alike. Emily Skinner and I are not the same height. We have different shoulders. We have different hips in different places. But people were convinced we were twins. That was a lot of work. Getting our weights to try to be together. . . . We shared a dressing room. It didn't make any sense to spend half hour [before the show] getting ready separately [to be joined together for the night]. It was perfect. We got to sit back-to-back, put on our makeup . . . even though it wasn't social hour, it was about being in the same room with her. Handling the score and the movement was unlike anything I've ever done. I've never been attached to anybody before, and they move differently. For example, there's a scene where we're fighting, and we're pulling each other around. We practiced who initiates a move. Why would you move first or why would I? You make all those decisions along the way because those little connective tissues pieces—no pun intended—those are the pieces that make the audience go, "Wow!" People still think the costumes were connected. They weren't.

So you and Emily approached the work similarly from the beginning?
Oh, yeah. The dynamic established itself early on. She's like my sister. I'm really grateful that she's still in my life because when I sing with her, I become my best self. I sound at my best. I think that we're in each other's life for a good reason, for a lifelong reason, and we have more to do together. That connection was there early on, and I was so grateful for that because we became a united front. But after eight hours of sweating up against the left side of someone's body, as sexy and amazing as she is, at the end of the day it was like, "See ya!" People want to think that we'd hang out all the time, but no, there was no way we would have survived if we did that. Time away is good. Onstage, it looked so casual but it was so sculpted. We were creating art with the way we held our bodies. It was true stagecraft. And it's because of the vision of Bobby Longbottom, our director and choreographer. Gregg Barnes's costumes were absolutely crucial to our performances. If we didn't have them, we wouldn't have been able to deliver the same performance. Bobby Longbottom basically would not let up until we looked identical. Getting there was really intense. Bobby choreographed The Rockettes. They are so perfectly precise, right? He [could be in] the back row and notice if my thumb wasn't flat against the back of my hand. And he's right. You do it and make it work. Those little things are the reason why people thought that we were twins, but getting to that point was real discipline. It was good for me. It heightened my awareness of that kind of thing. You have to always imagine that the audience is smarter than you and they can see everything. There are so many things we can do with our bodies if we really want to. Bobby made us look like dancers. He made us look like we were the real thing.

Did being "joined" and having to lean into that hip screw up your body at all?
Yeah! As a matter of fact, Emily and I both went to a guy, Ted Dugas—I called him Master Ted—and my God, I've had a lot of body work done and nobody ever did it like him. But the physical part of that show didn't beat me up. I felt challenged. It pushed me to what I was capable of doing. [But the many, many costume changes], and the numbers were full-on! At

the end of "Leave Me Alone," you back up and these panels come in [to block you from the audience. If you move two inches to the side, you'd be seen]. But each of us had three wardrobe people, six people on stage with us, behind these panels as we do a quick change. Three people strip her, three people strip me. Your job is to not do anything. You have to let them do it. You try to do something they'll (slaps her hand) and go, "Would you stop it? Stop trying to button your own shirt!" Everything's taken off—your wig, your costume, your jewelry, your shoes. And then everything is put on. It was pretty scary to be [changing] in the middle of the stage. You have to learn how to let those professionals [dressers] do what they need to do and not get in their way. And it's a matter of tick, tick, tick, tick, and then we're in the next scene. Three people each! Even though that's not something that you see ... that's teamwork! That's a skill that you have to learn and you only learn it by doing it. You get better and better at all that protocol. I got to have Norm Lewis and Hugh Panaro singing to my face. It doesn't get any better than these guys singing to your face. It was just heaven whenever Norm would sing "You Should Be Loved."

The show got great reviews but no audiences.
It wasn't about the show, it was about how people regarded the show. We were in trouble before previews, when the very first little piece of publicity came out in *New York Magazine*. It said, "Coming up this fall: *Side Show*. Not for the squeamish." I knew at that moment. And everyone knows that the poster is the most important thing before the show opens. It's the only thing there is. There had to be a little bit more money to put something else on the poster besides a stock photo of the back of someone's head. We got the best reviews of the season in *The Times* in a season where *The Lion King* and *Ragtime* opened. I read them all. None of those reviews were up [in front of the theater]. That was the hardest part of all because we were beautiful.

You received a joint Tony nomination.
I didn't know if we were going to get noticed at all, because we had closed. The Tony nomination felt like when you're running a marathon and people put their hands out [for high fives]. Natasha Richardson won for *Cabaret* and she should have. She was mind-blowing. So, we didn't win but it didn't really matter. I still felt just as good as if I had won. Once you get the actual award ... I can't ever complain about not being recognized or validated for my work. I'm so grateful because lots of other people deserve them. *Side Show* put me on a new level; she's an actor. That was major. It was a happy phase of my life.

Did you see the revival?
It wasn't *Side Show*. They made some structural changes, which were, I think—I'll come right out and say that they were bad—they were the wrong choices. They bring in Houdini, and Houdini gets his own song? What the fuck does Houdini have to do with the Hilton sisters' story? They should have asked us. We were the ones that actually saw the audience's response and experienced the show being received. When I went to see the revival, it was tough. I wanted to be there as an example of how to conduct yourself. It wasn't easy to go because that show wasn't like any other show I've done. It really felt like a relationship. When the show closed and I heard that people were doing it all over the place in different productions, it was like your lover is gone and you hear he's screwing everybody all over the world. People might roll their eyes at how dramatic that is, but that is how it felt. It was very personal. When I

went to the revival, I had to get some therapy first to go there with an open heart. And I did. I enjoyed it. It felt like I was watching my kids put on the show for me. I felt honored. But it wasn't *Side Show*. It boggles the mind how actors are underestimated as contributors. We are the people at the center of the frickin' piece. We know what this piece is. Why didn't you ask us? I was so pissed. I was so hurt. Of course I appreciate the actors and what they were doing. I was clapping for them. They were kind and as lovely as can be. But I think the original production was perfect. It just didn't get enough attention. I don't think there was anything wrong with it. It didn't need to be fixed at all.

After *Side Show* . . .

I took a little bit of a breather moment, going, "Where am I right now?" I was really liking how I was getting more auditions and people were taking me more seriously as an actor. But right after the show closing, I was like, "I gotta do something and ride on this a little bit." I had always looked up to Judy Kuhn, and she had put out a solo album. I wanted to do an album of standards and Emily and I . . . there was just so much magic happening when we sang together. I called the producer of Judy's album, Bruce Kimmel. We made "Duets," the first album [of two with Skinner]. People love that. That was my mother's favorite album. She loved the pairing of me and Emily. You know, people still call me "Emily." I did a production of *Clybourne Park* at Long Wharf and the reviewer called me "Emily Skinner." She wasn't in it! It used to really bug me because—middle child. I hated when people mistook me for one of my siblings. If somebody confused Emily for me, she'd just go, "Thanks," and sign my name. Anyway, after that I was just industrious about auditioning, trying to make ends meet, doing the New York thing. I knew that something else was going to come up.

You were asked to step into *Les Mis*.

They asked me if I wanted to rotate in for a year. "Yes!!!!" It was the perfect balm in so many ways right after *Side Show*. There I was, playing that role and hearing the music every night and basically killing it. I won't say this about any other role I've ever played, but Fantine . . . I'm perfect for that role. I get her. I was really happy. You know, you wash your face five times every show? First you put on regular, pretty girl makeup base, and then you immediately get it all dirty. That's your first look. Then you take all that off and you put on horror makeup, all dirty, and then take that off. And then you wash your face and you put on death makeup with hollowed-out cheeks. You die and then you wash all that off. Then you're barefaced with just dirt. You're a bullet boy. You spend most of the show like that. And then when everybody dies on the barricade, you go off and wash your face and put on a pretty girl face again. And then at the end of the show, you have to wash your face again. So after a while you realize you have to use Noxema because it doesn't cause any damage. You don't need to worry about all the other extra fancy stuff. Noxema. My last entrance, which is [singing] "Take my hand, and lead me to salvation . . . ," that part of the show is so low [vocally], "and you will be with God. . . ." To have that part be a beautiful vibrato sound is the challenge. You've spent the whole show belting at the top of your range. I'd stand stage right waiting for my entrance in my white gown and I'd go like this [massages her throat, attempting to physically place her larynx]. Betty Buckley taught me to do this, to just gently ease the larynx down to make sure that it's low enough to sing those low notes. You get one shot and it's the crucial moment of the show. You don't want to have a little frog down there. It worked every time. When I didn't do that, [the sound] would drop out.

You went from the gloom of *Les Mis* to the silliness of *Li'l Abner* at Encores!
That was a perfect role because I was still able to play the ingenue, but it was funny. It was really fun to be funny. *Li'l Abner* was all about Lea Delaria for me. There's so much mutual respect there and it started with that show. We love to sing together. It was really fun. Burke Moses played Li'l Abner and he was perfect. How could anybody be that hunky? Julie Newmar was in the cast playing the role she originated! I remember her walking up the stairs to the dressing rooms and saying, "My thighs are going to get huge." Cady Huffman carried a live baby pig on stage, like the size of a puppy. She's standing backstage, waiting to go on, and she says, "The pig just shit on me. What are you gonna do." That was a blast. Kathleen Marshall's Sadie Hawkins ballet was the whole reason to see that show. So good! I used to just hunker down in the corner and sit on the linoleum and watch everybody do that dance because it was incredible. We need more of that. I want to see dancers telling stories with their bodies and faces. So gifted. I felt so grateful to Kathleen for what she has committed her life to. People like her and Bob Avian and Susan Stroman, Jerry Mitchell, those people that just bring out that physical story. It seems to be not as common as it used to be, and I want to see more of it. I would never say I'm a dancer because it doesn't show enough respect to the people that are actually motherfucking dancers. I'm an actor who can make you believe I dance.

And then came *The Dead*.
I was so excited about that audition because it was at Playwrights Horizons. A smaller theater is my favorite place to work. I enjoy it more when I can see the audience and they can really see what I'm doing. The piece took place in Dublin, Ireland, at the turn of the last century and I have Irish roots, so to me, it was like I was playing my grandmother's mother. Richard Nelson was the director/playwright and I think that he got me right away. Most of what happened [to my character] in *The Dead* was unsaid, but it was huge. It was like the hidden part of an iceberg. Christopher Walken is one of my favorite actors, and once we started working together, I became obsessed with him. I went back and I watched everything that he'd ever done all over again. Once he realized that I was his audience, he was doing stuff for me all the time, trying to crack me up. He wore sweat pants to rehearsal and he would pull out the waistband and look down his pants and say, "Did you fuck my wife? I'm asking you, did you fuck my wife?" He doesn't even look up to see if I'm laughing. He just walks away. I live for this. Christopher Walken's doing racy jokes just for me! I used to sit in the wings and watch him. Free acting lessons! During the first week, Stephen Gabis, the dialect coach, gives us all little cards and cassette tapes. We're all hanging out in the green room and Chris is standing in the doorway, listening. We're talking about how we're excited for the dialects and he says, "They don't really expect me to speak in an Irish accent, do they? It's not like I'm going to fool anybody. I mean everybody knows I'm not Irish." We're all thinking, "He's got to be kidding." He was serious. He never did an Irish accent! That is spilling the tea but it's the truth and it's hilarious.

You were also sharing the stage with Sally Ann Howes and Marni Nixon.
Yeah! Talk about people that you can look up to! Women who have lived through so much! They are theater people. There's that texture of artistry that they carry with them. And they had chops! I loved being in the room with both of them. And Blair Brown? To be in awe of somebody.… It's an incredible feeling. Stephen Spinella! I was also looking up to him.

Everybody was really giving some good stuff in that show. The piece was really beautiful. That's my kind of show. It's mostly about what's not said. In the dining room scene, I'd watch Christopher Walken giving a speech and I was just gone. That was the most incredible acting experience I've ever had on stage. My back was to the audience so I was completely immersed in the situation. I felt so connected and it was mostly because I didn't have to say anything. Because then you can say anything you want internally. You can change it every day. It was such a sense of freedom.

And you were back onstage and sharing a dressing room with Emily Skinner again.
In that dressing room—the night that Elaine Stritch came to the show, we hear that she's coming backstage. You're like, half undressed, pin curls, in our very unglamorous dressing room with banquet chairs and old carpet. She blows into the room. Just like you would think, she was wearing a white men's shirt and black leggings and a trench coat. She just breezes in, past Christopher's room. I'd never met her. She sweeps in and in one movement, as she's saying, "Do you mind if I use your bathroom? Oh, what the hell, I'll just do it right here. I can't believe I made it through without passing out. I almost had a diabetic attack...." [As she is speaking] she puts her foot up on a chair, takes out a little alcohol swab, stabs herself in the thigh with a syringe, right through the pantyhose. The whole thing happens in like six seconds. I swear to you I am not exaggerating. You can see the color come back in her face, and then the introductions begin. "Hi, I'm Elaine. That was great. That was great." And she was gone. She didn't make it into the actual restroom. Christopher used to try to give us all these weird gifts that he would get from people. Like a pair of underwear that had [a prosthetic penis] attached to it. He's like "Do you want this?" "Um, no, I don't think I can use that. Maybe ask Emily." He's probably thinking, "I thought you were Emily." He would walk around the hallway in his tight black Fruit of the Looms. He would wander into the hallway in his underwear, stand in his doorway, then wander back inside. The piece itself really stirred the actor in me. There was a beautiful bubble that we were in. I felt like I was playing in a very safe place. The audience for *The Dead* needed to be really still and focused, really listening, and that's what they were doing. That makes you feel safe. I thought it was beautifully adapted. There's some real craftsmanship coming through. Molly was one of my favorite roles I've ever played. It was a really fun place for me to explore my inner monologue as an actor in front of an audience. And it was fun to explore a new relationship with Emily onstage because now I could see her whole face! I could see her walk away from me. There were a lot of things that we tried that were cut. You can always tell the song they're going to cut because it's the one they rehearse over and over and over. They are never satisfied. And then it's cut and you're like, "We just spent a week rehearsing this! OK, that's fine. Whatever." Actually, you do get over it because whatever you work on, if you've integrated it as an actor, even if it's cut you still remember it. The body remembers and it colors how you feel. There was a lot of that going on with *The Dead*. I love the experience of hammering out a new piece. It is kind of excruciating in a way, but it's the best. We had a beautiful set that transported you to another place in your imagination. It was just enough, but not too much. I had a Paul Huntley wig. It doesn't get better than that. Those final layers add the magic. Remember the tracing paper coloring books we had as kids? And you could look at a picture in layers? It's like that. All the layers that come together to make a performance. There is so much artistry of so many people involved.

What about your makeup? I mean, you paint your own face once a run gets going, but how do you arrive at the right look? Does someone do it for you to start?
This is the blurred line between what you bring as an artist to the role and what everybody provides for you. The wig is that, too. With Molly Ivers, he just copied my hair and then put it up so it looks like the same coloring, the same hair line. A person like David Bryan Brown or Paul Huntley, they know how to look at you and they know what your color palette is. They know how to make a wig that's going to look like it's your hair. They do it by hand. Makeup—most actors will probably take a class in school. You'll probably learn how to do a basic face, make the most of your best features and how to play down others. Then you're actually doing a job and somebody might give you makeup and brushes, everything you need. For a show like *Les Mis*, they give you the dirt, they show you how to do it, and they give you the wipes to take it off. And then there's what you do on your own with makeup. When you're a woman, you're used to doing that. Maria Verel designed the makeup for *Side Show* and she taught us. We had to age as the show went on. Not to look older, just more sophisticated. With *Next to Normal*, nobody really wore any makeup. I tried, but by halfway through the show I'd have cried it all off. We also used our own hair for *Next to Normal*. I don't think that's fair to the actor. Because now it's my job to make my hair look consistent every day and I didn't want that burden. I'm not a hair stylist, I'm an actor. In *American Psycho*, they plopped wigs on our heads and I'm like, "Where did this come from? A mohawk? No one told me I'd be wearing a mohawk." Don't you think that has something to do with how the character moves across the stage?

Take me back to makeup. So you have your idea about what the character looks like. Do you show up at costume parade [the first time the director and creative team see the cast in their costumes] with your idea of her look and then they tweak?
With *Sunset Boulevard*, there was a makeup designer and when we came to the wig fitting, we got all this makeup and brushes in a Ziploc bag. Your kit to do Betty Schaefer. He took about 25–30 minutes to do half of my face as Betty and he took a Polaroid of it [for my reference]. It was my job to do the other side. You have a palette and he shows you how to use tools. I was starting to see my face as a canvas. You start to lose the personal feelings you have about your face. You can do a lot of things to enhance the story with makeup.

After *The Dead* closed, you were cast in *The Rocky Horror Show*.
It was a kind of a wild ride with *Rocky*. I've never been in a show where the audience was encouraged to get wild. I used to think of the audience as the other cast member that you don't meet until the show. But as an actor when people are yelling at you … it's a process. That's the show. I was in my underwear onstage. So I ran six miles a day, six days a week. I had that baseline of Susan Sarandon's performance in the movie. She rocks. She didn't approach things in the regular way or safely. She wasn't the typical ingenue. [Director] Christopher Ashley is just such a fun person. He's got an infectious laugh and a great sense of humor. Jarrod Emick played Brad. He's a dreamboat. He was like my big brother and I love him. We had a great time. He taught me how to be funny in certain ways. I was definitely trying to find my footing. It was really hard not to yell back at the audience. But hearing somebody call you "slut" for a year starts to weigh on you. Water being shot in my face while I am singing. There

were a couple of times onstage when I was concerned about our safety because it was unpredictable. I am not trying to detract [from the audience participation]. That's the territory. But there was always a question mark: what's going to happen? It was a great company. We all got along really well. It was a good run.

And then, in 2002, you played Amy in *Company* as part of The Kennedy Center's Sondheim Celebration.

I did well with that role but I would like to go back and do it differently. It was a little one-note. Sometimes I can look back on things I've done, and I can say, "That's fine, but it might have been better if I had diced up a little bit more." Meaning more textured, more feeling or emotion coming out of the character. You only have so much rehearsal

I am surprised to hear you say that because yours was one of the most heralded performances from the entire Celebration.

It got a lot of buzz, yeah. The role is one of those roles. I'm not really trying to deflect my participation or my work. I thought it was a great show and it was cast with wonderful people. But it's one of those roles that, when it's well cast and it's a good production and you let the actor do what the actor wants to do, which is what Sean Mathias did ... I remember stopping the show with the number. The audience would just applaud and applaud and applaud and applaud. It was the longest applause I've ever heard. It was really great. Later that year I was asked to perform the number at The Kennedy Center Honors for Elizabeth Taylor. There I was, back in D.C., with my wedding dress and veil. When you sing for something like that, you sing to a track. It's not a live orchestra. The beginning of "Getting Married Today" is a vamp and when Amy wants to, she starts singing: "Pardon me, is everybody there? Because if everybody's there I want to thank you all for coming to the wedding. I'd appreciate you going...." On "appreciate," that's when the chord changes. So, with a track, you don't know for sure if you're with the music until that chord change. [A live orchestra would follow the performer's lead.] You wouldn't know you were off until it was too late. I was so terrified. Paul Simon's in the audience. James Taylor. Elizabeth Taylor. [Not to mention the president]. It was one of the scariest things I've ever done as a performer and that's saying a lot. Thank God I didn't fuck it up. Then when I finished, you don't get to enjoy it because you're like, "Thank God that's over!" I was in the staircase, going down to the dressing rooms, in my Amy outfit, my adrenaline going, sweating and crying, going, "Why do I put myself through this?" I hear somebody coming up the stairs and it's James Taylor with his guitar. There's nobody else around. He goes, "Hey, that was you just now on stage, wasn't it?" I was like, "James Taylor just watched me performing something and I didn't screw it up!" I just managed to nod. And then I blurted out, "I know every word to every one of your songs!" I had to get that little fan girl moment in there!

What can you say about rehearsing with Sondheim?

He walked in while I was rehearsing "Getting Married Today." I was hanging upside down from the counter. I was going through a phase of "try everything." Afterwards he came up to me and he had one note. He said, "Just sing the words." He's right, of course. Looking back on it, I could have done less. I still appreciate that note. I would like to go back and revisit *Company* someday and play Joanne.

Not getting married in *Company* at The Kennedy Center.
(Joan Marcus, courtesy of the Kennedy Center Archives).

The following year you were cast as Audrey in *Little Shop of Horrors*.

I was going to be going back to Broadway with *Little Shop*. It's the only show that I can think of that I've done where I signed two contracts before I went out of town, one for Coral Gables and one for Broadway. It was going to be the first time that my name was above the title. That still hasn't happened, by the way. It was one of the best companies I've ever worked with. We were doing really good work and I'm not really sure it was truly appreciated. While we were out of town, the producers decided that they wanted a new director [they fired Connie Grappo, who had been the assistant to original director Howard Ashman and married to original leading man, Lee Wilkof]. And, of course, that director [Jerry Zaks] wanted his own cast. We all had to re-audition and we were all replaced except for one of us [Hunter Foster]. Billy Porter was the voice of the plant. Reg Rogers was the dentist. You're going to improve on that? We were too real for the material or something. I started to get notes that my body language was doing this [caves in a bit, shoulders coming inward]. I'm like, "Yeah, I know. That's what I'm trying to do. I'm getting beaten up by my boyfriend. I'm in a cast. Audrey isn't fresh scrubbed." They told us at half hour [before a performance that they were recasting]. I cried my eyes out that night. We had signed the contracts! We weren't perfect. We were working out of town for $450 a week before taxes. If I was a new director, I would want my own cast. I wouldn't necessarily want the cast somebody else put together. But it broke my heart. The rug was just pulled out from underneath us. They had already bought a full-page color ad in *The New York Times*. The marquee had been put up with our names on it. And then they just changed their minds. This stuff happens sometimes. It's not about theater, it's about something else. It's about money or something else. We were doing great theater together. There were so many good actors in that company.

You bounced back with what would become your most significant role to date, Diana in *Next to Normal*. You started doing workshops in 2006, then off-Broadway and in Virginia in 2008, and then Broadway in 2009.

During rehearsal I remember thinking, "How far can we go with this?" Because I don't know what it's like to be her. I have never hallucinated. I've never taken a prescription pill. I'm not bipolar. I don't have any of those symptoms. I don't try to kill myself. I'm nothing like her. So I had no idea what to do. I just started throwing spaghetti all over the walls and thinking, "This is scary, but I'm in heaven right now. I can't believe I get to play somebody like this and discover that world." I realized that I am method because the only way for me to really know this character was to immerse myself in her. I mean, my family is crazy, but it's a different kind of crazy. It looked like I was completely enmeshed, but in fact, I was never more clear about the separation. Remember the movie *Somewhere in Time*? Where Christopher Reeve locks himself in the bedroom and just plays the tape over and over and over and over and over and wills his mind into another realm? Going back and forth and back and forth drains the life out of him. That idea was with me the whole time I was doing *Next to Normal*. I was doing mind over matter. It's just an absolutely phenomenal piece and it requires more than any actor ever expects. It asks you to go deep within yourself and the audience goes there with you. That guy over there just burst into tears and he looks like a linebacker. He is sobbing because of what he's watching. I credit [director] Michael Grief as the mirror side of my performance because without his perspective, I wouldn't have succeeded. I can't watch myself. I learned a lot about actor/director relationships during *Next to Normal*. I had no choice but to trust him in a way that I've never trusted a director. Diana took everything I had. It was an endless pit. There was no Alice. My approach to things changed. I was willing to do more than I was used to doing in order to do my job. I was possessed. It was coming from inside out. And it took so much of my daily twenty-four hours to reckon with everything. I was either playing her actively on stage, recovering from playing her, or getting ready to play her, every single day. It's all I did. No social life. I ate every meal alone. I couldn't participate in extra stuff with people. My instrument isn't a drum that I put in cases and in the closet; I take it everywhere I go. The self-care that was required to recover was the hardest part of doing the show. I had to put a sign on my door that said, "Don't knock on my door after half hour," because I was losing too much energy getting up and entertaining people. I was setting my own boundaries to take care of Diana. I was onstage all the time. I should have been leading the company but I couldn't. In order to do my job, which is to get myself together and do this. . . . I'm not going to say it's the reason why my second marriage ended but it didn't help. I was like, "Don't even ask me how my day is, I can't even talk right now. I'm sorry, Honey, I can't compute another question." Physically, the clock is ticking. You only have so many hours to put yourself back together. Vocal rest; putting in earplugs; ice on your throat; lay on racquetballs. You do it.

Do you think that's the fate of everyone who plays her?
I went through fire that nobody playing the role after me ever had to do. You can't compare the original performer with anybody that comes after. I did so much work for everybody that comes to play Diana. They don't have to hunt for her. I built this and you get to wear it. Make it fit you, but I built it. But I would never have to do that again because it's been done. You don't have to build the house again. I felt like the only way to deliver her was to go all the way past my fingertips. It came from the music because the music requires it. I never doubted what I was doing because it all came from the music. It's rock and roll. There are no other roles in musical theater that are equal to Diana yet. After *Next to Normal*, people didn't want to look at me anymore. I couldn't get arrested after I won my Tony. People thought I was Diana. It really hurt going through it because I had never sacrificed so much of my own personal life to tell a story. And I do feel like I made a sacrifice. Happily. That's my job. And it was my dream role. You drown in it. It couldn't have happened any sooner. It happened at the perfect time. You draw work into your life and the work creates your life. It doesn't surprise you anymore. But *Next to Normal* did surprise me because I didn't expect her to possess me. But I allowed her to. She was trying so hard to do it, and I was like, "Why should I resist this?"

Given how much the role took out of you, how did you negotiate the stage door? I am sure you wanted to be there for all of the people who really wanted to connect after being so moved.
Yes. I have utter respect for the audience. When I leave the stage door, add another forty-five minutes or an hour to the day. You are focused, listening. Strangers would hijack me. Take me by the elbow and gently pull you aside and say, "Here's my story." And they tell you the most intimate parts of their grief. A face you've never seen before, stained with tears. I was so happy because I wanted to see the audience as Alice after the show. I wanted to see their faces. The things that they would share! The most devastating details come out as real quick sound bites because whoever it is that's got me by the elbow telling me their pain thinks that they're the only one that has shame about their pain. But then that person goes and the next person does the same thing. Show after show after show, and it shows you that we're all

With Aaron Tveit (left) and J. Robert Spencer in her career-defining, Tony-winning, role, Diana in *Next to Normal*.
(Joan Marcus)

human. It's normal to feel ashamed of pain. But if I wasn't feeling well, I couldn't do the stage door because I can't live with just giving attention to two people and then going to my car. I just wouldn't come out the door. I'd leave some other way. Because it's not fair if the person in front is the one that gets attention. If I don't feel like I can talk to everybody, I don't go out.

I'm amazed that you had it in you to do it at all.
I was there for me. I was getting validation for my work. I can't get enough of that. I can never get enough validation for the work that I created, especially if I feel like I really, really worked hard. I was seeing transformed countenances. But until recently I was also really into helping people and people pleasing. I would sometimes get taken advantage of by fans. I would cross my own boundary as far as what I would give time-wise or information-wise to a total stranger. I was stalked. People followed me to the train. I had to fend for myself.

You took the show on tour.
I wanted to go on the road because it was my job to play her. Nobody knows her like I do and when the kids in Des Moines come to see *Next to Normal*, I want them to see me. I just wasn't comfortable with anybody else taking over the reins at that point. I learned a lot about myself in those years after I came off the road. I went through the darkest period of my life right after that. Both my parents died. My marriage ended. I ended up living alone for the first time in my life. I slept for years. My agent said that I told him, "I don't want to do another musical for a while." I don't remember saying that. I honestly have PTSD from *Next to Normal*, so I don't remember a lot of things. And I am still standing and stronger than I have ever been. I've

grown. I've expanded and I survived her. And that's the most beautiful part of *Next to Normal* to me. I survived Diana and became more Alice than ever. I had to use a lot of my personal soul to create her. We were creating hell.

Speaking of hell, your most recent Broadway show was *American Psycho*.
I was so happy to be playing a supporting role in the show. It's one of my favorite shows that I've ever done. I love the world that it lives in. I love that it's a mirror facing a mirror facing a mirror facing a mirror. There's always some different way to try it. I thought the company was terrific and Benjamin Walker was sublime. I think the score is underappreciated. The number where we were all in our bloody, nude-colored onesies, and we were doing modern dance—I never know what it looks like from the audience, but sometimes you don't care because you're just having so much fun. It was just so bizarre and so much fun. It was like performance art. The audience enjoyed it so much. It was like a party, a rave, for them. They were not afraid to respond and make noise. It was an ideal job. I was really sad when it closed.

It was a small role for a Tony winner. Did that factor into your thinking at all?
Well, it's only in the movies where the actors can take whatever role they feel like taking. That never happens in real life. The fact is it was a Broadway show. They could have said, "You're going to play the third spear carrier to the left." It's a Broadway show. It's fiction that anybody would say no to that. We have to have a job. How do you think we're going to pay our bills? There's no way that I would ever think about saying no to a Broadway show. I don't care what they want me to do, it's a Broadway show. I really don't care what anybody thinks, honestly.

During the COVID lockdown you kept busy. You did some streaming shows, including *The Waves* for Berkeley Rep.
A giant suitcase arrived with everything I needed to make a movie, including the slate. I performed the jobs of a whole crew. You find yourself doing all the assistant stuff and the stage management. It's a lot. There aren't enough hours. And you start to realize how much time you do really waste as an actor [in film] sitting around waiting for them to get the shot. But since I'm the one setting up the shot and assisting myself and coiling up everything and putting it away at the end of the day.... But fortunately I love this kind of stuff. I love gear. I'm not afraid to try stuff. You can't be afraid to push buttons and turn knobs. I discovered that's something that I could be happy doing. I was really into the gear.

What do you think you'd like your career to look like moving forward?
I want to be Angela Lansbury. I want to have my own TV series and be beloved enough to park in Shubert Alley. I know I can get that if I just hang in there. She's one of my heroes. And Bernadette Peters is the other one. If anybody ever really knew how much it takes for her to be that amazing.... She's disciplined! You have to be disciplined to have your voice sound like that! That's my most important thing now—to maintain and recover quickly, and know when to rest and when to leave. Our bodies, our emotions, our psyche ... it's all connected. But the body is what we see. So if you start to see imbalance in your body, it means that it's the last step before it starts to get bad. When you're a live performer, it is really just about the need to sleep and be quiet and drink water and eat broccoli. It's that simple. It's not some kind of magical thing you get from the doctor. People like Betty Buckley and Bernadette and

Patti—they've taught me how to look long-term at my physical commitment to being a performer. There are roles waiting for me. I have to believe that and I do believe it. That's just part of the deal—making my way to the new type. I was lucky to snag *Next to Normal* when I did because I'd probably be too old for her now and I was too young before that. [Sometimes you] feel rejected and worthless. It's never going to be just smooth sailing. It doesn't work that way. I have a nice little niche here that isn't going anywhere. I can see that now. But you have to believe it. My jobs used to overlap and now there's a whole new generation. But you do have to wait. It's a garden.

Sherie Rene Scott

November 2020

Prominently hanging above the couch in Sherie Rene Scott's living room is a brooding painting of Muhammad Ali, ready to swing. When I comment that he's not who I'd have expected to find, she directs my attention to another wall, on which the Dalai Lama's image presides. "I'm in between the two," she explains, before showing me framed Wonder Woman comics, adding still more layers to unpack in understanding her muses. And while it all seems a bit incongruous, it also all makes sense when one considers the multi-hyphenated life and career of Scott, who is an actor and singer, yes, but also a prolific writer and the founder of a record label, not to mention a divorced mother and a woman keenly aware of gender politics.

Raised in Kansas to parents she describes as "conservative, down-to-earth folks from Depression-era farms," Scott realized that she was different from everyone she knew. Not that she thought she was better, just different. And she somehow knew from a very early age that New York—a place she repeatedly calls her "savior," "a miracle," and her "truest steady relationship"—was the key. But performing in musicals was never the goal, it's just what happened. She read Eva Le Gallienne and studied at the Neighborhood Playhouse. For money, she sang backup for rock stars and on songwriter demos, developing a signature sound that served her well on Broadway in *Tommy*, *Grease*, *Rent*, and then, with a standout turn in *Aida*, where she honed what would become her trademark character: the slightly ditzy knockout with insecurities so exposed as to be simultaneously endearing and wince-inducing. Think of Cathy in *The Last Five Years*, Christine in *Dirty Rotten Scoundrels*, and most especially, the character of Sherie Rene Scott in *Everyday Rapture*, the "fictionalized autobiography" Scott penned with Dick Scanlan and for which they were both nominated for Tony Awards. Since then she's written two other pieces, *Piece of Meat* and *Two Hander*, which also feature fictional versions of her own story (the latter detailing her relationship with frequent co-star Norbert Leo Butz). She camped it up as Ursula, the sea witch, in *The Little Mermaid*; suffered through the one show she thinks she should have quit (*Women on the Verge of a Nervous Breakdown*); and starred in straight plays on and off-Broadway (*Landscape of the Body*, *The Front Page*, *The Portuguese Kid*, *Hamlet*, and *Whorl Inside a Loop*, an acclaimed play she also wrote with Scanlan). And then there was Sh-K-Boom Records, the label she conceived and founded with then-husband Kurt Deutsch. Sh-K-Boom and its offshoot, Ghostlight Records, were Broadway's first independent record labels and may prove to be Scott's most enduring creation, after her son, Elijah.

"I've never done this. This is kind of fucking my head up—in a good way," Scott says midway through our conversation, both hands flying to her head to scrunch her hair, something she does unconsciously and often. "To have to go back and look at all of this … I'm a little phobic about going backwards." Understandably. There's a lot of emotion as Scott talks. She tears up a few times, sometimes with awe at the kindness she remembers being shown, and sometimes at the admission that she spent a lot of her life giving up her own agency until she didn't do that anymore. But there's also a lot of self-deprecating humor, which Scott deploys expertly for her own enjoyment as much as mine. And she struggles to understand what her post-COVID-19 career might look like. "I'm open to seeing what my path is from here. I'm open. Because there's no possibility

A princess with a problem, in *Aida*.
(Joan Marcus)

right now, it's kind of opened up to every possibility. Transcendence is, like, a high bar to set for every aspect of your life, I guess. But I see people as more fearful as opposed to, 'What do we have to lose?' Let's push some more fucking boundaries."

Talking to you about you is particularly interesting because you've written several pieces in which you've depicted you, but not you. You keep crafting versions of yourself.

My co-writer, Dick Scanlan, and I love the idea that, in art, truth doesn't have to be factual. Sometimes you end up exposing more of yourself than you would have had it been all facts. Craft is more interesting to me than my story,

Sherie Rene Scott	
Tommy	Broadway, 1993
Grease	Broadway, 1995
Rent	Broadway, 1997
Over and Over	Washington, DC, 1999
Aida	Broadway, 2000
The Last Five Years	off-Broadway, 2002
Debbie Does Dallas	off-Broadway, 2002
Dirty Rotten Scoundrels	Broadway, 2005
The Little Mermaid	Broadway, 2007
Everyday Rapture	off-Broadway, 2009; Broadway, 2010
Women on the Verge of a Nervous Breakdown	Broadway, 2010

which is not interesting to me at all. Dick has always said, "the deeply personal is deeply universal." The more I can get to a personal experience rather than a personal story and craft that … the shared human experience is, I think, what we're all trying to get to in art.

And in doing that, are you keeping some of your actual story back for yourself?

Oh God, yes. I think I'm private but not secretive. Retaining your soul is obviously the most important thing in life. When all is said and done, that's what you're left with. Theater was always playing a character. It's that character singing, that character shaking her tits, that character with headlights on high beam. The character of the person who has my same name on stage loves to be center stage, loves the spotlight. She has no sense of ambivalence about it. She has no soul issue. All of those things that I constantly want to be a part of my work? That character doesn't have any of that. I can make her go through shit and it's more fun to watch this person, who thinks she has it all, be brought down to come back up again. It's the American way! The secret is I'm more fabulous in real life than I am onstage. I just don't want everybody to feel bad. I'm always writing stuff. I think I'm a writer masquerading as a singer and an actor.

You were born in Kentucky and you grew up in Kansas. What was your context for theater as something that you wanted to do?

That's still kind of a mystery to me. My dad had a great voice and played the guitar and harmonica. He would play Ozark songs. My mom was raised Amish Mennonite and only knew hymns. So it was a great mix. I began singing every single thing that I had ever heard on the radio or saw on TV. There was a children's theater that had started at the community center, so, for summer, they could put me there. Kids would write their own stories and put songs with them. That was my experience of theater—writing my own stuff and putting songs to it. At seven I was saying, "I'm going to go to New York to be an actor and a writer," and they were just like, "She does not know what she's talking about." I mean, no one [I knew] had ever been to New York. My parents had never flown in an airplane. My parents had never seen a play. I'd never seen a play. I think maybe in my mind I thought that Mary Tyler Moore lived in New York. But I knew there was no other thing for me. My mom said, "What do you want to be when you grow up?" And I said, "Respected by my peers."

How did you realize that being an actor was a conceivable option?
I really don't know where it came from. And it was a very painful thing because it was made fun of a lot. No one believed it was true. But it was true.

Were your parents supportive?
Yes, ultimately, very. And my mom especially sacrificed so much. But they just weren't interested in theater or the arts, or they didn't have the luxury of being interested; they worked a lot. My dad was older and had been in the military, in World War II, and my mom married him when she was nineteen. It was like I'd landed from another planet, honestly. I knew that as a kid. My parents were very earthy people and they would say that I was not in reality. I got that and I got that my chances in New York were very, very small. I knew I couldn't fuck around. I didn't have that luxury. And I knew I couldn't go home. I found my home the first time I saw New York City.

You spent a summer in New York at fifteen, right?
Yeah, I went to the American Academy of Dramatic Arts. I drove myself to Kansas City illegally, with my driver's permit, for the audition. And then when I got in and got here and I found out they graded by A's and B's, I was like, "This is bullshit! You can't grade art!" I'm pretty sure my parents thought I was going to be a stripper and never come back. As soon as I saw all the lights from the airplane I thought, "Each one of those lights means there's a person behind that light and every one of their stories is just as important as mine." It was so incredible. There'll always be a light on here. I feel much safer in New York than I did in Kansas.

That's interesting because New York in the early 80s was decidedly not safe.
I got mugged three times. But I knew that rough stuff would happen and I'd have to stay positive. And they were good muggings, civilized. I stayed at the Salvation Army Residence for Women and I was so lucky to get in there. I always knew it could go another way. The first hotel I stayed at was the Hotel Martha Washington, which allowed no men above the second floor. It was a whorehouse with literal pimps in yellow suits and purple hats in the lobby, but not above the second floor! It honestly felt safe. I saw my first Broadway show, *Agnes of God*, with Elizabeth Ashley, Amanda Plummer, and Geraldine Page. She was one of my idols. So good. My actual stigmatas exploded. But back to hookers. There used to be cars from East 28th to 30th on Madison and Park. They rotated in a circle around these hotels that were there. The women would go and talk to the drivers. We leaned out the windows from the Hotel Martha Washington and watched as our friends from the building would get into some of the cars. The first guy I ever kissed, Patrick O'Flanagan, was bringing me home one night and—you know how when there are steps [going below street level] there's a railing? You'd hear sounds of [heavy breathing, grunts] and you'd see the hands [of a woman engaging in intercourse] grasping the bars of the rail. I knew it was one particular girl because she had "love" and "hate" tattooed on her knuckles. I couldn't see but I could hear them and see a man's bald head. She'd be like, "Hey, Sheri." "Oh, hey, Theresa." I remember this exactly happened: "Can you get me a carrot cake at the Smilers?" This was a normal

night! "OK." Patrick was quiet for a little bit, and then, "You know her?" "Yeah, that's Theresa. She lives in my building." I just thought a lot of buildings had prostitutes in them. That was just how it was. "So, are we going to go to the Smilers and get her carrot cake?" And I'm like, "Yeah, of course." I never glamorized drugs or that life. I wouldn't smoke pot or do drugs. Broadway, in a way, saved my life because it was athletic. You couldn't smoke. You have to take care of your body. You have to perform eight times a week. It kept me behaving. That was my entrance into New York. I found my home. I went back to Kansas, worked hard to get into the Neighborhood Playhouse when I was eighteen, and when that happened I knew that was the key to the beginning of my life. They gave me a scholarship.

Did you work survival jobs?

I worked, before I came here, as a cocktail waitress, underage, in Kansas. That was the best way to make money in Kansas. I was horrible. I spilled so many drinks on people … but they didn't seem to mind [batting her eyelashes, flirting]. I had to pay for their dry cleaning out of my paychecks. Even so, I was able to save money before I came here. Then I worked at Banana Republic. I know how to fold clothes really well. And I worked at the Ritz Shoe Store selling shoes. It was during the time when AIDS was [spreading] and I'll never forget the day we were told we couldn't touch people, we couldn't put shoes on people anymore. I also worked at Penny Whistle Toys on Columbus Avenue. And I made money singing, doing demo tapes. I got involved in the rock and roll world, backup singing. That helped support me and was very informative. I always felt the two were separate—I'll be a singer and then I'll be an actor. Writer is like the point of the triangle. I didn't ever think of singing and acting going together in a musical for some reason. You weren't a serious actor if you were doing musicals. My singing teacher, Ron Shetler, started giving me lots of musical theater stuff to sing and he felt I had a real ability. I knew when I sang, it felt different. I could feel … a feeling that was different inside me. I think that's probably one of the things that led to my needing to have a character because—what it feels like to sing is—when you're doing it right, you're very exposed. I think when I'm at my best, utilizing the most of my craft, when I can serve the piece, and I'm also connected to it emotionally, it's like the sound of someone's soul. You can't hide behind that. I'm sure I wanted to give myself as many safe places to go [via a character] so that I could do that and offer whatever I had in that way, fully and honestly, and then go back to being funny or a little less exposed. I knew that singing was important for me. I just didn't put it together as eight shows a week, Broadway singing.

So how did you get there?

The guys who wrote *Hair*, Jerry, Jim, and Galt, got me my Equity card. They somehow heard me singing and then they cast me in the twenty-fifth anniversary of *Hair* at the United Nations. I sang a song with Donna Summer. I remember giving her my pantyhose because she got a run. Anyway, that led to getting *Hair* in Woodstock, New York. That was an Equity production and got me my Equity card, which I never even knew was a hard thing to get. Then some other jobs happened that were weird. I quit a job where they were paying $700 a week, but she'd [the producer, Adela Holzer] bring the money in bags of cash and I just felt like something was wrong. My parents couldn't believe it. $700 a week was just astronomical to them. She ended up going to jail, but I had quit in the first week and a half because I felt something was off. [The show, *Senator Joe*, closed on Broadway after two previews.] I did *Teenage Mutant Ninja Turtles* on tour. I thought I was doing a voiceover.

When I got it and I saw the schedule, I was like, "We're doing the voices at Radio City Music Hall? How does that work?" I couldn't believe that it was a live thing. And then I was like, "Wait a minute, I'm dancing with four turtles and a rat on stage?" But it was $1,500 a week. My dad started crying when I told him. When the Turtles came through Kansas City, the whole family was there, so proud. I was so embarrassed. I knew it wasn't where I wanted to go, but it certainly made them feel like I was not going to end up stripping. I had experiences like that, and then *Tommy* was the turning point. I auditioned for that six or seven times. Everybody in the cast [had done the tryout in La Jolla, except me]. I thought I found my home; rock and roll and musicals together? This is me! That was an amazing experience. I couldn't believe they were going to make us do eight shows a week. It took me a while to understand.

You had been in the city seven years! How was that your first understanding of a Broadway schedule?

I didn't know anybody that did it. When I heard we had understudies I just assumed that meant no one really does eight shows a week. That'd be insane. Remember, I used to ride my bike to the Quick Shop in Kansas and get the latest *New York Times* that was always at least three weeks late, just to see what the fuck was going on in the world. Even looking at this time, today, to see how easily misinformed people are, I totally get that because it is another world out there. There was a lot that I did not get. I'm sure I messed up a lot of things just out of complete ignorance and shyness. *Tommy* was huge and that was everything. It was heaven! Except for the sexual harassment. My direction for Sally Simpson was to bounce. In the audition: "Can you just kind of be really excited and just bounce up and down the entire time you're singing?" At the time I just thought this is part of it. My breasts were always a thing. I love them but I would constantly try to cover them to make people see me and not them. People said stuff about them all the time, like, "You'll never play Juliet with those bumpers." It made me work harder to sing and let my soul come out, to prove myself in other ways. I get that physically, this buys you something, but just as many times, physically, it cut me out of things. It would make people uncomfortable and their way of dealing with their discomfort was to diminish me. I knew that then and I think a lot of my energy went to managing that. I believed that the work would triumph.

What do you remember about rehearsing *Tommy*?

It kind of ruined me for everything else because the cast was a touchy-feely group. We would give group massages while we were getting notes. And we lay on each other's stomachs. It was so great. [Choreographer] Wayne Cilento got me dancing! Michael McElroy had to be like, "point your toes," when he lifted me by my waist, poor guy. I didn't know, I'd never been lifted up in a dance before. I could do one spin but then by the second one, I would always, like, spin out and end up offstage and the crew guys would have to push me back on. My dancing was a group effort. It was an amazing experience. And there was Pete Townshend and all the things that came with that: hanging out, going to play pool, singing in bars. I was sick half the time because we just never slept. I guess I was the party pooper because I behaved. I didn't know a lot of stuff that was going on.

You performed on the Tony Awards.

Did we?

I can't believe you don't remember that. I would have thought that would be a benchmark moment.

Especially for me because my only experience of the Tonys had been on a black and white thirteen-inch television in Kansas. But no. I remember everybody's astrology sign [but not my past]. This is my problem, I guess, and why people think I have a lack of ambition. *Tommy* was amazing and fun, but the laughs I had with the people and the times that we had creating [is what I remember]. Every time that music would start, everything else washed away. It was everything to me. Everybody was such an artist and it actually led to the idea to start the record label years later. I knew how talented my friends were. Alice Ripley was one of the first people we recorded. I had been offered all these record deals that I didn't want because I knew what a recording artist was from my experience as a backup singer. I knew that kind of life was just not for me. But I thought if we could do it ourselves and promote it … I was less interested in my own album than in creating a resource for other Broadway people. By then I knew Adam Pascal. And Michael McElroy had started the Broadway Gospel Choir [now Broadway Inspirational Voices]—his arrangement of "Joy to the World" was our first Grammy nomination. It was really important to me that those people were our first investments. [But back to *Tommy*,] we hung out all the time. We had slumber parties with the girls. Nobody had any time to have a personal life, which was fine. And then when I knew I had to move on, I auditioned for a show that I did not want to do: *Grease*. They offered me Sandy on the road, or I could take over from Megan Mullally as Marty on Broadway. I took over for Megan and that ended up being a really good experience. When I gave my notice [at *Tommy*], I was pulled aside by a producer who said, "If you leave, you'll never work again."

I'm interested in the fact that you left, given that you were so happy, to do a show you didn't like.

I learned the hard way that I'm not good when I don't believe in what I am doing. You have to believe in your show when you're in it, even when you know it's not going to go so well. You believe in each other and in the story that you're telling enough that you can go out there and do it. I knew that I didn't believe in *Grease* and what it was saying. But I knew that I needed forward movement. I never thought I was going to be doing musicals, so I thought I should do another one and see what it felt like. And again, I made lifelong friends there. And because I was in that show, I was able to do tons of readings during the day. That was a really good experience, meeting more people and seeing the whole world of creating work that was in development. And I knew I needed to make more money so I could go do things that I loved [that might pay less]. And I did; Randy Newman's *Faust* [in La Jolla], which never made it to Broadway. But it was something that I really loved. When you're out of town you make five hundred bucks a week. The goal was never to be famous or to be a star. I wanted to be famous only because that would lead to more influence so I could do more things for the community. There wasn't a goal of winning a Tony or anything. Maybe there should have been. But it was to do great work. How do I keep having the opportunity to do great work? It was really about the money putting me in a position so that I could make choices based on things I believed in. But it was really hard to articulate that at the time. I also did focus a lot on relationships and finding true love, probably to the detriment of my work. Relationships were more important to me than career achievements. Only later did I realize, "Oh, work has been kinder to me than most of my relationships. The one thing that has been honest with me is my work." The eight-show-a-week thing that I thought was keeping me from my life ended up being the one steady, honest thing in my life.

That was a huge realization. New York City's been the one true love that's always shown up for me. It's gone through hard times, but it always comes back. This city is a miracle.

You left *Grease* for *Faust*?

That started my new life in California for a time. Randy Newman was amazing and [director] Michael Greif is great. I loved that show very much and that's where I met my future ex-husband. I got a TV series and again my dad cried when I told him how much I would make. I was going to make more in six weeks than I had made in three years on Broadway. At first everything in L.A. seems so much easier, but over time you realize how much it's killing your soul. I just felt disconnected from people and from the pulse of the world. Then Michael Greif asked me to audition to replace Idina Menzel in *Rent*. I got the part and I think I sublet like twelve different New York apartments over nine months. Idina's understudy had gone on a lot. Remember, that's when people were sleeping on the streets [to get the daily rush tickets]. It was a phenomenon. Unbeknownst to me, they felt that the girl who was the understudy should have been given the role and so they were anti-me from the very beginning. I loved what Idina had done. I loved her voice and I knew that I would never compete with that. What I would do would be different just because I am different. But the fans just hated me. Starting with my first show, as soon as I would start "Over the Moon," the first two rows of the audience [the rush seats] got up en masse and walked out in protest. And there were cast members who wouldn't talk to me. I just thought, "This is what happens." I didn't say anything to anyone. The person playing opposite me was very mean and would say things before we had to kiss each other on stage. Every day. In her mind, she was being loyal to the understudy. I got that. I would just look forward to when people were nice to me. I didn't want to make a drama out of it. And watching the cool, funny Adam Pascal or Anthony Rapp or Norbert Leo Butz perform was great. Adam was the first person I'd seen on stage that could cry, tears coming from his eyes, and still sing beautifully. Michael McElroy came into the show. When the girl that was the understudy for Joanne, Shelly Dickinson, went on, we'd have so much fun. It was night and day. One Sunday, we had a really good show. The next morning in *The New York Times* there was an article about how replacements on Broadway can bring things to the shows that you haven't seen before and there was a big picture of me. It was a rave review. ["The most electrifying moment on Broadway these days is being supplied not by any above-the-title player, but by a pair of unknowns.... The sublime work by Ms. Scott and Ms. Dickinson is instructive for audiences and performers alike: replacement actors in hit shows need not be disappointingly wan facsimiles of their well-received predecessors. They can transform a piece in profound and unanticipated ways."] The stage manager put the review up on the callboard, which was unheard of. I knew that he did that to try to be like, "Everybody shut up." That's when the audience stopped leaving in the middle of my performance. It was just ironic that I was doing a show that I loved so much and it was all about love and yet some people were mean. When that all went away, it was good. But that was a hard time. I knew in my heart I could bring something to it. I felt like I could serve it really well and I could sing the shit out of it. I really believed in that show. It made me be better and I felt honored to be a part of it. The day that Taye Diggs got *How Stella Got Her Groove Back*, he was hiding, naked, in my and Marcy Harriell's dressing room, between the clothes on the rack. He popped out and was like, "I got the movie!" He ran around to every dressing room, naked, and we held the show. Everyone was rooting for him and cheering. Around then I also started readings for Disney for what was then called *Elaborate Lives*, not yet *Aida*. Disney had come to town and all of a sudden everything was ramped up a notch. For a reading we had a sound system and mics and they had water for us! Audra McDonald played Aida.

You left *Rent* to do *Elaborate Lives* in Atlanta.
The out of town was just an amazing experience. Heather Headley and I loved each other right away. She is a force of nature. They had all the Disney Imagineering guys who make the rides to do this amazing set of an origami pyramid that would open and close on three sides. It would sit on its chargers around the stage. It could open up and make all these different shapes. It was a great idea; they just couldn't figure out how to make it work. When it would charge it would charge in E flat [makes a humming sound]. Every time people would sing, it was really hard to keep pitches because you'd hear that E. Or it would get stuck and we'd do scenes with just our faces peeking out … hydraulic fluid would leak and people coming in for their entrances would slide on the jet fuel. Everybody was wonderful, but it just wasn't the right thing. The brilliant [designer] Bob Crowley reconceived the whole thing and it became a different experience by the time we went to Chicago.

Between Atlanta and Chicago you had time to do the Kander and Ebb musical, *Over and Over*, in Washington.
I replaced Bebe Neuwirth. I remember going to audition on the way to the airport to go on vacation. I auditioned for Kander and Ebb in person and they called me an hour later at the airport to say I got the job. [I had to go to D.C. immediately so] my husband went on vacation without me and I went to work, which is typical of the entire rest of our life. I knew that it was like, "We're not going to be able to get a star like Bebe, so let's just get somebody that's available and can get down to Washington by Tuesday." Sometimes they really are trying to find people that can fit in the costumes. I went in while they were in tech. They were sticking wigs on me while I was walking around the stage with a book in my hand. I loved the role and that piece and all the people very much. [Years later], after September 11, Kander and Ebb wanted me to go into *Cabaret*. They were like, "The show's probably going to close soon because of the attack. We don't care about a star, we want somebody we really want to do it in the role." I was so honored, I was crying. I knew I could knock it out of the park. The contract was coming to my apartment and my agent called: "Did you sign your contract?" "I didn't get it yet." "It's with your doorman! Run down!" As I got to the doorman, the messenger from Roundabout was literally taking it back. Gina Gershon [who had already done the role previously] had become available. It hurt but hey, the show stayed open. I'm not one to get angry about being replaced by stars—a lot of times it keeps shows open. Sometimes I wish I was more well-known so I could keep shows open, give people work. I think creating work for people is one of the greatest things we can do for each other.

After *Over and Over*, you went back into *Aida*, in Chicago.
That's when Adam Pascal came in. I was really happy to be involved. I got why it was important that I was a blond, white, Egyptian princess. You wouldn't look at me and think "Egyptian princess," but I got why I had to be that, so that we could really show [the racial difference between Amneris and Aida]. Right around that time, record offers started to come in. I knew I wasn't going to be a person that wanted to go and do a tour, but I did want to have the option of expressing myself. I just knew a regular label wouldn't be a good fit. And I knew people like Adam and Michael Cerveris did sell-out concerts of their own music on their nights off.

I knew that everybody was trying to express themselves. I thought, "I'm not interested in this deal. But you know what does interest me? Why don't we start a little record label on our own for all these people that I know are doing great work?" That excited me. I knew that there was a space in our community that wasn't being filled. Initially, it was for Broadway artists, bridging the gap between pop and theater. My view was that these people would be constantly working in theater and they would have a built-in audience. Them being in a show would be promoting their album. The key was being able to put my and the label's .com in my bio for *Aida*, which was unheard of at the time and I got so much agita from Equity. But Disney let me do it because I promised that Adam and my albums would be our first records. We recorded them while we were in tech for *Aida* on Broadway. We would run in the snow from doing 10 [hours] out of 12 at the theater to a studio. We hired the same producer, Joel Moss, for both. The big get would be if Disney let us sell the CDs with their other merchandise in the theater. They did. It wasn't like it was any money, of course, but it was a beginning. That was a real support. Tom Schumacher [at Disney Theatrical] was really supportive of me starting that record label. Sh-K-boom is a name that I didn't like, but I came up with it [it's the combination of the first initials of Scott and her then-husband, Kurt Deutsch]. I always kind of preferred my husband [as the face of the label] instead of me. I thought that he would really do well in this and I did feel that having a guy do it with me would make people take it seriously, take me seriously. So it all happened out of our second bedroom. The biggest thing I lived for was the Sh-K-Boom concerts that we did. It was basically all my friends. Everybody would get together and sing and that was a really dreamy situation. One of the things we did was a concert of Tom Kitt's and Brian Yorkey's *Feeling Electric* [which became *Next to Normal*]. I did it with Norbert and Greg Naughton, who I loved and who I set up with Kelli O'Hara [the two are still married]. Michael Greif [who went on to direct it on Broadway] saw it and he was like, "I don't get it." I knew that I didn't want to play that role because my psyche was very important to me and I knew that it would affect me as a person. There's no way that can't affect you. I was actually very conscious of that for Alice [Ripley, who played the role]. I actually made enemies in high places; I would talk to people in charge who were cultivating this constant treadmill of her during that show and I said, "This isn't healthy. Nobody can maintain this." Sometimes you speak up and it's a kill-the-messenger kind of thing. I understood what the price was. When all is said and done, you're at peace that you spoke up, and I always thought that if people are going to react poorly, better that I know that. If me speaking my truth is going to be the end, better it goes out with me having said something honest than me never having spoken up.

So that period, during *Aida*, was really fruitful for you.
And exhausting. I had a twenty-four-second costume change with three or four people changing my costume, head-to-toe. Now, whenever I write anything for myself, there will rarely be a costume change! By the time I left the show I had been playing the role much longer than the year on Broadway [between the workshops and the two out-of-town engagements]. I had to do something different. People forget that we're doing the exact same show, in the exact same position, every night. When I think I can't do it another time, I think, "I can do this. Maybe somebody in the audience today has cancer. This is going to make them feel good and they're going to be happy." That works for like two weeks, and then you're like, "Fuck that person with cancer." So then it's, "Somebody's child has cancer and I'm doing this show for them." And that maybe lasts three weeks or a month. Then you get to the point where you're just so over it you're like, "Why are all

these people with fucking cancer coming to see my show?" And that's what I love about New York: you still fucking have to do the show. You get mad that the audience is there. "Who are all these people ruining my life?" That's the beauty of theater.

You were cast in *The Last Five Years* that same year.
They sent me the tape and I remember sitting on my bed, listening and feeling like I could do it. I'd need training and to really focus, because I don't really sing like that. This was more legit. But I knew I felt it and that I could contribute something. I was learning about that Broadway/belty sound that they wanted, even though I kind of despised it. I also understood why people liked it. And I knew that I loved Norbert and that we would work well together. People would say [of the character, Cathy], "She's so insecure." That's a thing you'd only say about a woman. I was really aware of that. I didn't see her insecurity as being a bad thing. I saw it as being truthful to her given circumstances. I always felt confidence was overrated. Anybody can do confidence. Try doing vulnerable. Anybody that wasn't insecure was posing and I didn't want to be a poser. Because Norbert was in it, I felt very trusting, because I knew what kind of process I would have. I knew how he worked. We approach things similarly. We were really trying shit out. And I loved the idea of a female director, Daisy Prince. That's also when I went to the voice teacher, Joan Lader, full-on. I worked my ass off. I felt like, "I have to have this part," and I've never, ever, ever felt that way about anything. Like, it was important for my life. And then September 11 happened right around that time and everything stopped. And then we finally started rehearsals in January.

The show is so well loved now, but it only ran for a couple of months.
I was secretly prepared for that because I'd gone to a psychic, Tony LeRoy, in August, before September 11. It led to why we did the cast album. He was like, "I don't know what happens but something happens and everything just shuts down. It starts picking up next year. But from September to December, I would just go on vacation if you could. I can't figure out what it is, but everything is going to stop. It all falls down for a time." He kept saying "Fall down." I swear. I have the tape. He also said, "You're going to get this musical. But I'm going to tell you something that you can't tell anybody that's involved. But if you know this, you will be able to help people through and you won't be taken by surprise. It's going to close in May, just when it's building an audience. Downtown is dead. I don't know why but downtown is dead." And he said, "But there's something with your record label." And I was like, "Oh, we can't record the show because there are already deal options with big labels." He said, "They're all going to fall away and you need to be prepared to have a plan because you'll be the one left standing. And if you do this cast album, it'll be like a fine wine; people will be able to appreciate it as the years go on." So we got a plan together and we did end up doing the cast album. And when it closed, I wasn't devastated. I just believed in it. It was so beautiful. [Composer] Jason Robert Brown played [piano at] every show. So there was that pressure—the composer's always there. Just as I was getting a couple of things really in my body—there are usually times in a show where you're like, "God dammit, I want it in the pocket all the time. Why is it not in the pocket all the time?" So you find certain things that you're doing physically—you could stand up rather than sit down on the note because, "Oh! That's what's throwing me off." You don't know things like that until you're really in the run of it and I was just getting to that stuff. Norbert was going through a separation at that point. I wanted to be a friend to him but I also didn't want to take advantage on stage of something he was going through personally.

He told me that you would go to the Minetta Lane Tavern regularly and have these therapy sessions. As he described it, you were there for him.
I was surprised when I heard his version of what kind of friend I was, and I was really grateful for that because I always felt I wasn't experienced enough, I didn't have the words for how to help him through that time better. I was so comfortable and happy to talk to him about everything, but he said I never would talk about me. That's the thing that I'm learning to do. But I can't overestimate the importance of the experience of that show. It is done all over the world because of that cast album. I never sang from it again until Norbert and I sang together in *Two Hander* [the performance piece Scott wrote for herself and Butz in 2019].

Why?
Because it really meant something to me. It would minimize it for me. It felt wrong. Years and years I took a lot of grief about not singing from that show. I understood why people didn't get it. People just want you to make them happy and I love doing that. But some things are soul things I couldn't explain. Also, I'd never heard the phrase "No is a complete sentence" until way late in life so … there's that.

What was it like going to the revival or working on the movie?
The revival was great. Betsy Wolfe had done *Everyday Rapture* and I loved her so much. I loved her voice. And I loved Adam Kantor, too. I was thrilled. Betsy's such a great actress and so funny. She's much more beautiful than I was. I felt very self-conscious about my weight when I'd done it. She did all these different, new, amazing things that I would have never thought of doing. We'd asked for the movie rights [Scott and Deutsch] when we got the cast album. Then, in 2006 I had an audition for Richard LaGravenese for a film. I walk in the room and he starts jumping up and down. I look behind me to see what he's excited about. He says, "It's for you, it's for you! I listen to *The Last Five Years* every day in my car and I have wanted to meet you for so long! I have the whole movie in my head. My biggest dream is to do the movie." And I said, "Well, the record label that I half-own has the film rights, so if you want to talk after the audition, that'd be great!" And now I will read for the part of the ditzy best friend. I introduced him to my husband and removed myself from the discussion because I thought that would be awkward. Now I wouldn't do that. But at the time I thought we all had our best interests at heart. Women, if we do, like, three things, are seen as the least thing we do. So even though I started this record label and was an equal owner and then came up with the idea to do cast albums, I'll be seen as an actress. My future ex-husband had taken the out-front position as producer. Right as the movie was being filmed, things suddenly got really bad [in my marriage], so it was an odd experience.

You did the off-Broadway musical, *Debbie Does Dallas*, next.
I knew who was involved and I was so happy and excited to do it. It was showing how absurd and obscene it is [the way women are treated]. I could be totally fine taking my shirt off on stage because it served a purpose. It wasn't just because I was supposed to be hot. That makes me feel sick. But when it's for the first feminist porn musical, then yes! I was really excited to do that show even though I hated cheerleading. It's such bullshit and I always knew it, even as a kid. So sexist and stupid. I don't care how popular it is, I am not doing that. But we had to learn to cheer for that show. We were at the Jane Street Hotel, which is haunted. When the Titanic survivors came in to New York, that hotel was one of the places they put them, and several of them died there. The dressing rooms are at the very top of the building, so you'd

have to go through the actual hotel. We would walk down twelve flights of stairs in our little cheerleading outfits and several times people would be passed out in the hallway. It was a dump. A crazy, scary, fire hazard dump. It was fabulous. I really loved those girls and I loved that time. I loved the idea of it. It was saying something. I left the show early because I wanted to get pregnant and my ex-husband had devised a plan whereby I would have a week to get pregnant on our vacation, and then I go out to L.A. for pilot season and if I booked a pilot, I wouldn't be showing that much when we shot. Then I'd have the baby in September before the series started shooting and I'd have like two weeks off before going back to work. And I was like, "OK." That seemed like a normal plan at the time. And guess who got pregnant in a week? That was why I left *Debbie Does Dallas*. Then I had a miscarriage. On April Fool's Day. Hilarious, God. My manager dumped me two weeks later because I missed an audition after the miscarriage. "So what if you're sad. Go do it."

With Norbert Leo Butz (left) and John Lithgow (center) in *Dirty Rotten Scoundrels*.
(Carol Rosegg)

Thankfully, you got pregnant again. And at that same time you started work on *Dirty Rotten Scoundrels*?

The incomparable Jack O'Brien was the first person to cast me without needing me to audition, and he knew I was six months pregnant when I did the first reading of *Dirty Rotten Scoundrels*. The baby came soon after the second workshop. I never sang better. Being pregnant gives you a kind of grounded-ness. I was really open. It really helped me subsequently because I would try to imagine that feeling. That area is connected to the Earth. I had an emergency C-section which was fine. I was going to have a natural birth, but que sera. But a C-section is no joke! It's major surgery. I took my two-month-old to La Jolla [for the show] and the production put us up with an extra apartment for my parents to take care of the baby. That was great. I was just really tired. I loved that part. I am proud of being a part of so many new musicals and creating things from the ground up. By the time we went to Broadway, we were all really bonded. John Lithgow really set the bar in terms of how a star person should be. At Christmas he did drawings of the entire cast and crew. That's the kind of guy he is. You hate him because you're like, "I will never do as much for people as you do. It's impossible." Everybody was so funny and great and I just loved them all. And I loved my baby more and I was wanting to be with him any time I wasn't there. I get why back then there were so few new moms on Broadway; it's impossible. I was tired all the time. But I think you just find that you have more to give and more love. You can do more and you can be more and you want to be all things for people. I think that's what that time became. If ever there was a cast or a group of people that you would want to be all there for, it was that, and at the same time I needed to be all there at home, too. And then the Tony nominations. I was so happy to be involved, but I was like, "I can't wait to do this when I'm older and I don't have a baby!" Because [when the choice is] Tony luncheon or watch my kid play, I would watch my kid play. I wish I could have been in both places more. Who knows, maybe my work was better because I was just so, "go and do it." I would have to rest my voice, which is hard to explain to a toddler. The show itself couldn't have been a better experience. I was just exhausted. So when it became an option to do *Landscape of the Body* off-Broadway, I had to leave.

And then you went back to *Dirty Rotten Scoundrels*, with Jonathan Pryce and Brian d'Arcy James.

I didn't want to go back and do *Dirty Rotten*, but that's something I was made to do by my ex-husband. He still wasn't taking a salary from the label so we could put money into building more albums, so I had to go back in. I knew I was fortunate to even have the option. Around then is the first time I started questioning some things that didn't seem right or fair in my life. It was starting to dawn on me that I shouldn't be that tired. That was the first time that I ever went back into something and it was for the money. I knew I was lucky they wanted me back. Jonathan Pryce [who'd replaced Lithgow] was a dick, though. He's kind of irascible. I was so excited to work with him. He wanted me to do everything the same way every time. Whatever he needed I would try to do. It was just a totally different vibe. I love Brian d'Arcy James [who'd replaced Butz] and I wish I could have been in a better place for him. Anyway, during that time, they asked me to look at *The Little Mermaid*. Tom Schumacher had worked with me [on *Aida*] and I really appreciated what he was doing right from the get-go. He was trying to combine the opera world with something that was commercial. He was bringing in a director and a costume designer from the opera world to give it the grandeur and culture of opera. And the brilliant Doug Wright would be doing the book. This was highbrow stuff to aspire to. I also knew the cast would be very diverse. The sisters were going to be all different races. Ariel had a black dad, the beloved Norm Lewis, who I'd done *Tommy* with. I loved doing research and thinking about how to do this character. I decided that there's no way she wouldn't be a sexual being. I was thinking of Divine even before I knew that that was one of Howard Ashman's original inspirations. You're repulsed and yet you're drawn in at the same time. It is probably one of the roles that I didn't contribute to as much as I would have liked.

Why not?

I always felt part of an ensemble and I can see now how somebody who was not of that mindset could have fared better. The role wanted to be star turn. There are those performers—and now that I have worked with them, I know—that when the audience is out there, that's all that fucking matters. "It's just about me and I'm going to do my shit and nobody else here onstage matters." That is probably what people wanted to see. I always liked the idea of giving people what they didn't know they wanted, but it's on me, I didn't deliver as much as I wanted to. When you're in such a big production with a massive costume it was just never going to be—the costume designer spoke Russian and needed an interpreter. I remember getting fitted, being like, "How fast can we get it off when I have to go to the bathroom?" And they just shrugged. "You don't." Let me say one word to you: periods! Stuff like that took a lot of hours. I remember being late for an entrance because I was a getting WD-40 on my tentacles. The absurdity of it all. Like, you're having a really serious conversation with a castmate, then, "What are you, by the way? Oh, you're seafoam? OK. I didn't know what that costume was and we've been in this show for three and a half months. I had no idea. I thought you were a bubble." I wanted there to be a film crew backstage. Like, what the fuck is happening back here?

What was it like working in a costume that moved independently?

People forget when a new musical is happening, everybody has ideas about what they can do, and then if you can't do them, you're constantly changing until the day you open. With that costume there was a time when the tentacles all moved on their own with remote controls. That affects how you can dance. And the dance affects how you're expressing the song. And there are lines that only work if the tentacles move, so if they don't, you need to rewrite the line. That's why shows need time and go out of town. We went to Denver. We were in a five-thousand-seat opera house and we thought we were on track. But certain things can work in certain houses and not in others. I felt bad that I couldn't have done more to make myself better. I thought the show had heart and it was one of those times when heart didn't win the day. I saw that people were really trying hard. It was the best cast of people. Sierra Boggess is a great, great person and I wish I could have been there more for her at that time. [An actor fell from the set and was permanently injured.] It's a dangerous job and it's a fucking miracle when you think of how dangerous it is with sets moving and people flying in on sets and Rollies [many of the actors had wheels in their shoes to make them glide like fish] and trapdoors in the floor. It's like sports in that way; one little misstep in any game can be the end of your career.

Your dressing room at the Lunt-Fontanne was quite opulent.

I've never had that big of a dressing room. Usually it's the size of a closet. There was a pink tub that was put in by Elizabeth Taylor during *Private Lives*, and then Sting put in mirrors everywhere [during *The Threepenny Opera*]. Who the heck had time to take a bath? I didn't even take a shower in there. I had a baby to get home to.

You had a framed collage on the wall of all the people who inspired the character.
Richard the Third, Divine, Jerry Falwell, Leona Helmsley, Joan Collins, and Gloria Swanson. I watched *Sunset Boulevard* without the sound so I could see what they were having her do in silence. I definitely got "silent screen star." She knew her angles.

You thrust your shoulders out as you describe that, and you lead with your collarbone. Immediately that mid-Atlantic, geographically untraceable accent pops out.
Like when people go to London and they suddenly have an accent. Ursula learned the language of being a femme fatale. "I'm not bad, I'm just starving!" I watched a lot of *Absolutely Fabulous*, too.

You started writing *You May Now Worship Me*, which became *Everyday Rapture*, while you were in *Mermaid*.
For my first record, I wanted to write the liner notes as a character [named Sherie Rene Scott, but not me]. I wanted to imply in the liner notes that I had these sexual relationships with all the composers I'd worked with whose songs I was singing. So "Sherie Rene" had slept with Elton John, and Kander and Ebb, Pete Townshend … but nobody understood what I wanted to do. [Writer] Dick Scanlan was brought in to talk me out of it. But he actually understood what I was talking about and he really became a lifeline and a mentor. Probably one of the saviors of my life, honestly. He saw that I had something of value to offer as a writer. After that, we kept writing through the years. When I was in Williamstown when I was doing *Landscape of the Body*, I saw the Mr. Rogers documentary on PBS and I was so moved. I thought it could be hilarious for this character I'd been creating to have loved Mr. Rogers and also to have misinterpreted all of his songs as very sexual, very sex positive. Dick liked it and it became kind of a grounding section for *You May Now Worship Me* [a one-night benefit performance]. After that benefit was a success, Dick was the one who said, "If we add to it, I think we'd have a show." Having a big dressing room was a gift because we wrote what became *Everyday Rapture* backstage during *Little Mermaid*.

While you were in full costume?
Yes! It was so hard to get out of, I would just sit on a stool with this giant thing on because I couldn't fit in a regular chair. Crazy makeup and wig. It must have been beyond a sight. It was amazing having producers who supported the fact that I was doing their show and writing another one in the dressing room.

And that's when you came up with the notion of a "fictionalized autobiography"?
Dick saw there's an ambivalence I have about being on stage. There are people who really want to be center stage and are really comfortable with that. The writer in me is like, "this is fucking absurd," and so I have to make a character that can do that. You can tear them down so you can watch them fall apart and then piece themselves together again. The only thing that I really wanted in the show that really happened was my abortion. I wanted the character to have an abortion that was a good experience and that she doesn't regret. I was one of those lucky people that got pregnant the first time I had sex. The first thing I did after having an

abortion was say, "Thank you, God, for giving me this chance to have my life and living in a time where I can have this choice." I went to Kansas City and there were protesters calling me a murderer, and it all ended up being OK. The people there were amazing and it didn't hurt and I knew that when I was ready to have a kid, I would have a kid. I never told anyone at the time it happened and never really talked about it except when I shared with Dick that I was thinking of writing about it. That's one thing in the show that really happened and I wanted to talk about that because the reality of that situation is rarely discussed in a non-politicized way. I never regretted it. I regretted that I wasn't given the proper sex education. I regretted that I didn't have a good boyfriend at that time. I regretted that I didn't have people around that I could talk to about it. But I didn't regret the surgical procedure that I had.

How did you decide to incorporate other actors?
I didn't want to be alone. The idea of doing a one-person show is abhorrent to me. That's why it started with the title *You May Now Worship Me*, making fun of one-person shows as I was doing one. The Mennonettes [backup singers, plus another character] came in and it became a one-person show with four people. I really felt like I was part of an ensemble. The reason I got into theater was the people, not to do something alone. I'd had enough of that in my childhood. And then of course when Michael Mayer came on to direct, that lifted the whole experience in every way.

You left *Mermaid* to take *Everyday Rapture* to the next step?
You May Now Worship raised like $300,000 for Phyllis Newman's Women's Health Initiative. It became a show that we developed at Second Stage and the first time we did a run-through, the Second Stage people didn't get it. They just stared at us, no clapping at the end, and left. But then Dick and I believed in it even more. And it wasn't like, "I love my ugly dog," although I am the person who is going to love my ugly dog to the end of the earth. We knew it had heart. And it ended up going really well. I didn't read the reviews but I got the vibe.

And it moved to Broadway the next year when a slot at Roundabout opened unexpectedly. Had you been shopping it aggressively?
No, I would never get aggressive. People kept me out of that side of it because I had to do the show. I just knew that the reviews were good enough that they felt that we could move. But nobody wanted to take a chance with a no-name show. And then I'm in Florida, developing a new show, and I got a phone call. [Megan Mullally had quit the Roundabout's production of *Lips Together, Teeth Apart* abruptly.] They wanted to know if we could fill in. We'd have to go in eleven days or something. Michael was committed to *American Idiot*, so he couldn't be there as a director all the time. Dick would have to take a lot of the directing duties. They'd talk to each other every day. If Dick wasn't the kind of incredible person that he was and didn't already have the capabilities of being a director, we'd never have made it. He understood time, which is something I don't understand. What does eleven days mean? I couldn't think about any of that. We just had to do what we could do. But we did it and it was just magic. That cast and the musicians were all perfect, as well as the creative team, the crew, and everyone at the theater. When I got into the taxi on opening night after the party, I turned to my now ex-husband: "Did we get good reviews?" And he said, "You got raves." I just burst into tears. I had never cared about what kind of reviews I got for anything. There's nothing I can do about stuff like that except do the best work I can. But that one? Thank God! They

wanted to extend it, but by the end of the run I was just too tired. That's when I started taking sleeping pills for the first time. At some point, a good six hours of sleep end up being the best thing you can do for everybody. I need to sing? My voice sounds better when I sleep. I can't miss a show? I need to sleep. It becomes the lesser of evils.

That's quite a deal to make with yourself.
It's the same thing with the performance-enhancing drugs on Broadway. At every show you see, somebody's on steroids because their throat is raw. It's like, "I'll deal with this later when the show's over." It was the first time that I'd ever done anything like that.

You were nominated for Tonys for acting and writing.
I knew I didn't have a chance in hell of winning, so it was fun to just go to the party. And I was really proud of what we'd done. I was especially proud of the writing nomination because that had been years in the making. If I could dare say, "I'm proud"—because that was a word I never used because "pride cometh before a fall." But if I ever had that feeling of being proud, aside from my son, I'm proud that we did that. I really wanted the option to be able to keep writing. My next goal was to write something and not be in it. We sang on the Tonys and that was really fun. Being with Betsy and Lindsay [Wolfe and Mendez] made everything so much better. They are both so good. Dick said, when we were casting, that we needed two women who could hold a show in their own right. Each of them was so different and yet so special. And since then, they've both been able to hold shows in their own right.

You didn't get much time off because that very same year, you did *Women on the Verge of a Nervous Breakdown*.
I did a reading of *Women on the Verge of a Nervous Breakdown*. I didn't know [director] Bart Sher but I had worked with [composer] David Yazbek and [writer] Jeffrey Lane on *Dirty Rotten*. I just assumed that, as most readings go, I might hear about it again in like six months, after they work on it. They called and said they were doing another reading really soon after. I did that reading and again, I thought they were going to work on it. But then they said they were starting right away. Not even going out of town. I had thoughts and feelings about that that I shared with the team, but no one cares about your thoughts and feelings. You are a hired actor.

But as the leading lady, don't you have that right? Isn't that part of why they hired you?
People sometimes—especially men—don't like to be told that they need to rethink something. My feeling was that we didn't have enough time. I've done a lot of new musicals and I had done one really, really fast. Looking at the schedule, when you're taking us out of rehearsal for press, we had three weeks in the rehearsal room. The ending wasn't written, nor were the last few songs. Granted, I don't understand time, but I had a really strong feeling about this. I was assured that it would be OK. And the other thing that concerned me: I said, "Why are we all speaking in Spanish accents? You create the world and then everybody follows that world." They said, "It's not funny without the accents." And I was like, "Then we need to make it funnier." I didn't want to do it. I loved all those people and I wanted to work with them, but something felt really off, wrong. It felt horrible to have to say that. It was my first bad experience, honestly. I couldn't escape the situation. Every day you wake up and you think there's something you can do to help this, to make it better. I'm going to let

Woman on the verge of a nervous breakdown.
(Paul Kolnik)

go of yesterday and I'm going to go in with a fresh attitude. This is the day everything could change. At some point you realize there's nothing I can do about this situation. It's failing horribly and everybody's acting like it's wonderful. Weeks earlier, on the first day of rehearsal, everyone's like, "We know exactly what we're doing. We got it. We have it all planned out." So, I was like, "OK, I trust these people." First day: everybody talking, introducing everybody, a lot of bullshit. I'm thinking, "Please let us start in the afternoon and not lose any more time." By 3:00, Bart dismisses everyone except the women in the first number and it looks like we are going to finally start. Bart says, "So. What do you guys think we should do for the opening number?" I wanted to start crying. I was in shock. There was no plan. We sang the song standing. Then sitting. Then some of us standing, some sitting. And that was the day. It wasn't until way into it that I realized this was a show about women, written by men, that had no interest in hearing from a woman who wasn't going to give them great news about everything. I really, really tried and it just got worse and worse. It got to the point where we were on stage in front of paying audiences and stagehands were coming onstage, strapping us into harnesses because they couldn't figure out how to get us in the things to fly. Or … my bed that was on fire and was envisioned as this great, beautiful thing; I said, "Where's the fan to disperse the smoke?" "Oh, don't worry about the smoke." "Does the bed pull in the exhaust?" "Yeah, yeah, yeah." Then in the theater, they turn on the fire and I was like, "Where's the ventilation? Amazing! I don't even hear it!" I was so impressed that the fan wasn't making any noise. Bart says, "We didn't put a fan in there. But look up." They had opened the ceiling in the theater. "We're going to open the ceiling for five minutes every show?" Meanwhile, the lighting designer is walking by behind Bart, going, "Snow. Rain. Daylight." All the reasons why we couldn't open the ceiling. But I am made to feel like there's something wrong with me for complaining. I got onset asthma singing in a fire day after day. I had to get an inhaler, it was all so stupid and just didn't make sense. I would get direction about playing my subtext all the time and I was like, "I think I need some actual text." I'll work extra, I'll come in on my day off, I will do anything you want. I want to help this. I played a character who's stalking her lover, trying to find his other lover and I was told that men don't like it when women are angry. That's a quote. The character couldn't be angry. "What is she, then? She sets his clothes on fire!" "You just can't be angry."

Bart Sher is an accomplished director. He didn't see that you were struggling to find the character?
He didn't seem to. I tried everything he said. And there were other people that were able to take up a lot of time. There are certain actors that are like, "I'm not doing a bit of work in my own time. All of my work will happen in this rehearsal room or it will not happen at all." That's definitely a way of working. I've worked with people that have done that and that was the case in this show. But those people need a lot of time and especially one-on-one time with the director. And they're not going to say, "You know what? Let's talk about this on the phone later. I don't want to eat into everybody's time." At that point, I wasn't even judging it. I was noticing it. But it was cumulative over time. I was like, "What are people thinking? We're in week two and we don't have the first act done!" Of course, they ended up delaying previews several times, and every time they did, they looked at me in an angry way, like I witched it to happen. I always thought that all these people that I admired had something up their sleeve that I didn't know about. They were in charge. They had a plan. They said they did. I kept trusting that, but what I kept seeing in the room was different.

But at some point, you open. It's figured out.
It was never figured out. It was just patched together. People were fanning doors to clear the smoke. It was a real shame because a lot of the music was so fun and the cast was a great group of people. But theater is a top-down kind of operation and it became every-man-for-himself. Bart had never really done a new musical from scratch [he came aboard his one previous effort, *Light in the Piazza*, after it had had two out-of-town engagements]. He'd done revivals. When you're doing a new musical with a new book that's constantly changing . . . I knew how many changes there would be. I love collaboration but there was no structure for that. We tried and we were all game, but it kept adding up to nothing because there was no greater concept. And too many technical things. I could just see this disaster happening. I could just see it.

What did that mean for your performance?
I sucked. I didn't believe in it anymore. When I stop believing in something, I'm not good. I'm just not good. This was the one review I read, actually, because I wanted to see if it was as bad as it felt like it was. What he [Ben Brantley] said about me was very true; he said that I looked like I was thinking of what I was going to be ordering for dinner after the show. Not to mention that there was Patti LuPone. I remember moments that were just like, "What the fuck, Lady?" People that do horrible, mean things and get enjoyment out of it . . . she's definitely one of those people. In my experience, they always reframe it and find a way to justify it, but creating a toxic work environment is just one of the worst things you can do, in my opinion. Danny Burstein is just the greatest person in the world, and Stokes is the most amazing,

steady soul. But it was an incredibly painful experience and I couldn't make it better, and it's the worst feeling in the world when you can't have an effect on something no matter what you say or what you do. I was saying "Train wreck! Very expensive train wreck ahead!" and they treated me like an annoying party pooper. I felt really bad for the kids who were in their first show. It was the first time I ever thought I should have quit. Sometimes quitting is the best thing.

Since that time you've not done another book musical. Is that just the way it's gone or did that show keep you from doing that kind of work for a while?

There wasn't a musical that I really wanted to do. I wanted to work and write but not have to sing so that I could be a better mom and be in shape for my son. He was getting older and noticing my not being around. I wanted to focus more on plays. I started working with gentle genius Todd Almond and wrote *Piece of Meat*, which I was really proud of, and I was more involved with the record label. Dick gave me an opening night present for *Women on the Verge*; his friend taught in a men's maximum-security prison, and they wanted to do a personal narratives workshop. It was just the thing I needed to do. It was only supposed to be one class and it turned into three semesters over two years. I felt more respected and valued and ironically safer there than I did on a Broadway stage or in my own home a lot of the time. Going to prison kind of saved my life. Dick and I knew the experience had impacted our lives forever, and a couple of years later we realized it was something we had to write about. [They co-wrote *Whorl Inside a Loop*, which Scott starred in and Scanlan co-directed.] That's a really special show, with special people—I don't have the words for the greatness of that experience except that I hope it's not over.

I want to come back to the triangle you described, with writer at the top and singer and actor as the two points. After everything that you told me, how do you feel about that triangle and what you want now?

I want to work. I want to create work that I love with people that I love and believe in. Everything I've written was respected, appreciated. Whether it was your taste or not, it had something to say. I want to be able to use all my abilities to make something really great. I know that hasn't happened yet. There's still singing to be done. There's still writing to be done. I love creating things. I like utilizing the autobiographical form as an access point for the audience, so I can express this struggle with complex, private issues. But it really gets me going when it has a subversive aspect to it. Or maybe it feels subversive to me to bring out personal, spiritual thoughts and longings and make them funny and sexy and sing about them and then … BOOM … , make you feel things in your gut and heart in a way you didn't before. Maybe 'cause that's what I always wanted somebody to do for me—help me out with this human being thing, you know? This spiritual being having a human experience thing. That's what excites me. That's the kind of art I hope to make.

Kerry Butler

May 2008; January 2022

Ah, the madness of awards season. It's been described by many of the actors in this book, and while they all express gratitude for the honor, they concur that the month-long road to the Tonys isn't easy. Luncheons, media events, and fittings are squeezed into the punishing schedule of performing a show eight times a week, which is now being judged by Tony voters, adding to the daily pressure. On one of those days in heat of the 2008 Tony season, I shadowed Kerry Butler, a freshly minted nominee for her role starring (and skating) in *Xanadu*. It happened to be the same day that her first solo CD, *Faith, Trust and Pixie Dust* was released, so Butler was in the dual whirlwinds of awards season and album promotion. A sample day in the life of a leading lady:

6:08 a.m.: Two-year-old daughter, Segi, awakens, which means that Butler is awake, too.

10:00 a.m.: Physical therapist arrives at Butler's home to adjust her back, which she threw out earlier in the week.

11:15 a.m.: Arrive at Sardi's to shoot a video with John Lloyd Young as part of *Xanadu*'s Tony campaign.

12:30 p.m.: Associated Press interview in Butler's dressing room at the Helen Hayes Theatre.

1:30 p.m.: *Xanadu* half-hour.

2:07 p.m.: *Xanadu* performance. A perfect show despite Butler's back injury. She coughs out loud twice and sniffles once during the show, the only indications that she's fighting a cold.

3:50 p.m.: Immediately following autograph signing, a crew is on hand to tape another video for the show's Tony campaign. This one has Butler running down 44th Street from the stage door to Sardi's, stopping along the way to chat with Cady Huffman. Never once, as she runs, does she let on that her back is in pain.

4:15 p.m.: Press event for *Xanadu* outside of the theater. Cupcakes are for sale. Butler hawks cheerfully, but refrains.

5:00 p.m.: Butler is interviewed from the DJ booth of the Times Square Virgin Megastore. When asked unexpectedly to sing a cappella, she belts *Suddenly, Seymour*.

5:50 p.m.: Additional filming for the promotional video. Butler runs down 44th Street for three additional takes.

6:00 p.m.: Butler orders dinner from Zen Palate, quickly kisses her husband, Joe, who stopped by, and rests a bit.

7:30 p.m.: *Xanadu* half-hour.

8:06 p.m.: *Xanadu*.

9:52 p.m.: After greeting the day's second set of excited stage door fans, Butler heads home.

This is the life that Butler lived and lives, the one she coveted from the time she grew up in Brooklyn. It didn't take her long. After touring Europe in *Oklahoma!* fresh out of school, she was cast as the swing in *Blood Brothers* on Broadway. Leading roles in *Bat Boy*, *Les Misérables*, and *Beauty and the Beast* followed before her breakout success as Penny Pingleton in the smash hit *Hairspray*. *Little Shop of Horrors* was next, and then *Xanadu*, which she was performing at the time of our first conversation in 2008. We continued our chat fourteen years later in 2022. In the years between, Butler appeared in *Rock of Ages*, *Catch Me If You Can*, and then, after pressuring her agents to look for work in straight plays, she joined the starry *The Best Man* on Broadway, and the searing drama *The Call* off-Broadway. It was time, she thought, to play adult women, after a career that had specialized in girls. More recently she returned to musicals with *Disaster!*, *Clinton: The Musical*, *Mean Girls*, and *Beetlejuice*. The two-year-old daughter we talked about in 2008, Segi, is now in high school and has a sister, Sumaya. The whole family has given up the Upper West Side for a house with a yard in New Jersey. But while everything changes, it also stays the same. In both 2008 and 2022, Butler is relaxed and easygoing, her eyes regularly going wide with enthusiasm as she talks about anything that excites her. It's a big list. She looks remarkably unchanged and, in either decade, is an absolute delight.

Penny Pingleton is permanently punished. With Marissa Jaret Winokur (left) in *Hairspray*.
(Paul Kolnik)

How has it been navigating the craziness of awards season?

It is totally fun. I have to say I really like being nominated. I usually try to book out the mornings so that I have time with Segi. I try not to do anything before noon, and then I have the nanny come at 12:00. Thursday I have swim class in the morning with Segi, then I have the Tony luncheon, then the Lincoln Center filming that night. Friday I have an interview in Coney Island with Mo Rocca. It's pretty busy.

I always wonder if people in the throes of awards season have the time to take it in and really experience it. And I wonder if it's enjoyable or unbearable or both.

People have told me that they can't wait for it to be over, but I am really enjoying it so far. Luncheons are really easy to go to!

Kerry Butler	
Blood Brothers	Broadway, 1993
Beauty and the Beast	Broadway, 1995
Les Misérables	Broadway, 1998
Bat Boy: The Musical	off-Broadway, 2001
Hairspray	Broadway, 2002
Prodigal	off-Broadway, 2003
Little Shop of Horrors	Broadway, 2003
Miracle Brothers	off-Broadway, 2005
Xanadu	Broadway, 2007
Rock of Ages	Broadway, 2009
Catch Me If You Can	Broadway, 2009
Clinton: The Musical	off-Broadway, 2015
Disaster!	Broadway, 2016
Mean Girls	Broadway, 2017
Beetlejuice	Broadway, 2018

And they give you clothes.

I am not that into that. I'm very into clothes, so it's surprising. But when I get a dress, that ends up being a pain. I feel guilty if I take their time and I don't actually choose their dress. If I go [to a designer] I'm like, "Oh, they took out all of this stuff so I better take one of these dresses, even if I don't love it." I end up wearing something that I wouldn't normally. For the *Little Shop of Horrors* opening, I had this Dolce & Gabbana dress, which was nice but it ended up having stains all over it. It wasn't even clean! The wardrobe people from *Little Shop* were scrubbing it out on opening night. It's almost easier going to a store and choosing something that you love. I like buying things off the rack.

Do you feel like you are in a different place in your career, that you've arrived?

Yeah! I definitely feel like this changed things. I never would have thought *Xanadu* would have changed my career, but it has. I grew up doing car trips, singing along to Patti LuPone in *Evita*, so it's very, very exciting to be nominated with her. We did this whole Tony press conference and—a lot of times when I have done press conferences before, people are excited to see me but they are always looking over their shoulder to see who else is there. People were fighting over me this time and I was like, "This feels niiiiiiice!!!!!"

You also had the benefit of running in the show for a year before all of this.

Yeah, this is giving us a little boost. It's a little excitement. We got all of that scary, opening night stuff out of the way a year ago. So now I am just doing the show. Although it did get a little nerve-wracking when we knew the Tony voters were coming back. I felt all of this pressure because I got such good reviews. I didn't read them, but people told me that they were really good. I got nervous because now the expectations are that I had better be good.

I freaked myself out. I started forgetting my lines. It was awful. I was having panic attacks and stuff like that. But I'm better now. I was just worried for our show. I knew that they were counting on me a lot and that they needed the Tony nomination. I've been the lead in a show but it's never been where I've been in every single scene and really carried the show. It didn't stress me out in the beginning but it stressed me now, knowing how important it is, I was worried that I wouldn't deliver.

In a cast that's so small, does it feel hard being the only actor nominated?
Definitely. I definitely feel bad. But everyone has been so supportive. It doesn't feel weird at all. But I think our cast is so talented, I wish other people had gotten in.

Let's go back to the beginning. You grew up in Brooklyn. You saw *Annie* and fell in love with the idea of being onstage. Is it what you thought it would be?
It is and it isn't. I think when you are a little kid you think that Broadway is so glamorous. Everybody thinks that. But once you've been in it for a while, you see that it's not glamorous. There are cockroaches and mice all over, your dressing rooms are teeny tiny…. But performing in front of an audience is what I thought it would be. When you're little you think that when you're on Broadway everyone will know you and you'll be such a big deal. But it's not like that, either. I walk around and no one knows who I am. It's actually good because no one bothers me. I have my normal life and then I go do my show at night.

Your first big show was a tour of *Oklahoma!* It's interesting to me that you started with Ado Annie, a very big comedy role, before you made your mark with ingénues like Eponine and Belle in *Beauty and the Beast*. Was comedy always something that you wanted?
I found out in college that I could do comedy. Although after doing *Xanadu*, I feel ready to do a drama. I mean I LOOOOVE doing comedy, but sometimes there is nothing like singing a torch song to the audience. I am kind of in the mood to do that now. And Broadway has a short memory. They only think I can do comedy.

So, for your first show, you were out there touring Europe. What was that like?
It was great! In college, everyone wants to go see Europe and I got PAID to go see Europe. I was a lead so I got TWO bus seats!

Fancy!
Very fancy! You basically live on the bus. You put pictures up on the windows and stuff. We mostly went through Germany. We would move to a different city almost every day, so I got to see all of Germany. We would drive six or seven hours a day, so it was grueling, but it couldn't have been more fun. Sometimes we'd perform in high school auditoriums and sometimes we'd perform in front of 5,000 people. It was just whatever they booked. It was great. The audiences didn't speak English but we did the last song in German. "Oklahoma jede nacht, mein kleiner Liebling und ich…." They loved it! I'm sure they understood a little but most of the time we could tell that they did not speak English. It was also the first show in which I had to sustain a run. I ended up getting nodes on my vocal cords at the end. No air would come out. I was like, "What is going on?" They took me to an Italian doctor and he didn't speak any English. I was freaking out. I ended up having to leave the tour two weeks early.

How old were you?

Twenty-one. I was punching things on the phone: one beep for yes, two for no. For a whole month I did not talk at all. The nodes went down on their own and then I started studying with my voice teacher, Liz Caplan. Knock on wood, I never had problems again.

Was that the first time you started studying seriously?

Yeah. I studied belting, which I never had before. But it was great that it happened in my first show, because now I am super careful. I warm up for half an hour before every show. I know my voice inside and out. I'll know if I am straining. I know how to sing over a cold. It's good.

Do you have rituals that you need to do or you won't make it?

My voice teacher has me yodeling. That's something I have to do every day. And she has me sniff water. It's uncomfortable but it opens up your passages. That's my little trick.

After *Oklahoma!* . . .

I came back and I got *Blood Brothers*. I had spent a semester in England and I saw it there. No musical had ever affected me like that. I loved it. And then I heard it was coming to New York and I say to my agents, "You have to get me in for this! I love this show!" They were like, "Who is this kid?" but they got me in to the final callback with the producer. I sang "I Just Want to Be a Star" from *Nunsense* and the producer said, "Kerry, I think you will be [a star]." I had a callback that day and I ended up as a swing and then after six months they moved me into a role. I said in my audition, "I have to tell you that this is my all-time favorite show and I don't care if I'm in it or not. I'm just so excited that it's coming here because I want to see it again." And they were like, "Kerry, you'll be able to see it." I never got to play the part I understudied, Linda, and I am dying to play that part. And I'm dying to play Mrs. Johnston when I'm older. I think that's one of the best female roles. I love it when people don't care about what their voice sounds like, when they just go for the emotion. I was a swing, which means I wasn't actually in the show; you understudy a bunch of different people. So whenever I wasn't on, I was watching it. Every single night I would watch these amazing actors. They brought over six of the original cast from London and they were soooo good. I got to do the show with Petula Clark, Carole King, the Cassidy brothers . . . I had a crush on Shaun Cassidy growing up. And they were so nice! It definitely changed our show. It brought tons of people in. We had people trying to sneak into David's dressing room. All kinds of crazy stuff.

From *Blood Brothers*, you went to Belle in *Beauty and the Beast*.

Yeah. I did it in Toronto for eight months and then they moved me to Broadway. That was great because I am such a Disney fan. I auditioned for Broadway while I was in *Blood Brothers* and I didn't get it. I didn't even get past the casting director on that one and once that happens, your agents don't want to push for you anymore. I went to L.A. after *Blood Brothers* and I had new agents out there. They were like, "You are so perfect for *Beauty and the Beast*," so I flew myself back from L.A. just to go to the audition. I did terribly on the dance call, so I didn't get it. My agents said, "they love you but you need more time [to learn the dancing] than ten days to go into the show," which is the amount of time they give to put-ins. "But they want to use you somewhere else." I practiced. It was such a small little thing. You know that little can-can they do? It's nothing. But I am that uncoordinated. So I practiced every single day until my callback for Toronto and I got it! It ended up working out even better because

I had a full opening in Toronto. It's such a great city and they treat actors so well. There was tons of press in Canada. They moved me to Broadway after that and I did the show for like two and a half years.

As a Disney fanatic, was it incredible that you were a Disney princess?
Oh my God, I was so excited. I have videos of me on talk shows. I was going cuckoo. It was that Disney magic. It makes you feel like a little kid just being on that set. It was HUUUUUGE. Very, very exciting. And I was getting married at the same time! That was [almost] a deal breaker. [The producers] were like, "Well, maybe she can get married on a Monday and come back," and I was like, "No, I am going to have to take a honeymoon." So, we got that negotiated in there.

That would have been a deal breaker for you?
Yeah. You have to make family more important. That's how I live. I always trust that whatever's meant to be will be. I set limits and then I say, "Well, if they are not going to do that...." I just turned down a Broadway show recently because I have the baby and they didn't give me what I wanted. I said, "Well, then, that's it. It's not meant to be."

What did you want?
I wanted to bring Segi and Joe with me on the out-of-town tryout. I was going to have to be paid enough to afford that, but they couldn't go up and I was like, "Well, if it's meant to be maybe it will come back to me. And maybe it won't."

For somebody who has been called "the queen of readings" by *The New York Times*, to be able to just relax and say, "if it's meant to be" is pretty great.
Last year I did a reading of almost every show on Broadway that has a part I could play. I did five readings, one after the next. I did not get [cast in the shows]. And when I didn't, I was disappointed. You put the work in, you can't help but be disappointed with rejection. I was so close to being in *The Little Mermaid* and had I gotten *Little Mermaid* I never would have gotten *Xanadu*, and *Xanadu* has done much more for my career than *The Little Mermaid* would have done. Everyone knows I can do *The Little Mermaid*. That's not going to be a surprise. *Xanadu* put me on the map more because it's such a different kind of part. The only reason that it might be more fun to do Ariel than Kyra would just be because of the Disney perks. But other than that, Kyra is a much better part to play. It's much funnier. Ariel doesn't even talk for the second act! That's why you just have to trust that it will work out however it's meant to be. I was up for tons of stuff but it all works out the way it's meant to be.

Having that confidence and trust so that you can let go, is that freeing?
I see so many actresses, probably in your book, who never had a family and their career is everything. Your career is always going to disappoint you. I noticed with *Hairspray*, one minute you're on top and then they can't wait to rip you back down. If you believe the buzz and if you live by that, you are going to be miserable. You have to have something bigger in your life. In *Hairspray* everybody loved me, I was on the top. Then *Little Shop of Horrors* came along and people couldn't wait to rip me apart.

Who?

People in general. The internet chat boards. It's just human nature. People sometimes want people not to succeed. It's like, "You've had that one, now you've had enough. It's time for somebody else."

The "meant to be" attitude also jibes with your spirituality. What's it like to be religious in this business. Is there space for that?

Jack O'Brien [*Hairspray* director] used to give these amazing speeches. One of the things he said was that when you go to good theater it's like a religious experience. You get the audience to feel something and they are all feeling it at the same time. It's this magical thing. Everybody's laughing at the same time, everybody's crying at the same time. It's almost like you're shining your light on the audience and giving them the light that's in you. That's how I think of it. A lot of times I will go see an amazing performance by somebody and they might not believe in God at all, but I think that might be in their head because I'll clearly see God in them. I feel like maybe they are just fighting it because when they are onstage it's just coming out of them. I think it's around us a lot in theater. In almost all of the shows I have been in, we do a prayer circle before the show and people of different religions participate. We do it in *Xanadu* every night. We pray that we will be able to bless our audience. If people are sick in the audience, we pray that we will be able to give them the gift of laughter and healing. We did it on *Little Shop* and *Hairspray*, too.

I imagine it's really community building right before you go onstage together.

Yeah, it's really nice. And with *Xanadu* we had so many people getting injured that we were constantly coming together and praying for them. Luckily in theater, I didn't have to make big choices; there aren't too many things that would go against my religion. I don't have limits on what kind of roles I can take. You are supposed to be showing life. I loved doing *The Opposite of Sex*. That would certainly not be considered a Christian show, but it was showing basic Christian principles: to fall in love with the unlovable. My character, Dee, made all bad choices. She actually offends the audience. And the whole point is to come in with preconceived notions about homosexuality or teen pregnancy and have your eyes opened up. We're all just people and you can love everybody. You don't have to have blinders on. I can just relax because I know that God has a plan for me and I can just trust that plan. I never would have thought in a million years that *Xanadu* would have won me my first Tony nomination. God picks out my shows for me, he knows where I should go, and I just try to listen and follow.

Let's get back to your chronology. After *Beauty and the Beast,* was it like "Where can I go from here? How can it get better?"

A little bit. In this business you can't believe the hype. Like I said before, as soon as you're up on the top, you're down on the bottom. You still have to do your best on auditions. For a second there I was like, "I shouldn't have to audition, I'm the lead in a Broadway show." Things like that. And then you are quickly shaken back to reality. You have to be constantly working on your craft, you have to work just as hard as everybody else on your auditions. As great as it was, it didn't take me to a different level so much. And replacing isn't as big of a deal as originating.

Then was *Bat Boy* really exciting? That was your first time creating a leading role.
Yeah. I love creating shows. You are so much more free. It's so cool. I don't know about *Bat Boy*, but with *Hairspray*, I am sure that the girl [playing Penny] is doing all of these things that aren't in the script but that I put into the show. That's exciting. It's kind of neat to think you're passing the torch and now they are doing what I did.

Sometimes it's as minuscule as a gesture and it ends up in the stage manager's book because it's what you did.
In *Hairspray* there were scenes that I wasn't even supposed to be in, but I would start doing stuff on the side and they were like, "Oh yeah, you should be in that."

How did *Les Mis* happen?
I was doing *Beauty and the Beast* and I just auditioned for it. I always loved Eponine. I actually auditioned for Eponine when I was sixteen and made it through to the final callback for the original cast, but I was a kid and I hadn't done anything. But I could sing it. It was so exciting to finally get to do it after all of that time. I loved doing Eponine. I only got to do it for three months because I was replacing a girl who was going off to do something else and then coming back, but I loved doing that.

And then *Bat Boy*.
Yes, then *Bat Boy*. It's too bad that it never moved to Broadway. More people talk to me about that show at the stage door than anything else. People loved it. But September 11 happened and that really hurt that show.

How did *Hairspray* happen for you?
They had seen me in *Bat Boy* and they knew that they liked me. Then at my audition, I found a 50s song and turned it into a song that Penny would sing. I created this whole scene. [The role of] Penny was so tiny at the time of the reading. In the reading before, she had been cut out of the show, but then John Waters was like, "You can't cut Penny!" So I had maybe five lines for this audition. I got the reading and Jackie Hoffman was brought in at that same reading. They loved us and they started writing more and more stuff for us. They told us then that we would definitely be doing the Broadway show. The reading was amazing. When I am in shows, I never know [what it looks like]. You can never know as a performer, but with that show I knew it was going to be a huge hit. There was this excitement in the room and the music was so good. It was so new. It was an amazing experience. So much fun. From the very first lines, [audiences] were screaming. Huuuge laughter. Screaming after every number. It was unbelievable.

When *Hairspray* opened, it was a sellout and you were doing all of these appearances. Once all of that ends, is it a relief or a letdown?
It's a little bit of both. Sometimes you just want to get into the run because then you can focus on your own life and just do your show. Though with *Hairspray* it never died down. I was in it for a year and it was always exciting because we were the hot show that entire time. Everyone wanted us on every TV show. It was amazing. Really, really fun. But the show becomes your life. You don't end up talking to your friends. That's hard. Harvey Fierstein was a mom to

everybody. He and Dick Latessa were my original role models in a big way. Harvey had power and he used it to help out the ensemble. He'd stand up for everybody. And Dick Latessa would never complain. He wouldn't care about his dressing room; he would never miss a show … as soon as he felt anything [illness], he would eat five cloves of raw garlic and it would knock it out of his system. Now I do that. *Hairspray* definitely put me on the map. And I started going in for TV shows after that.

Do you want to be on TV?
I want to be a working actress and I'll do whatever it takes to achieve that. Sometimes you have to do TV to have longevity as a Broadway actress. It helps.

I am always interested in the young actors who choose to stay committed to theater as opposed to those who open in a show, get a lot of attention, and use it as their ticket to record a pop album, or go for a series.
If I am meant to go out there for something, I feel like God will get me in the perfect TV show. And I don't have to go out to L.A. for that. If I am meant to get that, it will come to me.

You said you don't read reviews. When did that start for you?
This year, for *Xanadu.*

Why?
Well, when I did *Little Shop*, I read the message boards a lot. It was very hurtful. When I got that show, my husband was like, "Kerry, it's a no-win situation. They will compare you to Ellen Greene. You will either do something completely different and people will be like, 'It's not Ellen Greene' or, 'She's just trying to be Ellen Greene and failing.' Either way you can't win with that part." He was almost like, "Don't do it," but it was a lead on Broadway. I am glad I did it. I loved doing that show and I love that music. But reading all of that stuff, people were mean. I would be the butt of jokes. So I just decided I was going to do my best. Even if they love you, [reviews] can get stuck in your head. It's like, "Oh this is the part that they love." If I promise myself that I am not going to read reviews then I don't put pressure on myself for the critics. That is what happened; I didn't put pressure on myself because I knew I wasn't going to read them.

You didn't have gnawing curiosity?
Yeah, I definitely was curious and people ended up telling me some stuff. I definitely wanted to know in general, good or bad. And I have read some of them now because they are up in front of the theater. But I wouldn't read them again. The bad ones always stay in your head. You can get nine amazing ones and one bad one, and that bad one will stay stuck in your head.

I think it takes discipline not to read them.
It's very freeing because you're not giving them weight. I read two reviews for a show right before our show opened. One talked about the music being the best music the critic had ever heard, and the other talked about the music being the worst. It's so subjective. It's not healthy for me to know what one person's opinion is. All I can do is my best and do the show I was directed to do. It's up to the director to find out what people like.

The part that would kill me is not knowing what is being put out in the world about the show that I am in. I want to know what the world is being told.
I know, but if it's bad, what are you going to do about it? It's different with your book because your product is finished. It's done. It's out there. What can you do about it? But I have to keep doing it night after night, knowing what they are saying. Somebody's review could influence my performance and that may not be what the director wanted.

During *Hairspray*, did you have a particular memory or moment that you loved?
We got to meet so many celebrities and I got to have pictures with so many people I love—Billy Joel, Mike Myers. Freddie Prinze Jr., Adam Sandler. It was very, very exciting. There were always celebrities coming backstage to meet us.

Was it hard to leave?
I was crying. I wasn't ready. But I had a great opportunity.

***Little Shop*. When I see someone take on a role I've seen played many times by someone else, it always feels off. I imagine that because Ellen Greene did the movie and people were so very familiar with her portrayal, it was as tough as Joe predicted it would be.**
Yeah. The people who went crazy for it were the people who had never seen it before. We had a lot of people who had never seen it.

How long did it take you to let go of that stuff and just do your show?
I had to from the very beginning. Jerry Zaks directed it and he will tell you exactly what he wants and what he doesn't want. He definitely did not want Ellen Greene's performance. And he didn't want that character to steal the show. He wanted his version to be more about Seymour. He didn't want me to do a voice. He wanted me to be more real and to play it as this woman who had had a really, really hard time and go more for the heart of the character.

How was that for you?
It was good but it was hard. I like to go for the comedy. But in many ways Jerry taught me a lot. I am still thinking about stuff he taught me. Not pushing for jokes. And I loved singing those Alan Menken songs. They can always make me cry. I really got into playing that part.

Since you are a self-described klutz, when you were offered *Xanadu* how did you not freak out about the skating?
I roller-skated when I was little, at birthday parties and stuff. I couldn't do tricks or anything. But when they asked me if I could skate, I was like, "Sure, I can skate." I didn't realize that there would be ramps on the stage! They put me in lessons and I actually took to it pretty quickly. I was able to skate backwards quickly and I got my arabesque. But that's when you're just focused on the skating. When we got into rehearsals, general blocking was so hard. The logistics of how I was going to get around: "I move on this foot, here, stop on this foot." My comedy is so physical and I couldn't do my comedy. I couldn't even think about acting. And then on top of that I had to dance on skates. In the beginning I was tap dancing on skates. The whole first month I thought I was going to be fired. I'd come home crying every night. Going through the choreography, just trying to get it into my body was the hardest thing. And being

a mom on top of that. But you do it. Now I feel like if I mastered that, I can do anything! It's hard being on stage the whole time. And the ramps were so scary at first. There's no railing. You can just skate right off of the stage into the audience. So, I feel like I'll never be, "Oh, I can't do that" ever again.

It couldn't have helped that your co-star went down early on. [James Carpinello, the original leading man, was injured during previews, forcing him from the show.]

Oh yeah, it was very scary. Not only did I have such a close bond with him, but then you are constantly in your head: "He's the best skater of all of us and if HE broke HIS leg, I am DEFINITELY going to hurt myself!" It's like constantly, "I'm gonna fall," all in your head playing over and over again.

How do you get out of that?

You have to keep talking to yourself, telling yourself you're fine, you're not going to fall. You have to override it.

That's interesting because unlike other things where when you do that you relax into it, here you can't.

Yeah, you can't let your guard down. But you get used to it. You get used to being super conscious.

How do you sustain a performance?

It's definitely hard. I started reinvestigating why I was saying the things I was saying. I needed to figure out why I am saying these lines again, mix it up a little bit, just to keep it fresh. That's important. You don't want to be walking through the show. Sometimes you will get on automatic pilot and just say your lines the way you are supposed to say them instead of actually thinking them through and living it. It's always good to go back to your notes and figure stuff out again.

Do you go back and re-rehearse a lot, just to keep all of the physical stuff sharp?

No. We really only rehearse when we have a press thing and the staging is going to be modified.

***Xanadu* must be a great show to be doing as a young mom, too.**

Yeah, it's only an hour and a half. It's the best. I can go home and play with her between shows.

What made you want to do an album?

I've always wanted to do an album and this seemed like the perfect time. We had just done the *Xanadu* cast album for PS Classics and they approached me about doing my own. I just couldn't get motivated to do it before, even though I wanted to. Everything just fell into place. All of the people we wanted were available. I was a little apprehensive about doing Disney songs even though, as you know, I love Disney. I wanted to make sure that it would have a wide audience because some people don't love Disney, believe it or not. We did it really quickly but I am really, really happy with the way it turned out. I love singing the songs. I really want to start doing concerts so that I can sing the songs around.

"You have to believe there is magic," in *Xanadu*.
(Paul Kolnik)

In 2009 you stepped into the cast of *Rock of Ages*. You told me once that that audience was unlike any other.
People were having sex in the audience, yelling things out, wasted. One guy came up on stage with two beers in his hands while I was singing a sad song. He was dancing. A brawl broke out in the audience one day. It was insane. Super fun, too, but crazy.

For it to have been super fun, did that mean you just had to let go and accept?
Yeah. You can't be precious. You can't be like, "I am singing here. How dare you!" I think my husband got more upset than I did. He was like, "My wife is singing up there! Be quiet!" People are passing their beers down the aisle while the show's going on.... It was different.

And for you, a Broadway baby, was singing that kind of music living a bit of a fantasy?
Totally! It was really fun singing that music and getting to belt like that. I'm so not cool, so getting to be in a show with cool people was great and a real stretch for me. A lot of times I'll play the good girl, so to be in a show that was so sexually over the top was fun. I loved it.

Then you had the opportunity to reunite with a lot of the *Hairspray* creators on *Catch Me If You Can*.
That was great. "Fly, Fly Away" is still my dream song. It wasn't written for me but I feel like I put my stamp on it. Tons of people sing it for auditions, so it's kind of cool to have a song that's like you're own "On My Own." And it was interesting to see the changes that the show went through. We had Terrence McNally as our book writer in Seattle and then they changed the whole direction of the show. Brian Yorkey came in and it was so interesting to see how a show transforms. I loved both versions, they were just very different.

When a show is transforming that dramatically, is it unnerving?
I just trust the creators. My part was completely changing every night of previews. I heard that one of our producers, Margo Lion, didn't want the women in the show to be weak, so she was really fighting for Brenda not to be portrayed as she was in the movie. But the problem was that the song was written for this mousy, meek girl, and then that's how she finds her voice. I was noticing that it wasn't going over the way it went over when Brenda was [weaker]. But I knew the creators had bigger things to think about, especially for Norbert Leo Butz, whose part was so different from what it had been. It's just very tense. You don't know which way is the better way to go. So, I didn't say anything until towards the very end of previews. We were about to open and I went to them with tears in my eyes: "I know how this song works, I don't know why isn't it playing well...." They really listened to me and rewrote it again. But it was really challenging because if the scenes are rewritten every single night of previews, I'm a different character, and then things land differently. One little piece of the puzzle affects everything else.

That kind of work always fascinates me. It takes multiple people having observations, living a moment, and piping up about it to keep fine-tuning and calibrating. Some would say that the calibration on that show wasn't successful. Did you feel that?
I thought that both versions were really smart, and I definitely thought this was the best music Marc Shaiman and Scott Wittman have written. It's one of the best scores around. But it's really hard to know. When they did the transition, they made the show much flashier, much

more like a Broadway show, but in the process they lost a lot of the heart. Before it was like a really deep father-and-son play. The scenes were gorgeous between Aaron Tveit and Norbert. I would sit on the side and cry. Then they made it very showy. Both versions were really entertaining. I think it could have used another out-of-town tryout. If they had done the new version and then brought in more of what Terrence was trying to do, I think that might have been the right way to go. It's hard to tell when you're in it. It seemed really fun and exciting. I really liked the changes when we were doing them.

Do you have a sense of why they abandoned McNally's approach?
I think they were following the reviews.

And they were facing the pressure of following up *Hairspray*. There was so much expectation.
That's what I think it was. I think they got beaten up because they came off of *Hairspray*.

Anything else you want to say to me about Jack O'Brien?
I would record his speeches because they were so inspiring. Every note session. He wouldn't give very specific notes, it would be more about what we're trying to do story-wise and what your part in that is. He's wonderful. Incredibly smart and kind. It was a really great gift to be directed by him. He gives you so much freedom. I hardly got any notes from him on *Hairspray*. He just let me do whatever I wanted.

You did some straight plays and then in 2016, you were part of the starry cast of *Disaster!*
Seth Rudetsky and I do a lot of concerts together. He was telling me about the show and I said to him, "Seth, everyone loves you. You could get tons of people to star in this show. I bet they would take less money than they normally do because they love you." And that's what ended up happening. He ended up getting his friends to star in the show. He just called people and asked them and I was one of them.

What was it like?
So much fun. *Disaster!* was like this gift that that came to me. Everybody in that cast has had pretty high highs and some low lows. We all know what this business is, so there was no ego. We were just there to have fun. No one needed to be the star. We were an ensemble passing the baton around, rooting for each other. That was really great. I've done shows with people where you can tell they are only thinking about how they're going to get their Tony nomination. None of that was going on here. Roger Bart would come up to me with suggestions about scenes he wasn't in. Some people wouldn't like that, but I appreciated it. I definitely learned stuff from him as a comedian. He's so, so funny and different every night. It would be really hard for me not to crack up on stage. And Roger and Kevin are best friends. They went to college together. Kevin would always be telling us jokes before the show. We were all helping each other. That's a really great environment, especially for a comedy. Everybody in that cast was like that. We would all help each other to make it better. That was one that lasted too short. We just couldn't find an audience and there wasn't the money to build the PR.

In 2018 you did *Mean Girls*.
They had asked me to audition for the workshops because [director] Casey Nicholaw hadn't worked with me before. My agent passed on it and didn't tell me. Then it was coming to

Broadway and Nell Benjamin, who wrote the lyrics, was like, "We understand why you don't want to audition but you're really everyone's top choice." And I was like, "What? I'll audition!" And I got it! But I had already been workshopping *Beetlejuice*. I had to negotiate to have an out in my *Mean Girls* contract to go do *Beetlejuice* on Broadway. I was doing the *Beetlejuice* workshop and rehearsing for *Mean Girls* at the same time, so *Mean Girls* let me miss a lot of rehearsal.

Did you feel overwhelmed or were you thriving?
It felt great! I loved doing *Mean Girls*. I felt bad about leaving [for *Beetlejuice*] because it was so much fun. It was a really great time. Tina Fey will just rewrite stuff, throw stuff out, constantly so creative and always working to try to better the joke. Nothing is precious. So that was really interesting to experience. And I loved working with Casey. He's so fun and so nice. He came up with really, really great things for the show. It was a tough decision to leave.

You yourself started your career playing teenagers in musicals, and now here you are surrounded by a new generation of young people. How was that?
I loved the girls and honestly, I couldn't do what they do. They are all triple threats. Tina said, "If we had done this ten years ago, you could have played any of those girls," but I wouldn't have been able to do that! They would come to me with questions about the business and things like that and I liked being a mentor. I have kids, and I'm used to being a mom figure, so I think I was a tiny bit, but more of a friend. A cool mom, maybe. When Halloween was coming up, we were talking about Halloween costumes and everyone's being kind of cagey. [It was clear that] they wanted to do costumes together and they weren't asking me. I was like, "Oh. OK." Then Halloween comes and they all dressed up as me in different shows!

You left to do the out-of-town tryout of *Beetlejuice* in Washington.
Yes, and it didn't get great reviews. I remember the audience loving it and getting huge laughs. I was thinking that I was in another show like *Hairspray*. And then the reviews came out. They did a big rewrite and really took all the notes, and in this case, they really got it right. It was a little too dirty and they made it just dirty enough where you can bring your kids. Kids love the show.

How was it being directed by Alex Timbers?
I adore him. He's just so creative and he has his hand on everything. He is such a perfectionist and so specific. He understands every department. Like, "I need a box light over here." He's not just working on the acting or the staging, he really gets every single thing the way he wants it. And he could not be nicer. I was really lucky these last few years having amazing, nice people to work with.

And then, just as the show was building up steam, it was forced to close.
It was shocking that *Beetlejuice* was going to close, but *The Music Man* wanted the theater. We had finally found our audience and it was selling like gangbusters. [Performing on] the Tony Awards was the [jolt] we needed. That put us on the map and made everyone start taking notice. People started buying tickets. Fans like I'd never seen at the stage door. The entire block

"You know what? I don't think we survived the crash!" With Alex Brightman (left) and Rob McClure in *Beetlejuice.*
(Matthew Murphy)

would be filled with kids dressed up in *Beetlejuice* outfits, screaming like we're rock stars. The fandom is intense. We had a few more months to go and then COVID happened [and the show abruptly closed on March 12]. It was crazy. We left thinking we were going to be off for two weeks and then it was completely over. Maybe like a month or two later they were like, "You can come back and get your stuff from the theater." Because of COVID restrictions we only had an hour to get all our stuff and you could only be in there with so many people, so we had scheduled times. I felt terrible because I left my room a mess because I had to get out. I was so nervous about going over my hour because I'm somebody who really follows the rules. Other people were sitting around chatting. And that was it. We didn't say goodbye. And then, literally years later, [we're coming back]. We didn't know until a few months ago that it was definitely going to happen. We were kind of at the peak when we closed, so who knows what is going to happen with this show. Hopefully, we'll be able to pick back up where we left off. It feels like there is excitement around it coming back. When you're opening a show, you never know if it's going to hit. We KNOW it's a hit! We know that people love it. So after two years of insecurity, to know that we have a second chance is really great. I have been offered other things that I have turned down because I haven't worked for two years and I have to make safe choices for my family now. I love doing *Beetlejuice* so it's not like I am sacrificing. But I can't go out of town and leave my family when I already have a job here. My daughter was the one who actually said that to me. She was like, "But Mom, why would you leave us when you have a job here?"

Are you able to feel like you are giving both your family and your career as much as you want to?

I love creating new roles. But when I make a decision for my family [instead of for a show], it will come back to me, whether it's in love from my family or some other amazing job. I'm doing this movie in Vancouver now, and [I'm asking myself] why leave to do a movie when I love doing theater so much? Why would I leave my family to do this?

So when you ask yourself that question, what do you answer?

I'm going to say I really want to focus on theater. Your agents and your managers are always pushing you to do TV and film because they want you to be a star, but there's nothing like theater. There's nothing like feeling that audience, and I completely missed that doing TV and film. I don't care about being famous. I love the consistency of theater. I love finding new ways to make the audience laugh and going on that ride with them. I feel very lucky that I've been able to keep going. I've always said, "I just want to be a working actor." I love the idea of regional theater where sometimes you're the lead, sometimes not. Some people will only do leads and once they've done that, they feel that they can't take supporting roles. I am not like that. I've always been happy with what I am doing. Sometimes I am just doing voice-overs and I am perfectly happy doing that. Sometimes I am starring in a Broadway show and I am happy doing that. It's all good as long I am a working actress.

Heather Headley

April, June 2022

"A professor of mine said to me, 'There's a difference between television performance and music theater performance,'" shares Heather Headley. "'Take a Coke bottle and you shake that Coke bottle. Shake it, shake it, shake it, shake it, shake it. For the movies and television, you shake it and you leave the bottle cap on, and then you perform. But for the theater you shake that Coke bottle and then you take that cap off and … BOOM!' That's exactly it. There's nothing else like it."

That soda explosion, the gush of a champagne bottle, the gallop of a horse set free, that's as apt a description as any of a Heather Headley performance. From the moment she's on-stage, she is almost feline: stately, still, contained, but percolating, poised, alert, and ready to pounce. And when she does unleash, it's with ferocity. In her Broadway debut, she was, in fact, a lioness, originating the role of Nala in *The Lion King*. She left that show for the next Disney on Broadway outing, tackling the title role in *Aida*. Ben Brantley, in his *New York Times* review, enthused, "She wears royalty as if it were a body stocking, right next to the skin, and it's easy to see why the other characters onstage sense that there is something that separates Aida from your run-of-the-mill slave. She has fire, self-possession and an uncompromising sense of purpose. And although she may have goddess-like attributes, she also gives off a purely human flesh-and-blood intensity … [Headley] is simply splendid. She not only has what is called It—that ineffable, sensual glow—but also a voice of stunning emotional variety and conviction. Anytime she sings, whether of memories of a lost girl-hood or of Aida's reluctance to take on a mantle of power, the show springs into vital life." She followed *Aida* with the starry, now-legendary *Dreamgirls* concert and then … moved to Chicago, where she focused on recording and starting a family. It took a dozen years for Headley to return to the theater, and *The Bodyguard*, in London's West End, may not have been a perfect show, but as a showcase for what Heather Headley brings to the table, it seemed tailor-made. In 2016 she returned to Broadway to replace Jennifer Hudson in *The Color Purple*. Brantley again raved: "Ms. Headley crackles with electricity from the get-go…. Her resplendent voice matches her mercurial character's every emotional shift." Most recently, at Encores!, she played The Witch in what was arguably the best-sung *Into the Woods* in that show's history.

Of all the women I spoke to for this book, pinning down time with Headley was the hardest. That's partially because she's filming the series *Sweet Magnolias* in Atlanta, but also because when she's not working, Headley is fiercely dedicated to her family and making sure that the time that she has goes to her husband, Brian, and their three kids, the youngest of whom is three. When we do steal some time, though, Headley is at ease and full of gratitude. She marvels at the career she's forged and the opportunities she's had, and confesses, wide-eyed, more than once, "Eddie, don't tell anyone, but I'd do it for free! But thanks for the check!"

"I think it pisses God off if you walk by the color purple in a field somewhere and don't notice it."
With Cynthia Erivo (right) in *The Color Purple*.
(Matthew Murphy)

As I understand it, the theater bug didn't hit you until Northrop High School, where you did *Camelot* and *Man of La Mancha* and then starred in *Funny Girl*. Did you have any interest in theater before that?
Before that I didn't have a name for it. It's like "I've always loved filet, I just didn't know this was what they called it." When I was growing up in Trinidad, our little church was kind of the rebel church because we had this drama group that would put on skits in town and in the street. My parents were pastors so I would always be there with them, I just didn't know it was called theater. The gentleman who introduced me to all of that, David Williams, just passed away. I sent a message saying, "This was the first introduction I had to the arts." He did that for thousands of children. And we always had a lot of Bollywood in Trinidad. I would watch these movies and, at some point in the film, they'd stop, dance, and sing. I just always thought, "Well, of course." Because in my head, you stop, dance, and sing whenever you need something. I mean I do it now! The first movie I saw was *The Sound of Music*. I got all dressed up. I remember what it did to me, even at that age. I remember crying. I remember going home and re-enacting it in my room. It taught me that children could be in these things and that when you couldn't speak anymore, you sang! So, I would say, I think [theater] was always in me, I just didn't have a word for it. Then, when I got to Northrop High School, they put the words "musical theater" onto my map. I really give a lot of credit to those guys in Trinidad for introducing me and opening my eyes to it, and then a lot of credit to my teachers at Northrop for starting to open that door and show me some things. *Camelot* was the first one. I was in the chorus and I really was not happy about that. I was like two months out of Trinidad! But let me tell you, in my life there have always been those *Camelot* experiences

where I had to sit in the wings or sit as the understudy, and I think it's necessary. Those are the times I learned the most. In my third year, Mr. Proctor, the drama teacher, came to me and he said, "You think your parents will be upset if you played a prostitute?" I was like, "WHAT?" I went home and I asked my mom and she said, "Well, if she has redeeming qualities." I went back and I said, "My mom says I can be a prostitute if she has redeeming qualities." In retrospect, I'm really honored and so happy about my teachers at Northrop because

Heather Headley	
The Lion King	Broadway, 1996
Do Re Mi	Encores!, 1999
Aida (Tony Award)	Broadway, 2000
Dreamgirls in Concert	Broadway, 2001
The Bodyguard	West End, 2012
The Color Purple	Broadway, 2016
Into the Woods	Encores!, 2022

they picked tough musicals with certain students in mind. *Man of La Mancha* is not an easy thing! With *Funny Girl*, I studied Barbra Streisand for a few months and it was a really great experience. I think I played the first Black, Jewish Fanny Brice.

You went on to Northwestern. And you were cast in *Ragtime* before you even graduated. How did that happen?

Sophomore year I got cast as Lorell in *Dreamgirls* at the Lincolnshire Theater. Angela Robinson was Deena and Felicia Fields was Effie. In retrospect, not the smartest thing I've ever done because I was doing my full load of school and then driving to the theater at night. My mother said [in a heavy Trinidadian accent], "Just don't fail." Because I had been getting A's. "If you bring me C's, I'll understand it. Just don't fail." I got my Equity card on that, which presented a little problem when I went back to shows at Northwestern. I'd joke, "Um, I need an Equity fifteen [minute break]!" Lincolnshire called me back the next year, my junior year, to do *And the World Goes 'Round*. That was with these really elite Chicago people, Kingsley Leggs and Greg Boynton. God bless them for casting me. My agent at that point was Janet Lower. The last day of junior year, Janet had set up two auditions. One was for the Lyric downtown. They were going to do a Christmas show with, like, 450 performances a weekend. You know how those are; they're just pumping them out. I was going to get like fifteen hundred dollars a week, which was 495 dollars more than I was making on work study, so I was like, "I'm in!" The other was for this show called *Ragtime*. I went to the first audition [for the Christmas show] and the director called me right up to the desk and said, "You have the part. We'll work around your school schedule." I had just gotten *Once on This Island* on the campus [for Fall semester], I was hanging out with the football players, I was gonna marry one in five years, it was fine. So, I called Janet and said to her, "I just got the part and I'm not going to go to this *Ragtime* audition. It is going to upend everything." Janet said to me, "I think you should go. It's for a big company, Livent. You're not going to get it. They're going to say you're too young and you're still in school. But it's important that they start seeing you." So I went. Whatever. I remember they were talking while I was singing, which is one of my great pet peeves. Everyone's talking and writing. At the end of it, I was like, [dismissively, annoyed] "Thank you," and I was leaving. They were like, "No, no, no! Wait! We're discussing how we're going to get you out of school and how we can get you to Toronto." No! No, no! No! I'm too young and you're not supposed to hire me! I have to go out with the football players tonight and they've never asked me to go anywhere before! I just got cast in *Once on This Island*! Life is good for me at Northwestern. I'm just here to sing for you so you know that I exist. Bye-bye!

But they're like, "No, you have to go to the callback." I said, "I can't. I am locking up my room at school [for the summer]." They called my agent and said, "You have a crazy person for a client. We're literally offering her a job and she's trying to run out of the room." I went back to Janet and she said, "Well, we are in a conundrum, aren't we? We have a little problem." I called my mother and—we were only three years out of Trinidad—and my mother was like, "I have no idea what to do. All I can do is pray for you. I think what you need to do is call every person that we know who knows about this stuff. And I'll just pray." So she started praying and I called all my professors, all my teachers, all my friends. I called everybody that had anything to do with the field and everybody said to go. So I packed up my things, crying the entire way. I just didn't know what was going to happen. *Ragtime* was another *Camelot* moment, one of the greatest *Camelot* moments of my life, watching everything. That was the cast of all casts.

Having been a decent-sized fish in a smaller pond, did you feel like a smaller fish in a bigger pond?

I was a piece of plankton. Even the chorus … these voices were ridiculous. Gold at every level. I don't want to downplay anything Northwestern ever did for me, but the training that I got within those six months of sitting in the wings, watching them work and learning from them, is invaluable. It's kind of like, if you're going to be a plumber, there's all the stuff that you can learn from the books, but at some point you've got to go out and apprentice. You're going to have to see it and feel it and learn how to keep your pants up. And that's what happened with me in *Ragtime*. I am incredibly grateful for those months when I just sat there. And Audra takes great care of her voice. She knows [when she should take a night off] and she's not insecure about that. So she would miss a few shows every now and then and I had the opportunity to be on stage with Brian Stokes Mitchell and Marin Mazzie and Peter Friedman. When you are onstage with people at that level, you straighten that back up. We're doing this! You come up to their level. It was a great time.

What do you remember learning specifically?

The plumbers are everywhere. You've got [composers] Stephen Flaherty and Lynn Ahrens! Seeing how musicals happen. One day it's [sings] "Daddy played piano, played it very well." And then the next day it's [sings it again with the last note changed]. "Oh! You can change it!" One of the things I learned from Audra at that time: she made it OK for me to bring all of my emotions to the stage. If I feel like crying, I can cry. Bring that all to the stage. I think I knew it before, but it was solidified that you bring everything to the table and if you have a good director, he'll cut it up and tell you. You bring it all, then the director says, "I don't need the filet and the shrimp and the scallops. Why don't you give me a little bit of shrimp, and filet? No scallops." I learned about the voice. There were two women: here was Marin Mazzie, God bless her, who'd walk on stage with her liver hanging out, dragging on the floor. And then [singing perfectly] "There was a time.…" But I'm watching your liver, dangling behind you! And then there's somebody like Audra who's very protective of her instrument. Audra might go into her room and [warms up] and if it's not right, we're not going to push it. And so to learn from those two … I had to find a happy medium for me. And learning how to be an ensemble member, how to be in the chorus—the etiquette of the chorus. I think there is an etiquette to being an understudy. I think a lot of times people come into a show and they're thinking, "I'm as good as you." And sometimes they are. But that's not relevant. Understand where you are. Understand your lead. You may not like it, but they may call out five minutes before the show. That's part of your job as an understudy. I was learning all of those things. There is a lot to be learned, not only on the stage, but off the stage.

A lot of people have talked about that. You get off the stage but you're not off the train.
It's always moving. And a lot of the time, we [actors] get all the credit. I'm down center with the lights on me. But I can't be a princess if I don't have a kingdom, and that kingdom is incredibly important. Every cast member, every chorus member, and all the bodies that are running in the back—the crew is so important. You think I am off the train but there's a Mack truck and a steamroller back stage. The crew has always been close to my heart. Without them, I am literally dead. Those guys take their jobs so seriously. There are so many things people don't see. When I was doing *The Bodyguard*, my dresser and I would literally never come back to the dressing room [because there were so many quick changes backstage]. My dresser Jenny took such great care of me. Once we left the dressing room, we were two fighters. As I crossed the stage glamorously, Jenny was running underneath it [to meet me on the other side with my next costume]. She'd make sure that all the dresses were placed in a certain way [for the fastest, easiest access]. I had one twenty-second change, going from jeans and a T-shirt to a gown. Change wigs. Everything. That train—it's a beautiful thing. Those are the things that I learned on the professional level.

You were directed and choreographed by Frank Galatti and Graciela Daniele? Were they different from what you'd experienced?
Nothing against the directors I had in Chicago, but this was like going to meet Spielberg. Graciela Daniele was a formidable force. There was just a steamroller in there. They brought in the best for that show. That show was ready to win every Tony until somebody said, "Have you thought about lions?" [*The Lion King*].

So, how did you end up with the lions?
I got a call from Janet. They snuck me into New York. I literally flew into New York on a Monday morning and back Monday night. Janet once again said, "You're not going to get this. But you should audition for Disney. They're going to say you're not right and that they can't get you out of the *Ragtime* contract, but it's good to be seen." So, I did it and then I got the call, "It's you." Janet, God bless her, sat with the contract one night and called me the next morning, like, before God woke up. She said, "I found a hole in your contract. If Disney buys you out of the contract, you can get out." She called Disney and [they agreed]. That started the biggest like mafia thing of my life! I remember walking down the streets of Toronto and a car drove up next to me. Window rolls down. "Hi! Garth Drabinsky wants to talk to you." He said, "You're a good understudy and we want to give you [the part] one day." I got talked to by every lead, every assistant director, every person. I'm going to try not to cry as I tell you this: Marin Mazzie called me into her room during intermission—and I had been going through great agita. My mom's like, "I can't help you. I don't know what to do. I'll pray." And, with all due respect, *Lion King*? Is this going to be like *Beauty and the Beast*? Will I have a mask over my face? Will I be in hair? How are you gonna put lions up there? I was thinking, "I can't do this." Marin calls me in, and this is a big deal. When a lead calls you into her dressing room at intermission? She says, "Sit." I'm thinking I did something wrong. She says, "On the record, and for the record, you need to stay here. We love you. You're a great understudy. You're

amazing at what you do, etc., etc. Off the record, you have to go." I still can't even deal with it right now [she tears up]. "You have to go. Sometimes you're not considered for leads when you're in an understudy position. You're not considered for leads until you leave and become your own lead. You're that talented and you're that good and you have to go. It doesn't matter if it works or not. You must go." I called Janet and said, "Marin Mazzie says I have to go." It was pretty much Marin's doing and one of the things I hold so close in my heart about that woman. I am indebted to her. I hope I can be that kind of mentor for someone someday. She was a great sweet, amazing woman. There was one other person: Stafford Arima [the assistant director] pulled me aside and said, "They are telling us we have to tell you to stay but you have to go. You have to go."

Before we get to *Lion King*, was there anything else you remember learning from those people by watching them?
I was always stunned by Brian Stokes. I call him "buttah" to this day. His voice is like butter. I was always interested in the way he held his body—the strength of it. And with Audra, you could watch her and see how she would act with her body [her shoulders collapse and turn in]. I loved watching that. I loved watching Peter Friedman, the delicacy of how he played a broken man. He wasn't scared to be vulnerable on stage. Those were moments that I pinpointed. Marin—how she could get that sound out! I learned nuances. In *Aida*, I used to have my body still, and then one little movement [she moves her hand slightly], when I do it, you'll notice. A lot of times we think we need to do a lot, even with notes, but it's in the stillness. You can control the audience's attention and where it goes. It's kind of what magicians do. In every show I do, I like to go watch it. I'll take a day if I'm not feeling well and I'll go watch the show, especially before we get into the run. It helps me to see how small I am in it. I love to see how small I am! You see all these beautiful things happening around you [that you don't see from the stage]. Somebody might be doing something beautiful, and because you're the lead and the light's on you the whole audience is [watching you]. So, if I can move your attention to her [looks over at the imaginary dancer], then you get to see what she's doing. You look over at that person and then the audience is like, "What's she looking at?" She's doing a jeté, I'm just standing here. Why are you looking at me? When I watch the shows, I have a greater appreciation for every cast member, and definitely the crew. I used to watch the opening of *The Lion King* all the time. Every time I felt like I was getting tired of the show, I would go watch the beginning and then you're like, "All right! Let's go!"

Let's talk about *The Lion King*.
I leave, not knowing what I am walking into.

And you go to New York, never having lived there.
And I had never seen a Broadway show. I bought a ticket to *The Life*. Lillias White got the Tony and I wanted to see someone at their best. I got dropped into New York and I didn't know how to take the train. If rehearsals started at 10:00, I'd leave the apartment at 8:30. I was carrying around mace because I thought everyone was going to kill me. My mother was like, "Don't go to New York and die." It was completely crazy and I walked into art at its highest. These South Africans [in the cast] were singing for murder. And then there was [director] Julie Taymor and [choreographer] Garth Fagan. I did not understand their brilliance until I had a moment, watching the show with Julie, and I got it all the way. It was in previews and

we were doing a press presentation. People were in black leotards. In the New Amsterdam Theater, there's a little cubby right off the side, stage right, where you can watch the show but an audience cannot see. So I went into that cubby and I sat because they were going to do the opening number. I was still kind of like, "I don't know if this thing's gonna work." Julie walked in. We weren't as close as we are now and I wasn't getting the whole vision of what she was doing. Julie was this woman that came into this very male environment, doing the costumes and designs and directing. I do think that Nala kind of represented that woman power to her. She had very, very specific ideas for Nala. I was trying to find this vision of hers and I couldn't see it. I was like, "I think I look crazy when I do that [does a head, shoulder, and body undulation]." The lights went down and the light hit the sunrise [set piece]. In the shadows, those giraffes started walking on. Tsidii La Loka came out and sang those first notes and I grabbed Julie's hand and started bawling through the whole thing. I will assure you that if that woman looks at her hand right now, there are dig marks from my nails, still embedded. I'm sure my nail is still in there and she carries it around. "That's from Heather Headley." I didn't let go. And at the end, I got it, and I was like, "We have the best show ever!" From then on, I made a promise to always watch the show. I cannot tell you how proud I am to be a part of that show, how honored I am to be one of the freshman class of that show. And I cannot tell you as a performer how proud I am of it as a singer, as an actress, and now as a mom. When I first got pregnant I decided I wasn't going to see that show until he was ready, so I did not watch it for seven years. I wanted to see it through his eyes. I wanted to experience what I saw those parents experience. So I have great affection for Julie Taymor and Garth Fagan and Disney. They live deep in my heart.

Talk to me about Garth Fagan and what you learned from him.
I was not capable of doing Garth's choreography. His choreography was on a different level. It was Ailey quality. Those girls who did it were at the highest levels. But he catered it to me and cut it around me. There are other choreographers that would be like, "It's this or nothing. You do this." Garth would come in and say, "I don't think that will work on her. Try this, Heather." And never did he make me feel that it was because I wasn't good enough. It was just like, "Here's the dress. We're going to tailor make it to you and make you shine." I'm so grateful to him for that. The South Africans came in and taught us about that music and that culture. They also taught us about their life and apartheid and what they had gone through. I learned click language, too. When they sang, they sang from the gut. There's nothing like it. So there was all that beautiful learning. Our cast was so diverse and so different. How amazing to share something that is now historical. It will go down as one of the greatest musicals of all time. If you had talked to me in Trinidad and told me that I was going to be part of one of the biggest musicals of all time, I'd be like, "Musical? What is that?" And here we are. So I am forever grateful to be a part of it. When you think about this stuff, it's really ridiculous. They could have picked any other person in the world. We forget that these shows just ask for one. The fact that it was me is beyond my brain.

It has to be, right? Or you'd get caught up in you. You just have to say "thank you" and do your work.
Yes. You do your work. That's my thing. You try to do your work. I think for all my life, I put blinders on. So when people say, "Oh, this is happening," I have no idea that it's happening until afterwards. I didn't read my reviews for *Aida*. I put the blinders on and I like it like that.

But with *Lion King*, the show exploded. You have to have known.

Yeah. It was like crazy. I would wear my *Lion King* jacket because I was proud of it. But in the time it took me to get from the Upper West Side down to the theater, I'd be accosted like twenty times: "Can you get me tickets?" We got a pin that I used to wear on my jacket: "I cannot get you tickets." Although I did such bad things with those tickets. For instance, I remember one time I moved into another apartment and I had no furniture. The guy who was supposed to deliver the bed calls and says, "I can't bring your bed today." I said to him, "I would love for you to bring the bed today because I'm doing a show and I need my rest." And he's like, "What show are you doing?" "*The Lion King.*" "[Sharp inhale] Can you get me tickets?" "I guess I could." It was hilarious. My husband was playing with the Jets at the time and we traded tickets. He'd call me up and be like, "I need four tickets." And I'd say, "Well, I need six tickets to your game for the crew." "OK, I'll give you six. Can you give me four?" So the crew would be going to Jets games and the Jets players would be coming to the theater. Everyone came to that show and that was another time that I figured out—I learned it in *Ragtime* a little bit—that I don't like to know who's in the audience. I don't want to know. They would announce it. It would be like, "Kofi Annan, Chris Rock, and Tom Hanks." And we'd all be like [if you must], "OK, bring Chris Rock back," or, "Hmm, we'll see Hanks." Everyone came to that show. Gorbachev! Michael Jackson. Steven Spielberg.

Being in the center of that as the female lead, doing all of the press, wearing those very heavy costumes, doing a long run, was that exciting? Overwhelming?

Scary. And not something that I'd been a part of. I was kind of thrust into it. There's a part of you that longs for the limelight. [But part of you is] kind of fighting, "Am I good enough? Did I do well enough? Do they hate me?" I always think that we performers have a little sickness.

In that show, I'd think it's easy to sort of diminish your own contributions. Because the thing that is really the star is Julie Taymor. It's all the design. You could talk yourself into a notion that they can plug in any human and, as long as they are wearing the costume, it'll work.

I think that's the case. I do believe that *The Lion King* is the star of *The Lion King* and Julie Taymor is its leading lady. And rightfully so. But that was one of the jobs—to make it and her work shine. We had a great cast: Max Casella, Tom Robbins, John Vickery, the hyenas, all of those people—it lifts it to a different level. But the show is still the star.

This was a show that was fraught with injuries because of those costumes and that choreography. How were you navigating that?

It was tough. We were all learning at the same time. So, for instance, my corset was made with African beads. It was incredibly heavy. The corsets that have come later, I'm told, are much lighter. My first corset was true Maasai, it was heavy. It hurt after a while. So, we had to learn that. My pants were, I think, dyed in Thailand and were incredibly expensive because that's all they knew at the time. Subsequent pants have been [made here]. My mask was heavy and there was a mic in it. So we had injuries. Necks were out. We had physical therapy between shows, before shows, and after shows. I think I still have issues from that time and I know I'm the least of the worries; the dancers danced on rakes and had jumps while carrying things. I know there are some people that are still hurting from the show, but I hope it's not awful.

What did that do for morale at the time? On the one hand, you've got this blockbuster and there's all that excitement, and on the other hand, people are getting hurt.
Yes. But I said this at the Tonys and I will say it here: I loved working for Disney and I will work for them for the rest of my life. Disney cared. So when somebody brought [a grievance] to their attention, they would try to address it and fix it. They tried their best to mitigate [issues causing injury.] It hurt me the least. The dancers! I think Max Casella had carpal tunnel and still does [from his Timon puppet].

Anything that you can say about Elton John?
I have great love for Elton John. Great gratitude. It starts in *The Lion King*. I remember him showing up and I'm not easily starstruck, but.... He sat in the room with us and gave notes. When I did *Aida*, he came twice a week for weeks. He'd bring his whole entourage. He'd be like [in a British accent], "Heather, I'll be back on Thursday with Larry Fishburne and Diana Krall. Fergie may come with me as well." I'm like, "OK, well, my friend, Pookie, will be coming. Can she sit with you?" And he would! He was there with us.

Between *The Lion King* and *Aida*, you did *Do Re Mi* at Encores!
One of my agents said, "They want you to audition for this. It is a really, really good thing to audition for." And needless to say, it was an amazing cast. Nathan Lane, Brian Stokes Mitchell, Randy Graff. [The last time] Brian Stokes and I had met [in Toronto's *Ragtime*], I was an understudy, he was the lead. Now I'm coming into it as a lead with him. It felt like a big deal. It was one of those moments where you feel this graduation. Not that *Lion King* was anything less, but now I am performing with Nathan Lane and Brian Stokes.

You're in the club.
Well, at least at the door. Maybe the bouncer won't kick you out. And I really believe that iron sharpens iron, so being in the presence of such people sharpens you. You have to come up. You better get good because you're playing with the big boys.

Did you? Did you grow and learn?
I think so. You always learn, but at the time, my head was so buried in it. My blinders are on. That's the kind of horse I am. I don't know. I hope I got better.

That was the first time you did a role not specifically written for a Black actor.
I love that casting. I want to play Maria [in *West Side Story*]. If it works. When I walk into any room, even if this role is written for maybe someone who doesn't look like me, I want to be so good in the audition and give you the best of me so much, that you question [for example], "Should Heather play Mother in *Ragtime*? Maybe she could." Even though it shouldn't happen, I want to go in there doing such a good job that I make you go, "Hmm. I didn't think of that but maybe she could." One time I got called to do a reading of *Sweeney Todd*. I remember trying to figure out what a Black woman would look like at that time. Why would she be in London? How would she be? It changes the whole thought process of it. I love

the opportunity to take on [non-traditional] casting and just have the roles be roles. We are forging paths here, but in order for that path to be forged, I have to do this exceptionally well. I have to bring a good mower out here, and a good machete, and cut. You go out there and cut the path amazingly and then everybody can walk down it.

How did *Aida* come to you? A phone call from your agent saying, "Disney wants to see you for this other thing?"
Yeah, and once again, "You're not going to get it. They are looking at known actresses who can sing and known singers who can act. They want to audition you as a 'Broadway person' to prove that a 'Broadway person' won't work for it." I think that's the best way for me to do things: without expectation. I'm just going to sing and leave. Whatever. I'm competitive enough to still do it, but I have the expectation that it won't happen. But I'm going to go in and try to make this a difficult decision for them. I auditioned and then got called back into this dark theater with Schumacher and Eisner and some of the other bigwigs at Disney. And then we got the call. And again, I'm just grateful to Disney because I know some of the other names they were looking at. But they saw something in me that I maybe didn't at the time. I am incredibly grateful that they gave me that opportunity. They pulled me out of *Lion King* and sent me to Atlanta and started that process.

This was your third new musical in a row, but the first that underwent such a significant overhaul during its development.
While we were in Atlanta, I think the show showed us a lot. I believe it was the first day of previews; Elton's there, the theater's full, we have this amazing pyramid that we're supposed to be living on, and that bad boy breaks. It just wets the stage with hydraulic fluid. All over the stage. The gentleman who did that thing was of the highest ilk. These were the men that were doing the rides at Disney [Disney's park designers, the Imagineers]. They were intent on making this thing work. One of them said to me, "Your job is from 8:00 to 10:00 every night and my job will be from 10:00 to 8:00 when you show up for it the next day." They were determined. The pyramid [had a hum] to it, like a "D note." I had to [really concentrate to find my note]. "This pyramid's off key!" The next night they came to me: "The pyramid's in a new key." "What? How'd you do that?" They would do stuff like that. But that first night [after the pyramid breakdown] we did the show on chairs [no staging] in front of the curtain. I think that's when they figured out we had a show. When a show is naked, you know if she has a good body or not, or if that body should be seen. And that's what it showed us because we got a standing ovation. People were crying and moved and actors did what they were supposed to. That's when it started moving in [a more minimalist] direction. We had a good run there, fixing things and moving things around. We closed the show and they had started giving us little hints the day before, that it might get messy the next morning. And the next morning it got messy. They fired everybody. Everyone was gone. Just Sherie Rene Scott and I remained. Sherie told me she had gone home and thrown up because it was so much. In that first version, by the way, Radames and Aida didn't die. Amneris saved them. Sherie and I went to the director and said, "They have to die. Disney's killed everyone. They killed Bambi's mother, they killed Mufassa, they've killed everyone for the good of the character who's learning. Radames and Aida—they have to die." There was a big ol' conversation and two scripts later, Radames and Aida were dead.

"Aida, Aida, All we ask of you is a lifetime of service, wisdom, courage . . . " In *Aida*.
(Photofest)

In the version where they were saved, what did they do next? I mean . . .
They went to Disney! "I just got out of the tomb and I'm goin' to Disneyland!"

I always wonder about actors who are in shows that are not working. Were you ever thinking, "What the hell am I in?" Or do you trust the creators to get there? Or is it both?
A bit of both. I knew we needed changes. I never was concerned about the story. I knew the story was working. I just felt the way the story was being set up physically was not there yet. But there was the feeling, "There's something here," whereas other times it can be, "Oh, we're in trouble." But the audience loved it. I think they tell you everything. If the audience is not handling it, then that's worse, but our audiences were responding to the show. So I knew there was something there. That's where Disney comes in and says, "We think that there is a change needed to make it better." Hence, a little hiatus. I went back to *Lion King* for three months. And I got some phone calls [with updates]. Disney was incredibly open with me, which I'm also grateful for because they didn't need to be. But "[director] Bob Falls is joining us." "OK." "[Playwright] David Henry Hwang is coming on." "OK." "[Designer] Bob Crowley." And then I got a phone call one day: "We've got your Radames. Adam Pascal." I was like, "Who's not going to want to look at him for a little bit? That's going to be fun." But I didn't know how our voices would get together. First day of rehearsals, Adam showed up exactly the way that I think they always wanted Radames: AC/DC shirt, ripped sleeves, five o'clock shadow. I was like, "Oh, yes. Hello, Captain. Take us away." I knew we could mold together. That's the beauty with voices and singing. A teacher always told me to listen to the other person and you meld that voice together. I just didn't know how much it would. And I didn't know personality-wise how it was going to work. I consider him one of my musical soulmates to this day. He could show up here right now and I'm sure we would be right back at it. He was the best.

I am guessing there was the expectation that you lead the company in a show that was an incredibly heavy sing and took a lot out of you. What was that like?
God was gracious to me. I had no children. I had no husband. I had no boyfriend. *Aida* became a boyfriend, she became everything. My aim was just to do my best and not get ripped by Ben Brantley in *The New York Times*.

And you did it!
I did! I found out later. My mother called me the next morning and tried to read the reviews to me. I wouldn't talk until like 5:00 p.m. She was leaving [to fly home after opening night] and she called from the airport. "Heather, hello, just making sure you're fine." I am making grunts, not talking. "OK. Well, I know you don't read reviews. I know you don't do that. But [at breakneck speed] *The New York Times* says this…." I'm like, "Mom! Stop!," trying to put the phone down! I just wasn't focused on that. I wanted to do a great job and lead the cast and to be a good cast mate. I'm sure at times I failed with that, but my goal was always to do the show properly. I will tell you this, and I don't want you to think I'm just making it up: I really, really do think that we have one of the greatest gifts ever. Singing is something I do in my bathroom. It's something I do around the house. It's something I do to make myself feel happy or to express myself when I am sad. You come along and say, "I will pay you to sing and I will sit in your audience and watch you while you do that." That is crazy. My mother worked. You know what I mean? My grandfather worked in a factory. Those are jobs. This is not a job! This is the opportunity to do something that is just natural to your body. So when you have that great gift of getting that opportunity, you better do

that right! Let's do it to the best of our abilities! So don't show up late for your entrance. Do it! Do it right! Let's get it done! Because these people [the audience] have jobs. We get the opportunity to take them away from that. My first memories are of me singing. And now you're going to put a light on me? On a stage? And people are going to come? I remember being in Japan and watching the art of the bow. It was out of respect; I bow to you out of great respect. That's how I feel when I bow. It's, "Thank YOU for coming here. You could've been anywhere else in this world and yet you sat here and listened to me sing." The bow is because I am honored that you would be here. And so with that said, I hope that those times that maybe I wasn't [the best leader] it was always, to me, for the show. I sometimes … am … less patient with understudies … because I was an understudy and because I understand the opportunity you have. My attitude is like, "You get to go on." The first two shows as an understudy I give you. Have fun. This is all about you. I go to understudies all the time and say that. "Let's do it. I'll move you around, I'll help," that kind of thing. But after that, you have to know. So those are the things that I can sometimes be a little less patient about. We're in multi-million-dollar projects. And people have paid two or three hundred dollars to come see us. So, I'll give you those first two, but we can't afford to do bad work after that.

I'm not even sure it's a question of bad; it's, here's how the director wanted it, here's where the light is focused, here's where the other actor is going to be, fit in!
And get there! We have to get there. This is the greatest opportunity. You just don't know who's in the audience.

Actually you do. You just said it: people with jobs who paid to be there and give themselves over to you.
Let's do it! And I am the first one to have fun on stage. I have pulled a few pranks. Lots of them. My problem is that I am not smart. I pull these pranks when I am playing the lead and I'm on stage the entire time. Then the crew is looking at me like, "you can't even defend yourself." So my dressing room has been topsy-turvy. Because it's always with the crew. I'm always pranking the crew. And they're just like, "Why are you playing with us? You're on stage for forty-five minutes. We have nothing else to do but come after you." I've tp'ed crew's rooms.… I got to the theater early in London just to tp the entire crew. There was toilet paper everywhere. The crew would look at me, "It's not gonna be good for you. It's gonna be ugly." I'm all for a good time. But with the [understanding] that this is serious and that it gets done properly. I'm not going to be up in your face or mean or anything, but I do expect that we do our best.

You say you don't read reviews, that you have your blinders on and focus on the work, but with the amount of media attention and awards that came your way, and invitations to perform at benefits and such, you have to have known that you were exploding. You were that season's performance to see.
It is tough and we try to temper that. Especially if you pull that blinder down a little bit and think, "Oh, it seems like I AM pretty cool." You have to try to temper it, especially for your castmates, who may not be getting that same attention. That's a hard line to toe. There can be survivor's guilt. Because you're thinking, "I really want this Tony," but it's hard. That morning of the *Aida* nominations, I always thought Sherie was better in the show than I was. The morning of the nominations [when I learned that Sherie and Adam weren't nominated], how do you go in the next day? That person is so happy for you but they're so disappointed. They put in work as well and we've been together for all this time. It's tough.

When I asked you about your own star power exploding, I didn't necessarily mean the glamour and awards of it all, I was really thinking about the weight. Audiences are not just coming for the show, they're coming to see Heather Headley in the show. Did you feel the responsibility of that?

Heck, yeah. I got the Tony on a Sunday night, Tuesday [following] was the scariest night of my life. I was scared out of my mind because at this point I now have a qualifier on my name that will be with me for the rest of my life: "Tony Award winner Heather Headley." I think I was more scared that night than any other night of doing the show. Because, like you said, there was this weight now. Even when I did London, I was so nervous because you have to live up to this thing. Now people are coming to see ... why? "Let me see why you got that Tony." You have to live up to that. Since that day, I feel that way all the time. You have to live up to it. You have to live up to Mandy Patinkin and Bernadette Peters and Brian Stokes Mitchell and Lillias White and Audra McDonald twenty times. All of these amazing performers that carry that moniker: Tony Award winner. It's a great weight and I am grateful for that weight. I want to always carry that weight with me. But that Tuesday, I remember feeling the weight. And Tony season is a lot. Disney gave me one of the greatest gifts in Chris Boneau, who was press agent to Disney at the time, and he walked me through that Tony season. And don't ever get it twisted: it is not fun all the time. There are a lot of parties and you have to show up and shake these hands. Chris was so great about walking me through all of it.

What about actually winning the Tony?

I still don't believe that it's here. It's downstairs right now and every now and then it's like, "Oh, it's still in my house. It wasn't a dream." I was up against some of the greatest: Audra, Marin Mazzie, Toni Collette, Rebecca Luker. I just didn't want to think that night. Badgley Mischka gave me a dress, my mom was my date, through it all my stomach's getting worse and worse and worse. I'm just like, "I'm going to throw up, but I'm gonna keep smiling." My mother said. "I feel like in my spirit, you're going to win," and I said, "Keep quiet!" My mother had gotten in trouble with me at the Drama Desks because when they called my name she jumped up and I was still seated, and she pulled my head into her belly—she was so excited—and pressed my face into her sequined dress, so when I went on stage, I had the imprint of the sequins in my face. I told her to be calm this time, so [if you watch the tape] when I win, you can see her [get really excited and then immediately subdue herself]. But when I heard them say that "H".... Eleven years before, we were coming from Trinidad, not knowing that Broadway existed or that this could be me. I always tell kids that my story is not the normal story. I'm grateful. I know people on Broadway who hit that pavement for decades and still.... When I was growing up as a child, I wanted to get a Grammy because that's what I knew about. So this Tony was just one of those things where your brain's not big enough to dream that big. And here it is. It was an out-of-body kind of experience and so much bigger than I was. I'm grateful to God for it and I'm still in shock by it. And I wanted it [not just for me], but for our show. I felt as though they overlooked us. There were only four musicals that year and one of them was *Contact*, which was a dance show. We didn't get nominated for [Best Musical], the rest of the cast didn't, it was just me, Elton, Bob Crowley [set and costume design], and Natasha Katz [lighting]. That show was my baby. It was my boyfriend. And my cast and crew were so cool and sweet with me. I wanted it, but I wanted it for everybody.

Did you have to live very carefully in order to maintain your energy and voice?

I always do. That's the tough part of Broadway. The slightest little cold, the slightest little phlegm changes everything. In *The Bodyguard* I was getting sick a lot in London because of new germs. There are some shows I can just barrel through. It's two songs or the songs are in the right place [vocally]. With *Aida*, I learned how to barrel through. You try to learn a way to do it unwell. If it means I need to lower the keys or to figure out how to mix it, there comes a point when you just have to learn how to sing it at 98 percent because some days you have to. But people are coming to hear you belt "Easy as Life." When I start doing a show, it becomes a lifestyle, and now that I have a family, they all have to come along for this lifestyle. When I did *Bodyguard,* I wouldn't speak until 4:00 or 5:00. I didn't speak to my child for almost a year, because I would only talk to him after 5:00. I don't go out after shows, I don't drink, I don't smoke, I try not to be near anybody smoking, I don't drink orange juice.... There's just this whole lifestyle that comes with it in order to maintain. That's what happened with *Aida*. I spent a lot of time in my apartment, waiting for 8:00 p.m. [And after a show] I am out of there. My husband and my children are waiting and I feel like I need to go give them my energy. Because I do think that [when I work] they lose out. They don't get all of me. And at the end of a show, I'm exhausted. I like to put it all on the stage. And I like it that way. It should be that way. There have been a few times that I've been in the box office because I wasn't [going on], maybe because I was sick or the Tonys, so I sat in the box office with my hat on, waiting for them to give me a seat. I would see people come in say, "She's not here? I came from Kansas with my sister!" And I'm like [in tortured tones], "I'll do it! I'm here! I'll go on!" Because I couldn't handle it.

That happened more than once?

Oh, yeah. I hated that feeling [of disappointing people]. But one night I was sick and I pushed through and did the show and after, my stage manager, Cliff, said, "To the car! Go!" This woman was at the stage door: "Can you please...." I wasn't talking and Cliff was saying, "Get in the car! Go sleep!" This lady wrote me this scathing letter. "How dare you," and "Who do you think you are?" I don't usually answer those kinds of letters but this time I wrote back. I said, "I think sometimes you guys don't understand, that there's a lot going on. I just want you to know that I did the show with a fever. They were trying to protect me from me and from you, to some extent." A lot of the time I do jump in the car and people don't really understand. You know what, though, I get it. You've spent money, you've brought your kids. It's a sacrifice.

In 2001, right after you left *Aida*, you joined Audra McDonald and Lillias White in the Actors Fund *Dreamgirls* concert.

The world changes literally two days after I leave *Aida*. My husband/boyfriend at the time—his birthday is September 11 and I said to him, "I want to be as far away from that theater as possible." Because for me, [being replaced in a show is] like watching somebody come and take your boyfriend. The audience comes in and they are OK with some other girl taking your boyfriend but I DON'T LIKE IT. So I said, "Get me as far away from that city as possible. I don't want to be there." When I left *Aida*—I like to leave shows when I still love them. I don't want to dislike the show. So I left *Aida* bawling. Monday, I am going to go to Chicago for his birthday and then we're going to head to New Orleans where I cannot hear anything, I don't know what's going on, and I hope that they are crying because I'm not there! And then the world completely changes and we're stuck in Chicago. Two weeks later, I'm supposed to do *Dreamgirls*. Audra was in L.A. LaChanze was nine months pregnant and they could not find her husband. I'm in Chicago and I won't fly. They're like, "You have to come back. We are going to do the show." Audra did the above-ground railroad; she was driving and people would pick her up in places and bring her to the next stop. Voices were tired, bodies were exhausted, because we literally had two or three days to come back into it and do it. Brian drove me. It was eerie driving down the West Side Highway. There were just pictures and pictures of people. And seeing the smoke! And then we started practicing. I just didn't know how this was going to be. But [on performance night] we heard them say, "Ladies and Gentlemen, *Dreamgirls*," and the audience went crazy. At that point I became angry. It was defiance. It was like, "We're going to go do a show! Here! Tonight! And we're gonna shut the place down!" And that's what happened. We were there for blood. We were there for LaChanze. We were there for every person that was down there. We were just going to perform and be hard and that's what happened. I popped cords. I left cords on that stage that I've never gotten back. I had to grow new ones. That's how deep it was. That's our boots on the ground—to perform for them and for two hours take their minds off the ugliness of what was happening outside. And so I remember thinking this is our chance, as we do this *Dreamgirls* concert. We're going to take your brains off of this for two and a half hours. It was quite the concert. It was so defiant. This you will not stop! This is New York and this is the theater and this is who we are! Such an amazing evening and I think one of the times in my life that I was aware of what was actually going on. I have had two or three of those that I was like, "OK, I'm going to live in this moment, right now." We had a good time! And with those ladies, Audra and Lillias! When they called me to do this, they said, "Hi. We want to invite you to be a part of *Dreamgirls* for The Actors Fund and we would like to offer you one of the lead roles." And I said [sounding very imperious, a bit like Joan Collins], "Oh darling. Thank you! I have always wanted to be Deena, Darling." And they said," Umm, no, we want you to be Lorell." And I was like [screaming at machine gun speed, a bit like Rosie Perez], "Lorell! I'm not Lorell! Why am I Lorell? I don't wanna be Lorell! I wanna be Deena." And they were like, "Um, we think you just passed the audition." Lorell was a lot of fun. And the last time I was with Audra I was her understudy and ... here we are.

There's rehearsal footage of Lillias singing "And I'm telling you . . ." and you throwing your shoe at her.
Yes! It goes back to iron sharpening iron. I love being around good metal. In the church in Trinidad, when you sang, the old ladies would say, "Don't let me throw my shoe at you!" It's like the highest honor to me to take your shoe off and throw it at somebody. I know that in other cultures that might be unusual, but in Trinidad ... I threw it at Sara Bareilles in rehearsal [for *Into the Woods*], too! You better not!

After *Dreamgirls* you took a twelve-year hiatus from the theater. What made you decide that *The Bodyguard* was the one you wanted to come back with?
Within that time we were looking at things, at what show would be right. For the first few years I did the record and everybody was focused on touring. I get a call from Joe Machota [Headley's agent]. We had been looking at scripts and he had been sending me things. My son was two years old at the time. There were many times that I was close to saying, "Let's do this or that show." But Joe has always been a good sounding board—my husband, too—the voice saying, "This might not be the one." So Joe called me one day and says, "I think I have something for you. I need you to sit down. How well do you know the music of Whitney Houston?" "Like the back of my hand. That's who taught me how to sing, to some extent. She and God. Send me the script." I remember thinking it was going to be a mess and falling

in love with it. God bless the producers over there: it took them something like seven years to get the rights to all of that music, because if you think of Whitney's music, it's all different writers. You have to go to Babyface and David Foster and Dolly Parton.... It was a task. I was going to say "no" to them in the beginning because it was London and we had a two-year-old, and I was like, "I can't do that." And then my husband said, "I think this is going to be amazing for you. This is the right thing." He and his mom sat me down and said, "We should do this. We will make this work." I get teary talking about it. My husband flew back and forth to London forty-four times over eleven months. He lived in jet lag. He made that sacrifice for us to be over there. We had an amazing nanny who nannied us both. It wasn't easy. There were many, many days I didn't talk. I wouldn't talk for most of the day, just to get through the show. And I got sick a few times there because the germs didn't work for me. Coming back for that show was because of Whitney, because right after I said yes, Whitney passed away. I called them back and I was like, "No, I don't want to do it now." They had to talk me into it.

How was it for you?
It was one of the hardest things I had to do. Emotionally, my husband wasn't there and even though I can be quite the loner, I missed my husband and I realized that he's such a part of even my performance life. I call him my "Joe Schmo." He's [not a theater junkie], he's my average Joe. He is the guy that I want to perform for. So I get to London and my Joe is not there. The cast was amazingly sweet and everything, but there's that emotional side of just being away from home. I think I put a lot on it because it was Whitney and I wanted to sing it perfectly. It was hard because it was fifteen or sixteen songs and [they were solos]. No chorus to help. As I mentioned I had the best dresser in the world: Jenny Carvell. She takes care of Dame Judi Dench now. Just a beautiful woman. She is the most giving, perfect dresser … I don't even know what to call it … helper/assistant. That's what she was. We were a team. She had a carpenter belt in case I needed Gatorade or Ricola or water … everything. Because I couldn't go back to the dressing room, I didn't have time. In the end, it was great.

Was it? Do you feel like you actually delivered what you wanted to do? Was it satisfying for you?
Yes, I got through it. I wish that I had gotten through it better. It was so vocally taxing and the way I was going to sing it was vocally taxing. If I could do it again, I would just tell myself, "You're OK." Because of those twelve years, I think I came back into it kind of trepidatious. Brian says to me, "Heather, you should be calmer and more confident now. The little girl that played Aida should be scared. You have done it and people know you and they know you're fine." And for some reason that scares me more because I feel like they now have expectations. One of my scariest performances was the Tuesday after the Tonys. I was going, "Oh my gosh, I have to live up to Antoinette Perry now! What if I can't?" So coming back after twelve years, I haven't done this in a while, I know I can and they're telling me it's good, and I'm fine. I think I was nervous about that and if I could go back, I would fix that part of it. I would say, "You're fine. You can do this. You got this." I did it, but I wish I could do it a little better—not the performance onstage, just the whole mindset.

Three years later you had another conversation with your husband about leaving Chicago for a period and coming to New York to do *The Color Purple*.
That summer my mom was getting married and I had a busy spring. I was really excited about just being home for the summer. [Again with the Joan Collins] "It will be amazing, Darling. I'll buy a hat and we'll go to the farmer's market!" And Joe Machota calls again. "Jennifer Hudson

has to leave *The Color Purple* a week after the Tony nominations come out. I know I tell you not to replace, but this is different and I need you to just look at it. We think this might be the right thing." I told him no. I said I wanted the summer off. He said, "OK, but at least come see it." I sent a message to them that I would pay for my own ticket and my flight because that's how much I was going to tell them no. And they were like, "No, we're still gonna fly you in." I said, "I'm going to bring my husband because we make these decisions as a family, and he should see it, just to see it." He sat in the theater and at intermission he was crying. He looked at me and said, "You're going to do this." I was like, "What? Wait, no! We came here to say no!'" By the end of it, Brian was, "We're doing it. We will do everything to make this work so that you can do this." And this is long before [director] John Doyle and I sat down to talk. So yeah, once again he sent me off. I think every few years he sends me off. I should look into that.

Talk to me about the John Doyle part of it.
John Doyle. I now have a little crush on him: an artistic and friend crush. Do you know that part of my contract was "John Doyle has to put you into the show," written in by Joe Machota? And I said to him, "This is not necessary." The resident director, Matt DiCarlo, was amazing and Matty was supposed to put me into the show, but they were like, "John Doyle has to come and work with you for at least two or three days." I was like, "Shouldn't the sticking point be money or something? Or my dressing room?" He's like, "No, the sticking point is going to be John Doyle." Part of me was thinking, "Come on, Joe, calm down with this." I thought Joe had gone crazy. And then John Doyle came over for those two days, and he would work with me by myself, and I was like, "Oh, this is why, this is why." I just adore him. He's one of the great directors of the theater. This man made a show naked, the most naked that the show could be, and what he did in doing that was highlight the show and the performers and the lyrics and the writing and the story. He also made the audience think. When I sat in that audience that day, I remember thinking, [Joan Collins] "These chairs are going to come rolling off and they will circle the perimeter of the theater, and then they will go back and the chairs will turn into people and they will be lit...." And the chairs just sat there. They never moved. I could not think of a better way to do that show.

You mentioned those couple of days in the rehearsal room with him. Can you elaborate on that? What in the process was revelatory for you?
His smartness about it. He was kind of like, "I want to strip down your hand movements," everything like that. Even the singing. If you notice, I think John Doyle did the smartest thing he could do for Cynthia Erivo and for the entire show. Cynthia, Jennifer Hudson, Danielle Brooks—amazing. Trust me, when I tell you that whole cast was thick with some of the best singers. They could blow the roof off that place if they wanted to. But he said, "No. You are going to calm it down, and when the time comes that we do blow it off, people will lose their minds." And that's what happened. For the first act and half of the second, there's nothing until Celie sings, "I may be poor. I may be Black. I may be ugly. But I'm heeeeere!" And the audience were laying in the aisles. I think that is incredibly smart and amazingly aware theatrically. You just ride that train and when the time comes, you burst through the clouds. I loved it. He understands the characters better than anyone else. He changed a few things when I came in, and I appreciated him for that. He said, "OK, you're going to fit into the same color dress but we're going to change it a little bit. I'll hem it here and I'll turn it there." I was grateful for that because there are not a lot of directors that would do such a thing. Normally you come in and

"I'm not good, I'm not bad, I'm just right." In *Into the Woods*.
(Joan Marcus)

you'll play what your predecessor played. John said, "I'm going to remake the dress for you. It'll be the same color, the same style, but we're gonna move it around for you." I was grateful.

How was the run for you?
It's tough going into a show when the person before you is loved, but this cast kind of came around me. Very much so. They were such a loving cast that it was easy to be there with them. Beautiful crew, amazing dressers. I enjoyed it, I really did. I think I took my husband's advice to go have fun, to try to just enjoy the process. And Shug was different for me because I had not played somebody like her. Sometimes you can look through your life, and … Aida is kind of me. Nala is me. Rachel [in *The Bodyguard*]? I can find me and other people I know, a little bit of my mom. Shug? Nobody. I'm trying to find somebody to base it off of and I'm like, "Why don't I know a Shug? I should know a Shug." So to create this woman who is deeply broken, but can still lift others up when she can…. She uses her body in certain ways. It was good for me to learn about her and to kind of make her my friend. I enjoyed her.

In 2022 you took on The Witch in *Into the Woods* at Encores! What made you say "yes" to that?
I spent my entire career running from Sondheim, I'm gonna be honest, just running from him. I found his music to be difficult. Sondheim is at the doctorate level and I don't know if I'll pass this class. I'm a [sings the notes] E, D, C kind of girl. I love a good C major chord. Sondheim is [all over the place] and I can't do it! It's so hard! [But, in 2015, I did *Into the Woods*] at the MUNY and I found myself in love with it. I think if we had to call out our top five musicals for all times, *Into the Woods* would be one of the five. It's so well written and it's such a beautiful story.

Your take on The Witch was highly unusual. You really went dark, avoiding almost all of the comedy.
I wanted to almost strip it of the fun, because I think a lot of people go into her with the funny parts. But for me, I think of her spending years waiting for this moment, maybe stalking these people, knowing their every move, knowing that these two people are the people she needs so that she can become better. She wants to become beautiful for herself and for the child. It's manipulative, sinister, urgent, depressed, and angry, and you [the Baker and his wife] have to go get this done for me in three days or else I've got wait another, maybe, fifty years to come out of this cage! And I don't need to be funny when you've got Neil Patrick Harris and Sara Bareilles and Ann Harada and Julie Lester handling that amazingly well for you—all these people who are at the top of their game. We don't need a funny moment [from me] there because these people—they'll do it. Let the cow handle that! I have the best cow ever! It's something that I learned in *Aida*; I remember saying to my mother, "Sherie's got all the funny moments." And my mother said," But that's not what you're supposed to do." And my mother's not a theatrical anything. "That's not what you bring to the show." I don't need to go for the laugh, just let me tell the story. I think sometimes the audience is expecting those laugh moments and I talked with [director] Lear DeBessonet and was like, "Well, what if we don't? What if we change it? What if we give them a laugh moment where they didn't expect it?" Because they know the show so well. "What does it look like if she's serious here?" You hear the line differently. I hope it worked. I love The Witch and she taught me a lot! There's that line, "I'm the witch," and I started thinking about that at the MUNY. "You're a liar and that one's a thief and you're all terrible. Why am I the bad guy?" And seriously, I don't think

she's that bad, and that's what I wanted the audience [to consider]. I wanted the audience to go, "Look, I wouldn't ask her over for tea or for a little bit of chicken, but I understand where she's coming from." And now, as a mother .... Two years ago, I locked my children up in a house for an entire year and nobody thought anything of it. The giant outside was COVID and I locked my children up for their own benefit. So, am I The Witch? That's what I did as a parent. Sometimes we go, "I don't want you to know about the big, dark, evil world." I loved cracking that side open. I was reading it through and thinking, "I would do the same thing if I knew that there were bad people out there and wolves that attack girls and princes that try to get you pregnant. If I can just keep you here being a child...." I didn't see her as a bad guy, I saw the parent in her. She loves Rapunzel with all her heart. It really has become one of my favorite musicals.

So given that, what was it like to walk away from it and not stay for the Broadway transfer?
Again, it's kind of like the boyfriend. Somebody else is coming into your house. But I had to say "no." I start filming in two weeks. And so did Denée and Neil Patrick. [Understandably] the producers couldn't wait. I love that cast! It was tough to have to say no. When they asked me, we talked about it: "Maybe I could do a week and then leave. We open the 27th and I'd have to leave on the fourth...." But you can't do that. You can't do that to the audience, and you can't do that to the show. It was not the right thing. I had to say no. But I think my boyfriend's in good hands.

What do you think you want now?
I want to do good work, work that changes people if I can. I'm standing on shoulders, shoulders of women, shoulders of Black women, shoulders of the Black people, shoulders of the theater greats, and now it's time for me to hoist. We have to hoist [young] people up. There was a time when that path wasn't even cut. People who came before us had to create a path and cut it out. And now there is a path and all I have to do is make sure it's cleaned up and give it my best so that other people can come behind me and will even have an easier time. Look at Joaquina Kalukango [who won the 2022 Tony Award for *Paradise Square*]! That path was laid so that she could do what she has done, but now she's added to it and the bar is raised even higher. The work I want to do is work that impacts people, that will change people. Everything I do I want to make sure that I can do it at my best. I think the theater is deserving of that and the good Lord, when he gives us these talents, I think that's what he wants—that we give the best of us. I don't expect it to be done; I hope to have many, many other chances to do shows and make people think. It's such a beautiful medium that we have, you know? You look in the audience and see people cry and laugh, and on days when the earth is completely shaken and taken away, and you don't understand what's going on with the giants in the sky—whether that giant be COVID or September 11—you could come into the theater and have your mind be taken away for two and a half hours. That I want to be a part of for a very, very long time. There's nothing like it. You plan things but that's not how it will go. And I'm Christian and I can say that in my life, everything that I planned the good Lord has come forth and done even bigger than I could ever have planned, so I have stopped trying to plan. Seriously. I mean ... you're not going to get me all sentimental and messy up in here today! It's been a good ride. It's been an elaborate life.

Karen Olivo

November 2020

As my conversation with Karen Olivo progresses, the entirety of which she conducts while standing, we come up with a list of people to whom Olivo owes cookies. There are the people who gave her couches to crash on when she first got to New York; Eden Espinosa, who mentored her through *Brooklyn*; the associate choreographer on *West Side Story*. Olivo claims she never thanked them properly. I don't believe her. Because, unless she's become another person altogether, Karen Olivo is one of the most self-aware, conscious, conscientious performers I have ever spoken to. Not much gets by her.

Born in New York and raised in Florida, Olivo was described, in a 2014 *New York Times* profile, as "the Broadway star who got away." If getting away means finding herself so that she could approach her work more healthily, Olivo admits to being guilty as charged. She moved to New York at the age of nineteen, having already secured a job in *Rent* during its first, meteoric year. The short-lived *Brooklyn* came next and then, in 2007, *In the Heights*, which became a sensation, moving to Broadway and cementing the careers of its creative team and several of its stars, who would go on to even greater fame with *Hamilton*. As Vanessa, the girl with big dreams and a bigger belt, Olivo played opposite Lin-Manuel Miranda, who has proven to be a constant throughout much of her career. Olivo loved *In the Heights* and left reluctantly, but when the offer to play Anita in the first bilingual production of *West Side Story* came her way, she couldn't refuse. She won the Tony but broke her foot, which led to a Hollywood detour and the series *Harry's Law*. It was during the off-Broadway run of *Murder Ballad* that Olivo took stock and decided that she needed to step away. "I leave behind the actor, and I start learning how to be me," she blogged, coinciding with a move to Madison, Wisconsin, to be with her now husband, Joe Uphoff, and his two children. She's happy there, teaching, sketching, throwing pottery, and living, with occasional sojourns back to the boards, including *tick, tick … BOOM!* At Encores! And a year as Angelica Schuyler in the Chicago production of *Hamilton*. Most recently, she was back in New York (and Tony nominated) with *Moulin Rouge*.

When COVID-19 abruptly shuttered *Moulin Rouge*, Olivo went back to Madison, where she's been anything but idle. In June 2020, Olivo and Espinosa formed AFECT (Artists For Economic Transparency), a not-for-profit that, according to its website, works "in response to the racism that is prevalent in the American theater." After our conversation, when Broadway reopened, she declined to return to *Moulin Rouge*, citing an industry in need of overhaul before she participates again. But there's plenty to keep her busy in Madison. Olivo teaches and has been performing locally, no longer limited to jobs that she's offered. She—and she alone—controls how she dispenses her gifts.

As I understand it, theater was part of your world from a very young age.
My dad started a theater company in the basement of our church, Agape Theater. I remember him putting me on stage at six because it was just a lot easier to know where I was. I was too young to be in the production, obviously. I didn't realize that theater was a thing that only certain people do. Everyone did it in my little six-year-old mind. This is just what life is.

"We got to show up as ourselves, not as a stereotype," said Olivo. With Robin de Jesús (left) and Lin-Manuel Miranda in *In the Heights*.
(Joan Marcus)

You must have realized that your peers were not in theater.
No. Truthfully. Even when we moved to Florida, he started a children's theater at the local community theater. And so everyone that I was surrounded with was always in the theater. I'm really an introvert, so when I went to school, I had like maybe one other friend. We didn't really have play dates. My parents were very strict, so it wasn't like I could just go and hang out with other kids. We were at the theater, working crazy hours at all times. I did sets, I did costumes, I even did concessions at one point. I just thought that that's what you did. My mother also did some stage managing, so I had both of them there. I never really got away from it.

At some point, it occurred to you to pursue it as a career.
I remember the exact moment. I was in a community theater production of *Magician's Nephew*. I had a little monologue in which I was supposed to be really menacing. I was advancing on the audience and talking about all the horrible things I was going to do, and I remember looking out and seeing all these adults staring at me, and I was like, "Oh, this is really cool. Nothing feels like this. They're all adults and they have to listen to me and they have to watch me. Yeah, I'm going to do this forever."

You went to Cincinnati College–Conservatory of Music and focused on music. What made you decide that that was going to be the thing that you were studying?
I didn't go to CCM with music in my mind. I was just an actor who could make sounds. I had no formal training. I was really rough around the edges, still learning basic breathing

techniques. My parents and a teacher of mine knew that if I stayed in Central Florida the likelihood of me amounting to anything would be pretty slim, and so they were trying to pluck me out and put me somewhere really far away. I come from a really low-income background with pretty heavy issues—mental health, abuse. This was my family's way of getting me started in something that I was passionate about. I had started to surround myself with people that were not going to help me further any kind of theatrical career.

So when you got to CCM, did you find yourself among peers, or would you say you were a little fish? Big fish? Medium fish?
Definitely a little fish. I had the least amount of training out of everyone in my

Karen Olivo	
Rent	Broadway, 1997; National Tour, 1998
Brooklyn	Broadway, 2005
Miracle Brothers	off-Broadway, 2005
In the Heights	off-Broadway, 2007; Broadway, 2008
Hair	off-Broadway, 2007
West Side Story (Tony Award)	Broadway, 2009
Murder Ballad	off-Broadway, 2012
tick, tick…BOOM!	Encores!, 2014
Hamilton	Chicago, 2016
Chess	Kennedy Center, 2018
Moulin Rouge	Broadway, 2019

class. I was also a woman of color. They all came from very different backgrounds. That was another thing—I realized that the abuses that I experienced in Florida—I didn't realize that everyone's life wasn't like that. Luckily, theater really did give me a place to put all of that and a place to refocus my brain and my attention. I was able to move through it. That's the kind of thing that would take someone down at nineteen. So yeah, I was definitely the little fish in a very big, big pond.

And yet, even with all that self-awareness of how good the program was for you, you left before you were done.
One of the things I remember being taught by my father from a pretty young age, living where I lived and being a woman of color, was that it's not going to be good enough that you're talented; "You're going to have to be the best brown girl in the room at all times." I always knew that I was going to have a different road than my white counterparts. It was the reality of my situation. Everything was about assimilation. There was no "be what you are and use your life experience." It was "how do we fit you in?" And when I got into the business, that didn't really change. Now, I think that that's different, but it was actually useful because I didn't go into the business disillusioned. And that's what actually made me leave. I knew that if I did not create opportunity for myself, I was not going to have the same outcome as my counterparts. I had to create my own way. I was a junior when *Rent* came out and I saw Daphne Rubin-Vega. I was like, "Oh if that's happening right now, I have to get out of Cincinnati and I have to go there. If those opportunities are happening, that's something that I need to be a part of." And then I ran as fast as I could.

You slept on the street for rush tickets and saw *Rent* on two successive nights.
I remember sitting in the front row, looking at my friend Chris Nichols, who had taken me there. I said, "I'm going to be in this show." He laughed and he was like, "Yeah, me too." And I was like, "No, no, no. I'm actually going to be in this show." And less than a year later, I was in that company performing on that stage.

Where did that come from? You felt, at the age of nineteen, that you had the chops?

Oh, I didn't think I had the chops. But I got to CCM with no formal training. My life has always been a little bit of "fake it till you make it." I knew I had enough—we call it "gana," which is the desire. I had such ambition and such a desire to be a part of it. Someone give me the shot and I will make up the difference. But that has been my entire life. Nothing has ever really been given to me. I pretty much fought for everything. Even though there's been a lot of luck, when the door opened, I was ready to walk through it.

That's not luck.

The luck would be the professor who saw me in high school and said, "I think you have something." He took me under his wing. That was lucky. I had nothing to do with that.

So does that mean that after seeing *Rent*, you decided, "I have to learn to belt like that and sing rock like that?"

Yeah. I remember sitting in my apartment, listening to "Take Me or Leave Me" and trying to figure it out. I didn't understand how Idina was making those sounds. I would play it over and over again. People must have hated me. I would just keep singing. I would change the shape of my mouth. I would try to envision my voice being in different places. I was learning my own technique. When I was at CCM, they wouldn't allow me to sing anything other than classical because I lacked technique and they were really afraid that I was going to ruin something [physically]. So I taught myself how to belt, but in my own way. I couldn't sound like Idina, so I would concentrate on hitting the notes with the same intensity, so I could at least match the dynamic. I created my own version of belting.

How did you end up auditioning?

My friend Chris Nichols was really resourceful. He found an open call in Toronto. We skipped school, got in his car, and we drove to Toronto for the open call. I made it to the finals and I remember Michael Greif looking at me, saying, "You're an American. Why are you here?" And I said, "I want to be in the show." They didn't cast me for that production, but shortly afterwards, the summer before my senior year, I got a phone call. I'll never forget it. "I'm with the company of *Rent* on Broadway. We would like to offer you a position. Can you get here in a month?" I was a swing. They had just lost one of their original swings.

And Norbert Leo Butz was the male swing?

Yeah. I actually went to New York not having a place to live. I relied on the kindness of some former CCM grads. They completely took me under their wing. I was such a knucklehead. I was really talented but it was evident that I was not prepared for so much.

***Rent* was at the peak of its crazy height. Most of the original cast was still there. What do you remember?**

I remember working really, really hard. No one had ever told me what being a swing was. I spent all day at rehearsal learning stuff. I ended up covering five of the six women. I remember being in rehearsal all day long and then coming home and looking at my script and playing the CD in my tiny little studio apartment, trying to do the blocking. All day long, every day.

Most schools don't really prepare people for the realities of the business, but growing up as you did, I imagine that a lot of that hard, practical work was familiar to you.
Absolutely. But I think the other thing that was the real driving force, is that when you're a kid that grows up with nothing and theater is the only thing that gives you intrinsic value, it becomes everything to you. So there was an element of, "If I can't succeed at this, then what am I?" It's a completely different mindset. It's not a hobby. It's "this defines me."

I think that's true for many young actors irrespective of background. It's the only thing you think you're made for, which can drive you but also can be toxic.
Absolutely. That was part of my decision to hit the pause button. Realizing that I am something other than an actor. Let me figure out what that is!

Do you also remember being in heaven? Thrilled every day?
Can I be honest with you? I was not enamored with the Broadway experience. I had this idea that it was going to be something very specific, and then I got there and I was like, "Oh, this is just the same as all the community theater productions I've ever done. It's just in a different place and you're paying me money." I thought it was going to be something grand, something mind-blowing, and I was going to feel elevated. It was the same work. It was the same slog—a slog I loved. But I was like, "Where is that other thing?" I was very sad about it, but once I got over it—I remember my first week there I cried.

But didn't you feel a higher level of professionalism and talent around you?
Yes. But I was expecting that I was going to change, and nothing within me changed. That's what I was hoping for—this thing that would make me feel this worth because I was here. That didn't happen and I needed that to happen. I needed to feel accepted and like I was worthy of the opportunity.

What else do you remember about the experience?
Being a swing, there is nothing like being in civilian clothing, sitting on the couch, eating a bagel, and hearing your name called over the loudspeaker: "Karen, you're Mark's Mom tonight." "Cool." And running up the stairs as fast as you can, throwing on clothes, being handed a mic as you step on stage. There's nothing like that. And that sense of community is amazing.

Wasn't the achievement, especially since you covered five roles, satisfying?
When you're thrown on, you're only thinking, "What is my part?" And afterwards, it's "What just happened?" It's always this idea that we did it together, especially with that show. That show felt like if we didn't all show up, we couldn't get the thing off the ground. I've never been able to stand outside [of that and pat myself on the back]. I just don't have that thing. Maybe that speaks to some of the issues that would arise later in my career. I actually went on a lot as Mark's Mom because Sherie Rene Scott [who was playing Maureen] had some injuries [her understudy, Christine Lee Kelly, went on and Olivo went on for Kelly]. It was a really good lesson for me to watch someone struggling to get back into a show but their body failing them, and it's one of the things that helped me decide to be an Equity deputy. I saw a lot of things that were happening to people's bodies. I realized that certain things were not safe and no one was saying anything. That informed my being an advocate.

At twenty years old? You took a leadership position as opposed to waiting to be led. That's pretty extraordinary.

But if you think about where I came from, it's not so out of the ordinary. It's all community-based. My company was going out into battle every night and things were not right for us. If you want us to perform and do our best, we need support. It just seems very logical to me.

Did you feel yourself growing as a performer?

Yes, absolutely! As a swing, you become a little bit of a magician and shape-shifter or else you don't succeed. I learned a lot about relationships. I learned a lot about who was ready to play and who was not. I learned a lot about the piece and what the piece is going to ask of you, and how you have to bring yourself to the piece regardless of what's happening. I know that show in my bones. I can hear that score and I can tell you exactly where I should be for any one of my characters.

So you could walk into it now?

Sadly, yes. It was my first show and it was the only time that I was ever a swing. I studied that thing like it was the Bible. It's in the hard drive. It's actually uncomfortable for me to hear it. Heart racing, sweaty palms.

Any other *Rent* memories?

You mentioned Norbert. I got to do understudy rehearsals with him as Roger. I remember being astounded by his capacity and his ability to drop in at a moment's notice, and for it to feel so real. I was like, "Oh, God, please, can I be Mimi to his Roger!" The day that it happened, I felt like my dreams were coming true. At intermission, I was in my dressing room with Shana Steele, and I said, "I think he loves me." And she was like, "No, Bitch. He's acting." He really was that good. I'll never forget that. It was one of the most incredible gifts I will ever be given.

They offered you the role of Mimi on tour.

Yeah, on the first national tour. The person who was contracted had to leave for eight to ten weeks and I got to do it. It was much harder than I thought. There's an ease to being a swing because it's not every night. You have to hold a lot of information and your impulses have to be really, really good, but I didn't yet have the framework for the longevity of playing a role. It became very difficult for me. My inability to show up consistently started to make me feel like I was less of a human. That was a really tough lesson for me, but super important. I wasn't ready to be in the spotlight.

Is that hindsight speaking, or do you think you knew that at the time?

At the time I always felt in over my head. I was working as hard as I could but there was just something—I think if you're going to be the lead in the show, you need a support system. There needs to be infrastructure for you. Especially when it's something like Mimi where you're as vulnerable as somebody can be. I knew something was missing. I couldn't have put my finger on it. I couldn't name it. But I knew I was not getting it. I was not sailing. I needed a mentor. I needed a partner who was supportive. I needed therapy to deal with some of my issues surrounding worth. When someone doesn't feel worth anything and you put them on a stage nightly in a spotlight, you're just rolling the dice. There's a lot of stuff that had not been dealt with and that's why I wasn't able to show up properly in the space.

For someone who describes themselves as not knowing a lot in your youth, you seem to have known some things pretty definitively. You knew to grab this show, and then you knew when it was time to leave after four years.

A basic principle that you know as an actor: you know when the scene is not working. Life is not that much different. Something was not clicking anymore. And I also knew in my heart that I needed to originate something. I could have stayed in *Rent* till it closed because I became very valuable. I knew all of my tracks. I could do any of them. But I decided I had to leave. I needed to do a little bit more of the regular actor thing: going to auditions, being rejected, and trying to find my own path. I needed to find the character that I was supposed to create.

You had four years of *Rent* money to live on. . . .

You would think!

Did you not?

No. I have never been great with money. I was a bartender. I was a hostess. I was the worst waiter in New York. I liked being an out-of-work actor. I felt like I was more creative during that time than any other time in my life. I was writing a lot. I was making a lot of art. There was so much inspiration during that time of being really poor.

Most actors feel at their most secure when they are working. You felt good and creative when you weren't. That's interesting.

I'm a child that was born in crisis. I understand when things are not working. When things are falling, I'm the person who's always level-headed and marches toward the problem to go fix it. When things start to become easygoing, without conflict, I would actually get bored and anxious. I'm used to fighting and clawing my way to get out of something.

So adversity was your comfort zone?

It really was.

And then you booked *Brooklyn*.

That was the first role that I ever originated. It was a five-person show, but there was only one supporting character and that was me. I learned so much. I learned that when you're creating something—and this is why I love creating something—you can bring so much more of yourself. I learned that bringing yourself to a character that you're creating is what's asked. It was so nice to feel like something was mine. I didn't know the feeling of creating something would feel that way. Both Ramona Keller and Eden Espinosa are friends to this day. I learned so much by watching them. Also watching them deal with stardom, how they showed up in public, polished. I was the kind of knucklehead who would just show up in a pair of sneakers and a T-shirt for a press event. They created a polished version of themselves and then they presented themselves. I was marveling how they could do it consistently, over and over again. It was a very important lesson. Even when you're showing up as yourself in this business, it's still a persona. It's not warts and all.

The show did not get good reviews. Were you aware of diminishing houses?
I remember feeling abandoned by the creative team when things did not go well. They had high hopes and they probably felt like they had let us down as well. But we had a family that was bigger than the cast, and then they were gone. We didn't see the director for quite some time and we were just out there by ourselves. We did notice houses diminishing. I remember it was hard to go out there and tell a story when we could tell our time was running out. It was a hard show. But we loved each other. That's really what got us through. We would gather before we entered and Cleavant Derricks was like, "Guys, let's do it for us." And we'd go out there and do it.

It closed after 284 performances.
It was a very hard thing for us because we really thought that people would enjoy it. It was before its time. A couple of years later, the concept of *American Idol* would take the entire world by storm, and we were doing it on stage years before that. There wasn't anything on Broadway at the time that I remember being that contemporary. I didn't have to go long without being employed. I was doing readings, but *In the Heights* was on my radar. Eden was actually doing a reading of it during *Brooklyn*. I remember her coming into my dressing room saying, "You need to get into that show." Shortly after we closed, there was an audition for the workshop and that became the next thing that I devoted the next four years of my life to. From a career perspective, that was the first time that I had mentors, people around me that were supporting me on- and offstage. The work that happened in *In the Heights* only happened because of that. That was the thing that I was really missing, and later on I would see that. It was also the first time that I was doing work with people that were all like me, that were like my brothers and sisters and cousins and parents.

When you say mentors, who? And in what way was that mentorship meaningful to you?
Andréa Burns—I would watch the way she would break down a scene. I would watch the questions that she would ask when they would give her a new scene: "Why? How does this further the plot? Where is the arc? If this scene happens and then I'm supposed to sing, what's the connective tissue? How do I reasonably get to singing?" Things about structure that no one had ever taught me. I was watching her do it. She was so important to me. And then having scenes with her—just understanding investment, understanding communication, understanding how she would lob the ball at me in a different way and I would have to catch it. It was like the finishing school that I needed with structure. She's a brilliant human being and a wonderful, wonderful educator. I'd seen other people ask questions, but I had never seen someone like me, a woman of color, in a space where obviously she felt confident enough to ask critical thinking questions. "How do we make this better?" I'd never seen anyone assert themselves in a space like that, and that's what showed me that it's OK to have these thoughts, and this is the way you're supposed to present them so that it's heard and people don't think you're aggressive or that you're a problem. All of the questions that she asked were based in, "How do I make this better? Help me make this better." It wasn't like, "This doesn't work. I don't like this." It was always, "Is there something in here that will elevate the scene and if it doesn't exist, how can we get it?" We pay millions of dollars for that and I had that person as my scene partner!

It's interesting to think about asking those kinds of questions when the writer [Lin-Manuel Miranda] is on stage with you.

I actually had two Usnavis to build with because Lin would sit in the house and watch Javier Muñoz perform. He'd go back and forth. We used to call Lin "The Touchstone" because it all emanates from him. You can't go wrong if you're close to him. If you match that mood, that energy, that intensity, you're good. And then, what I got from Javi when Lin would step away to write, was this incredible brain, and also, another scene partner like Andréa. They can dissect beats in one second. They can guide you. It was an embarrassment of riches, to have those two Usnavis. You won't find two nicer men.

You mentioned the feeling of being onstage with a lot of brown people.

Yeah. We were singing our music. We were moving to music that I'd heard my entire life. I didn't have to stretch myself to be in it. It was who I was. Vanessa is my younger self. At that time when I built it, I was Vanessa. I was still clawing, trying to get out of my circumstances. It's hard, actually, for me to watch productions of it, or even hear it, because it's like looking at a photo album of myself. It's kind of cringeworthy. A lot of things that I would say in rehearsal ended up being things that Vanessa said. There's a part that's quintessential Karen/Vanessa in "Carnivále," when Usnavi explains that he won the lotto and he's leaving for Puerto Rico. Vanessa and Sonny both have this line about being powerless. They are so angry that he's leaving. "What about us? How could you do this to us?" That's sort of like Vanessa/Karen's inability to see that this was a step up for someone. That reactive sort of thing is so Karen. Why are you angry? Don't be angry in this situation. It's just hard to see yourself when you haven't learned specific lessons. It's hard for me not to see the lessons that were to be learned.

Tell me about that creative team and being in the room with them.

They were all so young and kind of spitballing. It felt like a safe place to create. There was no one in the room that was supposed to know more than anybody else. We were all just sort of looking around going, "Who's got another idea? What could happen here?" And I think that that sense of community is what you saw on stage—people who built something together. They all rested on each other very heavily. Tommy [Kail] is not who he is now as a director. His true gift is being a facilitator. He's like an incredible chef. He knew exactly what kind of ingredient needed to be put with another ingredient, and the right amount. He knew the right people to put together. [Understanding] how people felt in the room was actually something that I clocked with him; he was constantly walking around, having side conversations with people, telling jokes, and getting to know everyone on this very specific level so that he could gauge a mood. He could see how the room was feeling, and when something didn't work, he was very quick to figure out how to fix that. I'd never seen anyone do that. He was very hands-on throughout the entire process. That's also the first time that I'd ever experienced collective gathering before we made work. We always circled up. It was a prayer and if there was something that was weighing you down, you'd put it in the circle and we would all carry it together. We had work to do to be there for each other. I'd never experienced anything like that, which is why I was able to do things that I didn't think I would ever be able to do.

Like what?

The things that I was not able to achieve in *Rent*: being in the spotlight and being able to sing a solo and not get so uncomfortable. Being an intuitive dancer as opposed to a technical dancer. I had confidence because there were people around me that if I made a misstep, they were [supportive] at every turn.

Speaking of which, you really had to dance. Where did that come from?

Andy Blankenbuehler. He was really patient. And he was really smart, putting Luis Salgado as my partner, guiding me. I promise you, you dance with Luis Salgado and all of a sudden you'll be like, "I actually think I'm really good." And I'm convincing you that I am the best dancer ever. Don't look at my feet, look at my face. Look how much I'm enjoying what I'm doing. If you look at the choreography, it's not very often that I'm left by myself. I'm with a very strong partner at all times.

I've heard you say that you knew at the time that the music was extraordinary.

Yeah, absolutely. I remember hearing the demo of "96,000." I picked up my phone and called my agent. "Sign me up. Get me in the room. I want to be a part of this." We knew that *In the Heights* was something that we loved. How often do you get to do a contemporary piece that is about your people, with your music, talking about your relationships? If we did not make the thing sail, if we did not bring it to its true potential in our own eyes, it would be a misrepresentation of what we were. People don't come to the theater to see Puerto Rican and Dominican and Colombian and Mexican people tell a story. And if we get you a come to this theater, and it doesn't show us, you'll walk away and you'll have the wrong perception about us. And we don't get a shot very often.

And you're speaking about developing the show for an off-Broadway audience. So the stakes were that much higher when you got the news that you were moving to Broadway and that many more people would see it.

That felt like the most ridiculous thing ever because we knew we loved it, we knew that it was important to us, but we never thought that everyone else would understand it or would want to see it on a larger scale.

You did *Hair* in between.

Ten days to learn *Hair* is a little insane, but working at the Delacorte was spectacular. Being able to make art on that stage in Central Park is unlike anything. I loved it. They brought it back the following summer for a full run [and then a Broadway transfer] but by that time we had gotten a theater and we were working on *In the Heights*.

How did Broadway feel different?

I remember our first day in the rehearsal room, one of our producers, Jeffrey Seller, said, "We know that we have something special, but can we make it better? That's the challenge here." So that's what we set out to do. We just kept trimming the fat until we could make it into something that was more representative of us, something that was going to create a better arc. We all had the same mindset and we were all there for the right reasons. There was no promise that people would receive it well. Doing something at 37 Arts is not the same as in a Broadway theater. I noticed the difference in Lin, in the sense that more pressure was put on him and there would be times where he had to stop being an actor and go be a producer or writer. I learned a lot from him, watching him navigate the press storm. Shortly after that, I would have to do the same thing, when I was in *West Side Story*. I didn't have a lot of experience with being the person that people were going to interview.

What specifically do you remember learning?

He always looked so calm during interviews. So pedestrian and casual. When I got to *West Side Story* and I had to do interview after interview, I remember calling him and being like, "I don't know what to do. I can't do one more interview." It's hard to talk about how you make art all day long and then go to the theater and actually do it. It puts this strange lens on it. And it also kind of robs you of the mystique, because you talked about how the sausage is made all day long. He said, "You know the ten questions they're going to ask you. Make truthful answers for those things and then just recite those answers every single time." Now I understand that's how you do it. You can't just bare your soul to every single person.

What was it like performing at the Tonys?

That's one of my favorite memories: us in the rehearsal on the Radio City stage. I remember us having to stand in our spot so they could light us. I actually have a picture of our backs looking out onto this empty Radio City Theater, and it's one of those pinch-me-moments. "I can't believe I'm here with this piece of art, with my family, and we're showing our world. We're sharing it with everyone." Nothing will ever top that feeling. We got to show up as ourselves, not as a stereotype, representing our families, our culture. I never would have thought that would happen.

Before we move away from *In the Heights*, I want to ask you about Priscilla Lopez.

Down at 37 Arts we all shared the same dressing room and sometimes she would tell us stories about *A Chorus Line* and how that was built. I remember her telling us on a number of occasions, "You don't understand the enormity of something like this when you're inside of it. It will take you years to really understand what you're a part of and the time will have already passed, so you have to cherish all of it as it's happening."

Was that ultimately true for you?

Yeah, when it comes to its scope and what it ended up doing. I know personally I cherished every moment of it. I didn't really let anything pass. I was not aware of how it was received on a wider scale because I was just so in love with it and the people. It was too personal.

But you left because *West Side Story* seemed like something you had to do?

You have to do it. I had run from that audition twice. They had called and I said, "Absolutely not. I'm not an idiot. I'm not going in for Anita." And then they called again when they were two weeks away from starting rehearsals. I was like, "I'm not touching that thing." It was a dancer role and one of the most well-known Puerto Rican roles. I revered it so highly [and it had been played by] ridiculous, ridiculous dancers. Performers that ... your face melts when you watch them dance. Whereas I have an issue transferring weight. I am not a dancer. So I was like, "I'm not doing that to myself." But the way that they posed it to me was, "We've seen everyone. Just come to the final callback we will teach you some of the choreography." So I showed up for the final callback. The thing that made me feel less insecure was that Lin was actually in my audition.

The self-described non-dancer dancing her way to a Tony Award in *West Side Story*.
(Joan Marcus)

Let's talk about Arthur Laurents. I understand that while he has a reputation for being difficult, it wasn't bad for you.

I was warned by lots of people. I don't know what it was. I really do believe that Arthur sensed in me a lack of confidence, and that's one of the things that I spoke about when I won the Tony Award. He was always pushing me: "I know you can do this." Knowing that the dance was so difficult for me and that I was not having the best experience with the choreographer [Joey McNeely], Arthur was always on my side. This version of *West Side Story* was a gift to Arthur's late partner, Tom. Tom always dreamed about doing a bilingual version of *West Side Story* and Arthur was at the end of his life and he knew it. He was like, "I want to give something to Tom." One of the things I remember so vividly in my audition with Arthur: he got up from his chair after I sang "A Boy Like That," and he was like, "I want you to sing this song from a place of love. You're not angry. You haven't been betrayed. You loved so deeply the person you lost and the person you're talking to. That's what's so painful; we see how much you love them both." And that's how we approached all of this. I'm assuming it was my ability to tap into that and go with him on that journey [that he appreciated]. The acting was never an issue. I love deeply and fiercely, I'm incredibly loyal, all of the components that you need to have—someone who is a fighter, someone who will do anything for the people that mean something to them—all of those things come naturally. And so he sort of let that be a guiding principle. I think that is why I stayed out of the line of fire. There was never a moment that I was complacent. I couldn't be complacent. There so much dancing! The Jerome Robbins choreography? I have nightmares about it still to this day. If you don't have technique, it is such an uphill battle. Not to mention, your body is just, "please stop doing this to me." Like with *Rent*, I was so focused, staying up all night, focused on getting it right.

Let's discuss the scene in Doc's when Anita is almost raped. That's a lot to do every night.
Yeah, the scene in Doc's was always going to be an issue for me because I'm a rape survivor. Looking back, I'm sure that there was a way for us to do that a little bit more holistically. I never felt like I was in danger. I really do give the choreographer credit; he waited until we really knew each other very well before we tried to mount that scene. I trusted those Jet boys implicitly. I knew that they had my back. They were such wonderful humans. It was the most of myself that I had ever really shown, in one of the most vulnerable experiences of my life. But I always felt held by those guys. I always felt supported. And luckily it was the last scene in the show for me. So, after that, I could go back and sort of pull myself together. I actually remember having a conversation with Lin about this because I was having such a hard time when we got into the run. I would come home so depressed and he was like, "You can't do that to yourself. You have to leave her at the theater. You have to leave what happens to you on that stage and be yourself again." He created a mix tape for me. It was called "Karen's Booty-Shaking Mix" or something like that, and when I would come offstage, I would put that on and, as I was getting dressed for the curtain call, I would dance to that music to remind me of who I actually was and how that had not really happened to me.

That's very kind. And wise. Especially for someone who was himself at the beginning of his own career.
I didn't even tell you—I was nervous my first day of rehearsal. That meet and greet is huge, the first time the whole company meets. I remember calling and saying, "Are you coming?" And he was like, "I don't necessarily need to, but I can if you want me to." And I remember seeing him there and he was like, "You got this." He was always a guiding, supportive friend, whenever possible.

Sondheim was around, too, wasn't he?
Only at the recording of the album. Arthur and Stephen did not get along. I remember a couple times, Arthur being like, "I hate the fucker."

You mentioned difficulty with the choreography and the choreographer.
It's taken me years of therapy and a lot of distance to be able to speak about it in these terms: Can you imagine being one of the few people that's allowed to mount Jerome Robbins choreography for the Broadway stage? And then one of the most important dancing characters is cast and that person is not a dancer? Can you imagine what that must be like [for the choreographer]? Because that's a reflection of your work.

You are showing tremendous compassion.
But it's the truth. I was definitely the kind of person that … my work gave me value. And I can only imagine that that's something that he was probably plagued with. His work would define him. He had an associate, Lori Werner, and she was the person that taught me the choreography. She was an incredible empath and a spiritual human being who was able to speak to me in terms of acting when it came to dance. I was able to hone my intuitive desire to be a storyteller into being a physical storyteller, and that's all Lori. What Joey lacked in grace and warm fuzzies, he made up for in the ability to know what his strong suit was. He knew he wasn't going to get to me. He knew he couldn't teach me what I needed to know because he came from a different school of thought.

He came from steps and technique, you came from heart. How did that manifest in the room. Was he frustrated with you? You with him?
I think it was mutual, for sure. I remember I had an injury and he was like, "What's going on? Why can't you work?" I think he had an idea that maybe I was lazy or I didn't have the kind of work ethic that he did. I mean, truthfully, no one does. If you're not a dancer, you don't understand putting your body through that kind of pain and torture daily. But he gave me the number of his acupuncturist. He said, "All of the greats go to this guy. He'll get you to a point where you can at least come back to rehearsal and move." That was a moment of kindness that he showed to me, but other than that, there was a lot of—dance is a dictatorship. There's only one brain in the room at any given time and it belongs to the choreographer. He comes from that very old school approach. I'd already had an experience that was so holistic and so supportive, and coming into this thing where I was like, "How come I don't have a say? You hired me for a reason"—I said that numerous times to Lori. "Why did he hire me? Why am I here if I can't do anything right for him?" That's a lot of my own work that I probably needed to deal with.

Did you feel like you got there?
Do I ever feel like I was the dancer that I had hoped I would be? Absolutely not. But I definitely felt like I was doing the work justice by the time we got to opening night. And it had a lot to do with my Shark girls. Lori explained to me that she had handpicked each one of them because they were all different in their styles and they came from different kinds of backgrounds. The two women [on either side of me in "America"], Yanira Marin and Tenairi Vazquez, were just unbelievable. I would sit and watch and she would be like, "Envision yourself between these two women." If I've learned anything from being a mover, it's that my follow skills are pretty good. If I can see you out of the corner of my eye, I can remember the next thing, and I can match my body to do whatever you're doing. So by putting me between these two ridiculous dancers, that's how I learned to have more confidence and how I had structure. But that was Lori's brain. She built a framework for me.

And you won a Tony.
I definitely didn't do it alone!

But you've also told me that you base a lot of your self-worth on your work. So winning . . .
Too big for me. Too big to really contemplate. I was so surprised that I won and then, as it was happening to me, I felt like I left a little bit. That persona stood in front of me and Karen was standing behind the persona going, "What's going on? How is this happening?" It pains me to say this, but I am an actor first and foremost, and that moment was so big that I had to act to get through it. If you watch it, it's me trying to produce something intelligent and the last bit is me falling apart. That last bit is actually me. And then I ran from the stage. It's one of the shortest speeches in the history of the Tony Awards. It was just still so unimaginable. I just realized that I can sometimes be really negative in the face of something incredibly positive, but [winning] posed a lot of obstacles for me. I had to be worthy of the title that was given to me. For a long time I wasn't able just to show up in the room and be myself. I had to be put together. Daphne Rubin-Vega called it "a happy death." It pushes you to a new level, and with that level comes chains. I'm stuck. My lack of self-worth was still prevalent throughout all of this. The only thing that was grounding

me in any sort of reality was the actual work itself. And then every door that I can imagine opened for me. After I won the Tony Award, I spent ten days in L.A. meeting every single producer, going to all the studio heads, you name it. It was a parade of doors opening. And I was like, "I want to go be Anita. I don't want to be in your TV show. I want to do the work that I've been working really hard to do."

What did that tell you?
That I'm somebody who likes to do the work. I don't need the fame. I mean, I live in Madison, Wisconsin. I'm not interested in celebrity. I'm about the work.

You stayed in *West Side* until the day you broke your foot.
I broke my foot because I didn't listen. I'd been told numerous times by the production stage manager and by the associate choreographer that the way I was leaving Doc's, because I was so frazzled, didn't look safe. I would sometimes be running through the door and shutting it at the same time. And sometimes my dress would just clear the door as it shut. They were like, "You have to slow down." But I didn't have the ability to stop myself. I'm not one of those actors who can compartmentalize, so every night I went through what I went through. And one day I went barreling through the door and it clipped me. It threw me off balance and I didn't put my foot down straight. The front of my foot snapped. It's called a Jones fracture, which is a typical dancer fracture. I tried to come back but my body wouldn't let me. I don't have a dancer body. I didn't have technique to lean on. They re-choreographed the show for me and I was about to go back in. We had a rehearsal and my foot was the size of an elephant's from not even a full show. My doctor was like, "Your foot is saying that it's not ready. And the chances are good that you could do more harm." I called the producers from a phone booth on 47th and 8th and I remember being doubled over, crying because I felt like I had failed my company and so many people. I failed Lori, failed myself. But I knew that I didn't have the facility to keep going. That's when I started to really look at TV and film because it was the only thing that I could do where I didn't have to move, and that's when *Harry's Law* [the NBC series on which Olivo co-starred for a season] happened.

You did get to revisit *West Side*, both in Salzburg and at the Hollywood Bowl. Was that satisfying?
Yeah, it was really lovely. I was much older, so I had more tools in the toolkit. It was an incredible experience. It didn't have this veil of sadness over it.

After *Harry's Law*, you did a straight play, *By the Way, Meet Vera Stark*, with Stephanie J. Block.
You can't be in a Lynn Nottage play and not do a lot of research, so I learned a lot about race and about the people who came before me. It was an education, for sure. I love Stephanie. She's the hardest worker. She takes copious notes, and she ticks every single box. I would marvel at the way that she would work. When the director gave her an adjustment, she would do exactly what they wanted. She produces. And she was also incredibly kind. So much fun.

That takes us to *Murder Ballad*.
That's a tough one. That's when I decided, "Oh, I gotta get out of here." *Murder Ballad* was immersive theater. There were no wings for me to hide in. I was being as honest and as

vulnerable as possible, and that's a really long time to be that vulnerable and naked in front of people. I had just divorced my second husband and I had not dealt with it. So, every night I was grieving in front of people. And by the end of it, I was like, "I have to stop doing this to myself." There was something about it that was so real and it was at my core. Having to tap into that stuff and relive it over and over—not only did it not feel safe, it felt like I was having an emotional and mental breakdown in front of people. I remember looking out at people being entertained as I was suffering. I'm crying uncontrollably and there are people smiling. I realized I had issues I had to fix.

The choice to step away from the thing you identified as giving you your identity is interesting.
I think the reason for stepping away had a lot to do with the fact that after *Murder Ballad* ended, we started negotiating for it to move. I decided that I wanted to be more hands-on with the negotiations, and so I got all of the information. It wasn't going through the filter of my manager. I negotiated my own contract and I basically negotiated all of the deals [for the four actors]. If you wanted one of us, you had to get all of us what we wanted. The show is so difficult for us, and I was like, "There's no way on Earth that I'm going to do this for what I was making. It costs me so much." Negotiations get kind of gross, and I started getting stuff back from the producers that made me feel like not only did they think I was not a good person, but that I lacked integrity. I remember reading an email and thinking, "Karen, why would you give that person your art?" Their integrity did not match my integrity. I've always had this weird thing about giving art for money, but when it came down to something that was going to cost me, I was like, "No. I'm not going to allow you to take advantage of me because I know you need me. I know you need me more than you're professing, and right now you're trying to bully me to get what you want from me." So I walked away, but luckily my cast mates got the deal that I had negotiated for them. And I started to look around and I was like, "I'm doing all of this for the wrong reasons. I need to care more about myself. I need something else to fill this spot. It can't just be the work that someone will give me." I felt so dirty and like I meant nothing to these people that I had a relationship with. So that was the reason for me stepping away. I was very aware of what the industry felt I was worth, and I realized I was relying on the industry to tell me what I was worth. It was the first time in my career that I was like, "I know I'm more than that." I needed my own touchstone and I didn't have one. So I built a family. I came to Madison and became a part of something that had nothing to do with what people would pay to see me on stage.

Did you see it as a pause, or did you see it as a stop?
I felt like it was a pause. I knew I needed to fix something and I was going to take the time that I needed to fix it. Everyone said it was a retirement, but it wasn't a retirement in my mind.

To have had the presence of mind to know that that's what you needed and then to give it to yourself is a very big deal.
If you think about where I started—I've always been a survivor. When you're that young and you have trauma in your life, the one thing you know how to do is to keep yourself safe. I realized that the transfer of my art for money was not helping me. It was actually making me worse. And so I removed it from my life. How can I keep myself safe in this moment in which I feel like my industry is betraying me?

You decided to go back briefly, to do *tick, tick ... BOOM!* at Encores!
Lin called me. When he told me I would be playing Susan, I was like, "Oh, that's actually what my life is right now." She got out of the city and was living a regular life. It was short, so I did it. Anything that Lin asked me to do I would have done.

Did it feel redemptive?
It felt great because I was making art with someone I trusted. Oliver Butler, our director, was a fantastic human being. It wasn't like it enticed me so much to come back. I remember thinking, "Yeah, I'm still going back home. That still feels better than any of this feels. This [Madison] is real."

A couple of years later, you took on *Hamilton*.
My husband rolled over in bed one day as he was scrolling through Twitter, and he said, "*Hamilton*'s coming to Chicago," which is a couple of hours away from us. I called Tommy and said, "Can I audition?" And he said, "No, you can't. You want to be in it?" And I said, "Yes." And that was it. I was a fan of *Hamilton*, and then I got to see how it was made. Kind of like with *Rent*. I was a fan of the show and then I got my shot.

You spent a year playing Angelica.
It was wonderful. It's a really hard show. I made a lot of really great friends. Chicago was a great place. It's where I started teaching more [at Northwestern]. I felt like me being on a stage wasn't gonna be enough, like I had to do something else. So I started teaching more regularly.

Did you feel like it was your job to lead the company?
I felt like everyone's mom a lot of times. I was a mama. And this was my first time doing a show and having an actual family. I was still trying to figure out how to be a remote parent. Truthfully, that a was harder job than being Angelica. The weight of that was taking all of my focus. Being Angelica in *Hamilton* in Chicago was [not everything to me].

So you had gotten to a place where being the lead in the big musical was no longer what was primary to you. That's a gift of a realization.
Yeah. I think the gamble of leaving New York and coming to Madison to find myself actually paid off in that moment. Those things didn't faze me as much. *Hamilton* opened up all these doors, but I was like, "I've got a family. I've got to figure out how to be a parent." The work is important but it became work all of a sudden. Not that I didn't give it its weight and I didn't do my best, but the thing driving me was keeping my family afloat. I'm still working on that balance.

When you left the show, you tweeted that you were leaving it to somebody else, and it sounded like you were stepping away from acting again.
When I was in *Hamilton*, I was watching all of these men [the creators] live their best lives with all of this material that really, really showed who they were. I was like, "I could do more." I needed more challenge, a life challenge. And one of the things that was a challenge for me was teaching. I was leaving so I could get my degree so that I could start teaching. I'd been asking the universe for something that really pushed me to do all of the things that I'm capable of doing. I started looking at schools and that's when *Moulin Rouge* happened. It was

"Every night was, 'Let's see if I can do it,' " said Olivo of *Moulin Rouge*.
(Matthew Murphy)

like, "Oh you wanted a challenge? You want to use every tool that you've amassed over your career? It's all wrapped up in this one thing. Are you going to try?" And so I put a pause on going back to school because I was like, "I did ask the universe for this incredible challenge and here it is." It's every tool I've ever used.

The role is, of course, demanding. But was it the most demanding thing you've done?
It was a struggle. I've never had to hold something on my shoulders like that. I had to do all of the press and be the face of it. It was still being formed, so I had to try to put my spin on it. It was a challenge on every single front. Did I meet the challenge? Yes, by the end. But it involved a big team: a trainer, a therapist, my dresser, the hair and makeup supervisors who walked every single step with me throughout every single offstage change [changing her costume as they moved]. We accomplished something really great. I think we pulled it off. I think we did the piece justice. I'd never worn costumes like that before; things that were handmade for my body, beaded over weeks by one person. All of the pieces that I get to wear are like museum pieces.

How does this leave you feeling in terms of your relationship to the business?
Satine is really close to who I am in real life: someone who's constantly fighting to keep the people that she loves afloat, not always making the right choices, fighting fiercely to keep her people together. That's kind of how I operate in life.

Was playing *Moulin Rouge* exhausting, exhilarating, or both?
All of the above. I'm not onstage for the first twenty minutes, so I would watch everyone take off, knowing that when I did start, I would not be able to stop until Satine died. I remember walking up the spiral staircase to get to the jump where I come down on the trapeze and being like, "Let's see if I can do it." Every night was "Let's see if I can do it." It was never a sure thing. Twice my standby went on for me during the show.

Are you eager to get back to it?
This time is happening for a reason. We need a pause to stop and think about what's going on. I'm not dying to get back because I know I'm supposed to be standing still in this moment.

In this moment, you've chosen to co-found Effect Change with Eden Espinosa. What made you decide to take that on?
I've felt like there have been issues with the industry not taking care of people, and one of the things that we noticed on this pause was that there was money that was given by a producer to 45's campaign. One of the things it made me realize was that my purchasing power and what I bring to the industry and how I make money was something that I had to be a little bit more aware of. I realized that I didn't know nearly enough about how Broadway was run. If I didn't know that, there's no possible way that students and people coming in can know what the structures are. There's a lot of inequity in there.

So what does an actor do about that?
You make a choice about whether or not you're going to align yourself with people who will give money to people who would take away your rights. What we're trying to do is get people to talk about stuff that they think is wrong. That's something that we've not done as actors. We

don't realize we have any agency in the room, or in our business. It's changing the way that we look at the interaction of art and commerce. We're actually stakeholders. If you know what the structure is and you know how things are going to go down, you have bargaining power. You can choose to work with people who do things equitably and you can you can seek those people out. The more we talk about structures and we talk about who does it right, and how things need to change—and luckily we see a lot of people are changing what they're doing— then you can put yourself in line with those people if you so choose. But now we don't have people just walking blindly into rooms. Effect Change is giving you a choice. It's saying, "Now you know and now you can do whatever you want."

I think that your willingness to say no to work is rare. There are not many people who do what you're doing.
The industry that I want to see is an industry filled with people who have a lot of integrity in their work and who are also thinking about social consciousness as they do it. I feel like I have to model that, in a way. If someone sees me do it, and knows that I don't have generational wealth, that everything I have I've built on my own, maybe they can do it as well. And that's the kind of work that I want out there. I want my industry to be more just in every capacity. I want people to love and revere the art that they make. Also, if I do something I don't believe in, I'm really shitty in it. I'm bad. I know that. So I don't want to put bad work out there. Don't do the things that you don't believe in.

What would you like to sink your teeth into next?
I want to teach people to go into our industry and be able to change it by their actions, and I want our industry to change because it's time for it to change. That's why I spend all my time teaching and working on this not-for-profit. That's it. Identify the need and then build a structure to change it. This is not going to happen overnight. But if we keep reminding the powers that be that these things really do need to change, and we don't get complacent, and we don't just start taking jobs, it's going to happen. We just can't give up.

Kelli O'Hara

October 2020; January 2021

It's no secret that the Broadway soprano is an endangered species. These days, leading ladies, more often than not, are called upon to belt their faces off like *American Idol* wannabees. But despite the odds, Kelli O'Hara, the epitome of a lovely, sincere leading lady, thrives. One might even say reigns. There are others who play in her sandbox, of course, with varying degrees of success. Pretenders to the throne. None of them sings on Broadway, in symphony halls, and in opera houses, as O'Hara does. And none of them has managed, as O'Hara has, to so successfully balance a career between musicals from the Golden Age and complex, challenging, new work. Every tried-and-true chestnut on her résumé is matched by daring pieces with risky commercial prospects.

O'Hara was raised in Elk City, Oklahoma. "My dad was born and raised on a farm and worked with his hands every day of his life," she says. "But he went back to law school when he was in his forties and that changed our lives. My mom did, too. She got her masters. I ended up going to a new school and meeting my voice teacher." That teacher was Florence Birdwell, the same woman who trained Oklahoma native Kristin Chenoweth. Like Chenoweth, O'Hara learned classically, with proper opera training. And like Chenoweth, O'Hara chose Broadway. Her New York debut was inauspicious, as a replacement in *Jekyll and Hyde*, which was followed by a poorly received production of *Follies*. But in *The Sweet Smell of Success*, O'Hara made an impression that was then sealed with *The Light in the Piazza*. As Clara, a young woman with an underdeveloped mind, O'Hara was charged with bridging a girl's simplicity and a woman's sensuality. She received her first of seven (to date) Tony nominations. *The Pajama Game* followed, in which she and co-star Harry Connick Jr. generated chemistry to rival DuPont. *South Pacific* minted her stardom and was followed by *Nice Work If You Can Get It* (a new show with an old-timey feel and a Gershwin score), *The King and I* (for which she won her Tony), *Kiss Me, Kate*, and high-profile concert stagings of *Carousel*, *My Fair Lady*, *Bells Are Ringing*, and *Brigadoon*. But in *The Bridges of Madison County* and off-Broadway, in *My Life with Albertine* and *Far From Heaven*, O'Hara took on dense works of contemporary composers. At this writing, she's thrilled to be working with *Piazza* creative team Adam Guettel and Craig Lucas in a piece written for her, *Days of Wine and Roses*. "I love the piece. It's going to be one of those that takes a few listens, believe me," she confesses. "It took a few just for me to even figure out how sing it. And that's high praise."

After she closed in *Kiss Me, Kate*, her husband, Greg Naughton, admitted to O'Hara that he'd read that her portrayal didn't quite work. Maybe not. It's not that she didn't shine as Lilli Vanessi, singing the glorious Cole Porter score sumptuously and frolicking with abandon, but O'Hara as a spoiled, insecure, temperamental diva strains credibility. She is just too … nice. O'Hara is thoughtful, kind, punctual, funny, witty, and totally comfortable in her own skin. If a diva's temperament lurks underneath, I didn't find it. While Lilli would give up anything for more applause, O'Hara is devoted first and foremost to her kids, and then to a life of creating. "I don't want celebrity, I want craft," she tells me. "I want respect as an artist. I know what

I can't do. But what I can do is try to find where I belong, where I can be useful and push myself in places where someone might not expect me to go."

A hundred and one pounds of fun. In *South Pacific*.
(Joan Marcus)

When did you first start singing?

When I was ten, my mom got me voice lessons. We would sing Disney music and the American Songbook. I was always singing. I was singing all over town. I knew that I loved it. I don't know what I thought I was going to do with it. But I knew that it was everything I was. Singing seemed to be the thing that made me find who I am. I was a small-town girl. I was chubby. I was probably annoying because I was singing and doing gymnastics. I think there was a part of me that wanted my own thing, that wasn't anybody else's. When I started to sing, I all of a sudden felt like that was my thing: my voice. I loved performing, but it had no reality to me. I went into college thinking, "I'll go to law school and be an entertainment lawyer." It wasn't until my first year of summer stock at Music Theater of Wichita, when I actually met people who lived in New York and worked on Broadway, [that I understood]. When I said to my parents, "I want to go into this," it must have seemed like outer space.

Kelli O'Hara	
Jekyll and Hyde	National Tour, 1999; Broadway, 2000
Follies	Broadway, 2001
Sweet Smell of Success	Broadway, 2002
My Life with Albertine	off-Broadway, 2003
Dracula	Broadway, 2004
The Light in the Piazza	Broadway, 2005
The Pajama Game	Broadway, 2006
South Pacific	Broadway, 2008
Bells Are Ringing	Encores!, 2010
Nice Work If You Can Get It	Broadway, 2012
Carousel	Lincoln Center, 2013
Far from Heaven	off-Broadway, 2013
The Bridges of Madison County	Broadway, 2014
The King and I (Tony Award)	Broadway, 2015; West End, 2018
Brigadoon	Encores! 2017
Kiss Me, Kate	Broadway, 2019
Days of Wine and Roses	off-Broadway, 2023

How did they react?

My mom is the one that I think was dreaming big for me before I knew it. She wasn't a stage mom. She had no idea about it. She put me in little dance classes, which I didn't stick with; piano classes, which I didn't stick with; but the minute I would say something like, "I'm going to try to go do this," she'd be like, "Yeah, you are! Do it! Absolutely, do it. We'll figure it out." And I think my dad just took her lead. After she had three kids, my mom was working full-time as a teacher and she went back and got her master's at night. Both of them [modeled] sacrifice to fulfill their dreams. If they had been like, "Well that's stupid, Kelli," who knows what would have happened? I was a do-gooder, I might have listened. But somewhere in my head it was instilled that you don't give up on dreams.

You have often credited your teacher, Florence Birdwell, with giving you your career.

Susan Powell, who had been Miss America, 1981, was from Elk City, my small town. I was five years old when she won and I remember her being held up as this princess. She came back to town and did this thing at the now Susan Powell Auditorium. I remember seeing her and something got inside me right then about learning to sing like her from [her teacher], the bird lady. That stuck with me. When we moved cities when I was sixteen, one of the ways my parents got me to go without kicking and screaming was because I would be able to take voice lessons with one of her students. And then when it came time to audition for Oklahoma City University, I never stopped thinking about her. She was the most different kind of person I had ever met. She really rubbed some people the wrong way. She was in Oklahoma, which is sort of a place where a lot of people do the same thing as each other. When you don't, it really stands out. But if you own it, then people sort of get out of your way. Mrs. Birdwell just owned herself. She owned it. She was loud and proud. I walk in the room with insecurities, wanting to be a perfectionist, and she's like, "No, Ma'am. Let's either get real or get out of here." And she changed my life. If you came in and were trying to sing a song that was completely insincere, she'd be like, "I don't think so. You can come back another time when you're ready." If I had a personal problem, let's get it. Let's figure it out.

Did she scare you?
That's what I'm most proud of, to be honest. A lot of students left her. The strong survived, and I'm most proud [she starts to tear up]—I can get emotional—I'm most proud that I stayed and I survived it. The way she worked was what I responded to. I knew that it was full of truth. I came in as a musical theater major and I didn't know what I was doing. She switched me to opera because I belonged there, I really did. By the time I got to my senior year I was sort of into it, but my heart started to kind of crumble and she knew it. I needed more of the catharsis of communication and expression. It wasn't just about singing perfectly technically. I'm sure that was hard for her as a technical voice teacher, but she was like, "You don't want to go [to graduate school] and so you won't." She ripped up my application and said, "You're moving to New York."

And you did.
New York was like the first time I ever felt really alive. I remember my first trip there without my parents. I went for spring break with a girlfriend. I remember running down Fifth Avenue with my backpack and I was going zoom, zoom, zoom, zoom [weaving between pedestrians]. I felt alive. I moved in September of '98. I didn't have a job. I lived on this person's couch. My parents were definitely helping me in those first few months. But Kristen Chenoweth rented a studio and got her two agents [to hear fifteen of us] from Birdwell Studio. And out of that group they called two of us. I got a couple of non-union jobs before they helped me book my first union job, which was the tour of *Jekyll and Hyde*. I do remember my agent telling me flat out, "Wear a tight sweater and short skirt to your audition." And I did. I didn't even think twice.

So there you were, out on the road . . .
It was a brand-new cast. Jerry Mitchell choreographed and David Warren directed. I made some of my best friends and I had a blast. I didn't think much about the musical itself. I came back because they stuck me in on Broadway. The girl in my ensemble track had gotten pregnant and all of a sudden, I was making my Broadway debut. By the time I got into it, the cast was ready to go. There was a lot of darkness. People were tired. I just shut my mouth but that was where the sadness came in. I rehearsed alone with the dance captain for a week and went into the show. That night we are upstage, curtain comes up. Nobody had said anything to me. John Schiappa tapped me on the leg and said, "Congratulations." I'll never forget that. It was the breath of humanity that I needed. And we're off. That was it. That was my Broadway debut and after a lifetime of sitting on a freaking cow patty, that hurt. I didn't realize it at the time,

but I think it humbled me. I think it set me up for understanding that the real things—you've got to really love and to not take for granted, because it's not always how you expect it. I don't mean to say that anybody was specifically mean or bad. People like Brad Oscar and Corinne Melançon were angels, mentoring me. It was more like I just didn't feel the love of theater.

How did you get through it?

I don't know how this happened or why they let me, but I somehow found my way backstage at *Fosse* [at the abutting Broadhurst Theater]. I would stand stage left and watch the show from offstage. Every night I would watch those glorious dancers. And to me at that time, that heart … maybe it was the music … it was so inspirational. I was mesmerized. And then I would run back and do my entrance. I think it's interesting and useful that the start of all my dreams coming true was not the joy that I wanted it to be.

When *Jekyll* closed, you went right into *Follies*.

I was ecstatic because I had learned that I had gotten *Follies* before we closed, so I knew that I was headed there. I was never a lifer, as they call them, in shows. I hated to do long runs. So the trajectory of those first several shows for me felt really right; I was hungry for something else the minute we opened. I was ready to get on to the next thing. I have learned, as someone who loves to learn, that long runs are very [instructive]. In *King and I*, I was often like, "I've just learned something new!" *Follies* wasn't received well, but it was such a beautiful group of people and it was beautiful to me. Judy Ivey [as Sally] played raw and broken so beautifully. They had the wrong key for her and two months into the run, they finally lowered the key and then she killed it. I loved the girls in the ensemble. I made some of my best friends to this day. Four of us still have Zooms every week. I was understudying three different parts. I really had fun. In the first scene, I walked [Joan Roberts on stage]. I was her escort into the party. I think Joan just sort of got it into her head that I would help her with many things, so there were a couple of days where, at the end of rehearsal, she said, "Go down to the street and get me a taxi." So I did. I did that for a few days before one of the assistant stage managers was like, "What are you doing? We can do that." And I was like, "Oh, well, I didn't mind." On the tenth anniversary, we had a reunion at Judith Ivey's house on the West Side. We all just loved each other. Joan Roberts walks in and by this time I had done a few shows. She was so sweet, saying things like, "I followed you, I'm so proud of you." She stays for a little bit and then literally, "Hey, go down and tell my driver I'm coming." I was like, "Absolutely! I'm on it." And I ran out the door and I got the driver.

Imagine if she absolutely knew the whole time the she shouldn't be asking you but was like "Well … I needed a cab!"

That would be my favorite possible version of this story! Betty Garrett was in the first-floor dressing room and she says, "I sat at this mirror when I was eighteen years old." She was eighty-three! I was really, really wild about that experience and it felt like my debut in a way. It felt like the way I thought it would feel. With *Follies* you had a bunch of people who were very happy to be there. I also saw a lot of humility. The leads were working so hard with such a desire to do well. It gave me this feeling of humanity, that we are all still working on it, still trying to be our best. [After the poor reviews] I remember Treat Williams saying, "We're a team, I'm proud of what we've built. Let's take this thing to the end and let's love it." And everybody was like, "Yes!" I learned early on how to be a leader. I learned it from Victoria Clark, Tom Hewitt, Brian d'Arcy James.… I'm grateful for it.

During *Follies* you auditioned for *Sweet Smell of Success*.
When I was doing *Phantom* at the Bridgeport Downtown Cabaret, I worked with a guy named Eric Michael Gillette. He said to me, "I'm working on a workshop of a new musical written by Marvin Hamlisch. There's a girl playing the part, but you're her to me." He gave me his entire script and score and he's like, "Just in case it ever comes back around." These auditions came up. They were going to move on from Lauren Ward, for whatever reason. It happens. I was understudying Lauren in *Follies*. And when I got to the final callback, the girl I was up against was Erin Dilly, who I was also understanding! We all talked about it, it was fine. [I got it] and was really excited. I thought, "This is it. I've just landed my first original Broadway role."

Marvin Hamlisch liked to tell the story of your audition.
I didn't know Marvin Hamlisch or what he looked like, and I certainly didn't know [lyricist] Craig Carnelia and [director] Nick Hytner. I couldn't get an audition. I was in tech rehearsals for *Follies*. [During lunch] I grabbed a cab, which at that time was unheard of because I didn't have any money. I race over there. I knock on the door. Nobody was there. No moderator. Marvin answered the door, but I didn't know who he was. I just told him, "I'm your Susan! You have to hear me. I have to have an audition. I didn't get an appointment but I came on my lunch break and you need to see me, please! I'm your girl." And he said, "Just a second." He closes the door and then he came back and he said, "OK, we're going to see you." Nick and Craig at the table. He said, "I'm going to play for you because the pianist went to lunch." I remember being like, "I don't care, just go!" I had to be back at rehearsal! He was playing my song. I snapped my fingers [she demonstrates, indicating he should pick up the tempo]. He sped up and I sang. They sort of looked at each other and said, "Would you look at these sides?" I stood out in the hall and looked at them for like five minutes and went back in. I left thinking that it went pretty well. I told my boyfriend at the time about it and he's the one that helped me discover that it was Marvin Hamlisch by showing me a picture! I proceeded to have a callback with Brian d'Arcy James. I had seen him in *Wild Party* and I thought to myself, "If I could ever work with him...." I think I probably was more excited about working with Brian d'Arcy James than the whole thing. I even remember thinking after the callback, "That's all I need, even if I don't get the job." Marvin was the most dear man. Years after the show, he called my parents to check on them after a tornado.

That show was another one of those mysteries—great artists working on great source material, but it's not coming together.
Sometimes I liken that whole experience to being in a straitjacket. It created a change in me. There were a lot of changes happening in Chicago that may or may not have been working, and then we stopped and we came back for this period of rehearsal and break before Broadway, and in that time crazy things changed. They just didn't know what to do with [my character]. I remember standing on stage with great sadness—being an actor that was looking outside my body at myself, not knowing what to do with myself. I just remember feeling not free. After that experience I learned that if I don't add to the project, if I don't add my voice, then I won't make anything better. I did have these pop-out moments of speaking up for myself a bit, but not enough. I sort of made my living off of lover stories. I love lover stories. I love love. I love playing being in love. I love being in love in life. [We were staging this number with Jack Noseworthy] and I remember Nick saying, "Stop touching him. You

look like you're mothering him." And I remember saying, "No, I don't. I know how to touch a man." I remember standing up for myself. I realized right there, "this is tough because the love relationship is not working for the director." After we opened in New York, I started getting notes and notes and notes. The stage manager would come into my room after half hour [which is strictly against Equity rules]. "You could stand this way, and you should probably wear your hat this way, and you shouldn't talk this way. . . ." I'd be in tears at Places. I wasn't protecting myself. I wasn't saying, "You need to get out of my room." No other stage manager was saying, "You can't be in there after half hour." I'd make my first entrance in a ball of insecurity, thinking, "I must be terrible. I must just be awful." And that's kind of how I remember it. That's how I remember the whole thing. . . . I got along really well with Jack and Brian and John [Lithgow] and Stacey Logan. We had a good time as a cast, but I felt the whole time like I was terrible. I don't remember being a sad sack, though; I remember straightening my back and getting out there and trying to do my best. You hope even though you're getting notes, the big picture is working. I wasn't in the number they did at the Tonys, so John Guare took me as his guest. It was the biggest thing! I borrowed my friend's dress. I was really living large. And then we got the closing notice. I was devastated. I'd planned for an entire year. I auditioned, randomly, for this John Kelly performance art piece with Radiohead music and people on rollerblades. We were going to go do it at Sundance Theater Lab. There was another musical [at Sundance] that they had half-finished and they said, "We just need another singer to play the sister-in-law." [Musical director] Ted Sperling had seen *Sweet Smell of Success* and said, "That girl Kelli O'Hara could play Franca." It was *The Light in the Piazza*. I never would have gone if *Sweet Smell of Success* had run. It was just a read-through of the first act, basically. Celia Keenan-Bolger, Mark Harelik, and Steve Pasquale were in it. We were just kind of seeing what it was, but I knew it was delicious. It was weird and different and I loved it.

But after three weeks at Sundance, you came back to New York. . . .
I went in for an audition to play a secondary part in this Ricky Ian Gordon/Richard Nelson piece, *My Life with Albertine*. Right then is when things clicked for me. That's strange to say because so few people got to see *My Life with Albertine*. But Ricky writes classically. I was doing a musical and it was serious and dramatic. I loved every second of it. He and Adam Guettel [composer of *The Light in the Piazza*] were also competitive and Ricky knew that I had worked with Adam and dated him.

You did?
Only for six weeks. We weren't right for each other. But I will sing his music till the day I die. When I started listening to some of Ricky's stuff, I thought, "This is my *Rent*! And if nobody comes I don't care. I want to act and play real characters who have something to say." *My Life with Albertine* gave me that. It was intellectual. And then I went back to Franca and by that time I felt like I was sort of off and running in a new way, with more classical singing. I went to Seattle [for *Piazza*]. It was all clouded with the fact that I was really, really in love [with future husband, Greg Naughton]. I went from there to a show in La Jolla and then straight to the Goodman in Chicago where we did *Piazza* again, except this time with Bartlett Sher directing, and the show became what it is. I was falling in love with it more and more. And then it stopped and we didn't know what it was going to do for a while. We came back from the Goodman and the creatives went back to the drawing board. They were looking at going to Broadway the next spring, so it was going to be a whole year. Frank Wildhorn's people called

me and said, "We want you to do *Dracula*," and I said, "I can't, I'm doing *Light in the Piazza* in the 2005 season," and they said, "We'll let you do both. You can leave in December." And, of course, they closed anyway. I thought to myself, "I'm going to play two leads in one Broadway season? Hell to the yes!"

In *Dracula*, you got to fly, suck blood, die violently on stage . . .
I absolutely did it! I actually had a really fun time except for the nudity debacle. It wasn't so much about the nudity; it was the fact that my agents weren't honest with me. When we were in rehearsal, Des McAnuff says, "OK, now your dress flies off." I had been told that it wouldn't. I said, "I'm sorry, there must be some misunderstanding." He sent everybody else to lunch and then he said, "I wouldn't have hired you. Your agents told us that you'd be fine with it." And [I later learned] they had. They said, "Oh, she'll get over it." And I did. I did get over it. But I moved on [from those agents]. They then tried to give me a bodysuit that had drawn pubic hair on it. It looked horrible and by that time I was like, "Forget it, I'll just do it." All the crew guys would stand at stage left and just stare. It was a different time, but I was the only woman in the discussion. At the end of the day, I did it. But you know what? I had just had a baby two months before we started *Bridges of Madison County*, and I was happy to be naked in that show. Just fat and leaking from my boobs. I was so happy about it because I felt like that was part of the story, not gratuitous. But in *Dracula*, I was having so much fun with all the special effects. I think we were all sort of having blind fun. And then I guess I got wind after the reviews came out that it was terrible. Nobody ever loves to do a show when the audience is diminishing. I knew that *Piazza* was on the horizon, so I was just biding my time. I made a living. I bought an apartment. Sometimes there are those jobs and then there are the ones that make you a better person. Everything leads to something else. Everything is useful. The experience with the nudity and making sure that my voice counts . . . that happened during *Dracula*. It ultimately led me to change agents, and in the next couple of years after, allowed me to choose projects more wisely.

By the time you got to *Piazza* on Broadway, you had moved to the role of Clara.
After Chicago, the conversation started happening that they were not going to have Celia do it. That was kind of a shock to everybody. Once Vicki Clark came on, I think it changed the way that Adam wanted to write the score. He wanted to change some things. They asked if I would come in and sing the role because they wanted to hear it in a different voice. Vicki and I had a conversation and we decided to go to them together and say no. Celia was Clara. They said, "OK, but Celia is not going to do it." Celia is a smart actress, but she also carries this innocence with her. Character-wise, they needed her to be a woman with the mind of a child. They needed the relationship to be sexual and chemical. What Celia brought was this beautiful child. They decided to do a nationwide search. I was asked to come back and sing again and, because they weren't going to go with Celia at all, Vicki and I talked and she said, "If it's going to be anybody, I would rather it be you because you've been here from the beginning. It's our family." I don't think everybody was on board with the idea of me doing it, but I did, and that same year Celia got *Spelling Bee*. I think that they all felt relieved by that, but they were the only ones relieved. The personal nature of it all was catastrophic for Celia, for Vicki, and for me. I never allowed myself to even think about that role until that moment, which was right before we started the Broadway rehearsals. I ended up playing Celia, and I say "Celia," not Clara. She had done the work. I ended up playing her. Adam changed a lot

of the melodies to go higher, he changed keys. That felt like mine. But ultimately, I didn't understand how to play her in my mind. I was doing my best. We did a reunion concert when I was forty and that night I said, "Now I know how to play Clara!" It was the first time I just knew how to let go. I wasn't trying so hard. I loved every second of that score but somehow, I couldn't fully enjoy it until that reunion.

I've heard you say that in the original run you didn't know how to do less, to just be simple.
No, I didn't. I didn't understand. I remember struggling with how to be simplistic. When I saw the show after I left, this young girl named Katie Clarke replaced me, and that's just how she was. I was wanting to play something. I studied blunt trauma to the head. Most people with blunt trauma—they can be sexual, they can be sort of childlike, but they're not going to be what Clara was. What they needed her to be was sort of a fictional thing. I remember during previews, Stephen Sondheim came. They asked for his notes and he said, "I need to see more of her affliction." We went back to the drawing board and I spent several days of rehearsal finding physical language that goes along with blunt trauma: grabbing my crotch, lifting my dress over my head like a seven-year-old. I did this for several shows. I took balls to the wall. But it was quickly deemed ridiculous because the boy would never understand that and would see that as strange. So they cut that out, but it left some physicalization that I did own.

Do you think that just having Sondheim's notes in your head was enough to alter your performance, even if you weren't actually behaving differently?
That's the way that Bart works. He wants to delve all the way into every single aspect. And then at the end of the day you strip it down and you have all these layers that you built on. If you had come to *South Pacific* in the first weeks of previews, it was the darkest show you'd ever seen. By the time we opened [we had scaled that all back, but it was in our heads].

In your Tony speech for *The King and I* you said that Bartlett Sher "made you fly." What makes working with him different?
He's one of the smartest people I know. He is also a master teacher and he wants to teach. If I ever said, "I don't think I should do that," he'd say, "OK, do what you want to do," and almost every time I'd come back to the way he was saying it. He allows for the self-journey. He doesn't plan everything out. Some directors will choreograph and stage everything [in advance] and have everything ready in a book. She'll arrive and say, "This is what you do." Bart will study the historical period [of the show], who was in power, what the politics were, what they wore, what the emotions were, individual storylines that happened, and then he'll come into the room and start the show. He has made no plan. And then he watches and listens and has lots of opinions. He says, "Here's where we are, let's learn about it." And then each of us comes and lives. We move in, and we play our parts. I could kill him sometimes. When I auditioned for *South Pacific*, do you know who the final three who were called back for the role of Nellie Forbush were? Victoria Clark, Kelli O'Hara, and Celia Keenan-Bolger. It was a very strange thing to do to an already tender situation between Celia, Vicki, and me. He's a funny, kind of emotional, all-over-the-place guy. He gives you freedom. He's also humble enough to listen and to say, "Well, I was wrong there." It's a relationship that I've gotten really, really comfortable with.

You said that you learned a tremendous amount from Victoria Clark.
Vicki is very strong, very vocal. She was just a force of unabandoned risk. She was mothering and nurturing and generous. I loved and admired her with every inch of my being. I was still at the age where I needed a lot of guidance and she was just incredibly generous. I cannot remember one moment of negativity with her in five years. I think it was important for her to create that offstage, so that once we got onstage, we would really be so intertwined. After I left, I went to *Pajama Game* and they were going to film *Piazza*. Adam said, "I want you to come back and do the film." Vicki Clark said, "No. I'm sorry. We won't be doing that." She had invested in Katie Clarke. She had been doing the show for over six months with another child. I do remember that choice and appreciating it, as much as it bothered me not to be in that film. She didn't want to upend their closeness that they had been working so hard to get. She invests fully. I really respect that.

Piazza **brought you your first Tony nomination.**
The concept of winning was not even part of my thinking. I was on the red carpet taking photos. My boyfriend was there with me. My parents flew in. But the concept of being disappointed by losing hadn't registered. The idea of the game of it literally didn't occur to me. I was unwilling to let that side of it in until *Bridges of Madison County*, when I sat down for the first time to talk about my Tony campaign, which naïvely, I didn't know existed. I couldn't believe it. It broke my heart. I just didn't think about . . .

Anything beyond meritocracy?
I guess I didn't want to. I wanted to believe that you do your work and you do the best you can. It wasn't until *Bridges*, a commercial production that was failing, that I understood the need to have a Tony for the production, to sell the show. On that show I had the pleasure of working with one of the most generous producers out there, Stacey Mindich. She threw a Tony luncheon for me and I got to invite my friends and family, and I remember being so moved by it. But I also noticed there were press people filming it. It had all been planned as a press event, which didn't diminish the joy, but I saw the pragmatic side of it.

The fact that it was a staged event, though, doesn't take away from the fact that the moment was real and the nomination was warranted.
I know that. But I will always think of these things differently and I don't want to stop and it's not because I'm naïve anymore. It's because I choose to want to keep loving this. Life is too short.

Do you dislike awards season?
I think things changed vastly after I had children. The way I wanted to live my life became harder. I don't have full-time nannies. I didn't have children so that they could spend all their money in therapy about me later, and I live every day with that concern. I noticed in the beginning, every single invitation felt like a joy. But then maybe by the third or fourth nomination, I started just being exhausted. I was also getting older. I'm waking up in the morning with my children, but then I might have six things in one day, be it an interview and it's hair and makeup and that sort of glamorous life, which I know is so delicious for fans. And this is another reason why I think I'm annoying: I don't want to find a dress. At least I don't today. I don't want to dress up. If a designer wants to loan me something, I'm so grateful, but I don't

want to go out and try to look for clothes and fancy shoes and put my hair and my makeup on. I want to work. I want to just dig deep inside and rip away and feel and cry and laugh and dissolve and disappear in things. I don't want to fancy myself up and come out and act big. But I think there are people who just love that. That's just a part of the game that I don't know how to play. I've played it. I played it for a long time. And during Tony season it's a little easier because you do get a little help. But you're also doing eight shows a week and then sometimes after the show you have to go to this function where you're selling the show to traveling companies, and then the next day you have a luncheon. And then you go back and do another show. And then the day of the Tonys is whack! You wake up at 6:00; you go to the dress rehearsal in full costume; you come back and try to get a little rest; you do a full matinee; you get into red carpet clothes; you go do the red carpet; you leave your seat and get back in costume; you do your number; you change back into red carpet; go back to your seat; lose; and then you're expected to go to the fancy parties and be gracious. It's not a complaint. I would never complain about these Tony experiences. I never dreamed about them, and I am grateful. As I look back over the seven times that I experienced these springs, they started to feel like some sort of tradition. The first couple of times I was nominated they had these luncheons in the Rainbow Room and it was a day of no press. They made a point of that. I was blown away by this place I landed in, this situation. I'm looking around the room, feeling like part of a club that I never could get into. Marian Seldes gets up and she reads this statement about what it means be a theater actor. They show a compilation of Tony Awards clips since their inception. I am bawling at Michael Jeter, Angela Lansbury.... All of a sudden, it's hitting me that I've been woven into this quilt. But a couple of years later, CBS is sponsoring, it's full press, it's downstairs at the Paramount, it's dark. It's filled with a million people, not just the nominees. You couldn't find anybody. They didn't show the video. Marian Seldes is dead. I remember thinking, "I'm not sure what I'm a part of anymore." That's a little bit of what changed for me. Not because it was getting old. Oh my gosh, never! I've been surprised to be nominated again and again. But my priority is changing. My children and my time are more valuable.

What made you decide you were ready to leave *Piazza*?
I had been working on *Piazza* for five and a half years. I told you I was not a lifer. We opened in April and I know it came as a shock that I would leave in December. [But I had the opportunity to do *The Pajama Game* and] I decided to do it. I got really excited about playing a ballsy lady. It was a big decision. I was mentally ready to figure out something else. I don't think I ever would have been considered for Nellie Forbush if I hadn't gone to do Babe. I took a huge pay cut to leave. But at that time in my life, that kind of stuff wasn't part of my decision-making. I was going to squeak by. I didn't have children. It was really just about finding that different thing to learn from.

The Pajama Game **was the first of several spunky roles and also the first of your several revivals.**
I was really anxious to stop playing the ingenue. When you're a young actress, you want to do something really rich and get out of the "looking pretty and saying nothing" stage. I was racing to get out of *Light in the Piazza* to get into something like *Pajama Game*, which doesn't seem that big of a leap, but at least the character was a woman. I was graduating into older things. I was not the vocal type [for the role] but back then I was willing to kind of scream if I had to. I did my best Doris Day imitation and I had the best time, the absolute

best time. I love everybody in that cast. Working with Harry Connick Jr. was like an artistic rollercoaster. Every night he would come by my room and say, "What do you want?" And I'd say, "Hillbilly," or "Classic rock," or something. There's a whole improv section on the piano during "Hernando's Hideaway" and he would change it every night to accommodate my request. Michael McKean and I would stand off stage every night and watch him play. He loved to improv. When we made the show album and my solo album, he said, "Why are you cutting off right where it says to cut off?"; or "Why are you singing straight quarters? Fuck it. Back phrase"; or "Come in early there." He changed the entire way I think about making music. He made me feel like a musician. It was so magical and so artistically fulfilling. There were all the rumors that we were having an affair. We weren't. I got engaged during the first week of rehearsals. I was deeply in love with Greg. The performance was a performance. And with Harry, every night was brand new. He had the lines that he said as Sid and he had the staging that he was given, but once that was sort of set in his body, never was a show going to be the same or he was going to be bored to tears. I loved every second of it. I could have definitely done that one for longer.

You returned to Lincoln Center with *South Pacific*.
South Pacific was sort of the beginning of something else for me, to be honest. I don't know why. Maybe it's because I got married and it felt a little different for me. In my head, my grown-up life was starting. The show was really special to me. I was raised by a mom who was the daughter of an Arkansas woman. I had Arkansas aunts and they love their Nellie Forbush. All the irony of that was completely lost on them. They all just love *South Pacific* and Nellie and they never really thought about her [racism]. I loved to play her because I realized that I wanted to be the vessel for that lesson. I knew that I knew Nellie Forbush, and I could do her justice and play her with a modicum of humanity. She needed to be a sympathetic character, but also had a horrible, horrible affliction—being such a racist. To be able to show her as a human being who had been carefully taught, wrongly, and needed to change, was ready to change, and be bigger than she was—I loved that. I was really proud of that production.

That was a long run for you.
I did it, and then I left because I was pregnant. I was like a whale doing cartwheels. I had my son and then I came right back into the show when he was about three months old. Then I left again, and then I came back to do the film that next summer. So I tried to get away with coming and going a little bit in that show. You don't always get to do that.

Do you think you returned to the role differently, having had time away from it?
I was probably just a little bit more emotional when I came back. I was a mom and also pumping backstage. I remember enjoying it very much when I came back, and remembering myself as a being other than a mother. I got to experience that role in two different ways, which was nice. My voice had changed. Your solar plexus separates and has to come back together later, but [it was] separated when I went back into the show. The chest resonance was gone.

Your next roles continued to take you away from lovely ingenues and to spunky spitfires. You did *Bells Are Ringing* at Encores! and then *Nice Work If You Can Get It*.
I loved just getting to be a goofball. I've tried to stretch myself and show different sides, but my M.O. will always be to go to the sincere. I'm not going to chew the scenery. Even in *Bells*

Are Ringing I'm probably going to go for the heart more than the comedy. People might want to come and just see balls-to-the-wall comedy and that's not going to be able to be me. But you know what? Some people are going to like it and some people aren't. But I'm glad to have had those opportunities to surprise some people. I had so much fun [in *Nice Work*]. I laughed more than I've ever laughed in my life—like, knees bucking laughter. And that was a good show to practice my [having a] voice. I remember having a lot of opinions. Not all were taken into consideration. They were still trying to figure out how to write the role and I think there were a lot of things that maybe never got solved, but they added a striptease number for me. I wanted to be a part of the hijinks.

At this stage of your career, you were appearing regularly with your name above the title. Do you remember feeling like a "certified leading lady of Broadway?"

I always think about how things maybe happen for a reason, and maybe sometimes they don't. I had done a little TV and film. I stopped because I had children, and then I started making the decision that TV wasn't for me. "I'm a theater person! And I'm proud of that! Just like Mary Martin and Barbara Cook. That's who I was meant to be." I remember being well aware that I had all these lead roles, and I was super excited about that and proud of myself, but I was always paired with a star. I couldn't sell the tickets alone. Matthew Broderick sold the tickets. Harry Connick Jr. sold the tickets. *South Pacific* sold the tickets. I'm going to get to work, but it's going to be on the coattails of someone. I also took great pride in the fact that I'm the girl who gets along with all of [the varying men]. I had great times with all of them. [But I started to ask myself], "Am I doing the right things for my career?" I decided to finally go in for a TV show. I wanted to do TV so that [I could gain name recognition] and get to do a play, or to get to carry my own show and not be the counterpart to the ticket-seller. It was very early in the game of *Nice Work If You Can Get It*. I got it. Big part. And the TV show—this is unheard of—was willing to shoot me only on Mondays so that I could still do this Broadway show. They would work around me. The *Nice Work* producers said "no" and threatened to sue me. I remember one of them literally calling me and saying, "Don't even worry about this. You'll get more TV. I think you should play Dolly Levi." I don't hold grudges, but I have been sour about that decision. Life would be different financially for me and my family. Not for nothing, and I am not saying he was right by a long shot—but I did get more TV later on and came to love the medium. When I was doing *King Lear* at The Public, I met the wonderful Arian Moayed who didn't even know I was a singer and wrote a show for me, *The Accidental Wolf*, which earned me an Emmy nomination. But the confining words of that *Nice Work* producer changed the way I felt about the kind of art I do and the way in which I wanted to make it. It's not fair to blame them for any of my career downfalls, but it hurt my feelings. My whole thing became, "I'm going to keep doing what I know how to do and what I've been allowed to do, which is bigger than every dream I've ever had: be on Broadway." But I also wanted to live my life. I got pregnant the next month. I remember the demand that I would do four months while I was pregnant. I was dancing all over those stairs. I can do that. I did it. I saw it through and everything. I look back on it with great affection and love and I actually miss the joy of it. But I do remember at that moment being ready to go. And then what happened after that was where the personal hits the professional as a woman. I felt like I really compromised *Far from Heaven* and almost *Bridges*. They had planned on doing *Bridges* at Williamstown that summer and I had to say, "I'm sorry, I'm pregnant." All their faces fell. They decided to go forward without me, which they had to. I was very, very upset not to be able to build that show and do it in Williamstown. After giving birth I only had two months to strap my boots on and try to figure out what it was going to be for Broadway. And *Far from Heaven* was just a blur. I had done the show the year before at Williamstown. I sometimes sort of cower when I think about how hard Scott Frankel and Michael Corey and Richard Greenberg worked on that, and to know that the whole thing was sort of colored in a different way by my pregnancy. I was very happy, of course, but also very insecure about how it was affecting the lives of these professional people. I felt guilty. I shouldn't have. But I definitely did at that time.

Why?

We worked on *Far from Heaven* for so long. I love that kind of art song. I was going to play this perfect housewife, vulnerable, her figure is just right. When we started, I wasn't showing quite as much. I was about five and a half months pregnant. But by the time we ended the run . . . I felt badly that somehow the center of the story was not what it was supposed to be. That's my own insecurity about it, because I want so much to do what's right for a character. I played the whole run carrying a child inside me, which changes everything. We bring so much of who we are to a role. It was a different role than it should have been. I have no regrets about any of it, but at the same time, I don't think the creators got what they had hoped for.

After you gave birth, you went right into *The Bridges of Madison County*.

I don't even remember exactly when it was that [composer] Jason Robert Brown called me with the idea. He said he always wanted to write his *Porgy and Bess*, his romantic opera. We went around together and sold it. It was an extraordinary process to be given that responsibility. Jason and I had a relationship from way back. I auditioned for the out-of-town production of *The Last Five Years* which Lauren Kennedy ended up doing. I got hired as the understudy. In the long relationship I have with my musical theater non-belt situation, I remember him following me out of the audition, and saying, "I feel like you take us there and then you just stop, you hold back." I don't think I owned the way I sing. I would sing some version of it, but then when it really wanted to go, I had no choice but to put it in head voice. It wasn't cohesive. Cut to *Bridges* and I said, "Well Jason, I don't think I sing the way that you like. I want to, but I don't, so what are we going to do? Are you going to write for me?" And he said, "Yes!" We did the first workshop, which was only partially finished, and some of those songs had that low, earthy feeling to it. [Sings] "What do you call a man like that," you know? That kind of stuff. The songs were staying in this kind of earthy, folky place, which I liked but it wasn't matching the emotion. I was like, "I don't know. I think I'm going to love this character, but I don't know about the singing." He came back for the next workshop and he decided to make her completely different for me. He used Francesca's Italian heritage, which lent itself to a classical feel. When I sing, it's how I feel, it's not how I hear. Every single thing he gave me to sing, all of a sudden, was just flowing out of me and it hadn't felt that easy. Pure feeling rather than placement. Ease of choice as a singer. He gave me a combination, the earthy and the soprano. Francesca wasn't about my looks or perceived looks or about being young. Quite the contrary. It just felt like a gift. You're not even thinking about what you're selling, you're just being. You're not overthinking it. I am not Francesca, but I was the granddaughter and daughter of farm wives. I know what it means to know a woman who was underfed in life. Incredibly smart women who didn't go towards themselves at all,

With Steven Pasquale in *The Bridges of Madison County*.
(Joan Marcus)

ever. I was deep inside her and then to be able to just open my mouth within that . . . I didn't think about much except just being in there. It was great. And I discovered this weird thing that was happening, and this is going to make me sound crazy: active awake meditation while on stage. I would be standing at the kitchen sink, saying my lines, completely in the moment. There was a drawer on the stage. I could open the drawer and, in my mind, see the contents of the drawer in my grandma's house. I know they were the contents when I was ten, but I hadn't thought about them in thirty years. I can't even explain it because I was completely inside the scene. It was the joy of finding myself on stage. I want to get back to it right away. That's where I feel the real joy and the real magic of owning who I am and what I do and being OK with messing up. It's all part of the messy pot. It takes so long to do that and I don't know if it was because I was exhausted and raw, but when you're raw and exhausted your brain gets out of the way. I haven't thought about it in a while and it's making me miss theater so much. It's awesome.

This time, you felt heard as the show was being built?
I had a lot of problems with *Bridges* and they didn't always listen to me. When I was eight and a half months pregnant, I had the ability to go watch it in Williamstown with my understudy, and I couldn't believe some of the things I saw. I was certain they would be gone by the time we opened on Broadway and they never ... I spoke up a lot. There were a lot of things about *Bridges* that I really truly loved, and then there were things about it that I never agreed about. I don't like the way American musical theater puts on country western people. It might be because I'm Southern. I don't feel like *Bridges* needed the cow. We don't have to have silly, cheesy laughs. We can actually trust the material. I did not like all the fluff. I think it undermined so much. But that wasn't my part. They give you allowance when it comes to what you are emoting and what you are feeling, but I'm not the dramaturg. I did not win those arguments. [But overall] it was one of the best experiences of my life.

You worked opposite Steven Pasquale in both *Far from Heaven* and *Bridges*.
I'm really glad that I did both of those shows with Steve because our relationship is so safe. During *Bridges*, I was postpartum and emotional and leaking—to find chemistry there for him was really, really something special. He took care of me during all that. And I think somehow, we both let it be part of the story that she was without sexuality for so long and it was reawakening. During that time it was special to be with someone I could trust.

Bridges had a disappointingly brief run.
I love work. I want to work all the time. But I had a brand-new baby and that trumped it. I was exhausted and so emotionally overwrought. I desperately wanted to be with her. Once I knew it was not a success and it was going to close, it killed me as an artist but I celebrated going home. Now that they're growing up, I don't feel like I've missed [too much]. I've tried not to stay away for more than twenty-four hours. You only get a minute when they're babies.

Is there a community of Broadway mothers? Do you compare notes with your peers?
All the time. There are so many women on Broadway that are mothers. We're all talking all the time. Audra McDonald and Ruthie Ann Miles and I have a text chain. I have a group of moms out here that are all Broadway girls and all we do is sit around and talk about our kids. I remember having a conversation with Christine Ebersole right when I was about to have my son. She was telling me about her pre-teenage kids and how they were mad at her because she was gone all the time. She was feeling like, "Hey, I've got to make a living. And I love what I do and I'm trying to teach them the importance of that." And then I saw her like seven years later and her kids were all out of the house. She grabbed me and said, "Don't make the same mistake. I missed them." I appreciated that so much. There are working mothers in every single part of the workforce, but there are several of us [Broadway women] who've pumped at the White House or were leaking on stage. A bunch of us were dancing or doing cartwheels while pregnant. We can't work once we're visibly pregnant. We actually sometimes get in trouble. You feel this major pressure about how your physical body is going to affect the kind of work you can give. We learn how to do it better through each other. Like, "I actually didn't take that

job because. . . ." Or, "I actually asked for provisions in my contract." They'll [make accommodations] if you push it. They'll let you have your kids in your dressing room [contractually]. I learned, "Oh, I should ask for that." They might say no, but I can ask because someone else got it. That sort of thing. There needs to be more information for young women to make decisions about how to have a life and a career. You just do it and hope for the best without a lot of information.

I can imagine that, no matter how you do it, you're always going to be questioning whether or not you did it well.
Every single day. I don't think it's that much different than other careers, but I think as parents, if we care at all, we just assume we're doing it wrong.

You were Tony-nominated for a sixth time with _Bridges_.
That was not a shining moment for me. It's not that I felt like I should have won because I saw _Beautiful_ . . . and Jessie's one of my favorite people in the world. But the Tony Awards themselves were so interesting because our show had closed. There was nobody going with me because Steve Pasquale was so horrendously left out. I actually still can't get over it because he's my favorite part of the show. I mean when you listen to the album, it's like, "More Steve! Pour it in a bottle and I'll drink it!" When your co-star isn't nominated and you're invited to this party, then you sort of feel left out in this weird way. You don't have your partner there. When you do a show, it's a team effort. You're happy to be there, but it's really the celebration of the work that's been done, so it feels like there's a side of you that's missing, this emptiness. And then you go back to work and you almost feel guilty for it. It feels selfish or something. [That year] I was sort of mourning the fact that that whole experience was over. Then the next morning at 7:00 a.m.—and by the way, I was still pumping—I had jury duty. It was pouring rain. I get up and go down to City Hall and I stand in the rain with my pumps on my shoulder. Keeping me humble. It's like the universe just saying, "Don't get too big for your britches."

How did _The King and I_ come into your world?
That was just a continuation of the whole Lincoln Center relationship. "OK, what should we do next?" At the time I thought it was going to be _My Fair Lady_. That's what my choice would have been. I actually loved _The King and I_ more than I thought I would. I underestimated it. I thought it was going to be safe, another sweet Rodgers and Hammerstein teacher. I didn't know the show. I didn't think about being on the ground, fighting with the King to stop the whipping of a young woman. Feminism. I took from it, over the three productions that I did, so much more than I ever expected. I am very grateful for all of those experiences put together. I think it was one of the first times that I stood on a stage with authority because the role called for it. I think it changed me as a person and as an actor and I am grateful for that.

It's interesting to me that you signed on if you were not excited by the role at first.
Well, I trusted the team. I also knew it would be extraordinary. I wanted to be studying a world that I didn't know. I love immersing myself in the realities of all the things I do. I knew that it would be handled really well. I had two very small children and I remember thinking, "This will be sort of easy to have children with." It was quite the opposite. It was a much heavier thing than I ever thought. It was three hours long. It was physically exhausting. I

remember underestimating its emotional difficulty. *Bridges* had been emotionally heavy, in a good way, but I didn't realize *The King and I* would be as complicated and complex as it was.

Rodgers and Hammerstein sort of fool us with "I Whistle a Happy Tune" at the top of the show. It's such a lovely, delightful little ditty, but when you consider the circumstances of the moment, it's really massive what this woman was doing.
Can you imagine going where she went with absolutely no knowledge? She shows up and is not given what she's promised, and she has a child with her. I remember building the whole entire role around being a protective mother who had no other options but to support her family this way. That put the weight into the piece for me, incredibly so. I was actually building a show around just protecting a child. It's interesting you pick that particular song because that's exactly where I started, with this great fear and this great false backbone. I think Anna's very easily played extremely done and complete. I had no desire to play her complete. I thought she was a very vulnerable and very, very scared woman. "I will protect you, I will let nothing happen to you. But we must do this because there are zero options." I haven't thought about in a while, but when I go back to talking about it, I get really into it again.

You mentioned "weight" and I immediately thought of the weight of the dress.
I had so many Annas that I would run to for advice. [They all said], "Mind your back." I'm like, "I am young and athletic." Oh my God, I practically lost my ability to walk most the time. That dress was forty pounds and you're whipping it in order to get that dance. I really did change my body. As you get older you get hurt more easily. *Kiss Me, Kate* killed my rotator cuffs. I have tendonitis. But I didn't have to go to the gym! It was a pretty good time. I could eat whatever I wanted.

You described Ken Watanabe as an explorer.
I can't really say to you, after five years, that I know Ken Watanabe because we have a language barrier. It is very much art imitating life. But as an artist, he was absolutely 100 percent dedicated and maniacally interested in searching and finding and trying to be better. When I did *Cosi Fan Tutte*, I was doing the entire thing in a language I don't speak. I know what I'm saying, but I don't quite know the nuance of how a person might be saying what they are saying to me. Ken was in a similar situation; he had his lines and I had mine, but would he notice if I changed my inflection? I think he was trying to be in that place. I loved that. I don't ever want to work with somebody who just wants to do the same thing every single time. It's like death to me. It's really in the minute choices. There was an admiration and respect that I think was mutual. We really stood on each other's abilities on stage.

That year, on your sixth nomination, you won the Tony.
Kristin [who had been nominated for *On the Twentieth Century*] won all the early awards. But at the Tony luncheon she whispered in my ear, "I want this to be yours." And it was. I took it from someone who deserved it. She should have won that year, but I celebrate the fact that I have it. When you win, at least in all of my times before, [the previous year's winners] host the pre-Tony show. So I win the Tony and sometime in the winter, a lovely friend of mine, a designer, Matthew Christopher, calls and says, "Gotta get you ready for the Tonys! I'm going to build you a dress!" I was excited. It's part of the win. You're with

the winner in the male category, having fun, and I thought Michael Cerveris and I were going to be up there. He builds me two dresses because he can't decide. Mid-May, my manager calls: "Unfortunately, they're going to go a different way this year." It was the year Anna Wintour had taken over. Every single presenter was a TV star who had done some Broadway. She was like, "That's fine, but at least her tickets for her and Greg . . . We don't have room for her this year." I had to call the designer and say, "I don't have anywhere to wear your beautiful dress that you made me for free because I'm not invited to the Tonys this year." The universe keeps you humble.

You played Anna on Broadway for a year. You came back to it again for London and then again for Tokyo. I'm wondering about what that experience was like for you coming to it anew.

The circumstances were so different each time, forcing me to find more and find more and find more. Every single time I walked away from the experience extraordinarily bettered by the situation, just really filled up—London for personal reasons and Tokyo for artistic reasons. In London the show was at the Palladium and I just felt an extraordinary opportunity, but then there was this weight of protection of my friend [co-star Ruthie Ann Miles was in a terrible accident in which she lost both her toddler and unborn child]. When Ruthie arrived, the show went out the window for me, in a good way. I had done my time and my work, and I found new things in the show every day. But it wasn't about that for me anymore. Ruthie became my reason for being on the stage. I don't even know what to say about her. I don't know what you do. And she's doing it every day of her life because there is no choice. It was so raw. There were days when literally, I would put my arm under her. She was still on a cane. Every single time that curtain came down we'd be on the floor in her room. She spent so much to get through it. She put herself completely into the role. When she stood on that stage, it was uber focus and richer than you can ever imagine.

Right before going to London, you did *Kiss Me, Kate*. Was that something that you were champing at the bit to do?

No, not at all. I wanted to do *Kiss Me, Kate* because of [director] Scott Ellis and the Roundabout and Will Chase. And here's one thing I don't want to get lost: I don't want to stop doing musical theater in a way that is just really fun. No, I don't want to stop doing Rodgers and Hammerstein, and no, I don't want to stop doing brand-new things. Whatever I do doesn't always have to be exactly what you expect of me or what you would rather me do. I knew that *Kiss Me, Kate* was just going to be fun and wild. And I felt like I was paying homage to Marin Mazzie. I know I'm not like Marin. The ballsy, sort of guttural thing she had, that's just not my thing. But I thought I could do it justice. I would do some of it in honor of her, and then I would try to find some new ways to do it. I try to look for the more human softness of things because that's what I can bring. I wanted "I Hate Men" to be more introspective. Whether that worked or not, I don't know, but you just take those chances because you're trying to make it yours. I did have a blast doing it. I loved working with [musical director] Paul Gemignani, I loved that cast. I loved being in a dance musical where I could watch those dancers. Every time I get to be in a musical comedy with big dance numbers, I feel lucky because I just love it. It's part of why I fell in love with musical theater in the first place. When the curtain goes up on *42nd Street*, I'm a mess.

A rare moment of quiet in the boisterous *Kiss Me, Kate*.
(Joan Marcus)

You said that you got hurt a lot during *Kiss Me, Kate*.
I always tend to say, "Yeah, I'll do the cartwheels." I love building it that way and I always see myself as really tough. But the whip—honestly, I think the dress was at fault. It had a cap sleeve and it was really tight. So [to crack the whip] I had to push it away every night. And then I'm on Will's back and I'm going like [flailing] this and I'm pushing up and I think I strained both rotator cuffs. It's just the repetitive motion. But *Kiss Me Kate* . . . I had a lot of fun.

You wore a hat that Marin wore in her production.
I asked for that. I asked Jason [her widower]. I wanted his blessing. I don't ever want to seem gratuitous or pandering. I really lost it when Rebecca Luker died [breaks into tears] because . . . I just can't explain what those women meant to me. I needed an example. I needed proof that I belonged here. [Growing up,] everybody thought I was crazy. They didn't think of the performing arts as a real thing. I moved up here and literally the first people I see are Marin and Audra. And then I see *Sound of Music* starring Rebecca. What they did for me—there was something about the contemporary nature of these women. They were strong, funny, sweet, good people. And they're gone. They're just gone off the Earth. I want to have them with me all the time. I can't believe they're gone.

Today, you are developing a new musical while also co-starring in a new TV show, *The Gilded Age*. Has doing TV altered what you think you want for your future?
I love the master class every time I walk into it. I'm literally doing scenes with Cynthia Nixon and Christine Baranski and Nathan Lane. I don't know how I got here. And I'm working on

a musical that I adore. My kids are great. My marriage is great. I'm trying not to feel guilty! I hope that I keep working and I get to do wonderful things. I used to think I needed work to be a ladder I was climbing. I don't anymore. Not that I've lost my ambition—that's the thing that can kill you. I definitely want to keep reaching, but the reach could be in other directions. Who cares who's watching? Could I someday play the mother in *August Osage County* when I'm older? Could I? Because I know her like the back of my hand. That kind of thing excites me. That's the ladder for me now. Or it was. The pandemic has altered me tremendously. It made me think, "Man, am I grateful that I built myself a world outside of my work!" My purpose at home is so clear. But my purpose also grew. We started to really talk about racial injustices in the theater community this year. Onstage, we've been telling the same stories for years, and I have been telling a lot them, but the stories need to change. I used to think the theater was so diverse and I was proud to be a part of that. We have such an opportunity—a mandate, actually, to rebuild in an environment where all of our stories are being told by all of the people, not just some of us.

Stephanie J. Block

July, August 2021; April, May 2022

In her speech accepting her Tony award for *The Cher Show*, Stephanie J. Block had a message for her daughter, Vivienne: "It's not about winning, little girl, it's about showing up, doing your best, loving all people, and finding joy along the way." If anyone has earned those sage words, it's Block. Because despite the well-deserved honor *The Cher Show* brought, Block's long résumé features more than its fair share of moments that looked like they'd catapult her career but—despite the excellence she brought—did not go as hoped or expected. A less formidable actor might have given up, and many in similar boats do. Block is not that actor. Again and again, she showed up, did her best, found her joy, and triumphed.

In early 2000, after a decade of paying her dues in regional theaters and theme parks in her native Southern California, Block came home one day to a call from the composer Stephen Schwartz, asking if she'd be available to participate in the development of a show he was working on about the witches of Oz. For two years, Block was *Wicked*'s very first Elphaba through every reading and workshop, poised to originate one of Broadway's most iconic roles. Until, that is, it was decided that they needed an experienced "name" to open the show. Idina Menzel was cast, with Block as her understudy. Block was crushed, but bounced back quickly, making her Broadway debut that same season as Liza Minnelli, in *The Boy from Oz*. She was a revelation, but aside from Hugh Jackman's star turn, the show was largely dismissed. Then she triumphed as Elphaba, originating the role in the *Wicked* national tour (and later on Broadway), to great acclaim and personal satisfaction, ready for the next challenge. It came in the form of the titular character in a big-budget new musical by the creators of *Les Misérables*. Block was, again, sensational, but *The Pirate Queen* was a fast flop, closing in two months. In 2008, *9 to 5* looked poised to hit, but it, too, did not meet expectations. After flawlessly replacing Sutton Foster in *Anything Goes*, Block received her first Tony nomination for the fantastic revival of *The Mystery of Edwin Drood*. Then, in the revival of William Finn's *Falsettos,* Block was Trina, the neurotic wife and mother, coping as the world she understands collapses around her. Block was daffy and heartbreaking, rock-solid and fragile, petty and magnanimous. She was Tony nominated for her efforts— and then, somewhat unexpectedly, *The Cher Show* in which Block didn't so much play the pop icon as embody her. In his *New York Times* review, Jesse Green said, "Not only does she ace Cher's vocal inflections and physical mannerisms, including the half-mast eyes, the arm akimbo and the dancing-from-the-hair-up hauteur, but she somehow integrates them into a portrait of a woman at odds with the very dream that sustained her." Block won the Tony, Outer Critics Circle, and Drama Desk Awards.

In 2020, Block was preparing for a new off-Broadway musical, *The Bedwetter*, when COVID hit. Like many a Broadway performer, she and her husband, the actor Sebastian Arcelus, decided to take a New York sabbatical, moving with Vivi to Northern California.

"I'm Cher, Bitches." *The Cher Show*.
(Joan Marcus)

She's happy there. And calm. I'd met Block several times prior to our conversations and always found her energy crackling and eager, ready to play. So when we spoke, she surprised me with her introspective, carefully considered ruminations. Maybe it was because of our collective moment of pause, or maybe it was being out of New York, but I suspect that at this stage of her career and life, Stephanie J. Block is no longer trying to prove anything to anyone. It suits her.

Stephanie J. Block	
The Boy from Oz	Broadway, 2003
Wicked	National Tour, 2005; Broadway, 2007
The Pirate Queen	Broadway, 2006
9 to 5	Broadway, 2008
Anything Goes	Broadway, 2011
The Mystery of Edwin Drood	Broadway, 2012
Little Miss Sunshine	off-Broadway, 2013
Falsettos	Broadway, 2016
Brigadoon	Encores!, 2017
The Cher Show (Tony Award)	Broadway, 2018
Into the Woods	Broadway, 2022; National Tour, 2023
Sunset Boulevard	Washington, DC, 2023

What's your first memory of performing in public?

I was seven years old, and I was the soloist at my First Communion. When I was little, I was always singing. I never stopped singing. It was my way to be seen and heard. As the younger sister of two, it was my way of saying, "I'm here too." I have a beautifully complicated relationship with music. My singing voice is my outlet, my badge of honor, my contribution—all intertwined … it's so much a part of my identity. Throughout the years, it's what has allowed me to stand up straight and say, "I'm worth something."

That puts a lot of pressure on your talent.

It does. Probably too much. It's popped up in my life in some unhealthy ways that I wasn't able to recognize until therapy. I always say, if you approach your art form in a healthy way, it's completely freeing. If you're hiding from yourself in this art form, if you're trying to disappear in your characters by avoiding life while making play, then you're in the danger zone. I was doing that, and I could keep that up for a while without recognizing that I was losing little shreds of who I was along the way. The first time I moved to New York—I think I was only there for maybe nine months—I was shape-shifting every time I walked into an audition. I would second-guess what I thought they wanted me to be. Every time I left the room, I was like, "I don't know what just happened." I was not feeling my own breath or truly hearing the words coming out of my mouth. Finally, I said, "I have to leave New York and work on … feeling comfortable being me." I had to come back home and figure out who I was and make sure I was staying true to myself regardless of place or situation. I was back in Southern California for another seven years until that cold call from Stephen Schwartz about the prospects of working on a new project, [that would later become] *Wicked*. And at the time of that phone call, I was ready. I tell students that our art form is a remarkable way to transport yourself, but if you completely *lose* yourself in the art, you're doing yourself a disservice. You have to make sure that the basic foundation of every character you build and every song you interpret has a piece of you.

That sounds very wise at twenty-two.
I had an incredible voice teacher, Jill Goodsell, from the time I was eleven, and she really helped shape me. She taught me to journal and to pay attention to the things around me. So even at twenty-two, my internal compass was pretty clear.

Did you train as an actor at all?
At a young age, my voice teacher had me write all the lyrics out in different colors and see what that brought out. She'd ask, "What emotion does that particular word elicit?" And then we would always break down the song: "What do you think is the most important word, or phrase, in the entire piece?" That core word or phrase needs to constantly be percolating when you're singing a song because that's what's defining the character for you, that's what you're connecting to. It's funny, I didn't know at the time it was acting training, but that's exactly what it was. And then I studied at the Orange County High School of the Arts and also privately. I would often work with a coach when preparing for auditions. I can remember going into an audition for Fantine [in *Les Misérables*], and they loved my voice. At the callback, the associate director said, "You sing beautifully, but I don't believe your pain." I have always remembered that. I have a tendency to hold onto certain comments—I take them, and I respond in action, like … "I'm going to do something about that, so nobody can ever tell me that again."

Thank God for feedback.
Thank God for feedback. Our knee-jerk reaction is to be defensive. I think that's because, as artists, we stand in such vulnerability. We open up our guts and somebody looks at us and says, "It's not enough." If you don't get defensive, there's a lot to be said for feedback. And if you do, you're in the wrong business. Notes, criticism, voices on social media … it never ends. So, you better be flexible, willing to take direction, all the while knowing who the hell you are in order to make it through.

So there you are, having racked up every regional credit in Southern California, and you get that phone call from Stephen Schwartz.
I was living in Studio City, California, and I had just finished performing as Natasha in *The Rocky and Bullwinkle Show* at Universal Studios. On my answering machine is a recorded message: "Hi Stephanie, this is Stephen Schwartz. I'm a composer. I wrote *Godspell*, *Pippin* …"—envision my jaw on the floor. "I'm in town creating a new musical. You were recommended to me. I would love to meet with you." A few days after that voice message, I walked into his Los Angeles apartment. He played me "As Long as You're Mine," "One Short Day," and "Making Good." We chatted a while. I sang a little bit of "Making Good," trying to sight-read, which is not my strongest skill. I remember learning it with him at the piano, making many mistakes, and him notating some of those mistakes. I also remember thinking, "Maybe I booked this gig,"—a gig that I assumed would just be a few exciting days of work. So, lo and behold, there I am, back in his apartment, working on those three tunes that would later be presented in a Universal Pictures conference room. Stephen was at the piano. Winnie Holzman, who wrote the libretto, had cue cards and was explaining the story scene to scene. And we sang. There were a lot of big-wigs with expressionless faces. As I can recall, they gave us very little reaction after that first presentation. And I left feeling as though I did the job I was hired for, to the best of my ability. The executives may not have shown their feelings about the piece, but Stephen and Winnie expressed their gratitude

and that was all that mattered to me. Then, subsequently, another phone call to continue expanding on the show. And then, several months later, another phone call … and then another … to continue working and presenting the latest revision of *Wicked*. That process remains one of the greatest thrills and, ultimately, one of the greatest "what ifs" of my life.

Since this was your first time having something created while you were in the room, do you remember thinking, "Oh, this is how it works?"
There are moments when you don't have enough information to ask the right questions or create assumptions about anything, and I think, in this case, that was a blessing. I could only see what was in front of me because I truly had no idea how it worked. So I would just show up as prepared as I could and try to knock it out of the park. I wasn't anticipating what might come next. Fast forward a year and a half later … when I'm doing the third or fourth reading of *Wicked*'s latest incarnation. Kristin Chenoweth is now sitting beside me playing Glinda, and we're in the thick of it. After that last round of presentations on the Universal lot, the executives sent me a cookie bouquet of all of *The Wizard of Oz* characters. They sent a gorgeous, congratulatory floral bouquet. I got a note from the president of Universal Pictures, telling me how remarkable I was in the part of Elphaba, and I have sweet Kristin saying, "You have nothing to worry about. If this goes as I think it will, they don't need Elphaba to be a star. With this material … ," she humbly went on to say, "and with me already having a Tony Award, that's all this needs." So, you start believing that narrative. I mean, expectations and assumptions aside, anyone would allow themselves to imagine, "Wow, I think I'm moving forward with this show."

You had every reason to believe that.
No one was handing me a contract, but, boy, was I picking up some cues and letting my imagination run wild with them. We know NOTHING is real until it's real. We know it's not real until you sign the contract, and even then … it's not real until the curtain goes up.

What did you learn from Kristin?
It's incredible to watch her. What she brings to life is far more than what's on the page. She's fearless, just lays it all out there. She never just dips her toe in and sees what might happen. Little mama dives in head first, and it either makes a huge splash or a belly flop. But in that moment, you understand what worked and what didn't. Big choices. God, I love to watch her work. It's a master class. She and I were attuned to each other during that final presentation. A great friendship developed. She would hold my hand for a good chunk of the reading. She knew what was on the line for me. I think she absolutely recognized *Wicked*'s tremendous future. And she was always lifting me up. When it came time for me to audition in New York, I called, and she squealed, "Oh, this is so exciting! You've gotta spend the night at my apartment, and bring some outfits…." I mean, it was a real Glinda and Elphaba moment. I was able to go on with her one time in *Wicked*'s pre-Broadway out-of-town tryout in San Francisco. I feel like I can remember most moments of that performance—the lights, the orchestra, the support of the entire cast and crew, the applause—but I'm not sure if I was actually in my body. I have no idea how those two and a half hours passed. Stephen Schwartz and Winnie Holzman were in the audience to see my performance. They came backstage after the show and said, "Go, do *Boy From Oz*, and, as soon as you're done, come back to us."

So during the San Francisco run of *Wicked* you knew you had *Boy from Oz*?
I did.

I have heard you say that the path that occurred was the path that was meant to be, and you understood that they wanted someone with more Broadway experience to open the show, but still . . .
Oh, I'm still affected. Let's be honest. *Wicked* is still everywhere. And it serves as a reminder of the aforementioned "what if." I can still walk through an airport and see somebody wearing a *Wicked* shirt and the "what-could-have-beens" come flying at me. To have been given the opportunity to helm such a world-renowned, massive blockbuster, well . . . deep down there's still a great sense of loss.

Backstage on the night she went on in *Wicked*'s San Francisco tryout.
(courtesy of Stephanie J. Block)

Given that, it's astoundingly brave ... or stupid ... that you decided that you could take on an ensemble role and stand by for Idina in the San Francisco run, because you're putting yourself in the room every day. Were you able to learn between licking your wounds?

There was work to do. And I'm a spiritual gal. I believe in God and in a higher being; I believe that there is a fate to my life, and I am a co-creator in that life, whether that's through paying attention or making thoughtful, prayerful decisions. And that was one of them. I mean, I knew I had to put my ego to the side. I knew I had to show up and be the best me that I could be. I had something to prove ... to myself and to all those who didn't believe I was ready. That decision got me back to New York. It got me a job and paid my bills. It's all a mitigated risk, a gamble. But you have to be willing to bet on yourself. The next pull of the slot machine could be it. And this was really just a big, grand next pull. But I learned a lot. I'd ask Idina for her insights and notes as often as I could—still allowing space for her to create. She was gracious in that regard, she really was. She was very open to me being as prepared as I possibly could be. I remember the conversation that Stephen [Schwartz] had with me when he told me the role of Elphaba wasn't going to go my way. "We don't know what this role is. This is going to be a hefty sing, so there is a possibility that you could be going on Wednesday and Saturday matinees." So that was what I was thinking in rehearsal: "Be ready! They better not catch you with your pants down."

And during that, *The Boy from Oz* came into your world. How did that happen?

Randomly. My agents called and said, "We know you're busy with *Wicked*, but do you happen to 'do' a Liza Minnelli?" I said, "I don't do a Liza Minnelli but I am very familiar with her work and her mother is my idol." The audition felt like a "have-to." The next pull of the slot machine, right? I went downtown on my lunch break from *Wicked* rehearsal in order to sing for casting and the creatives for *The Boy from Oz*. That night, I received another call: "Can you go back in on your lunch break tomorrow to dance?" That day I did not have time to do my lashes and hair, no time to change into my black pencil pants. I rushed into the callback wearing my schleppy rehearsal clothes and looking a little worse for wear. I was told later that I almost didn't get the role because of that, because I wasn't put together. Then, they called back and said, "We would love for you to have a work session with Hugh Jackman next Monday." The company of *Wicked* was scheduled to fly to San Francisco on that Monday, but I arranged to stay behind for that two-hour session with Hugh and catch a later flight. Auditioning with Hugh was so freeing because he was so fun and supportive. A half-hour after I left the room, my agents called and said, "Congratulations! Your Broadway debut will be playing Liza Minnelli in *The Boy from Oz*." I was reeling with excitement. It was only when I settled onto the plane heading to San Francisco to catch up with the company of *Wicked* that I thought, "Oh shit, how am I going to make this work? How does one play a real-life icon?" I can remember speaking to one of my dear friends, who is super effing smart, and he said, "Is this the way you want to introduce yourself to Broadway? As somebody who's not Liza Minnelli?" I remember thinking, "What does that even mean?" Now, looking back, I realize that the narrative of how you enter onto the Broadway scene is very important, but I certainly didn't know it at the time.

Do you think that you were handicapped by coming in as somebody else?

Look, I recognize that *The Boy from Oz* was an incredible opportunity. For one to make their Broadway debut as the female lead in a big-budget, highly anticipated musical starring opposite a mega-star like Hugh Jackman ... theoretically that is the perfect way to come onto the scene. But had I been cast as a fictional character, been given the chance to enter Broadway with all my own quirks and strengths, without having to manipulate my speaking voice, singing voice, gestures, and mannerisms to emulate Liza—I believe my path might have been very different. Playing Liza was a real challenge for me. The creatives and designers never stopped futzing with Liza's look, sound, and style. The character starts the show as a seventeen-year-old and ends the show in her late forties—doing all of this with less than an hour of total stage time. The initial idea was for my first entrance as Liza to be with a long wig and a schleppy sweater, which was very true to Liza at that age. It was meant to represent her hiding in the shadow of her mom, Judy Garland. I came out onstage and people seemed confused. "Who the hell is that? Is that supposed to be Liza?" So then the long wig was scrapped for Liza's signature mullet. Then, the team thought, "Well now she needs Liza's signature big eyelashes." But that wasn't staying truthful to who Liza was at that age. It all just spiraled from there … all because we kept contorting the look and style of her, resisting starting from a place of truth and allowing for the storytelling to take root. We catered, instead, to some sense of what our audience's expectations for Liza might be … and because of that, I was left spinning. It was actually Hugh, who finally put his foot down and said, "Stephanie knew who *her* Liza was. And now [with all this futzing and constant changes] we are both turned upside-down, and it's got to stop." Once all the creatives left, we were able to settle in and embrace these roles as our own. That's when the show really started to take off, in my opinion.

In what ways were they not allowing you to do the character as you had developed her?
Things like, "When I saw Liza perform at the Palace, she did this.…" And then another creative or producer would come up and say, "Well, yeah, she did do that, but when she worked with Kander and Ebb, she.…" And then, someone else's input would be, "Yeah, but what she's really known for is doing this.…" Everybody had and has their understanding of who Liza is to them, but it's subjective and personal and didn't serve the story we were trying to tell. I can even remember our director coming up to me in the middle of a run-through and whispering in my ear while I was acting in a scene, "Nobody loves you. Lorna is the favorite. Liza is nothing. You're fat. You're not what your mother expected." I can appreciate what he was trying to do, but those mind-games didn't help anything. I was never going to be THE Liza Minnelli because there is only one! There's a famous Judy Garland quote that says, "Always be a first-rate version of yourself and not a second-rate version of someone else." Irony at its finest, right? I can, now, look back fondly on those days because I learned so much from the experience and because you only get one debut. I also hold the cast and crew of *The Boy from Oz* so fondly. What an incredible group of people. But while in the throes of it all … it was a rocky creative process.

Once you opened, what was it like for you, running for a year?
That I loved. Going into the theater always felt holy to me. I made great friendships. I loved doing eight shows a week, being a part of the Broadway community. There was such a buzz before we opened, and then the [tepid] reviews came out and it took on a completely different energy backstage, onstage, in the house. Hugh was able to turn it around because he decided to break the fourth wall. He felt instinctively that that is exactly what this piece needed. That was Peter Allen's superpower and so he had to have that in his performance. And once he stood true to that, the whole show took flight. People effing loved it. *The Boy*

from Oz became less of a book musical and more of a theatrical experience. Hugh was our beacon, and he was the perfect example as to how to lead a show. To watch him from the wings, incredible. His work ethic, incredible. If ever I was feeling tired or the voice felt a little weak, I would just look out onto the Imperial stage and be inspired by his leadership, his stardom, and his stamina. After we opened the show, it was pure joy. People were fighting to get tickets.

You went straight from Oz to Oz.... Leaving *The Boy from . . .* to opening the first tour of *Wicked*.

Tour life ... I will attest that performing Elphaba on Broadway is far easier than performing her on the road, at least in my estimation. Opening up in every town was like mounting a new show, and that is exhausting. I had a new dresser at each theater, critics, press, and an opening night in every town, singing the National Anthem at football games, meeting with local city officials, doing morning shows after a five-show weekend, representing a new line of makeup at Sephora ... it was non-stop. And you do all of this while jumping from hotel to hotel, without the comfort of your own home.

The anticipation for that tour in each city must have been huge.

Yes. It was amazing! Hearing thunderous applause in a three-thousand-seat theater after "Defying Gravity" ends ... well, that is a sensation I will never forget or get over. The only other time I can remember feeling that palpable energy was at the opening night of *The Cher Show* when Cher, herself, walked onstage. A wall of sound knocked me off my center. Touring the country with *Wicked* for the first time, it felt a lot like that. I felt like a rock star.

And of course, being on the road led to your marriage.

I certainly *noticed* Sebastian. He was very talented. He had great integrity. He was always kind. He was the first to help anybody with their luggage on the bus or the plane. He was a good human. And of course ... you know, handsome ... that hair, that butt, those eyes. One day, shortly before I left the tour, Sebastian kept pacing in front of my dressing room door, which I always left open until I was painted green. He finally came in and said to me, "I can't pass your dressing room door one more time without telling you that you've changed my life. I feel like a different man because I've met you." He took a deep inhale/exhale and said, "OK, I'm going to go now." I was stunned. I thought, "What's happening right now?" I couldn't process the importance of what he was revealing to me in that moment. After I left the tour, Sebastian continued on for another nine or ten months. He would fly back to New York almost every Monday. That would lead to dinners, deep conversations, long walks around the city together, and, eventually, yes ... an engagement ring. We're now on our fifteenth year of marriage.

During the tour, *The Pirate Queen* came into your world?

My agents called and said, "They're really interested in you for this title role." I told them, "I don't think I can do it. Being on tour as Elfie is about as much as my voice and my stamina can handle." They called again and said, "What if we could get you into the final callback with [composers] Claude-Michel Schoenberg and Alain Boublil?" I finished the Sunday matinee, flew to New York that night to sing my guts out on Monday, and came back to the tour for the Tuesday night performance. I felt like the audition went well, although

Claude-Michel and Alain are very unique personalities and hard to read. Claude-Michel paces and intensely rubs his bald head as you perform his work and I always felt like, "Is he going to combust because he loves me, or is he going to combust because I'm completely destroying his material?" Alain is a little more gentle and tempered, but also difficult to read. They're French. I then got a call in December of 2005: "Could I fly to Ireland?" I thought it was going to be a chemistry test with a couple of UK actors. It was there I met the incredible Hadley Fraser. I believe there was also a partial orchestra that played through some of the material with us. I left Ireland thinking, "What the F was that? What a wild callback!" I came to find out that they had already cast me as Grace O'Malley! That information had not been passed to me. That whole experience would have been very different had I known I'd already won the role.

The title character in a new show by the composers of *Les Misérables* and *Miss Saigon*!
I know! Epic, right? The scope and spectacle of the show, the soaring anthems . . . I was swept up. I thought it was just beautiful. *The Pirate Queen* had so much potential. There were some incredibly powerful and thrilling moments. But the show was slow to start, taking us fifteen to twenty minutes to really grab the audience, and that was far too long. I knew in Chicago we still had a lot of work to do before Broadway. But I trusted [director] Frank Galati, Alain and Claude-Michel, and our lovely and generous producers, John McColgan and Moya Doherty [of *Riverdance* fame and fortune]. They were an incredible team. Moya and John were really big-hearted people who believed in Grace O'Malley's story and wanted to theatrically share their country's culture and heritage with Broadway, no matter the cost.

How was rehearsal?
There were a lot of changes between Chicago and Broadway. Good changes. Graciela Daniele joined the creative team, and I absolutely loved working with her. I remember being more tired than I ever had been. This role will never be matched as far as workload. I remember everybody getting ill during previews, except me . . . until . . . right before opening. I got hit hard. I had to take off a few shows, but, on critics' night, I had no option but to take the stage. I was on every over-the-counter medicine imaginable, as well as a shot of Prednisone. Fifteen minutes into the show, I began to sing my first solo, "Woman," and I could not finish the song. I had to "speak-sing" the ending. Knowing there were still about twenty more songs to come, the production stage manager prepared my understudy, Kathy Voytko, and she took over for the rest of the show. What an incredible feat, performed beautifully. I have great respect for Kathy. She's wonderful! Luckily—or maybe not so luckily—the producers had the critics come back, and the rest is history. As for opening night, my adrenaline got me through. It was a good night. Was it what I wanted it to be? No, but it was good. The reviews were not. Shortly after opening . . . one afternoon during fight call, a few of us saw Susan Stroman measuring the aisles and wings of our theater. She was prepping for *Young Frankenstein*. It was then we knew we were out. Still, we loved our show. We went out onstage every night loving each other, the story, and performing it with integrity. I have to say, to this day, I LOVE THIS COMPANY . . . so full of joy, heart, and wit. We would meet on stage at "Places" before every performance. We held hands, and gave each other the uplifting energy we needed as a company. The show was created with such love. Martin Pakledinaz, our costume designer, went to Ireland and brought back soil to be sewn into every hem of my costumes. He wanted Grace to carry her land with her. The lighting design by Kenneth Posner was a masterpiece. The

arrangements were incredible. So, I can look back at the piece fondly, while recognizing its flaws. Yeah, there were moments when the play was slow or perhaps overly dramatic. There were times it was hard to keep the audience with us. But I still think there were performances and elements in that show that should have been recognized and awarded. You cannot tell me those costumes did not deserve a Tony Award nomination that year. They were stunning! The leatherwork! The character of my father was named Dubhdara, which means "oak" in Gaelic, so when Marty was in Ireland, he went to oak trees and used chalk and silk to get the grain of the bark and incorporate it onto Dubhdara's clothing. For my undergarments, Marty and I felt it was imperative that every costume of Grace's had some sort of pant to ground me and remind me of my strength, except for my wedding dress … where I was being forced to marry, forced to be feminine. The audience would never know, but it changed the way I walked, stood, and sat. My every move was dictated by what the audience didn't see, which was underneath each costume. It was very difficult to see that level of artistry not be recognized. Hadley Fraser! Are you kidding me? His voice, his stage presence? He's a force! That man should have been recognized for his performance. Nobody within the New York theatrical structure seemed to even acknowledge that we were part of the 2007 Broadway season. I can't explain it, but it felt personal. From start to finish, with *The Pirate Queen*, there seemed to be forces at work that did not want it to succeed.

I had a conversation with Rachel York about *Victor/Victoria* and, no matter what one thinks of the show, ignoring the artistry of things like outstanding design—it's clear in those cases that there is a collective energy at play and you can't fight it. It's just that you weren't the narrative that season.
I'm never one to drink the Kool-Aid when I'm in a show. I'm never blind to a show's flaws because I am in the center of its creation. That's not how I operate. I really do have a very discerning eye. I know what hits, and I know what doesn't. But that doesn't mean the whole thing is crap and should be ignored. There were design elements that just were undeniable.

***The Pirate Queen* was your second Broadway show and you were the titular character. Did you feel the pressure of that?**
I was coming off a year on the road in a very successful run with *Wicked*. So when *The Pirate Queen* didn't happen the way we all envisioned or hoped, I carried the weight of that on my shoulders. If the show isn't well received and I'm onstage for two hours and fifteen minutes out of a two hour and thirty-five-minute play … how am I supposed to interpret that? It was a very emotional and disappointing time. But you just have to keep on keeping on with professionalism. All the other stuff plays out the way it plays out.

You've told the story before that David Stone [*Wicked* producer], even before you opened in New York, very matter of factly said, "Hey, I know you're going to be free very soon…."
Yup, that's exactly how the story goes. At least according to my memory. I was like, "Oh my gosh, are you kidding me? We haven't been given our closing notice yet. What does he know that I don't know?" Initially, I took the offer as an insult to *The Pirate Queen*. In reality, having that offer for *Wicked* and the timing of it all turned out to be a huge blessing. It afforded me a few months to breathe, to let my body recoup, and to plan my and Sebastian's wedding. I made my *Wicked* Broadway debut in the fall of 2007. I finally got to play Elphaba on the Gershwin stage … with my soon-to-be husband, who was playing Fiyero at the time. It was a bit poetic.

You've described your return to *Wicked* as a homecoming of sorts, but what else was it?
Oh, well, it was an ego booster, for one thing. The crowds went wild, and I loved it. I had missed that audience reaction more than I wanted to admit. Sharing the stage with Annaleigh Ashford was a pure and consistent joy. Sharing the stage with Sebastian was awesome, and I loved my star dresser, Kathe Mull. She is this healing, spiritual, ground-centering woman that changed how I look at the relationship between dresser and actor.

How?
I've had wonderful dressers before, but there's something about Kathe. It was like having a mother, teacher, therapist, life coach all in the room with you. I've asked her to come with me to many subsequent shows once I left *Wicked*. Every time, she's like, "Lady, I've got two kids. I'm in the happiest, 'government job' I've ever had. I adore you, but I'm never leaving this track [*Wicked*]."

Did you find stage door fan interactions rewarding at *Wicked*?
I have never experienced anything like it. I'm sure those who did *Rent*, *Jersey Boys*, *Hamilton* may have a similar sort of fervent fan base and loyalty. They're with you for life. To this day, I will see fans at my concerts or at the stage door of other productions, and they're like, "Look!" And it's a tattoo of me on their shoulder or back. Or they've taken samples of my handwriting and turned it into a tattoo. I can't tell you how many people are walking this earth with ink that either has my face or my handwriting on it. I literally say to them, "Are you sure you're gonna want that when you are fifty?" Now, I'm not sure what my stage door interaction will be moving forward. With COVID and social media, things have changed drastically.

Going into *Wicked* on Broadway, was it hard to let go of thinking about the path that might have been had you originated the role?
I gotta tell ya, that wasn't on my mind. Elphaba and I, we understand each other. Every moment I was on stage as Elphie … there was never a shred of doubt in my mind or body that I didn't belong there. I can't explain it, but I was meant to be a part of this story. I knew in my gut that Elphie and I aligned, and I loved her. A lot of the original cast members were still there in 2007, so it did feel like a coming home of sorts. It was a really, really great experience from beginning to end, other than the fatigue and constantly finding green makeup on my towels and pillowcases. I took my final bow in October of 2008 and blew my nose a month later and still found green. *Wicked* never really leaves you.

And that solidified your relationship with Joe Mantello, which leads us to *9 to 5: The Musical*.
It did. Between rehearsal time for the tour and working with him to prepare for Broadway, it did. Joe's quite a person, artist, and director to have in your corner. I received an email from him just a few days ago, and it's just a lovely thing to have those relationships beyond a specific project.

Take me into the rehearsal room and the space. There was a lot to live up to. The movie. Jane Fonda. Dolly Parton in the room.
Dolly Parton in the room is the most important sentence. Because of who she is and what she stands for and how she carries herself, you rise to the occasion. You are more professional,

kinder, polite. And what a beautiful space it is to have that sort of energy and intention coming into the room every day. Working alongside Allison Janney and Megan Hilty—the woman energy, the creating, the humor—it was just awesome. I loved going to work.

I once had the experience of spending a day with Whoopi Goldberg at Disney World. I realized, "Wow, everybody in this orbit right now is being deferential in a way that she's not asking for, but we are all just naturally doing it." Did you ever experience it that way with Dolly? Because that kind of deference can get in the way of the work.
Maybe the first few times she was in the room, but then you do become yourself, just your *best* self. I still felt a freedom to create and to make mistakes. That show was one where maybe I did drink the Kool-Aid, but I still look back and I go, "That's a cleverly crafted, fun, musical." It may not be a touchstone in the firmament of musical theater, but are you getting your money's worth? Is it delivering the same energy as the movie? Did Dolly write a really kick-ass score and was it delivered wonderfully by this cast? Yes, yes, and yes. You can feel the energy of an audience when their arms are crossed and people are like, "Prove it." And you can feel when people are leaning forward going, "We are in this! We can't wait!" And our audiences were in it. We had a lot of technical mishaps. It was a huge automated set with two dozen set changes. Out of town in Los Angeles, we had our superpower, which was Dolly Parton, at most of the shows. If things came to a screeching halt, she would go out into the house and do a mini-concert. The audience went wild. I think they were probably *hoping* for a mishap so that Dolly could come out. But did I ever see this show closing early on Broadway? No. This was the first time I went to Pottery Barn to buy dressing room furniture. "We're going to be at the Marquis for years." Skip to me, four months later, on the corner of Broadway and 45th with all my crap—Sebastian in a van coming to pick me up, so we could bring it all to storage.

Working with Dolly, what did you observe and learn as an artist?
I learned that being flexible, malleable, resilient is the best way to create. Dolly would bring in material, and Joe would say, "I love this … this works … I think that seems too general." Or, "Can we have an alternate verse for Judy here?" She'd go off to lunch, bring back a paper plate, and it would have new lyrics on both sides. "You choose," she'd say. And if those still weren't right, she'd grab somebody's old script page, sit down, and write some more. There was no ego or resistance. She would certainly speak her mind and say, "This is why I wrote it that way," but then Joe would say, looking at the larger picture, "If she says it here in Act 1, then there's no growth when she needs to say it here in Act 2." So, that sort of artistic maturity, emotional maturity, and flexibility with which she handled her side of the bargain was masterful to watch.

And that, of course, comes from knowing that you've got the goods. You're not going to be threatened by having to make an adjustment.
It was wildly fun to create in a room like that! [With Joe, our] input was always welcome. It wasn't always implemented, but it was welcomed. *9 to 5* afforded us a great space for our voices to be heard … and antics to be tried.

After *9 to 5* opened you released your solo album, *This Place I Know*, and you got to record with Dolly!
I did. That really happened! Writing the email to ask if she'd duet with me took a looooooong time to craft. We had built a friendly relationship by then, but I certainly didn't want her to

think that I was trying to ride her coattails or cross a line. It took her maybe ten minutes to respond. And she was the one that suggested "I Will Always Love You." We envisioned the arrangement to be one generation speaking to another, and, once we got into the flow of that, it was magical. I recorded the melody, and, later on, she came in to record her part. She would try some perfectly Dolly-esque harmony, and, from the booth, we would hear her voice saying, "No, that's not right." And then she'd try something equally as wonderful. We got to witness her process, and, much like when she writes lyrics, she goes with the flow and tries something new, making sure she gets it right. She was a dream, an absolute dream. She worked within what I was hoping to create with that track on the album. It goes back to what you said: when you've got the goods, what do you have to prove? She's just there, wanting to make any project the best it can be. And then she leaves, and her energy and her perfume stay in the room well after she's left.

Your next gig seemed unexpected: to take over Reno Sweeney in *Anything Goes*.
It had been about two years since *9 to 5*, but I kept busy with regional productions, like *They're Playing Our Song* in L.A., with Jason Alexander. I completed my album. I starred off-Broadway in Lynn Nottage's play *By the Way, Meet Vera Stark* and continued my concert work. Then, a phone call from my agents regarding *Anything Goes*. I assumed they meant interest for the national tour, but they said, "This is to fill in for Sutton Foster while she films a pilot. Do you think you can learn the show in ten days?" In my brain, I'm thinking, "OK, 9 a.m. to 6 p.m. every day for ten days. I can do it." I answer, "Yes." So, we schedule a work session with Kathleen Marshall. Did I consider myself a tapper? No. But I can tap. After doing regional theater for almost twenty years, I know the language of tap. But at that time, was my body conditioned to do whatever Kathleen Marshall was going to put it through in a rehearsal room? Yowza. I was not ready. She taught me, like, twenty bars of "Anything Goes," and there were a few things that weren't up to snuff. Like, my pullbacks weren't clean. I couldn't do the full splits. I still can't do the full splits; I will never be able to do the full splits. But the work session went well. Kathleen and I clicked and I got the job. Now, back to learning the show in ten days … I would be taught the show by stage management and the dance captain, Jennifer Savelli, to whom I owe a lot. Because those ten days went fast! There's no work on Monday because that's everyone's day off. I start rehearsals Tuesday. Wednesday, I would watch both shows. Thursday, I'd rehearse again. Friday, rehearsal and a costume fitting. Saturday, back to watching both shows. Sunday, no rehearsal. Monday, in for another costume fitting and to work with the musical director. Repeat Tuesday, Wednesday. And by Thursday, I was in the show. I believe, in total, it was twenty-three hours of rehearsal time.

Did Sutton walk you through it all?
Yeah. She was lovely, open, and generous. Over a coffee in between shows, she shared all the hints that would keep my body in order after such a demanding dance show. Things like, "I would advise you get Crocs to go home in, because you are not going to be able to walk." Or, "Order a crate of Zico Coconut Water for the hydration." She left me the coziest pillows to nap with in between shows. She took me through it. She left me affirmations on the dressing room mirror. She would lovingly check in every now and then. And she was right … when onstage, I could dance, but when offstage, I was too tired and achy to walk.

Working with Roundabout put you in good stead for *The Mystery of Edwin Drood*.
I was not really familiar with the show. I didn't know how fun it would be to be part of this multi-talented ensemble, where everybody tag-teams each other in and out. It was a show that I could have done for years and years because of the fun, the cast, and the changing endings. And because the work was spread pretty evenly between the cast, I could wake up and not freak out about my voice. I could have a life, go out to dinner afterward, knowing that I was still going to be OK the next day. There was a freedom that I hadn't really felt up until that point. Will Chase was a dream, and Chita was Chita effing Rivera. I love her. Our dressing rooms were across from one another, and our doors were always open. My dog, Macaco, who was in the show, would run from my dressing room to hers, and she would squeal with glee. I was gifted plenty of intimate moments between her and me. She taught me a lot about work ethic and discipline. She taught me how to welcome after-show guests with a really loving, timed-out, methodical system. She knows how to give—but still protect—her energy. Chita also taught me how to be the lead of a show backstage. Even with her certain seniority and her being a legend in this industry, she would look at me and say, "That's you. You're the lead of the show. You take care of it. This is your house. Clean your house." I wouldn't have necessarily chosen to take on that particular responsibility, but she urged me to . . . and I'm so glad she did.

You had the benefit of being the one character who didn't have to learn all the endings and then just come back at the end with the powerhouse finale.
I actually did have to learn the endings because, with every variation, there was choreographed action to shadow-play Edwin's death, depending upon how the audience voted that particular night. But then, yes, you're right, the show did end with the eleven o'clock number "Writing on the Wall." And being able to break the fourth wall and see people's expressions while singing lyrics about holding on to life, never giving up, nor taking any breath for granted, was life-affirming for me. I sing that song very rarely now. Close to the end of the run, Sebastian and I found out that we were pregnant. Eight or nine weeks into the pregnancy, I'm standing center stage delivering these powerful lines about what a miracle it is to survive each and every day . . . when I knew I was losing the baby. I had started cramping and bleeding midway through the song. It was one of those moments where I was floating above myself, knowing physically what was happening to me . . . torn between reality and performance. I feel like I should say more, but I can't.

After the show had already closed, you got nominated for a Tony.
It felt incredible. Every bit of it was a full-on celebration. Actually, two out of the three times I was nominated, I was able to enjoy the awards season experience in sort of a laissez-faire kind of way because I didn't have to juggle the hectic PR schedule and eight shows a week at the same time. It was wonderful to share that season with Will Chase, another Broadway journeyman, likewise receiving his first Tony nomination. I enjoyed every damn second. Another example of savoring every moment while also taking it in stride.

Your next show was *Little Miss Sunshine* at Second Stage.
That was a show that was a straight offer . . . from Lapine, no less. And when James Lapine just offers you a role, you say, "OK!" Because you know you're about to have the artistic ride of your life. At Second Stage, you work on the musical longer than you actually present it, and

I liked the idea of that, especially when you're going to be in a room with Lapine and [William] Finn. Because let's face it, with any off-Broadway contract, you're not making any real money, and you're not necessarily going to be thrust into stardom. I did love the source material of the movie, *Little Miss Sunshine*. I thought it was quirky and tender and hilarious. It's actually heartbreaking, too. And I always felt that I was those things. If there's material that would allow me to make wack-a-doodle choices the way I do in life, this would be the piece and these would be the creators. Now, I had heard rumor that James was not the easiest person to share a creative space with, that he purposely wants to take the polish off of people. Looking back, I almost think he assumed I had more polish to me than I actually did. But, when we got to work together, we just clicked. I have a theory: I think everybody's a bit crazy, and the question is, does your crazy match my crazy? There is something about James's crazy that matches mine … and vice versa. I understand him on a level that maybe I didn't with other directors in the past. He was the first director I considered extended family. And I never saw it coming, because I had been warned. It's funny hearing myself say the word "warned" because James believes in the exact opposite; don't be guarded, don't protect, be messy. Knowing him better now, I think that's all he's trying to do … to strip the actor of all their tricks and/or gimmicks that may have worked in the past. They are your crutches, and he wants you to walk without crutches, even if you fall smack dab on your face. With *Little Miss Sunshine* and *Falsettos*, he created a space that allowed us to be messy so that we could find a new … brilliance of sorts. I loved it. I love him. He does do some things that aren't necessarily orthodox in the school of theater. For example, he might bring you into a room at the end of week one or two of rehearsal and question you on your thoughts regarding the material, on fellow cast members' processes, on how you see your own growth up to this point, and where you think you want your character to land. It's really open, almost like a trap. And sometimes it's jarring. But he's trying to strip you down in order to find the simplicity and truth to everything—to get out of your own way, so you don't muck it up. He doesn't let you muck up your own truth, and that's a huge gift.

That would seem to set up the piece to really work well. That didn't happen.
In the commercial sense, maybe not. Perhaps we didn't allow the audience to participate enough, to satisfy their desire to clap, to release, to clean their palate and start again. There were so many different segues, beautifully unexpected musical dangling participles … just like there would be in life. It felt right for the tone of the piece. So, for those of us onstage, it did work really well, artistically. *Little Miss Sunshine* doesn't end with a big, red bow and everyone getting what they want. Audiences might have a hard time accepting that sometimes.

What about being in the room with William Finn, who's got such a different energy from James Lapine?
I admire and respect that kooky-kook genius. That man can write humanity better than most. His voice is singular. Nothing he writes is basic. Melodies go to places that you're not expecting them to go, and there is a reason why he does that. I'm not going to presume to understand that reason, but I certainly *feel* that reason when I'm singing his stuff. Bill's long-time musical director, Vadim Feichtner, would tell me, "You think you don't speak his language, but you interpret his stuff pretty damn great." When interpreting his music, an artist is plopped into his head and it's up to you to find your way out. I think it was where I was in life. Both times I worked with Bill and James, I was either trying to become a mother or had recently become a mother … and that's what I always tapped into—motherhood: the fear of

it, how everything becomes deeper. Your joys are higher; your sadness is lower. You're more fearful but more open; you're more anxious but have to be more steady. *Little Miss Sunshine* was all about showing up every day and tapping into those emotions. James and Bill allowed me to go through all of that. As did the cast. It really was like therapy, and it was supremely healing. Rory O'Malley and Will Swenson are gifts of human beings. Hannah Nordberg was a magical, effervescent child. When she wanted to twirl, she twirled; when she wanted to go potty, she went potty. It was marvelous to have a real kid in the room. But it really was one of those time periods where we were just doing the work at our own pace. And I don't know if that exists very much anymore—not worrying so much about the outcome or a tour or a cast recording. The only pressure cooker I was working under was trying to get pregnant, and I was able to use that playing Sheryl Hoover.

And it created relationships which led you to working on *Falsettos*.
Ah yes. Timing is everything. And with *Falsettos*, that timing got a bit complicated. It's almost like God and I made a pact before I was born: "Do not make my life too easy, or I won't work hard enough." So, news of the *Falsettos* revival is announced, but I had just given birth. Ta-da, a baby in January, and the call for *Falsettos* in February. I was not in any sort of space mentally, physically, or spiritually to be like, "Yes! Of course!" It was more like, "Are you kidding me? This is happening now?" I was ready to release the idea of Trina because of the timing, but Sebastian encouraged me to listen to the score again. He insisted actually. "I need you to really sit down and listen to the words that your character sings." Sebastian is one of those that believes all the dreams can come true for all the people. He wants Utopia for everyone, and he will do what he needs to do on his end so everybody feels happy and loved. He was

"I'm breaking down." In *Falsettos*.
(Joan Marcus)

literally figuring out how I could pump breast milk, he'd bring the baby to me, he was going to make it work for me. I'm the practical one that says, "I love that you're a dreamer. But, how are we going to map this out and realistically make this work?" Anyway, so I do listen to the recordings, and I start to weep because, now that I'm a mom, I see Trina. I really see her. I see her struggles and her wants. I look at Seb and say, "I don't know how we do this, but OK." Now, this call in February wasn't a straight offer, mind you. It was an interest and availability check. Then, an update from my agents: a call to say they want to cast Christian Borle and Andrew Rannells but that their schedules are not going to allow them to do it this season, so the project would be punted a year. After the initial confusion, my heart leaps because I get a year at home with my kid. Later that spring, the phone rings again. They send me a crapload of audition material. I have to take a red-eye to New York as I am in California visiting family, sing my songs, do my thing, jump through the hoops, get the job, and wait the year. I may not have known exactly how I felt about *Falsettos* walking into it, but I certainly know how I feel about it now and how I felt when we were creating it. Pinnacle. Absolute pinnacle. Lightning in a bottle. I think if you were to speak with any company of *Falsettos*, they might have a similar way of describing it. There's something about that show. You are connected in a way that I had never found and I don't know if I will ever again. The bond between Christian, Andrew, Brandon, Anthony, myself, and the entire cast is a forever bond. And "I'm Breaking Down" felt like a theatrical moment that if ever I were to put my stamp on musical theater, that would probably be my definitive moment.

Of everything you've done, do you feel that that's your moment?
For sure. A comedic song dripping with pain and angst, showing strength and vulnerability? I felt that if you took that piece of musical theater and dropped it anywhere, you'd know who this woman was and what she was made of. That was my moment.

Does it scare you that it might not get better?
No. I guarantee you: I'll be seventy and there will still be this sort of truth to *Falsettos* that was fucking magic in a bottle. No, it doesn't scare me that that could possibly be the pinnacle. To have in totality what that was—I never thought that could ever happen. In our industry, have you ever heard someone say that from soup to nuts it was a really extraordinary, almost perfect experience? I count myself lucky to be one of the few that can actually say that out loud. I don't know how to put it into words. You can do great work, you can do work that will transport people to a different place and time that gives them breath and joy, but "important" in musical theater—that's a rare breed, and *Falsettos* is really important. It's almost like a ministry of sorts, to go into the theater and deliver that piece night after night in the time that it was happening. Out in the world, people were divided and angry. Here, love was love was love. It's not going to get any better.

You got nominated again.
With *Drood* it was joy and relief; with *Falsettos*, there was a great satisfaction. And celebration. We closed in January, and everybody's mind in our industry is like a goldfish—quick to forget. Had *Falsettos* been running at the time of the Tony Awards, I think it could have had a different outcome. There could have been some wins. But it just felt so great for the four of us to have been acknowledged, to be reunited, and to hold hands through awards season. That was really, really special.

And then *The Cher Show* comes around.

Who the hell saw that one coming? Not me. The initial offer was simply for a reading of the show. But I was closing *Falsettos*, and I wanted to really be in the moment of what that was. I just wanted to marinate in those artistic juices. What I assumed was going to be the big, splashy, commercial *Cher Show* just didn't seem right for me at the time. Also, having played Liza, I knew the pitfalls of playing a living legend, and I didn't know if I wanted to go through that sort of process again. I really didn't think I was the right choice for it, honestly. The "No" came rather easily for those reasons. They went ahead and did that reading and then they came around again in spring. Still, I didn't have an interest. In the fall, another call. This time, [director] Jason Moore wanted to go to dinner and explain his vision for the show and see if I could connect with it. So we did, and he was an absolute delight. He spoke to all the right things: spirituality, not having to look or sound exactly like Cher, trying to create a play where Cher is every woman, and a sisterhood of three actors [each playing Cher at different stages of her life] sharing the stage together. The play's stage direction starts roughly like, "This piece is going to be like a moth in a cathedral, much like Cher." The way she thinks, the way she talks—she kind of bounces around. It's not linear. And then he started to talk about the connection between all three of the women and how it would be much like therapy. I coined the phrase "Cher-apy." We would talk to each other as the Star-Cher, the Lady-Cher, and the Babe-Cher. He really had a unique way of telling the story between this celestial being known as Cher and this human woman who went through all of the pitfalls that any woman might go through. So I said, "Yes," right then and there at the West Bank Café. The workshop would be for just a few weeks, and, at the end of it, we would present it to Cher. She herself would decide whether this was something she wanted to move forward. So we did that. It was myself, Lena Hall, and Micaela Diamond. Micaela was just out of high school, and she was not to be believed. It was fun—great fun—but also wildly intimidating. On the one hand, I was feeling empowered to be this character but didn't know if I was hitting all the marks that were expected of someone playing Cher . . . you know, the voice, the tongue, the gestures, the walk. At the end of those two weeks, we had two or three different presentations. The final one was for Cher. We were told she was going to arrive half an hour before anyone else so that we could meet with her and she could express whatever she wanted to share. I hid. I went upstairs into a dressing room. I didn't feel I could meet with her moments before the presentation and not have that meeting affect my performance. Cher apparently told a producer to come get me. She was very kind—spoke to me as a peer, and let me know she understood how vulnerable I must feel in this moment. I found it interesting that she, too, was self-protecting, wearing big ol' Aviator, reflector sunglasses and this huge—I'm not sure how to describe it—sombrero/fedora hat. She's got a big, black puffer jacket on, almost like she's wearing her armor. She's surrounded by a group of, like, ten to fifteen people. During the presentation, she's holding hands with the friend sitting next to her. There are tears coming from behind her Aviators, and she's applauding politely. And then that's it. She leaves. There are no congratulations; there are no hugs. She very quickly—not abruptly mind you—but smoothly and quickly leaves. And we all just kind of go, "Well, we'll see." When we get the A-OK to move forward, we make several changes to the show. We try to build upon the show in Chicago, but with the same concept as Jason presented to me at the West Bank Café—not having to look or sound exactly like Cher. So, the show opens with me in a dressing room with thirteen or fourteen other women, all of whom are dressed like Cher, and the audience has no clue what's happening. They don't know who's driving this boat. More changes had to be made. But we wanted to hold on to this very spiritual, universal way of telling her story ... while still hitting specific songs and wearing iconic costumes to let the audience know where we were in the timeline of her life. The show's original concept was that Cher was about to do a television special, and, in the minute before she steps on stage, her entire life flashes before her eyes in the vein of *The Sonny & Cher Show*. So the title "*The Cher Show*" takes on many meanings—it's not just a musical you're watching. You're also watching the show within the show within the show ... Cher is putting on the "show" that she's been living her entire life as if it were being filmed as a television special. Very meta. People weren't getting it. There were moments that felt ultra-deep and ultra-fulfilling, and there were moments that even I wasn't quite sure what was happening. The Chicago reviews came out, and Chris Brown at *The Tribune* gave some great advice as to what needed to be fixed. In between Chicago and Broadway, we changed 80 percent of the show in about a three-week rehearsal period. It was a fast and furious process. There were some very unhappy turns, some very open and heated discussions. I am very vocal in a rehearsal room, and Jason Moore and [writer] Rick Elice welcomed my thoughts. They were just awesome. They allowed me to have a seat at the table, and I made sure to make the most of it. When Cher would pop in, she would have very strong opinions, and the producers also had very strong opinions. Both Jeffrey Seller and Flody Suarez wanted to end the show in a big dance party. Less meta, more mega-mix. Talk about killing one version of a musical, and really giving birth to a whole brand-new one. Throughout the run, union rules just did not apply to Cher or this production, for that matter. Everything from Cher giving us notes at intermission to being on stage at 3:00 p.m. on opening night—still changing scenes and staging—to the show being videotaped from the back of the house so Cher could watch the tapes at home. Many rules were being broken. Cher is Cher, and she is not easy to say no to. I speak from experience.

When 80 percent of the show is changing, are you feeling invigorated, beleaguered, or both?
I will say both. Once we went with the new route of less meta and more mega dance mix, it was me who said there's no way that I can just *kind of* look and sound like her every now and again. If I'm popping up through the stage dressed in the "Turn Back Time" costume surrounded by sailors, then I can't *kind of* anything. So I got to work to find the balance between interpretation and impersonation. In rehearsal, I started to talk more and more like Cher. Jason said, "You can't do that. We've got to create a space where the audience knows you're an actress playing her so that it works [having three of you]. You are three very different actors that look different and embody her differently. If your Cher is too spot-on, it's not going to serve the play as a whole." What it kind of did, though, was connect us more with each other. Micaela, Teal [Wicks], and I started using the same exact hand gestures. Together, we found more and more moments where we could unify our performances, and our vocal inflections started to match. It actually allowed for *all of us* to become more authentically her. After experiencing Liza ... this time around, I just knew I had to trust my gut. And I feel very grateful that Jason Moore allowed me to follow my instincts. I think what we learned from Chicago was that the audience had to comfortably sit back in those first couple of minutes and trust me. I do believe that had I not popped up breaking the fourth wall, looking and sounding just like her, it would not have worked. I must say, popping up from below that stage—that will forever be the best entrance of my life.

Unlike when you played Liza, this time you had to impress your subject.
We were in previews in New York, and Cher wanted to meet with me for a note session at the Four Seasons Hotel on my day off. I called my agent and said, "I do not want to be disrespectful. I get one day off. I'm a mom to a young kid. I need this time. If she can come to the theater and meet me in my dressing room on Tuesday, I'll be there all day, and I will dedicate any time that she wants." Saying that was big for me. I'll be honest, I wanted Jason or stage management there, to hear her notes, to just have a third party in the room. But due to the timing of her visit, that wasn't possible. Next thing I knew … I was walking into my dressing room alone with Cher. She immediately took off her jacket and wanted to show me the way she walks. Now, we're already in previews, right? We've been receiving her written notes. I had been onstage as her for about two or three weeks, and now she was wanting something very different. She was wanting me to look different. She was wanting me to walk different. She was wanting me to speak different. I can only imagine how difficult it is to embrace someone playing you in the story of your life. I don't know if I could ever handle that with grace. So I listened intently. And then I finally said, "Cher, I hope you know that I love your body of work. In preparation for this show, I have learned more about you and gained great respect, but never did I consider myself an impersonator of yours. I'm just an actress. I'm a wife and a mom. I'm not looking to ride your coattails. I'm not looking to do anything other than just try to do the best job that I can. And I hope that you can see that I'm in a very vulnerable spot because we are already up and running. I have to be you in literally a few hours." And all of a sudden, she softened, and the energy in the room became very different. From that point on, our relationship became more … human. She was willing to share things about herself—the balance between her leather-wearing self and her feminine and delicate self. She wanted to show that she was not a victim. That there was hurt and betrayal, but she was a woman who had grown stronger because of that. We were talking to each other, woman to woman. It was real, honest, and tender. It was wonderful. She then proceeded to give me notes, based on a tape she had seen the night before. And I lovingly said, "I hope you know that the taped performances you're watching are never going to be what it looks and feels like when you're sitting in the audience and experiencing it in real time. You have to understand, if you're focusing on trying to replicate the beauty and the aesthetic of you, I can't fix that. Theater is theater, and it happens quick. I have literally twenty to thirty seconds to do a costume change. I've got nine people helping me make that change. My makeup is sweating off my face, and my wig is askew. And I still have to walk out onstage with the confidence you're showing me now. So what I could use your help with is how to embody your agency and your confidence … how to stand back and let people come to me, as you do. Anything that you can give me that can help me embrace that in myself, we're going to be golden." And that's when the conversation really started to take on a life of its own. It was then, I think, that she finally felt safe … with me … as her. But for the record, Bob Mackie did say I had her walk and her voice *down*.

How can Cher be objective about her own walk or sound? Speaking of, allegedly you found her voice using Crest White Strips?
Yeah, it was the Crest White Strips. That is not a joke. My family and I were vacationing in Cape Cod between Chicago and Broadway, and I was working on the revised script. I was trying to get a jump on it all because I knew what our rehearsal period was going to be like. So, I was bleaching my teeth and saying the lines out loud with my eyes closed,

trying to memorize them. I hear Seb say from the other room, "I don't know what you're doing, but you've found her voice." I was like [in Cher's voice], "Oh my God, I don't know what I'm doing, honey. I don't know what I'm doing. I'm just saying the lines." Previously, I'd been using a vocal positioning—almost like you're biting an apple. The back of your larynx is wide, your soft palate really high. But I wasn't hitting it. Some of the vowels sounded right, some of them were really wrong. With the Crest White Strips—I found that her sound is actually placed on the top gum. That's how I freaking found the voice. So every night, I just pretended I was bleaching my teeth, and then I could find it. [As Cher] Isn't that so crazy, babe?

Let's talk about wearing those thirty costumes and the weight of that, both literal and metaphoric.
Bob Mackie is a genius. I think that I had well over twenty costume fittings, which is completely unheard of in the Broadway world. Bob creates, and then he puts the fabric on your body and draws the design directly on that fabric, so he knows exactly where every bead on your body is going to be placed. Cher's body is not of this world. It's just not. Bob knew how to take a design that worked on Cher, put it on my body, which is a completely different shape and form, and still get a similar effect. He knew exactly where every line should be so that you saw the most flattering part of my abs, so that you saw the exact line of my leg, and that my shoulders looked glistening and toned. And then you add Kevin Adams's lighting design, and all of a sudden I've got a six-pack, right? It was a test for me because it's no secret that my confidence doesn't come from appearance. But somehow, when I looked in the mirror, all made up as Cher, it came together. I felt strong and beautiful. It was really empowering.

Let's talk about the Tony win.
It was one of those moments where I was fully in my body. I looked out into the audience, and I felt at home. I was with my people. I didn't feel like a stranger in a strange land. I didn't feel like a flash in the pan or that this moment was a fluke. After twenty years on Broadway, I had earned my place standing center stage at Radio City Music Hall accepting the Tony Award. And the true beauty of it was . . . I felt lifted up and supported by my peers.

Were you OK with letting the show go as it faded out?
After winning the Tony, I took a week's vacation. We were in Cape Cod and I was playing putt-putt golf with my family. I got a text from Cher that said, "Sorry to hear the news. I think you're wonderful." And I thought, "Oh crap, we're closing." I knew this was serious, as Cher usually communicates with lots of emojis. After the Tony, I got a heart, a medal, the strong arm, and some kissy lips, but this time, no emojis. I immediately picked up the phone to call general management to see what the future held. Of course, I didn't want to release it. I wanted to carry on with this role. But in my estimation, it had already been released by the powers that be.

In 2020, you moved your family to California. Looking forward, what do you want?
I want health; I want balance; I want what's best for my family. But if you're intimating about work . . . Sebastian and I have criteria before accepting any job: it either has to be joyful, artistic, or lucrative. If we can get two out of the three from a project, it's a no-brainer. We accept the gig. But we're always taking into consideration our daughter, Vivienne, and what is best

for her. That means constantly assessing, reassessing, assessing, reassessing. Earlier I mentioned that Sebastian is the dreamer of the family, always saying, "We can make this work!" I'm much more the practical one, saying, "OK, but we've got to map it out. Let's make a pros/cons list." His heart always leads with, "We can do it all," and mine leads from a place of, "I've gotta see the plan before I jump off the cliff." I know that I am my best self when I carve out time to cultivate my art and creative passions. So I have started a podcast, "Stages Podcast," with my dear friend and co-host, Marylee Fairbanks. Recording and helping to shape these incredibly personal and deep conversations with fellow artists and creatives has been wildly fulfilling during these COVID years. I want to continue to perform my solo concerts because I so enjoy interacting with my audiences … I just dig it so much. I want to be able to create new projects in New York when something really special comes across my or my agents' desks. I want to be able to say yes to limited runs knowing that Sebastian and I would be able to balance and arrange Vivi's schedule without disrupting too much of what's important to her. I don't know if a one- or two-year investment in a show can currently play out the way it has in the past. I actually have a hard time hearing that notion come out of my mouth. But we are in a new dawn, a new day. Looking back on the trajectory of my career, I take great pride in recognizing the feat of leading eleven Broadway and off-Broadway shows since 2003. I can't help but smile, get a little weepy, feel the weight of every decision and experience. Every show has helped shape me, and for that I am humbled and grateful. It has led me here, to this moment. The pandemic has reprioritized and rearranged a lot of performers' lives. So yes, we had the opportunity to relocate to Northern California and we took it. It has been quite a change. But it has also afforded me time and space to witness my child mastering crafts and skills in her own right. Our little family will make its way back East when the time is right. Trust me, I have learned by vast experience that timing is everything. Moving forward, I will continue with caution and mindful action because we're making choices for and with each other. And that feels right, important, and beautiful to me.

Adrienne Warren

April 2022

Of the more than sixty actors I spoke to for these books, a recurring theme is that no stage career is ever really calculated; people go from one show to the next, hoping for the best, and usually experiencing a series of peaks and valleys. Don't tell Adrienne Warren. Because from her debut onward, each of her performances has been a step up the ladder in what has been an astonishing trajectory. And even though she is at the relative beginning of her career, Warren is already at a pinnacle.

That's not unsurprising, actually, when one considers that Warren, the daughter of two athletic coaches, grew up with both discipline and competition rooted deeply within her. She was taught at an early age to play hard and win. Any conversation about her work is peppered with sports references and comparisons to training. She is, in fact, that rare theater kid who was also a jock. And basketball was the priority until an injury necessitated a pivot. She came to New York to study and nailed her first major audition, landing in the ensemble of the Encores! production of *The Wiz*. Before that show was even over, she was cast as Lorell in the national tour of *Dreamgirls*. Then, when that *Wiz* (and also *Hamilton*) creative team, Thomas Kail (director), Andy Blankenbuehler (choreographer), and Alex Lacamoire (musical director), along with Lin-Manuel Miranda, Tom Kitt, and Amanda Green (composers), began workshopping a new musical, they brought Warren along. *Bring It On*, a show about competing high school cheer squads, was a perfect match for Warren's athleticism. She not only sang and danced, but also flipped and flew, on national tour and then on Broadway. Then came *Shuffle Along*, a show featuring a veritable who's who of Black musical theater stars. It was Warren, however, playing a dual role, who walked away with a Tony nomination and a scrapbook's worth of superlative quotes. But nothing on Warren's résumé to date hinted at what she was about to unleash. In 2018 on London's West End, Warren stepped into the stilettos and spandex of Tina Turner in Turner's bio-musical, *Tina*. She was ferocious. In his *New York Times* review of the 2019 Broadway transfer, Jesse Green wrote, "In a performance that is part possession, part workout and part wig, Adrienne Warren rocks the rafters and dissolves your doubts about anyone daring to step into the diva's high heels." For her efforts, Warren took home the Tony, Drama Desk, and Outer Critics Circle Awards.

In conversation, Warren is an ebullient joy, full of light and laughter. She, in fact, laughs at almost everything, and speaks of some of her own experiences with a combination of wide-eyed disbelief and exuberance—until, that is, we discuss the demands *Tina* exacted and that Warren spent years fulfilling. It is then that the tears flow heavily. Warren is still coming to terms with the cost of delivering excellence at the levels she requires of herself. It's a lot to process, even as she takes pride in the achievement. Since *Tina*, Warren has starred in a miniseries, *Women of the Movement*, and shot an action film with Viola Davis, *The Woman King*. But onstage, how does one follow up something as Herculean as *Tina*? It's a conundrum that has plagued so many actors after indelible, singular portrayals. Fortunately, time, spirit, and chutzpah are on Warren's side.

Thrown, tossed, and flipped in *Bring It On*.
(Joan Marcus)

How did theater come into your world?
Accidentally. My parents took me to a production of *Once Upon a Mattress* at Hurrah
Players in Norfolk, Virginia, and I sat on my
mother's lap. I was six years old. I turned
around and looked at my mom and said, "I
want to do that." I remember that experience,
sitting in the audience, was unlike any experience I'd ever felt before. You get to be onstage
in front of people and bring them joy and happiness! So that's how it started. My parents,
being coaches, knew nothing about theater.

Adrienne Warren	
The Wiz	Encores!, 2009
Dreamgirls	National Tour, 2009
Bring It On	National Tour, Broadway, 2011
Shuffle Along	Broadway, 2016
Tina (Tony Award)	West End, 2018; Broadway, 2019

They were just fish out of water, trying to do the best they could to nurture their child. And
they did by letting me audition for the next Hurrah Players production.

Did you get in?
I did! I was a street rat in *Aladdin*. I didn't have any lines. I also forgot that I was afraid of the
dark and I was quickly reminded when we got into the theater. My mother made my costume. It was the beginning of everything. The Hurrah Players became family to me. Hugh
Copeland, the artistic director, became like a second father. I was around these incredible
human beings that were just filled with so much joy. It was a very different environment for
me than I was used to. I was raised in a family of educators and nurses. I was around athletes my whole life and it just felt different. It felt magical and I wanted to be around Hurrah
Players all the time as a kid. I wanted to be happy and have a good time and I associated that
with theater. I was still an athlete, playing basketball. I'd play basketball in our cul-de-sac
until the streetlight came on. My parents would beg me to come in. I was a guard and I ran
track in school. My trajectory was to be an athlete. I didn't think about theater as a professional career. I didn't know much about it. I think the only thing I really had that could even
give me an insider lens into that world was a VHS of *Cats*. My parents had seen it in a store
and were like, "I guess that's what she's into." They were doing the best they could!

For an athlete, *Cats* is actually a perfect bridge.
Exactly! I was obsessed with that VHS. I must have watched it at least three times a week.
My parents hate *Cats* because of me. I was obsessed. I was a big Tina Turner fan as well. The
second video they got me was a DVD of *Into the Woods*.

**For an athlete into theater, I can see some crossover that I imagine worked for you. Both require discipline, both are collaborative, team efforts, both require drilling and repetition.
But then theater gives you the freedom to experiment and play. Is that what sparked you?**
You're 100 percent right and I actually never had the opportunity to sit down and analyze it
this way. You're bringing up things for me that I'm like, "Yes! Of course that's it!" To this day
I approach my work as an athlete first because that is what I'm used to. I was an athlete first.
I will say that discipline has brought me so far. I auditioned for the Governor's School for the
Arts. It's like a *Fame* school. I always joked that if you couldn't belt a high C and kick your
face in three-inch heels, you might get kicked out. That discipline I subscribed to religiously.
It forced me to work so hard and I loved it. I stopped growing, so I couldn't be a guard at

University of Tennessee. I said, "You know what, I'll take everything that I learned and [apply it to theater]." And it has made me one heck of an artist because I approach my work like a lot of people don't. It's because I am a basketball player first.

At some point, you decided to pursue theater seriously.
I got hurt playing ball. I got a concussion and my dad was like, "I don't know, Kid. You might be done." But he could see the discipline that I was starting to put into theater. I was no longer in the gym shooting a hundred free-throw shots anymore because I had this new love. I was cheating on basketball with theater. My dad and my family are very much, "if you're going to do something, you're going to do it all the way." That is the Warren way. You are going to give everything you possibly have. And if you don't, you didn't run your race right. He saw that I was cheating on basketball and he was like, "Maybe this is what you need to lean into."

So at fifteen you went to the Governor's School. Did you feel like "I got this. I can do this."
Yes. Every day at 1:00 p.m., you leave your public high school and you go to Governor's School till five. Your day was long. And if you're doing a production, you might not get home till eight or nine. I loved it. I was around my friends who I grew up with at the Hurrah Players because Governor's School was a natural next step for those kids. My family are friends with their families. We were called the Hurrah-fia. We were very tight. My parents are still best friends with people we met at Hurrah Players.

These coaches who had no idea about theater . . .
Now they're on the board of Hurrah! They're on the board of the Arts Festival in Virginia. My mom became the executive director of the Governor's School for the Arts.

So you took your whole family with you.
I did!

And you came to New York.
My SAT scores were not high enough to get into NYU, even though I got into Tisch. So I went to Marymount. I was a horrible test-taker.

What was that like?
The beauty of going to a small school like Marymount was that I was really able to curate my experience and my education. I worked at the Little Gym on the Upper West Side, teaching kids somersaults. It was incredible. I saw Chita Rivera's last performance of *A Dancer's Life*. I had no money, so I ate hot dogs for the rest of the month. I didn't have a choice to not stay in school because my parents were educators. I was also surrounded by the music scene that is New York City—incredible. I would go to Iridium and these jazz clubs. It was this crazy experience where you're around all these people coming up. We were all kids just figuring it out. I fell in love with rock and roll, and somehow, some way I got tangled up with Jim Steinman. I ended up being in a Jim Steinman band with Rob Evan and being in Trans-Siberian Orchestra through that. This was all while I was in school. The first venue that I ever played in New York City was Joe's Pub with this rock and roll band. I was nineteen. My senior year, I convinced Marymount to let me go on a

very short holiday tour with Trans-Siberian Orchestra and to give me credit if I wrote a paper on it. I went on tour with this band, performing for 25,000 people in arenas every night for three or four months. My world was becoming so incredibly eccentric and exciting and strange. I had these theater ambitions, but I was becoming a rock and roll kid in New York City.

So how did you get back to the theater? Because it sounds like you were on a rock path.
My senior year, I was wearing leather pants and had straight black hair. But I thought I should start auditioning. I auditioned for the Encores! production of *The Wiz*.

Did you already have your Equity card?
I got my card at the Fox Theater in Atlanta, playing a Stepp sister in *Dreamgirls* with Jennifer Holliday. And I was the dance captain. I was the youngest person in the cast. But my deal with my parents was that I could only perform during the summers.

What do you remember about being in that rehearsal room?
I remember being a sponge. Our Deena was Cindy Herron from En Vogue. She was so beautiful. I was so in love with the rehearsal process and also very much in love with being a part of an ensemble. I could sit and watch Jennifer Holliday sing "And I'm Telling You …" over and over again. I never missed it. I would always run to the side of the stage and watch her do it. And when she leaves the stage every time she sings it, she has to grab someone and hold them. It was fascinating to watch someone leave their soul on the stage. I was watching one of our queens. This is what it takes. That was the first time I really saw the cost, if you allow yourself to go there as a performer. That's what it looks like at the finish line.

What specifically does that look like?
Pure exhaustion. You've given every part of yourself on that stage, for that moment, to tell that story. I'd never seen anything like that before.

You were also witnessing—and I don't mean to be unkind about this—someone who, for better and for worse—is attached to a role and a song for the entirety of her career. That role is her triumph and also her albatross. I am wondering if there was learning in seeing that woman, too, not just the performance.
A lot. I think I was a little too green and a little too excited to realize I was watching that part of it. I think I now know that I was also witnessing parts of the industry that can be really revealing about people.

Like?
As much as it means to her, she's holding on to it so much. What for? Is it bringing her joy? You start asking yourself questions. I think she was genuinely very proud of it. But I was a fly on the wall, watching the industry and how it works. How personalities blend and what it means to work together as a team. I was learning a lot. You don't leave an experience like hers and *Dreamgirls*, what it did to her career, what it did for her—you don't leave without wounds. Also, without a lot of joy. I think the more I learned about her journey with that show—she was so young [Holliday was nineteen when she was cast in the original production]! My heart can only look at her and see someone that may have been hurt. A fish out of

water and figuring it out. I don't know the psychology of things, but I can imagine that being transformative, and psychologically can probably alter you a little. I can't watch her do that and not feel so much joy and love and also—my heart. Thank you for the cost.

Let's get back to *The Wiz*. You go into your first New York audition and you book it.
I didn't necessarily come into the room terrified. The stakes weren't so high for me to get nervous because for me, the theater was always fun. It wasn't until later that I started to learn to get nervous. I was still green enough to just be enjoying myself and enjoying meeting new people. Then, as your career evolves and you come into more and more rooms, you're growing up and you realize, "Now, I'm supposed to feel anxiety." I didn't have that yet. I wasn't afraid to not work. I could call my band. I was interested in interior design. I would have been an intern. I was interested in so many things, I would just figure it out.

But you did book it! Did you feel like you belonged?
Yes! It was the first time I thought, "Whoa. This is right. Maybe I should lean into this more."

You had considered not leaning in more?
You're just not sure of your talent or yourself yet. You hope you can keep being in these rooms. You just don't know if people will give you opportunities. I couldn't believe the talent in the room I was in. I was in the ensemble and I understood Ashanti as Dorothy. I was on stage with some of the best dancers Broadway's ever had. And the best souls! When you're working with Andy Blankenbuehler, Lin-Manuel Miranda just comes in to a rehearsal because his boys are putting on a show. It was so cool. I was having the best time and the rehearsal rooms were electric.

So you come off that show and there's a *Dreamgirls* audition.
The audition actually happened during rehearsals and [director] Tommy Kail let me go. That never happens. But he let me go and he let me go to the callback. I showed up in black leather pants and a black shirt, straight hair. Nicole Valance, who worked for Jay Binder, pulled me into a corner and said, "For your callback you need to put a dress on, you need to push the babies up. Do your hair. *Dreamgirls*." I knew that, but I was in some rocker girl mindset. I honestly think it was another situation where I just came in and had fun. I never remember feeling nervous, just excitement and the honor of being in the Apollo Theater. I think that's what brought me the job. When I was ten years old at the Hurrah Players, there was a production of *Annie*. I told my mom I wanted to audition. "Mom, I want to be an orphan because I just want to do 'Hard-Knock Life.' " I just wanted to flip on beds like in the movie. It was a huge deal in our community. Girls came out of the woodwork. A hundred girls showed up to audition for this role. I just wanted to be an orphan. I had the best time in that room. We were doing "Hard-Knock Life," and we're throwing stuff on the ground and singing and I was with my friends. Then they announce the orphans at the mall on TV news. We're all standing there and they announce the names and I am so excited because this means my mom's going to get me pizza! There's a video of this somewhere. You can see me dancing around, so excited. They announce the Annie understudy, a lovely white girl. You can see me going, "Yes, I'm getting pizza!" And then they announce who's playing Annie and they say my name. I stop dancing and you see my face drop. And you see my mom's face drop because we had no idea that was coming. Didn't expect it, wasn't shooting

for it. Nothing. And I'm shaking because I know all these girls, and a lot of these girls are white. And I live in Virginia. I was the first Black Annie in the United States ever, and I needed protection. It was the first time it wasn't just fun anymore. But the *Dreamgirls* audition—that was fun.

And you get it.
I get it and I'm still doing *The Wiz*. Tommy Kail was like, "You're welcome." And that was really the beginning of everything. We played The Apollo, we went out on tour. That was the beginning of it for me. First lead role. And I'm now being seen by people in New York.

It's the beginning of a lot: your first long run, your first tour.... What was going through your head?
Honestly? It was getting through eight shows a week of singing Lorell. I realized how difficult this job can be. I remember tapping into my athletic discipline. I was like, "I can't do this, unless I set myself up for success. That means drinking my water, taking care of my body, taking care of my voice, all that that entails." Learning about warming up—because I was a rock and roll girl. We had like twenty-five costumes and wigs. That show is just insane with the costume changes. It's like leading lady bootcamp. I was around an incredible cast who were lovely. And I was also able to have fun, but it was lonely as well. It was the first time I was like, "I need to go home after the shows. I can't hang out with the cast." It was isolation. I was so tired. The three of us all had to.

You were also learning about maintaining a role.
That show was the first time I met the dresser that I usually work with, Kate. *Dreamgirls* showed me that if I really want to do this, I can't do it by myself. I desperately needed her. Dressers are your best friends, your psychologist, your ears, your light, your joy. Our partnership began there. And I learned that if I'm not careful, the isolation can sometimes muzzle me into not speaking up about my needs or not saying I need help. I was building up a wall around myself, unintentionally, just to get through singing that track eight times a week. *Dreamgirls* was also when I started getting close to stage crews. I have such an appreciation and admiration for them. They take this monster of a show [from city to city] ... I show up at the theater and it's all there. I found myself really bonding with those who worked in our crew. I started to learn truly about teamwork, and I became very aware of how big the team is that makes this monster machine work. I needed that. It was humbling. I know teamwork. Teamwork is comfort for me. So in moments where I did feel lonely, I would go and hang out with the crew. So, yes, you have to isolate so that you can produce a product, but you can't do it alone and I am not doing it alone.

After *Dreamgirls* you had some down time.
It was a very scary time. I didn't have work. I saved a lot of money on tour, as you do. I could always go to TSO and work with the band. It was a blessing to be able to have that. I wasn't doing survival jobs. I was auditioning, keeping myself up with classes. But I got really nervous. I'm a hustler, so if one thing's not working, I'm going to try something else, figure it out. I was going to make cellphone cases and sell them online! I was really into rhinestone cases with flowers and resin. I was really into my arts and crafts. I love interior design so I was talking to someone who knew someone about being an intern. And then *Bring It On* came around.

Before that, as you were exploring all these other options, was there sadness? Fear? Anger?
I could not come home without being a success. Maybe that's because my father was not the happiest when I came to New York for school. He was very nervous, as any father would be. I would get auditions to be in ensemble for things and I wouldn't take the auditions. My agent at the time was telling me, "You really have to set yourself up. If you start taking those jobs, then you will continue to get auditions like that. It's a path that you can get stuck in." I was very nervous about that. So I never took any of the auditions, which was terrifying.

So because you couldn't be a failure, you were looking at other things at which you could succeed?
Yes. I was so afraid of disappointing my father. I would tell my parents about auditions and my dad was like, "I don't understand why can't you take a job in the ensemble. You need money." "I know, but that's not the path. I just have to keep taking class, keep dancing, keep chipping away at it." It wasn't logical, but it was the only choice I gave myself. It was like once you become a leading lady you don't want to go backwards. Everything became about going backwards. That's when I started feeling the nerves. The stakes were much, much higher. Stakes that I put onto myself, that I created. I couldn't go backwards. Being a leading woman was like going to the championship game for me. It didn't mean I won, but I got there. I wasn't going to go back to my YMCA league. I come from a family that expects me to win if I'm in it. And so I was walking around, still do, working through it, with the mindset: it's go big or go home. I'm grateful for it right now because it made me work my tush off. But it was scary.

So you were willing to make Etsy phone cases before being in the ensemble.
Because, if I was going to make those Etsy phone cases, they were gonna be bomb! They were going to be number one on Etsy! It was always about being the champion of the thing that you're doing. That's not a step down; that's me doing another thing where I can be a champion.

But being an excellent ensemble member wouldn't have done it for you?
No. No matter how much I enjoyed being in an ensemble. I miss it to this day. Loved it.

It's interesting that you loved it but wouldn't let yourself do it.
I can only say that now after doing a lot of work in therapy. That cost me a lot. I'm grateful for it now because I'm here and my career is what it is, thank goodness. But I could have had a happier journey, I think, and a less lonely journey, if I allowed myself to find other avenues to get here.

So *Bring It On* . . .
Lin-Manuel Miranda was doing a reading of it and I was playing many characters. He got my name through Alex Lacamoire who was our musical director on *The Wiz*. I was just there, helping them with this reading. I was like, "You're telling me this show has Lin writing the music for one school and then Tom Kitt writing for the other school? [The show's plot hinges on a competition between two schools, one with mostly minority students and the other mostly white.] And it's a new piece? I'm here for it!" I had no idea what was ahead of us.

So your background as an athlete was coincidental? It wasn't why you were cast, it just gave you the tools to do it?

Yes! Which is very different. I am a dancer, I am an athlete, anything you ask me to do, I'm down for doing it. And we were all very young so we were like, "Sure, throw us from a building. we're fine." They were telling us that we'd have to stand on people's hands and I was terrified of heights. My mom happened to be painting my apartment in Harlem on a really, really tall ladder. I came home from one of the workshop rehearsals and she was like, "What's wrong?" "They had me on someone's hands today and I was shaking the whole time and I was crying silently." She's like, "Oh no, no, no! Get up on this ladder. You're going to stay on this ladder until you're not afraid anymore. Because you're gonna hurt yourself if you're afraid like this." So I got on that ladder and I just stayed there until the fear started dissipating.

But you did it. So you're playing Danielle, getting tossed around like a rag doll, you're a leading lady. What was that like?

Long. We started at the Alliance and then we toured before Broadway. It was the longest process and very painful physically. I was a basketball player! I was like the most opposite of a cheerleader. I got injured so much. We all did. We were very young, so we didn't really think about the impact it would have on our bodies, but people did not leave that show unscathed. There would be an ice line backstage after every show. You would go to a physical therapist's office and they would Saran Wrap ice to parts of our bodies, and then we would leave the theater. We would literally be leaving the stage door with ice Saran Wrapped to our bodies. That's how brutal it was. It wasn't like a heavy dance show. It's not like *Cats*. You're throwing people twenty-five feet in the air. It was absolutely insane. Looking back now, what was asked of us and how young we all were. . . . It was crazy and we were making it look easy.

I don't want to slam Andy Blankenbuehler, but when people are being asked to do crazy stuff eight shows a week, is that responsible?

It was a lesson in not being protected. We were in Charlotte, North Carolina, and I got a back injury. I could not walk and I was twenty-three. I'm on crutches. No one was there helping me. I was laying in my hotel room, screaming, crying, because I couldn't move my back. I was in so much pain and also feeling very guilty because, as a young person, you're scared you're going to lose your job. I was really not feeling protected and also getting bitter about that because I'm giving everything every single day. You've got to figure it out. You're in charge of figuring it out.

So is there a lesson in that? You've named the problem, but is there a lesson in how to do it differently? Or was it "that's the industry?"

That's what it was. That's the industry. That was the first time my parents were hot. That was the first time my parents got a lens into what I was really involved in. My dad became very protective after that. He knows that I'm going to approach roles 100 percent and sometimes that means I could get hurt. We all go through that in this industry. You get hurt and you find out that no one's there to rub your back or hold your hair when you're sick. Not a lot of people in power show up in those moments, but yet when you are able, they want you out there. That's the industry. I think there was a part of me that was like, "Oh, it's going to get better. We'll get to Broadway and it won't be like this. It's just because we're on the road and there's less access." You start making up excuses, because you can't believe it.

Like in any abusive relationship.

Yeah! This was actually the first time I learned to advocate for my cast. We would be staying in hotels that didn't have bathtubs to soak in and I so desperately needed that. In my twenties! If I need it, people who are doing far more than I am need it. How are we in the hotel rooms without bathtubs? How are we supposed to take care of ourselves? I started fighting back.

You're describing the feeling of working in an industry that is asking you to do the unsustainable. I am wondering if that gave you pause about what it means to do this.

I have thought about this quite a bit. Andy is an incredible choreographer and he is a dancer first. Dancers are some of the hardest-working people and they are not treated the way they should be treated. They are abused. As a dancer first and a choreographer, when you're putting together a new piece, you put together a room of the best dancers that are your friends. And it just so happens that those friends of Andy Blankenbuehler are some of the most singular, most talented storytellers with their bodies on this planet. It is Ariana DeBose, Ephraim Sykes, Daniel J. Watts.... You have that excellence in a room, creating this work with their bodies. And it is sustainable for some of those people! But those are the people building the tracks. I remember during *Bring It On* saying to Ari, "Can you do that eight times a week? Then get off the floor! Why are you showing him that you can do that?" We're in our twenties and you just want them to like you. You want them to invite you into the room again to create for the next thing, so that you can be in *Hamilton*. When you think about it like that, everyone's responsible. I had to learn that, because I was a person who said, "No it's cool. Throw me. I'll be good. Let me fall backwards and catch me on my back. I'm good." We're in an industry that glorifies and applauds you if you're exhausted.

So from what I'm hearing, *Bring It On* was a rough ride. But were you still happy?

Yes, I remember being at the Broadway Cares flea market at the autograph table sitting next to Brian Stokes Mitchell and I was losing my mind. He wrote on a poster, "Welcome to Broadway, Love, Stokes." I will never forget that. Moments like that happened. When Bernadette Peters invites you to Broadway Barks, it begins to fuzz out [the other stuff]. You begin to not feel the pain as much anymore. You're hobbling to the stage door because this is just what Broadway is. And that's when you are learning to love the abusive relationship of working in theater.

You're describing another version of what you saw Jennifer Holliday do, giving your all.

Yeah, and I just thought, "That's just what it is. So I'll continue hobbling along." And I hobbled for the next ten years.

You did have another slow period after *Bring It On*. Were you back to thinking about phone cases?

I did some work with TSO, and I started doing voice-overs around that time, commercial work. I did five pilots that no one has seen. I loved voice-over work because I was using my singer's ear. When they told me what they were looking for, I would think, "That emotion is evoked by this tone with this edge to it...." And that was the beginning of my learning how to do different people's voices. I became the voice of Maybelline, New York! Hustle, learn a new thing, and always be a student. I started taking TV and film class. It's about applying myself. That ended up sustaining me financially.

Making her mark with a cast of theater royalty in *Shuffle Along*.
(Joan Marcus)

So, how did *Shuffle Along* enter into your world?
There was this audition for a George C. Wolfe unknown project. I was asked to sing a jazz ballad. I got the job and had no idea what I was doing. That was the case for months. We did many workshops and had no idea what we were working towards. It would be myself, George C. Wolfe, and our musical director, Daryl Waters, in a studio, playing with my voice, trying to evoke emotion. What is it to sound like a bird? What does it sound like? We were finding [Warrens's dual roles] Gertrude and Florence, but I had no idea that's what we were doing. I was one of the only three people who was there for the entire process. I knew I was in a room working on something, and I knew there were a bunch of tap dancers in a room with Savion Glover tapping away. They also didn't know what they were doing. They were just creating. I remember thinking, "Savion Glover is giving me choreography!" I'm freaking out because I don't know what he's doing with his feet and I'm supposed to do it. It was all about the creation and this unknown journey. I just knew this journey was going to be exciting. It's almost better that I didn't know what I was doing. I'm literally walking into the room as a student. I'm much more willing and thrilled to jump off the artistic cliff. I wanted to create, I wanted to fly. I felt like I was flying every day, having no idea where I was going to land. I was growing my wings. I was blossoming in those rooms.

Eventually there is a script and a cast, and that cast is full of boldface names: Brian Stokes Mitchell, Audra McDonald, Billy Porter, Joshua Henry, Brandon Vincent Dixon. . . .
I was like the JV kid who had graduated to varsity. I will never forget the day George told me who the cast was. I almost was like, "I'm not going back in there. Nope." I was so nervous to pee because I didn't want to miss anything! I remember being very quiet. And I remember

studying Audra like a hawk. I was learning her process. How does she work? I was learning all of their processes. I knew they were singular, incredible talents, but to get an insight into their process and how they get that way? Every single day was the craziest master class you could ever imagine.

What were some of the things you picked up?
Ask a lot of questions. Come in prepared. Know about your characters. Know the history of the time period that you're working on, what's going on in the world. Everything is a part of that. It was fascinating to see all of them get into the psyche of their characters by asking questions. They never showed up in the room not prepared, even though you never knew what was going to happen because you're doing something with George C. Wolfe and every day could have been … who knows? I saw them be students of the process. No one knows how George C. Wolfe is going to move in a rehearsal room. And because of that, everyone has to be on their toes. It gave us all such camaraderie because at some point we were all out of our comfort zone, which was so beautiful. Probably not as beautiful to them, being the greats that they are, to feel uncomfortable in some ways.…

I don't know. Don't you think that all of them are at the stage of their careers that being stretched is exactly what they want?
Yeah, I would hope. It was a beautiful room. Even when an artist and George didn't necessarily agree on something, the way in which they got to the final product was always filled with so much respect and exploration and investigation. It was unbelievable to watch these artists.

You shared a scene with Audra.
I nearly threw up the day George told me that we were going to duet. I thought, "I can't sing on stage with her. No one's going to be paying attention to me." And also, how dare I? Very much imposter syndrome.

So how do you get through that? Just do the work?
And be present. I remember doing everything I possibly could to be present. I don't think I touched my phone very often when we were in rehearsals. I wanted to be there with her. I have snapshots in my mind of working with all of them. It was life-changing. There is no me without them. I was also learning that my heroes were human and I think I needed to know that. That allowed me to give myself some grace with my own striving for excellence all the time. *Shuffle Along* stretched me. It's so hard to articulate that whole process. I hadn't tapped in years, and there I was in a room with Savion Glover, who communicates with his feet. It is music. I challenged myself. I said, "If you are going to put me on 0 [front and center] in front of the best hoofers in our country," which our cast was—they were some of the most incredible dancers that I'd ever seen. I said, "I don't deserve to be on 0 unless I am given the choreography they are given." I asked him to give me their choreography and I showed up every morning and worked by myself to get it right. And I was the last to leave, working by myself, working on Florence's voice. I needed to step up to the level everyone else was. I don't think I had imposter syndrome about being in the room. I knew I deserved to be in the room because I was working in real time. I was earning it every day.

And it paid off.

Unexpectedly. I did not expect the attention, the Tony nomination. That got complicated for me. I was scared to come to work. I got a Tony nomination and Audra has six Tonys and this is her return to Broadway and she didn't. I didn't know if she was going to be mad at me or if our relationship would change. And she was the loveliest. So supportive during our process. And I began to learn more about her as a human being. It was also complicated because then I knew people were always going to expect something from me. Then I really couldn't go backwards. I was now becoming somewhat of a peer and I never really even thought of that before. So that was a shift. After I got my nomination I was hanging out at Glass House after the show. I love me some Glass House. Someone came up to me and said, "What are you doing here? You have a Tony nomination. You're supposed to go to Bar Centrale now." Suddenly it felt like I was not one of the ensemble anymore and I never would be again. "You're not one of us." It got complicated. I got a lot of joy in those spaces.

Did you take that on, or did you reject that?

I rejected it. But I still knew that people walked around thinking it. There were expectations. Especially as a young Black woman in this space. There aren't a lot of us.

I am going to go through all those boldface names about whom you have those snapshots. If you have a memory, a thought, a learning moment, let's free-associate. Brian Stokes Mitchell.

Stokes and I went to dinner on our break and he talked to me about the industry and navigating your way through it. I consider him like a governor of Broadway, so it was nice to sit down with the governor and talk about navigating the Broadway industry and community.

Joshua Henry.

Josh Henry would play his guitar all the time in his dressing room. And if you felt the urge to be artistic or have a jam session, you would just go to Josh's dressing room. The door is always open and he was always playing. You would create something or just listen to him sing, and who doesn't want to do that?

Billy Porter.

Billy had the coolest dressing room. I remember constantly wanting to go to Billy's dressing room just because the energy was going to be so warm.

Audra McDonald.

There was a moment during tech when I asked her—and I was terrified to ask this question, but I just did it—"Audra, if there's one thing you could tell your younger self, what would you say?" I'm not going to tell you the answer because it's mine, but she was so genuine and answered in a way that had nothing to do with career. And then also, she was pregnant. I had mentioned something about pizza. I said, "I just want pizza," and she was like, "That sounds like such a good idea!" And at the end of rehearsal, she'd ordered all these pizzas!

Brandon Vincent Dixon.
Brandon and George C. Wolfe are two peas in a pod, in the strangest pod. I remember Brandon just analyzing these characters and getting in there deep about the work and it was astonishing to watch. He's such a brilliant individual. Watching him work with George C. Wolfe and watching their bond … I was a fly on the wall anytime I saw the two of them speaking because I knew it was going to be incredibly insightful.

George C. Wolfe.
George saw something in me that I never remotely saw in myself. And I don't know how he saw it. I don't know how he trusted that I could do what I was able to do. He really believes in me. I view him as a mentor. I don't speak to him all the time, but if I ever have any ideas or anything to say, I'll shoot him an email and he always emails me back. I'm really grateful to know someone as incredible as him and to get to play with him. Working with him will always be one of the greatest honors of my life.

Savion Glover.
Savion put me through my paces. He has such a respect for his art form. I looked at him like a really tough coach. His associate, Marshall, was my godsend, because he became like my trainer. Marshall and I would rent out studios where he and I and I would just drill.

It all ended very abruptly.
I mourned the show. And it was history repeating itself in a way with that show [the original had all but vanished until this show, an examination of its creation]. It just disappeared. We didn't do an album. All of those artists were in a room together and the show just disappeared. That is wild. There is no guarantee. Enjoy creating as much as you can for as long as you can.

During *Shuffle Along*, you co-founded Broadway Advocacy. How did that happen?
The killing of Black bodies at the hands of police. We were all angry and sad. I went to a network advocacy meeting in Harlem on my way to work, thinking, "How can we get involved?" We just wanted the theaters to say something. No one was saying anything. They weren't even saying "Black Lives Matter." I was performing in a show about Black bodies performing to an audience of white faces. I was backstage, looking onstage at our Black cast. They were performing and tears were silently falling from their faces. Our pain wasn't being acknowledged and yet we were, per usual, giving, giving, giving, cost, cost, cost. When you're in an industry where most of the people with power, those people who can say something, are white, and they're not acknowledging your life mattering, it is traumatizing. So myself, Amber Iman, Britton Smith, Christian Dante, we started having meetings, trying to figure out what to do. We decided to produce a show called "Broadway for Black Lives Matter." That was the beginning of it. I got a *Non-Profit for Dummies* book and the Broadway Advocacy Coalition was born. I think the possibilities are endless. The trick really is to not be overwhelmed with your outreach. You can spread yourself so thin trying to help everyone and you don't end up helping anyone. We have to be very specific. It's now a full-blown not-for-profit with a staff, doing incredible work in the intersections of arts and advocacy. We are incredibly diverse in our approach and mission. Maybe that's what *Shuffle Along* was for.

The show's closing set you up for something altogether different.

I went to do a reading of *Tina* for the creators just to hear it. I thought I was reading the sister or something because I changed my body for *Shuffle Along*. I really wanted to have the body of a 20s flapper and I'd gotten rid of a lot of muscle mass. I was very small. I went to pick up the script and I asked, "Which role would you like me to read?" And they looked at me and they said, "Tina." Huh? I was stunned. I went back to the theater and I put the script on my table and I just stared at it. Like, "What are you? What is this?" Because this was so far away from what I was doing. At the table read, no one was supposed to sing. It was just for the words. The musical director, Nick, was in the room and was playing on the piano. He said, "Adrienne, if, you know any of these songs, feel free to sing a little." We got to, "We Don't Need Another Hero" and I love that song. So I sang it and I just remember seeing eyes coming up from the scripts. I was just going for it. I finished and everyone was kind of silent for a second. Then they clapped and we just kept going. And that's the only thing they had heard from me.

In fighting shape, and Tina Turner drag, in *Tina*.
(Manuel Harlan. Costume and scenic design by Mark Thompson)

I get a call to go to London to possibly be a part of a workshop of it. Scott Rudin doesn't let me leave *Shuffle Along* to do it, even though we've already been given our closing notice. So I'm missing it. It's gone. That's OK. They do that workshop. They end up calling me back for a workshop that I am available to do. I had just shot a pilot, so I was available for the workshop, but we knew I wouldn't be available for the show. I went into the workshop guns a-blazing. They didn't have choreography yet, but I studied Tina's dance moves and I started putting a little bit of something into it. I gave everything I possibly could. Tina came to that presentation along with all of the international producers. I end up getting a call saying that the pilot did not get picked up. An hour later I get a phone call from my agent, saying, "You're not moving to L.A., you're moving to London." I didn't even know I was still in the running.

When Tina was in the room, how did you manage to perform as her for her?
I didn't look at her. They asked me if I wanted to meet her beforehand and I said, "Absolutely not." I wanted to stay as far away from her as possible so that I could focus on my work. I also knew if I looked at her or I got to know her I would get so invested that I might have gotten lost. I would have started feeling the nerves and everything else. I do better when I'm able to just have fun and do my thing. I didn't look at her until I got to "Proud Mary." Because I also realized in not looking at her, I was missing an incredible moment: Tina Turner watching me play Tina Turner. So, I decided to look at her during "Proud Mary," and she was smiling and singing along.

You go to London. You who suffers from imposter syndrome. Were you doubting yourself?
Hundred percent doubting myself. A hundred percent. I was terrified. Shakin' in my boots. Who the heck wants to step into Tina Turner's heels? I'm gonna lose here. And I knew the show was going to be hard, but I didn't really know what I was signing myself up for. Just a lot of work. When I got the phone call, I was like, "Get to the gym immediately." And I did. I had three months in boxing class or with my trainer, jump roping constantly. I jump roped while singing "Proud Mary." Speed roping. That's how we trained: "Rocky" style. It was insane. I had washboard abs. I don't anymore. I was operating out of fear.

Other than physical preparation, what did you do?
Reading her books, watching her videos. Changing my diet. Anything you could possibly do. I started working with [vocal teacher] Liz Caplan. She became my voice whisperer and got me through the West End and Broadway.

How were those weeks of rehearsal?
So much fun because it was a new place with new people. I was really leaning into that, enjoying creating. I have such a great relationship with [director] Phyllida Lloyd because we worked so closely together to build this thing. I worked hand in hand with every single person on that creative team. Not a decision was made without me, without my insight, or without me in mind. It really felt like we were all on a team. That part of the journey was overwhelming and warm and great. When you have someone like Tina, that has been through what she's been through, no matter how hard the day at work is, you will never go through what she went through. I think I was carrying that with me for a lot. So even if I felt pain or something, I'd be like, "Yeah, but this ain't nothing. I don't have bruises on my face." For the piece, we wanted to show the exhaustion of her life and just how long this pain was in her. I couldn't leave the stage, because you would miss a part of the pain, which we didn't know we were doing at the time. Tina's on a train that she can't get off of. And then we

created an experience for the audience, watching the actress on a train that she cannot get off of. We didn't mean to do that.

So as it's happening, you realized that but you did it anyway?
Yes. I knew that I wanted the show to be succeed. I knew if it was going to succeed it was going to take all of me. It was not the healthiest environment for me. And I knew they wanted the show to go all around the world, and if it wasn't a success in London ... I was carrying around this pressure. I had to not just deliver excellence, I had to deliver something that no one had ever seen before. During previews, we got to the mega-mix at the end and I would run off-stage and throw up. The next day we'd try again and we'd cut back a verse. I would finish, come offstage and throw up. And then it would be like, "Did you throw up this time?" We were literally cutting back just enough so that I didn't get sick. I hadn't learned how to pace myself yet. I'm on a raked stage in three-inch heels and I didn't know how to pace myself.

What was Tina's involvement?
She wasn't coming to rehearsals. She came to two or three previews and came backstage to talk to everyone, but she didn't talk to me. And I knew at that point that I still had more work to do. I went to the dressing room and I cried. "She's not happy yet and I don't know what else to do." She called me that weekend and said, "Adrienne, I'm ready to talk now." It was about her, not about me. In that talk, she gave me her blessing. She gave Tina to me. She said, "I can be Anna Mae now. You can have her."

How do you ultimately learn to pace yourself? Just by doing it? "I hold back here so I can let go there?"
Yeah, and I had to do that on my own. There was no one that could really do that with me, although Phyllida and I did work hand in hand on so much of that performance. As well as Nick. But it was really about doing. People started calling me a superhero or a warrior. And then, in my head, I was like, "Am I? Am I supposed to keep going? Does that mean that even if I am hurt, I have to keep going because at the end of it, someone's going to applaud me because I kept going?" And then I would show up to work with sprained ankles and con-cussions and ... name the injury, I had it. I was learning in real time how to do this. I set an impossible standard that I had to give myself grace for. This was a thing that was built and was going to go all over the world and employ incredible Black women. They were going to have to do [what I created]. I didn't think that part through, and neither did Phyllida. In London, I was being a superhero at work and coming home alone and taking ice baths every day. [She tears up.] They bought an ice machine at the theater just for my ice baths. I wasn't really real-izing what I was taking home with me. The cost of it was revealing itself in such a major way. By the end, I was a skeleton. And there was still no guarantee that I was going to Broadway. My family and loved ones became increasingly aware of the toll. Creating this incredible job had given me so much, but it cost me so much as well. More than I could ever say.

It goes back to Jennifer Holliday and the cost of excellence. If you want to be this good, if you want to do what she did, if you want to give an audience your soul, it is a beautiful thing to do. It's art. But what is the cost, and are you willing to pay it? These are questions that probably still plague you.
What do you leave for yourself? What do you leave for your family? I had an uncle that died while I was in London and I couldn't go to his funeral. I couldn't leave and I really needed to be around my family. It changed how I approach my work from then on.

How?

I knew after that West End experience that no one was going to take care of me unless I take care of me. I learned that I have to ask for help. I learned that I'm the farthest from a super-hero. I learned that my spirit, my heart, my life is important and precious. And also that I don't have to go through—and I say "go through"—I recognize the privilege and the opportunities that I have. But I've also been asked to do things that no one has ever been asked to do. And I think there are a lot of people, especially people of color, who are asked to fly, to be superheroes, in order for them to be seen. If I look at my heroes, a lot of them were lonely. There is not greatness without some cost. And the culture of care in workplace is very important to me—the care of not just myself, but everyone in the building with me. I learned to be an advocate in my workspace. This is a business and it will be treated as such.

So you came to New York with this new understanding about what you needed to do for you. How did that change for your approach?

I was finally able to have fun. My dressing room door was open. I was very, very close with my cast. I became super protective of them. We had a ball. The cost was still the same physically, and I am still learning about when to say, "no," when to not go to work, when to take care of myself. I negotiated a wellness plan for myself for my Broadway contract. That included getting vitamin infusions and taking care of my body and keeping my trainer. Keeping Liz Caplan. Kate, my dresser, was with me. Everything that I learned, I finally was able to take it with me. That didn't mean it wasn't still just as hard and there's still crazy cost and it's still not equitable, but I was able to find Adrienne in my work. I'm learning to bring me and care about me. Being storytellers, we give ourselves to our work, to the characters. Imagine the healing we could do if we could also not forget about our hearts, our stories, our time.

You talk about advocating for other people and being aware of the rest of the cast and being a lioness, which I can totally see, mane and all. But how do you take that on when the demands of the role are so much?

I had to make room for it because I actually don't work well if I know that others are suffering. It creates for a better work environment for everyone. And I can't do that job without the support of everyone in the building—me personally. It may be different for other people. I work better in an environment where we're all striving for excellence together in a way that's working as a team. I've never not been like a team captain. It also takes me out of my isolation. I could do it without them, but I learned that I don't have to. And it makes it more fun as well.

It sounds like there was a huge reward between the London and the Broadway runs and that there were very different experiences.

Very, very, very different. My light was very dim when I left London. Firefly. Getting to the Broadway opening was, "Yes, we're doing this again." But it was also a major finish line for me.

The pandemic gave you a nineteen-month break and I'm wondering, when you came back to it, whether or not you came back differently.

When I came back, I had just finished shooting *Women of the Movement*. I had gained thirty pounds to play Mamie Till, so I freaked out because I had three months! I think because of Mamie and that experience, I had a perspective shift. I could close out this chapter and have a great time doing it. There was no pressure anymore. Have the most fun that you can.

Did you?

I really did. I didn't get back to my Tina body that I wanted to get. But we just went through a pandemic! Who cares! I'm alive! We're here! It was a full victory lap. The rest of the pressure was just noise. I deserve this lap, and I deserve to run it the way I want to run it and then I'm going to graciously bow out, happy to see the legacy of *Tina* all over the world.

How was it different doing it on your terms?

I just allowed myself to be human. I remember one day Kate ordered me Shake Shack after a show and I was just sitting there eating burgers and laughing, the happiest I could be. I was just being.

I think what you're describing is realizing that you are enough.

Yes. Not only did I not think I was enough when I got the job, not only did I not think I was enough for Tina Turner to approve me, not only did I not think I was enough for my producers to make me fight for my job every step of the way, I was never enough. So getting to come back—I'm enough. I remember sitting there at the Tonys. My parents were so nervous. And I think I was so nervous to disappoint everyone if I didn't win. I had done everything I could have possibly done. And if that wasn't enough, I was OK with this industry not thinking I was enough because I couldn't do more. I literally couldn't.

But you were, and you did win. So what do you want now?

I want to continue to create on both sides of the table. I am producing because I've learned so much about the care of a production and of people. I think that that can be more a part of this business. I know it can. It has to. And I want to take care of myself in all spaces as much as I can. I'm still learning to do that, and that's going to be a process for me. But in everything that I have done since *Tina*, I have found so much joy, peace. Even doing something as difficult as playing Mamie Till, I still had so much fun because I didn't forget about Adrienne. And if that was the lesson I was to learn, I'm really grateful for it. As a Black woman living in America, I'm constantly having to remind people that my life matters. I can't keep saying that if I don't actually treat myself as such. I don't know if I want to put my body through a theater schedule again right now. Not just my muscles and ligaments, my mind and my heart are still healing. Until a story compels me—I have to be pulled into it. Unless there's something that moves me, calling to me to be a part of it.... My relationship with musical theater—she and I are in couples therapy.

The industry is in need of some evolution, obviously. One has an opportunity to affect if one is there. That's not your job, necessarily....

If I can help it, I will never not be a part of this community. Whether that's through my Broadway Advocacy Coalition, through producing, ... I love this community with all my heart. We got work to do. But I fell in love with this because I was the kid with the *Cats* VHS and it gave me so much joy. I learned about myself and found my light in the theater. I'm not going anywhere. I just may be walking in different shoes. I like not knowing. It's cool.

Jessie Mueller

August, September 2020

Generally speaking, there are two types of leading lady on Broadway: one is either the soprano, playing the likes of Sarah Brown, Laurey, Amalia, and Glinda, or one is the belter, playing Adelaide, Ado Annie, Ilona, and Elphaba. Very rarely do the two meet in the same person, but such is the versatility and range of Jessie Mueller. Who else could belt out Jenna's searing "She Used to Be Mine" in *Waitress* and follow that up with Julie Jordan's pure soprano in *Carousel*?

I often ask people when the theater bug bit, but in Mueller's case, her childhood home was infested. Both parents and all three of her siblings are actors, cutting their teeth in the Chicago theater scene. In Chicago, most shows have predetermined limited runs of two or three months, tops, so it's not unusual for a prolific actor to amass a robust list of credits in a short span of time. Mueller played twenty leading roles in five years, including both the aforementioned Adelaide and Amalia.

Her casting in the Broadway revival of *On a Clear Day You Can See Forever* shocked no one more than Mueller, who auditioned in Chicago with no imminent intention to move to New York. Reviews were lukewarm, but rapturous for Mueller, who found herself with a Tony nomination and a slew of back-to-back leading roles in shows, including *Into the Woods*, *The Mystery of Edwin Drood*, and *Nice Work If You Can Get It*. But then came *Beautiful*. Mueller, as Carole King, was suddenly the Tony-winning toast of Broadway. In his *New York Times* review, Ben Brantley effused, "she steps confidently into the V.I.P. room of musical headliners.... When Ms. Mueller sings the show's title song she delivers something you don't expect from a jukebox musical. That's a complex, revitalizing portrait of how a very familiar song came into existence, and of the real, conflicted person within the reluctant star." She scored again with *Waitress*, and then again in *Carousel*, winning Tony nominations for both and the Drama Desk Award for the latter.

In an age when stars who are made on Broadway frequently leave the theater for more remunerative work, Mueller has stayed put on stage. But then, she doesn't especially perceive herself to be a star. "You might mean so much to someone and what you do might mean so much to someone," she told me, "But the person two seats down from you on the subway has no idea who you are. It's so beautifully leveling. You have to know what you're worth, but believing or subscribing to someone else's picture of who or what you are is just kind of insane to me."

You were in theaters from your earliest years. Your mom took you backstage when she was in *The Sound of Music*....
I thought that was magical. That was the first time that I'd ever been that close to a costume. At that point I thought it was so glamorous. I learned.

You spent many years happily and prolifically working in musical theater in Chicago.
I was really fortunate. That's what I wanted to do. I went to school at Syracuse University. So many of my friends that were there would go to New York and see shows. I had been to

In her Tony-nominated Broadway debut, *On a Clear Day, You Can See Forever*.
(Paul Kolnik)

New York and seen maybe two Broadway shows, *Miss Saigon* and *Jesus Christ Superstar*, but I'd grown up seeing Chicago theater all my life, so I just didn't feel I had a connection with New York. It was scary to me. It was a big, loud, expensive place and I didn't know anything about it. I wanted to go back to Chicago and work.

Did the shows you saw feel any different to you than what you knew from Chicago?
Oh, yeah. I had seen touring productions of Broadway shows. I remember seeing the huge *Show Boat* revival in the late 90s. I had never seen anything that big. I had never seen an opera. I definitely had that feeling of "Broadway"! The look of it. The stagecraft of it was so different. The other plays that I remember having that feeling about—my high school used to take trips to the Stratford Festival up in Ontario. I remember seeing shows there and being blown away, coming back to my hotel room and just—the teenaged, over-emotional

Jessie Mueller	
On a Clear Day You Can See Forever	Broadway, 2011
Into the Woods	off-Broadway, 2012
The Mystery of Edwin Drood	Broadway, 2012
Carousel	Lincoln Center, 2013
Nice Work If You Can Get It	Broadway, 2013
Beautiful (Tony Award)	Broadway, 2014
Waitress	Broadway, 2015
Carousel	Broadway, 2018
The Music Man	Washington, DC, 2019

feeling of like, "Oh my gosh, it's so good. I'll never be that good. I wonder if I could ever do something like that." That was a place I held in very high esteem.

Were you training at all in Chicago, or did it all come by learning as you went along?
I got really good training at Syracuse. I didn't really continue classes when I got back to Chicago. I was really lucky I got cast in the chorus of an Equity production right away. I just started working and I felt like I was learning a lot on the job. I still think so much of the job is just learning how to work with people. It's all about relationships. That's the stuff that I feel I got to learn in the [rehearsal] room early on, which was invaluable. Just sitting and watching. You train, you go to school, you take class and then you actually get into a rehearsal room. "Oh, this is what it's like! Somebody works like this and somebody else works like that, and the director asks for this and you take this much time for that, and then you take a lunch break"—just learning the fundamentals of how it actually works.

In Chicago, things have shorter runs. Actors therefore have the potential to end up in multiple rehearsal rooms in the course of a year. You were learning from several different directors and different companies in a concentrated amount of time.
That's totally true because I would do multiple shows. I was young, trying to pay my rent. I was doing a kids' show in the morning, another show at night, usually at the same theater, thankfully. But also, in Chicago, most of the musical theater houses are in the outlying suburbs. You're not necessarily in the city center like in New York. So, you'd be driving an hour each way. But you're right—shows run two, two and a half months there, so you want to book multiple shows a year if you're going to get your insurance and be able to pay your rent.

You also seemed to avoid being pigeonholed.
I had people who let me try things. [When I auditioned for a production of *Guys and Dolls* in Chicago] I went in to read for Sarah. My friend, Matt Raferty, who was directing, said, "Call me crazy, but would you look at Adelaide?" I was like "Sure," because growing up I always

thought I'd be the character actor. I love that stuff. He was the one that really had that idea. He knew that I was young for the part, but he was like, "If you're game I'm game." I said, "Yeah, I trust you." Maybe because the casting pool there is smaller, they don't pigeonhole people as much. They really do let people be flexible and have that versatility.

And you have a very flexible instrument . . .
A lot of that was learning on the job. I'd be like, "Yeah, sure, I could do that," and then have to go and figure it out.

You racked up quite a résumé, and you auditioned for *On a Clear Day* while you were still in Chicago.
I still don't know how my name got on that list. I really have to figure out that story. [Casting director] Jim Carnahan was coming through Chicago to cast the touring production of *American Idiot*. As I understand it, they also knew they had this *Clear Day* project. So I think that the understanding was, "Well, while we're in Chicago, why don't we check out the talent?" Somehow my name got on that list. When I went into the studio, it looked like I was the only one there for *Clear Day* because everybody else was all black nail polish and eyeliner, holding their guitars. I was walking in, in my little dress. I'm sure everyone looked at me and thought, "Poor thing." I'm still amazed the producers took the leap they did. Stuff like that doesn't happen very often. Jim said, "OK, OK, great. Can you come back tomorrow for a callback?" "I can't! I'm doing my friend's reading tomorrow." He was sweet. I don't ever remember him pressuring me or being like, "You know, this is important." He said, "All right, can you fly yourself to New York next week? That actually might work out even better because then the team will be there and they can see you."

So you did. And you sang with Harry Connick Jr.
I was a BIG Harry Connick Jr. fan, so I was quite nervous. But I walked in and there's this tall drink of water. He goes, "Hey, I'm Harry," with this big smile on his face, and he puts his hand out without skipping a beat. I just shook his hand and I was calm after that. It was so weird. That was my experience with him from there on out. He was just such a cool dude and he totally put me at ease. We read a couple scenes and then I think we sang the duet. I remember flying back home to Chicago. I love flying. I love looking out the window. My mind can get clear and peaceful. I remember having the feeling that this wasn't done. And I swear, my iPod was on shuffle and one of the songs that popped up was Harry's rendition of "This Time the Dream's on Me." What???? A bit prophetic! Then this week-long workshop came up and they asked if I was available because [the star they had been looking at] wasn't available. We did it at this studio where they mostly do dance stuff. It's always fun to see little ballerinas going up and down in the little iron-gate elevator. Then there was another call for a month-long lab. I had been told there was a possibility of me being the cover. I stayed on an air mattress with my one of my best buddies from high school who was living up in Harlem at the time. It was a fun, crazy, very hot month in New York City. Harry wasn't available for that workshop so Marc Kudisch did it. I didn't really know what this was going to be. I had never done a lab before. Toward the end of the lab, the producers called me out into the hall and were like, "You can't tell anyone, but we're going to give you the part." So I was kind of . . . [sings from *Into the Woods*] "excited and scared."

Did your first rehearsal room for a Broadway show feel different to you?

We were in New 42 Studios, right in the heart of Times Square. I learned, "Oh, this is where so many of the Broadway shows rehearse." It's like this pressure cooker of all these shows that are happening at the same time on different floors. There were a lot of young people in the show, several Broadway debuts. Harry had a totally different energy because he had done a show before, but this was the first one that was really on his shoulders. He was so amazing with me, so encouraging. Harry and David Turner and I would always start the days together dancing. There was this brilliant three-way cha-cha of sorts that we had to do in the show. We did that dance every single day. We just drilled and drilled. That was so fun.

What do you remember about [director] Michael Mayer?

He was so smart. I remember feeling like we were all always catching up to him. Michael's always a little in front of everybody. I think his mind is really, really quick. He was very sweet to me.

I heard you tell a story about Harry's monologue.

Harry had this epic monologue to start the show. In the last third of the show, he has another monologue, which is very similar to the first. He starts and the music is swelling because the reprise of "Too Late Now" is about to start, and I can tell that he's lost his place. He's gone back to the first monologue. I don't know if he knows [that he's doing the wrong scene]. It's about my time to sing and I did a "don't speak." I put my hand to his lips.... First, I tried to warn him with my body language. I didn't say anything, I just [covered his mouth] and came in singing "Too late now to forget your smile...." His eyes [went wide] and were like, "what are you doing?" And then [his face went "ohhhhhh" and he realized]. "I see!!!!"

Did you have the sense that the show wasn't fully working?

I don't think I did. Maybe that was my rose-colored glasses. A lot of the storytelling was really strong. Michael was really, really smart about the structure of it. We worked really hard. It was one of my first experiences trying it one way one night and then flipping the order of a scene, or rehearsing one version of a scene but not putting it in that night. I remember there was one change—we put in a new scene with new costumes. It changed from the Central Park ice skating rink to Coney Island. It was thrilling because it was such a challenge. It was just one of those moments I always dream that happened in the golden era; [she puts on an old time New York accent, something out of *42nd Street*] "We're gonna reset the scene tonight in Poughkeepsie and we'll put it in tomorrow on Broadway! I don't know how I'm gonna remember my lines, but gosh darn it, I'll try! Hand me the costume, I'll wear it! Come on, kids! I can do the part, yeah!" Everybody was so on board. That is one of the things I love about theater: you drink the Kool-Aid. Sometimes you know something's not working, for sure. And when you do know it, everybody knows it and you have to fight to try to do what you can. And you're just so friggin' busy. You're busy all the time so you can't see the forest for the trees. Sometimes that's why things don't end up working. You're so in it, you're so involved with it, you've been stewed in it for so long that you don't.... You need outside eyes. I never read reviews. I stopped reading reviews when I was in Chicago after a couple of my first plays. Even if they were positive, adjectives stuck in my brain and I got so heady about it. I still have not read the reviews for *Clear Day*. I just can't bring myself to do it. But you hear about it. You obviously know when something isn't working. I remember Harry taking me aside and saying, "I think we're struggling and I just want you to be prepared." And I really appreciated that. But no matter what, he was positive. He is one of the hardest-working people I've ever come across and he's so positive. You'd never hear him griping. You never heard him say, "I'm tired." Never. He was like our dad. He was going to take care of everybody. I got spoiled in a lot of ways. [It took me time to realize] you don't have to be superhuman. You have to show up and do your job and be honest and caring, but you're allowed to be tired. But I'm so grateful that I had that kind of behavior modeled for me. The show didn't last very long, but I had the time of my life.

When the show closed, did you go back to Chicago?
I stayed. I took a lot of walks in the park, thinking [about the future]. I cried A LOT. It was jarring and scary. "What do I do? What do I do?"

You got a Tony nomination.
In all honesty, it was so frightening to me. I didn't know what it meant. I didn't think I deserved it. The show was closed. I didn't have anyone from the show around me. I was like, "Why have I been singled out?" I was feeling so adrift, anyway. I didn't know what I was doing. As time went on, there were parts of it that I enjoyed and appreciated. But I felt intimidated by it. Like it was the first day of high school and I was walking into the cafeteria and didn't know who to sit with. I didn't know anyone. But everyone was very kind to me. I do remember that night—I don't like getting dressed up. I don't like getting my picture taken. That side of what I do is not what I'm most comfortable with. I just felt like I was going to show up to the ball and my dress was going to disintegrate and my coach would turn into a pumpkin surrounded by rats. "You don't belong here, Cinderella! You should be doing the drapes! Vacuum the carpet!" I look back on that period and I think I was trying to be what I thought people wanted me to be. By the time we actually got there, I thought, "Oh, this is cool. This is an honor." The community couldn't have been more welcoming. And I guess I did have this sense of "well, maybe I'm supposed to stay here, maybe there's momentum."

And there was. In fact, you had the opportunity to channel all of those Cinderella feelings into actually playing Cinderella! You did *Into the Woods*.
Yes! God was like, "Ha, ha! I know what I'll have you do next ... !" I've often thought, "do we just bring to the roles what we have at the moment, or do the roles come to us because of what we're ready for?" That's exactly what I felt like. [She starts choking up] I'd seen and loved that show and all of a sudden it was like, "I get her! I get Cinderella. I get it." Cinderella was all about "what I want most of all is to know what I want." To me, that was her in a nutshell, and that was something I related to for so much of my life. That was what the character was experiencing. A little bit of a wish or a wonder and then this amazing opportunity comes your way and everybody says, "this must mean everything to you!" And on the inside, she's thinking, "yes, but I don't know if it's everything I wanted it to be." There was that for me because there was so much that was unbelievably cool and there was so much that was different and strange and uncomfortable. I've never been great with change, and there was a lot of change. There was so much that changed so quickly in my life.

You worked with Donna Murphy, Denis O'Hare, Amy Adams, Chip Zien....
It was such a great cast. We had so much fun. I remember from day one of the table read, Donna was raring to go. She really set the tone. I feel like I'm always quite tentative at the beginning. I've learned that I really trust the process to be a process. I come in shy and I have to … I don't know … I come with a little baby skeleton and I have to build everything on top of it. But Donna knew what she wanted to do. I loved doing that show. I loved that process and I got to meet Amy. She and I got close during that. It was magical getting to do a show like that outside. There would be moments I'd sing to the birds and there'd be actual real birds flying over my head!

Was Sondheim around?
He came by a couple of times. I do remember I got a note from Mr. Sondheim. I was getting my wig on one day and that was sort of how I met him: head in a mirror because someone was putting a wig on me and he was kind of [behind me]. "Oh, hello." He basically said, "You can sing it more."—"On the Steps of the Palace"—"You understand the acting, but you can really sing it." "Yes. Sir."

That production also had trouble finding its footing. When it's not gelling like that, how does it feel?
I think I can start to sense what is working and what's not working. It just feels like you get to that part every night where maybe we didn't work on the scene enough, or we never cracked the code on this bit, or I don't know what I'm doing at this part of the song. Those moments feel technical. With the rest of it, you can soar and let it fly. Those moments, you gotta get through.

After that run, you went into another show with a big ensemble cast, *The Mystery of Edwin Drood.*
Andy Karl and I were like, "We're getting paid for this? This is insane." We had so much fun on that show. I just loved it. It was exhausting because it was a comedy and very high energy, but it was also unique because of the bits that would change every night. There was always something to keep it fresh.

Was working with Chita Rivera a learning experience?
I remember watching Chita from the first day, and coming into the theater every day and walking past her dressing room. She'd be on the floor stretching, in a split, every day as I walked past. Warren Carlyle was the choreographer and he was such a delight. He was the perfect kind of energy. It was just a really goofy room. People being stupid, basically. It's all these professionals, best of the best, cream of the crop, and everybody's just weird and wonderful and is being paid to goof off. It was just utterly delightful.

You would expect that Chita would be disciplined, but Will Chase told me that she was also a prankster.
She was! She's an awesome blend between discipline and naughty. Which is why she was perfect for that part—because she had that little glint in her eye. She was ready to have fun every day. You just got that sense, being around her, that she was always so grateful that this is what she got to do for a living. So disciplined. It was so cool to watch her work. The way

372 Here's to the Ladies

she walks across the stage, or works things out in the rehearsal room—she set the tone, in such a great way.

You were all playing music hall performers putting on a play, so there was lots of room for mugging and crossing the line. Was it a challenge keeping that consistency and not going over?
I think we were really lucky. It was casting. Everybody knew where that line was and had an innate understanding that we were all playing together. It was a really great ensemble in the truest sense of that word. Everybody knew how to set everybody up. No one was like, "this is my funny line." They also got as much joy out of setting up somebody else than for their own bit. It was really fun to figure that stuff out in the room. "How can we support this little bit over here?" As far as playing with the audience, that was the part that terrified me the most. In the beginning we had to come through the audience and talk to them. They plotted out our little sections and I ended up switching with Bobby Creighton at one point because I had the house seats section. So I would always walk into like, "Oh! Hello, Debra Messing!" It was always somebody famous and I got so intimidated. Bobby liked that way more than I did, so I was just was like, "we're switching." I got so thrown.

For your next job, you were sort of cast from the house at *Edwin Drood*.
Sarah Jessica Parker had seen *Drood*, and when they were casting to replace Kelli O'Hara in *Nice Work If You Can Get It*, she apparently told Matthew Broderick, "What about Jessie? She was funny." Which is funny to me because I don't understand how you would [make that leap] from what I was doing in *Drood* to *Nice Work*. People have been very generous to me. I don't know.

And before your replaced Kelli, you briefly co-starred with Kelli.
Yes! While I was doing *Drood*, we started the fast and furious two-week process of *Carousel*.

Things were really clipping along for you. Did you think that maybe you were not going to have to worry about a survival job, or was it more like today is fruitful but who knows about tomorrow?
I always feel like the latter. I think that's common. And I grew up around that, too. But I remember on my birthday walking through the Lincoln Center campus, going to rehearsal for *Carousel* before my nighttime show at *Drood*. I remember having a moment of like, "Holy shit! You're going to rehearse at Lincoln Center to sing with the New York Philharmonic, and then tonight you get to go do your Broadway show on your birthday! You're doing it!" Getting to work with Kelli was a really wonderful experience. John Rando directed and I think we had two weeks or ten days to put it all together. I remember getting into the room and just realizing who I was in a room with—Nathan Gunn, Stephanie Blythe, Kelli—and being like, "Oh boy, what have I gotten myself into." I was going to have to really step it up. But that was a wonderful experience. And man, it was fast and furious. But I just loved it. It almost felt like high school, because you have like two weeks to rehearse and then you get a weekend of shows and that's it. Poof, it's gone.

Did you find yourself connecting to Kelli, not just as someone who you were about to replace, but as someone in the business who you might want to emulate?
She's really funny and she's really down to earth and she's a little naughty, too. I love that combination. I don't see how anybody could not get along with her. She's just so likable. Very

easy to talk to. But also, getting to watch her up close on stage and working in the rehearsal room, I was just kind of awed by her ease. She's this tiny little petite thing and there's so much voice. And it's just effortless the way it comes out. It's incredible to me. There's no tension. She doesn't force things. By the time I got into rehearsals for the *Nice Work* replacement, we already had a bit of a relationship and it made that transition so easy. That whole thing was a whirlwind. I think I learned that show in ten days and she was like, "Any time you want to shadow me backstage, or come hang out and watch the costume changes.... Anything I can do to help ease the transition...." She and her pal, Fran Curry, who was dressing her at the time, really walked me through that whole thing.

That was your first time replacing and joining a company that had cohered. What was that like for you?
That was wild. The whole idea of replacements was very foreign to me because, as we talked about, in Chicago you run a show for two or three months. [I was aware of] the effect I was having on other people who had built the show with other artists and personalities, and now I was coming in. You want to bring what you bring, but you don't want to be like a stick in everyone's bicycle wheel. You have to do what was constructed. You have to work upon that skeleton. Also because of the time constraints, it's not like you have time to explore [much]. There's a little bit of plug and play. I rehearsed most of that show with stage managers, and then I had a couple of sessions with Kathleen Marshall for one of the numbers. The amazing dance captains taught me all the dance stuff. I'm not a dancer. They were so patient with me. It was really fun, too. I had so much to learn in such a short time that there was no time to worry about it. There was no time to judge myself. I don't remember the first time I went on at all. I remember Fran, who was dressing me, was like, "You're not going to remember this. Just get ready. You're going to feel like you're shot out of a cannon but I'm gonna be there for you. 'Right foot in the shoe, left foot in the shoe. Give me your right arm....' We'll get you dressed." Matthew was so kind. Any time I messed up, he freakin' loved it! His eyes would get so wide and all, "Hee, hee, hee, what's coming? How are you gonna fix it?" The glee in his eyes!

You didn't have to audition.
Yeah, that was wild. On the marquee, Kelli and Matthew were above the title, so they wanted to put my name with Matthew's. I felt really uncomfortable with that. It was like "Matthew Broderick and some girl you've never heard of" or "Matthew Broderick and NOT Kelli O'Hara." It felt like I cheated. I was looking around like, is anyone going to notice that I didn't really earn this? It felt really weird to me, really weird.

And you had Kelli's dressing room.
She was right on deck level, right off of stage right. They put in a bathroom for her. She left me this beautiful white couch and a couple of art pieces. It felt very fancy to me. The company was so sweet and kind and welcoming. It's a lot of change and upheaval and everybody was really on board.

Was that true in terms of filling in as a leader of the company, too?
I got the feeling that Kelli had a very open-door policy and wasn't precious about time alone. I was trying to fit the tone that had been set up: Matthew's room was where people went after the show to have a cocktail. I very much looked to him as the leader of the company.

"You're beautiful as you feel." In *Beautiful*.
(Joan Marcus)

That show closed a few months later. Did you know *Beautiful* was coming?

I remember auditioning for *Rocky* and *Beautiful* while I was in *Nice Work*, so those seemed like maybe some possibilities for work coming up. I remember reading about *Beautiful* and thinking, "Wow, that could either be really cool or a disaster," because it seemed like the most un-Broadway thing—the opposite of razzle-dazzle and jazz hands. By the time my agent called with the offer, I was very confused because I had heard that Carole was nervous for this to happen and she wasn't really involved. I remember saying, "I don't feel comfortable unless I know that this has her blessing." My agent helped set up a call with Sherry [King's manager and daughter]. I was trying to figure out how to say, "I'm so honored that you guys have come to me but I don't feel comfortable moving forward unless I know that Carole wants this to happen and that she wants this story told." I already started to feel a really intense responsibility for the task at hand. After that conversation, I felt like I had more clarity that Carole definitely did believe in the project. She was blessing it, but she basically needed to keep her distance. The story goes that [Carole had heard that a musical was being developed and] when Sherry took over as her manager, one of the first things on the list of what needed to be done was "kill the Carole King musical." So Sherry went to an early reading and then came back to her mom and was like, "I don't think you should kill this. This could be really good." [Then] they were doing another presentation and Carole watched the first act. At the break she told Sherry, "Please tell them they're amazing and they're doing an awesome job, but this is just too hard for me to watch. I have to leave."

Did they want you to try to sound like her?

Funnily enough, no one on the team really spoke about it, so I took the reins on how I wanted to craft the sound. One of the first things I did was take out vibrato. On the cast recording, if I go back and listen to it, it sort of sounds different to me in terms of where I felt I ended up later in the run. I was always kind of working on it because I wasn't trying to do a mimicry. I knew that I couldn't. She has such a unique voice, and as I started to work on it, I just went on a deep dive and gobbled up all the information I could. I listened to everything I could find and watched every interview. I remember trying to get really technical too early, trying to analyze her voice too soon. And then I remember just thinking, "Hang on, you're not ready for this. You gotta just listen and absorb it. Listen for the vibe and how it makes you feel." In the end, that was something I could connect with more. Why do people love her? What is it that you feel when you listen to her? There was just an extreme authenticity to her. I never felt like there was anything between her heart and the sound that came out of her mouth. She was a vessel for her spirit, and her soul just came right out. I think that's why people responded to her in the way they did. In some ways that was freeing, and in some ways it was frightening because it was like, "Oh great, just do that. Just figure THAT out." I was always fine-tuning the technical stuff. "Oh, that's what she does there!" Or, "She does that sort of shaping of her mouth." We have very different instruments. Her cords are different, the structure of her face is different. So sometimes I had to lean more into her phrasing than her sound or tone. But I love that stuff. I find that so fascinating. I've always been fascinated by people's voices and accents and stuff like that. I loved doing that work.

Were you doing the same kind of work to capture her physicality?
Oh sure. I'm a very visual person, so I collect a lot of pictures. I always get an album together. I visualize things when I'm working on a project or a character. I had so many photos on my phone! One of the things I always remember going back to was her smile, especially when she was performing. It just kind of beamed out of her. The wigs and costumes, by the amazing Chuck LaPointe and Alejo Vietti, respectively, did a ton of the work. That long wig was just amazing. If Carole and Beyoncé had a baby—man, I loved that wig.

You were now a leading lady....
Yeah, how did that happen? We went out of town to San Francisco. There was so much working and reworking and tweaking things. Anika Larsen and Jarrod Spector and I got very close and fell in love with [the people we were playing]. We really felt like we had a responsibility because they were all living artists.

What was it like when you finally got to meet Carole?
[It was the first day of rehearsals in New York after the San Francisco run.] And it was a surprise! Jarrod Spector and I saw her down the hallway at the rehearsal hall and thought, "WHAT?" She got into an elevator and he and I got into a separate one. It was like a meet-cute from a romantic comedy. The elevator doors opened and there she was! I think I just started to cry. I was overwhelmed. I had spent all this time studying this person and trying to feel aligned with her. There she was standing in front of me and I was thinking, "I know I don't ACTUALLY know you and I have no right to hug you. I don't want to be overly familiar, but...." She just looked right at me and folded me into her arms.

You had the presence of mind to realize that even though you had gotten intimate with Carole the character, that's not Carole the woman.
Yes! I feel like I know you, but I know that I don't. I know what I think I know of you. She said [to the cast], "I just wanted to show up. I've heard such amazing things from friends who saw

the show in San Francisco. I wanted to thank you all for the amazing work you've been doing, and I wanted you to hear it from me about why you haven't met me until now." I felt like I already understood, because the more I got to know about her … of course she wouldn't want to watch a musical about herself. That is not who she is. That's sort of the essence of her character. That made total sense to me, but it was very cool of her to show up and say, "I am so behind you," but also just be really honest and vulnerable. It wasn't until a couple of months later, after we opened, that she surprised us and came to the show. She literally had a wig and glasses on in the audience so nobody would recognize her. We do our bows and Jarrod Spector is making the Broadway Cares/Equity Fights AIDS speech and he's doing a bang-up job. We got to the point where he was like, "… and food banks and hospice care …" and people were going "Wow," and I thought, "We are gonna raise some money tonight! People are really into this speech!" And then I realize it's because Carole King is walking on from stage right. I saw Jarrod literally double over like the breath went out of him before I realized [what was happening]. He couldn't believe it. He just collapsed in half with this look of delight and awe and surprise and shock on his face, and then there she was. I was trying not to poop my pants or cry. And I was trying to catch her eye, like, "Are we cool?" Because she had just seen me attempt to portray her life! She met my eyes and she just gave me the biggest hug. My belly was in my feet. My bottom just dropped out. She got three people to each bid ten grand for her to sing "You've Got a Friend." I remember her saying something like, "It was so fascinating to watch you portray my younger self because I got to see me the way other people have described me to myself." I was so in shock. … I wanted to know everything about what she thought and I was also terrified to hear what she thought. She was totally gracious about it and very moved.

Was it odd to you that she hadn't come to opening night?
Not at all. With what I had learned about her as a person, I understood her not coming to opening. I don't want to go to openings!

Do you not like going to opening night?
Sometimes I've had really fun opening nights. I don't love all the press. I don't love getting dressed up. It's usually at the end of the week, too. So, it's like you've done your week of work and then you've got to work for three or four more hours. Opening night is not for the cast and crew. It's for everybody else, for the investors. And that's really important. But to me, it's an extended work week. Openings on Broadway are fantastic and exciting and all that. But it's a responsibility.

I have heard similar things said about Tony nominations; as wonderful as it is to be nominated, it's responsibility and pressure to represent the show optimally.
That's how I see it. Certainly, the first time through it felt like a complete whirlwind. It's like, "Wait, I have to find another dress to wear [for each event]? I can't wear the same thing?" Now I've had the blessing of working with some wonderful stylists. I'd rather spend money on food and travel. I can appreciate beautiful clothes, but I like it much better when someone's like, "Would you like to borrow this?" Like Cinderella. And then just give it back.

When you have a spring opening …
It stacks up. Rehearsals and previews and changes and opening and Tonys. It's amazing anyone survives. People are on steroids. Doctors are coming to give everyone flu shots.

Everyone's drinking potions to try to get through their performances. Everyone's kind of running on empty. I'm convinced there is a better way to structure things. I totally understand that it is part of our job to market the show, but if the marketing of the product is causing the actual product to suffer … how could we make that better? I don't understand everything a producer does. I don't expect a producer to understand everything I do. But at some point, shouldn't we all get in a room and talk about this? Sometimes it just feels like no one's explained what the other does and there's this huge impasse.

How did it feel as the leading lady?
I really felt a lot of comfort because I felt like I was representing Carole. I never really felt like it was about me. I could always default to Carole. I could always talk about Carole. That's why people were coming to the show. I wasn't a known name or entity.

But as soon as the show opened, you became a known entity. It wasn't just the show that was hot; you were. Fans were lining up at the stage door. People were sending you gifts.
I was kind of tickled by it, but I also found it really overwhelming. The first time I remember getting a picture someone had drawn of me, I was like, "What???" What that person is responding to, hopefully, is the magic that's created. The person doesn't know me. It's all through a lens, through a camera, or through stage lights. It's through an illusion that a bunch of people are creating together. There's the stage, there's the audience, and there's the magic in the middle. They're responding to that magic. I put [my performance] out in the universe, and then whatever the audience is bringing to it and whatever I put out meet in the middle. I'm a spiritual person. That's God. That's being a vessel. There's a part that maybe I have control of, but there's a part that I don't have control of, and that's the beauty of it. If someone writes me a letter about something they felt or experienced, that is bigger than me. And that's also something they were a part of. Sometimes meeting a fan, if they say, "I love you," or, "You're my favorite," I try to take it in and say, "Thank you so much," but to me, it's more like, I'm so glad you were touched by the performance or the songs moved you. It's about being a part of something bigger. That was my first experience of people putting it all on me and I was very uncomfortable with that.

So how do you deal with that?
In the beginning I would get the letter and look at it and then put it aside. I didn't know how to answer it. I didn't know if I was supposed to answer it. People were getting very personal and I didn't know whether I should respond. All of a sudden, it was like there was this other responsibility that I had, and I felt uncomfortable. It was very weird. There were a couple of instances later in my career where I had some scary moments with people whose behaviors were becoming unhealthy and trying to get a little too close. Sometimes I think people mistake the vulnerability of a character for a performer's vulnerability. The superfans can form an unhealthy attachment. If someone writes you and you write back and then they write you again and then they start to think that they're your friend and they know you, that can get to be a slippery slope. There are people that are really respectful and when I or another performer have been a part of creating something that has deeply affected them, that's the best! That's why I wanted to get into this. I have had that experience with a performance and been like, "Oh my God, that just made me feel so much. I wonder if I could ever do that for someone." But I have had moments where I can tell people want something from me that is not appropriate or healthy for me or them. It's been a learning curve. Your instincts get better.

When it's unhealthy, what do you think they want?

I get really concerned for these young fans, especially with social media. There's so much you go through as a young person. There are so many intense emotions. I get very concerned about people attaching importance to performers that they see, because I think they get caught up in the illusion of the performer. They say things like, "You're so perfect. I want to be just like you." And I want to say, "Honey, I'm a mess. You don't want to be me, you want to be you. You might like or admire this one part of your perception of my personality, but don't get caught up in thinking that someone else is perfect." There's a lot of poison in social media. I get very concerned. It started with *Beautiful* and then certainly with *Waitress*, a lot of young, vulnerable women I met were in bad relationships. When I was doing *Carousel*, I was having trouble keeping up with fan mail. My wonderful dresser, Lolly, said, "Jess, maybe writing out their feelings was good for them, whether or not you write back. You do what you can, but hopefully knowing that someone heard their feelings, maybe that's gift enough." It meant a lot to me to think about it that way. I don't know how people deal with fandom and stardom. I think it's really unnatural.

You went back to the Tonys for *Beautiful*. Was it fun this time?

It was more fun. I had a little bit more of an idea of what was required and expected, and I had more help. Two of the ladies that were on our press team, Molly and Chelsea, were amazing. They were just so helpful with everything. They helped set up fittings. Molly helped make me a calendar of all the things I had to be at. "We're going to find an outfit for each one, so you know what you're wearing. We're going to get this all laid out." I felt a little bit more prepared. And I felt a little bit less like the new kid at school. I felt like I proved myself a little bit more. I felt really proud of my work. So I guess in some ways I felt like I could own being there a little bit more. But look at the people I was in the category with! That was insane [Sutton Foster, Idina Menzel, Kelli O'Hara, and Mary Bridget Davies]. And then it happened. It was the right role at the right time. There was just something that fit about it. And the fact that I got to meet Carole and have that influence in my life at that point, to learn about her growing into her fame and artistry while I felt like I was being asked to grow into my artistry and more of a public persona than I had ever experienced before … I felt like I could kind of watch her and see how she did it. She was very much a role model at that time for me. It felt like she had given me this huge gift. [She tears up.] It really felt like that. It was nothing that I ever thought would happen. But I guess that's the beauty of it, too. I was really proud, the proudest that I've been.

Why does this make you choke up?

Because I've always had a hard time owning my wins. Balancing modesty or humility with owning what I was bringing to the table. But that was one of those moments where, on a very different scale, the world was telling me, "Yeah, you do this. You do this in your way. You, Jessie, have been given certain gifts." I guess that's why I get choked up. That's always been hard for me. *Beautiful* and the Tony win … but even just the process of going through *Beautiful* and realizing how Mark Bruni, the director, trusted me. I was regarded as a legitimate practitioner in that room. That was really cool. I really like the work, and the fact that people respected me at that level was really big for me. I wasn't a kid playing at it anymore. I remember getting to the *Beautiful* party [on Tony night] and everyone was so happy for me. That was a really generous group. As a little kid, I used to draw a lot. We would have these drawing contests in grade school. You'd win a teddy bear. I won a bunch of years in a row and I remember everyone getting mad at me. So, I think, you know, formative childhood memories … somewhere in my little brain I had sort of carved out that me succeeding meant someone else was lacking. I know now, thank the Lord, that is not always the case.

What made you decide to leave the show?
I was cooked. I was so exhausted. I think I stayed six months after my contract. I'd never done a show that long. It was a year longer than any show I'd done. My back was always crazy. Vocally I stayed pretty strong, but I was always doing a ton of physical therapy. And I didn't really know how to do the work for that long. I felt like I wasn't doing it in the way that I wanted it to be done anymore. Maybe I was getting a little stale and maybe it was time for somebody else to do this. I was burnt out. My attitude wasn't as positive because I was so tired and I was really aware of that because again, I felt like I was supposed to be the leader of this company and I just didn't have much extra energy.

Was it weird when your sister ended up in the role?
That was whackadoo for both of us. We had a lot of conversations about it. She was like, "My agent keeps calling me about auditioning. I can't tell if this is a good idea or a terrible idea." I really give her a lot of credit because she talked to me about it, she was open about it. I got to see her do it in Chicago and then on Broadway. I was kind of like, "What is this going to be like?" Lights come up and it was weird because I know what it feels like to be inside that picture, but then I was seeing the picture with the clothes and the hair.… But she started and I was like, "Oh, OK, cool! This is the way Abby's gonna do it." She killed it. She absolutely killed it.

Let's talk about *Waitress*.
I first got approached about *Waitress* right before we opened *Beautiful*. They were doing the workshop. I heard Sara Bareilles's demos and I was floored, but also at a point where I couldn't handle it. I couldn't do a workshop all day and then do the show at night. I had to tell my agent, "Please tell them that I'm so interested, but I just can't swing it with the schedule right now." Thank God it came back around again. There was another reading. I was still in *Beautiful* at the time [but had settled into the run and] at that point I couldn't say no again. I just fell in love with it. [We did the try-out at A.R.T. in Cambridge and] that was a great way to spend a summer. We felt like we were at summer camp. I was surprised how powerful that show was for people. I was very proud of it because we all cared deeply. It was a lot of work. But we just felt like the heart and soul of it was so precious that it needed to be kept pure, it needed to be fought for, and I think that a lot of people responded to that. It was this great rough-and-tumble group of flawed people on stage, and as an audience member you could relate to that.

What was the rehearsal room like?
It was very collaborative. There were so many moving parts because it was a new show. Sometimes when you are working on something new, it can be hard to suss out why it's not working if it's not working. Is it because what is written is not working? Or we don't know how to play it? Or how to stage it? It's not like when you're doing a revival and you can change the interpretation or the lighting or the staging but you can't really change a scene. Everyone also

had the sense of wanting to honor what Adrienne Shelly had created for the original screen-play. She wrote and directed the film and she was tragically murdered just before it went to Sundance. It was awful. So there was this feeling around the whole thing, this spirit to it. Her work was having another life. Similar to *Beautiful*, we felt like we had this responsibility to uplift and uphold. I felt like we had this bigger picture to honor. We would always come back to that, especially when it got hard, because there were days it was so fucking frustrating. There were so many props. [Director] Diane Paulus said, "We have to make this feel like a working, breathing diner." So, on top of trying to figure everything else out, it's like, so and so still needs the plate and it's got to have this food on it. Eric, who plays the cook, has to figure out when to start cooking . . . there were so many moving parts. We were brain dead. If something worked, you'd have to remember what you did and replicate it eight times a week. But I remember that Sara was so jazzed about the whole thing. She wanted to be at every rehearsal. She was fascinated, I think, by the process of how this was going to be made, so she was in the room. A lot of emotion, frustration, a lot of elation. It's like, "Oh my God, it's working and people are moved by it!" It was an intense period. And then we got to Broadway and it wasn't like we were starting over but there were changes and some new cast. We changed the opening number I don't know how many times. At one point we cut it entirely. Diane wasn't precious about stuff. I remember opening night felt incredible. That felt like such a win.

You had this big showpiece song to hit every night. Were you ever self-conscious about it or worried about getting there?
The show was structured so well, I didn't feel like I had to do a lot of muscling to get there. The character is led so beautifully to that moment. You start the show, you get on the train, and all of a sudden, you're at "She Used to Be Mine" station and you've kind of picked up all the pieces you need to make your journey there. Also, it's about being stripped down and vul-nerable and messy, so I knew I didn't have to be perfect. That all being said, I was terrified of that song during rehearsal. I was so self-conscious about it. I didn't want to touch it. I hadn't gotten through it. I couldn't sing it yet. Any time it came up in rehearsal, I was like, "Diane, can we work on it tomorrow?" I remember just wanting to hide.

You got another Tony nomination.
We were always joking we got invited to the Hamiltons that year. And the Pulse shooting happened the week before. It kind of took all the BS out of the room. Everybody was so glad to be there in an environment celebrating a community that I felt had always been [about inclusion]. Everybody was just glad to be alive and safe. We were mourning. There was this higher purpose that had taken over the whole show. Everybody's speeches were all about in-clusivity. And *Hamilton*. Thank God that show came along when it did.

You already expressed that you don't like having pictures taken, so what was it like having your picture on top of taxis and on billboards all over the city?
I cried the first time I saw the key art. I was very uncomfortable. I was like, "Who's that sup-posed to be? That doesn't look like Jenna." I understand that it needs to be marketable and they explained that they wanted it to be a mix between the character and me. I was so dolled up. I was like, "she doesn't look like a waitress. It looks like she went to the beauty parlor and then came in for her shift. Can we please do something to make her look like a working girl Can you put a pencil behind my ear or something?" They ended up photo-shopping it in! I don't think

anyone noticed, but it made a big difference to me. Oftentimes my first reaction to seeing a picture of myself is not great. But that was the first time I'd ever experienced anything like that and I was just very confused. By the time it started to go up all over the city, I was much more comfortable. I remember when the big one went up in Times Square and I was like, "That's my face! I can live with that! Look at all the hair pieces they put in. That looks nice."

You described leaving *Beautiful* feeling burnt out. When you left *Waitress*...
It was pretty much the same. I was so exhausted. I wasn't healthy. I wasn't in a good mental place. My body was exhausted. Near the end I found out I had an allergy to gluten. I was having all these body aches and mood swings during most of the run. I had been throwing flour in the air and singing. We switched to gluten-free flour and it made a huge difference. I was not in peak shape for that one. And afterward I really realized how much of a dark place I had to be in for that show. Just exploring really bottom of the barrel stuff, being in the mindset of an abused woman for two years will take a toll. The bounce back from that was long. It took a long time to feel like I was ready to do anything again.

Was doing the show not an overall joyous experience?
There were parts that were ridiculously joyous. I adored doing the show, and I loved it and I loved all the people. I have made some of my best and lifelong friends during *Waitress*. But it was also fucking hard. It just took a lot out of me, and everything else in my life had to revolve around that.

So you bounced back from two years as an abused woman by ... doing *Carousel* and playing another abused woman!
Can you believe it? I never would have planned it. But looking at those experiences, *Carousel* was one of the best Broadway experiences I've ever had. It was joyous. I was really careful about what I wanted to do next and thank the Lord I had a choice. I was trepidatious. I'd done the show several times before, but I'd never done Julie. I never really felt like I understood her. When I got to play her, I was like, "I have got to stop thinking about Kelli O'Hara, because it's never going to be sung better." I just had to get over that hurdle. I almost laughed the day I had my first music rehearsal with [musical director] Andy Einhorn. I was like, "Wait, Andy ... I only sing one-and-a-half songs? This is incredible!" Talk about how shows were written versus how they are written now! I look back to the rehearsal room in *Waitress* and I was so gung-ho. "I don't need to leave the stage. I can do this and then run over here...." I didn't have the wherewithal to know what I was getting myself into, I think. It's not "woe is me," I just think it's fascinating looking back now—I had one pee break in the whole show. That was it. [In *Carousel*] Lindsay Mendez and I used to eat chips while Josh Henry was singing his guts out. We're like, "Man, this is a good gig!" It was also really a chance to enjoy the atmosphere backstage again and to be backstage with people. It was an incredible group. Josh was a big part of that. He was an amazing leader. We would circle up before every performance and just take hands. He'd pick someone for a word of the day and that was the day's focus. Everybody just felt really strongly about what we were doing. It was an interesting blended group because there were a lot of people from the ballet world and Renée Fleming was coming from the opera world. Everybody had such an appreciation for what people were bringing to the table. Sort of an awe. I was in awe of the dancers. "How can you do that?" They were magical to me.

Tackling one of the all-time greatest musical theater moments, "the bench scene," with Joshua Henry in *Carousel*.
(Julieta Cervantes)

As someone who had never seen your work in Chicago, I was really surprised by your casting because I did not know you had that legit soprano voice. Was showing that part of the motivation for doing it?

Yeah. In looking for the next thing, I do have an eye out for something different or something challenging. I want to keep people guessing. I knew I'd get to do something vocally that a lot of people hadn't seen me do before. It was a big challenge vocally because I hadn't sung like that in so long. And Andy wanted things big and grand. We really felt we were being stretched. Initially it felt very disconnected to me. There was a disconnect between the scenes and the songs. I felt like I was putting something on when I was singing to achieve the sound he was after. It took time to get comfortable with making sound that way again.

When you say "he wanted it grand," that's what the music calls for, right? What else do you think he was asking for?

I think it also has to do with the production of sound, how much they wanted to lean or not lean on the mic. They wanted us to produce a lot of sound. There are definitely ways of lessening the grandeur of it, making it breathier or something as simple as the shaping of consonants. Easing into notes rather than starting everything right on the breath. A more operatic approach, which I hadn't really done since college. That was also [director] Jack O'Brien's vision. The set design was very classic. Jack was really interested in exploring the larger scope of the story, the spiritual aspect of it. So, to me, it made sense that there was sort of a vastness to it. There was no easing into anything. You had to commit, especially with the singing, but even with the speaking.

What do you want to say about working with [director] Jack O'Brien?

I love working with Jack. He was soft and tough at the same time. After we opened, he was teasing me about how long it took me to find the character. I think he was on to something. We had so much time in that process, we were almost spoiled. Jack famously says, "How much time does it take to put up a show? It takes how much time you've got." If you've got two weeks, it takes two weeks. If you've got two months, it's going to take two months and you're going to use all that time. I decided to really work hard to not push or put flesh on a thing that didn't have any skeleton yet. I was waiting and watching. I was also scared. I remember we didn't touch "If I Loved You" for a long time. I kept being like, "We can wait on that." It was like "She Used to Be Mine." "Let's do that next week." I was really intimidated by it. It's one of the best love scenes in musical theater ever written. I didn't want to fuck it up. It wasn't until we really started to pick it apart ... we staged and re-staged that thing I don't know how many times. It might have been twenty times. Jack would be like, "I think we can keep digging." Jack is so smart. He's so smart. The moments that I remember the most with him and am so grateful to him for are the moments in the second half where Billy dies. Julie is over his dead body and the guidance he gave me there, the encouragement to really just ... wait, wait, wait, wait, wait, wait, wait, wait. Stave off any grief, stay in shock for as long as possible. I really trusted him. He would talk to me differently than he would talk to Josh or Alex or Renée because he knows what he needs from you and me is going to be different. He might [give me a direction today] but with you, he might plant a seed and let it marinate and let you work, and then address it on Tuesday. Or he knows, "I know that needs to be fixed, but they're not ready for it yet." So he won't tell you. He won't give you [the note] until you're ready. There are only a few people I have worked with who are like that. I think that is such a big deal. You feel really safe in his room. You feel like you're in good hands. I always knew we were taken care of. I always knew there was someone driving the ship. He has the most vast vocabulary I have ever experienced. I'd be like, "I would love to do that thing if you tell me what it means."

How did it feel to have *Carousel* close so prematurely?
I could have done that longer. I think everybody could have. It was heartbreaking for a lot of folks because there were a lot of Broadway debuts and they were having such a wonderful time. Some of us had been seeing the warning signs. There were light houses, people's agents were checking in. It wasn't a shock to me.

Next you went to Washington and did *The Music Man*.
Yeah, to work with Mark Bruni again. I was like, "Let's do it again as adults." There was so much at stake for both of us the first time. He's so positive and calm. He had the best attitude. Putting together something like that in two weeks can be such a shit show. His attitude made it really delightful. My whole goal for that was to have fun. I used to watch that movie as a kid. My neighbors had a copy and I used to go over and knock on the door, "Can I borrow *The Music Man*?" And even though I knew it was too fast, I was not sure I'd ever get the chance to do it again. Norm Lewis was so much fun! Everybody worked their butts off and did a great job. I had never worked at The Kennedy Center and I really wanted to. I'm really glad I did it.

What is it that you think you want now?
Voiceover for animation! [Other than that] ... as crazy and confusing and emotional as this pandemic has been, it has been an opportunity to craft some sort of life—a day-to-day life that doesn't have to do with eight shows a week or doing press. I think that's been so good for me because I've been able to reassess and re-engage in parts of my life that I have been absent from, even if it's something as seemingly silly as cleaning my house on a regular basis or cooking again. It's been so interesting to look at my life, sometimes on a daily basis, and think, "How do I want to spend my time today?" When it comes to a project—does this need to be seen, does this need to be heard? That's really important to me. [I want to do TV and film but] I think I will always want to come back to the theater. It's part of me. I will still always sit out in the house during tech if I'm not being used. Like I'm back in high school and I have a free period and I can run to the theater. I'm at home with my people.

Marin Mazzie

As told by: Lynn Ahrens (lyricist, *Ragtime*), Becky Ann Baker (co-star, *Merrily We Roll Along*), Jason Danieley (husband and co-star, *Next to Normal*), Judy Kuhn (peer), David Loud (musical director and conductor, *And the World Goes 'Round*, *Ragtime*), Brian Stokes Mitchell (co-star, *Ragtime*, *Kiss Me, Kate*, *Kismet*, *Man of La Mancha*), Martin Moran (co-star, *Doonesbury*, *Big River*, and *Spamalot*), Donna Murphy (co-star, *Passion*), Kelli O'Hara (peer), Molly Ranson (co-star, *Carrie*), Christopher Sieber (co-star, *On the Twentieth Century*, *Spamalot*), Joseph Thalken (musical director), Valerie Wright (co-star, *And the World Goes 'Round*), Karen Ziemba (co-star, *And the World Goes 'Round*, *Bullets Over Broadway*).

On September 19, 2018, the sidewalks of 45th Street between Broadway and Eighth were so jam-packed with people on both sides of the street they were spilling out into the gutters, obstructing oncoming traffic. The throngs weren't on their way to the theater or lining up at a stage door. They just stood, eyes cast upward at the marquees of the block's seven theaters. At 6:45 p.m., just as the last of the sky's light was receding, the bulbs and neon illuminating the theaters went dark, as they did at every Broadway playhouse. On those of the marquees with digital capability, an image appeared: a serene, luminous face framed by a thick, blonde mane, and the words, "In Memory of Marin Mazzie. October 9, 1960–September 13, 2018." The crowd erupted into spontaneous, robust applause, sustaining their cheers and appreciation for the entire minute of this tribute. One block over, at the Broadhurst, company members of *Anastasia* stood on the fire escape waving sunflowers, Mazzie's favorite. On 41st Street, at the Nederlander Theater, where Jason Danieley, Mazzie's husband, was appearing in *Pretty Woman*, the marquee's montage of Mazzie photos was punctuated with the phrases "Funny Woman," "Fierce Woman," "Modern Woman," and "Strong Woman." When it was over, people didn't move. They weren't ready. Friends, fans, former colleagues, and strangers alike lingered, telling stories and jokes, sharing memories, and celebrating the life of one of Broadway's most beloved contemporary figures.

Marin Mazzie was born in Rockford, Illinois, to parents who loved musicals. Their vast collection of cast albums worked their magic on Mazzie, who began taking singing lessons at twelve. She graduated from Western Michigan University in 1982, majoring in theater, and in 1984 found herself touring the country in the musical *Doonesbury*. Back in New York, a quick succession of replacement roles followed (*Big River*, *Into the Woods*, *And the World Goes 'Round*) before Mazzie landed her breakout role. In Sondheim and Lapine's 1994 *Passion*, she was a revelation as Clara, a voluptuous rival to Donna Murphy's plain, sickly Fosca, competing for and defining variations on love. Mazzie was Tony-nominated for her efforts, as she was again for her next show, *Ragtime*. In that musical, full of plot and characters vying for audience attention, Mazzie's Mother had arguably the show's most profound arc, going from stifled repression to acceptance and loving empathy. Late in the second act, when she stood alone on stage and unleashed the searing "Back to Before," she never failed to stop the show. *Kiss Me, Kate* followed, with Mazzie exploring the spectrum's opposite end; the restraint she showed in *Ragtime* gave way to wild abandon, as she and Brian Stokes Mitchell mined comedy gold. Mazzie earned yet another Tony nomination. She teamed with Mitchell again in 2002 in *Man of La Mancha*, replacing Mary Elizabeth Mastrantonio, and again in the Encores! production of *Kismet*. In 2006 she stepped into *Spamalot* and then in 2010, the short-lived play *ENRON*. Later that same year, she and Danieley took over the leading roles in *Next to Normal*, a show about a family fracturing as they cope with the wife's bipolar depression. Mazzie called the show among the most rewarding she had done. In 2012, Mazzie headlined an off-Broadway production of the infamous Broadway flop *Carrie*, which failed to redeem the show, but showcased Mazzie's incredible range. In 2014, she was the outrageous and soused diva Helen Sinclaire, in another disappointment, Woody Allen's *Bullets Over Broadway*. It was on opening night of the 2015 Encores! production of *Zorba!* that Mazzie learned she had ovarian cancer. She fought hard, performing on concert stages, often with Danieley, as frequently as she could while undergoing treatment. In 2016, she triumphantly replaced Kelli O'Hara in what would be her final musical, *The King and I*. The headline of Ben Brantley's *The New York Times* review? "How to Keep a Musical Great? Call Marin Mazzie."

Mazzie was very public about her diagnosis, determined to help others, if she could, with her story. And she performed to the end, appearing in 2018 in Terrance McNally's play, *Fire and Air*, even as she underwent exhausting treatments. "Singing involves the interconnection of mind and body. It has always been healing for me," she told *The New York Times* in a 2017 interview with Susan Gubar. "It makes me feel extremely alive, whether I am playing a character or in concert. 'Live in the moment' or 'life is a gift': I always believed that, but never before felt the power of life and love, of an outpouring from my husband, family and community." That same outpouring was so palpably on display during that balmy September marquee dimming.

Indelibly hating men, with Brian Stokes Mitchell in *Kiss Me, Kate*.
(Photofest)

It was after that event that I found myself on the phone with Norm Lewis. I told him that I had actually spoken to Mazzie about participating in the first of my Broadway books, *Nothing Like a Dame*. She had agreed to do it, but our schedules did not align in time and then, once I embarked on this one, I was too late. "Do it anyway," implored Lewis. "Talk to people about her, since you can't talk to her." I didn't know if it would work, but I did know that I very much wanted to honor Mazzie and contribute to the telling of her story. So, what follows is a departure from every other chapter in this book. You'll hear not from Mazzie herself, but from those she worked with and loved. I asked people, as much as possible, to stick to witness accounts. What did you see? What did she tell you? What did you share? The speakers didn't always address those questions head-on, but universally they all answered another one: what did Marin Mazzie give?

Marin Mazzie was born in Illinois to loving parents. She went to Catholic school and described having a happy childhood.

Marin Mazzie	
Where's Charley?	off-Broadway, 1983
Doonesbury	National Tour, 1984
Big River	Broadway, 1985
Into the Woods	Broadway, 1989
And the World Goes 'Round	off-Broadway, 1991; National Tour, 1992
Passion	Broadway, 1994
Out of This World	Encores!, 1995
Ragtime	Broadway, 1998
Kiss Me, Kate	Broadway, 1999; West End 2001
Man of La Mancha	Broadway, 2003
Kismet	Encores!, 2006
On the Twentieth Century	Broadway, 2005
Spamalot	Broadway, 2006
Next to Normal	Broadway, 2010
Carrie	off-Broadway, 2012
Bullets Over Broadway	Broadway, 2014
Zorba!	Encores!, 2015
The King and I	Broadway, 2016

KAREN ZIEMBA: Her father was a real liberal activist. He really was not afraid and she learned from that. And she lived that life too. She was such a loving, open person and always wanted everybody to feel comfortable. Her dad was quite an exemplary man. A really good cook, too! She was influenced by him a lot. His whole outlook on life, she really took on. She walked the walk. She had such a wicked sense of humor that she was really fun to be around. Her mom and dad were very much that way, too.

BECKY ANN BAKER: I met her the summer she was getting her Equity card at The Barn Theater [Michigan]. *Unsinkable Molly Brown*. She was in the chorus but she was creating a very lively character with a full back story. My first impression of her was that she had a lot going on in the smallest of roles imaginable. We did *A Chorus Line* the summer of '85 at the Barn as well. I was playing Cassie and Marin was Morales. They had her in this dark, dark wig. She was so clearly a white girl. It was hilarious. Baroness Morales. She and Scott Burkell and Jonathan Larson had this wonderful cabaret show out of The Barn. They had been apprentices together for two seasons and they had written this entire club act with John's music. And when they first got to New York, they performed it at places like Don't Tell Mama. It was great. So for the first many years, we would sit in my living room and sing through John's early, early work. I think they were called "J. Giltz." It was very funny stuff. We'd all go see them at whatever little cabaret they were in.

Mazzie made her New York debut at the Equity Library Theater in *Where's Charley?* Her first big production contract was the national tour of *Doonesbury*, a show based on Garry Trudeau's comic strip that flopped on Broadway, but toured nonetheless.

MARTIN MORAN: We were kids. There was such an excitement at being employed, and she was very, very new. We both were. But she was like a ball of sunshine. We'd sit on the bus, chatting away. We had signed nine-month contracts but we closed suddenly in Los Angeles, five weeks into our run. We all were really sad. What I remember about Marin was how comforting she was. She said, with absolute confidence and absolute surety, "You know, it's going to be completely fine. It's all great. We're going to get the next thing and it's going to be fine." I didn't believe that. But indeed, she got *Merrily We Roll Along* in La Jolla within weeks, and I went home and booked this weird off-Broadway show where I met my husband, Henry Stram, who I've been with for thirty-seven years. When I was a waiter at Joe Allen, Kathy Bates said to me [in this business], "You need to have the heart of a child and the head of a bullet." Marin had the heart of a child and, in the most beautiful sense, the head of a bullet. She just knew [to stay on target] and you could feel that about her all those years ago.

Mazzie made her Broadway debut in 1985, as a replacement for the female lead in *Big River*.

MARTIN MORAN: I was understudying all the boys and they asked me to concentrate on Huck Finn even though I was told that Daniel Jenkins never misses. I'd only had the job for a couple of weeks and, lo and behold, Danny was struggling with a cold and I got a call that he was out. I ran to the theater and Marin was absolutely my anchor. She showed up for the understudy rehearsal, even though [she didn't have to]. She was like, "What do you want? Chicken soup? Chicken soup sound good? With some Saltines? I'll bring it to your dressing room." I went on that night and in the next couple of shows and she was just glorious supporting me. She was beautiful as Miss Mary Jane and we had a wonderful time. She befriends everyone immediately. She's just naturally a leader and a company member. She was this ball of support, the furnace you go to, to warm your hands. We had so much fun being on Broadway together.

JASON DANIELEY: During *Big River* she was called "Burperina." She could burp the alphabet with Carol Woods. They would burp "Happy Birthday." And she had this bawdy side, flashing her tits to the chorus during a quick change. There was this levity that not everybody has when they're the star.

BECKY ANN BAKER: She could belch an entire song. She could fill in enough air in her gut to be able to do it! It was gift. She could also get her whole fist in her mouth when she was younger!

JASON DANIELEY: She has small fists. And a big mouth.

BRIAN STOKES MITCHELL: She was a champion belcher. She could do that and then do these incredibly sophisticated, deep performances. That's a rare and wonderful person and my kind of person, I gotta say. She did not take herself seriously, but she was absolutely seriously committed to the work.

After a stint as Rapunzel in the original Broadway production of *Into the Woods*, Mazzie played Beth in another production, *Merrily We Roll Along*, at the Arena stage in 1990.

BECKY ANN BAKER: Marin, Mary Gordon Murray, and I shared a dressing room and it was always the best time ever. After a show we get this "Bang! Bang! Bang!" on the door. We're like, "Just a second, just a second." And then, we hear "Bang! Bang! Bang!" again. Really impatient. "It's Steve!" [Sondheim] We were all totally naked, but he was wanting to move on to other people. "Let him in. Let's go." I'll always remember the naked Sondheim moment.

In 1991, Mazzie replaced Karen Mason in the hit off-Broadway Kander and Ebb revue, *And the World Goes 'Round.*

DAVID LOUD (MUSICAL DIRECTOR): My impression of Marin at that time was that she came to New York mousy and not sure who she was, really, except she had this voice. And then she decided she was going be a leading lady, so she became blond and a little bit more buxom, and transformed herself to somebody who matched her voice. But by the time I met her, she had figured out who she was. She auditioned for *And the World Goes 'Round* and she was gorgeous and funny, and we just snapped her up. We couldn't get enough of her.

BECKY ANN BAKER: She definitely made a transformation, but she was always that person. She just knew she had to physicalize it. Of course she had her breasts done and, as was typical of Marin, she was very out about it. She would say to me, "I feel like my hips don't match my bust. If I can just get the balance right, I'm going to have this great body." And sure enough.... I think we threw her a party to reveal the breasts. Marin was always beautiful facially. Just stunning. She just had that perfect little nose and her skin was flawless. She could be that stunning, sexy woman, but she's also had just the most common sense of humor ever. Her sense of humor was hilarious and rude and down and dirty.

VALERIE WRIGHT: I'd never really met anyone like her. I was the understudy, so I watched her from the back of the house for a year and that was a tremendous learning experience. Marin had so many unbelievable gifts. She had an inner strength and a vulnerability, all at the same time. She could be a broad and she could be elegant and she could be hilarious and she could be heart-sinking.

KAREN ZIEMBA: She just had this kind of carriage about her. She had beautiful posture and this big, big smile. She fit in really well right away. There was a lot of laughter in that dressing room. And, of course, her vocal chops were just tremendous. She was very generous on stage. She'd look at you, not always out front. She stepped up to that plate beautifully because she wasn't insecure.

DAVID LOUD: Her "Colored Lights" was totally different from Karen Mason's. It was a much sunnier, more sort of California girl kind of experience. She could do that California girl thing very easily. And her "Ring Them Bells" was also very different from Karen's. Marin's was this triumph over the world. Her joy was so big.

JOSEPH THALKEN: There was one moment during the show where she would turn around and she'd always wink up at me where I was playing second keyboard. I looked forward to that.

KAREN ZIEMBA: She didn't miss shows. She was one of those. One of those old pros. Her voice was trained so well that she knew how to work around it if she ever felt a little like tickle or something.

VALERIE WRIGHT: Marin could really drink. We would go out and drink and the next day I would be sort of stumbling.

DAVID LOUD: Marin liked her wine. It never interfered with her show. Except once. We were in Chicago and the swing was from Chicago. She wanted to go on and Marin said, "I'll take the night off." The swing went on, and then the other girl who she covered was heaving, vomiting in the bathroom. The stage manager went and found Marin, who was eating with some friends at a nearby restaurant. When I say "eating" I mean "drinking." He said to her, "You have to come back and go on in the show!" [The first number she joined was "The Rink"] which meant that she had to come on in roller-skates. So, there I am in the pit. I see she's bright red in the face. At least three margaritas in her, laughing at the top of her lungs, going, "Hey! Hey!" waving to the audience. She comes on, roller-skating really fast, starts doing, like, a warm-up circle. She never stopped laughing the entire time. It's a miracle that nobody got hurt. They sobered her up during intermission. There was coffee and probably a shower involved.

VALERIE WRIGHT: It was quite honestly, one of the funniest things I have ever been involved with. Marin was having the best time. There was no guardrail or anything. I mean, at any time any one of us could have gone careening off into the orchestra! There she was, just having the time of her life.

JASON DANIELEY: Someone she knew, I don't remember how, had been diagnosed with AIDS and he came to see her that night. He passed like maybe a few months later. Her friend needed to see her and it meant so much to him. She believed that [her going on that night] was meant to happen.

In 1993, Mazzie was cast in a workshop of a show that changed everything for her. In Sondheim and Lapine's *Passion*, she was Clara, a beautiful married woman, having an affair with Giorgio (Jere Shea), with whom the sickly Fosca (Donna Murphy) is in love.

DONNA MURPHY: On the first day of rehearsal, they called our very small company at staggered times. [Before I went in] I was watching a little bit through the glass window of the door. She was singing at the piano with Peter Gallagher who was doing the workshop with us. I remember just looking at her—actually, I could hear her before I could see her—and I remember thinking, "That is gold. That sound is golden." And then I looked in the little window and I thought, "Oh my God, she is golden!" She had this long, long, long hair down to her butt, she looked to be a little bit tanned. She just looked golden. I had very, very short brown hair at the time and no makeup. I was dressed in my baggy black skirt. She was wearing a cute, short summer skirt and platform sandals and a little tank top. She looked sassy and gorgeous and golden. I felt a little bit like Fosca! "She's so beautiful. And I feel so ... not." But that passed super quickly because I opened the door, and she looked over, and she went "Donna Murphy!!!" And she opened her arms and wrapped me in the biggest hug. I just knew that we were going to be friends in a way that was going to go way beyond the show. In that first week, we often had lunch together. We sat out at the fountain at Lincoln Center. She told me about having worked with Steve and James before. She said, "But I don't pretend to know James. I'm a little nervous about him." James was quiet and not easy to read. And then we talked about family, and boyfriends, and husbands. There was a very easy, natural flow to our connection and communication. Having become friendly with so many friends of Marin's over the years, I've heard that from a lot of people. She was very open-hearted and had a great sense of humor about herself. And she was extremely hardworking and ambitious. [During rehearsal] I remember watching her and Peter and thinking how glorious the two of them were together. Occasionally, I will write in my script notes: "N.A.N."— "No Acting Necessary." Watching the two of them together, which Fosca would not have ever had the opportunity to do, she could only imagine it, I thought, "She [Fosca] couldn't have imagined anything more beautiful—and terrifying and depressing—than what I'm watching and listening to right now. It's rapturous. It's beauty on every level and connection." Donna the human was in awe and Donna the actress playing Fosca was [stunned]. Steve's notes to us were so brilliant: they were about the music, but also about the acting; why there was a quarter note rest as opposed to a half note rest and why there was an accelerando. I've worked with amazing composers, but I'd never heard anyone be that specific. Marin and Peter took the notes beautifully. James was very insistent on people remaining in the rehearsal space. He wanted people to remain in the room whether you were in the scene or not, so we were watching each other. I was so close to her in that rehearsal, and I would think, "Is there any part of her body that is tense?" There seemed to be such an ease about her, and that's so unfair to say because I know how hard she was working. Peter cracked me up and he definitely cracked Marin up. She was bawdy and fun. We were secure enough in our friendship and our working relationship that I remember that when I was getting more press opportunities than she was, she said, "I'm frustrated! I wish I had more press opportunities." I would say, "Honey, you're just not unattractive enough!" But she always said, "It's not that I'm jealous. I'm so happy for you. I just wish I could have some more of it, too."

MARTIN MORAN: I can remember how happy she was, when *Passion* was happening. That was a game-changer.

JASON DANIELEY: Jere Shea and his wife were having twins. He'd been stressed opening a show that didn't feel like it was working and James and Steve were using Jere as a scapegoat, kind of putting undue pressure on either his part or his performance. He was really under a lot of stress and his back went out. [The show begins and] he lays there with Marin straddling him, completely naked. He wears a flesh-colored dance belt and he must have put some Tiger Balm on his back and got some on his dance belt. She gets on top of him, completely naked, just before the curtain goes up. She started feeling a tingling down there and then a burning sensation. She said all she could hear in her head was [singing to the tune of "City of Fire" from *Sweeney Todd*] "Pussy on fire! Pussy on fire!" As soon as she got offstage they did a whore's bath with Wet Wipes.

DONNA MURPHY: There was a lot of concern for Marin's feeling of being safe backstage before the top of the show. We had the best stage manager, the goddess of stage management, the late Beverley Randolph. Once you've worked with Beverley, you don't want to work with anybody else. Beverley protected everybody. Marin really appreciated the amount of respect, but she also had an incredible sense of humor about the absurdity of being nude in bed with another actor.

In 1997, Mazzie was cast in *Ragtime*, the epic musical by Lynn Ahrens, Stephen Flaherty, and Terrence McNally, based on E. L. Doctorow's novel. Mazzie was Mother, a privileged, conservative woman from New Rochelle who is awakened to the world's realities.

LYNN AHRENS: Prior to *Ragtime* she had done a tour called *Music of the Night* that Garth Drabinsky produced. [When her contract was up] she didn't want to renew and he was furious with her, absolutely furious. And so, when *Ragtime* started to audition, he refused to bring her in. We went through I don't even know how many women auditioning for the show. We just couldn't find anybody who quite embodied that character and who quite could sing that song. And finally, he kind of grudgingly allowed her to be brought in. She sang "Back to Before" and we all fell on the ground. She just had it at that moment. Garth knew it, we all knew it, but getting her there was tough.

JASON DANIELEY: That company was like a family and Mother was probably the role that meant the most to her over her career and her life because of Mother's journey. She found a great responsibility to tell this woman's story as fully as she could. She was good friends until the day she died with all of those people. I heard her say, when somebody asked her if she would ever consider returning to Mother, "Only if everybody else did."

DAVID LOUD: They all went up to Canada for a year to develop that show, which was a huge sacrifice. And they all wanted to come back with certain things. Marin got her "Back

"We can never go back to before." With Mark Jacoby in *Ragtime*.
(Photofest)

to Before" moment. Barefoot, alone on stage. They all had to fight for that stuff. It was intense. She made sure that Mother worked, and that we never lost track of her. It was very important to her to make Mother's journey as big as Coalhouse's journey and Tateh's journey. They all had to advocate for their characters.

JASON DANIELEY: She'd get up early and swim miles and then go to rehearse. She always referred to [director] Frank Galati as sort of a Buddha figure. He's like a mountain, not only because he's a heavy, big guy, but he sits there like an immovable mountain. He flows with his spirit. He gives you the gentlest sentence about something and it just explodes your mind. One of the things that Frank shared with Marin was a very small book of meditation. She would read it before every performance during *Ragtime* and *Kiss Me, Kate*. There was this deepening of her spiritual awareness. She grew up Catholic and she did not believe in the dogma of the Catholic church. That was kind of the beginning of a spiritual awakening that she continued to up to the day she died.

LYNN AHRENS: In the early previews, "Back to Before" was getting a [tepid] reaction. I thought, "This is crazy, this is a really good song and we have an incredible performer doing it. Why is it not getting a better reaction?" Well, [behind her] the sky was gray, just after a storm; she was wearing a beautiful sea green dress; her hair was blown by the wind; she had been staged to start singing the song looking offstage to where Father had just left, very far upstage. So, we had a big convene with the creative team and we all discussed it. In the end, [lighting designers] Jules Fisher and Peggy Eisenhaur made the sky go from gray to a rising sunrise. There was a boardwalk railing and [set designer] Eugene Lee said, "The railing goes up and down. I could just have it go down at the right moment during the song." And then I said to [director] Frank Galati, "Could you just turn her around so she starts singing downstage, and then have her walk toward us?" And he said, "Absolutely." [Costume designer] Santo Loquasto changed her dress to white. And the wig department made the wig tighter, with just a couple of loose tendrils. [From then on] she stopped the show every night. And once it started working, it was amazing. I don't know how many times I've heard her sing that song, but it was never the same twice. Some nights she was tearful, some nights joyful, some nights angry and passionate. . . . She just kept finding new stuff in it.

BRIAN STOKES MITCHELL: [The entire original company] got left in Canada when they were promised that we were going to be up there for three months and then we were going to come down and open in some American town, probably Los Angeles or Chicago, and then we would all open in New York. Well, about two months into the run, people started getting calls, and I think Marin was one of them: "Hey, I hear they're opening a company in Los Angeles. Am I right for your role?" That was the first that our company heard about it. So, of course, that put the company in a tizzy. Marin had been working on workshop after workshop after workshop, creating this particular role. Somebody else was going to get to do the American premiere of the show. So that was really, really disheartening. I had right of first refusal for Los Angeles in my contract, but the rest of the company had to do this terrible year in Toronto. It was winter there and it was dark and somebody else was opening their show and doing their roles that they had created. That was a very disheartening, disappointing thing for the company.

DAVID LOUD: She knew what she had to do in that number. It wasn't easy for her to do. Saturday night and Sunday afternoon were not the best times to come see "Back to Before." She could get scratchy and tired by the end of the week. But I think she knew from the beginning that that was her big moment, and she knew how to do it and built it. She felt that she did it differently every night and, in her mind, there were different things each night. But musically, it was very consistent. It always felt fresh. I don't think she ever phoned anything in in her entire life. There was a night the nursemaid dropped the [prop] baby on its head. So what do you do? The nursemaid picks up the baby, looks at him, and says, "He all right," and tries to exit. Marin couldn't let it go! She had to see about that baby! She was fussing over it. She couldn't just let the nursemaid go, which was [perfectly in character] but, of course, ruined the scene!

KELLI O'HARA: The month I moved to New York City I had this friend who was one of the company managers for *Ragtime* and I saw it eight times. I saw Marin Mazzie and Audra McDonald and it changed my path. Years later when we would hang out, I would act like we were peers but inside I was like, "That's Marin Mazzie!" I was coming out of an opera degree and I thought I was relegated to the classic Broadway, Rodgers and Hammerstein, Lerner and Loewe sort of thing—which I love and I continue to do. But all of a sudden here was this woman, playing this feminine, strong mother, making a choice to help another mother, breaking molds and breaking boundaries, standing on her own two feet—the husband's gone—and even naming it: "You're away and we're never going to go back to the way we used to be, when I just let you make all my choices." Then shortly thereafter I saw her do *Kiss Me, Kate*. She's angry, she's saying, "Fuck men and their behavior," and she is doing it in soprano! I thought, "This is a whole different take on my whole story. I didn't see it before." That's why representation and example and inspiration are so important. From then on, in everything I did, I thought, "How do I give this more balls? How do I give this more backbone?" In everything I ever saw Marin do, she just carried a strength, but also a sexuality that she was not ashamed of. She never apologized for her beauty, or her power, or the way she looked, her sexuality. She just worked it.

VALERIE WRIGHT: When she was doing *Ragtime*, she called me she said, "I hemorrhaged a vocal cord." It happened onstage. She just started coughing and she couldn't stop coughing when she came offstage. She coughed up blood. She couldn't go back out. Sees the doctor and she has to go on complete vocal rest for two or three weeks. So, she and Jason came up to Connecticut where I was doing *Redhead*. We spent the weekend together, but she couldn't talk. She would mouth her sentences, but Jason couldn't understand one thing. I was like, "I got this. She said she wants the salmon."

JASON DANIELEY: During *Ragtime*, Marin started taking voice lessons from Arthur Levy. We got his name through Audra. She would touch base with Arthur for each show, specifically. The way she vocalized for *Kiss Me, Kate* was different than for *Carrie* or *Next to Normal*. And she was regimented: the door would be closed at half hour and she'd have her vocalese and her reading that she would do to get herself to "that place." But after a show we were at Joe Allen, often having a couple glasses of wine.

In 1999, Mazzie was reunited with Brian Stokes Mitchell in the Broadway revival of *Kiss Me, Kate*.

BRIAN STOKES MITCHELL: When Marin and I were doing *Ragtime*, of all the people in the cast, Marin was the person that I knew the least. We had almost no scenes together, so, as a result, we rarely saw each other in the rehearsal hall, because she was rehearsing her thing and I was rehearsing my thing at another time. And then, even when we were onstage, our shows were opposite; when I was down in the dressing room, she was onstage. So, we didn't see each other very much. And because *Ragtime* was an exhausting show for both of us, we didn't go out and party afterwards and we didn't spend social time together. When *Kiss Me, Kate* came up, I got on the phone with her and I said, "Marin, we need to go out to lunch because I feel like I don't really know you. We just haven't had the time." So, we had a lunch and we talked about a lot of the terrible things about *Ragtime*. At the end of the lunch, we made a little pinky swear to each other. I said, "Marin, let's have a great time doing this show. It's going to be a lot of fun. Let's just promise, between you and me, to have the most fun ever." And we absolutely did have the most fun ever on that show. We would say that to each other before the show. "Let's have the most fun ever." And we did, every single night.

JASON DANIELEY: She worked her tail off to nail the Shakespeare. The thing that she learned from [director] Michael Blakemore is that you know where the jokes are, but you're not going to get the laugh every night. The more you try to nail that laugh, the less chance that you're going to actually get the laugh because you're working too hard. Everyone would be going for the joke and he'd say, "No, tell the story." That was big for her.

BRIAN STOKES MITCHELL: The thing that I hated the most about *Kiss Me, Kate* was being slapped about eight times a show. Marin walloped me! I mean, those were not fake slaps. It got to the point, where the cast would hang out offstage and listen to how big the slap was. They started holding up signs, like at the Olympics: 9.3! 9.7! I got more than a few tens! She was always so apologetic afterwards.

JASON DANIELEY: She did say that playing Lili, she got all of her frustrations out onstage, so she came back home to me sweet and docile. It wasn't entirely true, but it's a good story.

DAVID LOUD: Her "I Hate Men" was so funny, with that big face of hers. It's hilarious. She could be icy Nordic goddess, she could be the girl next door, she could be Hollywood glamour. She could be Lucille Ball. She was just so versatile. And it was all done with this joy.

BRIAN STOKES MITCHELL: She was working on multiple levels. There are not too many people who have that ability to be zany and also be really sophisticated in their comedy and in their choices. That speaks to her intelligence, that speaks to her powers of observation and again, her artistry. I mean, it takes a really smart person to do comedy. And she was fiercely smart. Curious, and funny and kind, and connected.

JASON DANIELEY: She was corseted and drinking a lot of water because she was onstage all the time. She'd have to make dashes to the bathroom and pee. And Burperina would show. [Does an amazingly loud and long burp]. And then you'd have to enter after just hearing that.

Mazzie took *Kiss Me, Kate* to London's West End and then joined Mitchell in *Man of La Mancha*, replacing Mary Elizabeth Mastriantonio.

JASON DANIELEY: They wanted Marin to play it originally, but she was in London, doing *Kate*. She grew up singing to her parents' albums and one of them was *Man of La Mancha*, wearing her mother's blue nightgown and using her purple hair brush as a microphone. Playing a character that had been raped and abused, shut down to any possibility of hope but being open to what Don Quixote was offering her, his heart, meant a lot to her. That was very important.

After *La Mancha* closed, Mitchell and Mazzie were paired up yet again, for the Encores! production of *Kismet*.

BRIAN STOKES MITCHELL: I think Marin had a photographic memory. I remember going in for the second or third rehearsal and she already had the role memorized. She claimed it was because she had done the role before. I don't ever, ever recall her going up. Ever. And I think that's because she had this incredible mind. She's the person that I performed the most with. Her professionalism, her voice, her talent, her skill, her energy.... She was always amazing, always good. She was always on. She was one of those performers who's constantly trying to find better ways to do it. She was never like, "OK, I've nailed the song." She's just one of those actresses that's constantly exploring, trying to improve, and it's why I loved her so much. Her mind was always working.

In 2005, Mazzie appeared in a one-night Actor's Fund performance of *On the Twentieth Century*, featuring Douglas Sills, Jo Anne Worley, and Christopher Sieber.

CHRISTOPHER SIEBER: She could be an intimidating figure if you didn't know her. When I first saw her in rehearsal, she was this goddess. She commanded the room [with her presence]. She had the thing, the IT thing. You couldn't keep your eyes off of her. Walking into rehearsal, she seemed so at ease. We had like four days to put up this enormous show and she was probably screaming inside, like all of us, but she was just nose to the grindstone. Whenever you worked, she was always very, very focused on the material and the task at hand. And then when you were on a break, that's when the real Marin really came out; the sweet, kind, funny, self-deprecating like crazy, Marin. That made me relax, playing opposite her. As far as a comedy partner goes, she was so gung-ho about everything that we did. She was so amazingly easy to work with. She could read my mind—she was that good. And generous with the stage, letting other people do their thing and shine.

Mazzie stepped into the cast of *Spamalot* in 2006, replacing Sara Ramirez as The Lady of the Lake.

MARTIN MORAN: It was so much fun, but it was a struggle for her initially. She didn't necessarily want to be taking over a role rather than creating one. But we got to play with Mike Nichols! When Marin came into the show, along with Jonathan Hadary, after a bit of time Mike was like, "This isn't it. I want to meet with you." I remember her being scared: "Oh my God, it's not working and Mike is calling us." Mike helped her unleash her best instincts and [the idea of] not adding to what is there. He's famous for that: don't put a hat on a hat. I remember how initially upset she was and then how instantly thrilled she was to be engaged with him—"Oh my God, it was so great, he's so smart!"—the excitement of the work.

CHRISTOPHER SEIBER: Mike Nichols always told us that it's OK to surprise your fellow actors, just don't go crazy. And that's exactly what she did to me. She was surprising me. I knew the part like the back of my hand, but it was so refreshing and joyous with her. I learned a different way to approach the song and approach my character. It was eye-opening. You feel like a little kid on a playground. "Oh great. Yeah! Let's do that! Let's try it!" She played with me and I played with her and it just worked.

JASON DANIELEY: That show was like going to Disney World. She'd get to do the silliest things, wear the greatest costumes, and play with tried-and-true theater actors. Marty Moran's dressing room was next to Marin's. She would go in there during intermission. There was a book that Marty had been reading called *As It Is*. Eastern philosophy as the guiding overall principle. She's going out there saying and doing all that great comedy and then backstage she's with Marty, really poring over these ideas of the hereafter. That book is still in her nightstand. She would read it all the time.

CHRISTOPHER SEIBER: Right before we come on for "The Song That Goes Like This," we had about fifteen seconds [after a costume change]. About four or five seconds before the doors opened and it was entrance time, she would go [makes horrible, phlegmy, hacking sounds], clearing her throat. Just getting things out. If she spat, I wouldn't have been surprised. And then she'd say, "Let's go."

In 2010, Mazzie and Danieley took over the lead roles in *Next to Normal*, playing Diana and Dan, a married couple who had lost their son and were coping with that loss and Diana's worsening bipolar depression.

JASON DANIELEY: That was super challenging. Marin would have to wake up, preparing herself to be sad. But as soon as we took our final bow and walked offstage, she'd slap me on the ass and we'd go to Joe Allen's. Glass of wine, and liver and onions. She just would drop it. It was a great tight-knit company. Every time we would go to the stage door we'd meet people who were bipolar, who had parents who are bipolar, who had children who died at an early age—all that catharsis made it so important. We felt like we were able to be a part of helping other people. It was so rewarding in that way. We would always go out the stage door and meet everybody. We stayed there as long as there was someone there, because you didn't know if there was some really shy person who wanted to [talk].

Mazzie starred opposite Molly Ranson in the off-Broadway production of *Carrie* in 2012.

MOLLY RANSON: I was so nervous. It was my first big role. I always perceived Marin as having this very regal presence, but in person she is completely disarming and approachable. She was completely there for fellow actors and artists in a way that I think is extremely rare and genuine. That was my experience of her from the first time I met her. And she really encouraged me to speak up and have a voice. There was a lyric in the song "Carrie" that was not resonating with how I understood the character. Carrie was fantasizing about what her life could be, and one of the lyrics had to do with wearing a shorter dress. I was like, "I don't think that that's her main concern." I talked to Marin about it and she was like, "Say something. Talk to them." She taught me to speak up and that's something that I've held on to throughout the rest of my career. [Onstage] she was always alive and present in each moment. I wish I could say I learned to do that from her, but I still think, "How DID she do that?" She was so just viscerally emotional in each scene. The night of the Drama Desk Awards, I was really nervous. I felt like I was not in good voice that day and I didn't want to sing. She was like "You're doing it. That's it." She was such a maternal presence for me. And continued to be after the show. She was one of the people I would call if I had a horrible audition experience and needed to cry to someone.

Just as when she went from *Ragtime* to *Kiss Me, Kate*, swinging from serious drama to rollicking comedy, in 2014 Mazzie followed up *Carrie* with *Bullets Over Broadway*, based on Woody Allen's hit film. The show, though eagerly anticipated, was not well received and closed after 156 performances.

JASON DANIELEY: That was a very challenging road because Stro [Susan Stroman] wanted her to play the part. She auditioned just to do the workshop. No one was getting guarantees for Broadway. So, the workshop was kind of like a big audition.

BECKY ANN BAKER: When they did the workshop, everyone else was offered the Broadway production. Marin had to wait. That was a really difficult time for her.

JASON DANIELEY: On the last day of the workshop, Stro said, "You're going to do it." So, that was big pressure. You were just putting it all on the line.

DONNA MURPHY: The only time I ever heard her complaining about a work situation was during *Bullets Over Broadway*. They put her through a gazillion auditions for it while they were talking to this person and talking to that person, and then ultimately, they gave her the role and she was glorious. But she was disappointed that the show was not as well received as she'd hoped it would be. She worked really hard to get that job. She always worked hard. She always worked her butt off. There's no situation that she didn't, and still had a great time doing it. I was hanging out in her dressing room after a performance and she had other guests. I watched her being so gracious. I thought, "God, I'm watching a queen! This woman knows how to receive." Her feet were so firmly planted on the ground. She was so connected to the Earth. At the same time, there was this goddess-like quality about her that didn't remove her from other people, but drew people towards her. She radiated.

KAREN ZIEMBA: She set an example for Zach Braff. He had to come up to her level. He was great, but I think her professionalism and the way she took everything in stride.... The shit hit the fan a couple of times, when costumes had to be changed or the set wouldn't move off the stage ... and she took everything in stride. I think she was an incredible example. He really, he rose to the occasion, and I think a lot of it had to do with her. In the theater, you have to do it for each other. She had that in spades. What a great person to play opposite. Not everybody does it. Some people are more selfish than that. She was generous. Marin's door was always open. But she was one of those people that didn't hang around in her dressing room a lot. She was always walking around, standing in the wings, and when you do that, you are around everybody else and you are checking in with everyone.

JASON DANIELEY: That was such a heartbreak. It opened and closed. You put every ounce of positive energy into making it work. Marin was fifty-three. You don't know how many roles you have coming up.

BECKY ANN BAKER: I remember talking a lot with her about the younger women coming up through the ranks. All of a sudden, you're struggling to get the roles that you feel like you can do as well as anybody. This business is terrible, and I remember having some heartbreaking talks with her when she hadn't gotten a part, or I hadn't. Those conversations where you just let it all out. In this business you only feel like you're as good as the job that's coming up or that you currently have.

JOSEPH THALKEN: I remember one time there was an article in *The New York Times* about the big Broadway performers, the big women divas. She was not mentioned. We had a rehearsal that day and she was just a little sad about that. It was a moment of vulnerability about her career that I had not heard her express before.

JASON DANIELEY: It frustrated me beyond belief that Marin didn't get a nomination for that. She was fine with it. That aspect of the business had less and less importance to us. It kind of set us up, mentally, for when she was diagnosed: life is the most important thing. All of the drama about roles and shows and awards doesn't mean anything. We're all going to die. We want to have a good life, and if it's successful, that's great. The most important thing for both of us was our marriage and our love and our relationship. If that was strong, which it always was, then we had succeeded. It was easier at that point to go, "That really sucks. Oh well." And that's basically when the engine just fell out of the car and Marin was diagnosed.

In 2015, on the opening night of the Encores! production of *Zorba!*, Mazzie was diagnosed with stage four ovarian cancer. She had liters of fluid drained from her that afternoon and performed that night.

CHRISTOPHER SEIBER: The way she found out her diagnosis and the way she dealt with it, the strength, the courage, the sense of humor she had was so admirable. She continued to work and was still Marin. She just had this new thing that was happening to her.

JASON DANIELEY: [In *Zorba!*] she couldn't take her big Marin Mazzie breath. She had to kind of position her body in a way so that she could take the deepest breath that she could. The show was all about seizing life. It was buoying.

DONNA MURPHY: When Marin was diagnosed, she reached out to Shawn [Murphy's late husband, Shawn Elliott] who was, to his knowledge, at that time, cancer-free after treatment for cancer in 2012, as one of her guides. He'd been treated at Sloan-Kettering and that's where she was being treated. He was so amazed by how she talked about it. She called chemo her "healing therapy." And then, when he was not feeling well that summer and was diagnosed with a new cancer, he asked me not to tell Marin because she had just had a big surgery and was doing well. Unfortunately, she found out because shortly after that, the four of us were all in the emergency room at Sloan-Kettering together. It was early fall. And I was upset because seeing her there, I knew something was wrong that I didn't know about before that moment. And I was also upset because I know now that she knows Shawn is sick, and he's very upset. We all just kind of helped each other. Jason and I would go back and forth between their rooms at the hospital. She was as astounding in the hospital as she was onstage. She had it down. She had her rituals and the things she needed to have with her. She was always talking to me about Shawn and asking how could she help him. Some days they were having chemo at the same time and they would talk to each other. Shawn decided, "If Marin is calling it her 'healing therapy,' I'm going to call it my healing therapy."

JASON DANIELEY: I'm at the theater [in *The Visit*], not wanting to tell anyone necessarily, but knowing that I could talk to Roger Rees [who himself was also dealing with cancer]. We immediately became this family through cancer. Everything was just kind of happening for both of our families. She called her chemotherapy "healing therapy" just to change the vernacular, and she considered singing [to be] healing therapy. We went to the Fairmont Hotel in San Francisco and we did our act and we talked about it being healing therapy for her. [During the show] we talked about her journey, trying to share, the same way that we shared at that stage door at the Booth, with people who are going through a difficult time in their lives. It was important to make something positive or at least experience something positive from what we were going through.

DONNA MURPHY: There had been this sense of self that was getting stronger and more powerful as she was playing these different leading ladies, and also with the range of what she was doing. I was very aware of the very formidable woman that she was becoming and owning. Her spirit was somehow just becoming larger. We talked a lot about this after she was diagnosed with cancer. She'd been seeing a therapist for a while and she said, "I didn't realize how much of the work I was doing was really to prepare me for what was ahead." Because the woman who was diagnosed—the woman she was—was, of course, devastated by that diagnosis. But at the same time, she was so ready to take it on as a warrior that got on a stage that night and sang "Life is what you do while you're waiting to die." She also refused to tell people initially that she was diagnosed with stage four. In the letters and emails that she sent, updates to the people she chose to share with, you came away educated, [tearing up] you came away inspired, you came away more enlightened about how to live your life. All of that had been developing in her. There was always a light about her, but there was also a gravitas that was developing. She embodied so many qualities and she just kept growing as a human. She was a very disciplined person. She exercised and swam and worked out with trainers. She really enjoyed it, too. And she was very careful about what she ate. Very health-minded. Every time I would see her in these different roles, I could see how she was just expanding her range and humanity and spirit.

JOSEPH THALKEN: We had a concert somewhere in the Berkshires and I think it was the first performance we did after she started treatment. She wore a wig. She hadn't gone totally public with what had happened. Shortly after that, she thought, "F it! This is what it is." And the wig came off.

KAREN ZIEMBA: It was very eye-opening for me to see how open she was about the truth of her illness. Most people I have known that had cancer or any kind of illness keep it under wraps because of the business and the way people view you. She really came out truthfully and said, "This is what's going on with me." She fought it and she worked. It was almost like it fueled her.

DONNA MURPHY: She always said "singing is healing to me." So whenever she could grab a concert—if she was going to start another treatment protocol, she would ask herself and her doctors, "Can I squeeze this concert in before I start that protocol? Could it cost me time? What might the singing give me?" Because she felt it was healing. She had doctors who supported and understood her as an artist. They understood how important that part of her was, and how she could contribute to her own health and healing.

MARTIN MORAN: We talked a lot about counting our blessings that we live where we live, that we do what we do. Our conversations were fueled by wine, fueled by good food, and in the later years, fueled by nature and quietude and trees and birds. This was something that we deeply shared. Marin was on a spiritual path, and that was a huge part of negotiating the biggest mystery of all: that we will die. That she was gravely ill. She was searching for peace and acceptance of exactly the life she was having. That's what we always talked about. Can we accept life as it is? Trust that some higher, mystery ... power ... God ... the universe ... is guiding? The practice is to trust that moment to moment.

In 2016, with her cancer in remission, Mazzie replaced Kelli O'Hara in the Lincoln Center Theater production of *The King and I*.

BECKY ANN BAKER: She had a meeting with the director that didn't go the way she thought it would, and she thought she might not be doing that show. She thought she was coming in for them to discuss her doing it and instead it became a discussion of, "Do you think you can do this?" It had nothing to do with the cancer at all. She walked out of that meeting, instead of feeling excited about doing the project, furious. Furious that she had to go through that. And I remember her agents jumping on Lincoln Center and then Lincoln Center jumping on Bart Sher. That wasn't what she thought she was there for—to discuss whether or not she could do it. I don't think anyone goes through this business without having those kind of heartbreaks. It's that rollercoaster. It was just a mind-blowing performance.

DONNA MURPHY: She was spectacular! She had such a quiet and then not-so-quiet power. I didn't know that during that time the cancer came back. She was an astounding Mrs. Anna. No shame to anyone else, but maybe the most astounding.

KELLI O'HARA: I learned from her performance. I can't see myself performing on the out-side. And when I do, I want to put my head in a hole in the ground. We process how we feel so deeply, but performing is very different for people. Some people are more introspective; they're feeling so much inside, but that doesn't make a great stage per-former. And I will admit that I've always felt like what I was feeling on the inside was never expressed enough. Whereas Marin had a great ability to be more demonstrative on the stage. She takes the stage. She always did. So, when I saw her performance—just watching her taking the stage—and her clip was much faster than mine because I like to sit in something and sort of wallow in it. There's great power and control in tempo and clip. I appreciated her efficiency in playing the role. I believe that in certain spots, that efficiency awards you and makes the slow down more powerful. Her performance was powerful and wasn't so precious. That was my biggest note from it: "Trust that you've built all the layers of feeling and we can move forward." So, when I went to London [with the show, after having seen Mazzie's performance], there was an efficiency about it, while using all the things that I knew from doing it over a whole year. I could add a little bit of her tempo and efficiency.

JASON DANIELEY: She was tapped into something that other people, thankfully, aren't tapped into: this brush with their mortality. Every song meant something different, and the joy was even more joyous because she was in remission. When she sang "Hello, Young Lovers," she opens a heart locket and the props people had put my picture in there. So singing "I had a love of my own"... she knew that she had a love of her own. For me as well. Just as the song says: "Don't be sad for me because he's not here, I had that." It doesn't make life easy, but at least I know what that is. Signs started coming toward the end of her run and then the rest of 2016 was utter hell. We couldn't get the pain managed. She had a fentanyl patch and they just kept increasing, increasing. She's laying on this couch while I'm decorating the Christmas tree. Couldn't eat. In 2017 they got the pain medication right. We had concerts, we went to Paris, she did Terrence's play. The symptoms started coming back during *Fire and Air*.

Throughout the run of *Fire and Air*, Mazzie's condition worsened, necessitating several missed performances. But whenever she could be there, she was on.

KELLI O'HARA: There was this big thing at Carnegie Hall where they honored Bartlett Sher and me. We got to pick who performed for us and I picked different people out of all my shows: Matthew Broderick, Danny Burstein, Paulo Szot, Steven Pasquale, and I asked Marin and Rebecca Luker and Judy Kuhn to do a trio of "Make Someone Happy," which is my song. She weighed like eighty pounds. I just sat in the box and wept. There she was standing in the middle, right before she died. That both she and Becca are gone now is un-believable to me. Marin was so strong, and then she wasn't.

BECKY ANN BAKER: We would try to relieve Jason every now and then and spend the night at the hospital, one of the friends. Even doing that with her, there were always moments of joy despite the fact that she was failing so badly physically. She was so much fun. When I think of Marin, the first thing I think of is laughter. Belly laughing with her.

JASON DANIELEY: She was on oxygen. We had to get certain things, like a chair with wheels and commode for next to the bed because it was difficult to get all the way to the bath-room. The night before she passed, she said, "I'm scared." I said, "I am too." And she said, "It's not about you."

JUDY KUHN: Their relationship was so beautiful. She loved him so much. They had such a beautiful professional partnership and romantic partnership and that was a beautiful thing to witness.

Marin Mazzie died on September 13, 2018.

JASON DANIELEY: We never wanted to be away from one another. I always wanted to be with her.

VALERIE WRIGHT: About three months after she passed away, I said to Jason, "Why don't we get her girlfriends together?" Jason went through all her stuff and he said, "Everything that I don't really have a place for, I'm going to put out on the dining room table and I want everyone to take whatever you want." So we stood around that dining room table for like forty-five minutes and we all just found ways to put off taking something because it seemed so final. But once we started, it felt so good. I have earrings. I have two jackets. I have scarves. I wear so much of her stuff. And I think there's something very profound about that. Honestly, having that stuff on me, around me, has made me feel like she's still around, and I talk to her.

LYNN AHRENS: I have my Marin scarf and my Marin earrings and my Marin bracelet that I actually gave to her. She had showed me how to tie a scarf a particular way, so I do that with her scarf.

DONNA MURPHY: When Marin passed there was more than one of us saying we'd lost our best friend. Because of the way she loved people, because of the fun you had with her,

"I had a love of my own." Mazzie's final musical, *The King and I.*
(Paul Kolnik)

because of how intimate the relationships were.... And I don't mean that she was casual about having intimate relationships. I just know that I wasn't the only person who called her my best friend. I have many truly wonderful friendships that have come from shows I've done. But to do a show where you start out not knowing a person at all, and at some point you find that you're doing it with your best friend—it was incredible. It's never quite happened like that again.

JASON DANIELEY: I had a plaque put on a seat at Lincoln Center, M101. It says, "You were my sky, my wind and my stars and my ocean," from *Ragtime*, and "So in love with you am I," from *Kiss Me, Kate*.

MARTIN MORAN: She said, "See? Trust life." She said it all the way along, including when life was leaving her.

KELLI O'HARA: She's not gone because I'm telling you, I have made choices with my behavior and my treatment of younger people coming up because of the way she mentored me. So, it lives. You pass it forward. Thank God. In this business, you can either champion people, or you can eat yourself alive with resentment or concern, or jealousy, and the biggest gift she probably gave me is that she just didn't do any of that shit. We were at galas together, doing our makeup, talking about things and—it's the difference [between] giving me a lot of advice and saying, "Oh sweet girl," versus, "Hey, what do you think about this?" That was Marin. No condescension. She had a little bit more self-worth than the rest of us. [When I did *Kiss Me, Kate* in 2019] I had her in my mind. I wanted to carry her on. I wanted to do that show because I said to myself in 1999, "One of these days I want to do that show. I want to be strong like Marin." She was going to be with me no matter what, but for me to start the show wearing her hat [O'Hara wore the hat that Mazzie had worn for her entrance in the 1999 production] ... I was going to put that hat on every day and look in the mirror and be like, "Let's go, friend. Let's do this thing." She made me stronger every single night. We become actors because we're trying to find something that's not us. If I want to be powerful and strong as an actor, who do I pull from? What sense memory? What method? Well, my method was Marin Mazzie. I wanted to have her hat on my head.

CHRISTOPHER SEIBER: Her professionalism was unbelievable. If she deemed something [she did as] unprofessional, she would say, "I'm so sorry. That was so unprofessional of me." She had such high standards for herself. When you were with her, you were her friend. She always had time for you.

JOSEPH THALKEN: She was a great collaborator. Very honest about her opinions, about keys, about the feel of what she wanted, but also very open to suggestions. She wasn't someone who sang everything exactly the same way every night. That said, she was incredibly reliable. I can't remember one time where she went up on her lyrics.

DAVID LOUD: She was so masterful and so versatile. She was just always good. And I don't think that came from directors or teachers. I think it was just inside her. And it was never that hard for her, either. She knew what to do, and she did it. She never "angsted" over her performance. She had a knowledge of how things had to be. Marin was not a question asker. She just knew how to make it good.

JUDY KUHN: I had the great fortune of singing with her on some concerts. She was just the warmest, kindest, egoless, most generous person you ever want to come across, especially in show business. She was so extraordinarily talented and beautiful and yet so humble. That night of that Carnegie Hall thing where I sang with her and Audra, I was really ill. I had a fever, I was sweating, I had this terrible sore throat. It was horrible. She and Audra both just took such good care of me, bringing me tea and making sure that I felt OK and that I was calm, reassuring me that everything would be OK. It was just so sweet.

JASON DANIELEY: She had no ego with her talent. She had talent in spades. "Put me in, coach. I can catch the pop flies. I can field the grounders." She knew that she could do it and had a calm confidence without bravura or unnecessary, diva-like behavior.

LYNN AHRENS: She was always willing to try anything. She was game. Very daring. In everything she did there was always a sense of experimentation. She was so fluid and so fast, so fearless.

Kelli O'Hara [who is scheduled to play Mazzie's role in the original cast reunion concert of *Ragtime*]: I'm shaking in my boots, but I consider myself the very, very best choice. And the reason why is because I will be a placeholder. [Tears up] We can't have Marin, so we need the wax figure, cardboard cutout, and I'm your girl. I can't sing it like her, but I will be there representing her. And I know that she would bless it. As an insecure performer, I'm dying. But I'll be twice as strong because it won't just be me up there for sure.

DONNA MURPHY: She and I were both trying to get pregnant around the same time and we each had our journeys with that, which did not result in either of us giving birth to a child. And then my husband and I decided to pursue adoption. I'll never forget after we brought Darmia Hope home, how present Marin was in so many ways. She sang Maury Yeston's "New Words" at Darmia's welcoming ceremony at the UN Chapel. Darmia, who was seven and a half months old, looked straight at her and never took her eyes off her for the entire song. It was unbelievable. Then Marin took her to see Santa for the first time! And Marin and her mother, "Mama Donna," came to our home and brought us all of these beautiful heirloom baby blankets that had been made for Marin by relatives of hers. I have every one of them. The only tears were mine. The generosity, the love, and her sense of celebration for Shawn, Darmia, and I.... She'd already been through her own journey with Jason, had come to a decision, and, with full embracing of her middle name—Joy—just experienced this with us.

MARTIN MORAN: What she gave herself, and us all the while, to the best of her ability, was the gift of NO FEAR.

JASON DANIELEY: We were sounding boards for each other on whatever project the other one was working on. I knew and heard where she was coming from on most everything. She believed that I could do anything. And that's one of the things that's extraordinarily difficult since she passed. Can I do this anymore? I know I am capable, but that solid pillar of support is no longer there. Our time here is so fleeting. And what we do as stage actors is here and gone. As time goes, I think we all just kind of disappear like dust in the wind. But I'm hopeful that through books and people who can speak in such warm and glowing terms of her leadership, that people might strive, not only be an actress like Marin and to be as diverse as she was, but that her empathy and compassion for human beings, and the kinds of stories that she liked to tell, will be her legacy.

Acknowledgments

In the acknowledgments of *Nothing Like a Dame* and *A Wonderful Guy*, I mentioned the village it took to make those books happen. The township keeps growing with people to whom I am incredibly indebted.

Jennifer Keller is my reality touchstone to the extent that I have a connection to reality. She has a bullshit meter like no one else and an intelligence that leaves me dumbfounded and humbled. She once again served as a constant sounding board, occasional proofreader, and the best dispenser of tough love that I could ever ask for. Her contributions to the ways I approach these conversations were invaluable.

Melinda Berk proofread this book's every word and many that, thanks to her, aren't included. For a third time, she showed unwavering support, objective perspective, and perpetual good humor.

There are a number of friends and colleagues whose help to me included their feedback and ideas, and there are others who jumped in to help me reach out to some of the book's more elusive subjects. And there are some wonderful people who work with or are married to this book's women, and who dealt with my myriad communications. Thank you to:

Sebastian Arecelus, Laura Benanti, Erich Bergen, Christian Borle, Nicole Dancel, Jeffrey Epstein, Melissa Errico, Raúl Esparza, Charlie Finlay, Catherine Guiher, Tom Kirdahy, LaChanze, Adam LeGrant, Norm Lewis, Terrence Mann, Andrea Martin, Louise Martzinek, Billy Masters, Brian Stokes Mitchell, Ryan Oboza, Michael Paternostro, Erica Tuchman, Jack Upton, Michael Urie, and George Youngdahl.

Then there are the people who worked directly on the book.

Rob McQuilken at Massie & McQuilken is the agent and cheerleader I'd recommend to absolutely anyone.

Norman Hirschy and his team at Oxford University Press could not have been more encouraging when I said I wanted to do a follow-up to *Nothing Like a Dame*, and they made the process so incredibly easy. I am grateful to have a home at Oxford.

The photographers whose images grace these pages and the licensing staff at Photofest and the New York Public Library were incredibly helpful and generous. Thank you, Julieta Cervantes, Manuel Harlan, James Higgins, Paul Kolnik, Joan Marcus, Matthew Murphy, Carol Rosegg, Craig Schwartz, Deen van Meer, and the good people at the New York Public Library and at Photofest.

And of course, thank you to all of the women whose words fill these pages. Their generosity of time, spirit, humanity, dish, and even friendship is what you hold in your hands.

Finally, my family. My parents exposed me to Broadway musicals from the time I was five, not knowing that they'd created a monster. But once that die was cast, they were nothing but supportive. My sisters, too, tolerated my incessant playing of cast albums. My nieces tolerate those less but they still adore me, whether or not I earn it. And then there are the spouses and partners who love me even though it isn't a biological imperative. Thank you all for believing in me, Ann, Donald, Arlene and Rona Shapiro, Emma Morgan, David Franklin, and Noa and Hallel Shapiro-Franklin.

Index

For the benefit of digital users, indexed terms that span two pages (e.g., 52–53) may, on occasion, appear on only one of those pages

Figures are indicated by *f* following the page number